VISUALIZING

PSYCHOLOGY

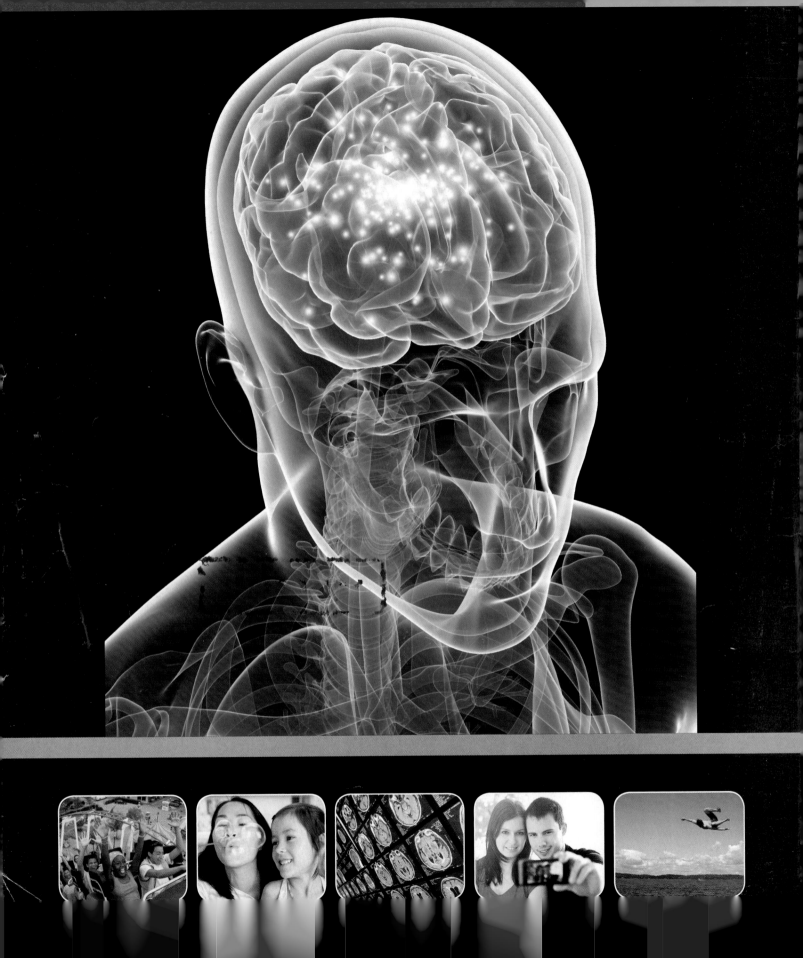

VISUALIZING
PSYCHOLOGY

SECOND CANADIAN EDITION

Karen Huffman
Palomar College

Alastair Younger
University of Ottawa

Claire Vanston
Capilano University

WILEY

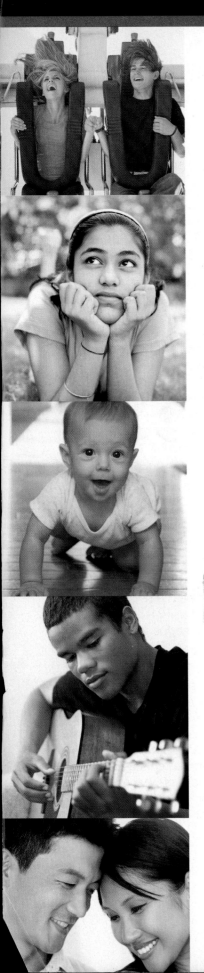

Vice President and Publisher: Veronica Visentin
Acquisitions Editor: Rodney Burke
Marketing Manager: Patty Maher
Editorial Manager: Karen Staudinger
Production Manager: Tegan Wallace
Developmental Editor: Gail Brown
Editorial Assistant: Luisa Begani
Layout: cMPreparé
Creative Director: Harry Nolan
Cover Design: Harry Nolan
Senior Design: Maureen Eide

Cover Credits: Main Image: © IngramPublishing/iStockphoto
                      Filmstrip from left to right: © PureStock/SuperStock/Corbis; © Chris Bernard;
                      © Jason Woodcock; © Aleksandar Nakic; © Mike Chan
Copyright page credits: Mike Kemp/© RubberBall/Alamy; ©Vikram Raghuvanshi/iStockphoto;
                      © Brian McEntire/iStockphoto; © Ariel Duhon/iStockphoto; © Nicolas Hansen/iStockphoto

This book was set in Baskerville by cMPreparé. Printed and bound by Quad Graphics.

Copyright © 2013 John Wiley & Sons Canada, Ltd.

Library and Archives Canada Cataloguing in Publication
Huffman, Karen
    Visualizing psychology/Karen Huffman, Alastair Younger,
Claire Vanston.—2nd Canadian ed.
Includes bibliographical references and index.
ISBN 978-1-118-30080-0
    1. Psychology—Textbooks. I. Younger, Alastair II.
Vanston, Claire III. Title.
BF121.H784 2012   150   C2012-904220-X

Printed and bound in the United States of America.
1 2 3 4 5 QG 17 16 15 14 13

John Wiley & Sons Canada, Ltd.
6045 Freemont Blvd.
Mississauga, Ontario L5R 4J3
Canada

Wiley Visualizing

How Is Wiley Visualizing Different?

Wiley Visualizing is based on decades of research on the use of visuals in learning (Mayer, 2005).[1] The visuals teach key concepts and are pedagogically designed to **explain**, **present**, and **organize** new information. The figures are tightly integrated with accompanying text; the visuals are conceived with the text in ways that clarify and reinforce major concepts, while allowing students to understand the details. This commitment to distinctive and consistent visual pedagogy sets Wiley Visualizing apart from other textbooks.

Wiley Visualizing's images are not decorative; such images can be distracting to students. Instead, they are purposeful and the primary driver of the content. These authentic materials immerse the student in real-life issues and experiences and support thinking, comprehension, and application.

Together these elements deliver a level of rigour in ways that maximize student learning and involvement. Wiley Visualizing has proven to increase student learning through its unique combination of text, photographs, and illustrations, with online video, animations, simulations, and assessments.

(1) Visual Pedagogy. Using the Cognitive Theory of Multimedia Learning, which is backed by hundreds of empirical research studies, Wiley's authors create visualizations for their texts that specifically support students' thinking and learning—for example, the selection of relevant materials, the organization of the new information, or the integration of the new knowledge with prior knowledge.

(2) Authentic Situations and Problems. *Visualizing Psychology*, Second Canadian Edition benefits from an array of remarkable photographs, illustrations, media, and film. These authentic materials immerse the student in real-life issues in psychology, thereby enhancing motivation, learning, and retention (Donovan & Bransford, 2005).[2]

(3) Designed with Interactive Multimedia. *Visualizing Psychology* is tightly integrated with *WileyPLUS*, our online learning environment that provides interactive multimedia activities in which learners can actively engage with the materials. The combination of textbook and *WileyPLUS* provides learners with multiple entry points to the content, giving them greater opportunity to explore concepts and assess their understanding as they progress through the course. *WileyPLUS* is a key component of the Wiley Visualizing learning and problem-solving experience, setting it apart from other textbooks whose online component is mere drill-and-practice.

Wiley Visualizing and the *WileyPLUS* Learning Environment are designed as a natural extension of how we learn

To understand why the Visualizing approach is effective, it is first helpful to understand how we learn.

1. Our brain processes information using two main channels: visual and verbal. Our *working memory* holds information that our minds process as we learn. This "mental workbench" helps us with decisions, problem-solving, and making sense of words and pictures by building verbal and visual models of the information.

2. When the verbal and visual models of corresponding information are integrated in working memory, we form more comprehensive, lasting, mental models.

3. When we link these integrated mental models to our prior knowledge, stored in our *long-term memory*, we build even stronger mental models. When an integrated (visual plus verbal) mental model is formed and stored in long-term memory, real learning begins.

The effort our brains put forth to make sense of instructional information is called *cognitive load*. There are two kinds of cognitive load: productive cognitive load, such as when we're engaged in learning or exert positive effort to create mental models; and unproductive cognitive load, which occurs when the brain is trying to make sense of needlessly complex content or when information is not presented well. The learning process can be impaired when the information to be processed exceeds the capacity of working memory. Well-designed visuals and text with effective pedagogical guidance can reduce the unproductive cognitive load in our working memory.

---

[1] Mayer, R.E. (Ed.) (2005). *The Cambridge Handbook of Multimedia Learning*. Cambridge University Press.
[2] Donovan, M.S., & Bransford, J. (Eds.) (2005). *How Students Learn: Science in the Classroom*. The National Academy Press. Available at http://www.nap.edu/openbook.php?record_id=11102&page=1

Wiley Visualizing is designed for engaging and effective learning

The visuals and text in *Visualizing Psychology*, Second Canadian Edition, are specially integrated to present complex processes in clear steps and with clear representations, organize related pieces of information, and integrate related information with one another. This approach, along with the use of interactive multimedia, minimizes unproductive cognitive load and helps students engage with the content. When students are engaged, they're reading and learning, which can lead to greater knowledge and academic success.

Research shows that well-designed visuals, integrated with comprehensive text, can improve the efficiency with which a learner processes information. In this regard, SEG Research, an independent research firm, conducted a national, multisite study evaluating the effectiveness of Wiley Visualizing. Its findings indicate that students using Wiley Visualizing products (both print and multimedia) were more engaged in the course, exhibited greater retention throughout the course, and made significantly greater gains in content area knowledge and skills, compared with students in similar classes that did not use Wiley Visualizing.[3]

The use of *WileyPLUS* can also increase learning. According to a white paper titled "Leveraging Blended Learning for More Effective Course Management and Enhanced Student Outcomes" by Peggy Wyllie of Evince Market Research & Communications, studies show that effective use of online resources can increase learning outcomes. Pairing supportive online resources with face-to-face instruction can help students to learn and reflect on material, and deploying multimodal learning methods can help students to engage with the material and retain their acquired knowledge.

[3]SEG Research (2009). Improving Student-Learning with Graphically-Enhanced Textbooks: A study of the Effectiveness of the Wiley Visualizing Series.

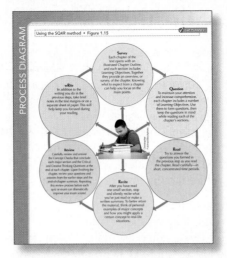

Using the SQ4R method (Figure 1.15) A logical progression of visuals and graphic features directs learners' attention to the underlying concept. The arrows visually display processes, helping us recognize relationships.

Ready for responsibility? (Figure 9.12) Images are paired so that students can compare and contrast them, thereby grasping the underlying concept. Adjacent captions eliminate split attention. When we must divide our attention between several sources of different information.

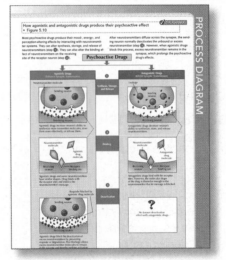

How agonist and antagonist drugs produce their psychoactive effect (Figure 5.10) Textual and visual elements are physically integrated. This eliminates split attention.

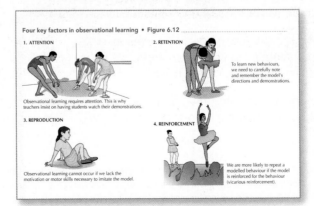

Four key factors in observational learning (Figure 6.12) This matrix visually organizes abstract information to reduce cognitive load.

Guided Chapter Tour

How Are the Wiley Visualizing Chapters Organized?

Student engagement is more than just exciting videos or interesting animations—engagement means keeping students motivated to keep going. It is easy to get bored or lose focus when presented with large amounts of information, and it is easy to lose motivation when the relevance of the information is unclear.

Each Wiley Visualizing chapter engages students from the start

Chapter opening text and visuals introduce the subject and connect the student with the material that follows.

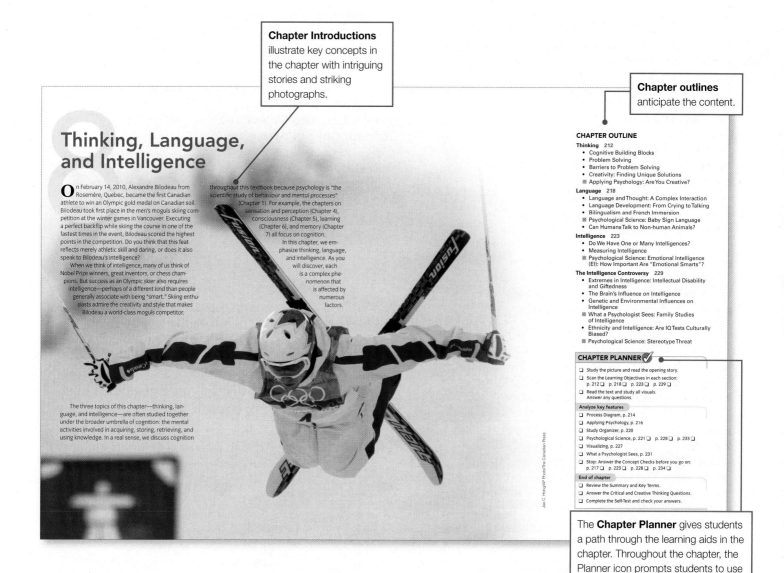

Chapter Introductions illustrate key concepts in the chapter with intriguing stories and striking photographs.

Chapter outlines anticipate the content.

Thinking, Language, and Intelligence

On February 14, 2010, Alexandre Bilodeau from Rosemère, Quebec, became the first Canadian athlete to win an Olympic gold medal on Canadian soil. Bilodeau took first place in the men's moguls skiing competition at the winter games in Vancouver. Executing a perfect backflip while skiing the course in one of the fastest times in the event, Bilodeau scored the highest points in the competition. Do you think that this feat reflects merely athletic skill and daring, or does it also speak to Bilodeau's intelligence?

When we think of intelligence, many of us think of Nobel Prize winners, great inventors, or chess champions. But success as an Olympic skier also requires intelligence—perhaps of a different kind than people generally associate with being "smart." Skiing enthusiasts admire the creativity and style that makes Bilodeau a world-class moguls competitor.

The three topics of this chapter—thinking, language, and intelligence—are often studied together under the broader umbrella of cognition: the mental activities involved in acquiring, storing, retrieving, and using knowledge. In a real sense, we discuss cognition throughout this textbook because psychology is "the scientific study of behaviour and mental processes" (Chapter 1). For example, the chapters on sensation and perception (Chapter 4), consciousness (Chapter 5), learning (Chapter 6), and memory (Chapter 7) all focus on cognition.

In this chapter, we emphasize thinking, language, and intelligence. As you will discover, each is a complex phenomenon that is affected by numerous factors.

Jae C. Hong/AP Photo/The Canadian Press

CHAPTER OUTLINE

Thinking 212
- Cognitive Building Blocks
- Problem Solving
- Barriers to Problem Solving
- Creativity: Finding Unique Solutions
- ■ Applying Psychology: Are You Creative?

Language 218
- Language and Thought: A Complex Interaction
- Language Development: From Crying to Talking
- Bilingualism and French Immersion
- ■ Psychological Science: Baby Sign Language
- Can Humans Talk to Non-human Animals?

Intelligence 223
- Do We Have One or Many Intelligences?
- Measuring Intelligence
- ■ Psychological Science: Emotional Intelligence (EI): How Important Are "Emotional Smarts"?

The Intelligence Controversy 229
- Extremes in Intelligence: Intellectual Disability and Giftedness
- The Brain's Influence on Intelligence
- Genetic and Environmental Influences on Intelligence
- ■ What a Psychologist Sees: Family Studies of Intelligence
- Ethnicity and Intelligence: Are IQ Tests Culturally Biased?
- ■ Psychological Science: Stereotype Threat

CHAPTER PLANNER ✓

- ☐ Study the picture and read the opening story.
- ☐ Scan the Learning Objectives in each section: p. 212 ☐ p. 218 ☐ p. 223 ☐ p. 229 ☐
- ☐ Read the text and study all visuals. Answer any questions.

Analyze key features
- ☐ Process Diagram, p. 214
- ☐ Applying Psychology, p. 216
- ☐ Study Organizer, p. 220
- ☐ Psychological Science, p. 221 ☐ p. 228 ☐ p. 233 ☐
- ☐ Visualizing, p. 227
- ☐ What a Psychologist Sees, p. 231
- ☐ Stop: Answer the Concept Checks before you go on: p. 217 ☐ p. 223 ☐ p. 228 ☐ p. 234 ☐

End of chapter
- ☐ Review the Summary and Key Terms.
- ☐ Answer the Critical and Creative Thinking Questions.
- ☐ Complete the Self-Test and check your answers.

The **Chapter Planner** gives students a path through the learning aids in the chapter. Throughout the chapter, the Planner icon prompts students to use the learning aids and to set priorities as they study.

Wiley Visualizing guides students through the chapter

The content of Wiley Visualizing gives students a variety of approaches—visuals, words, interactions, videos, and assessments—that work together to provide a guided path through the content.

Process Diagrams provide in-depth coverage of processes correlated with clear, step-by-step narrative, enabling students to grasp important topics with less effort.

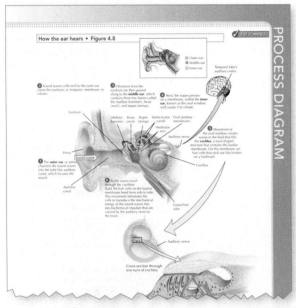

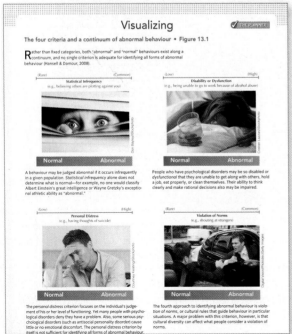

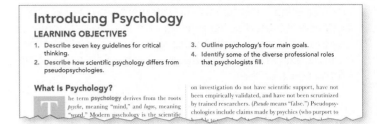

Learning Objectives at the start of each section indicate in behavioural terms the concepts that students are expected to master while reading the section.

Coordinated with the section-opening **Learning Objectives**, **Concept Check** questions at the end of each section allow students to test their comprehension of the learning objectives.

CONCEPT CHECK · STOP

1. What are the four goals of psychology?
2. Why are critical thinking and empirical evidence so important to scientific psychology?
3. What professional fields might psychologists work in?

Author Podcasts accessed via QR codes expand on key concepts or topics to further enhance student understanding and illustrate the real-world relevance.

Evolutionary Psychology: Natural Selection Drives Behaviour and Mental Processes

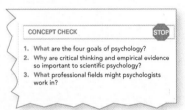

For an interesting discussion on this topic, scan to download the author's podcast.

Evolutionary psychology is based on the premise that many behavioural commonalities, from mating to fighting, emerged and remain in human populations today because they helped our ancestors (and their descendents) survive and reproduce. This perspective stems from the writings and research of Charles Darwin (1859), who theorized that environmental forces

Visualizing features are multipart visual sections that focus on a key concept or topic in the chapter, exploring it in detail or in broader context using a combination of photos, diagrams, and data.

Applying Psychology helps students relate psychological concepts to their own lives and understand how these concepts are applied in various sectors of society, such as the workplace.

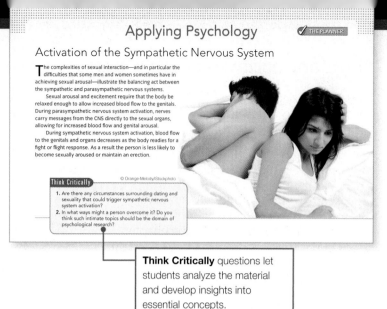

Applying Psychology ✓ THE PLANNER

Activation of the Sympathetic Nervous System

The complexities of sexual interaction—and in particular the difficulties that some men and women sometimes have in achieving sexual arousal—illustrate the balancing act between the sympathetic and parasympathetic nervous systems.

Sexual arousal and excitement require that the body be relaxed enough to allow increased blood flow to the genitals. During parasympathetic nervous system activation, nerves carry messages from the CNS directly to the sexual organs, allowing for increased blood flow and genital arousal.

During sympathetic nervous system activation, blood flow to the genitals and organs decreases as the body readies for a fight or flight response. As a result the person is less likely to become sexually aroused or maintain an erection.

© Orange-Melody/iStockphoto

Think Critically

1. Are there any circumstances surrounding dating and sexuality that could trigger sympathetic nervous system activation?
2. In what ways might a person overcome it? Do you think such intimate topics should be the domain of psychological research?

Think Critically questions let students analyze the material and develop insights into essential concepts.

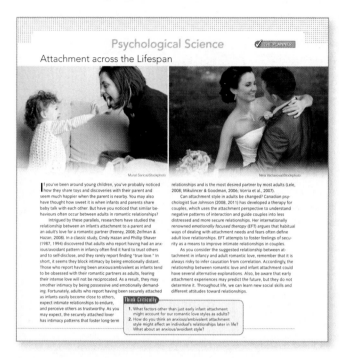

Psychological Science ✓ THE PLANNER

Attachment across the Lifespan

Murat Sarica/iStockphoto   Nina Vaclavova/iStockphoto

If you've been around young children, you've probably noticed how they share toys and discoveries with their parent and seem much happier when the parent is nearby. You may also have thought how sweet it is when infants and parents share baby talk with each other. But have you noticed that similar behaviours often occur between adults in romantic relationships?

Intrigued by these parallels, researchers have studied the relationship between an infant's attachment to a parent and an adult's love for a romantic partner (Feeney, 2008; Zeifman & Hazan, 2008). In a classic study, Cindy Hazan and Phillip Shaver (1987, 1994) discovered that adults who report having had an anxious/avoidant pattern in infancy often find it hard to trust others and to self-disclose, and they rarely report finding "true love." In short, it seems they block intimacy by being emotionally distant. Those who report having been anxious/ambivalent as infants tend to be obsessed with their romantic partners as adults, fearing their intense love will not be reciprocated. As a result, they may smother intimacy by being possessive and emotionally demanding. Fortunately, adults who report having been securely attached as infants easily become close to others, expect intimate relationships to endure, and perceive others as trustworthy. As you may expect, the securely attached lover has intimacy patterns that foster long-term

relationships and is the most desired partner by most adults (Lele, 2008; Mikulincer & Goodman, 2006; Vorria et al., 2007).

Can attachment style in adults be changed? Canadian psychologist Sue Johnson (2008, 2011) has developed a therapy for couples, which uses the attachment perspective to understand negative patterns of interaction and guide couples into less distressed and more secure relationships. Her internationally renowned *emotionally focused therapy* (EFT) argues that habitual ways of dealing with attachment needs and fears often define adult love relationships. EFT attempts to foster feelings of security as a means to improve intimate relationships in couples.

As you consider the suggested relationship between attachment in infancy and adult romantic love, remember that it is always risky to infer causation from correlation. Accordingly, the relationship between romantic love and infant attachment could have several alternative explanations. Also, be aware that early attachment experiences may predict the future, but they do not determine it. Throughout life, we can learn new social skills and different attitudes toward relationships.

Think Critically

1. What factors other than just early infant attachment might account for our romantic love styles as adults?
2. How do you think an anxious/ambivalent attachment style might affect an individual's relationships later in life? What about an anxious/avoidant style?

Psychological Science emphasizes the empirical, scientific nature of psychology by presenting expanded descriptions of current research findings, along with explanations of their significance and possible applications.

What a Psychologist Sees highlights a concept or phenomenon that would stand out to psychologists. Photos and figures are used to improve students' understanding of the usefulness of a psychological perspective and to develop their observational skills.

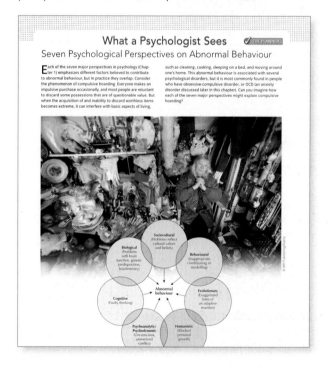

What a Psychologist Sees ✓ THE PLANNER

Seven Psychological Perspectives on Abnormal Behaviour

Each of the seven major perspectives in psychology (Chapter 1) emphasizes different factors believed to contribute to abnormal behaviour, but in practice they overlap. Consider the phenomenon of compulsive hoarding. Everyone makes an impulsive purchase occasionally, and most people are reluctant to discard some possessions that are of questionable value. But when the acquisition of and inability to discard worthless items becomes extreme, it can interfere with basic aspects of living,

such as cleaning, cooking, sleeping on a bed, and moving around one's home. This abnormal behaviour is associated with several psychological disorders, but it is most commonly found in people who have obsessive-compulsive disorder, or OCD (an anxiety disorder discussed later in this chapter). Can you imagine how each of the seven major perspectives might explain compulsive hoarding?

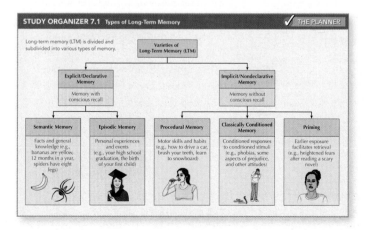

STUDY ORGANIZER 7.1   Types of Long-Term Memory ✓ THE PLANNER

Long-term memory (LTM) is divided and subdivided into various types of memory.

Varieties of Long-Term Memory (LTM)

Explicit/Declarative Memory — Memory with conscious recall

- **Semantic Memory** — Facts and general knowledge (e.g., bananas are yellow, 12 months in a year, spiders have eight legs)
- **Episodic Memory** — Personal experiences and events (e.g., your high school graduation, the birth of your first child)

Implicit/Nondeclarative Memory — Memory without conscious recall

- **Procedural Memory** — Motor skills and habits (e.g., how to drive a car, brush your teeth, learn to snowboard)
- **Classically Conditioned Memory** — Conditioned responses to conditioned stimuli (e.g., phobias, some aspects of prejudice, and other attitudes)
- **Priming** — Earlier exposure facilitates retrieval (e.g., heightened fears after reading a scary novel)

Study Organizers present material in a format that makes it easy to compare different aspects of a topic, thus providing students with a useful tool for enhancing their understanding of the topic and preparing for exams.

Student understanding is assessed at different levels

Wiley Visualizing with *WileyPLUS* offers students lots of practice material for assessing their understanding of each study objective. Students know exactly what they are getting out of each study session through immediate feedback and coaching.

The **Summary** revisits each major section, with informative images taken from the chapter. These visuals reinforce important concepts.

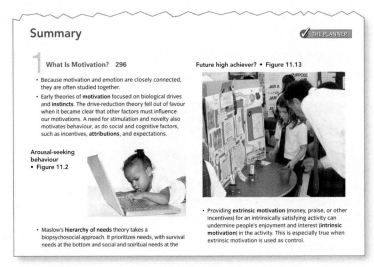

Summary

✔ THE PLANNER

1 What Is Motivation? 296

- Because motivation and emotion are closely connected, they are often studied together.
- Early theories of **motivation** focused on biological drives and **instincts**. The drive-reduction theory fell out of favour when it became clear that other factors must influence our motivations. A need for stimulation and novelty also motivates behaviour, as do social and cognitive factors, such as incentives, **attributions**, and expectations.

Arousal-seeking behaviour • Figure 11.2

Future high achiever? • Figure 11.13

- Providing **extrinsic motivation** (money, praise, or other incentives) for an intrinsically satisfying activity can undermine people's enjoyment and interest (**intrinsic motivation**) in the activity. This is especially true when extrinsic motivation is used as control.

- Maslow's **hierarchy of needs** theory takes a biopsychosocial approach. It prioritizes needs, with survival needs at the bottom and social and spiritual needs at the

Critical and Creative Thinking Questions

1. Do you think there are emotions that might be a product of our evolved instincts (such as anger or fear), and other emotions that are a product of our culture or society (such as guilt or embarrassment)? Is it possible to "learn" emotions from parents and elders?

2. Think about Maslow's hierarchy of needs. Have you ever fulfilled certain higher-level needs without having sufficiently met lower-level needs?

3. Is obesity an eating disorder? Do you think it is more genetic than environmental, or more environmental than genetic? How do you think culture and historical time period influences eating and hunger?

4. Are intimate topics, such as sexual pleasure, arousal, and orgasm, the domain of psychological research? Does psychology go too far when it looks at such private and personal aspects of the human experience?

5. If you were going out on a date with someone or applying for an important job, how might you use the four theories of emotion to increase the chances that things will go well?

6. Have you ever felt depressed after listening to a friend complain about his or her problems? How might this be explained by the facial-feedback hypothesis?

7. Why do you think people around the world experience and express the same basic set of emotions? What evolutionary advantages might help explain these similarities?

Critical and Creative Thinking Questions challenge students to think more broadly about chapter concepts. The level of these questions ranges from simple to advanced; they encourage students to think critically and develop an analytical understanding of the ideas discussed in the chapter.

Visual end-of-chapter **Self-Tests** pose review questions that ask students to demonstrate their understanding of key concepts.

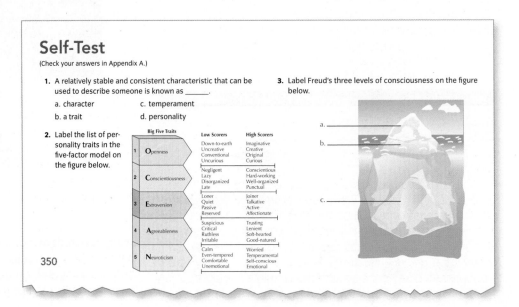

Self-Test

(Check your answers in Appendix A.)

1. A relatively stable and consistent characteristic that can be used to describe someone is known as _____.
   - a. character
   - b. a trait
   - c. temperament
   - d. personality

2. Label the list of personality traits in the five-factor model on the figure below.

Big Five Traits	Low Scorers	High Scorers
1 **O**penness	Down-to-earth Uncreative Conventional Uncurious	Imaginative Creative Original Curious
2 **C**onscientiousness	Negligent Lazy Disorganized Late	Conscientious Hard-working Well-organized Punctual
3 **E**xtroversion	Loner Quiet Passive Reserved	Joiner Talkative Active Affectionate
4 **A**greeableness	Suspicious Critical Ruthless Irritable	Trusting Lenient Soft-hearted Good-natured
5 **N**euroticism	Calm Even-tempered Comfortable Unemotional	Worried Temperamental Self-conscious Emotional

3. Label Freud's three levels of consciousness on the figure below.

a. _____
b. _____
c. _____

350

Why *Visualizing Psychology*?

People are complicated and diverse. We think differently, act differently, and feel differently from one another. Our behaviour differs from one day to the next. We do things for reasons we can explain and often for reasons we cannot. As we age, our views and perspectives change, and we feel differently about the world around us. Across evolutionary time, we have changed as a species—with our expanding frontal lobes came new skills, more complex thought, and more diverse behaviours. These, and a wide variety of related topics, constitute the domain of psychology. We study humans (and non-humans), their similarities, differences, and peculiarities; why they do things and how they think and feel. The study of psychology truly is the study of the human experience. *Visualizing Psychology*, Second Canadian Edition, invites you to explore this remarkable area and learn about a field that has interested people since they first began to wonder about themselves and the world they live in.

Unique Approach

As you might expect, the compelling nature of psychology has attracted the attention of millions of readers, along with a multitude of psychology books. So, what makes *Visualizing Psychology* unique? Why did we write this book? The answer is simple—we believe this book does psychology differently. First, we think that *active learning* and *critical thinking* (two closely related concepts), in conjunction with meaningful, relevant, and engaging examples, are key ingredients to true understanding and lifelong learning. Therefore, we have developed and incorporated a large set of active learning and critical thinking pedagogical tools designed to help you with the material. We have also taken a keen interest in providing examples that are relevant to students. Moreover, in developing the book, we subjected it to the critical eye of student focus groups in a variety of campuses across Canada. Many of their insights have been incorporated into the book, and we are most grateful for their participation.

As the name implies, *Visualizing Psychology* is unique in its focus on visuals. Students today are different from those of 10 or 20 years ago. Most have been raised with bright, high-definition screens, rapidly projecting vivid images and displaying abundant information. These screens let you quickly and readily look at our colourful world and its inhabitants. This textbook acknowledges you as a new breed of learner. It includes all the basic content of a post-secondary psychology text, but enhances the information with an educationally sound and carefully designed visual art program. We have chosen images that we want you to find engaging, relevant, and sometimes even a bit provocative. Our visuals are current, interesting, and new. We wanted visuals that you would not find in other psychology textbooks. In addition, each chapter contains a unique *Visualizing* feature and *Process Diagram* that present a key concept and then explore it in detail using a combination of illustrative photos or figures. As you read

through the text, we encourage you to take full advantage of these and other special study tools, including *Learning Objectives, What a Psychologist Sees, Applying Psychology, Psychological Science, Study Organizers, Concept Checks,* and *Summaries*. Take a look at the Guided Chapter Tour for samples of these special features.

This textbook is intended to serve as a broad overview of the entire field of psychology. *Visualizing Psychology*, like most other survey textbooks, contains a large number of unfamiliar terms and complex concepts. We understand that the language of psychology is new to all but the most seasoned scholars, and we have used care with our terms and definitions to make them uncomplicated and clear. Unlike some other textbooks in psychology, this one is written for every student, and not just those intending to major in psychology.

As you can see, we feel passionate about psychology and about our textbook. We believe that psychology is indeed the finest discipline. The study of psychology offers us all an incomparable window into not only the human experience but also the world that sustains us. As you will see, psychology offers many keys to understanding people and what they think and do. We're eager to share our passion for psychology with you, so let's get started.

Organization

While psychology is renowned for its diversity, if you're like most introductory psychology students, you probably think of psychology as primarily the study of abnormal behaviour and therapy. You'll be quite surprised to discover that our field is much larger, richer, and variable than just these two areas. To organize such a diverse and complex field, our book is divided into 15 chapters that are arranged in a "micro" to "macro" fashion. Generally, we tend to move from the smallest element of behaviour (the neuron and neuroscience) out to the largest (the group, culture, and social psychology). Here is a brief summary of the major topics we explore in each chapter:

- **Chapter 1** discusses the importance of critical thinking, describes psychology's history and its different theoretical perspectives and fundamental questions, and explains how psychologists go about answering those questions.
- **Chapter 2** explains the evolutionary, neural, and other biological bases of behaviour, and lays the groundwork for further discussions of biological foundations that appear in later chapters.
- **Chapter 3** examines interactions among stress, health, well-being, thinking, and behaviour.
- **Chapters 4** through **8** present aspects of cognition (thinking), including sensation, perception, consciousness, learning, memory, language, and intelligence. These chapters examine both typical cognitive processes and cases in which thinking goes awry.

- **Chapters 9** and **10** explore human development across the lifespan, from prenatal development to the post-retirement years, including physical, cognitive, social, moral, and personality development.
- **Chapters 11** and **12** discuss processes and qualities that are integral to our most basic experiences and interactions with one another: motivation, emotion, and personality.
- **Chapter 13** begins by discussing what constitutes abnormal behaviour and how psychological disorders are identified and classified. We discuss the major disorders, their symptoms, how they develop, and, finally, how psychological disorders vary across cultures.
- **Chapter 14** describes and evaluates major forms of therapy, organizing them into three groups: insight therapies, behaviour therapies, and biomedical therapies. We also discuss the different types of therapists and counsellors in Canada who provide psychological help.
- **Chapter 15** discusses how we think about, feel about, and act around other people. In this chapter, we explore a range of social psychological phenomena, from perceptions of others' intentions, to romantic attractions, to prejudice and discrimination, to aggression and bullying.

The **Statistics Module and Psychology** (Appendix B) is a stand-alone section that introduces you to the powerful tools psychologists and other researchers use to analyze their research findings.

New to this edition

Preparation for the second Canadian edition began with a thorough evaluation of the contents of the previous edition by a number of expert reviewers, including students and other users of the text. The main suggestions were to incorporate new research developments, to include features on emerging "hot topics" in various areas of psychology, and to reorganize some textual material to increase readability. We have been responsive to their insightful and invaluable feedback, while maintaining the approach and framework used by *Visualizing Psychology*. Key changes for this edition are as follows.

Contemporary Focus and Student Engagement

Photos, figures, diagrams, and other visuals have been carefully examined and revised to increase their diversity and overall effectiveness as aids to learning, while continuing to engage students and provoke thought. We have presented features, discussions, and examples—many of which are accompanied by critical thinking questions—that are directly relevant to students and that reflect our commitment to student engagement, comprehension, and learning.

To further engage students and generate discussion, each chapter includes a QR code for accessing our podcast on a key concept or topic from a chapter. With these podcasts we take students beyond the classroom and offer a personal and engaging discussion to illustrate the real-world relevance and application of psychology in everyday life.

A central aim in revising this edition was to include expanded coverage of current hot topics in psychology. Some of these topics are bullying and cyber bullying, the effects of alcohol and tobacco on prenatal development, IQ testing, baby sign language, herbal remedies for treating psychological disorders, virtual reality therapy in the treatment of phobias, effects of videogame and media violence on aggression, attachment across the lifespan, eating disorders, gay marriage, human sex differences, stress and well-being, and psychoactive drug use.

Content Revision

This edition has been thoroughly revised and updated in an effort to present the most recent available data and findings in Canadian and international research in psychology, and to provide expanded coverage of key topics and concepts. As a result we have added more than 800 new references throughout this edition. Some examples of key content revisions include:

In Chapter 2 Neuroscience, Evolution, and the Biology of Behaviour, we have added a section outlining the structures of the central nervous system involved in support and protection. As well, because many students often find neural signalling a challenging concept to grasp, this entire section was carefully reviewed and updated for clarity, accuracy, and comprehension.

In Chapter 5 States of Consciousness, we have added content on myths about sleeping and dreaming and on common myths about alcohol consumption, as well as new information on federal regulations involving the packaging and sale of energy drinks and the access and availability of the prescription opiate OxyContin.

In Chapter 10 Lifespan Development II: Social and Personality Development, we have added a section on siblings and peers, as well as a discussion of divorce in Canada, along with recent data on children's continued contact with their fathers following divorce.

In Chapter 11 Motivation and Emotion, we have included new examples of the severe consequences of anorexia nervosa and a new discussion on leptin and its relationship to obesity. A discussion on famous sociologist Alfred Kinsey and his controversial research has been added, and we have also included the most current national census data on same-sex marriage and same-sex cohabitation in Canada.

In Chapter 13 Psychological Disorders, we have included new Canadian data on the incidence of depression, bipolar disorder, schizophrenia, and substance abuse. We have presented a number of well-known cases of Canadian celebrities who have been open about their psychological problems, such as songwriter and musician Matthew Good. We have also included the example of convicted murderer former colonel Russell Williams.

In Chapter 15 Social Psychology, we have included new material on the connection between physical attractiveness and popularity. We've expanded our discussion of bullying and victimization and included a new discussion of the growing problem of cyber bullying.

How Does Wiley Visualizing Support Instructors?

Wiley Visualizing

The Wiley Visualizing site hosts a wealth of information for instructors using Wiley Visualizing, including ways to maximize the visual approach in the classroom and a white paper titled "How Visuals Can Help Students Learn," by Matt Leavitt, instructional design consultant. Visit Wiley Visualizing at www.wiley.com/college/visualizing.

WileyPLUS

This online teaching and learning environment integrates the entire digital textbook with the most effective instructor and student resources to fit every learning style. With *WileyPLUS*:

- Students achieve concept mastery in a rich, structured environment that's available 24/7.
- Instructors personalize and manage their course more effectively with assessment, assignments, grade tracking, and more.

WileyPLUS can be used with or in place of the textbook.

Wiley Custom Select

Wiley Custom Select gives you the freedom to build your course materials exactly the way you want them. Offer your students a cost-efficient alternative to traditional texts. In a simple three-step process, create a solution containing the content you want, in the sequence you want, delivered how you want. Visit Wiley Custom Select at http://customselect.wiley.com.

Media and Supplements

Visualizing Psychology is accompanied by an array of media and supplements that support the textbook to form a pedagogically cohesive package. Features and visuals from the text are incorporated into the media and supplements. For example, a Process Diagram from the book may appear in the *Instructor's Resource Guide* with suggestions on using it as a PowerPoint in the classroom or it may be the subject of a short animation.

Book Companion Site

www.wiley.com/go/huffmancanada

All instructor resources (the Test Bank, Instructor's Resource Guide, PowerPoint presentations, and all textbook illustrations and photos in jpeg format) are housed on the book companion site (www.wiley.com/go/huffmancanada). Student resources include self-quizzes and a **free** online study guide.

Videos

A collection of videos, including CBC videos, has been selected to accompany and enrich the text. These videos and animations illustrate and expand on a concept or topic to aid student understanding. The textbook's Media Integration Guide provides a description of each video and animation along with questions to further develop student understanding. Videos and animations are available in *WileyPLUS*.

PowerPoint Presentations
(Available in *WileyPLUS* and on the book companion site.)

A complete set of highly visual media-integrated PowerPoint presentations is available online and in *WileyPLUS* to enhance classroom presentations. Tailored to the text's topical coverage and learning objectives, these presentations are designed to convey key text concepts, illustrated by embedded text art.

Image Gallery

Photographs, illustrations, and other visuals from the text are online and can be used as you wish in the classroom. These files allow you to easily incorporate them into your own customized PowerPoint presentations.

Test Bank
(Available in *WileyPLUS* and on the book companion site.)

The Test Bank contains approximately 1,200 test items, including multiple-choice and essay questions that test a variety of comprehension levels. The Test Bank is available in two formats: online in Word files and as a computerized Test Bank. The easy-to-use test-generation program fully supports graphics, printed tests, student answer sheets, and answer keys. The software's advanced features allow you to create an exam to your exact specifications.

Instructor's Manual
(Available in *WileyPLUS* and on the book companion site.)

The Instructor's Manual provides a summary and outline of each section in the chapter. It includes suggestions for in-class activities, lecture extenders, discussion points for critical and creative thinking, and suggestions for additional resources (videos, websites, and books) for the chapter. Also included are suggestions for using the visuals throughout the chapter.

Wiley Faculty Network

The Wiley Faculty Network (WFN) is a global community of faculty, connected by a passion for teaching and a drive to learn, share, and collaborate. Their mission is to promote the effective use of technology and enrich the teaching experience. Connect with the Wiley Faculty Network to collaborate with your colleagues, find a mentor, attend virtual and live events, and view a wealth of resources all designed to help you grow as an educator. Visit the Wiley Faculty Network at www.wherefacultyconnect.com.

About the Authors

Karen Huffman is a professor of psychology at Palomar College in San Marcos, California, where she teaches full-time and serves as the Psychology Student Advisor and Co-Coordinator for Psychology Faculty. Karen received the National Teaching Award for Excellence given by Division Two of the American Psychological Association (APA). She also was recognized with the first Distinguished Faculty Award for Excellence in Teaching from Palomar College, and an Outstanding Teaching award from the University of Texas at Austin. Karen's special research and presentation focus is in active learning and critical thinking, and she has presented numerous online seminars and workshops throughout the United States, Canada, and Puerto Rico. Karen is the author of Wiley introductory psychology texts, including *Psychology in Action* and *Living Psychology*.

Alastair J. Younger is a professor of psychology at the University of Ottawa. He received his B.A. in psychology from Carleton University in Ottawa in 1976, after which he studied clinical and developmental psychology at Concordia University in Montreal, completing his M.A. in 1979 and his Ph.D. in 1984. He is registered as a clinical psychologist with the College of Psychologists of Ontario and is a member of the Canadian Psychological Association and the Society for Research in Child Development. He is co-author of the first three Canadian editions of *Child Psychology* (Wiley). In addition, he has authored more than 15 student study guides for courses in introductory psychology, child psychology, and abnormal psychology. He has been a professor at the University of Ottawa since 1985, where he is currently Director of Undergraduate Programs in Psychology. He coordinates the introductory psychology courses at the University of Ottawa in both English and French and has taught courses in child psychology, theories of development, social development, and research methods and ethics. His research focuses on children's peer relations, especially shyness/withdrawal and aggression in children.

Claire Vanston is a psychology instructor at Capilano University in North Vancouver, British Columbia. She earned her B.A. (Hons.) in Psychology in 1997, and completed a Master of Science in biological psychology in 2000, and a Ph.D. in 2005. She has been the recipient of four national-level research scholarships and is a published experimental psychologist. She is also the owner and director of Evidence-Based Education (www.drclaire.ca), a B.C. business that offers school-based elementary and high school sexual health/puberty curriculum. She has authored nearly a dozen post-secondary student study guides and instructor manuals in psychology and human sexuality. Dr. Vanston has taught courses for many years at Capilano University and elsewhere in the areas of introductory psychology, biological psychology, human neuropsychology, lifespan development, research methods, and human sexuality. She is a mother of daughters, a consummate educator (and learner), and a devout fan of the CBC show *Dragons' Den*, and is described by her students as "not your average psych prof."

Acknowledgements

Professional Feedback

Throughout the process of writing and developing this text—both the first and second edition—and the visual pedagogy, we benefited from the comments and constructive criticism provided by the instructors listed below. We offer our sincere appreciation to these individuals for their helpful review:

Margie Bader, *Seneca College*
Cheryl Berezuik, *Grand Prairie Regional College*
Judy Berger, *John Abbott College*
Rena Borovilos, *Humber College*
Cindy Chisvin, *Seneca College*
Kimberley Clow, *University of Ontario Institute of Technology*
Kriten Deuzman, *Algonquin College*
Jill Esmonde, *Georgian College*
Renee Ferguson, *Georgian College*
Robin Gagnon, *Dawson College*
Stephane Gaskin, *Concordia University*
Tom Hanrahan, *Canadore College*
Ralph Hofmann, *Durham College*
Sue Honsberger, *Algonquin College*
Naomi Kestenbaum, *Seneca College*
Linda Lysynchuk, *Laurentian University*

Colleen Mahy, *George Brown College*
Dawn More, *Algonquin College*
Luigi Pasto, *John Abbott College*
Susana Phillips, *Kwantlen Polytechnic University*
Ruth Rogers, *Durham College*
Jonah Santa-Barbara, *Mohawk College*
Donald Sharpe, *University of Regina*
Joel St. Pierre, *Mohawk College*
Karen Taylor, *NorQuest College*
Karen Tee, *Vanier College*
Mary Trant, *Seneca College*
Jessica Trinier, *Seneca College*
Paul Valliant, *Laurentian University*
Stephen White, *Champlain College*
Frank Winstan, *Vanier College*
Daniel Yepes, *Seneca College*

Special Thanks

Thank you to the team at Wiley for your commitment to excellence and your professionalism. Very special thanks to Gail Brown, our developmental editor, who worked tirelessly to transform our ideas into this beautiful book—without your patience, conscientiousness, commitment, and expertise, this book would not be what it is. We also owe heartfelt thanks to our Acquisitions Editor, Rodney Burke—it is your vision and effort that has continued to drive and direct this project.

We also thank Dawn Hunter and Laurel Hyatt for their editorial and proofreading contributions, which were very much appreciated.

Our sincerest thanks are also offered to those who worked on, and contributed to, the wide assortment of supplements and ancillaries: Madeleine Côté, Dawson College (Instructor's Resource Guide); Jill Esmonde, Georgian College (Instructor's Resource Guide); Ralph Hofmann, Durham College (PowerPoint presentations and student practice quizzes); and Dawn More, Algonquin College (PowerPoint presentations and student practice quizzes). In addition, a heartfelt thank you to Deanna Durnford for coordinating them all.

All the writing and production of this book would be wasted without the energetic and dedicated sales and marketing staff. We wish to sincerely thank the marketing team and sales representatives for their tireless efforts on behalf of this book.

From Alastair Younger: To my wife, Manal—thank you for all your wonderful ideas and advice as we discussed the content of each chapter, and for your encouragement and steadfast support throughout the production of this book. To my son Daniel—thank you for your special insight into the world of college students and for taking the time to discuss ideas with me. To my daughter Melanie—thank you for inspiring many of the creative examples that I used in this book and for always being so supportive.

From Claire Vanston: Thanks first to all my students—you are my source of inspiration. To Jennifer Sorochan—your ability to identify and find those elusive references made my job so much easier. And to my family: Dwayne, I could not have done this without you and your unwavering support. Thank you for the time, understanding, and patience you always unconditionally offer me. Bianca and Alex, thanks for understanding that I need to be more than a Mum, and Sophie, Jerry, and Rian—this book is for you.

Scott Hailstone/iStockphoto

Bartosz Hadyniak/iStockphoto

Contents

Kristian Sekulic/iStockphoto

Darryl Dyck/The Canadian Press

© RubberBall/Alamy Limited

© AP/Wide World Photos

Tetra Images/Getty Image

Blend Images/Superstock

jjmm888/iStockphoto

Scott Dunlap/iStockphoto

Mark Bowden/iStockphoto

gaspr13/iStockphoto

Edward Mallia/iStockphoto

Tanya Constantine/Photographer's Choice

digitalskillet/iStockphoto

a-wrangler/iStockphoto

Visualizing Features

Process Diagrams

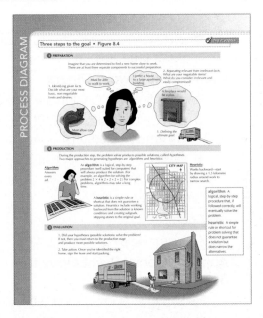

WileyPLUS

WileyPLUS is a research-based online environment for effective teaching and learning.

WileyPLUS builds students' confidence because it takes the guesswork out of studying by providing students with a clear roadmap:

- what to do
- how to do it
- if they did it right

It offers interactive resources along with a complete digital textbook that help students learn more. With *WileyPLUS*, students take more initiative so you'll have greater impact on their achievement in the classroom and beyond.

or more information, visit www.wileyplus.com

WileyPLUS

SECOND CANADIAN EDITION

VISUALIZING
PSYCHOLOGY

Introduction and Research Methods

1

What might compel a person to willingly dangle hundreds of feet above the ground? What binds mothers—human and non-human alike—to their young? How can chronic stress contribute to serious health problems, such as cancer and heart disease? Why are men and women so sexually different? What happens when ancient cultural practices and evolved tendencies collide with the demands of modern living? All these questions, and countless more, are the province of psychology.

Psychology is a dynamic field that affects every part of our lives. It encompasses our most private thoughts, our relationships, our physiology, our politics, our gut feelings, and our deliberate decisions. It examines complex interactions that affect us at every level, from the cellular to the cultural, across evolutionary time and into the future. It truly is the study of the human experience. Psychology encompasses not only humankind but also our non-human compatriots—from sea snails and pigeons, to cats and chimps.

Psychologists work in an incredible range of areas, perhaps more than you might realize. In addition to studying and treating abnormal behaviour, psychologists study sleep, dreaming, stress, health, drugs, personality, sexuality, motivation, emotion, learning, memory, childhood, aging, death, love, conformity, intelligence, creativity, and much, much more.

CHAPTER OUTLINE

CHAPTER PLANNER ✔

- ❏ Study the picture and read the opening story.
- ❏ Scan the Learning Objectives in each section:
  p. 4 ❏   p. 9 ❏   p. 13 ❏   p. 17 ❏   p. 27 ❏
- ❏ Read the text and study all visuals.
  Answer any questions.

Analyze key features

- ❏ Psychological Science, p. 7
- ❏ What a Psychologist Sees, p. 11
- ❏ Study Organizer: p. 12 ❏   p. 18 ❏
- ❏ Process Diagram: p. 14 ❏   p. 19 ❏   p. 28 ❏
- ❏ Visualizing, p. 24
- ❏ Applying Psychology, p. 29 ❏
- ❏ Stop: Answer the Concept Checks before you go on:
  p. 8 ❏   p. 12 ❏   p. 17 ❏   p. 24 ❏   p. 30 ❏

End of chapter

- ❏ Review the Summary and Key Terms.
- ❏ Answer the Critical and Creative Thinking Questions.
- ❏ Complete the Self-Test and check your answers.

Jacob Sjöman Svensson/iStock

Introducing Psychology

LEARNING OBJECTIVES

1. **Describe** seven key guidelines for critical thinking.
2. **Describe** how scientific psychology differs from pseudopsychologies.
3. **Outline** psychology's four main goals.
4. **Identify** some of the diverse professional roles that psychologists fill.

What Is Psychology?

The term **psychology** derives from the roots *psyche*, meaning "mind," and *logos*, meaning "word." Modern psychology is the scientific study of **behaviour** and **mental processes**. Behaviour is anything we do—from sleeping to eating to rock climbing. Mental processes are our private, internal experiences: thoughts, perceptions, feelings, memories, hopes, and dreams (**Table 1.1**).

> **psychology** The scientific study of behaviour and mental processes.

For many psychologists, the most important part of the definition of psychology is the word *scientific*. Psychology places very high value on empirical evidence and critical thinking. We have included a detailed discussion of both these terms later in this chapter. First, we want to differentiate psychology from its cheap imitator: pseudopsychology.

Be careful not to confuse scientific psychology with pseudopsychologies, which may claim to be scientific but on investigation do not have scientific support, have not been empirically validated, and have not been scrutinized by trained researchers. (*Pseudo* means "false.") Pseudopsychologies include claims made by psychics (who purport to be able to read thoughts and foretell the future), palmistry (reading people's character from the markings on their palms), psychometry (determining facts about an object by handling it), psychokinesis (moving objects by purely mental means), astrology (the study of how the positions of the stars and planets influence people's personalities and affairs), and other similar fields (**Figure 1.1**).

Psychology Is about Critical Thinking; Life Is about Critical Thinking

In his book *Challenging your Preconceptions: Thinking Critically about Psychology*, Randolf A. Smith (2002) begins the preface with the heading you have just read (Smith, 2002). In his book he outlines seven essential

For an interesting discussion on this topic, scan to download the author's podcast.

Test your knowledge of psychology   Table 1.1

Answer true of false to the following statements:

1. The best way to learn and remember information is to study it intensively during one concentrated period.

2. Most brain activity stops during sleep.

3. Subliminal persuasion is a powerful way to influence our behaviour.

4. Punishment is the most effective way to permanently change behaviour.

5. Eyewitness testimony is often unreliable.

6. Polygraph (lie detector) tests can accurately and reliably reveal whether a person is lying.

7. Behaviours that are unusual or that violate social norms indicate a psychological disorder.

8. People with schizophrenia have two or more distinct personalities.

9. Similarity is one of the best predictors of long-term relationships.

10. In an emergency, as the number of bystanders increases, your chance of getting help decreases.

Answers: 1. False (Chapter 1). 2. False (Chapter 5). 3. False (Chapter 5). 4. False (Chapter 4). 5. True (Chapter 6). 6. False (Chapter 11). 7. False (Chapter 15). 8. False (Chapter 13). 9. True (Chapter 13). 10. True (Chapter 15).

"The Amazing Randi" • Figure 1.1

Do you believe there is such a thing as psychic power? James Randi, magician and director of the James Randi Educational Corporation, has dedicated his life to educating the public about fraudulent pseudopsychologies. Along with the prestigious MacArthur Foundation, Randi has long offered $1 million to "anyone who proves a genuine psychic power under proper observing conditions" (About James Randi, 2002; James Randi Educational Foundation, 2008). We discuss Randi and his prize further in Chapter 4.

Alan Diaz/AP/The Canadian Press

critical thinking
The ability to accurately analyze information and be able to draw rational, fact-based conclusions based on the empirical evidence provided.

guidelines for critical thinking, listed below. The term **critical thinking** is defined as the ability to accurately analyze information and be able to draw rational, fact-based conclusions based on the empirical evidence provided. This type of thinking is not only required for psychology but is also essential for everyday life. Every day we are bombarded with advertising claims, news reports, anecdotes, and apparent facts provided by "experts," all purported to be truths. Critical thinking allows us to evaluate these claims.

1. *Critical thinkers are flexible and can tolerate ambiguity and uncertainty.* The process of scientific discovery is neither linear, nor perfect, nor quick. Understanding the world and the people in it takes time and patience. Critical thinkers appreciate that it takes many studies to understand a psychological phenomenon. Seldom does one single study solve the problem or answer the question. Critical thinkers also acknowledge there is diversity and variation in most areas. They resist the urge to neatly compartmentalize the world, and always appreciate that knowledge has grey areas more often than black and white ones.

2. *Critical thinkers can identify inherent biases and assumptions.* A **bias** occurs when a belief prevents fair judgement on an issue. An **assumption** is something taken for granted to be true. It takes skill to identify biases and assumptions in claims and even greater skill to identify them in ourselves. We

bias When a belief prevents fair judgement of an issue.

assumption Something taken for granted to be true.

are much less likely to question evidence or statements that fit with an existing belief than those that do not. For example, the statement "yoga improves concentration" is much more likely to be accepted without question than the statement "raspberry ice cream improves concentration." The former fits with our general beliefs. Although we are much more likely to question the latter statement, we should question *both* claims.

3. *Critical thinkers are sceptical.* Critical thinkers must maintain an air of cautious suspicion when evaluating the claims of others. If it sounds too convenient, too good, or too simplistic to be true, then it probably is. Never accept anything on authority; insist that claims be supported with **empirical evidence**. This is evidence obtained from experimentation, formal observation, or measurement (usually in the

empirical evidence Information acquired by formal observation, experimentation, and measurement by using systematic scientific methods.

form of research studies). Be careful of statements that appear to be derived from received wisdom. It is perfectly okay to ask, "How do you know that?" Base your decision on the response to that question. Be wary of such responses as "everybody knows" or "my friend/mom/aunt/teacher told me." Neither are empirical sources.

4. *Critical thinkers separate facts from opinion.* A major difference between scientists and non-scientists is that scientists are trained to ignore opinions and look for quality evidence. The standard of evidence in psychological science is empirical evidence. Opinions, urban myths, old wives tales, good stories, and TV shows are not empirical sources and are therefore not valid forms of scientific evidence. Likewise, critical thinkers do not fall into the trap of *argument by anecdote*, which is when the evidence provided is a personal story or word-of-mouth description. Simply because someone told you it worked for them is not evidence that it has worked. Often in first-year college and university courses students are challenged when general psychological principles and findings contradict their personal experiences and beliefs. If this happens to you, look for the empirical evidence.

5. *Critical thinkers do not oversimplify.* Although simple explanations are often appealing, and many of us want to find solutions to problems quickly, the world generally does not work that way. People, their thinking, and their behaviours are complex, diverse, and ambiguous. Scientific questions are often complicated. Psychological problems are not solved in one hour of therapy, or before the next commercial break (as some afternoon TV shows would have you believe). Critical thinkers understand that although simple explanations can be appealing, they are often too simple to be correct.

6. *Critical thinkers make logical inferences.* If your friend told you he was going to school at 8 a.m. today when he normally leaves at noon, you might infer he wanted to study, go to the library, or work on a project. Your logical inference follows on from the information given. It would not be logical for you to infer your friend was going to school early because he was going to be teleported to Jupiter. Similarly, critical thinkers use logical inference processes in their own thinking and in evaluating the claims of others. If it sounds weird, inconsistent, or illogical, then ask more questions.

7. *Critical thinkers examine the available evidence.* This is probably the most important of all seven guidelines. Good critical thinkers generally use this one the most. Because empirical evidence is the general standard used to evaluate claims, ideas, and information, if

Not all evidence is empirical • Figure 1.2 ___

As this cartoon humorously illustrates, critical thinking requires a skill in evaluating the quality of the evidence provided.

Sources of empirical psychology evidence
Scholarly journal articles
Psychology textbooks

Sources that should be verified
Websites
News programs
Newspapers
Documentary TV shows

Sources that should not be used to make empirical claims
Anecdotes
Urban myths
Old wives' tales
Fables and legends
Horoscopes
Television shows, including sitcoms

someone cannot support a claim with some proof, the statement should be discounted. If you are in doubt, ask questions and always look at the quality of the evidence (**Figure 1.2**).

Probably by now you are getting the idea that psychologists are not just therapists and counsellors but are a much more diverse group. This is indeed the case. Psychologists work as researchers, teachers, and consultants

The Fundamental Goals of Psychology

Scientific psychology has four basic goals: to describe, explain, predict, and change behaviour or mental processes through the use of scientific methods. Let's consider each within the context of aggressive behaviour.

Psychologists usually attempt to describe, or name and classify, particular behaviours by making careful scientific observations. Description is usually the first step in understanding behaviour and mental processes. For example, if someone says, "Men are more aggressive than women," we would ask what is meant by the term *aggressive*. Does aggressive mean angry? Prone to yelling? Likely to throw the first punch? Scientific description requires specificity in terms.

An explanation addresses why a behaviour or mental process occurred. To explain a behaviour or mental process, we need to discover and understand its causes. One of the

nature-nurture controversy
Historical dispute over the relative contributions of nature (heredity) and nurture (environment) in the development of behaviour and mental processes.

most enduring debates in science has been the **nature-nurture controversy** (Gardiner & Kosmitski, 2005; McCrae, 2004). To what extent are we controlled by biological and genetic factors (the nature side), or by environment and learning (the nurture side)? Today, almost all scientists agree that most psychological, and even physical, qualities reflect an interaction between nature and nurture. For example, research indicates that there are numerous interacting causes or explanations for aggression, including culture, socialization and learning, genes, nervous systems, and high levels of testosterone (e.g., Bjorklund & Pellegrini, 2011; Bushman & Huesmann, 2010; Dodge et al., 2008; Rhee & Waldman, 2011).

After describing and explaining a behaviour, an event, or a mental process, psychologists try to predict the conditions under which it is likely to occur in the future. For instance, knowing that excessive alcohol consumption leads to increased aggression (Tremblay, Graham, & Wells, 2008), we might predict that more fights will erupt in places where alcohol is consumed such as in clubs and bars. We discuss this Canadian study in more detail in Chapter 15.

The final goal of psychology is to change behaviour. To psychologists, change means applying psychological knowledge to prevent unwanted outcomes or to bring about desired goals. In almost all cases, change as a goal of psychology is positive. For example, psychologists help people stop addictive behaviours,

Yuri Arcurs/123RF.com

improve their work environments, learn better, become less depressed, improve their family relationships, control their temper, and so on.

Think Critically

Why might psychologists be interested in describing, explaining, predicting, and changing internal mental processes, such as the emotion expressed here? Isn't actual behaviour more relevant? Why or why not?

Areas of specialization in psychology   Table 1.2

Area of Specialization	What a Psychologist Does
Biopsychology or neuroscience	Investigates the relationship among biology, behaviour, and mental processes, including how physical and chemical processes affect the structure and function of the brain and nervous system
Clinical psychology	Specializes in the evaluation, diagnosis, and treatment of psychological disorders
Cognitive psychology	Studies mental processes, including thought, memory, intelligence, creativity, and language
Counselling psychology	Overlaps with clinical psychology, but practitioners tend to work with less seriously disturbed individuals and conduct more career and vocational assessments
Developmental psychology	Studies human growth and development from conception until death (womb to tomb)
Educational and school psychology	Studies the process of education and works to promote the intellectual, social, and emotional development of children in the school environment
Experimental psychology	Examines processes, such as learning, conditioning, motivation, emotion, sensation, and perception, in humans and other animals. (The term *experimental psychologist* is somewhat misleading because psychologists working in almost all areas of specialization also conduct research.)
Forensic psychology	Applies principles of psychology to the criminal justice system, including jury selection, psychological profiling, and so on
Gender and/or cultural psychology	Investigates how men and women and different cultures differ from one another and how they are similar
Health psychology	Studies how biological, psychological, and social factors affect health and illness
Industrial/organizational psychology	Applies the principles of psychology to the workplace, including personnel selection and evaluation, leadership, job satisfaction, employee motivation, and group processes within the organization
Social psychology	Investigates the role of social forces and interpersonal behaviour, including aggression, prejudice, love, helping, conformity, and attitudes
Evolutionary psychology	Studies behaviour and mental processes as products of natural selection and evolutionary change

in academic, business, industrial, and government settings, or in a combination of settings (**Table 1.2**). For more information about what psychologists do—or how to pursue a career in psychology—visit the websites of the Canadian Psychological Association (CPA; www.cpa.ca), the American Psychological Association (APA; www.apa.org), and the Association for Psychological Science (APS; www.psychologicalscience.org).

CONCEPT CHECK STOP

1. **What** are the four goals of psychology?
2. **Why** are critical thinking and empirical evidence so important to scientific psychology?
3. **What** professional fields might psychologists work in?

The Origins of Psychology

LEARNING OBJECTIVES

1. **Describe** the different perspectives represented by the early psychologists.
2. **Identify** a fundamental difference between the psychoanalytic and behaviourist perspectives.
3. **Explain** the central idea underlying the biopsychosocial model.

hd I had to • — indeed me 2

Although people have always been interested in human nature (think about why you took this course), it was not until the first psychological laboratory was founded in 1879 that psychology as a science officially began. As interest in the new field grew, psychologists adopted various perspectives and made decisions on the "appropriate" topics for psychological research and the "proper" research methods needed to investigate them. These diverse viewpoints and subsequent debates have shaped and cultivated the psychology we know today.

A Brief History of Psychology

Wilhelm Wundt [VILL-helm Voont; (1832–1920)], generally acknowledged as the father of modern psychology, established the first psychological laboratory in Germany in 1879. Wundt helped train the first scientific psychologists and wrote one of psychology's most important books, *Principles of Physiological Psychology*, which was published in 1874.

Wundt and his followers were primarily interested in how we form sensations (from our senses), images, and feelings. Their chief methodology was termed *introspection*, which involved monitoring and reporting on our inner world or conscious experiences (Goodwin, 2011). Edward Titchener, one of Wundt's students, brought his ideas to North America. Titchener's approach, now known as **structuralism**, sought to identify the basic building blocks, or structures, of thoughts through introspection, and then determine how these elements combine to form the whole experience. Just as we understand carbon dioxide by considering its components—carbon and oxygen—structuralists believed they could unravel the complexities of consciousness by understanding its component parts. Because introspection could not be used to study animals, children, or more complex mental disorders, structuralism failed as a working psychological approach. Although short-lived, structuralism established a model for studying mental processes scientifically. In fact, James

Mark Baldwin, who in 1889 established the first psychological laboratory in Canada at the University of Toronto, was influenced by this approach, having completed some of his graduate training in Germany with Wundt (Cairns & Cairns, 2006; Wright & Myers, 1982).

Structuralism's intellectual successor, **functionalism**, studied how the mind functions to help humans and other animals adapt to their environment. This early form of psychology was interested in why mental processes existed in the first place and their adaptive significance to the organism. It's no surprise to learn that functionalism, led by American William James (**Figure 1.3**), was strongly influenced by Charles Darwin's theory of evolution by natural selection (Chapter 2) (Green, 2009). Although functionalism also eventually declined, it expanded the scope of psychology to include research on emotions and observable behaviours, initiated the psychological testing movement, and influenced modern education and industry.

William James (1842–1910) • Figure 1.3

William James broadened psychology to include the study of animal behaviour, the influence of biological processes, and observable behaviours. His book *Principles of Psychology* (1890) was the first textbook in psychology and took him 12 years to write.

© Bettmann/Corbis Images

During the late nineteenth and early twentieth centuries, while functionalism was prominent in the United States, the **psychoanalytic school** was forming in Europe (Gay, 2000). Its founder, Austrian physician Sigmund Freud, believed the human mind contains a province hidden from conscious awareness where urges, wishes, and drives reside, which could influence thinking and behaviour. According to Freud, this region, called the *unconscious*, would cause psychological problems when conflicts arise between "acceptable" behaviour and "unacceptable" unconscious sexual or aggressive motives (Chapter 12). The theory provided a basis for a system of talk therapy known as *psychoanalysis* in which a specially trained psychoanalyst helps the patient gain insight into the conflicts hidden in the elusive unconscious (Chapter 14).

Freud's non-scientific approach and emphasis on sexual and aggressive impulses have long been controversial, and today few strictly Freudian psychoanalysts are left. But the broad features of his theory profoundly influenced psychotherapy and psychiatry.

In the early twentieth century, another major perspective appeared that dramatically shaped the future course of psychology. Unlike earlier approaches, the **behaviourist perspective** emphasizes objective, observable environmental influences on overt behaviour. Behaviourism's founder, John B. Watson (1913), vociferously rejected the practice of introspection as a method of research, and the notion that unconscious forces could influence behaviour. Instead, Watson adopted Russian physiologist Ivan Pavlov's concept of *conditioning* (Chapter 6) to explain behaviour in terms of observable stimuli (in the environment) and observable responses (behavioural actions).

Most early behaviourist research was focused on learning, and non-human animals were ideal subjects for this research. One of the best-known behaviourists, B. F. Skinner, was convinced that behaviourist approaches could be used to "shape" human and other animal behaviour. Therapeutic techniques rooted in the behaviourist perspective have been most successful in treating observable behavioural problems, such as anxiety and phobias (Chapter 13) (**Figure 1.4**).

Although the psychoanalytic and behaviourist perspectives dominated North American psychology for some time, in the 1950s a new approach emerged, the **humanistic perspective**, which stressed human qualities of *free will* (voluntarily chosen behaviour) and *self-actualization* (a state of self-fulfillment to achieve our highest potential). According to Carl Rogers and Abraham Maslow, two

B. F. Skinner (1904–1990) and the conditioning box he developed • Figure 1.4 _____

B. F. Skinner was one of the most influential psychologists of the twentieth century. He believed that by using basic learning principles to shape human behaviour, we could change what he perceived as the negative course of humankind. He developed the conditioning box (shown here) to study behaviour and its consequences.

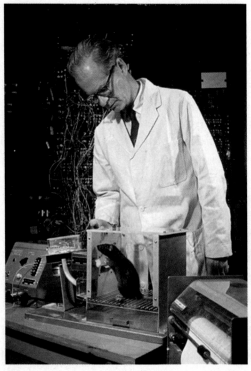

Nina Leen/Time & Life Pictures/Getty Images

central humanist figures, all individuals naturally strive to develop and move toward self-actualization. Like psychoanalysis, humanist psychology developed an influential theory of personality and a form of psychotherapy (chapters 12 and 14). The humanistic approach also provided the foundation for a contemporary research specialty known as *positive psychology*—the scientific study of optimal human functioning (Snyder, Lopez, et al., 2011).

One of the most powerful influential modern approaches, the **cognitive perspective**, recalls psychology's earliest years by emphasizing thoughts, perceptions, and information processing. Modern cognitive psychologists, however, study how we gather, encode, and store information by using our vast array of mental processes. These include perception, memory, imagery, concept formation, problem solving, intelligence, reasoning, decision-making, and language. Many cognitive psychologists employ what is called an *information-processing approach*, likening the mind to a computer that sequentially takes in information, processes it, and then produces a response (Chapter 7).

During the last few decades, scientists have explored the role of biological factors in almost every area of psychology. Using sophisticated tools and technologies, scientists who adopt this **neuroscientific or biopsychological perspective** examine behaviour through the lens of genetics and the biological processes of the brain and nervous system.

The **evolutionary perspective** stresses natural selection (Chapter 2), adaptation, and the evolution of behaviour and mental processes. This perspective seeks to understand human and other animal behaviour in terms of its evolutionary past. Because natural selection favours behaviours and traits that confer a reproductive or survival advantage, traits and preferences that are with us today provide clues to our ancestral history. Similarly, knowledge and theories of our ancestral past help us understand our modern behaviour and mental processes.

Finally, the **sociocultural perspective** emphasizes social interactions and cultural determinants of behaviour and mental processes. Although we are often unaware of their influence, such factors as ethnicity, religion, occupation, and socio-economic class have an enormous impact on our mental processes and behaviour.

Early schools of psychological thought, such as structuralism and functionalism, have almost entirely disappeared or have been blended into newer, broader perspectives. Contemporary psychology reflects seven major perspectives: psychoanalytic/psychodynamic, behaviourist, humanistic, cognitive, neuroscientific/biopsychological, evolutionary, and sociocultural (**Study Organizer 1.1**). Yet the complex behaviours and mental processes humans and other animals exhibit require complex explanations. That is why most contemporary psychologists do not adhere to one single intellectual psychological perspective. Instead, a more integrative, unifying theme—the **biopsychosocial model**—has gained wide acceptance. This model views biological processes (e.g., genetics, the nervous system, and evolution), psychological factors (e.g., learning, thinking, emotion, personality, and motivation), and social forces (e.g., family, school, culture, ethnicity, social class, and politics) as interrelated, inseparable influences (see *What a Psychologist Sees: The Biopsychosocial Model*).

> **biopsychosocial model** A unifying theme of modern psychology that considers biological, psychological, and social processes.

What a Psychologist Sees

✓ THE PLANNER

The Biopsychosocial Model

Look at the young person in this photo. What might be the cause of her emotional arousal? Now look at the next photo, which shows her within a broader context. With this "bigger picture" (the immediate surroundings, her parents' guiding influence, and her culture's enthusiasm for exciting sporting events) in mind, can you better understand why she might be feeling and behaving as she is? The biopsychosocial model recognizes that there is usually no single cause for our behaviour or our mental states. For example, our moods and feelings are often influenced by genetics, hormones, and neurotransmitters (biology), our learned responses and patterns of thinking (psychology), and our socioeconomic status and cultural views of emotion (social).

Tim Mantoani/Masterfile

Perspectives

Psychoanalytic/ Psychodynamic

Major Emphases

Unconscious processes, unresolved past conflicts, and interpersonal relationships

Paula Connelly/ iStockphoto

Behaviourist

Objective, observable environmental influences on overt behaviour

Ilya Stcherbakov/iStockphoto

Humanistic

Free will, self-actualization, and human nature as naturally positive and growth-seeking

Jacob Wackerhausen/iStockphoto

Cognitive

Thinking, perceiving, problem solving, memory, language, and information processing

Vikram Raghuvanshi/iStockphoto

Neuroscientific/ Biopsychological

Genetics and biological processes in the brain and other parts of the nervous system

Jana Blašková/ iStockphoto

Evolutionary

Natural selection, genetics, adaptation, and evolution of behaviour and mental processes

Warwick Lister-Kaye/iStockphoto

Sociocultural

Social interaction and the cultural determinants of behaviour and mental processes

kali9/iStockphoto

The Biopsychosocial Model
The biopsychosocial model combines and interacts with the seven major perspectives.

CONCEPT CHECK   STOP

1. **Which** early schools of psychological thought are reflected in modern perspectives?

2. **Why** did structuralism decline in popularity?

3. **What** modern perspective views biological, psychological, and social forces as interrelated influences on behaviour?

The Science of Psychology

LEARNING OBJECTIVES

1. **Compare** the fundamental goals of basic and applied research.
2. **Describe** the scientific method.
3. **Identify** how psychologists protect the rights of human and non-human research participants and psychotherapy clients.
4. **Explain** why research with non-human animals is valuable.
5. **Explain** why plagiarism is ethically wrong.

In science, research strategies are generally categorized as either basic or applied. **Basic research** is typically conducted in universities or research laboratories by researchers who are interested in advancing general scientific understanding, and testing theories. Complementing basic research is **applied research**. Applied research can be conducted either outside or inside the laboratory, and its goal is to change existing real-world problems by using research results.

Basic and applied research often interact, with one building on the other. For example, after basic research identified how chronic sleep deprivation impairs performance, more applied research showed how sleep extensions (that is, getting more sleep) improve both reaction time and mood in people (Kamdar, et al., 2004). Findings like this have important implications for sports medicine and industrial psychology.

> **basic research**
> Research conducted to advance scientific knowledge and test scientific theories.
>
> **applied research**
> Research designed to solve practical real-world problems using research findings.

The Scientific Method: An Organized Way of Discovering

Like scientists in any field, psychologists follow strict, standardized scientific procedures so that others can understand, interpret, and repeat or retest their findings. Most scientific studies involve six basic steps (**Figure 1.5**). The **scientific method** is cyclical and additive, and scientific progress comes from repeatedly challenging and

> **scientific method**
> A systematic and orderly procedure for understanding and learning about the world.

revising existing theories and creating new ones. When different scientists, using different participants in different settings, can partially repeat, completely repeat, or *replicate*, a study's findings, there is greater confidence in the accuracy of the results. If the findings cannot be replicated, researchers look for explanations and conduct further studies. Similar to a jigsaw puzzle, scientific discovery involves putting together many little pieces of information to reveal the whole picture.

Ethical Guidelines: Protecting the Rights of Others

The largest professional organization of psychologists in Canada is the Canadian Psychological Association (CPA). Its first objective is to improve the health and welfare of all Canadians. This objective is achieved by a mandate to promote excellence in psychological research, psychological education, and psychological practice. The CPA outlines four ethical principles, listed in order of weight, intended to guide Canadian psychologists and others in the field of psychology who counsel and help people:

> Principle I: Respect the dignity of all people.
> Principle II: Provide responsible caring.
> Principle III: Demonstrate integrity in relationships.
> Principle IV: Be responsible to society.

In research settings, psychologists and other scientists must also adhere to important principles, many of which are enshrined in Canadian and international legislation.

Respecting the rights of human participants

One of the primary principles governing research with human participants requires a researcher to obtain a

The scientific method • Figure 1.5

THE PLANNER

Step 1
Literature review
The scientist conducts a *literature review,* reading what has been published in major professional, scientific journals on her subject of interest.

Cycle continues

Cycle begins

Step 6
Theory
After one or more studies on a topic, researchers generally advance a *theory* to explain their results. This new theory then leads to new (possibly different) hypotheses and new methods of inquiry.

Step 2
Operationally defined hypothesis
The scientist makes a testable prediction or *hypothesis* about how one factor or variable interacts with another. To be scientifically testable, the variables must be *operationally defined*—that is, stated very precisely and in measurable terms.

SCIENTIFIC METHOD

Step 5
Peer-reviewed scientific journal
The scientist writes up the study and its results and submits it to a *peer-reviewed scientific journal.* (Peer-reviewed journals ask other scientists to critically evaluate submitted material before publication.) On the basis of these peer reviews, the study may then be accepted for publication.

Step 3
Research design
The scientist chooses the best *research design* to test the hypothesis and collect the data. He or she might choose naturalistic observations, case studies, correlations, surveys, experiments, or other methods.

Step 4
Statistical analysis
The scientist performs *statistical analyses* on the raw data to describe, organize, and numerically summarize them. Additional statistical analyses are performed to make inferences from the study to the more general population. This allows the researcher to determine whether the findings support or refute the hypothesis.

© Image Source/Corbis

Informed consent • Figure 1.6

Research participants must be fully informed about the nature of a study, including the potential risks involved, before agreeing to participate. Do you think informed consent helps or hinders quality scientific methodology? Why?

> **informed consent**
> A participant's prior agreement to take part in a study after being told what to expect.

research participant's **informed consent (Figure 1.6)** *before* initiating an experiment. The researcher must fully inform the participant as to the nature of the study, including any physical risks, discomfort, or unpleasant emotional experiences. The researcher must also explain to the participant that he or she can refuse to participate in the study and can withdraw from the research even after the study has started.

One of the outcomes of informed consent is that participants are aware of the purpose of the study. This can often change the actions of the participants and they may not respond naturally in the research setting. Therefore, the CPA acknowledges the need sometimes for some minor deception in certain research areas. When deception is used, important guidelines and restrictions apply, including **debriefing** participants at the end of the experiment.

> **debriefing**
> Informing participants after a study about the purpose of the study, the nature of the anticipated results, and any deception used.

CPA guidelines also stipulate that all information acquired about people during a study must be held confidential and not published in such a way that individuals' privacy is compromised.

Finally, an institutional research ethics board must first approve all research that uses human participants conducted at a college, a university, or any other reputable institution. Most scholarly journals in North America will not publish a study without a statement from the researcher confirming the research was compliant with its in-house institutional research board decisions (American Psychological Association, 2010). If a Canadian researcher receives federal money to help fund the costs of his or her research, the researcher must comply with the ethical rules of the federal funding agency. Should a researcher violate the ethical rules, his or her funding can be cancelled (Canadian Institutes of Health Research, 2011).

Respecting the rights of non-human animals

Although they are involved in only a small percent of psychological research (American Psychological Association, 1984), non-human animals—mostly rats, mice, and fish—have made significant contributions to almost every area of psychology, including the brain and nervous system, health and stress, sensation and perception, sleep, learning, memory, and emotion (Charney & Nester, 2011; Grippo, 2011; Lupien et al., 2009; Matos et al., 2011; McKinney, 2001; Mogil et al., 2010; Nielsen et al., 2012;

Non-human animal research • Figure 1.7

Although guidelines provide instructions for the care, housing, and socialization of animals in non-human animal research, the issue remains hotly debated.

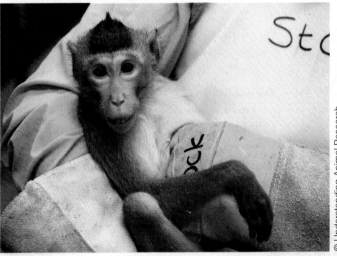

© Understanding Animal Research

Winters et al., 2010; Zelinski et al., 2010). Non-human animal research has also produced significant gains for animals themselves—for example, by suggesting more natural environments for zoo and lab animals and more successful breeding techniques for endangered species (National Research Council, 1991; Pro-Test, 2006) (**Figure 1.7**).

The Canadian Council on Animal Care (CCAC) (www.ccac.ca) supervises research involving non-human animals. The mandate of the CCAC emphasizes both high ethical standards and research excellence (Canadian Council on Animal Care [CCAC], 2005). The CCAC provides clear guidelines for the use of animals in research, testing, and teaching (it has no jurisdiction over animals used for human consumption). Its guidelines contain instructions on how to care for research animals, including such factors as housing, diet, socialization, transportation, veterinary care, anaesthesia, and surgical procedures (CCAC, 2005). Should researchers violate these guidelines, they risk losing their federal funding. Each year the CCAC publishes summary documents on its website that include statistics regarding the numbers of animals used in biomedical research in Canada, the types of species used, and the types of procedures conducted. As with human research, all animal research must be approved *before* the study's inception by an institutional animal care committee. This committee compares the proposed research to the CCAC guidelines to ensure compliance. Any non-compliant proposals must be changed or the research cannot be conducted.

While the ethical debate surrounding the use of non-human animals in research is ongoing and has been a topic of considerable media attention (Burghardt, 2009; Conn & Rantin, 2010), it is often overlooked that psychologists do, in fact, take great care with their research animals. Researchers also actively search for new and better ways to protect animals (Appiah, 2008; CCAC, 2005; *Guidelines for Ethical Conduct*, 2008). For example, the CCAC requires researchers to test their proposed research against the three Rs when using research animals (Russell & Burch as cited in CCAC, 2005): *reduce* the numbers of animals used in research; *replace* animals with other types of research models wherever possible, and *refine* experiments such that animal suffering and discomfort is minimized.

Respecting the rights of psychotherapy clients Like psychological scientists, therapists must also maintain the highest of ethical standards and uphold their clients' trust. All personal information and therapy records must be kept confidential, with records being available only to authorized persons and with the client's permission. However, the public's right to safety ethically outweighs the client's right to privacy. If a therapist believes a client might harm herself or himself or others, the therapist is legally required to report the information. In general, a psychologist's primary obligation is to protect client disclosures (Sue & Sue, 2008). Clinicians who violate the ethical guidelines risk severe sanctions and can permanently lose their licences to practise (Canadian Psychological Association, 2000).

Plagiarism: the dark side of research In most artistic and academic arenas, individuals who create and publish documents own these works as part of their intellectual property. It is the same in research. When researchers publish a study, idea, or theory they have created, they must be acknowledged or credited when anyone discusses or uses their research. In psychology, we acknowledge the work of another by using citations. In the text, these typically include the name of the authors and the year of publication of the work in parentheses following the discussion of the work. Citations are then listed in full in the References section at the end of the document. A person who does not acknowledge the work of another with proper citations and references is guilty of **plagiarism**. Plagiarism is a form of academic dishonesty and a serious ethical violation. It is generally uncommon in most research areas, but with the electronic age, it has become more common among post-secondary students (Badge, Cann, & Scott, 2007; Şendağ, Duran, & Fraser, 2012). While most students do not plagiarize, some do. A variety of factors have been shown to foster this form of cheating, such as poor academic skill, time-management issues, ineffective deterrence, or simply student ignorance (Park, 2007). Despite the explanations, however, there is no acceptable excuse for plagiarism.

> **plagiarism**
> A form of academic dishonesty in which a person takes credit for the work or ideas of another person or fails to cite a source or idea.

Psychology as a discipline that has helped but also harmed Although psychology has done a great deal to help improve the quality of life for many, in the past psychology has also inadvertently harmed people. For example, it was psychologists who developed and administered the first intelligence tests. Although these tests have served many valid and useful purposes, IQ scores have also been misused to legitimize racial and cultural bigotry, force sterilizations, and justify mass murder (Blanton, 2003; Murdoch, 2007; Tilley et al., 2012). Another example of inadvertent harm can be seen in the work of psychoanalyst Frieda Fromm-Reichmann, who gave us the early, and incorrect, theory that mothers could cause their children to become schizophrenic. The *schizophrenogenic* mother was described as a dominant, overprotective, and rejecting mother who, by her behaviour, could induce psychosis

in her child (Dworin & Wyant, 1957; Harrington, 2012; Hartwell, 1996). This explanation persisted for a number of years, and caused untold guilt and stress for many families (Parker, 1982). Psychologists have also supported surgical procedures that while creating more compliant mental health patients, in many cases also resulted in their permanent brain damage (Baker & Pickren, 2007).

While psychology does not have a perfect track record as a helping profession, it is a discipline that is self-critical (Danziger, 1994) and does attempt to ultimately undo some of the harm it has caused. Sadly, it is often only in hindsight that these mistakes are identified. Consider this point as you read the chapters in this text. Is there a current therapy, theory, or procedure about which future generations of psychologists might say, "That hurt a lot of people—what were they thinking back then?"

CONCEPT CHECK STOP

1. **What** is the primary purpose of basic research? Of applied research?

2. **How** do scientists generate and refine hypotheses?

3. **What** is informed consent? Debriefing? Confidentiality?

4. **What** procedures are in place to protect human and non-human research participants?

Research Methods

LEARNING OBJECTIVES

1. **Explain** why only experiments can identify the cause and effect underlying particular patterns of behaviour and mental processes.

2. **Differentiate** the independent variable from the dependent variable.

3. **Describe** the three types of descriptive research.

4. **Explain** how correlational research identifies relationships between variables.

5. **Explain** what is meant by the statement "correlation is not causation."

6. **Identify** some important research methods used in biological studies.

sychologists draw on four major types of psychological research: experimental, descriptive, correlational, and biological (**Study Organizer 1.2**). All have advantages and

disadvantages, so most psychologists use several methods to study a single problem. In fact, when multiple methods lead to similar conclusions, the accuracy of research findings is strengthened.

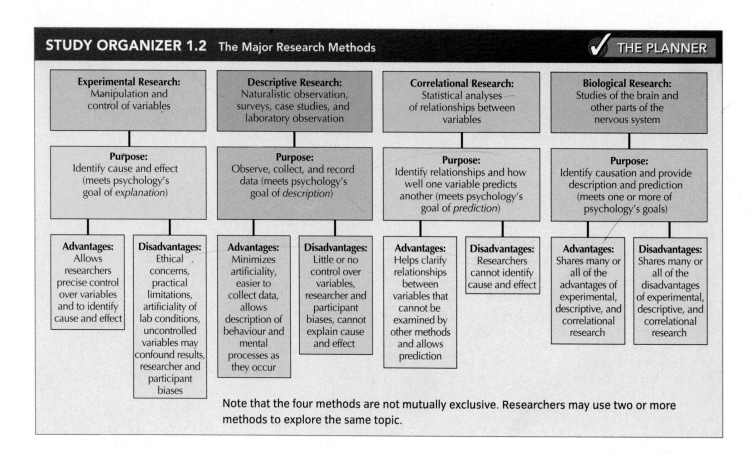

Experimental Research: Manipulation and control of variables	Descriptive Research: Naturalistic observation, surveys, case studies, and laboratory observation	Correlational Research: Statistical analyses of relationships between variables	Biological Research: Studies of the brain and other parts of the nervous system

Purpose: Identify cause and effect (meets psychology's goal of *explanation*)

Purpose: Observe, collect, and record data (meets psychology's goal of *description*)

Purpose: Identify relationships and how well one variable predicts another (meets psychology's goal of *prediction*)

Purpose: Identify causation and provide description and prediction (meets one or more of psychology's goals)

Advantages: Allows researchers precise control over variables and to identify cause and effect

Disadvantages: Ethical concerns, practical limitations, artificiality of lab conditions, uncontrolled variables may confound results, researcher and participant biases

Advantages: Minimizes artificiality, easier to collect data, allows description of behaviour and mental processes as they occur

Disadvantages: Little or no control over variables, researcher and participant biases, cannot explain cause and effect

Advantages: Helps clarify relationships between variables that cannot be examined by other methods and allows prediction

Disadvantages: Researchers cannot identify cause and effect

Advantages: Shares many or all of the advantages of experimental, descriptive, and correlational research

Disadvantages: Shares many or all of the disadvantages of experimental, descriptive, and correlational research

Note that the four methods are not mutually exclusive. Researchers may use two or more methods to explore the same topic.

Experimental Research: A Search for Cause and Effect

The most powerful research method is the **experiment**, in which a researcher manipulates and controls the experimental variables to determine cause and effect. Only through an experiment can researchers isolate and examine a single factor's effect on a particular behaviour. That's because the only way to discover which of many possible factors has an effect is to experimentally isolate each one. As illustrated in **Figure 1.8**, an experiment has a number of critical components, including an **independent variable (IV)**, a **dependent variable (DV)**, an experimental group, and a control group. See **Table 1.3** for help with understanding the difference between the independent and dependent variable.

experiment
A carefully controlled scientific procedure that determines whether variables manipulated by the experimenter have a causal effect on the experiment result.

independent variable (IV)
A variable that is manipulated by the experimenter to determine its effect on the dependent variable. The IV is the cause variable.

dependent variable (DV)
A variable that is measured; it is affected by (or is dependent on) the independent variable and is the outcome or *effect* variable.

Differentiating the independent variable from the dependent variable Table 1.3			
IV	Independent variable	Cause variable	Manipulated by experimenter
DV	Dependent variable	Effect variable	Measured by the experimenter

As a memory aid, remember that *dependent* starts with the letter *d* and *data* (that are measured and then collected by the experimenter) also starts with the letter *d*.

Experimental research design • Figure 1.8

To test the hypothesis that watching violent television shows increases aggression, experimenters might randomly assign children to one of two groups: **experimental group** participants, who watch a prearranged number of violent television programs, and **control group** participants, who watch the same amount of television, except the programs that they watch are nonviolent. (*Having at least two groups—a control group and an experimental group—allows the performance of one group to be compared with that of another.*)

experimental group The group that receives the experimental manipulation.

control group The group that does not receive the experimental manipulation but is treated the same way as the experimental group in all other areas.

Experimenters then observe the children and count how many times—say, within one hour—each child hits, kicks, or punches a punching bag (an operational definition of aggression).

Hypothesis
"Watching violence on TV increases aggression."*

↓

Participants are **randomly selected** from the population and **randomly assigned** to the experimental group or control group.

Experimental Group | **Control Group**

Independent Variable (IV) (Violent or nonviolent program)

Dependent Variable (DV) (Number of times child hits the punching bag)

Groups Compared

*If this were a real experiment, we would operationally define the type and amount of violent TV and what is meant by "aggression." In this example, aggression is defined as the number of times the child hits the bag.

The goal of any experiment is to learn how the dependent variable is influenced by (or depends on) the independent variable. Experiments can also have different *levels* of an independent variable. For example, consider the experiment testing the effect of TV violence on aggression described in Figure 1.8. Two experimental groups could be created, with one group watching two hours of mixed martial arts fighting and the other watching six hours; the control group would watch only nonviolent programming. Then a researcher could relate differences in aggressive behaviour (DV) to the *amount* of violent programming viewed (IV).

In experiments, all extraneous variables (such as time of day, lighting conditions, and participants' age and sex) must be held constant across experimental and control groups so that they are exactly the same between the two groups. This ensures these **confound variables** do not affect the groups' results.

> **confound variables** Nuisance variables that can affect the outcome of the study and lead to erroneous conclusions about the effects of the independent variable on the dependent variable.

In addition to the scientific controls mentioned (e.g., operational definitions, a control group, and controlling of confound variables), a good scientific experiment protects against potential sources of error from both the researcher and the participants. Experimenters can unintentionally let their beliefs and expectations affect participants' responses, producing flawed results. For example, imagine what might happen if an experimenter breathed a sigh of relief when a participant gave a response that supported the researcher's hypothesis. One way to prevent such **experimenter bias** from destroying the validity of participants' responses is to establish objective methods for collecting and recording data. For example, an experimenter might use computers to present stimuli and record responses.

Another option is to design a **double-blind study** in which neither the researcher nor the participant knows which group received the experimental treatment. In a **single-blind study**, only the researcher knows who is in the experimental and the control groups, but the participants do not (**Figure 1.9**).

Participants can also add error or bias into an experiment. First, **sample bias** can occur if the sample of participants does not accurately reflect the composition of

Single-blind versus double-blind study
• Figure 1.9

Participant   **Experimenter**

Single-blind study
The experimenter knows who is in the experimental versus the control groups and the participants do not.

Double-blind study
Neither the experimenter nor the participants know who is in which group.

the larger population that they have been drawn from. For example, in psychology, critics have argued that the subject pool used for most of our research has been biased because it has historically used either young, white male post-secondary students or young, white male rats (Henrich et al., 2010). This is not to suggest these mammals are interchangeable as research subjects, of course. One way to minimize sample bias is to randomly select participants who constitute a representative sample of the entire population of interest. Logically, this process is called **random selection**. Once the sample has been obtained, assigning participants to experimental groups by using a chance, or random, system, such as a coin toss, also helps prevent sample bias. **Random assignment** ensures that each participant is equally likely to be assigned to either the experimental group or the control group.

> **random selection** Everyone in the population of interest has an equal chance of being in the sample.
>
> **random assignment** Everyone selected to be in the study has an equal chance of being put in either the control group or the experimental group.

Bias can also occur when participants are influenced by the experimental conditions. For example, participants may try to present themselves in a good light (the **social desirability response**) or deliberately attempt to mislead the researcher. This type of bias is especially common with controversial research topics, such as infidelity, drinking and driving behaviours, illegal drug use, and cheating (Krumpal, 2011; Steenkamp et al., 2010). Researchers attempt to control for this type of participant bias by allowing respondents to answer anonymously (de Jong et al., 2010; van de Mortel, 2008).

Descriptive Research: Formal Observation and Recording

> **descriptive research** Research methods used to observe, record, and describe behaviour (without making cause-effect explanations).

We all watch others, think about their behaviour, and try to explain and understand what we see; but in conducting **descriptive research**, psychologists do it systematically and scientifically. The key types of descriptive research are naturalistic observation, laboratory observation, surveys, and case studies. Most of the problems and safeguards discussed for the experimental method also apply to these non-experimental techniques.

When conducting **naturalistic observation**, researchers systematically measure and record a subject's behaviour, without trying to manipulate anything. Many settings lend themselves to naturalistic observation, from supermarkets to airports to schools and outdoor settings.

The main advantage of naturalistic observation is that researchers can obtain data about a behaviour in the environment where and when it naturally occurs, rather than behaviour that might be a reaction to a potentially artificial experimental manipulation. But naturalistic observation can be difficult and time-consuming, especially if the behaviour occurs infrequently, or the research subjects are rare or remote (**Figure 1.10**). If a researcher wants to observe behaviour in a controlled setting, **laboratory observation** has many of the advantages of naturalistic observation but with greater control over the variables. In this type of observation the psychologist brings participants into a specially prepared room in the laboratory and, while hidden from view, observes the behaviour of the participants (**Figure 1.11**).

Naturalistic observation • Figure 1.10

Canadian primatologist Dr. Biruté Galdikas, shown here with orangutans, studied them in the jungles of Borneo. Before her, field research scientists knew very little about this species of great apes (Orangutan Foundation International, 2011). Studying behaviour in its natural environment allows behaviour to unfold naturally and without interference.

© A & J Visage/Alamy

Laboratory observation: Observing behaviour in a controlled setting • Figure 1.11

With laboratory observation, researchers can watch behaviour unfold within the confines of a preorganized space. Why is this researcher observing the children's behaviour through a window from outside the room?

Jeffrey Greenberg/Photo Researchers

Surveys • Figure 1.12

When conducting surveys, researchers often use questionnaires and short interviews to gather data from a wide range of people. Under what conditions would you be willing to participate in such research? Do you think the research topic might influence participation rates?

Psychologists use **surveys** (Figure 1.12) to measure a variety of psychological behaviours, thoughts, interests, and attitudes. The survey technique includes tests, questionnaires, polls, and interviews. One key advantage of surveys is that researchers can gather data from many more people than is possible with other research methods. Unfortunately, surveys have a number of disadvantages: most surveys rely on self-reported data, and not all participants are completely honest. In addition, if the survey topic is a bit edgy or personal, those who volunteer to participate and form the survey sample may not be representative of the larger population. Human sexuality research is plagued by this **volunteer effect**, where those who participate tend to be more liberal and sexually active than those who do not (Gaither et al., 2003; Wiederman, 1999). Surveys also suffer the problem of large non-

response rates. Sometimes those who choose not to participate outweigh those who do. If it takes 20 different requests to get one participant, the results of the survey might not reflect the larger population, and the results could be biased. Finally, although they can help predict behaviour, survey techniques cannot explain causes of behaviour.

What if a researcher wants to investigate porphyrophobia (fear of the colour purple) or metrophobia (fear of poetry)? In such cases, it would be difficult to find enough participants to conduct an experiment or to use surveys or naturalistic observation. For rare disorders or phenomena, researchers try to find someone who has the problem and then study him or her intensively. Such in-depth studies of a single research participant are called **case studies** (Figure 1.13).

Correlational Research: Identifying Relationships

We all know that certain things go together—for example, hot weather and fewer clothes; higher annual income and more toys; height and weight; candy and dental cavities; and so on. Researchers can formally observe and measure these types of relationships by using a non-experimental technique called **correlational research**. Correlational research determines what the degree of relationship (or correlation) is between two variables. As the name implies, when any two variables are correlated, a change in one is accompanied by a change in the other.

> **correlational research** A research method in which variables are observed or measured without manipulation to identify possible relationships between them.

By using the correlational method, researchers measure participants' responses or behaviours on the variables of interest. Next, the researchers analyze their results by using a statistical formula that gives a **correlation coefficient**. This is a numerical value that provides two pieces of information: the *strength* and the *direction* of the relationship between the two variables. Correlation coefficients are expressed as a number ranging from +1.00 to –1.00. The sign (+ or –) indicates the direction of the correlation, positive or negative

An early case study • Figure 1.13

In 1848, a railroad worker named Phineas Gage had a metal rod (6 kg, 3 cm in diameter, and 1 m long) blown up through the front of his face, through his brain, and out the top of his head. Amazingly, Gage was not knocked unconscious and was soon up and moving around. Moreover, he didn't receive any medical treatment until 11/2 hours later. However, Gage suffered a serious personality transformation. Before the accident, he had been capable, energetic, and well liked. Afterward, he was described as "fitful, capricious, impatient of advice, obstinate, and lacking in deference to his fellows" (Macmillan, 2000, p. 13). Women were instructed to not remain long in his presence in case his frequent fits of profanity might offend their sensibilities (Damasio, 2006). Gage's injury and recovery were carefully documented and recorded by his physician, Dr. J. M. Harlow. As Gage's story illustrates, the case study method offers unique advantages—a researcher could never do such an experiment nor find any volunteers willing to participate in the experimental group (the group that would receive the penetrating brain injury). The case study does have some research limitations, including a lack of generalizability to the larger population and inadvertent bias in recording the case study details.

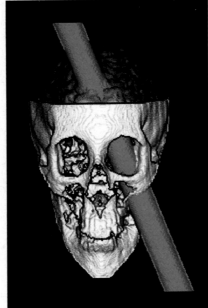 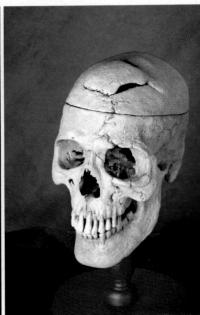

From H. Damasio, T. Grabowski, R. Frank, A.M. Galaburda, A.R. Damasio (1994). The return of Phineas Gage: Clues about the brain from a famous patient. Science, 264:1102–1105. Dornsife Neuroscience Imaging Center and Brain and Creativity Institute, University of Southern California.

The Image Works

(**Figure 1.14a**). The closer the number is to –1.00 or +1.00, the stronger the relationship. Both +1.00 and –1.00 are the strongest possible relationships. Thus, if you had a correlation of +.92 or –.92, you would have a *strong correlation*. By the same token, a correlation of +.15 or –.15 would represent a *weak correlation*. Correlation coefficients close to zero are often interpreted as representing no relationship between the variables, and such is the relationship between breaking a mirror and years of bad luck. A "no-relationship" relationship is relevant, because when we think variables go together and they don't, it can foster superstitious beliefs (Diaconis, 1985; Hutson, 2008). Correlations can be represented numerically with the correlation coefficient, but they can also be represented graphically in a **scatter plot** (Figure 1.14a).

Correlational research is an important research method for psychologists, and understanding correlations can also help people live safer and more productive lives. For example, correlational studies have repeatedly found high correlations between birth defects and amount of alcohol consumed by the pregnant mother (Bearer et al., 2004–2005; Gunzerath et al., 2004). Research findings like this enable us to make predictions about relative risks and fosters more informed decisions as consumers of medical and other information (**Figure 1.14b**).

People do not always understand that a correlation between two variables does not mean that one variable is causing the other to happen (**Figure 1.14c**). Some critics of global warming research have argued that the evidence in its support is based on correlational rather than experimental research and therefore does not establish cause and effect (Kampen, 2011; Solomon, 2008). This is a very valid point from a research method perspective. Although correlational studies do sometimes suggest possible causes, only the experimental method manipulates the independent variable under controlled conditions and can therefore support conclusions about cause and effect.

Biological Research: Ways to Describe and Explore the Nervous System

Biological research studies the brain and other parts of the nervous system to examine the physical processes that are involved in our mental processes and behaviour.

> **biological research** Scientific studies of the brain and other parts of the nervous system.

The earliest explorers of the nervous system dissected the brains of cadavers (deceased humans) and conducted experiments on other

Visualizing

Correlations • Figure 1.14

a. Three types of correlation Each dot on these graphs (called *scatter plots*) represents one participant's score on two factors, or variables. (Note: For simplicity we have not included unit values on the graph axes.) ▼

Salary — Years of Education

In a positive correlation, the two factors vary in the same direction.

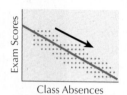

Class Absences — Exam Scores

In a negative correlation, the two factors vary in opposite directions—that is, as one factor increases, the other factor decreases.

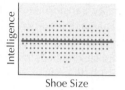

Shoe Size — Intelligence

Sometimes no relationship exists between two variables. This is a zero correlation.

b. Pregnancy and smoking Research shows that cigarette smoking is strongly correlated with fetal harm. The more the mother smokes the greater the risk of damage to her fetus (Chapter 9). Is this a positive or negative correlation? ▶

© Chris Carroll/Corbis

c. Correlation is not the same as causation Ice cream production and sexual assaults have a strong positive correlation (+.84). Does this mean eating ice cream causes men to sexually assault women? Or does sexual assault cause an urge to eat more ice cream? Obviously not! Instead both are being caused by a third variable—summertime or warm weather, when days are longer and people are outside more. ▶

Superstock RF/Superstock

---

animals by using *lesioning* techniques (systematically destroying brain tissue to study the effects on behaviour and mental processes). By the mid-nineteenth century, this research had produced a rudimentary map of the nervous system, including some areas of the brain. Early researchers also relied on clinical observations and case studies of living people who had experienced injuries, diseases, and disorders that affected brain functioning. The case study of Phineas Gage was one such example. Modern researchers still use these methods, but they also employ other techniques to examine biological processes that underlie our behaviour (**Table 1.4** on next pages). Recent advances in digital technology and scientific machinery have led to various ways to image the living brain, which can be used in both clinical and laboratory

settings (Haller et al., 2005). Most of these methods are relatively *non-invasive*—that is, their use does not involve breaking the skin or entering the body.

CONCEPT CHECK STOP

1. **How** do psychologists guard against bias?
2. **Which** type of psychological research involves observing participants' behaviour in the real world?
3. **What** is the difference between a positive and a negative correlation?
4. **What** does it mean to call a procedure *non-invasive*?

Critical and Creative Thinking Questions

1. Scientific psychologists are among the least likely to believe in psychics, palmistry, astrology, and other paranormal phenomena. Why might that be?

2. This chapter noted how one goal of psychology is to attempt to change undesirable behaviours or mental processes. What human behaviours do you think could be modified by applying the first three psychological goals?

3. Which psychological perspective would most likely be used to study and explain why some animals, such as newly hatched ducks or geese, follow and become attached to (imprinted on) the first large moving object they see or hear?

4. Why is the scientific method described as a cycle, rather than as a simple six-step process?

5. Imagine that a researcher recruited research participants from among her friends, and then assigned them to experimental or control groups based on their sex. Why might this be a problem?

6. It is not uncommon for the media to incorrectly report research correlations as though they are cause-and-effect relationships. Why are these types of errors particularly troubling to scientific discovery?

7. Which modern methods of examining how the brain influences behaviour are non-invasive?

8. What do you think keeps most people from fully employing the active learning strategies and study skills presented in this chapter?

9. Why is critical thinking important in everyday life?

Self-Test

(Check your answers in Appendix A.)

1. Psychology is defined as the _____.
   a. science of conscious and unconscious forces on behaviour
   b. empirical study of the mind
   c. scientific study of the mind
   d. scientific study of behaviour and mental processes

2. The goals of psychology are to _____.
   a. explore the conscious and unconscious functions of the human mind
   b. understand, compare, and analyze human behaviour
   c. improve psychological well-being in all individuals, from conception to death
   d. describe, explain, predict, and change behaviour and mental processes

3. Whereas Edward Tichener was associated with the structuralist school of psychology, William James was a _____.
   a. humanist
   b. psychoanalyst
   c. functionalist
   d. behaviourist

4. Which of the following individuals is referred to as the father of modern psychology?
   a. Sigmund Freud
   b. B. F. Skinner
   c. Wilhelm Wundt
   d. Abraham Maslow

5. Which of the following research questions would interest a psychologist from the behaviourist perspective?
   a. Is there a correlation between self-esteem and anxiety?
   b. Does crowding influence acts of aggression?
   c. Is depression related to intelligence?
   d. Can motivation be increased by positive self-talk?

6. The biopsychosocial model refers to _____.
   a. an integrative, unifying psychological perspective
   b. a means of maximizing your learning by incorporating a variety of modalities into your studying
   c. an early school of psychology
   d. an offshoot of the behavioural perspective

7. The term *basic research* is best defined as research that _____.
   a. is basic to one field only
   b. is intended to advance scientific knowledge rather than being done for practical applications
   c. focuses on questions that are simple rather than complicated
   d. solves basic problems encountered by humans and animals in a complex world

8. When researchers can specify the conditions under which a behaviour or event is likely to occur, they have accomplished which psychological goal?
   a. explanation
   b. influence
   c. description
   d. prediction

9. Identify and label the following six steps in the scientific method: choose the best research design to test the hypothesis; after more studies, advance a theory to explain the results; perform statistical analysis; conduct a review of the literature; make a testable prediction; write up the study and its results and submit the study to a scientific journal.

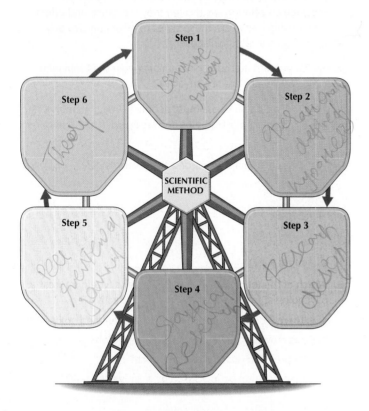

10. What does debriefing involve?

    a. interviewing subjects after a study to find out what they were thinking during their participation

    b. explaining the purpose of the study, anticipated results, and deception used when the study is over

    c. disclosing potential physical and emotional risks, and the nature of the study before it begins

    d. interviewing subjects after a study to determine whether any deception was effective in preventing them from learning the true purpose of the study

11. _____ are manipulated; _____ are measured.

    a. Dependent variables; independent variables

    b. Surveys; experiments

    c. Statistics; correlations

    d. Independent variables; dependent variables

12. A researcher has developed a new treatment for smoking that combines hypnosis and acupuncture. He randomly assigns participants to two groups and administers his new treatment to one group, while the other group receives no treatment. He measures the number of cigarettes participants smoke in the two weeks following the treatment. This study is best described as _____.

    a. experimental

    b. correlational

    c. laboratory observation

    d. naturalistic observation

13. What is the dependent variable in the previous study?

    a. the two groups of participants

    b. the two weeks following treatment

    c. hypnosis and acupuncture

    d. the number of cigarettes smoked

14. A researcher conducts a study assessing the frequency of aggressive acts displayed by Grade 2 students in the schoolyard during recess. What type of research would the researcher likely employ?

    a. a case study

    b. naturalistic observation

    c. an experiment

    d. laboratory observation

15. The best definition of a double-blind study is research in which _____.

    a. nobody knows what they are doing

    b. neither the participants in the treatment group nor those in the control group know which treatment is being given to which group

    c. neither the researcher nor the participants are aware of who is in the experimental and control groups

    d. two control groups must be used

16. Which of the following are generally considered to be sources of empirical evidence?

    a. websites

    b. scholarly journal articles

    c. news programs

    d. personal anecdotes

17. Who supervises the use of research animals in Canada?

    a. the research institution where the animals are housed

    b. the Canadian Council on Animal Care

    c. the Canadian Psychological Association

    d. the Canadian Wildlife Association

18. The number that indicates the direction and strength of the relation between two variables is referred to as a _____.

    a. correlation score

    b. positive correlation

    c. scatter plot

    d. correlation coefficient

19. List the six steps of the SQ4R study method.

20. Rebecca studies for her psychology course by carefully considering how different concepts of human behaviour are related, by thinking about examples and applications of such behaviour, and then by continually reviewing this material afterward. What study skill is Rebecca using?

    a. massed practice   c. time-management

    b. overlearning   d. distributed practice

THE PLANNER ✓

Review your Chapter Planner on the chapter opener and check off your completed work.

Neuroscience, Evolution, and the Biology of Behaviour

"**Y**ou have to be mental to be a fighter pilot" (Murray, 2010) is the title of an article in *Canadian Air Force Journal*. For the nearly 60 Canadian men and women who hold this job, is being "mental" a critical component of their job description? While psychologists typically don't use this term, most would agree there is a cluster of cognitive and perceptual skills that are essential for piloting a CF-18 Hornet jet. At any moment in time combat pilots must negotiate vast amounts of information provided by numerous visual displays and auditory input (see image of pilot helmet displays on facing page), as well as rapidly changing surroundings, potential ground and air threats, weapons targets, speed, and aircraft navigation—all in high-stress situations with nauseating gravitational forces. One study identified more than 200 elements important for safe and tactical in-flight fighter operations (Endsley, 1993). For pilots, each element requires a brief moment of attention and an immediate decision to react, store, or ignore. At air speeds of more than 1,500 kilometres per hour, split second decisions must be correct or the consequences and loss immeasurable.

Fighter pilots are an exceptional example of the power and versatility of the human nervous system. What parts of their brain allow them to rapidly detect, prioritize, and integrate such vast amounts of information? Are their brains wired the same as ours? Are their reflexes faster? In this chapter, we will look at the biological processes that make it possible for combat pilots—as well as the rest of us—to detect, organize, and respond to the massive influx of external and internal stimuli that compete, every second, for the brain's attention.

CHAPTER OUTLINE

CHAPTER PLANNER ✔

❑ Study the picture and read the opening story.

❑ Scan the Learning Objectives in each section:
   p. 38 ❑   p. 42 ❑   p. 49 ❑   p. 56 ❑

❑ Read the text and study all visuals. Answer any questions.

Analyze key features

❑ Process Diagram: How Neurons Communicate: Communication *within* the Neuron, p. 44 ❑   p. 45 ❑

❑ What a Psychologist Sees, p. 47

❑ Study Organizer 2.1, p. 46

❑ Psychological Science, p. 53

❑ Applying Psychology, p. 55

❑ Visualizing, p. 64

❑ Stop: Answer the Concept Checks before you go on:
   p. 42 ❑   p. 49 ❑   p. 55 ❑   p. 65 ❑

End of chapter

❑ Review the Summary and Key Terms.

❑ Answer the Critical and Creative Thinking Questions.

❑ Complete the Self-Test and check your answers.

Our Genetic Inheritance

LEARNING OBJECTIVES

1. **Summarize** how genetic material passes from one generation to the next.

2. **Understand** the various approaches that scientists take to explore human inheritance.

3. **Describe** how natural selection and genetic mutations help explain behaviour.

Hundreds of thousands of years of evolution have contributed to who we are today. Our ancestors foraged and scavenged for food, fought for survival, and passed on some traits that were selected for and transmitted down through vast numbers of generations. How do these transmitted traits affect us today? For answers, psychologists often turn to **behavioural genetics** (the relative involvement of genes and environment on our behaviour and mental processes) and **evolutionary psychology** (how our current behaviours and mental processes can be understood in terms of the evolution of our species).

> **behavioural genetics** The study of the relative contributions of genetic influences and environmental factors on behaviour and mental processes.
>
> **evolutionary psychology** A branch of psychology that studies the ways in which natural selection and evolution can help to explain behaviour and mental processes.

in pairs, with one gene of each pair coming from each parent. For some traits, such as blood type, a single pair of genes determines what characteristics you will possess. But most traits are determined by a combination of many genes.

When the genes in a pair for a given trait differ, the outcome depends on whether the gene pair is *dominant* or *recessive*. A dominant gene expresses (or shows) its trait whenever the gene is present. In contrast, the gene for a recessive trait will normally be expressed only if both genes in the pair are recessive.

It was once assumed that such characteristics as eye colour, hair colour, and height were the result of either one dominant gene or two paired

Behavioural Genetics: Both Nature and Nurture Contribute Differentially

Ancient cultures, such as the Egyptians, Indians, and Chinese, believed the heart was the centre of all thoughts and emotions. We now know that the brain and the rest of the nervous system are the driving force behind our psychological life and our physical being. This chapter introduces you to the field of **neuroscience** and *biopsychology*, the scientific study of the biology of behaviour and mental processes. In this chapter we will discuss genetics and heredity, the nervous system, and the functions of each part of the brain.

> **neuroscience** An interdisciplinary field that studies how biological processes interact with behaviour and mental processes.

No one really wants to think about his or her parents having sex, but it obviously did happen and at the moment of your conception, your mother and father each contributed 23 *chromosomes* to begin the process of making you. Some chromosomes have thousands of genes on them and others have fewer than a hundred, but all are necessary to make a human being (**Figure 2.1**). Like chromosomes, genes operate

Hereditary code • Figure 2.1

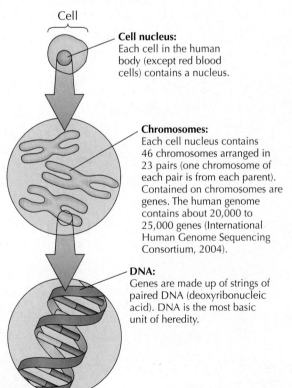

Cell nucleus: Each cell in the human body (except red blood cells) contains a nucleus.

Chromosomes: Each cell nucleus contains 46 chromosomes arranged in 23 pairs (one chromosome of each pair is from each parent). Contained on chromosomes are genes. The human genome contains about 20,000 to 25,000 genes (International Human Genome Sequencing Consortium, 2004).

DNA: Genes are made up of strings of paired DNA (deoxyribonucleic acid). DNA is the most basic unit of heredity.

recessive genes. But today most geneticists believe that each of these characteristics is *polygenic*, meaning they're controlled by multiple genes. Many polygenic traits, like height and intelligence, are also affected by environmental and social factors (**Figure 2.2**). How do scientists research human genetic inheritance? To determine the influences of heredity and environment on complex traits, such as aggressiveness, intelligence, and sociability, scientists rely on indirect methods, such as twin, family, and adoption studies, and using studies of genetic abnormalities.

Psychologists are especially interested in the study of twins because twins have a uniquely high proportion of shared genes. Identical (*monozygotic*—one ovum) twins share 100 percent of the same genes, whereas fraternal (*dizygotic*—two ova) twins share, on average, 50 percent of the same genes, just like any other pair of siblings (**Figure 2.3**).

Because both identical and fraternal twins have the same parents and develop in a similar environment, they provide a valuable "natural experiment" in which genetic and environmental influences can be teased apart. If genes influence a trait or behaviour to some degree, identical twins should be more alike than fraternal twins on that

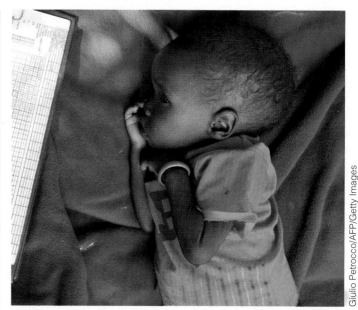

Giulio Petrocco/AFP/Getty Images

Gene-environment interaction • Figure 2.2

Children who are malnourished may not reach their full potential genetic height or maximum cognitive ability, as good nutrition is essential for normal physical and brain development. Can you see how environmental factors interact with genetic factors to influence many traits?

Identical and fraternal twins • Figure 2.3

Darryl Dyck/The Canadian Press

Kevin Mazur/WireImage/Getty Images

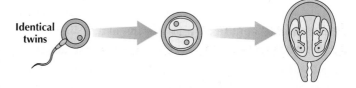

Identical twins

a. Monozygotic, or identical, twins develop from a single ovum fertilized by a single sperm. They share the same sex and the same genetic makeup.

Fraternal twins

Same or opposite sex

b. Dizygotic, or fraternal, twins are formed when two separate sperm fertilize two separate ova. They can be the same or opposite sex and share some of the same genetic makeup.

trait or behaviour. Twin studies have provided a wealth of information on the relative effects of heredity on behaviour. For example, studies of intelligence show that identical twins have almost identical IQ scores, whereas fraternal twins are only slightly more similar in their IQ scores than are non-twin siblings (Bouchard, 2004; Plomin, 1999). This difference suggests a genetic influence on intelligence.

Psychologists in the field of behavioural genetics also study entire families. If a specific trait is inherited, blood relatives should show greater trait similarity, compared with unrelated people. Also, closer relatives, such as siblings, should be more similar than distant relatives. Family studies have shown that many traits, such as intelligence and sociability, and psychological disorders, such as depression, do indeed run in families.

Studying families with children who have been adopted provides valuable information about inheritance for researchers. If adopted children are more like their biological family than their adoptive family on some trait, then genetic factors probably had the greater influence. Conversely, if adopted children resemble their adopted family even though they do not share similar genes, then environmental factors may be more influential.

Finally, research in behavioural genetics explores disorders and diseases that result when genes malfunction. For example, researchers believe that genetic or chromosomal abnormalities are important factors in Alzheimer's disease and schizophrenia (Borenstein et al., 2006; O'Tuathaigh et al., 2006), and the sequencing of the entire human genome has identified the genes responsible for many disorders, such as muscular dystrophy and cystic fibrosis (Edelman et al., 2011; Emery, 2002).

Findings from these four lines of inquiry (twin studies, family studies, adoption studies, and genetic abnormalities) have allowed behavioural geneticists to estimate the heritability of various traits. *Heritability* is the degree to which individual differences are a result of genetic, inherited factors rather than differences in environments. If genes contributed nothing to trait differences, they would have a heritability estimate of 0 percent. If trait differences were completely due to genes, they would have a heritability estimate of 100 percent. Bear in mind that heritability estimates apply to the *differences* seen in traits people have and not the actual traits per se. For example, a height heritability estimate would calculate the relative genetic contribution of differences between the shortest and tallest person in a population (**Figure 2.4**). Because heritability estimates are derived from population values,

JGI/Jamie Grill/Blend Images/Getty Images

Height and heritability • Figure 2.4 _____

Height has one of the highest heritability estimates—around 80 to 90 percent (Plomin, 1990; Silventoinen et al., 2008). However, it's impossible to predict with certainty a single individual's height from a heritability estimate because we each inherit a unique combination of genes, and heritability estimates are based on groups as a whole. The same is true regardless of whether the trait in question is athletic ability, intelligence, depression, or the risk of developing cancer. What other factors might have contributed to the difference in height between the mother and daughter in this photo?

they do not apply to individuals. That is to say, we do not speak of a heritability estimate for a single person.

As we've seen, behavioural genetics studies help explain the role of heredity (nature) and the environment (nurture) in our individual behaviour. To increase our understanding of genetic dispositions, we also need to look at universal behaviours that have been transmitted to us from our evolutionary past.

Evolutionary Psychology: Natural Selection Drives Behaviour and Mental Processes

For an interesting discussion on this topic, scan to download the author's podcast.

Evolutionary psychology is based on the premise that many behavioural commonalities, from mating to fighting, emerged and remain in human populations today because they helped our ancestors (and their descendents) survive and reproduce. This perspective stems from the writings and research of Charles Darwin (1859), who theorized that environmental forces

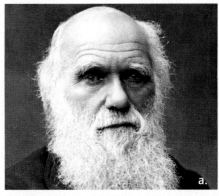  

Bob Thomas/Popperfoto/Getty Images   Ralph Lee Hopkins/National Geographic Stock   Frans Lanting/National Geographic Stock

Charles Darwin and natural selection • Figure 2.5

Despite popular belief, Charles Darwin (a) (1809–1882) was not the first to propose the concept of evolution. The theory of evolution—the process of genetic change in a population—predated Darwin by many years (his grandfather Erasmus Darwin had written about it in the eighteenth century). What Darwin did was to propose the mechanism by which evolution occurs, that is, through natural selection. Darwin noted that across a wide range of inherited (genetic) trait variation, those traits that confer a survival or reproductive advantage for an individual will gradually increase in the population (Darwin, 1859). Look at the images of these two finches. These finches evolved from a common ancestor. The beak of the large ground finch (b) is big for cracking large seeds, and the beak of the i'iwi finch (c) is long and curved to extract nectar from flowers. The genes of those birds with beaks that were slightly better adapted to getting food in their local environments slowly increased in the population and ultimately gave rise to these two finch species from the common ancestor.

natural selection
The mechanism by which those genetically linked traits that confer a survival or reproductive advantage for an organism will increase in a population.

preferentially select traits that are adaptive to the organism's survival. This process of **natural selection** occurs when a particular genetic trait gives an individual a survival and reproductive advantage over others of the same species (**Figure 2.5**). Some people mistakenly believe that natural selection means "survival of the fittest." It is not necessarily the fittest (or strongest) who survive; rather, it is those who can adapt best to their environment and make the greatest genetic contribution to succeeding generations. What really matters then is *reproduction*, that is, the survival of the *genome* (an organism's entire genetic complement). Because of natural selection, the individual with the most adaptive traits will be more likely to live long enough to pass on his or her genes to the next generation.

When we think of natural selection, we often think of its effects in terms of anatomy. For example, a beneficial gene or gene combination might cause an organism to run a little faster, have better vision, or use food or oxygen more efficiently. But natural selection also acts on behaviour—genes influence what we do and how we act, and if those genes confer a behaviour that is adaptive, that behaviour will also increase in a population.

Studying the influence of natural selection on behaviour is more difficult than studying its influence on physical characteristics; unlike anatomical adaptations, behavioural effects generally do not leave much in the fossil record. This inconvenience has not deterred evolutionary psychologists and others, however, and many examples of behavioural adaptations both within our own species and across the rest of the animal kingdom have been identified. The caterwauling and loud mewing made by female cats to advertise their sexual receptivity is one such example, as is the demand of a dead insect "gift" in exchange for mating access by some female spiders. That female deer and moose "prefer" males with the largest antlers (**Figure 2.6**) is another example of an evolved behavioural adaptation (LeVay & Baldwin, 2012). In our own species are numerous other examples. Research has shown men and women prefer faces that are more symmetrical, and this variable is a reliable indicator of good genes and good health—both critical for reproductive success (Jones et al., 2001; Little et al., 2008). Similarly, humans typically have few offspring, and we care for our young for an extended period of time. Compare this to the parenting behaviour of salmon or sea turtles, which have large numbers of offspring and provide little or no parental care.

Evolutionary psychologists consider human parenting and infant attachment behaviour to be one of a number of *universal behaviours* (Bowlby, 1969/1982; Brown, 2000). That is, it is present in all cultures no matter where in the world we grew up. Universal behaviours have particular significance: not only are they are very old (they appeared in the ancestral human line long before we dispersed around the

My, those are sexy antlers • Figure 2.6

Well perhaps not to you, but for a female moose those big antlers are irresistible. Research has shown that female moose prefer and are more likely to mate with males with large antlers (Lincoln, 1992; Malo et al., 2005). Darwin (1859) called this preference *sexual selection*—the evolution of traits (such as big antlers) based on either mate preference, or competition for mates. Across evolutionary time those traits that were preferred by mates (usually the female) or provided a competitive advantage for getting a mate (usually the male), increased in the population. Another consequence of sexual selection is that preferred traits become more and more pronounced across millennia. If big antlers are sexy for female moose, then bigger antlers will be sexier and preferred even more. This preference can trigger an evolutionary runaway effect where a particular trait becomes exceptionally prominent. The large and elaborate tail feathers of the peacock compared to the drab appearance of the peahen is one such example of this phenomenon. How do you think sexual selection might explain the male size advantage seen in many mammalian species?

planet and took the behaviour with us) but to be with us today, they must also have an adaptive genetic basis.

Genetic mutations help explain the evolution of behaviour. It's likely that everyone carries at least one gene that has mutated or changed from the original. This was probably also true of ancestral humans (called Hominins) and other organisms. Most genetic mutations are disadvantageous or have no effect, but very rarely, a mutated gene will confer a behavioural advantage. When this happened in the past, it might have caused an ancestral human to be more aggressive, vigilant, receptive, or careful. If the gene then provided a reproductive advantage, he or she would be more likely to pass on the gene to future generations. Then through evolutionary time, this advantageous genetic mutation will spread in the population. An advantageous genetic mutation doesn't guarantee long-term survival. A well-adapted population can quickly perish if its environment suddenly changes. This is because environments select for adaptive traits; if environments change, the trait may no longer be adaptive.

CONCEPT CHECK STOP

1. **What** is the difference between a dominant and a recessive trait?

2. **What** does knowing the heritability of a trait tell us about that trait?

3. **What** is evolution by natural selection?

4. **How** are heredity and evolution linked to human behaviour?

Neural Bases of Behaviour

LEARNING OBJECTIVES

1. **Describe** how neurons communicate throughout the body.

2. **Explain** the role of neurotransmitters.

3. **Compare** and contrast the functions of neurotransmitters and hormones.

neuron A nervous system cell that receives and conducts electrochemical impulses.

glial cell A nervous system cell that supports, nourishes, insulates, and protects neurons.

Your brain and the rest of your nervous system consist of billions of **neurons**. Each one is a tiny information-processing system with thousands of connections for receiving and sending electrochemical signals to other neurons. Each human body may have as many as one *trillion* neurons. (Be careful not to confuse the term *neuron* with the term *nerve*. Nerves are large bundles of axons—defined below—outside the brain and spinal cord.)

Neurons are held in place, supported, nourished, and nurtured by **glial cells**. Glial cells surround neurons and perform a variety of tasks, including cleaning up and insulating one neuron from another so their neural messages aren't scrambled. Glial cells also have a wide

The structure of a neuron • Figure 2.7

Arrows indicate direction of information flow: dendrites → cell body → axon → terminal buttons of axon.

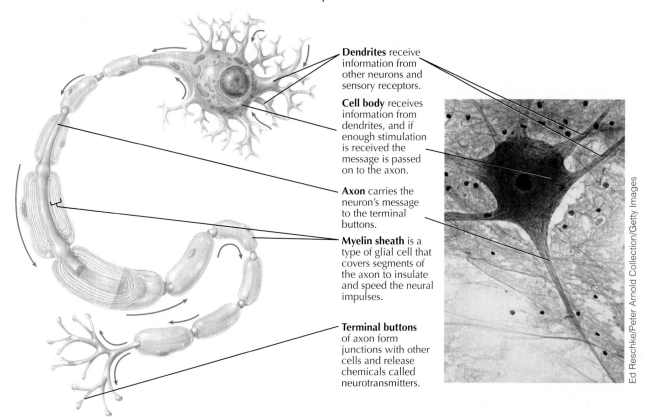

Dendrites receive information from other neurons and sensory receptors.

Cell body receives information from dendrites, and if enough stimulation is received the message is passed on to the axon.

Axon carries the neuron's message to the terminal buttons.

Myelin sheath is a type of glial cell that covers segments of the axon to insulate and speed the neural impulses.

Terminal buttons of axon form junctions with other cells and release chemicals called neurotransmitters.

Ed Reschke/Peter Arnold Collection/Getty Images

array of other duties, such as playing a direct role in nervous system communication and speed of neural signalling (Arriagada et al., 2007; Wieseler-Frank et al., 2005; Zillmer et al., 2008). It was once thought that glial cells were rather uninteresting and they did not garner much research attention, but this is no longer the case. Newer research suggests they play an important role in learning and memory formation (Ikeda & Murase, 2004), and diseases such as Alzheimer's and Parkinson's (Salmina et al., 2010; Yokoyama et al, 2011). Glial cells are also critical for the formation of the embryonic nervous system. Without glial cells to guide immature neurons, they would not end up in the correct parts of the brain.

No two neurons are identical, but most share three basic features: **dendrites**, the **cell body**, and an **axon** (**Figure 2.7**). To remember how information travels through the neuron, think of these three in reverse alphabetical order: *dendrite → cell body → axon*.

How Do Neurons Communicate?

A neuron's basic function is to transmit information throughout the nervous system. Neurons communicate in a type of electrical and chemical language. The process of neural communication begins within the neuron itself, when the dendrites and cell body receive electrical messages. These messages move along the axon in the form of a neural impulse or **action potential** (**Figure 2.8**).

A neural impulse travels along a bare axon at only about 10 metres per second. This is much slower than the speed at which electricity moves through a wire. Most mammalian axons, however, are enveloped in glial cells that provide a fatty insulation. This insulation is called a **myelin sheath**. The sheath blankets the axon, except in places called *nodes* where the myelin is very thin or absent. In a myelinated axon, the neural impulse moves about 10 times as fast as on a bare axon. This is because the action potential jumps from node to node rather than travelling along the entire length of the axon membrane.

Communication *within* the neuron (**Figure 2.8a**) is not the same as communication *between* neurons (**Figure 2.8b**). Within the neuron, messages travel electrically.

action potential
The voltage change across an axon membrane when an impulse is transmitted.

myelin sheath The fatty insulation that segmentally wraps an axon and serves to speed neural transmission.

How neurons communicate: Communication *within* the neuron • Figure 2.8a

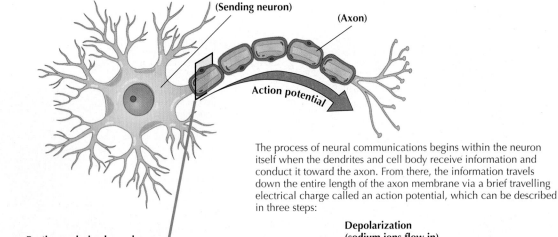

(Sending neuron)

(Axon)

Action potential

The process of neural communications begins within the neuron itself when the dendrites and cell body receive information and conduct it toward the axon. From there, the information travels down the entire length of the axon membrane via a brief travelling electrical charge called an action potential, which can be described in three steps:

Resting, polarized membrane

Depolarization (sodium ions flow in)

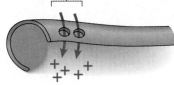

❶ Resting potential

When an axon is not stimulated, it is in a polarized state, called the *resting potential*. While "resting," the fluid inside has more negatively charged atoms and molecules (called ions) than the fluid outside. This occurs because the axon membrane is selective permeable (it restricts the flow of some types of ions but not others) and because special pumps embedded in the membrane (called *sodium-potassium pumps*) pull potassium ions in and pump sodium ions out of the axon. These two effects result in the fluid inside the membrane being about 70 millivolts more negative than the fluid outside the axon membrane. Just like a tiny battery, this charge difference is a store of potential energy.

❷ Action potential initiation

When an "at rest" axon membrane is stimulated by a sufficiently strong signal, it produces an *action potential* (or depolarization). This action potential begins when the first part of the axon opens channels embedded in the axon membrane, and positively charged sodium ions rush through. The additional sodium ions change the previously negative charge inside the axon to a positive charge—thus depolarizing the axon.

(potassium ions flow out)

Depolarization

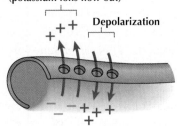

Flow of depolarization

Action potential

Action potential

Action potential

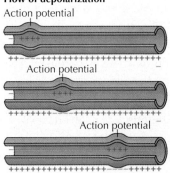

❸ Spreading of action potential and repolarization

The initial depolarization (or action potential) of Step 2 produces an imbalance of ions in the adjacent axon membrane. This imbalance causes the action potential to spread to the next section. Meanwhile, another set of channels in the axon membrane of the initially depolarized section open, and potassium ions flow out. This allows the first section to repolarize and return to its resting potential. Triggering the action potential is a digital decision—yes or no; on or off. It will only be generated at the top end of the axon if there is sufficient stimulation. If not, it does not start. This is called the *all or nothing law*. Once generated, the action potential always travels at the same speed. Weaker stimulus does not generate a slower action potential. The strength of the stimulus input is recorded in the nervous system by the number of action potentials in a unit of time—stronger stimuli generate much higher volleys of action potentials.

❹ Overall summary

As you can see in the figure above, this sequential process of depolarization followed by repolarization transmits the action potential along the entire length of the axon, from the cell body to the terminal buttons. Think of it like an audience at an athletic event doing "the wave." One section of fans initially stands up for a brief time (action potential). As this section sits down (resting potential), the "wave" then spreads to the next adjacent sections.

How neurons communicate: Communication *between* neurons • Figure 2.8b

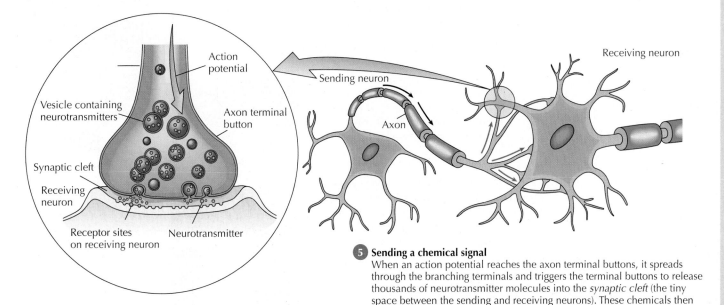

5 **Sending a chemical signal**
When an action potential reaches the axon terminal buttons, it spreads through the branching terminals and triggers the terminal buttons to release thousands of neurotransmitter molecules into the *synaptic cleft* (the tiny space between the sending and receiving neurons). These chemicals then move across the synaptic cleft and attach to receptors on the membranes of the receiving neuron. In this way, they carry the message from the sending neuron to the receiving neuron.

6 **Receiving a chemical signal**
After neurotransmitters diffuse across the synaptic cleft, they bind to the membrane of a specific receiving neuron. Each receiving neuron gets large numbers of neurotransmitter messages. As shown in the photo, the terminal buttons from thousands of other nearby neurons almost completely cover the cell body of the receiving neuron. Neurotransmitters deliver either excitatory or inhibitory messages, and the receiving neuron will produce an action potential and pass along the message only if the number of excitatory messages outweighs the number of inhibitory messages (in a process called *summation*). Why do we need competing messages? Like an accelerator and brake on a car, your nervous system needs similar on (excitatory) and off (inhibitory) mechanisms. By using these two switches, your nervous system manages an amazing balance between overexcitation, leading to seizures, and underexcitation, leading to unconsciousness and death.

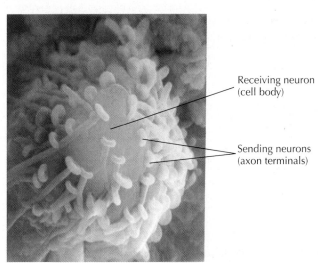

E. Lewis, Y. Zeevi, and T. Everhart

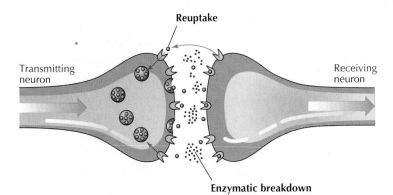

7 **Dealing with leftovers**
Neurotransmitters do not remain attached to their receptors forever—they bind and release. When unbound they are either taken back up into the terminal buttons of the sending neuron for breakdown and recycling (a process called *reuptake*) or are destroyed right in the synapse by a variety of degradation enzymes.

Neurotransmitter	Behaviours and Mental Processes Affected
Serotonin (5-HT)	Sleep, mood, appetite, sensory perception, temperature regulation, memory, learning, sexual behaviour, pain suppression, and impulsivity. Low levels associated with depression.
Acetylcholine (ACh)	Muscle action, cognitive functioning, attention, memory, rapid-eye-movement (REM) sleep, and emotion. Low levels are associated with Alzheimer's disease.
Dopamine (DA)	Voluntary movement, attention, working memory, learning, and positive emotions. Excess DA is associated with schizophrenia, and too little, with Parkinson's disease. Also plays a role in addiction and the reward and pleasure systems in the brain.
Norepinephrine (NE)	Learning, memory, dreaming, emotion, eating, alertness, wakefulness, and reactions to stress. Low levels of NE are associated with depression, high levels with agitated, manic states.
Epinephrine	Emotional arousal, memory enhancement, and metabolism of glucose necessary for energy release.
Gamma aminobutyric acid (GABA)	Muscle tone and neural inhibition in the central nervous system. Tranquilizing drugs, such as Ativan or Xanax, increase GABA's inhibitory effects and thereby decrease anxiety.
Endorphins	Feeling of wellbeing, pain suppression, orgasm, memory, and learning.

© Marilyn Nieves/iStockphoto

© Toby Creamer/iStockphoto

© Aldo Murillo/iStockphoto

© H-Gall/iStockphoto

neurotransmitters Chemicals that neurons release across the synaptic cleft in response to the arrival of an action potential, which affect other cells, including other neurons.

But messages are transmitted chemically from one neuron to the next. The chemicals that transmit these messages are called **neurotransmitters**. (**Study Organizer 2.1** discusses some of the better-understood neurotransmitters.)

Researchers have discovered hundreds of substances that mimic or inhibit neurotransmitters. These substances regulate a wide variety of physiological processes. See *What a Psychologist Sees: How Toxins and Drugs Affect Our Brain*, for a description of some of these effects.

Studying the brain and its neurotransmitters will help you understand some common medical problems. For example, we know that decreased levels of the neurotransmitter dopamine are associated with Parkinson's disease, whereas excessively high levels of dopamine appear to contribute to some forms of schizophrenia. And low levels of the neurotransmitter acetylcholine are associated with symptoms of Alzheimer's disease.

While neurotransmitters have been made famous for their role as chemical messengers in the synapse, many are also produced and utilized by the body. For example, the intestines produce significant quantities of serotonin (Gill et al., 2008; Verhoeckx et al., 2011), and epinephrine is synthesized in the adrenal glands.

What a Psychologist Sees

How Toxins and Drugs Affect Our Brain

Poisons, toxins, and mind-altering (psychoactive) drugs have their effect in the nervous system by interacting with neurotransmitter systems.

Examples of antagonists to acetylcholine include most snake venom and some poisons, such as botulinum toxin. Botulinum is a highly poisonous naturally occurring substance, but when used in tiny doses in the form of Botox®, it is effective in treating migraines and excessive sweating. It is also used for cosmetic purposes to improve the appearance of frown lines and crow's feet wrinkles. Another example of an acetylcholine antagonist is curare, a plant toxin that has been widely used by South American hunter-gatherer peoples as an arrow poison. When the curare-tipped arrowhead breaks the skin, it paralyzes the respiratory muscles and the animal quickly dies by asphyxiation.

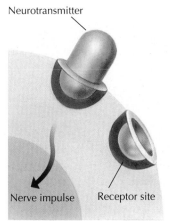

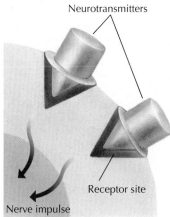

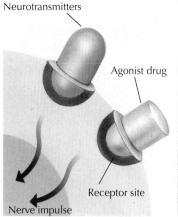

© aspireimages Royalty-Free/Inmagine.com

a. and b. Normal neurotransmitter activity
Like a lock that needs a specific key, receptor sites on receiving neurons' dendrites and cell bodies recognize particular neurotransmitters by their distinctive shapes and affinities. Neurotransmitter and other molecules without the correct shape won't fit a particular receptor, so they cannot stimulate the receiving neuron.

c. Agonist drug
Agonist drugs, such as the poison in the black widow spider or the nicotine in cigarettes, are similar enough in structure to a certain neurotransmitter (in this case, acetylcholine) that they can mimic its effects on the receiving neuron.

d. Antagonist drug
Some antagonist drugs block neurotransmitters like acetylcholine. Because acetylcholine is vital in muscle action, blocking it paralyzes muscles.

Some of the better-known brain chemicals are the endogenous opium-like peptides, commonly known as **endorphins** (a contraction of *endogenous*, meaning "self-produced," and *morphine*). These nervous system chemicals mimic the effects of opium-like drugs, such as morphine and heroin: they elevate mood and reduce pain. One of their evolved purposes may be to permit an injured organism to get out of harm's way without being distracted by pain (Machelska et al., 1998; Randall & Rodgers, 1988). They also affect memory, learning, blood pressure, and appetite, and are produced by the brain in a variety of circumstances, such as when we eat spicy food, fall in love, or have an orgasm (Bodnar, 2011).

Hormones: A Broadcast Communication System

You've just seen how the nervous system uses neurotransmitters to rapidly transmit messages across synapses to have widespread effects throughout the body. A second type of communication system exists. This second system is made up of a network of glands called the **endocrine system** (**Figure 2.9**). Rather than neurotransmitters in synapses, this system uses **hormones** in blood to carry its messages (see **Figure 2.10**).

> **hormones**
> Chemicals synthesized by endocrine glands that are released into the bloodstream to bind to target tissues and organs, producing bodily changes or maintaining normal function.

The endocrine system • Figure 2.9

This figure shows the major endocrine glands, along with some internal organs to help you locate the glands.

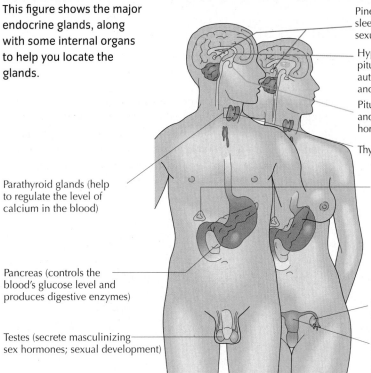

Parathyroid glands (help to regulate the level of calcium in the blood)

Pancreas (controls the blood's glucose level and produces digestive enzymes)

Testes (secrete masculinizing sex hormones; sexual development)

Pineal gland (helps regulate sleep cycles and body rhythms; sexual development)

Hypothalamus (controls the pituitary gland; controls the autonomic nervous system and the endocrine system)

Pituitary gland (influences growth and lactation; also secretes many hormones that affect other glands)

Thyroid gland (controls metabolism)

Adrenal gland (arouses the body, helps respond to stress, regulates salt balance and some sexual functioning)

Ovaries (secrete feminizing sex hormones; sexual development)

Placenta (in pregnancy, synthesizes hormones and transports oxygen and nutrients to the fetus)

Why do we need two communication systems? • Figure 2.10

You can think of neurotransmitters as individual e-mails (or BBMs, text messages, or Twitter DMs). Neurotransmitters deliver messages to specific receptors across specific synapses, which other neurons nearby probably don't "overhear." Hormones, in contrast, are like a global e-mail message (or a Facebook status update) that you send to everyone in your address book or friends list. Endocrine glands release hormones directly into the bloodstream.

The hormones travel throughout the body, carrying messages to any cell that will accept them (that is, it has the appropriate hormone receptors). Hormones also function like your global e-mail recipients forwarding your message to yet more people. For example, a small part of the brain called the hypothalamus releases hormones that signal the pituitary gland, which then stimulates or inhibits the release of other downstream hormones.

Neurotransmitters send individual messages

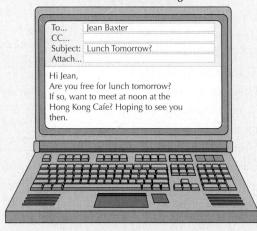

To... Jean Baxter
CC...
Subject: Lunch Tomorrow?
Attach...

Hi Jean,
Are you free for lunch tomorrow? If so, want to meet at noon at the Hong Kong Cafe? Hoping to see you then.

Hormones send global messages

To... Friends; family; co-workers
CC...
Subject: Party!
Attach...

Hi Everybody,
Jean Baxter and I are hosting a party on Saturday night at 9 p.m. Please come, and tell your friends!

The endocrine system is controlled by the hypothalamus and it has several important functions. It helps regulate long-term bodily processes, such as growth and sexual characteristics. For example, if testosterone were to be blocked or removed from a healthy young man, his genitals would get smaller and his sex drive would decrease (Brett et al., 2007). Canadian researcher Doreen Kimura and others believe the sex differences seen in cognitive tasks such as the female advantage seen in object location tasks and the male advantage in spatial navigation are caused in part by the effects of testosterone and other hormones on the developing brain (Kimura, 2004; Halpern, 2012). Hormones also maintain ongoing bodily processes (such as digestion and elimination), and they control the body's response to emergencies. In times of crisis and arousal, the hypothalamus sends messages through two pathways: the neural system and the endocrine system (primarily via the pituitary gland). The pituitary gland sends hormonal messages to the adrenal glands, which sit on top of each kidney and are shaped similar to a Hershey's chocolate kiss. The adrenal glands then release three hormones: *cortisol*, a stress hormone that boosts energy and blood glucose levels; *epinephrine* (often marketed as Adrenaline); and *norepinephrine*. These last two hormones also serve as neurotransmitters, but they have different functions in the endocrine system.

CONCEPT CHECK

1. **What** are the major parts of a neuron?
2. **Why** is myelin important?
3. **How** does an action potential start and then move along an axon?
4. **What** is the difference between a drug that is an agonist and one that is an antagonist?
5. **What** important functions does the endocrine system serve?

The Organization of the Nervous System

LEARNING OBJECTIVES

1. **Identify** the major components of the nervous system.
2. **Explain** how the spinal cord initiates reflexes.
3. **Explain** why research investigating neuroplasticity and neurogenesis are important.
4. **Describe** the opposing roles of the sympathetic and parasympathetic nervous systems.

The human nervous system is a spectacular example of high-speed information detection, processing, integration, and output. It is faster and more powerful than any computer ever built (although supercomputers are catching up) and more complex than any software ever developed (Whitworth & Ryu, 2009). The functional unit is the neuron—and some would argue also glial cells—but at the macro level it is much larger than the sum of it neural parts. Our nervous system contains all that we think, feel, believe, wish, aspire to, and do.

The nervous system is divided and subdivided into several branches (**Figure 2.11**). The main part of our nervous system includes the brain and a large bundle of nerves that form the *spinal cord*. Because this system is located in the centre of your body (within your skull and spine), it is called the **central nervous system (CNS)**.

The second major part of your nervous system includes all the nerves outside the brain and spinal cord. This **peripheral nervous system (PNS)** carries messages (action potentials) to and from the central nervous system to the periphery of the body.

> **central nervous system (CNS)** The brain and spinal cord.
>
> **peripheral nervous system (PNS)** All other neurons connecting the CNS to the rest of the body.

Central Nervous System (CNS): The Brain and Spinal Cord

Although the central nervous system (CNS) is incredibly versatile and remarkably powerful, it is also incredibly fragile. Unlike neurons in the PNS that can regenerate and

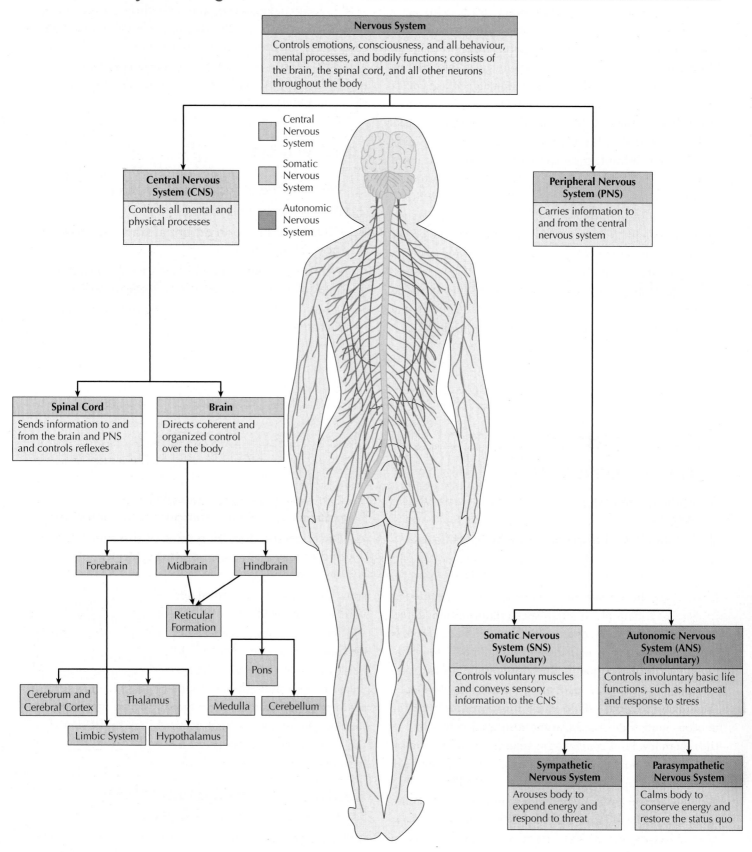

Nervous System

Controls emotions, consciousness, and all behaviour, mental processes, and bodily functions; consists of the brain, the spinal cord, and all other neurons throughout the body

Central Nervous System

Somatic Nervous System

Autonomic Nervous System

Central Nervous System (CNS)

Controls all mental and physical processes

Peripheral Nervous System (PNS)

Carries information to and from the central nervous system

Spinal Cord

Sends information to and from the brain and PNS and controls reflexes

Brain

Directs coherent and organized control over the body

Forebrain

Midbrain

Hindbrain

Reticular Formation

Cerebrum and Cerebral Cortex

Thalamus

Pons

Medulla

Cerebellum

Limbic System

Hypothalamus

Somatic Nervous System (SNS) (Voluntary)

Controls voluntary muscles and conveys sensory information to the CNS

Autonomic Nervous System (ANS) (Involuntary)

Controls involuntary basic life functions, such as heartbeat and response to stress

Sympathetic Nervous System

Arouses body to expend energy and respond to threat

Parasympathetic Nervous System

Calms body to conserve energy and restore the status quo

require less protection, serious damage to neurons in the CNS is usually permanent. However, new research is revealing the brain is not as "hard wired" as we once thought. Scientists once believed that after the first few years of life, humans and most animals are unable to repair or replace damaged neurons in the brain or spinal cord. We now know that the brain is capable of lifelong **neuroplasticity** and **neurogenesis**.

neuroplasticity The brain's remarkable malleability to reorganize and change its structure and function across the lifespan.

neurogenesis The process by which new neurons are generated.

Neuroplasticity: Changing in the brain's architecture Rather than being a fixed, rigid organ, the brain is capable of changing its structure (anatomy) and function (physiology) through usage and experience (Deller et al., 2006; Kinsley & Lambert, 2008; Mateer & Kerns, 2000; Romero et al., 2008; Rossignol et al., 2008). It was once thought that this malleability occurred only during childhood and that by puberty the brain was fixed in its permanent adult form and function. Now, decades of research have shown the brain has the lifelong capacity to reorganize its neural pathways in response to new experiences and to compensate for lost function after damage. It is this dynamic rewiring that makes brains so wonderfully adaptive. It is also this adaptability that makes it possible for us to learn a new sport, computer game, or foreign language.

Neuroplasticity is the mechanism by which our brain can structurally and functionally modify itself following a stroke or brain injury (Taub, 2004; Ward & Frackowiak, 2006; Wolf et al., 2008). Canadian researchers Brian Kolb and Ian Whishaw have shown in a number of primate and rodent experiments that the mammalian brain does modify itself in response to trauma and experience (Kolb & Whishaw, 2009; Kolb, Muhammad, & Gibb, 2011; Mychasiuk, Gibb, & Kolb, 2011). Other research has also shown that aspects of a healthy lifestyle, such as exercise and fitness, can also induce neuroplasticity (Colcombe & Kramer, 2003; Lui et al., 2009), yet another beneficial reason to work out!

The idea that changes in neuronal architecture could account for changes in learning, thinking, and behaviour was first demonstrated in the 1940s by Dr. Donald Hebb (1904–1985) (**Figure 2.12**). A Canadian psychologist and the principal pioneer of neuropsychology, Hebb's description of how the brain and its neural signals can account for the higher functions of the mind and consciousness was extremely influential. He believed the human conscious

Chris F. Payne/McGill University Archives, PR000387

Donald Hebb • Figure 2.12 _____

experience could be described in terms of patterns of neural signals (Hebb, 1949). Hebb suggested that neurons that are simultaneously active (as is the case when we learn to do something) would tend to become associated with each other, such that activity in one would facilitate activity in the other (Hebb, 1949). Repeated stimulation—such as happens when we practise a new skill—ultimately strengthens the synapses, and associated neurons fire more readily, translating into the output of acquiring the new skill. At the time, the idea was revolutionary; scientists had long wondered how the 1.5-kilogram gelatinous organ in our heads could initiate behaviour; interact with the environment; and form cohesive thoughts, ideas, and beliefs. Hebb's early work gave psychology the basic mechanism of synaptic plasticity. Many of Hebb's ideas remain with us today and have been subsequently supported by numerous research studies.

Neurogenesis: The making of new neurons A process related to neuroplasticity is neurogenesis—the generation of new neurons. The brain continually replaces lost cells with new ones. These cells originate deep within the brain and migrate to become parts of specific circuitries. The source of these newly created cells is neural **stem cells**—rare,

stem cells Precursor (immature) cells that can develop into any type of new specialized cells; a stem cell holds all the information it needs to make bone, blood, brain—any part of a human body—and can also copy itself to maintain a stock of stem cells.

immature cells that can grow and develop into any type of cell in the nervous system. Their fate depends on the chemical signals they receive (Abbott, 2004; Kim, 2004; Vaillend et al., 2008). Stem cell research has come a long way since the 1960s, when it was first described in transplanted mouse bone marrow cells by Canadian scientists Ernest McCulloch and James Edgar Till (Becker, McCulloch, & Till, 1963). These special cells are now used for a variety of purposes, such as bone marrow transplants. Clinical trials that have used transplanted stem cells to replace cells destroyed by strokes, Alzheimer's, Parkinson's, epilepsy, stress, and depression show their tremendous potential in treating neural disease and spinal cord injury (Chang et al., 2005; Fleischmann & Welz, 2008; Hampton, 2006, 2007; Leri et al., 2007).

Does this mean that people paralyzed from spinal cord injuries might be able to walk again? Indeed, this is the great hope for the future, and much research is currently directed at realizing this eventuality, but we are still a long way from it. At this time, neurogenesis in the spinal cord appears to be minimal. However, one line of research is exploring the possibility of transplanting embryonic stem cells into damaged areas of the spinal cord. Researchers have transplanted embryonic stem cells into a damaged rat spinal cord (Jones et al., 2003; Kerr et al., 2010; McDonald et al., 1999; Niclas et al., 2011). When the damaged spinal cord was viewed several weeks later, the implanted cells had survived and spread throughout the injured cord area. More important, the rats also showed some movement in the previously paralyzed parts of their bodies. Similar findings have been reported by other research teams (Feng et al., 2008; Hatami et al., 2009; Rossi et al., 2010). Preliminary human clinical trials have shown that some spinal nerve regeneration can occur after a spinal cord injury has been treated with cell-growth-promoting substances (Wu et al., 2008; Lunn et al., 2011; "First Patient Dosed," 2011).

In the adult mammalian brain, neurogenesis occurs most predominantly in two deep brain regions: the hippocampus and a specialized area lining the lateral ventricles (see the next section for a discussion of these two regions). Most of these neurons die soon after they are born, but some of them continue to grow and integrate themselves into surrounding neural tissue (Gage, 2002; Ming & Song, 2005). It's currently unclear what purpose these new neurons serve, but research suggests a role in learning and memory (Deng et al., 2010; Gould et al, 1999). Aging and stress seem to reduce neurogenesis (Kuhn et al., 1996; Snyder et al., 2011), and exercise, some antidepressant medications, and

The workings of the spinal cord • Figure 2.13

Reflexes provide an evolutionary advantage. If messages had to travel all the way to the brain before they could be acted on, an organism might react too slowly and be fatally wounded.

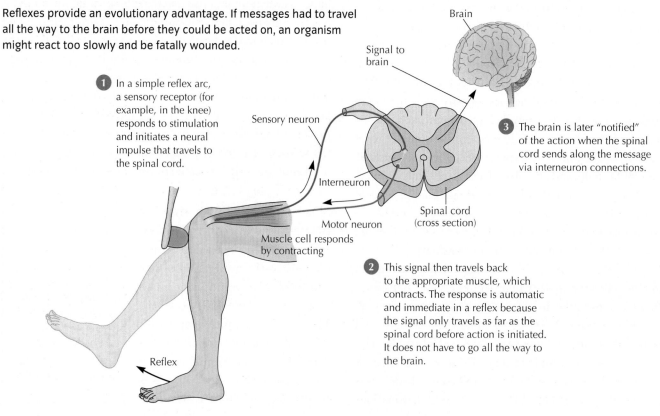

1 In a simple reflex arc, a sensory receptor (for example, in the knee) responds to stimulation and initiates a neural impulse that travels to the spinal cord.

Sensory neuron

Interneuron

Motor neuron

Muscle cell responds by contracting

Reflex

Brain

Signal to brain

Spinal cord (cross section)

3 The brain is later "notified" of the action when the spinal cord sends along the message via interneuron connections.

2 This signal then travels back to the appropriate muscle, which contracts. The response is automatic and immediate in a reflex because the signal only travels as far as the spinal cord before action is initiated. It does not have to go all the way to the brain.

Psychological Science

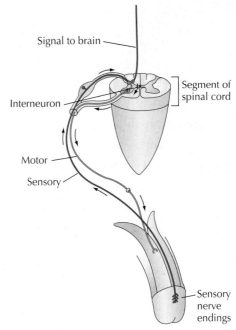

The Brain Isn't Necessary for an Erection

Direct tactile (touch) stimulation of the penis or clitoris can trigger an erection. This occurs because of a spinal reflex that forms a loop from the genitals to the spinal cord and back. Sensory nerve endings in the genital area detect the tactile stimulation, and this information is then conveyed to the spinal cord. Nerves then transmit the output signal back to the penis or clitoris, and this signal causes the changes in blood flow in the genitals that account for an erection. Although the spinal cord does send sensory information onward to the brain, this role is not essential. People with spinal injuries that sever communication between the lower regions of the spinal cord and the brain can usually achieve erection with tactile stimulation alone.

Signal to brain

Segment of spinal cord

Interneuron

Motor

Sensory

Sensory nerve endings

---

stimulating experiences seem to increase it (Stone et al., 2011; Van Bokhoven et al., 2011; Wu et al., 2008). A key area for researchers to now address is discovering the relevance and implications of these early findings.

The spinal cord Beginning at the base of the brain and continuing down the middle of the back, the spinal cord carries vital information from the rest of the body to and from the brain. The spinal cord doesn't just relay messages. It can also initiate some automatic behaviours on its own. We call these involuntary automatic behaviours

> **reflexes** or **reflex arcs** Involuntary automatic behaviour initiated by the spinal cord in response to some stimulus.

reflexes or **reflex arcs** because the response to the incoming stimuli is automatically "reflected" back (**Figure 2.13**).

We're all born with numerous reflexes, many of which fade over time. But even as adults, we still blink in response to a puff of air in our eyes, gag when something touches the back of our throat, and urinate and defecate in response to pressure in the bladder and rectum. Reflexes also influence our sexual responses. Certain stimuli, such as touching the genitals, can lead to clitoral and penile erection (see *Psychological Science*). But to experience passion, sexual thoughts, and emotions, or to get aroused by sexy sights or sounds, the sensory information must ultimately include the brain.

Peripheral Nervous System (PNS): Connecting the CNS to the Rest of the Body

The main function of the peripheral nervous system (PNS) is to carry information to and from the central nervous system. It links the brain and spinal cord to the body's senses, muscles, and glands.

The PNS is subdivided into the somatic nervous system and the autonomic nervous system. In a kind of "two-way street," the **somatic nervous system (SNS)** first carries sensory information to the CNS and then carries messages from the CNS back to the skeletal muscles (**Figure 2.14**).

The other subdivision of the PNS is the **autonomic nervous system (ANS)**. The ANS is responsible for involuntary tasks, such as heart rate, digestion, pupil dilation, and breathing. Like an automatic pilot, the ANS can sometimes be consciously

> **somatic nervous system (SNS)** Subdivision of the peripheral nervous system (PNS). The SNS transmits incoming sensory information and controls the skeletal muscles.

> **autonomic nervous system (ANS)** Subdivision of the peripheral nervous system (PNS) that controls involuntary functions of tissues, organs, and glands. It is subdivided into the sympathetic nervous system and the parasympathetic nervous system.

The relationship between sensory and motor neurons • Figure 2.14

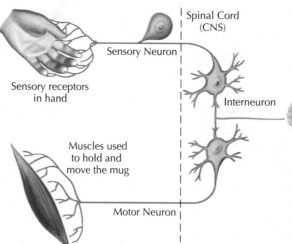

Spinal Cord (CNS)

Sensory Neuron

Sensory receptors in hand

Interneuron

Muscles used to hold and move the mug

Motor Neuron

For you to be able to function, your brain must communicate with your body. This is the job of the *somatic nervous system*, which receives sensory information, sends it to the brain, and assists in the brain's response. *Sensory neurons* carry messages to the CNS. *Motor neurons* carry messages away from the CNS. *Interneurons* communicate within the CNS and link up the sensory inputs and the motor outputs. Most of the neurons in the brain are interneurons. What *type* of communication do you think occurs across interneurons within the CNS?

overridden. But as its name implies, the autonomic system normally operates on its own without conscious effort (autonomously).

The autonomic nervous system is further divided into two branches: the sympathetic and parasympathetic, which tend to work in opposition to regulate the functioning of organs, like the heart, the intestines, and the lungs (**Figure 2.15**).

During stressful times, either mental or physical, the **sympathetic nervous system** mobilizes bodily resources to respond to the stressor. This emergency response is often called the fight-or-flight response. If you saw an angry black bear lumbering toward you, your sympathetic nervous system would, among other things, increase your heart rate, respiration, and blood pressure; stop your digestive and eliminative processes; and release hormones,

Actions of the autonomic nervous system (ANS) • Figure 2.15

Stress, high activity, fight or flight

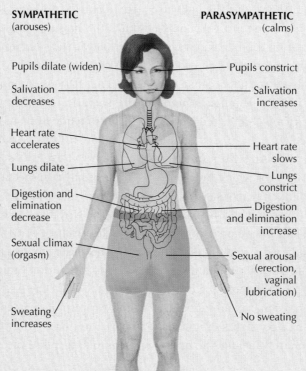

SYMPATHETIC (arouses)

- Pupils dilate (widen)
- Salivation decreases
- Heart rate accelerates
- Lungs dilate
- Digestion and elimination decrease
- Sexual climax (orgasm)
- Sweating increases

PARASYMPATHETIC (calms)

- Pupils constrict
- Salivation increases
- Heart rate slows
- Lungs constrict
- Digestion and elimination increase
- Sexual arousal (erection, vaginal lubrication)
- No sweating

Relaxation, low stress, rest and digest

Applying Psychology

Activation of the Sympathetic Nervous System

The complexities of sexual interaction—and in particular the difficulties that some men and women sometimes have in achieving sexual arousal—illustrate the balancing act between the sympathetic and parasympathetic nervous systems.

Sexual arousal and excitement require that the body be relaxed enough to allow increased blood flow to the genitals. During parasympathetic nervous system activation, nerves carry messages from the CNS directly to the sexual organs, allowing for increased blood flow and genital arousal.

During sympathetic nervous system activation, blood flow to the genitals and organs decreases as the body readies for a fight or flight response. As a result the person is less likely to become sexually aroused or maintain an erection.

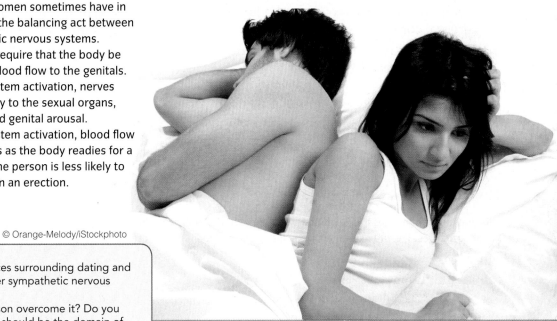

© Orange-Melody/iStockphoto

Think Critically

1. Are there any circumstances surrounding dating and sexuality that could trigger sympathetic nervous system activation?
2. In what ways might a person overcome it? Do you think such intimate topics should be the domain of psychological research?

---

such as cortisol, into the bloodstream. The net result of sympathetic activation is to get more oxygenated blood and energy to the skeletal muscles and to prepare you to deal with the stressor—whether you defend yourself (fight) or escape (flight).

The sympathetic nervous system provides an adaptive, evolutionary advantage. Early in evolution, when an organism faced a dangerous predator or an aggressive intruder, it had only two reasonable responses: fight or flight. This evolved automatic mobilization of bodily resources is still essential today. However, non-life-threatening events, such as traffic jams and pressing deadlines, also activate our sympathetic nervous system. As the next chapter discusses, ongoing sympathetic activation to such chronic stressors can damage health and well-being.

In contrast to the sympathetic nervous system and its fight or flight response, the **parasympathetic nervous system** functions to rest and digest. It is responsible for returning the body to its normal functioning by slowing heart rate, lowering blood pressure, and increasing digestive and eliminative processes. In non-arousing activities (such as reading, texting, or talking on the phone), this branch of the nervous system is involved in energy storage and conservation. Understanding the complementary processes involved in the autonomic nervous system can provide some useful insights into common problems. (See *Applying Psychology* for one such example.)

CONCEPT CHECK

1. **What** are some of the important roles of the spinal cord?
2. **How** are neurogenesis and neuroplasticity different?
3. **What** are the tasks of each subdivision of the peripheral nervous system?

A Tour through the Brain

LEARNING OBJECTIVES

1. **Identify** the major structures of the hindbrain, midbrain, and forebrain, and of the cerebral cortex.

2. **Summarize** the major roles of the lobes of the cerebral cortex.

3. **Describe** what scientists have learned from split-brain research.

4. **Explain** why it's a mistake to believe that the right brain is usually "neglected."

5. **Describe** some examples of localization of function in the brain.

 e begin our exploration of the brain at the lower end, where the spinal cord joins the base of the brain, and move upward toward the front of the skull. As we move from bottom to top, vital reflexes, like breathing, generally give way to more complex mental processes, like making social judgments and planning (**Figure 2.16**).

The human brain • Figure 2.16

This drawing summarizes the key functions of some of the brain's major structures. The brainstem, which includes parts of the hindbrain, midbrain, and forebrain, provides a handy geographical landmark.

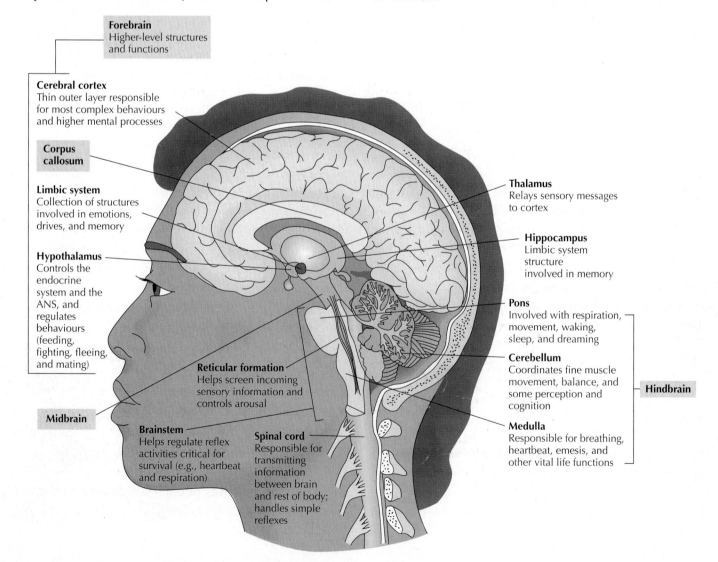

Forebrain
Higher-level structures and functions

Cerebral cortex
Thin outer layer responsible for most complex behaviours and higher mental processes

Corpus callosum

Limbic system
Collection of structures involved in emotions, drives, and memory

Hypothalamus
Controls the endocrine system and the ANS, and regulates behaviours (feeding, fighting, fleeing, and mating)

Midbrain

Reticular formation
Helps screen incoming sensory information and controls arousal

Brainstem
Helps regulate reflex activities critical for survival (e.g., heartbeat and respiration)

Spinal cord
Responsible for transmitting information between brain and rest of body; handles simple reflexes

Thalamus
Relays sensory messages to cortex

Hippocampus
Limbic system structure involved in memory

Pons
Involved with respiration, movement, waking, sleep, and dreaming

Cerebellum
Coordinates fine muscle movement, balance, and some perception and cognition

Medulla
Responsible for breathing, heartbeat, emesis, and other vital life functions

Hindbrain

Lower-Level Brain Structures: The Hindbrain, Midbrain, and Parts of the Forebrain

The billions of neurons that make up the human brain control most of what we think, feel, and do. Certain brain structures are specialized to perform certain tasks, a process known as **localization of function**. However, most parts of the brain perform integrative, interdependent functions.

> **localization of function**
> Specialization of various parts of the brain for particular functions.

The hindbrain The **hindbrain** includes the medulla, pons, and cerebellum and functions collectively to generate most of your vital bodily processes. When this region is damaged or deprived of oxygen, the consequences for the individual can be catastrophic (**Figure 2.17**).

The **medulla** is effectively an extension of the top of the spinal cord, carrying information to and from the brain. It also controls many essential automatic bodily functions, such as respiration and heart rate, so damage to this brain region is often fatal. But for your medulla you would also not be able to swallow, vomit, or defecate—all clearly essential functions.

The **pons** is involved in respiration, movement, sleeping, waking, and dreaming (among other things). The pons also has a role in relaying sensory information from the periphery to higher brain structures. For example, auditory information first enters the brain at the level of the pons.

The cauliflower-shaped **cerebellum** at the back of the brain ("little brain" in Latin) is, evolutionarily, a very old structure. It coordinates fine muscle movement and balance. The cerebellum also has the rather interesting task of taking a sequence of movements that always runs in the same order and packaging them as a single automatic output. While executing complex martial arts moves or acrobatic movements nicely illustrate the cerebellum at work, it is best demonstrated when a person is learning to drive a standard transmission car. For most, this process is initially very difficult, requiring tremendous concentration to get the clutch, gas, and gear change in the correct order. After a bit of practice, however, the driver is able to change gears effortlessly, without being distracted by music, conversation, or other variables: the cerebellum has tuned into the repetitive behaviours involved in the gear-changing process and runs them as a single smooth behaviour. This ability then frees up higher brain regions to do more complex tasks, such as concentrating on road conditions and other drivers (and not changing radio stations, searching for music, or texting friends!).

Damage to the brain • Figure 2.17

Isaiah May was born in Alberta on October 24, 2009. During a long and difficult labour the umbilical cord became wrapped around his neck, cutting off the supply of oxygen to his brain. After doctors examined Isaiah they determined his brain damage was both severe and irreversible and he would soon die. But Isaiah survived, and for the next two months he continued to grow and develop. Despite these positive signs his medical team believed Isaiah was brain dead. He had no evidence of brainstem function and could not survive without the aid of a ventilator to manage his breathing. On January 13, 2010, the hospital wrote a letter to his parents stating they were taking him off his ventilator. Isaiah's parents, Rebecka and Isaac May, applied to the courts for an injunction to stop the actions of the hospital. Court of Queen's Bench Justice Michelle Crighton requested both parties find an independent expert to assess the severity of Isaiah's brain damage. Ultimately, based on advice from two neonatal specialists the Mays agreed to remove Isaiah from the ventilator and he died on March 11, 2010 (CBC News, 2011a; Hanon, 2010). In Canada and many other countries, brain death is defined, in part, as the irreversible loss of all brainstem functions, including the capacity to breathe. It is deemed equivalent to the death of the individual (Canadian Neurocritical Care Group, 1999). Under this definition a person can be brain dead even though the heart continues to beat.

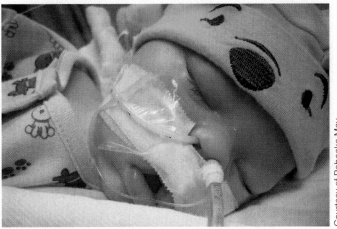

Courtesy of Rebecka May

The midbrain The **midbrain** helps us orient our eye and body movements to visual and auditory stimuli, and works with the pons to help control sleep, temperature regulation, and level of arousal. When you are visually tracking a moving object, it is the midbrain—among other regions—that is active.

Running through the core of the hindbrain, mid-brain, and brainstem is the **reticular formation** (RF). This diffuse, long, finger-shaped network of neurons filters incoming sensory information and alerts the higher brain centres to important events. It also regulates pain signals and body movement.

The forebrain The **forebrain** is the largest and most prominent part of the human brain. It includes the thalamus, hypothalamus, limbic system, cerebrum, and cerebral cortex (**Figure 2.18**). The first three structures are

located near the top of the brainstem. The cerebrum is wrapped above and completely around the other three structures, and the cerebral cortex (discussed separately in the next section) is the outermost layer of the cerebrum. (*Cerebrum* is Latin for "brain" and *cortex* is Latin for "covering" or "bark.")

The **thalamus** receives input from nearly all sensory systems and directs the information to the appropriate cortical areas. It may also have a role in learning and memory (Bailey & Mair, 2005; Ridley et al., 2005). Because the thalamus is the brain's major sensory relay centre to the cerebral cortex, damage or abnormalities can cause the cortex to misinterpret or not receive vital sensory information. Interestingly, brain-imaging research has linked thalamus abnormalities to schizophrenia, a serious psychological disorder involving problems with accurate sensory processing (such as hearing) and perception

Structures of the forebrain • Figure 2.18

Cerebral cortex
Governs higher mental processes

Hypothalamus
Controls the autonomic nervous system, the endocrine system, and motivated behaviours, such as eating and sex

Limbic system
Functions in memory and regulates fear and other emotions

Thalamus
Integrates input from the senses

(Chapter 13) (Andreasen et al., 2008; Byne et al., 2008; Clinton & Meador-Woodruff, 2004; Preuss et al., 2005).

Beneath the thalamus lies the kidney-bean-sized **hypothalamus** (*hypo* means "under" or "below"). It is the control centre for many essential survival behaviours, such as hunger, thirst, sex, and aggression (Hinton et al., 2004; Williams et al., 2004; Zillmer, et al., 2008). It controls the autonomic nervous system and the body's internal environment, including temperature control, which it achieves by controlling the endocrine system. Looking as if it is dripping from the bottom of the hypothalamus is the *pituitary gland*. The pituitary is often wrongly referred to as the master endocrine gland, but this gland is actually a slave to the hypothalamus. On instruction from the hypothalamus, it releases hormones that activate the other endocrine glands in the body. The hypothalamus influences the pituitary in two ways: (1) through direct neural connections and (2) by releasing its own hormones into the blood supply to the pituitary.

An interconnected group of forebrain structures, known as the **limbic system**, is located roughly along the border between the cerebral cortex and the lower-level brain structures.

In general, the limbic system is responsible for emotions, learning, and memory and includes the *hippocampus* and the *amygdala* (some neuroanatomists also include parts of the thalamus, the hypothalamus, and the pituitary in the limbic system). The amygdala has been a major focus of research interest in the limbic system, particularly its involvement in aggression and fear (Asghar et al., 2008; Carlson, 2008; LeDoux, 1998, 2002, 2007). Another well-known function of the limbic system is its role in pleasure and reward (Dackis & O'Brien, 2001; Olds & Milner, 1954; Torta & Castelli, 2008). Even though limbic system structures and neurotransmitters are instrumental in emotional behaviour, the cerebral cortex also tempers and modulates emotion in humans.

The hippocampus is important in long-term memory and spatial navigation. It is one of the first brain regions to be affected in people with Alzheimer's, and this is probably why early symptoms of the disease involve memory loss and disorientation, which progressively worsen (Dhikav & Anand, 2011).

Neuroanatomy of Protection and Support

The brain and spinal cord are protected and supported by a number of structures. Enclosing the entire CNS

The supporting and protective structures of the CNS • Figure 2.19

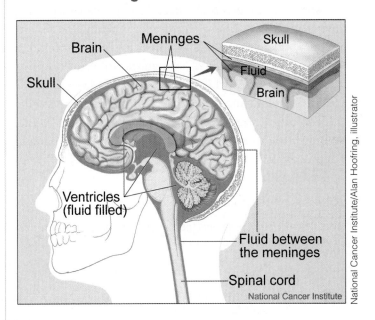

National Cancer Institute

National Cancer Institute/Alan Hoofring, illustrator

are three layers of membranes or **meninges** (**Figure 2.19**) that align closely with the surface of the brain and spinal cord and offer structural support and protection. The CNS is also protected and cushioned by *cerebrospinal fluid* (*CSF*), which circulates around the CNS and fills four spaces inside the brain called *ventricles*. Cerebrospinal fluid is constantly being made, circulated, and removed from the CNS. If the passage of outflow is blocked, CSF accumulates inside the skull, leading to brain swelling and a condition known as hydrocephalus ("water" and "head" in literal translation). This serious condition can cause enlargement of the head, convulsions, mental disability, and sometimes death.

> **meninges** The triple-layered set of membranes that envelope the CNS to provide support and protection.

The Cerebral Cortex: The Centre of Our Higher Processing

The grey, wrinkled **cerebral cortex** is responsible for most of our complex behaviours and higher mental processes. It plays such a vital role in our sense of self that many

> **cerebral cortex** Thin surface layer on the cerebral hemispheres that regulates most complex behaviour, including processing sensations, motor control, and higher mental processes.

consider it the essence of our subjective experience of life and the embodiment of exactly who we are.

Although the cerebral cortex is only about three millimetres thick, it's made up of approximately 30 billion neurons and nine times as many glial cells. It contains numerous wrinkles called *convolutions* (think of a crumpled-up newspaper), which allow it to maximize its surface area while still fitting into the restricted space of the skull.

The full cerebral cortex and the two cerebral hemispheres beneath it closely resemble an oversized walnut. The deep valley, or *fissure*, down the centre marks the left and right *hemispheres* of the brain. The hemispheres make up about 80 percent of the brain's weight. They are mostly filled with axon connections between the cortex and the other brain structures. Each hemisphere gets signals from and controls the opposite side of the body.

The cerebral hemispheres are divided into eight distinct areas or lobes, with four in each hemisphere (**Figure 2.20**). Like the lower-level brain structures, each lobe specializes in somewhat different tasks—another example of localization of function. However, some functions are shared between the lobes.

Lobes of the brain • Figure 2.20

Divisions between the brain's four lobes—frontal, parietal, temporal, and occipital—are marked by visibly prominent folds or valleys.

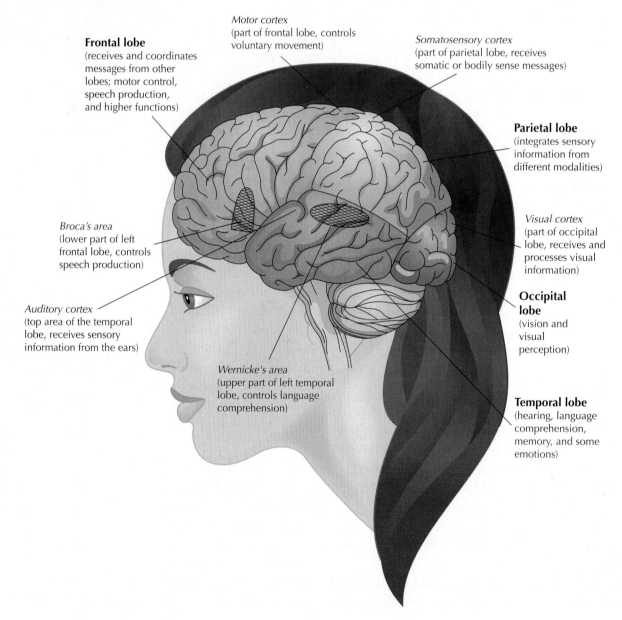

Frontal lobe
(receives and coordinates messages from other lobes; motor control, speech production, and higher functions)

Motor cortex
(part of frontal lobe, controls voluntary movement)

Somatosensory cortex
(part of parietal lobe, receives somatic or bodily sense messages)

Parietal lobe
(integrates sensory information from different modalities)

Visual cortex
(part of occipital lobe, receives and processes visual information)

Occipital lobe
(vision and visual perception)

Broca's area
(lower part of left frontal lobe, controls speech production)

Auditory cortex
(top area of the temporal lobe, receives sensory information from the ears)

Wernicke's area
(upper part of left temporal lobe, controls language comprehension)

Temporal lobe
(hearing, language comprehension, memory, and some emotions)

Accidental evidence of specialized brain functions? • Figure 2.21 _____

In 1998, construction worker Travis Bogumill was accidentally shot with a nail gun near the rear of his right frontal lobe. Remarkably, Bogumill experienced only an impaired ability to perform complex mathematical problems. This case study is consistent with experimental research showing that the frontal lobes and short-term memory are responsible for mathematical calculations, reasoning, problem solving, and thinking about future rewards or actions (Evans, 2003; Hill, 2004; Neubauer et al., 2004). What symptoms do you think he might have experienced should the injury have been to his left frontal lobe?

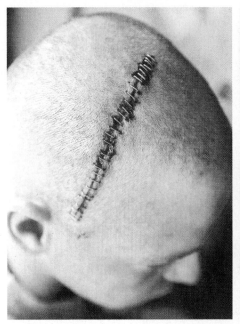
Jeff Thompson/AP Photo/Eau Claire Leader-Telegram

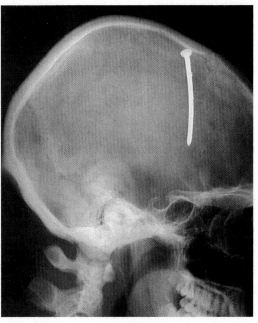
Jeff Thompson/AP Photo/Eau Claire Leader-Telegram

The frontal lobes The large **frontal lobes** coordinate messages received from the other three lobes. An area at the very back of the frontal lobes, known as the *motor cortex*, initiates all voluntary movement (which is different from the largely automatic motor tasks performed by the cerebellum). In the lower left frontal lobe lies *Broca's area*. In 1865, French physician Paul Broca discovered that damage to this area causes difficulty in speech production but not language comprehension. This type of impaired language ability is known as *Broca's aphasia*. The frontal lobes also control most of the higher functions that distinguish humans from other animals, such as thinking, personality, emotional judgments, and memory. Abnormalities in the frontal lobes are often observed in patients with schizophrenia (Chapter 13). As seen in the case of Phineas Gage (Chapter 1) and in other research, damage to the frontal lobe affects motivation, creativity, self-awareness, initiative, reasoning, and suitable emotional behaviour. Our ability to function normally and respond appropriately in social situations is also a function of the frontal lobes (**Figure 2.21**).

The parietal lobes, the temporal lobes, and the occipital lobes The **parietal lobes** interpret bodily sensations, including pressure, pain, touch, temperature, and location of body parts. A band of cortical tissue along the front of the parietal lobe, called the *somatosensory cortex*, receives information about touch and other skin and visceral senses (**Figure 2.22**). In the 1940s Canadian neurosurgeon Dr. Wilder Penfield was instrumental in mapping the human cortex while developing a surgical treatment for epilepsy. In what was coined the "Montreal Procedure," patients were given a local anaesthetic so they would be conscious throughout the operation. While Penfield probed the brain, the patient described the sensations he or she was experiencing. This allowed Penfield to accurately locate and remove the location of the seizure activity. More than half of his patients were cured of epilepsy as a result of this procedure. This technique also allowed Penfield to create accurate maps of the sensory and motor areas of the brain, showing their connections to the various organs and limbs. These maps are still used today (Library and Archives Canada, 2008).

The **temporal lobes** are responsible for hearing, language comprehension, memory, and some emotions. The *auditory cortex* (which processes sound) is located at the top front of each temporal lobe. This area processes incoming

Body representation of the motor cortex and somatosensory cortex • Figure 2.22

These drawings represent a vertical cross-section taken from the left hemisphere's motor cortex and right hemisphere's somatosensory cortex. If body areas were truly proportional to the amount of tissue on the motor and somatosensory cortices, our bodies would look like the oddly shaped human figures draped around the outside edge of the cortex. Notice that the most sensitive regions of the body and the regions of the body that have the greatest fine motor precision (such as the fingers and the lips) have the largest representations on the motor and somatosensory strip. This is superbly illustrated by clay homunculi ("little men") made to demonstrate the relative space body parts occupy on the motor and sensory strips. Newer research suggests the discrete mapping of the fingers onto the motor cortex may in fact be a bit of an oversimplification. It seems the representation of the fingers actually mingle and overlap, suggesting a more accurate motor homunculus would look like a naked little man wearing mittens. Moreover, the body part position on the cortex appears to be organized according to the behaviours to be performed rather than simply as a static map of the individual body parts (Afshar et al., 2011; Graziano, 2006).

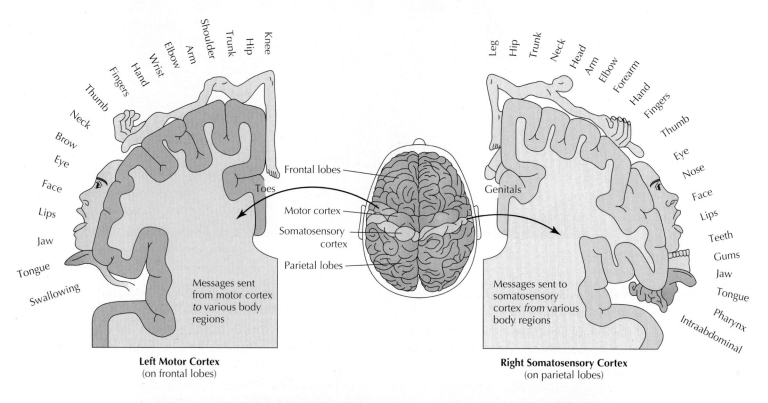

Left Motor Cortex
(on frontal lobes)

Right Somatosensory Cortex
(on parietal lobes)

Messages sent from motor cortex *to* various body regions

Messages sent to somatosensory cortex *from* various body regions

Frontal lobes
Motor cortex
Somatosensory cortex
Parietal lobes

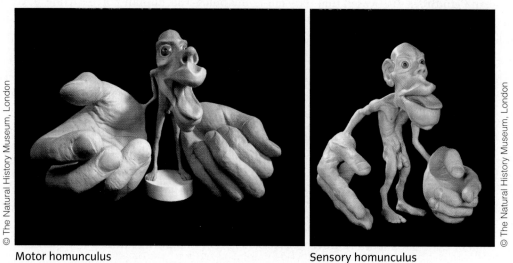

Motor homunculus

Sensory homunculus

© The Natural History Museum, London

sensory information and sends it to the parietal lobes, where it is combined with other sensory information.

An area of the left temporal lobe, *Wernicke's area*, is involved in language comprehension. About a decade after Broca's discovery, German neurologist Carl Wernicke noted that patients with damage in this area could not understand what they read or heard. Their speech was often unintelligible, containing made-up words, sound substitutions, and word substitutions. Interestingly, they could speak quickly and easily as if their utterances were clear and meaningful. This syndrome is now referred to as *Wernicke's aphasia*.

The **occipital lobes** are responsible primarily for vision and visual perception. Damage to the occipital lobe can produce blindness, even though the eyes and their neural connection to the brain are perfectly functional.

The association areas One of the most popular and enduring myths in psychology is that we use only 10 percent of our brain. This myth might have begun with early research showing that approximately three quarters of the cortex is *uncommitted* (that is, it had no precise, specific function when stimulated by weak electrical current). This suggested to early researchers that it didn't do anything important—a neural spare tire, for want of a better term. Abundant research has now shown these areas are not at all dormant. They are clearly involved in interpreting, integrating, and acting on information processed by other parts of the brain and cortical lobes. They are called **association areas** because they associate, or connect, various areas and functions of the brain. The association areas in the frontal lobe, for example, help in decision-making and task planning. Similarly, the association area right in front of the motor cortex is involved in the planning of voluntary movement before it occurs.

Two Brains in One? Split-Brain Research

We mentioned earlier that the brain's left and right cerebral hemispheres control opposite sides of the body. Each hemisphere also has some separate areas of specialization. (This is another example of *localization* of function, yet it is technically referred to as *lateralization*.)

Early researchers believed that the right hemisphere was subordinate to the left, or non-dominant, and had few special functions or abilities. In the 1960s, landmark research with *split-brain* patients began to change this view.

The primary connection between the two cerebral hemispheres is a thick, ribbon-like band of axons under the cortex called the **corpus callosum** (see Figure 2.16). In some rare cases of severe epilepsy, when other forms of treatment have failed, surgeons cut the corpus callosum to stop the spread of epileptic seizures from one hemisphere to the other. Because this operation cuts the major communication link between the two hemispheres, it reveals what each half of the brain can do in isolation from the other. The resulting research with split-brain patients has profoundly improved our understanding of how the two halves of the brain function.

If you met and talked with a split-brain patient, you probably wouldn't even know he or she had had the operation. The subtle changes in split-brain patients normally appear only with specialized testing (**Figure 2.23**).

Dozens of studies on split-brain patients, and newer research on people whose brains are intact, have documented several differences between the two brain hemispheres. In general for most adults, the left hemisphere is specialized for language and analytical functions, while the right hemisphere is specialized for non-verbal abilities, such as art and music (**Figure 2.24**). Interestingly, left- and right-brain specialization is not usually reversed in left-handed people. About 68 percent of left-handers and 97 percent of right-handers have their major language areas on the left hemisphere. This suggests that even though the right side of the brain is dominant for movement in left-handers, other skills are often localized in the same brain areas as for right-handers.

What about the popular conception of the neglected right brain? Courses and books directed at "right-brain thinking" often promise to increase your intuition, creativity, and artistic abilities by waking up your "neglected" and "underused" right brain (e.g., Brady, 2004; Edwards, 1999). This myth of the neglected right brain arose from popularized accounts of split-brain patients and exaggerated claims and unwarranted conclusions about differences between the left and right hemispheres. Research has clearly shown that while lateralization is present, the two hemispheres communicate with each other across the corpus callosum and work together in a coordinated and integrated way. Simply said, you cannot get by without your right or your left hemisphere (so don't leave home without them).

Visualizing

Split-brain research • Figure 2.23

Experiments on split-brain patients often present visual information to only the patient's left or right hemisphere, which leads to some intriguing results. For example,

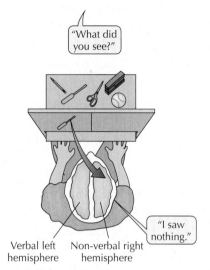

"What did you see?"

"I saw nothing."

Verbal left hemisphere   Non-verbal right hemisphere

a. When a split-brain patient is asked to stare straight ahead while a photo of a screwdriver is flashed only to the right hemisphere (via the visual system), he will report that he "saw nothing." This is because the information has not been presented to the verbal left hemisphere.

"With your left hand, pick up what you saw"

b. However, when asked to pick up with his left hand what he saw, he can reach through and touch the items hidden behind the screen and easily pick up the screwdriver. This is because the right hemisphere knows what it saw, but it cannot speak it. When given the opportunity to show what it saw by touch, it instructs the left hand to pick up the screwdriver.

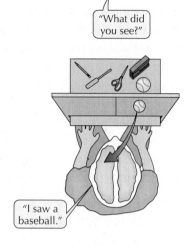

"What did you see?"

"I saw a baseball."

c. When the left hemisphere receives an image of a baseball, the split-brain patient can easily name it.

Assuming you have an intact, unsevered corpus callosum, if the same photos were presented to you in the same way, could you name both the screwdriver and the baseball? Can you explain why? The answers lie in our somewhat confusing visual wiring system:

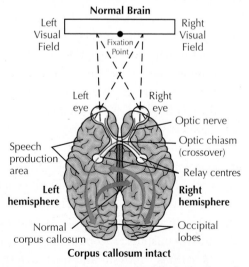

Normal Brain

Left Visual Field — Fixation Point — Right Visual Field

Left eye — Right eye — Optic nerve

Speech production area — Optic chiasm (crossover)

Relay centres

Left hemisphere — **Right hemisphere**

Normal corpus callosum — Occipital lobes

Corpus callosum intact

d. As you can see, our eyes connect to our brains in such a way that, when we look straight ahead, information from the left visual field (the blue line) travels to our right hemisphere, and information from the right visual field (the red line) travels to our left hemisphere. The messages received by either hemisphere are then quickly sent to the other across the corpus callosum. So yes, with an intact corpus callosum you can easily name both the screwdriver and the baseball.

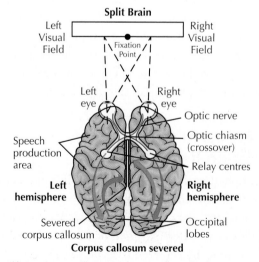

Split Brain

Left Visual Field — Fixation Point — Right Visual Field

Left eye — Right eye — Optic nerve

Speech production area — Optic chiasm (crossover)

Relay centres

Left hemisphere — **Right hemisphere**

Severed corpus callosum — Occipital lobes

Corpus callosum severed

e. When the corpus callosum is severed, and information is presented only to the right hemisphere, a split-brain patient cannot verbalize what he sees because the information cannot travel to the opposite (verbal left) hemisphere to be stated out loud.

Functions of the left and right hemispheres • Figure 2.24

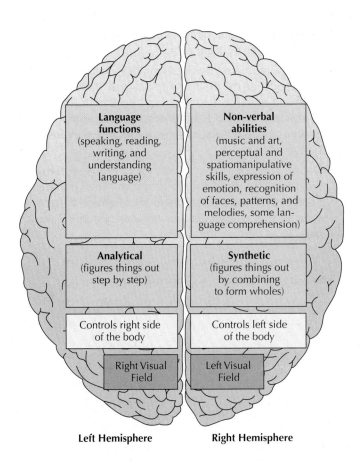

Language functions (speaking, reading, writing, and understanding language)

Non-verbal abilities (music and art, perceptual and spatiomanipulative skills, expression of emotion, recognition of faces, patterns, and melodies, some language comprehension)

Analytical (figures things out step by step)

Synthetic (figures things out by combining to form wholes)

Controls right side of the body

Controls left side of the body

Right Visual Field

Left Visual Field

Left Hemisphere   Right Hemisphere

In general, the left hemisphere specializes in verbal and analytical functions; the right hemisphere focuses on non-verbal abilities, such as spatio-manipulative skills (the ability to locate and manipulate objects in three-dimensional space), art and musical abilities, and visual recognition tasks. Keep in mind, however, that both hemispheres are activated and rapidly share information when we perform almost any task or respond to any stimuli.

CONCEPT CHECK STOP

1. **What** are the main parts of the hindbrain, the midbrain, and the forebrain?
2. **What** are the primary functions of each of the four lobes of the cortex?
3. **Why** is the hypothalamus important?
4. **How** do Broca's aphasia and Wernicke's aphasia differ?
5. **What** are the findings of research with split-brain patients?

 THE PLANNER

Summary

1 Our Genetic Inheritance 38

- **Neuroscience** studies how biological processes relate to behavioural and mental processes.

- Genes (dominant or recessive) hold the code for inherited traits. Scientists use **behavioural genetics** methods to determine the relative influences of heredity and environment (heritability) on complex traits.

- **Evolutionary psychology** suggests that many behavioural commonalities emerged and remain in human populations through natural selection because they were adaptive and improved survival and reproductive success.

Hereditary code • Figure 2.1

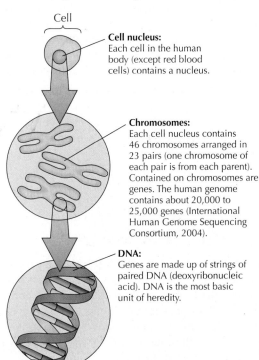

Cell

Cell nucleus: Each cell in the human body (except red blood cells) contains a nucleus.

Chromosomes: Each cell nucleus contains 46 chromosomes arranged in 23 pairs (one chromosome of each pair is from each parent). Contained on chromosomes are genes. The human genome contains about 20,000 to 25,000 genes (International Human Genome Sequencing Consortium, 2004).

DNA: Genes are made up of strings of paired DNA (deoxyribonucleic acid). DNA is the most basic unit of heredity.

2 Neural Bases of Behaviour   42

- **Neurons**, supported by **glial cells**, receive and send electrochemical signals to other neurons and to the rest of the body. Their major components are **dendrites**, a **cell body**, and an **axon**.

- Within a neuron, a neural impulse, or **action potential**, moves along the axon.

How neurons communicate: Communication *within* the neuron • Figure 2.8a

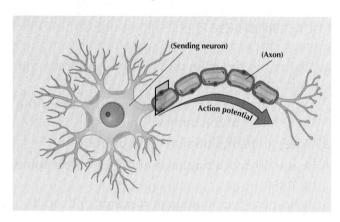

(Sending neuron)

(Axon)

Action potential

- Neurons communicate with each other by using **neurotransmitters**, which are released at the synapse and bind to receptors on the dendrites and cell bodies of receiving neurons. Neurons receive input from many synapses, some excitatory and some inhibitory. Hundreds of different neurotransmitters regulate a wide variety of physiological processes. Many poisons, toxins, and drugs act by mimicking or interfering with neurotransmitters.

- The **endocrine system** uses **hormones** to broadcast messages throughout the body. The system regulates long-term bodily processes, maintains ongoing bodily processes, and controls the body's response to emergencies.

3 The Organization of the Nervous System   49

- **The central nervous system (CNS)** includes the brain and spinal cord. The CNS allows us to process information and adapt to our environment in unique and versatile ways. The spinal cord transmits information between the brain and the rest of the body, and initiates involuntary **reflexes**. Although the CNS is very fragile, recent research shows that the brain is capable of lifelong neuroplasticity and **neurogenesis**. Neurogenesis is made possible by **stem cells**.

- The **peripheral nervous system (PNS)** includes all the nerves outside the brain and spinal cord. It links the brain and spinal cord to the body's senses, muscles, and glands. The PNS is subdivided into the **somatic nervous system (SNS)** and the **autonomic nervous system (ANS)**.

- The ANS includes the **sympathetic nervous system** and the **parasympathetic nervous system**. The sympathetic nervous system mobilizes the body's fight-or-flight response. The parasympathetic nervous system returns the body to its normal functioning.

The nervous system • Figure 2.11

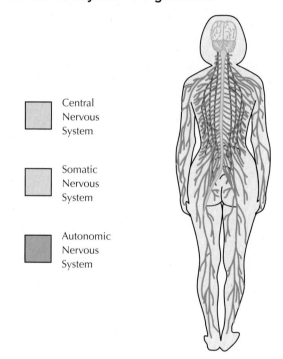

Central Nervous System

Somatic Nervous System

Autonomic Nervous System

4 A Tour through the Brain   56

- The brain is divided into the **hindbrain**, the **midbrain**, and the **forebrain**. The brainstem includes parts of each of these. Certain brain structures are specialized to perform certain tasks (**localization of function**).

- The hindbrain (including the **medulla**, **pons**, and **cerebellum**) controls automatic behaviours and vital reflexes.

- The midbrain helps us orient our eye and body movements, and helps control sleep and arousal. The **reticular formation** runs through the core of the hindbrain, midbrain, and brainstem.

- Forebrain structures (including the **thalamus, hypothalamus**, and **limbic system**) integrate input from the senses, control survival behaviours, and regulate the body's internal environment, emotions, learning, and memory.

- The **meninges**, cerebrospinal fluid, and ventricles support and protect the brain and spinal cord.

- The cerebrum and **cerebral cortex** are part of the forebrain and govern most higher processing and complex behaviours. It is divided into two hemispheres, each controlling the opposite side of the body. The **corpus callosum** links the hemispheres. Each hemisphere is divided into **frontal, parietal, temporal**, and **occipital lobes**. Each lobe specializes in somewhat different tasks, but a large part of the cortex is devoted to integrating actions performed by different brain regions.

- Split-brain research shows that each hemisphere performs somewhat different functions, although they work closely together, communicating through the corpus callosum.

The human brain • Figure 2.16

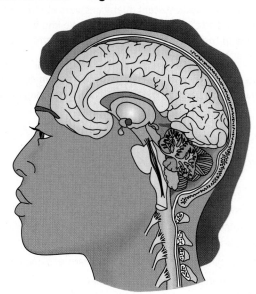

Key Terms

- action potential p. 43
- association areas p. 63
- autonomic nervous system (ANS) p. 53
- axon p. 43
- behavioural genetics p. 38
- cell body p. 43
- central nervous system (CNS) p. 49
- cerebellum p. 57
- cerebral cortex p. 59
- corpus callosum p. 63
- dendrites p. 43
- endocrine system p. 47
- endorphins p. 47
- evolutionary psychology p. 38
- forebrain p. 58

- frontal lobes p. 61
- glial cell p. 42
- hindbrain p. 57
- hormones p. 47
- hypothalamus p. 59
- limbic system p. 59
- localization of function p. 57
- medulla p. 57
- meninges p. 59
- midbrain p. 58
- myelin sheath p. 43
- natural selection p. 41
- neurogenesis p. 51
- neuron p. 42
- neuroplasticity p. 51

- neuroscience p. 38
- neurotransmitters p. 46
- occipital lobes p. 63
- parasympathetic nervous system p. 55
- parietal lobes p. 61
- peripheral nervous system (PNS) p. 49
- pons p. 57
- reflexes or reflex arcs p. 53
- reticular formation p. 58
- somatic nervous system (SNS) p. 53
- stem cells p. 51
- sympathetic nervous system p. 54
- temporal lobes p. 61
- thalamus p. 58

Critical and Creative Thinking Questions

1. Imagine that scientists were able to identify specific genes linked to criminal behaviour, and it was possible to remove or redesign these genes. Would you be in favour of this type of gene manipulation? Why or why not?

2. In considering gene–environment interaction, what are some ways in which you are very similar to your parents or your siblings? What ways are you very different? Can you think of environmental factors, such as events and experiences, that might contribute to this variation?

3. Why is it valuable for scientists to understand how neurotransmitters work at a molecular level?

4. What are some everyday examples of neuroplasticity? That is, describe some ways the brain is changed and shaped by experience.

5. Which part of the nervous system allows you to type on your keyboard and which part allows you to recognize that it is indeed a keyboard beneath your fingers?

6. As neuroscience continues to understand the marvels of the human nervous system, many answers about the causes of disease and disorders are revealed. We know the many benefits of these findings in helping to treat and cure, but can you think of any disadvantages?

7. When you experience different emotions, from anger to pleasure, what system of the brain is active? Imagine if neuroscience could surgically change this system so that we only felt positive emotions. What would be the advantages and disadvantages of this type of manipulation?

8. If you were in a car accident that damaged your left temporal lobe, what type of behavioural and cognitive deficits would you experience?

Self-Test

(Check your answers in Appendix A.)

1. Behavioural genetics is the study of _____.
   a. the relative effects of behaviour and genetics on survival
   b. the relative effects of heredity and environment on behaviour and mental processes
   c. the relative effects of genetics on natural selection
   d. how genetics affects correct behaviour

2. Evolutionary psychology studies _____.
   a. the ways in which humans adapted their behaviour to survive and evolve
   b. the ways in which humankind's behaviour has changed over the millennia
   c. the ways in which humans can evolve to change behaviour
   d. the ways in which natural selection and adaptation can explain behaviour and mental processes

3. This is a measure of the degree to which a characteristic is related to genetic, inherited factors.
   a. heritability
   b. inheritance
   c. the biological ratio
   d. the genome statistic

4. The term _____ refers to the evolutionary concept that those with adaptive genetic traits will survive and reproduce and their genes will spread in the population.
   a. natural selection
   b. evolution
   c. survival of the fittest
   d. all of these options

5. Label the following parts of a neuron, the cell of the nervous system responsible for receiving and transmitting electrochemical information:
   a. dendrites
   b. cell body
   c. axon
   d. myelin sheath
   e. terminal buttons of axon

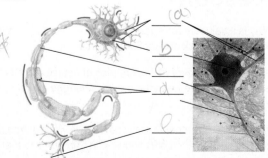

6. Your textbook defines the *action potential* as _____.
   a. the likelihood that a neuron will take action when stimulated
   b. the tendency for a neuron to be potentiated by neurotransmitters
   c. a neural impulse that carries information along the axon of a neuron
   d. the firing of a nerve, either toward or away from the brain

7. Why is the myelin sheath so important for proper neural functioning?
   a. Myelin allows neurotransmitters to travel smoothly from the dendrites to the cell body.
   b. Myelin allows significantly faster neural communication.
   c. Myelin allows neurotransmitters to travel smoothly from the cell body to the axon.
   d. Myelin supports the fundamental metabolic, life-sustaining functions of the neuron.

8. Which of the following neurotransmitters would be released if we experienced a severe and painful injury, such as a broken bone?
   a. serotonin, as it helps with pain relief
   b. dopamine, as it helps us feel less stressed during traumatic situations
   c. norepinephrine, as it helps with recovery
   d. endorphins, as they help with pain relief

9. Too much of this neurotransmitter appears to be related to schizophrenia, whereas too little may be related to Parkinson's disease.
   a. acetylcholine
   b. dopamine
   c. norepinephrine
   d. serotonin

10. Chemicals that are manufactured by endocrine glands and circulated in the bloodstream to change or maintain bodily functions are called _____.
    a. vasopressors
    b. gonadotropins
    c. hormones
    d. steroids

11. Label the main glands of the endocrine system:

a. pineal

b. pituitary

c. adrenal

d. thyroid

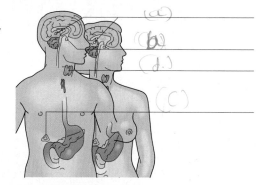

12. The central nervous system _____.

a. consists of the brain and spinal cord

b. is the most important nervous system

c. includes the automatic and other nervous systems

d. all of these options

13. The peripheral nervous system _____.

a. is composed of the spinal cord and most of the peripheral nerves

b. is less important than the central nervous system

c. is contained within the skull and spinal column

d. includes all the nerves and neurons outside the brain and spinal cord

14. The _____ nervous system is responsible for fight or flight, whereas the _____ nervous system is responsible for maintaining calm.

a. central; peripheral

b. parasympathetic; sympathetic

c. sympathetic; parasympathetic

d. autonomic; somatic

15. Driving on the highway late one night, Jason's car nearly collided with another vehicle. The sudden shock of this near-fatal experience made Jason's heart rate increase dramatically, his breathing quicken, and his entire body break into a sweat. Which division of the nervous system was activated by this experience?

a. the sympathetic nervous system

b. the peripheral nervous system

c. the parasympathetic nervous system

d. the central nervous system

16. Label the following structures or areas of the brain:

a. forebrain

b. midbrain

c. hindbrain

d. thalamus

e. hypothalamus

f. cerebral cortex

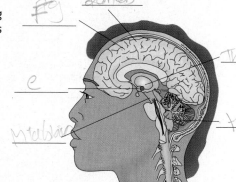

17. Label the four lobes of the brain:

a. frontal lobe   c. temporal lobe

b. parietal lobe   d. occipital lobe

18. A serious car accident has left Jasmine with the inability to speak normally (she can still understand everything said to her, however). She also has difficulty with many simple, everyday cognitive tasks. Which part of her brain has likely sustained the most damage?

a. the frontal lobes   c. the hindbrain

b. the left hemisphere   d. the limbic system

19. Identify the following functions of the brain with either the left or right hemisphere.

a. language function, _____ hemisphere

b. nonverbal abilities, _____ hemisphere

c. control of left side of the body, _____ hemisphere

d. control of right side of the body, _____ hemisphere

20. What has newer research shown regarding the bodily representation on the motor and somatosensory cortex?

a. Only men have these structures.

b. The representation of the fingers mingle and overlap.

c. The most sensitive regions have the largest representation.

d. All of the above.

> **THE PLANNER** ✓
>
> Review your Chapter Planner on the chapter opener and check off your completed work.

Well-Being, Stress, and Coping

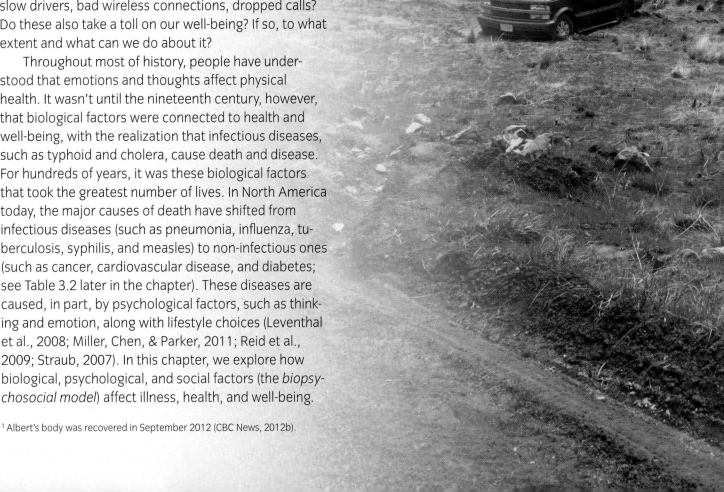

In March 2011, Rita and Albert Chretien left their home in British Columbia to drive to a trade show in Las Vegas. En route, their vehicle got stuck in mud on a logging road in northeastern Nevada. After being stranded for three days, Albert left to find help, taking the GPS with him. Rita remained with the vehicle. She would stay there, alone, for the next seven weeks, surviving on sandy water from a nearby pool, fish oil pills, some candy, and small quantities of trail mix. During her ordeal, she lost 13 kilograms but maintained remarkable mental strength. She attributed her amazing coping skills to her faith, a commitment to keeping busy, and being willing to wait it out until rescuers arrived. Local hunters found Rita early in May. (CBC News, 2011b)[1]. For Rita, this was undoubtedly the most stressful time in her life. Many would not have been able to endure such physical and psychological hardship. How does such extreme stress affect people's health and well-being? How do people cope, and why do some people cope better than others? What about life's more trivial aggravations: slow drivers, bad wireless connections, dropped calls? Do these also take a toll on our well-being? If so, to what extent and what can we do about it?

Throughout most of history, people have understood that emotions and thoughts affect physical health. It wasn't until the nineteenth century, however, that biological factors were connected to health and well-being, with the realization that infectious diseases, such as typhoid and cholera, cause death and disease. For hundreds of years, it was these biological factors that took the greatest number of lives. In North America today, the major causes of death have shifted from infectious diseases (such as pneumonia, influenza, tuberculosis, syphilis, and measles) to non-infectious ones (such as cancer, cardiovascular disease, and diabetes; see Table 3.2 later in the chapter). These diseases are caused, in part, by psychological factors, such as thinking and emotion, along with lifestyle choices (Leventhal et al., 2008; Miller, Chen, & Parker, 2011; Reid et al., 2009; Straub, 2007). In this chapter, we explore how biological, psychological, and social factors (the *biopsychosocial model*) affect illness, health, and well-being.

[1] Albert's body was recovered in September 2012 (CBC News, 2012b).

CHAPTER OUTLINE

CHAPTER PLANNER ✔

- ❏ Study the picture and read the opening story.
- ❏ Scan the Learning Objectives in each section:
  p. 72 ❏   p. 78 ❏   p. 83 ❏   p. 88 ❏
- ❏ Read the text and study all visuals. Answer any questions.

Analyze key features

- ❏ Applying Psychology p. 74 ❏   p. 84 ❏   p. 86 ❏
- ❏ Study Organizer, p. 75
- ❏ Process Diagram p. 76 ❏   p. 77 ❏   p. 89 ❏
- ❏ What a Psychologist Sees, p. 80
- ❏ Psychological Science, p. 83
- ❏ Stop: Answer the Concept Checks before you go on:
  p. 78 ❏   p. 82 ❏   p. 88 ❏   p. 91 ❏

End of chapter

- ❏ Review the Summary and Key Terms.
- ❏ Answer the Critical and Creative Thinking Questions.
- ❏ Complete the Self-Test and check your answers.

Jarbidge Wilderness, Albert and Rita Chretien vehicle as located. Elko County Sheriff's Office: Elko, Nevada.

Understanding Stress

LEARNING OBJECTIVES

1. **Describe** some common sources of stress.

2. **Explain** how the body responds to stress, immediately and over the long term.

3. **Review** the three phases of the general adaptation syndrome (GAS).

nything that places a demand on the body can cause **stress**. The trigger that prompts the stressful reaction is called a **stressor**. Stress reactions can occur in response to internal cognitive stimuli, such as chronic worrying, or external (environmental) stimuli, such as ongoing loud noise (Sarafino, 2008; Straub, 2007).

> **stress** The body's non-specific response to any demand made on it; the physical and mental arousal to circumstances that we perceive as threatening or challenging.
>
> **stressor** An event that places demands on an organism that tax its resources.
>
> **eustress** Pleasant, beneficial, or curative stress.

Pleasant or beneficial stress, such as moderate exercise or winning a competition, is called **eustress**. Stress that is unpleasant or objectionable, as might occur when a person is stuck in a traffic jam, is called **distress** (Selye, 1974).

Sources of Stress

Early stress researchers Thomas Holmes and Richard Rahe (1967) believed that any life change that required some adjustment or compensation in behaviour or lifestyle could cause some degree of stress (**Figure 3.1**). They also believed that exposure to several stressful events within a short period could have a direct and detrimental effect on health.

To measure the relationship between change and stress, Holmes and Rahe created and administered a Social Readjustment Rating Scale (SRRS) and then asked people to check off those life events they had experienced in the previous year (**Table 3.1**).

The SRRS scale is an easy and well-used tool to measure stress caused by life change. Cross-cultural studies have shown that most people rank the magnitude of stressful events in similar ways (De Coteau et al., 2003; Scully et al., 2000). The SRRS is not perfect, however. For example, it shows only the correlation between stress and illness; it does not show that stress actually causes illness and

Seven major sources of stress • Figure 3.1

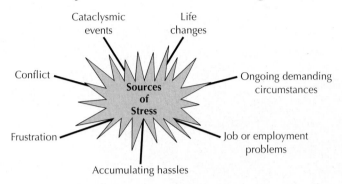

disease. Moreover, not all people respond to life's challenges in the same way, and not all stressful situations arise from a single devastating event, such as the death of a loved one. Significant stress can arise from ongoing demanding circumstances. These **chronic stressors**, such as being in an abusive relationship or living with crime and poverty, can be significant too. Even the stress of low-frequency noise is associated with measurable sleep disturbances and hormonal and cardiac changes (Waye, 2004; Waye et al., 2002). Academic achievement can also be chronically stressful as meeting assignment deadlines and exam pressures, and getting good grades requires considerable thought and energy. As you will notice when you read through this chapter, we evolved in a way that lets us deal with acute stress but not with chronic, ongoing stressors. These stressors, however, often typify life today. The original SRRS from 1967 is now quite old and has been improved and updated by other researchers. The scale we present here is the newer version (Hobson et al., 1998).

Perhaps the largest source of chronic stress for many is work. People often experience stress associated with keeping or changing jobs or with job performance (Moore et al., 2004). The most stressful jobs are those that make great demands on performance and concentration but allow little control, creativity, or opportunity for advancement (Smith et al., 2008; Straub, 2007) (**Figure 3.2**).

Stress at work can also cause significant stress at home, not only for the worker but for other family members as well. In our private lives, divorce, child and spousal abuse, alcoholism, and money problems can also place severe stress on all members of a family (Aboa-Éboulé, 2008; Aboa-Éboulé et al., 2008; DiLauro, 2004; Luecken &

Measuring life changes   Table 3.1

Social Readjustment Rating Scale (SRRS)

Holmes and Rahe (1967) and others (Hobson et al., 1998) believe that higher scores on the SRRS are correlated with greater risks of illness and disease. Below is the list of life events derived from their scale that require some readjustment and are therefore believed to cause stress. Life events are listed from most to least stressful. Each life event has an associated numerical value (not reprinted here) with the death of a spouse/partner having the highest score of 100. Values then decrease down the list.

Life Event

1. Death of a spouse/partner
2. Death of a close family member
3. Major injury/illness to self
4. Detention in jail or other institution
5. Major injury/illness to close family member
6. Foreclosure on loan/mortgage
7. Divorce
8. Being the victim of crime
9. Being the victim of police brutality
10. Infidelity
11. Experiencing domestic violence/sexual abuse
12. Separation or reconciliation with spouse/partner
13. Being fired/laid off/unemployed
14. Experiencing financial problems/difficulties
15. Death of a close friend
16. Surviving disaster
17. Becoming a single parent
18. Assuming responsibility for sick or elderly loved one
19. Loss of, or a major reduction in, health insurance/benefits
20. Self/close family member being arrested for violating the law
21. Major disagreement over child support/custody/visitation
22. Experiencing/involved in auto accident
23. Being disciplined at work/demoted
24. Dealing with unwanted pregnancy
25. Adult child moving in with parent/parent moving in with adult child
26. Child developing behaviour or learning problem
27. Experiencing employment discrimination/sexual harassment
28. Attempting to modify addictive behaviour of self
29. Discovering/attempting to modify addictive behaviour of close family member
30. Employer reorganization/downsizing
31. Dealing with infertility/miscarriage
32. Getting married/remarried
33. Changing employers/careers
34. Failing to obtain/qualify for a mortgage
35. Pregnancy of self/spouse/mate
36. Experiencing discrimination/harassment outside the workplace
37. Release from jail
38. Spouse/partner begins/ceases work outside the home
39. Major disagreement with boss/co-worker
40. Change in residence
41. Finding appropriate child care/daycare
42. Experiencing a large, unexpected monetary gain
43. Changing work positions (transfer, promotion)
44. Gaining a new family member
45. Changing work responsibilities
46. Child leaving home
47. Obtaining a home mortgage
48. Obtaining a major loan other than home mortgage
49. Retirement
50. Beginning/ceasing formal education
51. Receiving a ticket for violating the law

Which occupation is associated with more psychological distress and poorer mental health? • Figure 3.2

Canadian research addressing mental health in the workplace has shown poor working conditions, psychological demands (such as hectic work and conflicting demands), and job insecurity are risk factors for the development of chronic psychological distress, but job skill level and decision-making autonomy are not (Cohidon et al., 2010; Marchand & Blanc, 2011). Based on these findings, in which of these two occupations might you expect to find higher levels of worker distress?

Aaron Vincent Elkaim/The Canadian Press

Lemery, 2004; Orth-Gomer, 2007). In addition to chronic stressors, the minor **hassles** of daily living can pile up and become a major source of stress. We all experience many minor hassles in a day, such as project deadlines, annoyances (gas prices), organizational irritations (conflicting exam schedules), and inconveniences (people walking too slowly in front of us).

Some researchers have shown that daily hassles can be as significant as major life events in creating stress (Kraaij et al., 2002; Kubiak et al., 2008). Being a victim of a violent crime is indeed a very stressful event, but the accumulation of daily hassles can also trigger significant stress reactions. In fact, scales, such as the Hassles and Uplifts Scales (Kanner et al., 1981), have been developed to assess the health impact of the stresses of everyday living. *Applying Psychology: What Are Your Major Hassles?* gives you the opportunity to compare your daily hassles with those of students who participated in a research study on the topic.

As with hassles, **frustration** can cause stress. Frustration is the negative emotional state often associated with a blocked goal. The more motivated we are to attain a goal, the greater the frustration experienced when the goal is blocked.

Stress can also arise when we experience **conflict**—that is, when we are forced to make a choice between at least two incompatible alternatives. The three basic types of conflict are shown in **Study Organizer 3.1**.

The longer any conflict exists or the more important the decision, the more stress a person experiences. Generally, approach-approach conflicts are the easiest to resolve and produce the least stress. Avoidance-avoidance conflicts are usually the most difficult because all choices lead to unpleasant results.

Probably one of the most dramatic causes of severe stress is surviving a cataclysmic event, such as the earthquake, tsunami, and nuclear incident that occurred in Japan in 2011 (**Figure 3.3**). These types of stressors occur very quickly and wreak havoc on the lives and well-being of many people. For survivors and their families, these events are often remembered as the most stressful time in their lives.

Applying Psychology

 THE PLANNER

What Are Your Major Hassles?

List the top 10 hassles you most commonly experience, then compare your answers to the following:

	Percentage of Times Checked
1. Troubling thoughts about the future	76.6
2. Not getting enough sleep	72.5
3. Wasting time	71.1
4. Inconsiderate smokers	70.7
5. Physical appearance	69.9
6. Too many things to do	69.2
7. Misplacing or losing things	67.0
8. Not enough time to do the things you need to do	66.3
9. Concerns about meeting high standards	64.0
10. Being lonely	60.8

Source: Kanner, A. D., Coyne, J. C., Schaefer, C., & Lazarus, R. S. (1981). Comparison of two modes of stress measurement: Daily hassles and uplifts versus major life events. *Journal of Behavioral Medicine*, 4, 1–39.

Type	Description	Example
Approach-approach	The person must choose between two or more favourable alternatives. Either choice will have positive results; the requirement to choose is the source of stress.	You must choose between two jobs: one that involves travel to an exotic location and one that pays very well.
Avoidance-avoidance	The person must choose between two or more unpleasant alternatives that will lead to negative results no matter which choice is made.	You must choose between missing a critical assignment deadline and missing an important job interview.
Approach-avoidance	The person must choose between alternatives that will have both desirable and undesirable results. Such situations lead to a great deal of ambivalence.	You want to spend more time in a new intimate relationship, but that means you won't be able to see your friends as much.

In the book (and film) *Sophie's Choice*, Sophie (played by actress Meryl Streep) and her two children are sent to a German concentration camp. A soldier demands that Sophie give up either her daughter or her son, or else both children will be killed. Obviously, both alternatives will have tragic results. What kind of conflict does this example illustrate?

Cataclysmic events, stress, and recovery • Figure 3.3

Mr. Sugawara sits in a cardboard-divided government shelter he shares with his wife. In the aftermath of the devastating earthquake and tsunami that struck Japan, victims waited for aid and tried to cope with the devastation and stress of losing loved ones, their homes, and their possessions. The earthquake and tsunami killed nearly 16,000 people and damaged the Fukushima Daiichi nuclear power plant, causing the worst nuclear disaster since Chernobyl in 1986. More than a year later, over 3,000 people were still listed as missing. How does a community recover from such immeasurable loss? Do you think it might be easier or more difficult to cope with a major stressor when shared by a large number of people?

Reacting to stress: An interrelated system • Figure 3.4

When stressed, the sympathetic nervous system prepares an organism for immediate action—to fight or flee. Parts of the brain and endocrine system are then activated to maintain our arousal. How does this happen?

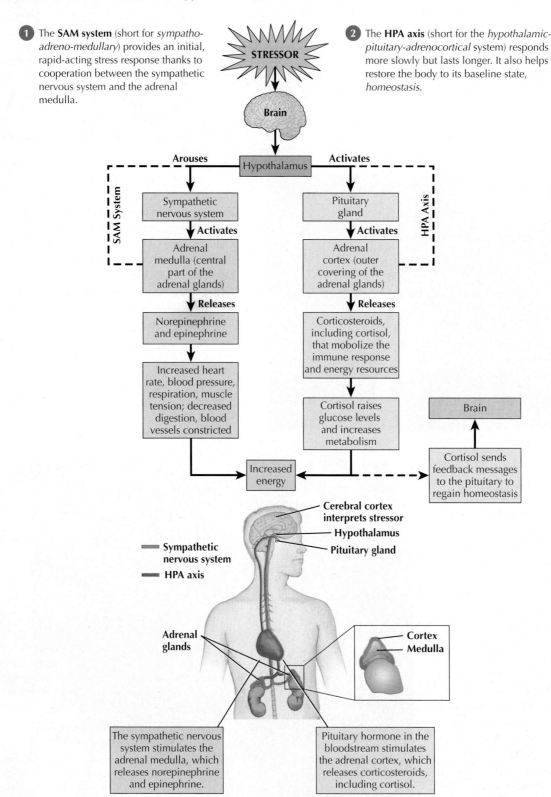

1 The **SAM system** (short for *sympatho-adreno-medullary*) provides an initial, rapid-acting stress response thanks to cooperation between the sympathetic nervous system and the adrenal medulla.

2 The **HPA axis** (short for the *hypothalamic-pituitary-adrenocortical* system) responds more slowly but lasts longer. It also helps restore the body to its baseline state, *homeostasis.*

STRESSOR

Brain

Arouses → Hypothalamus ← Activates

SAM System

Sympathetic nervous system
↓ **Activates**
Adrenal medulla (central part of the adrenal glands)
↓ **Releases**
Norepinephrine and epinephrine
↓
Increased heart rate, blood pressure, respiration, muscle tension; decreased digestion, blood vessels constricted

HPA Axis

Pituitary gland
↓ **Activates**
Adrenal cortex (outer covering of the adrenal glands)
↓ **Releases**
Corticosteroids, including cortisol, that mobolize the immune response and energy resources
↓
Cortisol raises glucose levels and increases metabolism

Brain

Increased energy ⟷ Cortisol sends feedback messages to the pituitary to regain homeostasis

Cerebral cortex interprets stressor
Hypothalamus
Pituitary gland

═══ Sympathetic nervous system
━━━ HPA axis

Adrenal glands

Cortex
Medulla

The sympathetic nervous system stimulates the adrenal medulla, which releases norepinephrine and epinephrine.

Pituitary hormone in the bloodstream stimulates the adrenal cortex, which releases corticosteroids, including cortisol.

The general adaptation syndrome (GAS) • Figure 3.5

While commonly used today, the word and meaning of *stress* is a relatively new addition to medical and psychological vocabulary. It was first coined by Dr. Hans Selye [SELL-yay], a twentieth-century pioneer in stress research. Selye was born in Vienna but came to Canada as a young man, where he began his professional career at McGill University in Montreal. It was there he began researching stress and its physi-

general adaptation syndrome (GAS) Selye's three-part generalized model of how organisms react physiologically to stressors.

ological effects. One of his most influential contributions is the **general adaptation syndrome (GAS)**, described below (Selye, 1936). Selye was a tireless and committed researcher and dedicated his life to understanding the physiological basis of stress, publishing more than 1,700 articles and 39 books on the subject. He was made a Fellow of the Royal Society of Canada and a Com-

panion of the Order of Canada, and received honorary fellowships in more than 60 scientific societies. He was nominated for a Nobel Prize in Physiology or Medicine 10 times (Loriaux, 2008).

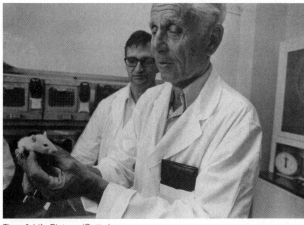

Time & Life Pictures/Getty Images

Note how the three stages of this syndrome (*alarm, resistance,* and *exhaustion*) focus on the biological response to stress—particularly the "wear and tear" on the body with prolonged stress. As a critical thinker, can you see how the alarm stage corresponds to both the fight or flight response and the SAM system, whereas the resistance and exhaustion stages are part of the HPA axis?

1 Alarm Reaction (SAM system)
In the initial stage your body recognizes the threat and prepares for action. This stage is associated with strong physiological and psychological arousal analogous to our evolved flight or fight reaction.

2 Stage of Resistance (HPA axis)
If the stressor remains, your body attempts to endure the stressor and enters the resistance phase. During this stage your body attempts to regain homeostasis and repair any damage. Physiological arousal remains higher than normal, but it can level off somewhat as you adjust to the threat.

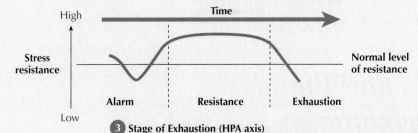

3 Stage of Exhaustion (HPA axis)
Long-term exposure to the stressor eventually leads to the exhaustion phase if the resistance is not successful. In this phase, you become more susceptible to illness and disease as your body is no longer able to mount an effective response to the chronic stressor. Selye maintained that when this occurs, some people develop *diseases of adaptation*—stress-related disorders, such as heart disease, depression, high blood pressure, and allergic reactions.

A. Operti/American Museum of Natural History Library

◄ **Stress in ancient times**
As shown in these ancient cave drawings, the fight-or-flight response triggered by the sympathetic nervous system was adaptive and necessary for early human survival. Today, it often occurs as a response to ongoing stressful situations from which we cannot fight or flee. This ongoing, reactive, low-level arousal is detrimental to our health and well-being and contributes to disease states, such as cancer and heart attacks (Aboa-Éboulé et al., 2008; Ben-Eliyahu et al., 2007).

How Stress Affects the Body

When threatened we have evolved a remarkable system to cope with and respond to a stressor. During times of stress, your body undergoes several physiological changes that are activated by two major pathways from the brain to the body—the **SAM system**, and the **HPA axis** (**Figure 3.4** and **Figure 3.5**).

Cortisol, a key element of the HPA axis, plays a critical role in the long-term effects of stress. Prolonged elevation of cortisol has been linked to increased levels of depression, post-traumatic stress disorder (PTSD), memory problems, unemployment, and drug and alcohol abuse (Ayers et al., 2007; Bremner et al., 2004; Johnson et al., 2008; Sarafino, 2008). Perhaps most important, increased cortisol is directly related to impairment of immune system functioning. When the immune system is compromised, we become more susceptible to opportunistic infections (these are infections that we can normally resist) such as the viruses that cause colds. With lowered immune function, we are also at an increased risk of developing a number of other diseases, including bursitis, colitis, Alzheimer's disease, rheumatoid arthritis, and periodontal disease (Cohen et al., 2002; Cohen & Lemay, 2007; Dantzer et al., 2008; Gasser & Raulet, 2006; Segerstrom & Miller, 2004).

Knowledge that psychological factors can influence both the nervous system and the immune system upset the long-held assumption in biology and medicine that infectious diseases are "strictly physical." The clinical and theoretical implications of this relationship are so important that a new field of biopsychology has emerged called **psychoneuroimmunology**—the study of the interaction among the mind, the nervous system, and the immune system.

> **psychoneuro–immunology** The interdisciplinary field in which researchers study the interaction among the mind, the nervous system, and the immune system.

CONCEPT CHECK STOP

1. **What** are the three types of conflict that can cause stress?
2. **What** is the HPA axis?
3. **How** does chronic stress affect the immune system?
4. **What** occurs during the exhaustion phase of the GAS?

Stress and Illness

LEARNING OBJECTIVES

1. **Explain** why an immune system compromised by stress might be more vulnerable to cancer growth.
2. **Describe** the personality trait that can influence how we respond to stress.
3. **Describe** the key symptoms of post-traumatic stress disorder (PTSD).
4. **Explain** how biological and psychological factors can jointly influence the development of gastric ulcers.

As we've just seen, stress has a dramatic effect on the body. This section explores how stress is related to four serious illnesses: cancer, cardiovascular disorders, post-traumatic stress disorder (PTSD), and gastric ulcers.

Can Stress Cause Cancer?

Cancer is the leading cause of death for adults in Canada (Statistics Canada, 2012; see **Table 3.2**). It occurs when a particular type of immature body cell begins rapidly dividing unchecked and then forms a mass or tumour that invades surrounding healthy tissue. Unless destroyed or removed, the tumour eventually damages organs and ultimately causes death. More than 100 types of cancer have been identified and they appear to be caused by an interaction between environmental factors and genetic predispositions.

In a healthy person, when cancer cells start to multiply, the immune system checks the uncontrolled growth

Leading causes of death, by sex, 2009		Table 3.2	
Both sexes	**Rank**	**Number**	**%**
Total, all causes of death		**238,418**	**100.0**
Malignant neoplasms (cancer)	1	71,125	29.8
Diseases of heart (heart disease)	2	49,271	20.7
Cerebrovascular diseases (stroke)	3	14,105	5.9
Chronic lower respiratory diseases	4	10,859	4.6
Accidents (unintentional injuries)	5	10,250	4.3
Diabetes mellitus (diabetes)	6	6,923	2.9
Alzheimer's disease	7	6,281	2.6
Influenza and pneumonia	8	5,826	2.4
Intentional self-harm (suicide)	9	3,890	1.6
Nephritis, nephrotic syndrome, and nephrosis (kidney disease)	10	3,609	1.5

Source: Statistics Canada. (2012a). Leading causes of death, by sex, 2009. Retrieved from www.statcan.gc.ca/tables-tableaux/sum-som/l01/cst01/hlth36a-eng.htm.

by attacking and killing the abnormal cells (**Figure 3.6**). Because ongoing stress causes the adrenal glands to release hormones that can suppress immune function, a compromised immune system is less able to contain the development of aberrant cell growth, which can ultimately

The healthy immune system in action
• Figure 3.6

Stress can compromise the immune system, but a healthy immune system can readily deal with invaders, as shown here. The round red structure is a leukemia cell. Yellow killer cells are attacking and destroying the cancer cell. The killer cells are a type of white blood cell produced by the immune system known as T-lymphocytes.

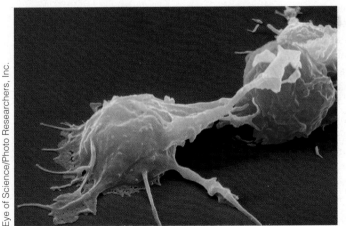

Eye of Science/Photo Researchers, Inc.

give rise to cancers (Ben-Eliyahu et al., 2007; Chida et al., 2008; Kemeny, 2007; Miller et al., 2008; Sood et al., 2010).

We might be able to reduce our risk of developing cancer by making changes that reduce our stress levels and enhance our immune systems. For example, researchers have found that interrupting people's sleep significantly decreased the number of their *natural killer cells*, a type of immune system cell (Fondell et al., 2011; Irwin et al., 1994). After a normal night's sleep, these cells are redistributed throughout the immune system, and immune function is enhanced (Besedovsky et al., 2012).

Most of us have learned from a young age that we can reduce our chances of developing cancer by eating fruits and vegetables, but a few studies have found little connection between fruit and vegetable consumption and reduced risk of cancer (Aune et al., 2011; Key, 2011; Michels et al., 2000; Schatzkin et al., 2000). Don't compost your salad just yet though. More convergent and causal evidence is needed to draw strong conclusions in this area.

Stress and Cardiovascular Disease

Cardiovascular disease, which includes heart disease and stroke, kill tens of thousands of Canadians every year (Statistics Canada, 2012a; see Table 3.2). Ongoing stress is a major contributor to cardiovascular disease and death (Chida & Steptoe, 2010; Dimsdale, 2008; Menezes et al., 2011). *Heart disease* is a general term for all disorders that eventually affect the heart muscle and lead to heart failure. *Coronary heart disease* occurs when the walls of the coronary arteries thicken, reducing or blocking the blood supply to the heart. Symptoms include *angina* (chest pain caused by insufficient blood supply to the heart) and *heart attack* (death of portions of heart muscle tissue). A *stroke* occurs when there is a disruption of blood supply to the brain. It is often caused by a blockage but can be caused by a leakage of blood into surrounding neural tissue. Factors beyond our control, such as the genetic complement we were born with, contribute to the risk of developing one of these conditions (Dastani et al., 2010; Kibos & Guerchicoff, 2011; Nemer et al., 2008), but there are a number of controllable factors as well. These include ongoing stress, smoking, certain personality characteristics, obesity, a high-fat diet, and lack of exercise (Aboa-Éboulé, 2008; Ayers et al., 2007; Sarafino, 2008).

Recall that when the body is under stress, the autonomic nervous system releases epinephrine and cortisol into the bloodstream. These hormones increase heart rate and release fat and glucose from the body's stores to give muscles

Media Bakery

Sarah M. Golonka/Getty Images

Controllable risk factors for premature death • Figure 3.7

Cancer, heart disease, and stroke are the leading causes of death for Canadians, but among young adults, suicide and accidents are the biggest killers. Why do you think these types of age-related differences exist? How much control do we have over our longevity?

a readily available source of energy. If no physical fight-or-flight action occurs (and this is often likely in our modern lives), the fat that was released into the bloodstream is not burned as fuel. Instead, it can adhere to the walls of blood vessels. These fatty deposits are a major cause of blood supply blockage, which causes heart attacks (Blumenthal & Margolis, 2009; Keo et al., 2011; Mathiesen et al., 2011).

For young adults heart disease is not one of the leading causes of premature death. In this age group, suicide and accidents top the list (**Figure 3.7**).

The effect of stress on well-being also interacts with personality factors. Have you ever wondered why some people survive in the face of great stress (personal tragedies, demanding jobs, an abusive home life) while others do not? Suzanne Kobasa was among the first to study this question (Kobasa, 1979; Maddi et al., 2006; Vogt et al., 2008). By examining male executives who were experiencing high levels of stress, she found that some people are more resistant to stress than others because of a personality factor called

What a Psychologist Sees

 THE PLANNER

The Personality Trait of Hostility

Among personality traits, the strongest predictor of developing heart disease is *hostility* (Krantz & McCeney, 2002; Mittag & Maurischat, 2004). In particular, the constant stress associated with cynical hostility—being hypervigilant and constantly being "on watch" for problems—is linked to poor physiological outcomes, such as higher blood pressure, heart attacks, and production of excess stress-related hormones. People who are hostile, suspicious, argumentative, and cynical tend to have more interpersonal conflicts. These can heighten autonomic activation, leading to increased risk of cardiovascular disease (Boyle et al., 2007; Bunde & Suls, 2006; Eaker et al., 2007). While most of us do not suffer from this form of cynical hostility, getting angry does seem to affect us physiologically, so when you find yourself irritated with another driver, a friend, or family member, remember your anger might be more detrimental to your health than just getting you red in the face.

Exactostock/SuperStock

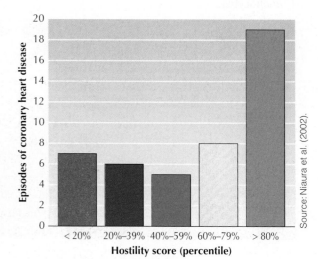
Source: Niaura et al. (2002).

hardiness, a resilient type of optimism that comes from three distinctive attitudes.

First, hardy people feel a strong sense of commitment to both their work and their personal life. They also make intentional commitments to purposeful activity and problem solving. Second, these people see themselves as being in control of their lives, rather than as victims of their circumstances. Finally, hardy people look at change as a challenge to overcome and not as a threat to their well-being. As outlined in *What a Psychologist Sees: The Personality Trait of Hostility*, other personality variables have been implicated in stress effects and well-being.

Smoking, obesity, and lack of exercise are also important contributory and controllable factors associated with heart disease and stroke. Smoking restricts blood circulation, and obesity stresses the heart by causing it to pump more blood to the excess body tissue. A high-fat diet, especially one that is high in cholesterol, contributes to the fatty deposits that clog blood vessels. Lack of exercise contributes to weight gain and prevents the body from obtaining important exercise benefits, including strengthened heart muscles, increased heart efficiency, and the release of endorphins and neurotransmitters, such as serotonin, that alleviate stress and promote well-being.

Post-Traumatic Stress Disorder (PTSD): Unforgettable Anxiety and Suffering

One of the most powerful examples of the effects of severe stress is **post-traumatic stress disorder (PTSD)**. Children and adults can experience the symptoms of PTSD, which include feelings of terror and helplessness during the trauma, and recurrent flashbacks, nightmares, impaired concentration, and emotional numbing afterward. These symptoms may continue for months or years after the event. Some victims of PTSD self-medicate with alcohol and other drugs as a way to relieve their emotional pain and ongoing suffering. This approach often compounds their problems

Fred Chartrand/The Canadian Press

Coping with extreme trauma • Figure 3.8

Roméo Dallaire, now a retired Canadian lieutenant general, was head of the United Nations (UN) Peacekeeping Force during the 1994 conflict in Rwanda. While there, he witnessed the gruesome slaughter of more than 800,000 Tutsis and Hutus by Hutu extremists in the space of about 100 days. The genocide and the unspeakable horrors Dallaire encountered in Rwanda left him battling depression, substance abuse, and PTSD for years afterward, culminating in a suicide attempt in 2000. He has since received treatment and now speaks openly about PTSD and his recovery process.

and harms valuable interpersonal relationships (Kaysen et al., 2008; Sullivan & Holt, 2008).

During the Industrial Revolution, workers who survived horrific railroad accidents sometimes developed a condition very similar to PTSD. It was called *railway spine* because experts thought the problem resulted from a twisting or concussion of the spine. Later, doctors working with combat veterans referred to the disorder as *shell shock* because they believed it was a response to the physical concussion caused by exploding artillery. Today, we know that PTSD is caused by any exposure to extraordinary stress (**Figure 3.8**).

PTSD's essential feature is *severe anxiety* (a state of constant or recurring alarm and fearfulness) that develops after experiencing a very traumatic event, such as learning about the violent or unexpected death of a family member, experiencing war first-hand as either a soldier or a civilian, or being a victim of or witness to violence (American Psychiatric Association, 2002). **Table 3.3** summarizes the primary symptoms of PTSD and offers five important tips for coping with traumatic events.

Identifying PTSD and coping with crisis   Table 3.3

Primary symptoms of post-traumatic stress disorder (PTSD)	Five important tips for coping with crisis
• Re-experiencing the event through vivid memories or flashbacks • Feeling "emotionally numb" • Feeling overwhelmed by everyday situations • Having diminished interest in performing normal tasks or pursuing usual interests • Crying uncontrollably • Isolating oneself from family and friends and avoiding social situations • Relying increasingly on alcohol or drugs to get through the day • Feeling extremely moody, irritable, angry, suspicious, or frightened • Having difficulty falling or staying asleep, sleeping too much, and experiencing nightmares • Feeling guilty about surviving the event or being unable to solve the problem, change the event, or prevent the disaster • Feeling fear and a sense of doom about the future	1. Recognize your feelings about the situation and talk to others about your fears. Know that these feelings are a normal response to an abnormal situation. 2. Be willing to listen to family and friends who have been affected and encourage them to seek counselling if necessary. 3. Be patient with people. Tempers are short in times of crisis, and others may be feeling as much stress as you are. 4. Recognize normal crisis reactions, such as sleep disturbances and nightmares, withdrawal, reverting to childhood behaviours, and trouble focusing on work or school. 5. Take time with your children, spouse, life partner, friends, or co-workers to do something you enjoy.

Colin Perkel/The Canadian Press

Source: American Counseling Association (2006) and adapted from Pomponio (2002).

Stress and Gastric Ulcers

Beginning in the 1950s, psychologists reported evidence that stress can lead to ulcers—painful lesions to the lining of the stomach and upper part of the small intestine. Correlational studies found that people who live in stressful situations develop ulcers more often than people who don't live with stress. Numerous experiments with laboratory animals have shown that stressors, such as shock or confinement to a very small space, can produce ulcers (Andrade & Graeff, 2001; Bhattacharya & Muruganandam, 2003; Gabry et al., 2002; Landeira-Fernandez, 2004).

The relationship between stress and ulcers was generally accepted until researchers reported that a particular bacterium (*Helicobacter pylori* or *H. pylori*) was also associated with ulcer formation. Most people with ulcers have the *H. pylori* bacterium in their stomachs, and it has been shown to damage the stomach wall. However, approximately 75 percent of normal control subjects' stomachs also have the bacterium. This suggests that ulcers are not purely the result of an infection by *H. pylori* and that other factors—psychological factors—must also contribute. It seems that the bacterium can cause ulcers, but they develop more readily in people whose systems are compromised by stress.

Studies of the amygdala (a part of the brain involved in emotional responses) show that it appears to play an important role in gastric ulcer formation as well (Aou, 2006;

Tanaka et al., 1998). It seems that stressful situations, which activate the amygdala, cause an increase in stress hormone synthesis and hydrochloric acid secretion, along with a decrease in blood flow in the stomach walls. This combination leaves the stomach more vulnerable to attack by the *H. pylori* bacteria. Behaviour modification and other psychological treatments, along with antibiotics, have been shown to be effective in treating patients with ulcers.

The connection among stress, bacteria, and ulcer formation is yet another example of how biological, psychological, and social forces influence one another (the biopsychosocial model) (Overmier & Murison, 2000).

CONCEPT CHECK	

1. **How** does stress suppress the immune system?
2. **Which** personality trait is most strongly related to heart disease?
3. **What** are the components of psychological hardiness?
4. **What** is the primary feature of PTSD?

Health Psychology

LEARNING OBJECTIVES

1. **Explain** what health psychologists do.
2. **Review** the challenges in preventing teenagers from smoking.
3. **Describe** what the term *binge drinking* means.
4. **Describe** the risks associated with a sedentary lifestyle.

Health psychology is the study of how biological, psychological, and social factors affect health and illness. One of the roles of the health psychologist is to reduce psychological distress and unhealthy behaviours (*Psychological Science: What Does a Health Psychologist Do?*). In this section, we consider three unhealthy behaviours that contribute to premature death and disease states: tobacco use, excessive alcohol consumption, and an inactive lifestyle.

health psychology
The study of how biological, psychological, and social factors interact in health and illness.

Tobacco: A Well-Known Noxious Substance

Most people today know that smoking is bad for their health and that the more they smoke, the more at risk they are. This has not always been the case. When considering the substances to outlaw in the Canadian Opium and Drug Act of 1911, policymakers excluded tobacco because it was not considered to be a habit-forming drug (Alexander, 1990). Today, we know that tobacco use endangers both smokers and those who breathe in second-hand smoke. It is no surprise that most health psychologists and medical professionals are interested in preventing smoking and getting those who already smoke to stop (*Applying Psychology: Preventing Teenage Smoking*).

The first puff on a cigarette is rarely pleasant, so why do people ever start smoking? The answer is complex. First, smoking usually starts when people are young. According to the *2008–09 Youth Smoking Survey* sponsored by Health Canada, 23 percent of young people in grades

---

Psychological Science

✓ THE PLANNER

What Does a Health Psychologist Do?

Health psychologists are interested in how people's lifestyles and activities, emotional reactions, ways of interpreting events, and personality characteristics influence their physical health and well-being.

As researchers, they are particularly interested in the relationship between stress and the immune system.

As practitioners, health psychologists can work as independent clinicians or as consultants with physicians, physical and occupational therapists, and other health care workers. The goal of the health psychologist is to reduce psychological distress and unhealthy behaviours. They also help patients and families make critical decisions and prepare psychologically for surgery or other treatment.

Health psychologists educate the public about health maintenance. They provide information about the effects of stress, smoking, alcohol, and lack of exercise, and about other health issues. In addition, health psychologists help people cope with chronic problems, such as pain, diabetes, and high blood pressure, as well as unhealthful behaviours, such as anger expression and lack of assertiveness.

The Canadian Psychological Association has a health psychology section that connects individuals in the field and provides research and clinical information. You can access its website at www.cpa.ca/aboutcpa/cpasections/healthpsychology.

Alexander Raths/iStock

Think Critically

1. How might a health psychologist help a patient coping with HIV (the virus that causes AIDS)?
2. What biological, psychological, and social factors would need to be addressed in this case?

Applying Psychology

Preventing Teenage Smoking

For adolescents, the negative long-term health consequences of smoking often seem trivial compared with its short-term social rewards and the addictive, reinforcing properties of the nicotine. Because of this mindset, many smoking-prevention programs focus more on the immediate problems associated with smoking, such as its detrimental effects on sexual function (see right). Films and discussion groups are often used to try to educate teens about peer pressure and media influences, as well as to help them refine their decision-making and coping skills. Unfortunately, the effect of such psychosocial programs on reducing smoking is small (Hatsukami, 2008; Pierce, 2007; Vijgen et al., 2008). To have even a modest effect, these programs must begin early and continue for many years. To reduce the health risk and help fight peer pressure, most schools ban smoking in college and university buildings. The rising cost of cigarettes—now averaging $10 per pack in most provinces and territories—may also deter many young people from smoking. For a person who smokes a half a pack a day, the annual cost is more than $1,800.

WARNING

TOBACCO USE CAN MAKE YOU IMPOTENT

Cigarettes may cause sexual impotence due to decreased blood flow to the penis. This can prevent you from having an erection.

Health Canada

Health Canada. Licensed under Health Canada copyright.

Think Critically

1. Why do you think teenagers tend to disregard the health risks associated with smoking, even when they are aware of the risks?
2. Do you think the cost of cigarettes is a sufficient deterrent to teenagers' smoking? Can you think of a more effective deterrent?

---

6 through 9 report experimenting with some form of tobacco product; for grades 10 to 12, this number has increased to 55 percent (Health Canada, 2010). Peer behaviour and imitation of celebrity role models (such as actors and musicians who smoke) are particularly strong factors in young people's decision to begin smoking. Perhaps cigarettes that are marketed to appear less harmful might make them more attractive to some people (**Figure 3.9**).

Second, nicotine is addictive; once a person begins to smoke, they experience a biological need to continue. Nicotine addiction appears to be similar to cocaine and alcohol addiction (Brody et al., 2004). When a person inhales tobacco smoke, the nicotine quickly increases the release of acetylcholine and norepinephrine in the brain. These neurotransmitters (see Chapter 2) increase alertness, concentration, memory, and feelings of pleasure. Nicotine also stimulates the release of dopamine, the neurotransmitter that is most closely associated with the reward centres of the brain (Fehr et al., 2008; Yang et al., 2008). Finally, smokers learn to associate smoking with pleasant things, such as good food, relaxation, friends, enjoyable social activities, and sex. These associations make quitting even harder as the smoker now has to break the connection between these pleasurable activities and smoking.

In addition to these social and psychological associations, smokers also learn to associate the act of smoking

"Natural" cigarettes? • Figure 3.9

An increasingly health-conscious public has generated a demand for healthful alternatives to foods and other items that have traditionally contained significant quantities of chemicals and additives. Cigarettes are no exception. In Canada and the U.S. there are now new tobacco products that are being marketed as natural and organic. Although some brands contain more tar and nicotine than conventional cigarettes, they have none of the additives ordinarily found in tobacco products (Kezwer, 1998). What effect do you think this type of product might have on consumers? Do people think they are making a more healthful choice if they switch to an organic, all-natural cigarette? What are products like this appealing to?

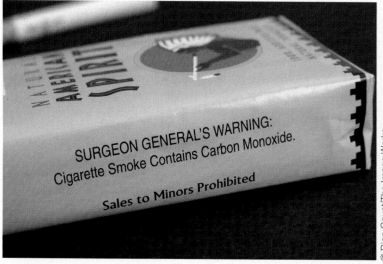

NATURAL AMERICAN SPIRIT

SURGEON GENERAL'S WARNING:
Cigarette Smoke Contains Carbon Monoxide.

Sales to Minors Prohibited

with the "high" that nicotine gives them. When smokers are deprived of cigarettes, they go through an unpleasant *withdrawal*. Nicotine relieves the withdrawal symptoms, so ongoing smoking is reinforced.

The best way to reduce the number of smokers is to stop people from ever taking that first cigarette. As a way to discourage both smoking and young people from starting smoking, the Canadian Tobacco Act prohibits the sale of cigarettes to minors and the display of cigarettes in stores. It also bans cigarette advertisements on television, radio, and in Canadian magazines (American editions of many magazines available in Canada do not have to comply with Canadian law, however). In addition, all cigarette packets sold in Canada are required by law to carry an anti-smoking statement. As of 2010, 20.8 percent of Canadians continued to smoke—a percentage that has been steadily decreasing. On average, more Canadian males than females smoke.

In 2010, British Columbia had the lowest smoking prevalence (17.4 percent) and Nunavut had the highest (54.4 percent). The remaining provinces had percentages between 18 and 24 percent, and the territories had percentages much higher. All provinces have experienced a large drop in smoking prevalence since 1985 (**Figure 3.10**).

Some people find that the easiest way for them to stop smoking is to suddenly and completely stop. However, the success rate for this "cold turkey" approach is extremely low. Even with medical aids, such as nicotine patches, gum, or pills, it is still very difficult to quit. Any program designed to help smokers break their habit must combat the social rewards of smoking, the social bonds among smokers, the paired associations, and the physical addiction to nicotine (Koop et al., 2004).

Some smoking cessation programs combine nicotine replacement therapy with cognitive and behavioural techniques. This approach helps smokers identify stimuli or situations that make them feel like smoking and then change or avoid them (Brandon et al., 2000). Smokers can also be trained to refocus their attention on something other than smoking or remind themselves of the benefits of not smoking (Taylor et al., 2000). Behaviourally, they might cope with the urge to smoke by chewing gum, exercising, or chewing a mint after a meal instead of lighting a cigarette. Some prescription medications have been shown to make quitting smoking easier. Buproprion (Zyban or Wellbutrin) is an antidepressant that has a useful side effect of reducing nicotine cravings, and varenicline tartrate (Champix), makes smoking feel less enjoyable (Jorenby et al., 1999; Tonstad et al., 2006).

According to the Canadian Lung Association, there are five interventions that advertisers claim help smokers quit, but they have not been proven to work. These are acupuncture, acupressure, electrostimulation, laser therapy, and hypnosis. The Canadian Lung Association recommends a person checks with their doctor before spending money on these therapies (Smoking and Tobacco, The Lung Association, 2011).

Smoking rates by province and territory, 2011 • Figure 3.10

Smoking rates in Canada have been steadily decreasing since the mid-1980s. Still, rates are quite variable across Canada. What do you think might account for this national variation?

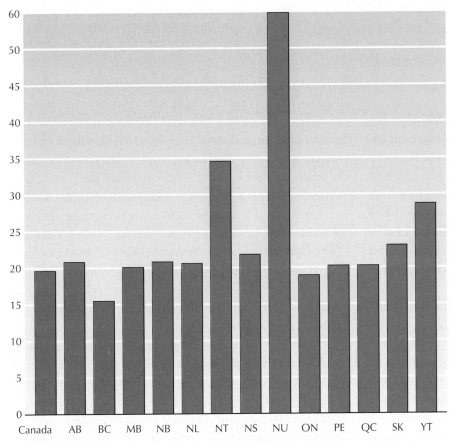

Note: Population aged 12 and over who reported being a current smoker.

Source: Statistics Canada. (2012b). Smokers, by sex, provinces and territories, 2011. Statistics Canada, CANSIM, table 105-0501 and Catalogue no. 82-221-X. Data retrieved from www.statcan.gc.ca/tables-tableaux/sum-som/101/cst01/health74b-eng.htm.

Applying Psychology

 THE PLANNER

Do You Have an Alcohol Problem?

In our society, moderate consumption of alcohol is generally considered acceptable. However, some people abuse alcohol. To assess your own drinking behaviour, place an X next to each of the symptoms below that best describes your current drinking behaviour.

Seven Signs of Alcohol Dependence

_____ Significant drinking occurs regularly, sometimes to the point of almost continuous daily consumption.

_____ Drinking is given a higher priority than other activities, despite its negative consequences.

_____ More and more alcohol is required to produce behavioural, subjective, and metabolic changes; large amounts of alcohol can be tolerated well.

_____ Even short periods of abstinence bring on withdrawal symptoms, such as sweatiness, trembling, and nausea.

_____ Withdrawal symptoms are relieved or avoided by further drinking, especially in the morning.

_____ The individual is subjectively aware of a craving for alcohol and has little control over the quantity and frequency of intake.

_____ If the person begins drinking again after a period of abstinence, he or she rapidly returns to the previous high level of consumption and other behavioural patterns.

Source: World Health Organization (2008).

Sean Locke/iStockphoto

Think Critically

1. Why is it important to determine whether you have an alcohol problem?
2. In what ways might alcoholism be a greater social problem than addiction to heroin or methamphetamines?

Alcohol: Use versus Abuse

According to the 2004 Canadian Addiction Survey, while almost 80 percent of Canadians 15 years and older drink, most of their alcohol consumption is at moderate levels and is not considered harmful. (Canadian Centre on Substance Abuse, 2004). Alcohol has been shown to have a number of beneficial effects, including a lowered risk of heart disease (Arriola et al., 2010; Ramstedt, 2006; Rehm et al., 2010). The primary problem with alcohol is what it can do when consumed in large quantities. This is when it harms our health and well-being.

According to the Canadian Centre on Substance Abuse (2007), alcohol is number three on its list of risk factors for disease, disability, and death. At 9 percent, alcohol is just behind tobacco (12 percent) and high blood pressure (11 percent). The American Medical Association (2008) considers alcohol to be the most dangerous and physically damaging of all drugs. After tobacco, it is the leading cause of premature death in the United States and most European countries (Abadinsky, 2008; Cohen et al., 2004; Maisto et al., 2008). Excessive alcohol consumption causes serious brain damage (Crews et al., 2004). In Korsakoff's syndrome, brain damage is caused by a lack of the B vitamin thiamine. It is commonly seen in chronic alcoholics as they often have poor eating habits and alcohol aggravates the stomach lining, impeding the absorption of some vitamins (Thomson, 2000). Individuals with Korsakoff's syndrome retain normal IQ but present with such symptoms as amnesia, disorientation, confabulation, lack of insight, and apathy (Kolb & Whishaw, 2009; Oscar-Berman, 1980). Alcohol consumption increases aggression, which helps explain why it's a major factor in many murders, suicides, spousal assaults, incidents of child abuse, and accidental deaths (Levinthal, 2008; Sebre et al., 2004; Sher et al., 2005).

Most people are now aware of the major risks associated with drinking alcohol and driving: heavy fines, loss of driver's licence, jail time, serious injuries, and death. The effects of heavy alcohol consumption during a single bout can also be fatal. Because alcohol depresses neural activity throughout the brain, if blood levels of alcohol rise to a critical level, the brain's respiratory centre stops functioning and the person dies. This progression

Binge drinking • Figure 3.11

Unfortunately, some college and university students believe that heavy drinking is harmless fun and a natural part of post-secondary life. But excessive alcohol consumption, such as binge drinking, carries serious health consequences and can be fatal. While you have probably not engaged in the form of "drinking" shown in the picture, have there been occasions when your alcohol consumption met the criteria for binge drinking? Do you think these amounts are too high, too low, or about right? Why?

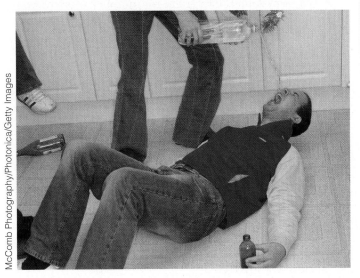

McComb Photography/Photonica/Getty Images

---

binge drinking When a man consumes five or more drinks in a row or a woman consumes four or more drinks in a row on at least three occasions during the previous two weeks.

is why **binge drinking** can be so dangerous (**Figure 3.11**).

Nearly 9 percent of Canadians have reported binge drinking, and the majority of them are young men between the ages of 15 and 24 (Flegel et al., 2011). Binge drinking is of particular concern on college and university campuses. A survey of Canadian campuses by the Centre for Addiction and Mental Health found in 2004 that 32 percent of undergraduates drink at a dangerous level. Ten percent of those surveyed reported having experienced an alcohol-related assault, 9.8 percent reported alcohol-related sexual harassment, and 14.1 percent reported having unplanned sex because of their alcohol consumption (Binks, 2008).

College and university administrators are increasingly aware of the problems of binge drinking and other types of alcohol abuse. For example, Queen's University in Ontario suspended its homecoming celebrations for two years because excessive drinking and its consequences had become too serious a problem to ignore (Binks, 2008;

Flegel et al., 2011). Many institutions are developing policies and programs that go beyond traditional educational programs to include the physical, social, legal, and economic environment on post-secondary campuses and the surrounding communities (Kapner, 2004).

Inactivity: The Risks of a Sedentary Lifestyle

The *Canadian Community Health Survey 2009* has estimated that approximately 50 percent of Canadians are inactive, meaning they participate in no formal exercise program. Another study put this number as high as 62 percent (Craig et al., 1999). For many Canadians the only exercise they get is walking to and from the vehicles that take them to work or school and home again. Research has shown a strong relationship between time spent watching television or using the computer and obesity in both men and women (Statistics Canada, 2008) (**Figure 3.12**).

A sedentary lifestyle increases the risk of developing a number of diseases and disorders, including obesity, type II diabetes, some cancers, heart disease, and premature death. Research has estimated the direct health care costs attributable to physical inactivity in Canada at about $2.1 billion per year (Katzmarzyk et al., 2000).

What you are doing while relaxing might matter • Figure 3.12

The same study that identified a link between time spent watching television and computer use and obesity in men and women found no such association between reading and obesity (Statistics Canada, 2008). All three activities are sedentary, so what might explain the different findings?

© Big Cheese Photo LLC/Alamy

In 2010, the Public Health Agency of Canada consulted with national stakeholders, including health experts and health organizations, to support the development by the Canadian Society for Exercise Physiology (CSEP) of new physical activity guidelines for all Canadians (Public Health Agency of Canada, 2011). To achieve health benefits, CSEP recommends adults should accumulate at least 150 minutes of moderate- to vigorous-intensity aerobic exercise per week in bouts of 10 minutes or more. CSEP also recommends bone- and muscle-strengthening exercises at least two days per week and emphasizes that more physical activity provides greater health benefits (Canadian Society for Exercise Physiology, 2011).

In the life of a busy student, sometimes it's difficult to find time to exercise or go to the gym. Here are some simple ways to increase your activity levels when on campus:

- Park away from a building entrance in a parking lot. Spots farther away from a building entrance are usually more readily available, and you gain the exercise benefits of walking a few minutes more.
- Use the stairs rather than an elevator or escalator. If this is difficult for you, start by taking the stairs when you are going down.
- Avoid using automatic door buttons. You use more muscles by pulling or pushing a door than by simply tapping a door opener.
- Get up and walk around during the break in your class, and if time allows, go outside. A 10-minute class break can allow for a small bout of exercise.
- Walk whenever possible: between classes, to the cafeteria, to the library, or to the lecture hall.
- Use a pedometer to track the number of steps you walk. Aim for 10,000 steps each day.
- Visit the school gym and see what fitness classes are offered. These are a healthful and smart way to fill time between classes.

CONCEPT CHECK

1. **Why** is it so difficult for people to quit smoking?
2. **What** are some key indicators of problem drinking?
3. **What** are some of the risks associated with a sedentary lifestyle?

Managing Stress and Maximizing Well-Being

LEARNING OBJECTIVES

1. **Compare** emotion-focused and problem-focused forms of coping.
2. **Explain** the role that interpretation plays in shaping our responses to stressors.
3. **Review** some major resources for combating stress.

Because we can't escape stress, we all develop strategies to deal with it. Sometimes these approaches are effective and beneficial, and other times they are maladaptive to overall well-being.

Coping with Stress

coping Adaptive or compensatory strategies designed to reduce the effects of a stressor.

Simply defined, **coping** is an attempt to manage stress in some effective way that minimizes its negative effect on the body and mind. It is not one single act but a process that allows us to deal with the various stressors when they present themselves. Not all forms of coping are effective. Sometimes when confronted with a stressor a person simply gives up and withdraws. Some blame themselves or lash out at other people. Many use self-indulgence strategies, such as partying with friends to avoid the stress caused by a looming final exam period. While these strategies may help people feel better in the short term, none of them work in the long term because they don't facilitate change or reduce the effects of the stressor on general health and well-being.

No coping strategy *guarantees* a successful outcome but effective coping strategies share some common features: identifying the stressor and evaluating potential options, realistically appraising the problem, recognizing and managing emotional reactions, and minimizing the negative effects stress can have on the body. Our level of stress generally depends on both our interpretation of and our reaction to the stressors (**Figure 3.13**).

Cognitive appraisal and coping • Figure 3.13

Research suggests that our emotional response to an event depends largely on how we interpret the event.

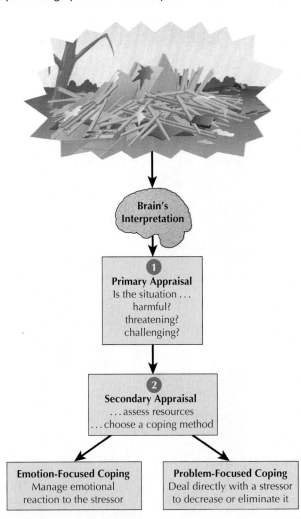

Brain's Interpretation

1 Primary Appraisal
Is the situation . . .
harmful?
threatening?
challenging?

2 Secondary Appraisal
. . . assess resources
. . . choose a coping method

Emotion-Focused Coping
Manage emotional
reaction to the stressor

Problem-Focused Coping
Deal directly with a stressor
to decrease or eliminate it

© AP/Wide World Photos

© AP/Wide World Photos

People often combine *emotion-focused* and *problem-focused* coping strategies to resolve complex stressors or to respond to a stressful situation that is in flux. In some situations, an emotion-focused strategy can allow people to step back from an especially overwhelming problem. Then they can reappraise the situation and use the problem-solving approach to look for solutions. Can you see how each form of coping is represented in these two photos?

Resources for healthy living   Table 3.4

Health and exercise	Exercising and keeping fit help minimize anxiety, depression, and tension. The healthier a person is, the better they can cope with stress. Exercise also improves cardiovascular efficiency and increases strength, flexibility, and stamina.

Vasko Miokovic Photography/iStock

Positive beliefs	A positive self-image and attitude can be especially significant coping resources. Even temporarily raising self-esteem reduces the impact of anxiety caused by stressful events. Similarly, remaining hopeful can sustain a person in the face of severe odds. Consider Rita Chretien in the chapter-opening vignette.

Ariwasabi/iStock

Social skills	People who acquire social skills (such as knowing appropriate behaviours for certain situations, knowing conversation starters, and expressing themselves well) suffer less anxiety than people who do not. In fact, people who lack social skills are more at risk for developing illness than those who have them. Social skills not only help us to interact with others but also to communicate our needs and desires, enlist help when we need it, and strive to decrease hostility in tense situations.

Rich Legg/iStock

Social support	Having the support of others helps offset the stressful effects of divorce, the loss of a loved one, chronic illness, pregnancy, physical abuse, job loss, and work overload. When we are faced with stressful circumstances, our friends and family often help us take care of our health, listen, hold our hands, make us feel important, and provide stability to offset the changes in our lives.

R. Eko Bintoro/iStock

Control	Believing that you are in charge of your own destiny is an important resource for effective coping. People with an **external locus of control** feel powerless to change their circumstances and are less likely to make healthy changes, follow treatment programs, or positively cope with a situation. Conversely, people with an **internal locus of control** believe that they are in charge of their own destinies and are therefore able to adopt more positive coping strategies.

Dagmar Heymans/ iStockphoto

Material resources	Money increases the number of options available for eliminating sources of stress or reducing the effects of stress. When faced with the minor hassles of everyday living, chronic stressors, or major catastrophes, people with money and the skills to effectively use it generally fare better and experience less stress than people without money.

Courtney Keating/iStock

Relaxation	There are a variety of relaxation techniques. Biofeedback is often used in the treatment of chronic pain, but it is also useful in teaching people to relax and manage their stress. **Progressive relaxation** helps reduce or relieve the muscular tension commonly associated with stress. To use this technique, patients first tense and then relax specific muscles, such as those in the neck, shoulders, and arms. This technique teaches people to recognize the difference between tense and relaxed muscles.

Sanjay Deva/iStock

Sense of humour	Research shows that humour is one of the best ways to reduce stress. The ability to laugh at ourselves, and at life's inevitable ups and downs, allows us to relax and gain a broader perspective. The physical action of smiling and laughing, in and of itself, improves mood and well-being.

Quavondo/iStock

Emotion-focused forms of coping are emotional or cognitive strategies that change how we view or feel about a stressful situation. For example, suppose you were refused

emotion-focused forms of coping
Coping strategies based on changing one's perceptions of stressful situations.

a highly desirable, well-paying job. You might reappraise the situation and decide that the job wasn't the right match for you, that you weren't ready for it, or that the time commitment was too large.

Emotion-focused forms of coping that are accurate reappraisals of stressful situations and that do not distort reality may alleviate stress in some situations (Giacobbi et

problem-focused forms of coping
Coping strategies that use problem-solving strategies to decrease or eliminate the source of stress.

al., 2004; Patterson et al., 2004). Many times, however, it is necessary and more effective to use **problem-focused forms of coping**, which deal directly with the situation or the stressor by coming up with practical solutions to eventu-

ally decrease or eliminate it (Bond & Bunce, 2000). These direct coping strategies include the following:

- identifying the stressful problem
- generating possible solutions
- selecting the appropriate solution
- applying the solution to the problem, thus eliminating the stress

Resources for Healthy Living

A person's ability to cope effectively depends on the stressor itself—its complexity, intensity, and duration—and on the type of coping strategy used. It also depends on available resources. Eight important resources for healthy living and stress management are health and exercise, positive beliefs, social skills, social support, control, material

resources, relaxation, and a sense of humour. These are described in **Table 3.4**.

The strong federal support for healthy living is evident by the wealth of resources and information provided by Health Canada. Among other things, the agency encourages individuals to do the following:

1. Eat nutritiously by choosing a variety of foods from all the food groups, as suggested by *Eating Well with Canada's Food Guide*.

2. Build a circle of social contacts to create a supportive environment of people who care for you and respect you.

3. Stay physically active to keep your body strong, reduce stress, and improve your energy.

4. Choose not to smoke.

5. Put an end to other negative lifestyle practices.

By making healthy living choices, a person has a better chance of maintaining and improving not just physical health but mental health as well. Also, a healthy lifestyle results in less illness and morbidity in old age and the final years of life (Hubert et al., 2002).

For an interesting discussion on this topic, scan to download the author's podcast.

| CONCEPT CHECK |  |

1. **Why** would it sometimes be useful for people to combine coping strategies?

2. **Why** is exercise important for counteracting stress?

3. **How** can social skills protect us against stress?

Summary

 THE PLANNER

1 Understanding Stress 72

- **Stress** is the body's non-specific response to any demand placed on it. Pleasant or beneficial stress is called **eustress**. Stress that is unpleasant or objectionable is called **distress**. Stress can be caused by a

variety of factors, such as catastrophes, life changes, intolerable situations, the accumulation of minor **hassles**, **frustrations**, and **conflict**. There are three basic types of conflict: **approach-approach conflict**, **avoidance-avoidance conflict**, and **approach-avoidance conflict**.

- The **SAM system** and the **HPA axis** control significant physiological responses to stress. The SAM system prepares us for immediate action; the HPA axis responds more slowly but lasts longer. The understanding that psychological factors influence many disease states have created a new field of biopsychology called **psychoneuroimmunology**.

- The **general adaptation syndrome (GAS)** describes the body's three-stage reaction to stress. The phases are the initial alarm reaction, the resistance phase, and the exhaustion phase (if the resistance to the stressor was not successful).

Reacting to stress: An interrelated system
• **Figure 3.4**

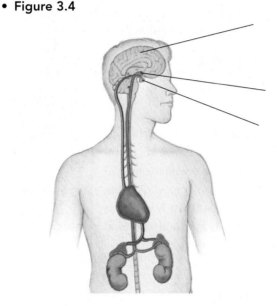

2 Stress and Illness 78

- Stress makes the immune system less able to resist infection and increases the possibility of cancer development.

- Increased stress hormones can cause fat to adhere to blood vessel walls, increasing the risk of heart attack. Having the personality trait of hostility amplifies the risk of stress-related heart disease.

- Exposure to extraordinary stress can cause **post-traumatic stress disorder (PTSD)**, a type of severe anxiety that is characterized by flashbacks, nightmares, and impaired functioning.

- Stress increases the risk of developing gastric ulcers among people who have the *H. pylori* bacterium in their stomachs.

What a Psychologist Sees: The Personality Trait of Hostility

3 Health Psychology 83

- **Health psychology**, the study of how biological, psychological, and social factors affect health and illness, is a growing field in psychology.

- Most approaches to helping people quit smoking include cognitive and behavioural techniques to aid smokers in their withdrawal from nicotine, along with some form of nicotine-replacement therapy.

- While moderate alcohol consumption has beneficial effects, excessive alcohol consumption is a significant factor in premature death and can cause brain damage. Alcohol also seems to increase aggression. Although many college and university students believe that heavy drinking is a harmless part of post-secondary life, administrators are becoming increasingly aware of the problems associated with alcohol abuse.

- A sedentary lifestyle is harmful to general health and is a contributing factor in a variety of disorders and diseases. Health Canada has recommended a number of strategies to improve daily activity levels.

Applying Psychology: Do You Have an Alcohol Problem?

- Our level of stress generally depends on both our interpretation of and our reaction to stressors. **Emotion-focused forms of coping** are emotional or cognitive strategies that change how we view a stressful situation. It is often more effective to use **problem-focused forms of coping** strategies—actual practical solutions to reduce or remove the stressor. People often combine problem-focused and emotion-focused coping strategies to resolve complex stressors or to respond to an ongoing stressful situation.

- Eight important resources for healthy living and stress management are health and exercise, positive beliefs, social skills, social support, control, material resources, relaxation, and a sense of humour. An in-depth look at

control tells us that having an **internal locus of control** is a healthier way to manage stress than having an **external locus of control**.

Cognitive appraisal and coping • Figure 3.13

Key Terms

- approach-approach conflict, p. 74
- approach-avoidance conflict, p. 00
- avoidance-avoidance conflict, p. 74
- binge drinking, p. 87
- chronic stressors, p. 72
- conflict, p. 74
- coping, p. 88
- distress, p. 72
- emotion-focused forms of coping, p. 91

- eustress, p. 72
- external locus of control, p. 90
- frustration, p. 74
- general adaptation syndrome (GAS), p. 77
- hardiness, p. 81
- hassles, p. 74
- health psychology, p. 83
- HPA axis, p. 78
- internal locus of control, p. 90

- post-traumatic stress disorder (PTSD), p. 81
- problem-focused forms of coping, p. 91
- progressive relaxation, p. 90
- psychoneuroimmunology, p. 78
- SAM system, p. 78
- stress, p. 72
- stressor, p. 72

Critical and Creative Thinking Questions

1. What are the major sources of stress in your life? Are any of these stressors of the more pleasant type (eustress), or are they all unpleasant (distress)?

2. Imagine your life with absolutely no stressors at all. Is this a life you would want? Why or why not?

3. If you are experiencing a period of high stress, what could you do to avoid becoming ill from the various stressors?

4. Controllable risk factors for premature death include risky behaviour, such as texting while driving. What effect, if any, do you think legislation and legal penalties might have on this and other types of risky behaviour?

5. Why are smoking-prevention efforts often aimed at adolescents?

6. Everyone knows physical activity improves health and well-being, yet so many people get little or no exercise. What motivational factors do you think contribute to this dichotomy?

7. Which forms of coping do you most often use? Do you use primarily emotion-focused methods or problem-focused forms when dealing with stress?

8. Which of the resources for stress management seem most useful for you? Are there any others you would add to this list?

Self-Test

(Check your answers in Appendix A.)

1. The physical and mental arousal to situations that we perceive as threatening or challenging is called _____.
   a. distress
   b. eustress
   c. stress
   d. stressor

2. Vikram has recently become a father and moved to a different city to start a high-paying job, both positive things, in his view. What type of stress is Vikram likely to experience with these changes?
   a. distress
   b. chronic stress
   c. eustress
   d. none of the above

3. Holmes and Rahe (1967) and others believe that higher scores on the SRRS are correlated with greater risks of having which of the following?
   a. ulcers
   b. heart disease
   c. disease and illness
   d. cancer

4. Which of the following is one of the largest sources of *chronic* stress for adults?
   a. birth
   b. work
   c. bad relationship
   d. moving

5. Which occupation is associated with psychological distress and poorer mental health?
   a. police officers
   b. firefighters
   c. truck drivers
   d. machine operators

6. In an *approach-approach conflict*, a person must choose between two or more goals that will lead to _____, whereas in an *avoidance-avoidance conflict*, a person must choose between two or more goals that will lead to _____.
   a. less conflict; no conflict
   b. frustration; hostility
   c. a desirable result; an undesirable result
   d. effective coping; ineffective coping

7. Lisa must decide whether to spend the night with old friends in town for a short visit, or stay home and work on her major term paper due the next day. What type of conflict is Lisa likely experiencing?
   a. an approach-approach conflict
   b. an approach-avoidance conflict
   c. a eustress-distress conflict
   d. an avoidance-avoidance conflict

8. Label the structures on the diagram.
   a. hypothalamus
   b. pituitary
   c. cerebral cortex
   d. adrenal glands

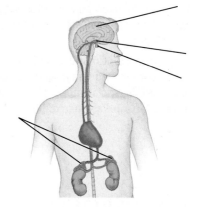

9. Which of the following is the field that studies the interaction among the mind, the immune system, and the nervous system?
   a. psychosomatology
   b. neurobiology
   c. biopsychology
   d. psychoneuroimmunology

10. Research suggests that one particular personality trait, illustrated in this photo, is *most* associated with heart disease. What characteristic is this?
    a. cynical hostility
    b. road rage
    c. intense ambition
    d. time urgency

11. People who experience flashbacks, nightmares, and impaired functioning following a life-threatening or other horrifying event are suffering from which of the following?
    a. a psychosomatic illness
    b. post-traumatic stress disorder
    c. a nervous breakdown
    d. depression

12. Which of the following is *not true* of health psychology?

    a. It studies the relationship between psychological behaviour and physical health.

    b. It studies the relationship between psychological behaviour and illness.

    c. It emphasizes wellness and the prevention of illness.

    d. It typically does not include working with people who have chronic or long-term problems.

13. The effects of nicotine on the brain are related to the release of which of the following?

    a. glutamate

    b. serotonin

    c. dopamine

    d. all of these options

14. At several parties in the past couple of weeks, Arash consumed five drinks in a row and his girlfriend consumed four drinks in a row. This means that _____ met the definition for binge drinking.

    a. Arash

    b. his girlfriend

    c. both Arash and his girlfriend

    d. neither Arash nor his girlfriend

15. Approximately what percentage of the Canadian public is inactive?

    a. 15%–25%

    b. 50%–65%

    c. 65%–80%

    d. 75%–80%

16. How much activity does the Canadian Society for Exercise Physiology (CSEP) recommend per day?

    a. 30 minutes

    b. 45 minutes

    c. 60 minutes

    d. 90 minutes

17. Which of the following activities is *not* correlated with obesity in men and women?

    a. reading

    b. working on a computer

    c. watching television

    d. reading and watching television

18. *Emotion-focused forms* of coping are based on changing your _____ when faced with stressful situations.

    a. feelings

    b. perceptions

    c. strategies

    d. all of these options

19. Hue-Linh generally deals with stressors in her life by considering possible solutions to the problem, choosing the most appropriate solution, and then actually using the solution to deal with the issue. What does Hue-Linh appear to have?

    a. a high level of intrinsic motivation

    b. an external locus of control

    c. an emotion-focused coping style

    d. a problem-focused coping style

20. Research suggests that people with a higher _____ adopt better coping strategies than those with a higher _____.

    a. external locus of control; internal locus of control

    b. internal locus of control; external locus of control

    c. emotion-focused coping style; problem-focused coping style

    d. problem-focused coping style; emotion-focused coping style

THE PLANNER

Review your Chapter Planner on the chapter opener and check off your completed work.

Sensation and Perception

Imagine that your visual field were suddenly inverted and reversed so that things you expected to be on your right were on your left, and things you expected to be above your head were below it. No doubt you would have trouble getting around. Imagine pouring a cup of coffee or taking notes in class. Do you think you could ever adapt to this distorted world?

To answer that question, about a hundred years ago, psychologist George Stratton (1896) wore special lenses for eight days. For the first few days, Stratton had great difficulty navigating in this environment and coping with everyday tasks. But by the third day, his experience had begun to change—things were easier to do. By the fifth day, Stratton had almost completely adjusted to his strange perceptual environment and his expectations of how the world should be arranged had changed significantly. As Stratton's experiment shows, we are able to adjust even our most basic perceptions by retraining our brains to adapt to unfamiliar physical sensations, creating a newly coherent world.

This chapter focuses on two separate, but inseparable, aspects of how we experience the world: sensation and perception. The boundary between these two processes is not precise but they are generally defined as follows: sensation is the process of receiving, translating, and transmitting raw sensory data from the external and internal environments to the brain. More simply, it is the gathering up of the information provided from our senses. Perception is the higher-level process of selecting, organizing, and interpreting sensory data into useful mental representations of the world. It is what we do with the sensory information we get in order to understand the world and our experiences. While these definitions might seem a bit dry and boring, the beauty and magic of the concepts come alive in the examples.

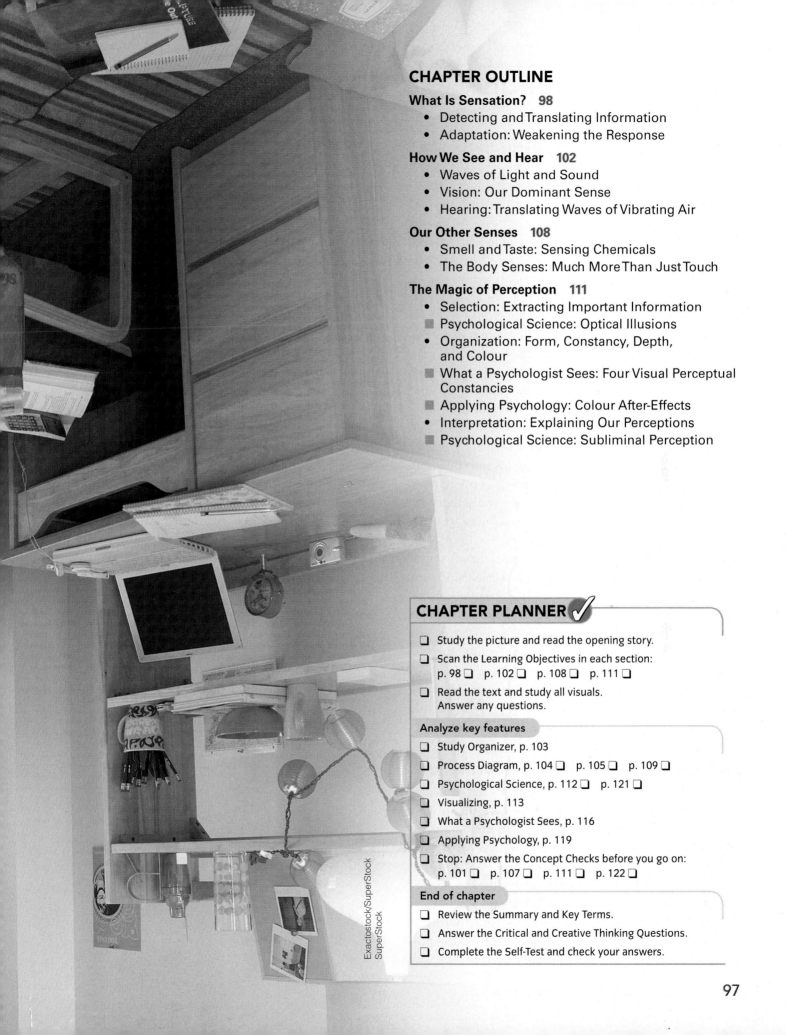

CHAPTER OUTLINE

CHAPTER PLANNER ✔

- ❏ Study the picture and read the opening story.
- ❏ Scan the Learning Objectives in each section:
  p. 98 ❏   p. 102 ❏   p. 108 ❏   p. 111 ❏
- ❏ Read the text and study all visuals.
  Answer any questions.

Analyze key features

- ❏ Study Organizer, p. 103
- ❏ Process Diagram, p. 104 ❏   p. 105 ❏   p. 109 ❏
- ❏ Psychological Science, p. 112 ❏   p. 121 ❏
- ❏ Visualizing, p. 113
- ❏ What a Psychologist Sees, p. 116
- ❏ Applying Psychology, p. 119
- ❏ Stop: Answer the Concept Checks before you go on:
  p. 101 ❏   p. 107 ❏   p. 111 ❏   p. 122 ❏

End of chapter

- ❏ Review the Summary and Key Terms.
- ❏ Answer the Critical and Creative Thinking Questions.
- ❏ Complete the Self-Test and check your answers.

Exactostock/SuperStock
SuperStock

What Is Sensation?

LEARNING OBJECTIVES

1. **Describe** how raw sensory stimuli are translated and conveyed to the brain.

2. **Explain** how the study of thresholds helps to explain sensation.

3. **Describe** why adapting to sensory stimuli provides an evolutionary advantage.

4. **Identify** the factors that govern pain perception.

The word *sensual* is often used in a sexual context, but its actual meaning is more closely related to the first section of this chapter. *Sensory* and *sensual* both mean *relating to the physical senses* (*Webster's Revised Unabridged Dictionary*, 1913) and not necessarily in a sexual way. Consider how patient S described his sensory experiences to famous physician and psychologist Alexander Luria (1968): when presented with a high-pitched tone (such as the sound of a flute), patient S reported, "It looks like fireworks tinged with a pink-red hue. The color feels rough and unpleasant, and it has an ugly taste—rather like that of a briny pickle" (Luria, 1968). Patient S was describing his rare condition known as *synesthesia*, which means "mixing of the senses." People with synesthesia routinely blend their sensory experiences. They may "see" temperatures, "hear" colours,

> **sensation** The process of receiving, translating, and transmitting raw sensory data from the external and internal environments to the brain.

or "taste" shapes. For those of us with normal, unblended **sensations**, we might consider Patient S as having spectacular sensual experiences far richer than our ordinary senses. But even for us, our sensory systems are quite spectacular, effortlessly processing vast amounts of incoming sensory information and converting them to the language of our nervous system—the action potential.

Detecting and Translating Information

Before a brain can translate any stimulus into a neural signal, there must be a mechanism for detecting it. Our eyes, ears, skin, and other sense organs all contain special cells called receptors, which receive and process sensory

> **sensory transduction** The process by which a physical stimulus is converted into neural impulses.

information from the environment. For each sense, these specialized cells respond to a distinct stimulus, such as sound waves or odour molecules. During the process of **sensory transduction**, the receptors convert the stimulus into neural signals, which are then sent to the brain. For example, with hearing, tiny receptor cells in the inner ear convert the vibrations from sound waves into electrochemical signals. These signals are carried by neurons to the brain, where specific sensory neurons detect and interpret the information. How does our brain, entombed in the skull without direct access to the world, differentiate between sensations, such as sounds and smells? Through a process known as **labelled lines**, in which different physical stimuli are interpreted as distinct sensations because their neural impulses activate specific receptors and travel by different routes to arrive at different places in the

> **labelled lines** The way the brain interprets the type of sensory information based on its neural origin in the body and its destination in the brain.

brain (**Figure 4.1**). Taste is somewhat more complicated (Erickson, 2008), but in general, we can make this claim about sensory pathways to the brain.

Sensory processing within the brain
• Figure 4.1

Neural impulses travel from the sensory receptors to various parts of the brain.

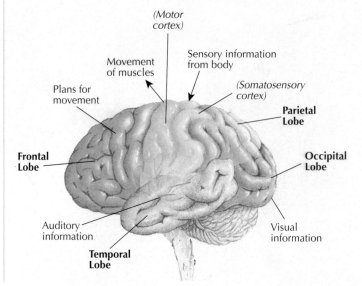

(Motor cortex)

Movement of muscles

Sensory information from body

Plans for movement

(Somatosensory cortex)

Parietal Lobe

Frontal Lobe

Occipital Lobe

Auditory information

Visual information

Temporal Lobe

Dogs with jobs • Figure 4.2

A dog's superior sense of smell makes it extremely valuable for identifying olfactory stimuli undetectable to humans. For this reason, specially trained dogs provide invaluable help in sniffing out plants, drugs, money, cadavers, and explosives; tracking offenders; and assisting in search-and-rescue operations. Why do you think the ancestral relatives to dogs evolved such an enhanced sense of smell?

Species have evolved a range of sensory receptors that are uniquely adapted to their environment. Sensory systems that were advantageous for survival and reproduction were preferentially selected by the organism's environment. Through evolutionary time, these systems were enhanced and diverged based on the different selective pressures ancestral species faced. This explains the incredible range of sensory diversity seen across species today (**Figure 4.2**). Although humans have remarkable sensory systems that are uniquely adapted to our world, we cannot sense ultraviolet light as bees can or detect infrared heat radiation from warm-blooded animals as some snakes do.

Adaptation: Weakening the Response

Imagine that friends have invited you to come meet their new cat. As they greet you at the door, you are overwhelmed by the potent odour of cat urine. "How can they live with that smell?" You think. "Can't they smell that?" The answer lies in a well-known sensory phenomenon called **sensory adaptation**. When a stimulus is presented constantly over time, the sensation in the sense receptors often fades or disappears.

Sensory adaptation makes sense from an evolutionary perspective. We can't afford to waste attention, time, and neural energy

> **sensory adaptation**
> Repeated or constant stimulation decreases the number of sensory messages sent to the brain from the sense receptors.

on unchanging, normally unimportant stimuli. Imagine how big your head would have to be to hold a brain that registered and recorded every sensory event around you. Tuning out repetitive information helps the brain cope with an overwhelming amount of sensory stimuli and allows it the time and space to pay attention to change. Researchers have long been interested in studying the subtleties and nuances of our sensory systems (**Figure 4.3**).

Measuring the senses • Figure 4.3

How do we know exactly what humans can see, hear, feel, or smell? The answer comes from research in *psychophysics*, the study of the relationship between events in the physical world and our psychological experiences of them. Researchers study how the strength or intensity of a stimulus affects us. Consider this example:

- To test for hearing loss, a hearing specialist uses a tone generator to produce sounds of differing pitches and intensities.
- You listen over earphones and indicate the earliest point at which you hear a tone. This is your absolute threshold, or the smallest amount of a stimulus needed to correctly detect the stimulus half the time.
- To test your difference threshold, or just noticeable difference (*JND*), the examiner gradually changes the volume and asks you to respond when you notice a difference.
- The examiner then compares your thresholds with those of people with normal hearing to evaluate whether you have a hearing impairment, and if so, by how much.

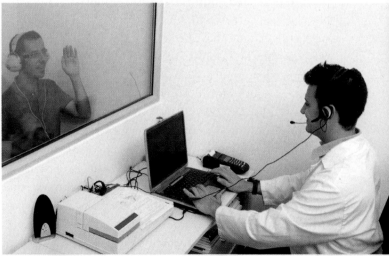

Although some senses, like smell and touch, adapt quickly, we never completely adapt to visual stimuli or to extremely intense stimuli, such as the odour of ammonia or the pain of a bad burn. From an evolutionary perspective, these limitations on sensory adaptation aid survival: they facilitate learned avoidance behaviour and encourage protective self-care when injured.

If we don't adapt to pain, how do athletes keep playing despite painful injuries? As you will see, pain has a significant psychological component. The nervous system produces its own natural painkillers, synthesized in the pituitary and hypothalamus, called **endorphins** (see Chapter 2), which help to manage and minimize pain.

Pain is initially detected by special sensory receptors

> **nociceptor**
> A special type of sensory receptor that signals the spinal cord and brain in response to potentially damaging stimuli.

called **nociceptors** found both inside and on the body. From here, information about pain is sent to the brain via two different pathways, signalling two different types of pain. The sharp, localized pain experienced as a result of a cut travels along myelinated fibres to the spinal cord and then onward to the thalamus and cortex. This fast pathway allows the organism to respond rapidly and reflexively to quickly withdraw from the painful stimulus. The slower, unmyelinated pathway travels via the spinal cord to the brain and interacts with the limbic system to convey emotion. It's activation of this slower pathway that signals dull, throbbing, or burning pain, along with the misery and crying that often co-occurs with a painful injury.

The experience of and reaction to pain are not automatic or rigid. They can be greatly influenced by expectations, age, sex, fatigue, and emotions. This psychological element of pain is evident when we are distracted from our pain and the discomfort temporarily disappears. Likewise, placebo medications with no active ingredient given to unsuspecting patients have been shown to have powerful pain-relieving effects (Fuentes et al., 2011; Puhl et al., 2011).

How does our nervous system intercept incoming pain messages? McGill University psychologists Ronald Melzack and Patrick Wall (1965) proposed the influen-

> **gate-control theory** The theory that pain sensations are processed and altered by mechanisms within the spinal cord.

tial **gate-control theory** to explain this mechanism. According to this theory, the experience of pain depends partly on whether the neural message can get past a "gatekeeper" in the spinal cord. Normally, the neural gate is kept

open either by impulses coming down from the brain, or by sensory messages, such as touch and pressure, coming from the body. When tissue is damaged, the pain signal travels along the two pain pathways mentioned above, passing through the open gate, and informing the brain. The result is the subjective experience of pain.

According to the gate-control theory, messages from the brain can also close the pain gate, thereby preventing the subjective experience of pain. These neural signals can be triggered by a number of psychological factors, such as expectancy effects, emotion, and cultural influences. It is via this mechanism that injured athletes and wounded combat soldiers can carry on despite what would normally be excruciating pain (**Figure 4.4**). When we are soothed by endorphins or distracted by competition or fear, our experience of pain can be greatly diminished. Conversely, when we get anxious or dwell on our pain, we can intensify it (Roth et al., 2007; Sullivan, 2008; Sullivan et al., 1998). Ironically, well-meaning friends who ask chronic pain sufferers about their pain may unintentionally reinforce and increase it (Jolliffe & Nicholas, 2004).

The power of the nervous system in inhibiting pain • Figure 4.4

The body's ability to inhibit pain perception sometimes makes it possible for athletes to play through painful injuries. MMA Champ Randy Couture broke his left arm while deflecting a high kick from opponent Gabriel Gonzaga in 2007. Despite the injury, Couture continued to fight and won the Ultimate Fighting Heavyweight Championship (UFC) by technical knockout later in the third round. Do you think this remarkable ability to ignore pain is learned through life and experience, or is it genetically based?

Jon P. Kopaloff/Getty Images

Mirror therapy can reduce phantom limb for some people
• Figure 4.5 _____

Often phantom limb pain is reported as burning, stabbing, or shooting pain, or as though the lost limb is actually frozen in an excruciating position. If the brain perceives the lost limb to be present, often the phantom pain subsides. By using mirrors, it appears to the patient that the limb is still present. This visual feedback is believed to retrain the brain to reconstruct a new

map of the body, including the lost limb (Ramachandran et al., 2009; Ramachandran & Altschuler, 2010; Weeks et al., 2010). With an intact representation of the body, the brain no longer registers the amputated pain sensations. Why do you think this therapy works?

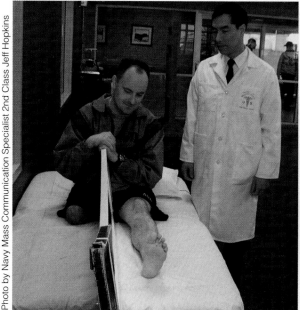
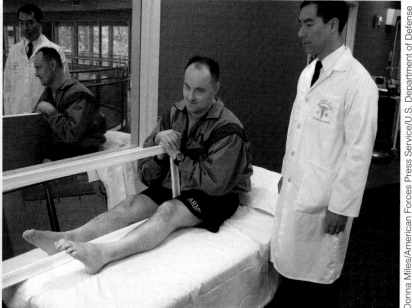

Research also suggests that the pain gate may be chemically controlled, that a neurotransmitter called *substance P* opens the pain gate—pain is felt—and that endorphins close it—pain is reduced (Lee et al., 2009; Zubrzycka & Janecka, 2000). Other research (Melzack, 1999; Vertosick, 2000) has shown that when normal sensory input is disrupted, the brain can generate pain and other sensations on its own. Amputees sometimes continue to feel pain (and itching or tickling) long after a limb has been amputated. This *phantom limb pain* occurs because neurons send conflicting messages to the brain. The brain interprets these messages as pain because it arises in the area of the spinal cord responsible for pain signalling. When amputees are fitted with prosthetic limbs and begin using them, phantom pain generally disappears (Crawford, 2008; Gracely et al., 2002), but not always. For some amputees the phantom pain can continue for years

(Desmond & MacLachlan, 2010; Hunter et al., 2008). An innovative approach to managing phantom pain is to "trick" the brain into thinking the amputated limb is still present. This manipulation is achieved with the use of mirrors (**Figure 4.5**).

CONCEPT CHECK 🛑 STOP

1. **How** do we convert sensory information into signals the brain can understand?

2. **Why** would we want to limit the amount of sensory information that we receive?

3. **Why** is such a vast range of sensory systems seen across species?

4. **What** factors govern pain perception, management, and suppression?

How We See and Hear

LEARNING OBJECTIVES

1. **Identify** the three major characteristics of light and sound waves.

2. **Explain** how the eye captures and focuses light energy, and how the eye converts light energy into neural signals.

3. **Describe** the path that sound waves take in the ear.

4. **Summarize** the two theories that explain how we distinguish among different pitches.

Waves of Light and Sound

Even the most complex visual and auditory experiences depend on our basic ability to detect light and sound. Both light and sound move in waves, similar to the movement of waves on the ocean (**Figure 4.6a**).

Light waves are a form of electromagnetic energy, and different types of waves on the *electromagnetic spectrum* have different wavelengths (**Figure 4.6b**).

In contrast to light waves, which are particles (tiny packets) of electromagnetic energy, sound waves are caused by air molecules moving in a particular wave

Illustrating differences between light and sound waves • Figure 4.6

a. Watching a fireworks show is one way you've probably learned that light travels much faster than sound. But light also travels differently from sound, which must pass through physical material to be heard. The speed of light is always 300 million metres per second no matter what it passes through. Sound travels through air at 344 metres per second at 21°C. But if you were observing fireworks under fresh water, you'd notice a shorter gap between the burst of light and the arrival of the sound—in water, sound will travel at a speed of about 1,500 metres per second, which is about five times its speed in air.

Sjoerd van der Wal/iStockphoto

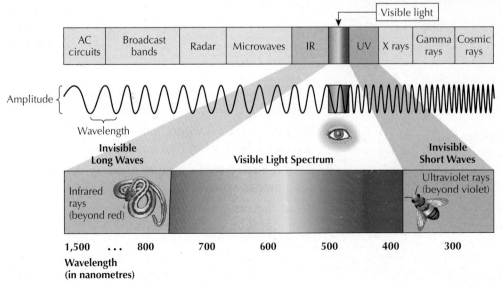

b. The human eye can see only visible light, a tiny part of the full electromagnetic spectrum. We perceive visible light with a short wavelength as blue, visible light with a medium wavelength as green or yellow, and visible light with a long wavelength as red. Recall that honeybees can detect very short ultraviolet wavelengths, and some rattlesnakes can detect very long infrared wavelengths.

Physical Properties	Wavelength: The distance between successive peaks	Wave amplitude: The height from midline to peak (or midline to trough)	Range of wavelengths: the mixture of waves
	Long wavelength/low frequency (the number of waves per unit of time)	*Low amplitude/low intensity*	*Low range/low complexity*
	Short wavelength/high frequency	*High amplitude/high intensity*	*High range/high complexity*
Vision (Light Waves)	**Hue**: Short wavelengths that are higher frequency are perceived as bluish; long wavelengths that are lower frequency are perceived as reddish.	**Brightness**: Great amplitude produces more intensity and bright colours; small amplitude produces less intensity and dim colours.	**Saturation**: Wider range produces more complex colour; narrow range produces less complex colour.
Audition (Sound Waves)	**Pitch**: Shorter wavelengths that are higher frequency are perceived as high-pitched sounds; long wavelengths that are lower frequency are perceived as low-pitched sounds.	**Loudness**: Great amplitude produces louder (more intense) sounds; small amplitude produces soft sounds.	**Timbre**: Wider range produces more complex sound with a mix of multiple frequencies. Narrower range produces less complex sound with one or a few frequencies.

pattern. The waves originate when a vibrating object, such as vocal cords or guitar strings, compress the air molecules (push them together) and then decompress the air molecules (spread them out), resulting in a particular wave pattern. This wave pattern moves away from the vibrating object, propagating the sound wave. Sound waves can be created in any substance in which particles can be compressed and decompressed—even slightly—such as water or steel.

Both light waves and sound waves vary in wavelength, amplitude (height), frequency, and range—each with a distinct effect on vision and hearing, or audition, as shown in **Study Organizer 4.1**.

Vision: Our Dominant Sense

Most structures in the eye are involved in capturing and focusing light and converting it into neural signals to be interpreted by the brain, as shown in **Figure 4.7**.

Learning what the visual system does with light helps us understand some visual peculiarities. For example, small abnormalities in the eye sometimes cause images to be focused in front of the retina (nearsightedness, also called myopia) or behind it (farsightedness, or hyperopia). Corrective lenses or laser surgery can correct most such visual acuity problems. During middle age, most people's lenses lose elasticity and the ability to adjust or accommodate for near vision, a condition known as presbyopia. This problem is usually treated with corrective lenses.

If you walk into a dark movie theatre on a sunny afternoon, you won't be able to see at first. This is because in bright light, the pigment inside the rod photoreceptors bleaches, making them temporarily non-functional. It takes a second or two for the rods to become functional enough to see. This process of *dark adaptation* continues for 20 to 30 minutes. Light adaptation, the adjustment that takes place when you go from darkness to a bright setting, takes 7 to 10 minutes and is a property of the cone photoreceptors.

Hearing: Translating Waves of Vibrating Air

The sense of hearing, or audition, has a number of important functions, from alerting us to the dangers around us, to facilitating communication with others. The ear has three major sections that function as shown in **Figure 4.8**.

How the eye sees • Figure 4.7

3 Behind the iris and pupil, the muscularly controlled *lens* focuses incoming light into an image on the light-sensitive *retina*, located on the back surface of the fluid-filled eyeball. This is the process of accommodation, in which the lens changes shape to focus images on the retina. Note how the lens reverses the image from right to left and top to bottom when it is projected onto the retina. The brain later reverses the visual input into the final image that we perceive.

2 The light then passes through the *pupil*, a small adjustable opening. Muscles in the *iris* allow the *pupil* to dilate or constrict in response to light intensity or emotional factors.

1 Light first enters through the *cornea*, which helps focus incoming light rays.

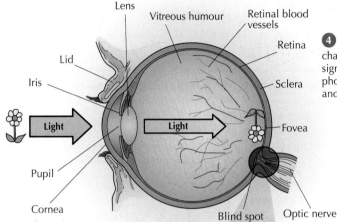

4 In the **retina**, light waves are changed into neural signals (visual transduction) by photoreceptors called rods and cones.

5 The **fovea**, a tiny pit filled with cones, is responsible for our sharpest vision. When we focus directly on an object, the image falls on the fovea.

6 **Rods** are photoreceptors that detect white, black, and grey and are responsible for peripheral vision. They are most important in dim light and at night.

10 After exiting the eye, neural messages travel along the optic nerve to the brain for further processing.

9 At the back of the retina lies an area that has no photoreceptors at all and therefore absolutely no vision. In this **blind spot**, blood vessels and neural pathways enter and exit the eyeball.

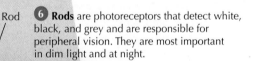
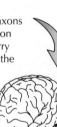

7 **Cones** are photoreceptors adapted for colour, daytime, and detailed vision. They are sensitive to many wavelengths, but each is maximally sensitive to red, green, or blue.

Optic nerve (consists of axons of the ganglion cells that carry messages to the brain)

Visual cortex

8 Rods and cones generate neural signals that send their messages to the brain via activation of the bipolar and ganglion cells.

Do you have a blind spot?

Everyone with vision does. To find yours, hold this book about 30 cm in front of you, close your right eye, and stare at the X with your left eye. Very slowly, move the book closer to you. You should see the worm disappear and the apple become whole.

How the ear hears • Figure 4.8

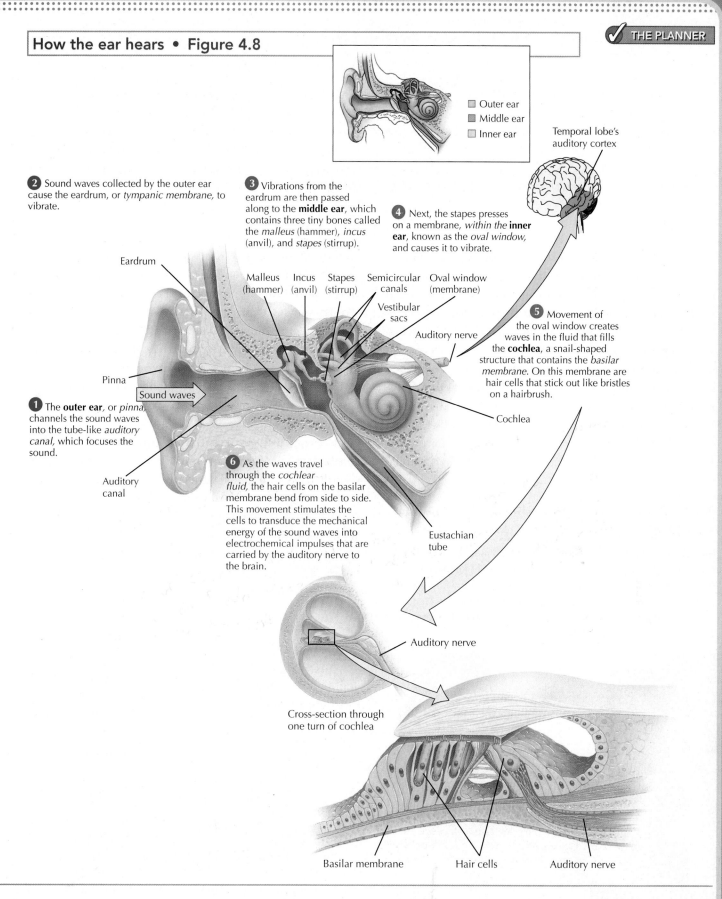

☐ Outer ear
■ Middle ear
☐ Inner ear

2 Sound waves collected by the outer ear cause the eardrum, or *tympanic membrane,* to vibrate.

3 Vibrations from the eardrum are then passed along to the **middle ear**, which contains three tiny bones called the *malleus* (hammer), *incus* (anvil), and *stapes* (stirrup).

4 Next, the stapes presses on a membrane, *within the* **inner ear**, known as the *oval window*, and causes it to vibrate.

Temporal lobe's auditory cortex

Eardrum

Malleus (hammer)   Incus (anvil)   Stapes (stirrup)   Semicircular canals   Oval window (membrane)

Vestibular sacs

Auditory nerve

5 Movement of the oval window creates waves in the fluid that fills the **cochlea**, a snail-shaped structure that contains the *basilar membrane*. On this membrane are hair cells that stick out like bristles on a hairbrush.

Pinna

Sound waves

1 The **outer ear**, or *pinna,* channels the sound waves into the tube-like *auditory canal,* which focuses the sound.

Cochlea

Auditory canal

6 As the waves travel through the *cochlear fluid,* the hair cells on the basilar membrane bend from side to side. This movement stimulates the cells to transduce the mechanical energy of the sound waves into electrochemical impulses that are carried by the auditory nerve to the brain.

Eustachian tube

Auditory nerve

Cross-section through one turn of cochlea

Basilar membrane   Hair cells   Auditory nerve

How the ear distinguishes among sounds of different pitches		Frequency	Pitch	Example
Theory				
Place theory	Hair cells are stimulated at different locations along the basilar membrane.	High frequency	High-pitched sounds	A squeal, or a child's voice
Frequency theory	Hair cells fire at the same rate as the frequency of the sound.	Low frequency	Low-pitched sounds	A growl, or a man's voice
Place and frequency theory	Hair cells fire at the same rate as the sound frequency on different locations of the basilar membrane.	Mid-range frequencies	Mid-pitch sounds	A rustling, or a scrunching sound

The mechanisms determining how we distinguish among sounds of different pitches (low, medium, and high) differ depending on the frequency of the sound (**Table 4.1**). According to **place theory**, different high-frequency sound waves (which produce high-pitched sounds) maximally stimulate the hair cells at different locations along the basilar membrane. Hearing low-pitched sounds works differently. According to **frequency theory**, low-pitched sounds cause hair cells along the basilar membrane to bend and fire neural messages (action potentials) at the same rate as the frequency of that sound. For example, a sound with a frequency of 90 hertz would produce 90 action potentials per second in the auditory nerve. Mid-range frequencies are coded by both location on the basilar membrane (place theory) *and* temporal pattern (frequency theory; see **Figure 4.9**).

Whether we detect a sound as soft or loud depends on its intensity. Sound waves with high peaks and deep valleys produce loud sounds; those that have relatively low peaks and shallow valleys produce soft sounds. The relative loudness or softness of sounds is measured on a scale of *decibels* (dB) (**Figure 4.10a**).

Hearing loss can stem from two major causes: (1) **conduction deafness**, or **middle-ear deafness**, which results from problems with the mechanical system that conducts sound waves to the inner ear (such as a perforated eardrum), and (2) **nerve deafness**, or **inner-ear deafness**, which involves damage to the cochlea, hair cells, or auditory nerve (such as hearing loss caused by ongoing loud noise) (**Figure 4.10b**).

Although most conduction deafness is temporary, damage to the auditory nerve or hair cells is almost always irreversible. The only treatment for severe nerve deafness is a small electronic device called a *cochlear implant*. If the auditory nerve is intact, the implant bypasses hair cells to stimulate the nerve directly. Currently, cochlear implants produce only a rudimentary approximation of hearing, but the technology is improving. Rather than repairing the damage, it is best to protect your hearing in the first place. This can be achieved by avoiding exceptionally loud noises and wearing earplugs when such situations cannot be avoided.

conduction deafness (middle-ear deafness) Deafness resulting from problems with the mechanical system that conducts sound waves to the inner ear.

nerve deafness (inner-ear deafness) Deafness resulting from damage to the cochlea, hair cells, or auditory nerve.

Mosquito ringtone: Can you hear me now?
• Figure 4.9

Stealthy teenagers now have a biological advantage over their teachers: a cellphone ringtone that sounds at 17 kilohertz—too high for adult ears to detect. The ringtone is an ironic by-product of another device that uses the same sound frequency. That invention, dubbed the Mosquito, was designed to help shopkeepers annoy and deter loitering teenagers.

Slobodan Vasic/iStockphoto

How loud is too loud? • Figure 4.10

a. The loudness of a sound is measured in decibels, and the higher a sound's decibel reading, the more damaging it is to the ear. Chronic exposure to loud noise, such as loud music or heavy traffic—or brief exposure to really loud sounds, such as a stereo at full blast, a jackhammer, or a jet engine—can cause permanent nerve deafness. Disease and biological changes associated with aging can also cause nerve deafness. Accumulating research has shown many young adults have the volume on their MP3 player (iPods, etc.) in the loudness range that causes nerve deafness and ultimately damage hearing (Keppler et al., 2010; Muchnik et al., 2012; Portnuff et al., 2011; Torre, 2008). ▼

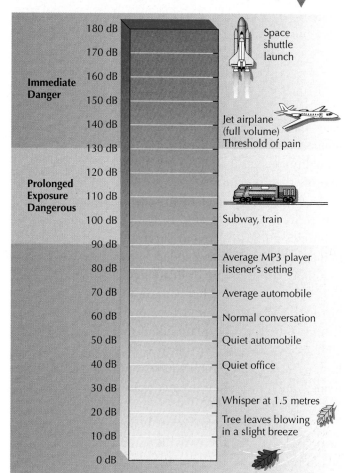

Tim Mosenfelder/Getty Images

 b. The Who held the Guinness World Record since 1976 for the loudest rock concert, with a documented loudness of 126 dB measured at 32 metres from the speakers. Pete Townshend and Roger Daltry both report significant nerve damage hearing loss caused by their prolonged exposure to this type of loud music. Incidentally, Guinness World Records no longer recognizes this category as it doesn't want to promote activities that cause hearing loss.

Turning down the volume on your MP3 player is one easy way to protect your hearing and reduce your chances of deafness later in life. Paying attention to bodily warnings of possible hearing loss, including a change in your normal hearing threshold and tinnitus, a whistling or ringing sensation in your ears, are also important in avoiding hearing loss.

CONCEPT CHECK STOP

1. **What** are rods and cones responsible for and where are they found?

2. **Why** do middle-aged people often need reading glasses?

3. **What** are the three major parts of the ear?

4. **What** are the types of deafness?

Our Other Senses

LEARNING OBJECTIVES

1. **Explain** the importance of smell and taste to survival.
2. **Describe** how the information contained in odour molecules reaches the brain.
3. **Identify** the locations of receptors for the body senses.
4. **Explain** the role of our vestibular and kinesthetic senses.

Vision and audition may be the most prominent of our senses, but the others—taste, smell, and the body senses—are also essential for gathering information about our environment.

Smell and Taste: Sensing Chemicals

Smell and taste are sometimes referred to as the *chemical senses* because they both involve chemoreceptors that are sensitive to certain chemical molecules. Smell and taste receptors are located near each other and often interact so closely that we have difficulty separating the sensations; think about how your sense of taste was diminished the last time you had a bad nose-congesting cold.

Our sense of smell, olfaction, is a remarkably useful, sensitive, and very old sense. In vertebrates, the sense of smell evolved long before vision and hearing, and it's the most universal sense employed by living organisms (Haddad et al., 2008). Humans possess more than 1,000 types of olfactory receptors, allowing us to detect more than 10,000 distinct smells (lemon, nutty, musty, smoky, etc.) (**Figure 4.11**). With this sensitivity you might predict that we would be very good at recognizing different odours, but this is not the case. People have a difficult time matching names to smells, although women tend to be a little better at it than men (Kobal et al., 2000).

For millennia organisms have used the sense of smell not just to detect food but also for communication. Pheromones are compounds found in bodily scents and fluids

For an interesting discussion on this topic, scan to download the author's podcast.

that can affect behaviour, such as signalling threat, courtship, and sexual behaviour. While pheromone research is far more conclusive in insect species, some research evidence suggests that these chemical odours might be able to change sexual behaviours in humans (Savic, Berglund, & Lindström, 2007; Thornhill et al., 2003) or influence menstrual cycle synchronicity in women who live together (McClintock, 1971). Other research findings challenge these results, arguing that humans do not have this capacity (Hays, 2003) and that menstrual cycle synchronicity is an artifact of poor research methodology (Schank, 2001; Strassmann, 1999). Although research does not as yet have a clear answer on the presence or effects of pheromones in our species, investigators do agree that human sexuality and its influences are far more complex than that of other animals.

Today, the sense of taste, gustation, might be the least critical of our senses. In the past it probably contributed significantly to our survival. Evolutionarily, the major function of taste, aided by smell, was probably to help us avoid eating or drinking harmful substances. Because many plants that contain toxic chemicals taste bitter, an organism would be more likely to survive if it finds bitter-tasting plants distasteful (Cooper et al., 2002; Kardong, 2008; Skelhorn et al., 2008). Conversely, humans and other animals have a preference for sweet foods, which are generally not poisonous and are good sources of energy.

Evolutionary psychologists believe the heightened taste sensitivity seen early in pregnancy may be an adaptation to prevent a pregnant woman from ingesting substances that might be harmful to her developing fetus (Bayley et al., 2009). As with the sense of smell, women generally have a keener sense of taste than men (Michon et al., 2009). In our ancestral past, women assumed much of the food preparation responsibility, where a well-developed gustatory and olfactory sense would have increased the chances of detecting rancid or toxic food.

The sense of taste varies across the lifespan. Children's taste buds are replaced more quickly than adults' taste buds—about every seven days. As we age, taste bud replacement occurs more slowly. Because children have abundant new taste buds compared with adults, they often dislike foods with strong or unusual tastes. Many food and taste preferences are also learned from childhood

How the nose smells • Figure 4.11

THE PLANNER

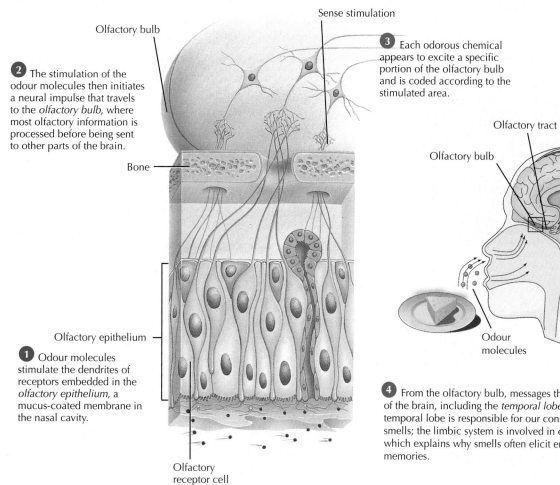

Sense stimulation

Olfactory bulb

2 The stimulation of the odour molecules then initiates a neural impulse that travels to the *olfactory bulb*, where most olfactory information is processed before being sent to other parts of the brain.

3 Each odorous chemical appears to excite a specific portion of the olfactory bulb and is coded according to the stimulated area.

Bone

Olfactory epithelium

1 Odour molecules stimulate the dendrites of receptors embedded in the *olfactory epithelium*, a mucus-coated membrane in the nasal cavity.

Olfactory receptor cell

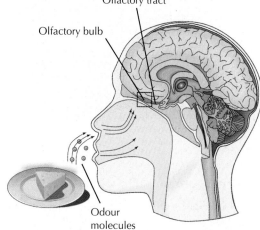

Olfactory tract

Olfactory bulb

Odour molecules

4 From the olfactory bulb, messages then travel to other areas of the brain, including the *temporal lobe* and *limbic system*. The temporal lobe is responsible for our conscious recognition of smells; the limbic system is involved in emotion and memory, which explains why smells often elicit emotion-laden memories.

experiences and cultural influences, so that one person's delicacy can be a source of revulsion to others. For example, most New Zealand and Australian children enjoy the flavour of Vegemite: a thick, black, savoury spread that looks very similar to axle grease. It is typically spread thinly on toast or crackers but is also used in cooking as a flavour enhancer. Most Canadians who have tried it dislike both the flavour and the texture of Vegemite, primarily because they were not exposed to its strong taste during childhood.

When we take away the sense of smell, we can sense five distinct tastes: sweet, sour, salty, bitter, and umami. *Umami* means "delicious" or "savoury" and refers to sensitivity to an amino acid called glutamate (Chandrashekar et al., 2006; McCabe & Rools, 2007). Glutamate is found in meats, meat broths, and monosodium glutamate

(MSG). It is this flavour in soya sauce that makes it so appealing.

Taste receptors respond differentially to food molecules of different shapes. The major taste receptors (taste buds) are clustered on our tongues within little bumps called *papillae* (**Figure 4.12**).

The Body Senses: Much More Than Just Touch

The senses that tell the brain how the body is oriented, where and how the body is moving, and what it touches or is touched by are called the body senses. They include the **skin senses**, the vestibular sense, and the kinesthetic sense.

Taste sensation • Figure 4.12

When we eat and drink, liquids and foods dissolved in saliva flow over bumps on our tongue called papillae and into pores where the taste buds are located. The taste buds contain the receptors for taste. When these receptors are activated they trigger neural impulses that travel to the cortex via the thalamus.

Surface of the tongue magnified about 50 times

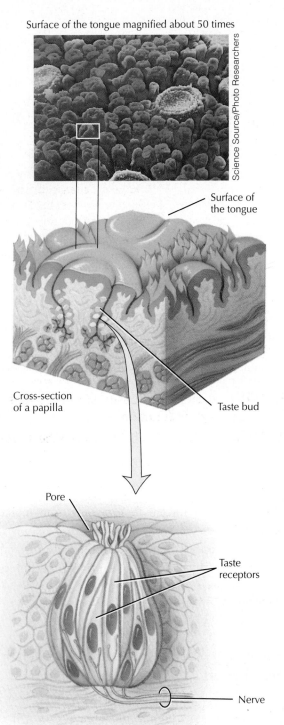

Science Source/Photo Researchers

Surface of the tongue

Cross-section of a papilla

Taste bud

Pore

Taste receptors

Nerve

A taste bud

Our skin is sensitive to touch (or pressure), temperature, and pain (**Figure 4.13a**). The concentration and depth of the receptors for each of these stimuli vary. For example, touch receptors are most concentrated on the face, genitals, and fingers and less so on the back and legs. As you manipulate something with your fingers, pressure receptors in the skin register the indentations made by the object. For blind people, a heighted sense of touch allows them to read Braille. Learning to develop the sensitivity necessary to detect and differentiate the small raised dots on a page is an example of neuroplasticity (Chapter 2). Repeatedly performing this task changes the architecture of the blind person's brain as they learn to read with their fingers (Merabet & Pascual-Leone, 2010).

Some receptors respond to more than one type of stimulation—for example, itching, tickling, and vibrating sensations seem to be produced by light stimulation of both pressure and pain receptors. We have more skin receptors for cold than for warmth, and we don't seem to have any receptors for hot at all. The sensation of hot occurs when the cold and warm receptors are simultaneously activated (Craig & Bushneil, 1994).

The **vestibular sense** is responsible for balance—it informs the brain of how the body, and particularly the head, is oriented with respect to gravity and three-dimensional space. When the head moves, liquid in the *semicircular canals*, located in the inner ear, moves and bends hair cell receptors. At the end of the semicircular canals are the vestibular sacs, which contain hair cells sensitive to the specific angle of the head—straight up and down or tilted. Information from the semicircular canals and the *vestibular sacs* is converted to neural impulses that are then carried to the appropriate section of the brain (**Figure 4.13b**).

Kinesthesia is the sense that provides the brain with information about bodily posture, orientation, and movement. Kinesthetic receptors are found throughout the muscles, joints, and tendons of the body. They tell the brain which muscles are being contracted or relaxed, how our body weight is distributed, where our arms and legs are in relation to the rest of our body, and so on (**Figure 4.13c**). Parkinson's disease is a degenerative disorder of the CNS characterized by significant loss of dopamine neurons in the brain. As the disease progresses it increasingly interferes with the kinesthetic sense, making it more and more difficult for the affected person to stand, walk, or sit (Wright et al., 2010).

The body senses • Figure 4.13

a. The skin senses are vital. Skin not only protects our internal organs but also provides our brains with survival and attachment information. Both humans and non-human animals are highly responsive to physical contact and touch. ▼

Mike Kemp/© RubberBall/Alamy

Sean/Kilpatrick/The Canadian Press

Roy Toft/National Geographic Stock

▲ **b.** Part of the thrill of amusement park rides comes from overloading the vestibular sense. This sense is used by the eye muscles to maintain visual fixation, and sometimes by the body to change its orientation. We can also become dizzy or nauseated if the vestibular sense is overloaded by boat, airplane, or automobile motion. Random versus anticipated movements increase chances of motion sickness, explaining why the driver of the car is generally the least likely to get sick. Children between ages 2 and 12 years have the greatest susceptibility to motion sickness, and it tends to decline with age.

▲ **c.** Without his finely tuned kinesthetic sense to provide information about his bodily posture, orientation, and movement, Canadian snowboarding Olympic gold medallist Jasey-Jay Anderson would be on his way to the hospital rather than the winner's podium.

CONCEPT CHECK **STOP**

1. **Why** are our senses of smell and taste called the chemical senses?

2. **What** are the three basic skin sensations and what are their functions?

3. **How** do the vestibular and kinesthetic senses differ?

The Magic of Perception

LEARNING OBJECTIVES

1. **Describe** the relationship among selective attention, feature detectors, and habituation.

2. **Summarize** the factors involved in perceptual interpretation.

3. **Describe** the limitations of subliminal perception.

While sensation is the process of receiving and translating raw sensory data from the environment, **perception** is the process of selecting, organizing, and interpreting the sensations into useful mental representations of the

> **perception** The higher-level process of selecting, organizing, and interpreting sensory data into useful mental representations of the world.

world. More simply, perception is the meaningful interpretation of our sensations. Certainly, sensation is remarkable, but the real power and creativity of the nervous system is showcased in perception. It is our perceptual system that makes the world feel real, cohesive, and

Psychological Science

Optical Illusions

Illusions are either a false impression produced by an interpretation error in the perceptual process or by an actual physical distortion, such as in desert mirages. Illusions provide psychologists with a tool for studying the normal process of perception. Drawing a illustrates the *Müller-Lyer illusion*. The two vertical lines are the same length, but psychologists have learned that people who live in urban environments usually see the one on the right as longer. This is because they have learned to make size and distance judgements from perspective cues created by right angles and horizontal and vertical lines of buildings and streets.

Magnetic Hill (in image b) near Moncton, New Brunswick, is a famous example of an optical illusion. When a car is in neutral and facing what appears to be downhill, it will begin to roll backward—that is, the vehicle seems to be rolling uphill. This happens because the slope of Magnetic Hill is an optical illusion

and the obstructed horizon confuses the perceptual system as to the correct grade of the slope. In image c (*i*) it appears as though square A is much darker than square B. That is not the case, A and B are exactly the same shade of grey (see proof in image c *ii*). Our brain perceives the difference because it compares the target square with those around it and enhances the contrast. Also, our visual system tries to correct for shadows cast by objects to determine colour consistently (in this case, the shadow is being cast by the green cylinder). This is also known as *colour constancy* (see below).

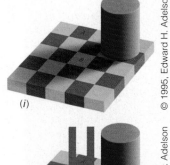

(*i*)

(*ii*)

c. Checkershadow illusion

© 1995, Edward H. Adelson

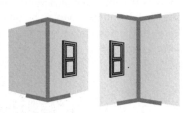

a. Müller-Lyer illusion

b. Magnetic Hill illusion

Tourism Moncton

Think Critically

1. Why do you think optical illusions are so interesting to look at? Could it have something to do with the way our brain pays attention to incoming stimuli that challenges the fluidity of our sensory and perceptual systems?
2. Why do you think clothing with vertical stripes makes a person look leaner than clothing with horizontal stripes?

---

meaningful. Normally, our perceptions fluidly interact with our sensations. When they do not, the result is an *illusion*. See *Psychological Science: Optical Illusions*.

Selection: Extracting Important Information

In almost every situation, we encounter more sensory information than we can reasonably pay attention to. Three major factors help us select and focus on some stimuli and ignore others: **selective attention**, **feature detectors**, and **habituation** (**Figure 4.14**).

Certain basic mechanisms for perceptual selection are built into the brain. For example,

selective attention Filtering out distractions and attending only to important sensory messages.

feature detectors Specialized brain cells that respond only to certain sensory information.

habituation The tendency of the brain to ignore environmental factors that remain constant.

through the process of selective attention (see **Figure 4.14a**), the brain picks out the information that is important and relevant and ignores the rest (Folk & Remington, 1998; Kramer et al., 2000).

In humans and other animals, the brain contains specialized cells, called feature detectors, that respond only to certain sensory information (see **Figure 4.14b**). There are feature detectors for all sorts of visual stimuli, such as lines, edges, shapes, and movement. The further along the visual system, the more specialized are the feature detector neurons (Hubel & Wiesel, 1979; Hinton, 2010). Monkeys and humans also have feature detectors that respond maximally to faces (Freiwald et al., 2009;

Visualizing

Selection • Figure 4.14

Ryan McVay/Photodisc/Getty Images

a. Selective attention

▲ When you are in a group of people, surrounded by various conversations, you can still select and attend to the voices of people you find interesting. An example of selective attention occurs with the well-known *cocktail party phenomenon:* have you ever been at a noisy party but been able to suddenly tune into a conversation when you hear someone mention your name?

Medford Taylor/National Geographic Stock

b. Feature detectors

▲ Cats possess cells, known as feature detectors, that respond to specific lines and angles (Hubel & Wiesel, 1965, 1979). Researchers found that kittens reared in a completely vertical world fail to develop the ability to detect horizontal lines or objects. Conversely, kittens restricted to only horizontal lines cannot detect vertical lines. A certain amount of interaction with the environment is necessary for feature detector cells to develop normally (Blakemore & Cooper, 1970).

© VStock/Alamy

c. Habituation

After some time, these young women's brains will begin to ignore the sensations of their braces. (Sensory adaptation will also occur at the level of the sensory receptor.) ▶

Tsao & Livingstone, 2008) Deficits in feature detectors in the temporal and occipital lobes can produce a condition called prosopagnosia (*prospon* means "face" and *agnosia* means "failure to know") (Barton, 2008). People with this condition can recognize that they are looking at a face, but they cannot say whose face it is, even if it is the face of someone they know. Similarly, they might see their own face in the mirror but do not recognize themselves.

Other examples of the brain's ability to filter experience are evidenced by habituation. The brain is "prewired" to pay more attention to changes in the environment than to stimuli that remain constant. For example, when braces are first applied or when they are tightened, they can be uncomfortable. After a while, however, awareness of the pain diminishes (**Figure 4.14c**). Note the difference between sensory adaptation, in which the diminished response occurs in the sense receptors, and habituation, in which the diminished response occurs further along the perceptual pathway in the brain.

As advertisers and political operatives well know, people tend to readily select stimuli that are intense, novel, moving, contrasting, and repetitious. For sheer volume of sales (or votes), the question of whether you like the ad is irrelevant; what matters is whether it gets your attention.

Organization: Form, Constancy, Depth, and Colour

Raw sensory data are like the parts of a clock—they must be assembled in a meaningful way before they are functional and useful. Our perceptual system organizes sensory data in terms of form, constancy, depth, and colour.

Form perception: What is it? Gestalt psychologists were among the first to study how the brain organizes sensory impressions into a *gestalt*—a German word meaning "form" or "whole." They emphasized the importance of organization and patterning in enabling us to perceive the whole stimulus rather than perceiving its discrete parts

as separate entities. The Gestaltists proposed several laws of organization that specify how people perceive **form** (**Figure 4.15**).

The most fundamental Gestalt principle of organization is our tendency to distinguish between figure (our main focus of attention) and ground (the background or surroundings).

Occasionally, it can be difficult to distinguish the figure from the ground, as can be seen in **Figure 4.16a**. This is known as a reversible figure. Your perceptual system alternates what it sees as the figure.

Like *reversible figures*, *impossible figures* help us understand perceptual principles—in this case, the principle of form organization (**Figure 4.16b**).

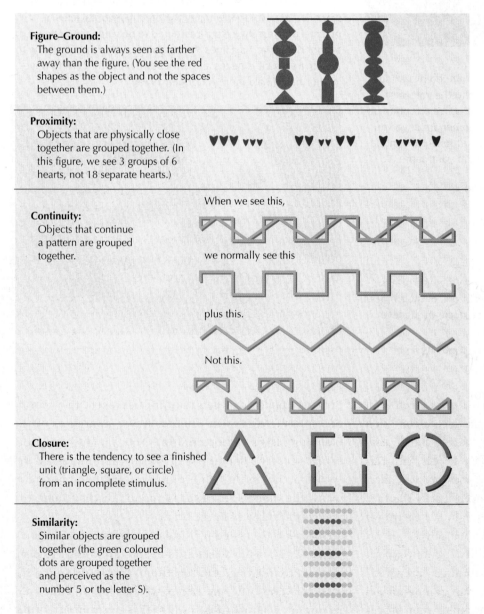

Figure–Ground:
The ground is always seen as farther away than the figure. (You see the red shapes as the object and not the spaces between them.)

Proximity:
Objects that are physically close together are grouped together. (In this figure, we see 3 groups of 6 hearts, not 18 separate hearts.)

Continuity:
Objects that continue a pattern are grouped together.

When we see this,

we normally see this.

plus this.

Not this.

Closure:
There is the tendency to see a finished unit (triangle, square, or circle) from an incomplete stimulus.

Similarity:
Similar objects are grouped together (the green coloured dots are grouped together and perceived as the number 5 or the letter S).

Gestalt principles of organization • Figure 4.15

Figure-ground, proximity, continuity, closure, and similarity are shown here, but the Gestalt principle of contiguity cannot be shown because it involves nearness in time, not visual nearness. Although the examples of the Gestalt principles in this figure are visual, each principle applies to other modes of perception as well. You probably have experienced aural figure and ground effects; for example, in a lecture, when there was a conversation going on close by you. You might have found it difficult to sort out background sounds from those you wanted to focus on. This is especially difficult if the conversation is interesting or the lecture is boring or difficult.

Reversible and impossible figures
• Figure 4.16

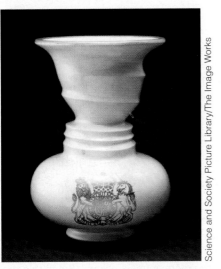

a. This Silver Jubilee vase of Queen Elizabeth (right side) and Prince Philip (left side) demonstrates alternating figure-ground relations. In one view the faces are perceived as the figure and in the other view the vase is the figure.

b. When you first glance at this famous print by Dutch artist M. C. Escher, you detect specific features of the stimuli and judge them as sensible figures. But as you try to sort the different elements into a stable, well-organized whole, you realize they don't add up—they're impossible. There is no one-to-one correspondence between your actual sensory input and your final perception.

Constancy: Keeping sensations understandable See *What a Psychologist Sees: Four Visual Perceptual Constancies* for a discussion of four perceptual constancies.

Depth perception: How far away is it? In our three-dimensional world, the ability to perceive the depth and distance of objects—as well as their height and width—is essential. Imagine trying to parallel park or cross the road without the ability to perceive distance and depth. We usually rely most heavily on vision for this perception, but we also use other senses, such as hearing.

Depth perception is primarily learned through experience. However, research using an apparatus called the *visual cliff* (**Figure 4.17**) has shown that some of depth perception is present from very early in postnatal development.

One mechanism by which we perceive depth relies on having two forward-facing eyes to produce **binocular cues**; the other involves **monocular cues**, which work regardless of eye placement.

Visual cliff • Figure 4.17

Crawling and newly walking infants hesitate or refuse to move to the "deep end" of the visual cliff (Gibson & Walk, 1960 Lin et al., 2010; Witherington et al., 2005), indicating that they perceive the difference in depth. (The same is true for baby animals that walk almost immediately after birth.) Even 2-month-old infants show a change in heart rate when placed on the deep versus shallow side of the visual cliff (Banks & Salapatek, 1983; Ueno et al., 2011).

What a Psychologist Sees

Four Visual Perceptual Constancies

As noted earlier with sensory adaptation and habituation, we have evolved to be particularly alert to change in our environment. However, for some perceptions we also depend on some consistencies. Without this perceptual constancy, our world would be totally chaotic. There are four basic perceptual constancies:

1. Size constancy. Although the more distant zebras in the photograph appear much smaller than those nearby, we perceive them as similar in size because of size constancy. According to this principle, the perceived size of an object remains the same even though the size of its image on the retina changes. Interestingly, size constancy, like all constancies, appears to develop from learning and experience. Studies of people who have been blind since birth and then have their sight restored find they have little or no size constancy (Sacks, 1995).

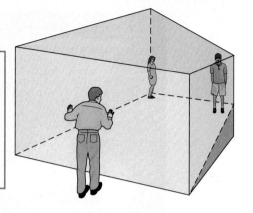

perceptual constancy The tendency for the environment to be perceived as remaining the same even with changes in sensory input.

The Ames room illusion is based on the unusual construction of the room, and our perceptual constancies have falsely filled in the wrong details. To the viewer, peering through the peephole, the room appears normal. But in this specially constructed room, the trapezoidal shape and sloping ceilings and floors provide misleading depth cues. Because our brains mistakenly assume the two people are the same distance away, we compensate for the apparent size difference by perceiving the person on the left as much smaller.

Several Ames room sets were used in *The Lord of the Rings* film trilogy to make the heights of the diminutive hobbits appear correct when standing next to Gandalf the wizard.

2. Shape constancy. As a coin is spun, it appears to change shape, but we do not get confused by this, and still perceive it as the same coin because of shape constancy.

In this photo, the person on the right appears to be much larger than the person on the left. The illusion is so strong that when the left person walks to the right corner, the observer perceives them to be growing, even though that is not possible. How can this be?

3. Colour constancy and **4. Brightness constancy.** We perceive the clothes we wear as having a relatively constant hue (or colour) and brightness, despite the fact that brightness of light varies indoor to outdoor, and conditions of illumination change during the day. A red dress in the morning light still appears to be a red dress at sunset.

Sadi Ugur OKÇu/iStockphoto

© Moviestore Collection Ltd/Alamy

© Michael Doolittle/Alamy

Nadezhda Kulagina/iStockphoto

Retinal disparity • Figure 4.18

a. Stare at your two index fingers a few centimetres in front of your eyes, holding the tips about half a centimetre apart. Do you see the "floating finger"? Move your fingers farther away and the finger will shrink. Move them closer and it will enlarge.

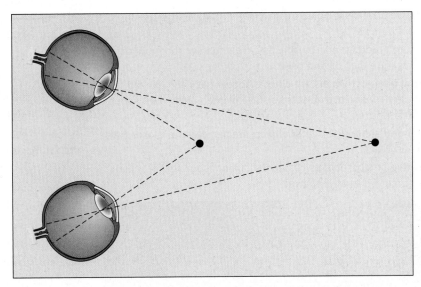

b. Because of retinal disparity, objects at different distances project their images on different parts of the retina. Far objects project on the retinal area near the nose, whereas near objects project farther out, closer to the ears.

One of the most important binocular cues for depth perception comes from **retinal disparity** (**Figure 4.18**). Because our eyes are about 6.5 centimetres (or two and a half inches) apart, each retina receives a slightly different view of the world. You can demonstrate this yourself by seeing what happens when you hold your finger up at arm's length and then alternatively open and close each eye while looking at your finger. Your finger seems to jump from side to side. When we look at an object, the brain fuses the different images received from each retina into one overall image in an effect known as *stereoscopic vision*.

As we move closer to an object, a second binocular cue, **convergence**, helps us judge depth. The closer the object, the more our eyes are turned inward. The resulting amount of eye-muscle tension assists in interpreting distance (**Figure 4.19**).

The binocular (two eyes) cues of retinal disparity and convergence are inadequate in judging distances longer than about a football field. Luckily, we have a number of monocular cues available separately to each eye.

Retinal convergence • Figure 4.19

When looking at an object that is very close, our eyes are turned so far inward we appear "cross-eyed."

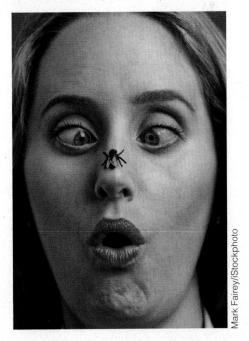

Mark Fairey/iStockphoto

Monocular cues • Figure 4.20

Linear perspective: parallel lines converge, or angle toward one another, as they recede into the distance.

Interposition: objects that obscure or overlap other objects are perceived as closer.

Relative size: close objects cast a larger retinal image than distant objects.

Texture gradient: nearby objects have a coarser and more distinct texture than distant ones.

Aerial perspective: distant objects appear hazy and blurred compared with close objects because of intervening atmospheric dust or haze.

Light and shadow: brighter objects are perceived as closer than darker objects.

Relative height: objects positioned higher in our field of vision are perceived as farther away.

Imaginechina via AP Images

The 3D pavement art in **Figure 4.20** contains several monocular cues. Can you identify which ones?

Two additional monocular cues are accommodation of the lens (discussed earlier) and motion parallax. In accommodation, muscles that adjust the shape of the lens as it focuses on an object send neural impulses to the brain that interprets the signal to assist in distance perception. Motion parallax is the phenomenon that occurs when we are moving; close objects appear to whiz by whereas farther objects seem to move more slowly or remain stationary. This effect can easily be seen when you look out a window while travelling by car or train and lampposts seem to zoom past, while distant buildings move by much more slowly.

Colour perception: The vividness of vision

Our colour vision is as remarkable as our ability to perceive depth and distance. Humans may be able to discriminate among 7 million different hues, and research conducted in many cultures suggests that we all seem to see essentially the same coloured world (Davies, 1998). Furthermore, studies of infants old enough to focus and move their eyes show that they are able to see colour nearly as well as adults can (Clifford et al., 2009: Knoblauch, Vital-Durand, & Barbur, 2000; Werner & Wooten, 1979).

Although we know colour is produced by different wavelengths of light, the actual way in which we perceive colour has been the subject of more than 150 years of scientific debate. There are two theories of colour vision: the trichromatic (three-colour theory) and the opponent-process theory. The **trichromatic theory** (from the Greek word *tri*, meaning "three," and *chroma*, meaning "colour") was first proposed by Thomas Young in the early nineteenth century and was later refined by Herman von Helmholtz and others. It seems we have three "colour systems," as they called them: one system that is maximally sensitive to red, another maximally sensitive to green, and another maximally sensitive to blue (Young, 1802). The proponents of this theory demonstrated that mixing lights of these three colours could yield the full spectrum of colours we perceive. Unfortunately this theory has its flaws. One is that it doesn't explain *colour after-effects*, a phenomenon you can experience yourself in the *Applying Psychology: Colour After-Effects* feature.

The **opponent-process theory**, proposed by Ewald Hering later in the nineteenth century, also has the three colour systems, but he suggested that each system is sensitive to two opposing colours—blue and yellow, red and green, black and white—in an "on-off" fashion. In other words, each colour receptor in our visual system responds either to blue or yellow, or to red or green, with the black-or-white systems responding to differences in brightness levels. This theory makes sense because when different-coloured lights are combined, people are unable to see reddish greens and bluish yellows. In fact, when red and green lights or blue and yellow lights are mixed in equal amounts, we see white.

> **trichromatic theory** The theory that colour perception results from mixing three distinct colour systems: red, green, and blue.

> **opponent process theory** The theory that colour perception is based on three systems of colour receptors, each of which responds in an on-off fashion to opposite colour stimuli: blue or yellow, red or green, and black or white.

Applying Psychology

Colour After-Effects

Try staring at the dot in the middle of this colour-distorted flag for 60 seconds. Then stare at a plain sheet of white paper. You should get interesting colour after-effects—red in place of green and white in place of black—giving you the Canadian flag you are most familiar with. Do the same thing with the image of the model. What colours do you now see in her outfit and nose?

What happened? This is a good example of the opponent-process theory. As you stared at the figure, the green area stimulated only the green channel of the red-green opponent colour cells. Continuous stimulation fatigued the green channel, whereas the unstimulated red channel was not fatigued. When you looked at the piece of white paper, the white stimulated both the red and the green channels equally. Because the green channel was fatigued, the red channel fired at a higher rate and you therefore saw a red after-effect. Without first staring at the white dot, the red and green receptors would have cancelled each other out and you would have seen white when you looked at the white paper.

Svetlana Braun/iStock

Think Critically

In what kinds of situations do you think colour after-effects are likely to occur?

In 1964, research by Paul Brown and George Wald showed we do have three types of cones in the retina, each responding optimally to red, green, or blue. This confirmed the central component of the trichromatic theory. At nearly the same time, R. L. DeValois (1965) was studying electrophysiological recording of cells in the optic nerve and optic pathways to the brain. He discovered that cells respond to colour in an opponent fashion in the optic nerve, thalamus, and visual cortex. The findings reconciled the once-competing trichromatic and opponent-process theories. Now we know that colour is processed in a trichromatic fashion at the level of the cones in the retina, and in an opponent fashion at higher neural levels in the optic nerve, thalamus, and cortex.

Colour-deficient vision Most people perceive three different colours—red, green, and blue—and are called *trichromats*. However, a small percentage of the population has a genetic deficiency in the genes that code for either the red-green system, the blue-yellow system, or both. Those who perceive only two colours are called *dichromats*. People who are sensitive to only the black-white system are called *monochromats*, and they are totally colour blind. If you'd like to test yourself for red-green colour blindness, see **Figure 4.21**.

Colour-deficient vision • Figure 4.21

Are you red-green colour blind? People who have a red-green deficiency have trouble perceiving the number in this design. Although we commonly use the term colour blindness, most problems are colour confusion rather than colour blindness. Furthermore, most people who have some colour blindness are not even aware of it.

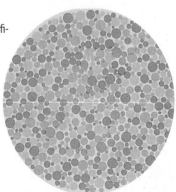

Interpretation: Explaining Our Perceptions

After selectively sorting through incoming sensory information and organizing it, the brain uses this information to interpret, explain, and make judgements about the external world. This final stage of perception—interpretation—is influenced by several factors, including perceptual adaptation, perceptual set, frame of reference, and bottom-up or top-down processing.

George Stratton (1896) and his special lenses experiment, discussed in the chapter opener, illustrates the critical role that *perceptual adaptation* plays in how we interpret the information that our brains gather. Without his ability to adapt and change his perceptions to a new and skewed environment, Stratton would not have been able to function. His brain's ability to adapt to new incoming stimuli allowed him to create coherence out of what would otherwise have been sensory chaos. The ability to do this is an example of perceptual adaptation.

Our previous experiences, assumptions, and expectations also affect how we interpret and perceive the world by creating a *perceptual set*, or a readiness to perceive things in a particular way—in other words, we largely perceive what we expect to perceive. For example, if you are speeding and see a parked sedan up ahead, you might ease off on the gas and slow down. This is because you are more likely to perceive it as an unmarked police car, rather than a pulled-over vehicle. Perceptual set is one of the factors that influence the interpretation of incoming sensory information (**Figure 4.22**).

Finally, recall that we began this chapter by discussing how we receive sensory information (sensation) and work our way upward to the top levels of perceptual processing (perception). Psychologists refer to this type of information processing as **bottom-up processing** (also known as feature analysis). In contrast, **top-down processing** begins with higher, top-level processing involving thoughts, previous experiences, expectations, language, and cultural background and works down to the sensory level (**Figure 4.23**).

Science and ESP So far in this chapter, we have talked about sensory input provided to our eyes, ears, nose, mouth, and skin. But is it possible for some people to perceive things that cannot be perceived by using the usual sensory channels? Is there such a thing as **extrasensory perception (ESP)?** People who claim to have ESP profess to be able to read other people's minds (telepathy), perceive

© Trinity Mirror/Mirrorpix/Alamy

Perceptual set: Is it a log on the water or the Loch Ness Monster? • Figure 4.22

Imagine yourself driving along the road beside Loch Ness in the Scottish Highlands at dusk. This large, very deep freshwater lake near Inverness is most famous for the alleged sightings of the Loch Ness Monster or "Nessie." How might your perceptual system interpret this image if you saw it out your car window as you drove by? Is it a log floating on the water or is it the legendary monster? How you perceive it depends in part on your previous assumptions and expectations about the existence of the monster. If you believe in Nessie, then that is what you probably will think you have seen.

objects or events that are inaccessible to their normal senses (clairvoyance), predict the future (precognition), or move or affect objects without touching them (psychokinesis).

Scientific investigations of ESP began in the early twentieth century in a number of countries around the world, and some work on the subject continues today. After nearly a hundred years of research on the topic, the results have overwhelmingly found no conclusive evidence for ESP.

Bottom-up, top-down • Figure 4.23

When first learning to read, you used bottom-up processing. You initially learned that certain arrangements of lines and squiggles put together represented specific letters. You also realized that these letters combine in memorable chunks to make up words. When you read a sentence, you would look at and read every word (think of how a child sounds when they read a sentence out loud).

Now, yuor aiblity to raed uisng top-dwon $prcessoing mkaes it psosible to unedrstnad thsi sntenece desipte its mnay mssipllengis.

Psychological Science

 THE PLANNER

Subliminal Perception

Is the public under siege by sneaky advertisers bombarding us with subliminal (literally, "below the threshold") messages that can undermine our intentions and influence our buying behaviour?

Can you lose weight, stop smoking, or relieve stress by listening to subliminal recordings that promise to solve your problems without you having to pay attention or exert any effort? It is possible to perceive something without conscious awareness (Aarts, 2007; Boccato et al., 2008; Cleeremans & Sarrazin, 2007). For example, in one study the experimenter briefly flashed one of two pictures subliminally (either a happy or an angry face) followed by a neutral face. They found this subliminal presentation evoked matching unconscious facial expressions in the participants' own facial muscles (Dimberg, Thunberg, & Elmehed, 2000).

You really must come for a ride in...

The **VAUXHALL LIGHT SIX** WITH INDEPENDENT SPRINGING

Mary Evans Picture Library/ONSLOW AUCTIONS LIMITED

Despite this result and considerable evidence that *subliminal perception* occurs, does it mean that such processes result in *subliminal persuasion*? That is, is subliminal perception the same as subliminal persuasion—can we be manipulated to do things we are not aware of? Based on considerable research over many decades, the answer to this question is a very clear no. While subliminal stimuli can be detected in a variety of circumstances, at best, it has a minimal (if any) effect on consumer thinking and behaviour and no effect on citizens' voting behaviour (Begg, Needham, & Bookbinder, 1993; Dijksterhuis et al., 2005; Karremans et al., 2006). As for subliminal self-help recordings, you're better off with old-fashioned, tried-and-tested, conscious methods of self-improvement.

A now-classic Canadian media test of subliminal persuasion was conducted in the 1950s. During a popular Sunday night CBC television show called Close-up, viewers were flashed a subliminal message more than 300 times. When asked to guess what the message was, around 500 people wrote in and about half reported feeling hungry or thirsty during the show. Not one writer got the message correct. The subliminal message was simply "telephone now" ("Phone Now," 1958).

Think Critically

1. Why do you think humans developed the capacity for subliminal perception?
2. What role might subliminal perception play in everyday life today?

For example, a number of studies, including a meta-analysis of 30 studies that used good scientific controls, reported absolutely no evidence of ESP (Francis, 2012; Hyman, 2010; Milton & Wiseman, 1999, 2001; Valeo & Beyerstein, 2008).

Probably the most important criticism of both experimental and casual claims of ESP is their lack of stability and replication. These are core requirements for scientific methodology and general scientific acceptance (Hyman, 1996). Even offering a $1-million prize was not a strong enough inducement to encourage any self-proclaimed psychics to demonstrate their ESP abilities to the scientific community. As mentioned in Chapter 1, the James Randi Educational Corporation offered this prize to anyone who could demonstrate any paranormal event under proper scientific observation conditions. To date, despite many hundreds of applications, no one has ever passed even the preliminary test (Wagg, 2008). The corporation stopped offering the prize in March 2010, stating that many other international organizations are now offering similar and larger prizes. If you are interested in applying to one of

these organizations, a list can be found at the *Skeptic's Dictionary* online (http://skepdic.com/randi.html). The offer of large cash prizes to anyone who can demonstrate ESP is not new. In 1922 *Scientific American* offered two $2,500 prizes for anyone able to demonstrate evidence of psychic abilities. A number of people applied, but no one won those prizes either (*Skeptic's Dictionary*, 2012).

Why do so many people continue to believe in ESP? One reason has previously been mentioned—our motivations and interests often influence our perceptions, driving us to selectively attend to things we want to see or hear. In addition, the subject of ESP often generates strong emotional responses. When individuals feel strongly about an issue, they sometimes fail to recognize the faulty reasoning underlying their beliefs.

Belief in ESP is particularly associated with failures in critical thinking (Chapter 1). For example, people often fall victim to the *fallacy of positive instances* (also known as the *confirmation bias*) (Chapter 8), noting and remembering events that confirm personal expectations and beliefs and ignoring non-supportive evidence. This fallacy of positive instances may explain why some people play the lottery despite the overwhelming odds against winning. For these people, repeatedly seeing other winners on television or in the newspaper confirms that they too could also win. Finally, human information processing often biases us to notice and remember the most vivid information—such as a detailed (and spooky) anecdote or a heartfelt personal testimonial. A powerful or vivid personal story is far more memorable and convincing for many than a large collection of "dry" negative scholarly findings on the subject.

CONCEPT CHECK STOP

1. **What** are the processes that allow us to pay attention to some stimuli in our environments and ignore others?
2. **What** kinds of cues do we use to perceive depth and distance?
3. **What** factors cause some people to believe in ESP?

Summary

✓ THE PLANNER

1 What Is Sensation? 98

- **Sensation** is the process by which we detect stimuli and convert them into neural signals (**sensory transduction**). **Labelled lines** are the mechanism by which different physical stimuli are interpreted by the brain as distinct **sensations**.

- In **sensory adaptation**, sensory receptors in the body fire less frequently with repeated stimulation so that, over time, sensation decreases.

- The absolute threshold is the smallest amount of a stimulus needed to detect a stimulus half the time, and the difference threshold, or just noticeable difference, is the smallest change in stimulus intensity that a person can detect.

- **Nociceptors** detect painful stimuli and then send the information to the spinal cord and brain via two different pathways. According to the **gate-control theory**, our experience of pain depends partly on whether the neural message gets past a "gatekeeper" in the spinal cord.

Measuring the senses • Figure 4.3

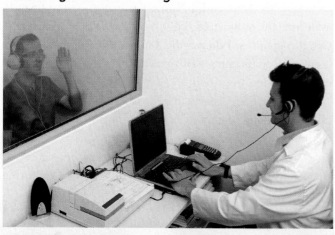

2 How We See and Hear 102

- Light and sound move in waves. Light waves are a form of electromagnetic energy, and sound waves are produced when air molecules move in a particular wave pattern. Both light waves and sound waves vary in length, height, and range.

- Light enters the eye at the front of the eyeball. The cornea protects the eye and helps focus light rays. The iris provides the eye's colour, and muscles in the iris dilate or constrict the pupil. The lens further focuses light, adjusting to allow focusing on objects at different distances. At the back of the eye, incoming light waves reach the **retina**, which contains photoreceptors called **rods** and **cones**. A network of neurons in the retina transmits neural information about light to the brain.

- The **outer ear** gathers sound waves; the **middle ear** amplifies and concentrates the sounds; and the **inner ear** changes the mechanical energy of sound into neural impulses. The frequency and intensity of the sound wave determine how we distinguish among sounds of different pitches and loudness, respectively.

How the eye sees • Figure 4.7

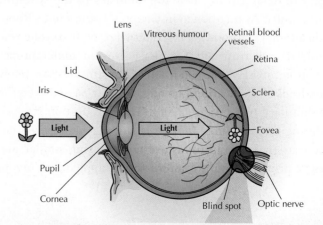

3 Our Other Senses 108

- Smell and taste involve chemoreceptors that are sensitive to certain chemical molecules. In olfaction, odour molecules stimulate receptors in the olfactory epithelium in the nose. The resulting neural impulse travels to the olfactory bulb, where the information is processed before being sent elsewhere in the brain. Our sense of taste (gustation) involves five tastes: sweet, sour, salty, bitter, and umami. The taste buds are clustered on our tongues within the papillae.

- The body senses tell the brain how the body is oriented, where and how it is moving, and what it touches. They include the **skin senses**, the **vestibular sense**, and **kinesthesia**.

The body senses • Figure 4.13b

4 The Magic of Perception 111

- **Perception** is the process of selecting, organizing, and interpreting incoming sensations into useful mental representations of the world. **Selective attention** allows us to filter out unimportant sensory messages. **Feature detectors** are specialized cells that respond only to specific sensory information. **Habituation** is the tendency of the brain to ignore stimuli that remain constant. People tend to automatically select stimuli that are intense, novel, moving, contrasting, and repetitious.

- To be useful, sensory data must be assembled in a meaningful way. We organize sensory data in terms of form, constancy, depth, and colour. The **trichromatic theory** accounts for colour vision processing in the retina and the **opponent-process theory** accounts for processing in the brain and optic nerves.

- Perceptual adaptation, perceptual set, and **bottom-up** versus **top-down** processing affect our interpretation of what we experience. Subliminal stimuli, although perceivable, have a minimal effect on thinking and behaviour.

- Despite considerable scientific evidence against its existence, many people continue to believe in ESP.

What a Psychologist Sees: Four Visual Perceptual Constancies

Key Terms

Critical and Creative Thinking Questions

1. Sensation and perception are closely linked. What is the primary distinction between the two? What happens when the fluidity of these two systems is disturbed?

2. If we detected and attended equally to all incoming stimuli, the amount of information would be overwhelming. What sensory and perceptual processes help us reduce and manage incoming sensory information?

3. Knowing that humans adapt to some types of pain, why is it that people can sometimes tune out painful injuries?

4. How might optical illusions contribute to a belief in ESP?

5. What senses would likely be impaired if a person were somehow missing all the apparatus of the ear (including the outer, middle, and inner ear)?

6. When we have a bad cold, why do you think our ability to taste food is severely diminished? What is it that prevents proper taste perception when our sense of smell is compromised?

7. As we age, the ability to hear high frequency sounds deteriorates. Other than the examples used in the text, what advantages and disadvantages could this confer to young adults?

8. Can you explain how perceptual sets might contribute to the development of prejudice or discrimination?

Self-Test

(Check your answers in Appendix A.)

1. Sensory transduction is the process of converting _____.
   a. neural impulses into mental representations of the world
   b. receptors into transmitters
   c. a physical stimulus into neural impulses
   d. receptors into neural impulses

2. Labelled lines refer to how _____.
   a. people can reduce their dependence on a single sensory system by developing their ESP
   b. the eye processes visual information before it gets to the thalamus
   c. the brain interprets the type of sensory information by attending to its neural origin and destination in the brain
   d. the sensory receptors can reduce environmental sensations by physically preventing your sensory organs from seeing, hearing, and so on

3. You walk into a nightclub and the music is playing at a comfortable volume. Although the DJ has been slightly increasing the volume for the past hour, you actually only notice this perceptual change when he drastically increases the volume for a particular song. Which perceptual process is illustrated here?
   a. psychophysics   c. sensory deterioration
   b. absolute threshold   d. difference threshold

4. A martial-arts fighter breaks his wrist during a title fight, triggering a surprisingly brief sensation of pain. He is able to continue, eventually overcoming this setback to win the fight. Research suggests _____ facilitated the initial feelings of pain, while _____ blocked the feelings of pain so he could continue on and ultimately win the fight.
   a. serotonin; endorphins

   b. substance P; endorphins
   c. phantom limb pain; dopamine
   d. endorphins; substance P

5. Identify the parts of the eye, placing the labels on the figure below:

blind spot	lens	sclera
cornea	optic nerve	vitreous humour
fovea	pupil	
iris	retina	

   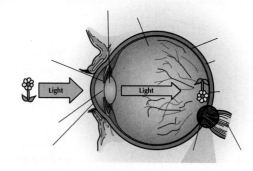

6. What is the visual acuity problem that occurs when the lens focuses an image in front of the retina?
   a. farsightedness   c. myopia
   b. hyperopia   d. presbyopia

7. When you eat a steak, what taste sensation gives it its savoury quality?
   a. salty   c. MSG
   b. bitter   d. umami

8. Identify the parts of the ear in the following figure.

auditory canal
auditory nerve
cochlea
eardrum
incus

malleus
oval window
pinna
stapes
semicircular canals

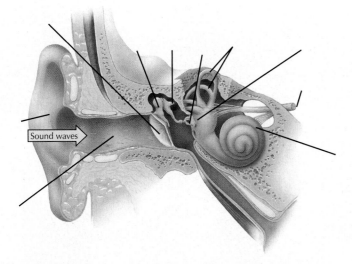

Sound waves

9. Chronic exposure to loud noise can cause permanent _____.

   a. auditory illusions   c. nerve deafness

   b. auditory hallucinations   d. conduction deafness

10. Which brain region is responsible for why some smells can elicit such powerful emotion-laden memories?

   a. the limbic system   c. the olfactory bulb

   b. the temporal lobe   d. the cerebral cortex

11. Why is it that children generally dislike foods with strong or unusual tastes?

   a. Their brains are undeveloped.

   b. Their taste buds are replaced more quickly than the taste buds of adults.

   c. Their parents also dislike the same foods.

   d. Their taste buds are replaced less quickly than the taste buds of adults.

12. Touch receptors are most densely concentrated on the _____.

   a. genitals   c. legs

   b. back   d. All of the above

13. Identify which of these photos, 1 or 2, illustrates

   a. vestibular sense: photo _____

   b. kinesthetic sense: photo _____

1.

2.

14. The *cocktail party phenomenon* is an example of _____.

   a. sensory adaptation   c. selective attention

   b. sensory habituation   d. feature detecting

15. In a(n) _____, the discrepancy between figure and ground is too vague and you may have difficulty perceiving which is figure and which is ground.

   a. illusion   c. optical illusion

   b. reversible figure   d. hallucination

16. The tendency for the environment to be perceived as remaining the same even with changes in sensory input is called _____.

   a. perceptual constancy

   b. the constancy of expectation

   c. an illusory correlation

   d. Gestalt's primary principle

17. The theory of colour vision proposed by Thomas Young that says colour perception results from mixing three distinct colour systems is called the _____.

   a. tricolour theory   c. colour constancy

   b. trichromatic theory   d. opponent-process theory

18. The following illustration is an example of _____.

   a. top-down processing

   b. frame of reference

   c. subliminal persuasion

   d. perceptual adaptation

19. A readiness to perceive in a particular manner is known as _____.

   a. sensory adaptation   c. habituation

   b. perceptual set   d. frame of reference

20. Which explanation is one of the reasons given in the textbook to account for why so many people believe in ESP?

   a. failures of good information

   b. failures of education, particularly high school math

   c. failures of media sources to provide accurate and reliable information

   d. failures of critical thinking

THE PLANNER ✓

Review your Chapter Planner on the chapter opener and check off your completed work.

States of Consciousness

Archaic folklore in North Harbour, Newfoundland, tells of an old hag or *ag rog* who enters a person's room at night just after they have fallen asleep and restrains them with such force they cannot move, speak, or breathe. Despite strenuous effort, the victim is unable to break the hold of the old hag. One of her victims described his experiences with her as "The outside door opened … and I wondered who was comin' in bein' so late. Then I saw a woman all in white come across the kitchen. She came around the stove and came over to me. Then she put her arms out and pushed my shoulders down. And that's all I know about it. She 'agged me'" (Ness, 1978, p. 126). For other victims of "agging" the reports are similar; a malevolent being enters a bedroom just as the victim is falling asleep and pins them down. The unfortunate sleeper remains paralyzed until the old hag eventually leaves. Victims report great fear and anxiety and often sweat profusely during and after the encounter. When it is suggested they were dreaming, her victims are emphatic—they were wide-awake and fully conscious when she assaulted them.

It seems old hag is just one of a number of nocturnal terrors that harass people as they fall asleep. In other cultures the figure is a devil, a ghost, or even a fat little demon, as seen here in this famous painting by Henry Fuseli. For their victims, these creatures are vividly real; for scientists they represent a neural malfunction known as sleep paralysis that can occur as we cross the divide between waking and sleep.

In this chapter, we discuss the mysterious concept of consciousness and its various alternate states. We begin with a general overview of consciousness and then explore the way it changes when we sleep and dream. We discuss how we alter it with drugs and other chemicals, and why these experiences are often desirable and pleasurable. Finally, we explore two alternative routes to altered consciousness: meditation and hypnosis.

The Nightmare, oil on canvas by Henry Fuseli. Detroit Institute of Arts, USA/Founders Society purchase with Mr. and Mrs. Bert L. Smokler/and Mr. and Mrs. Lawrence A. Fleischman funds/The Bridgeman Art Library.

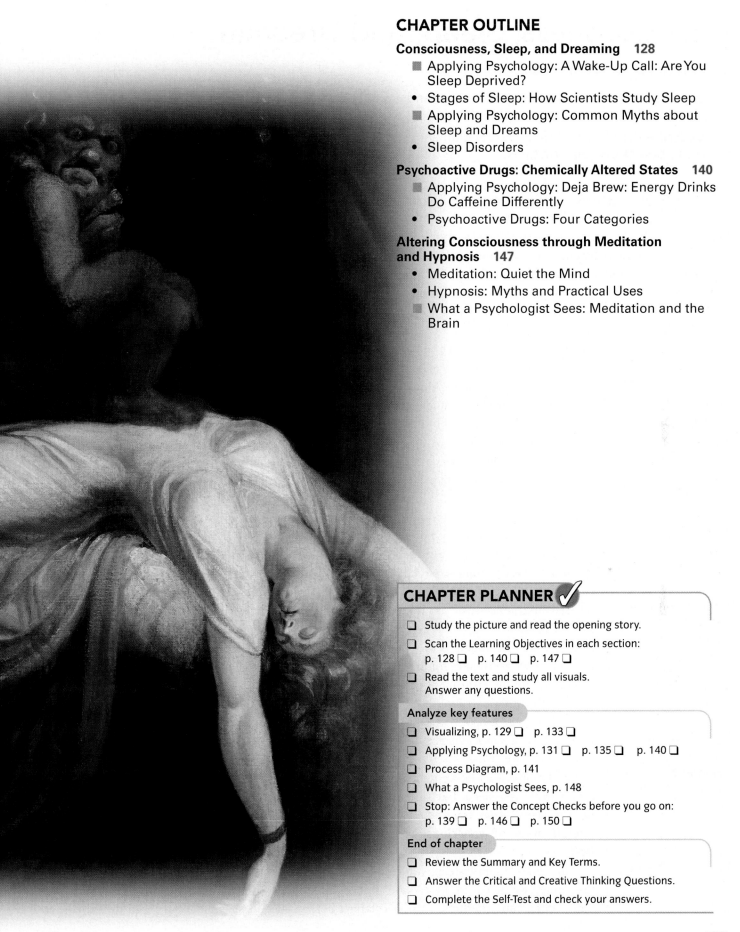

CHAPTER OUTLINE

CHAPTER PLANNER ✓

- ❏ Study the picture and read the opening story.
- ❏ Scan the Learning Objectives in each section:
  p. 128 ❏   p. 140 ❏   p. 147 ❏
- ❏ Read the text and study all visuals. Answer any questions.

Analyze key features

- ❏ Visualizing, p. 129 ❏   p. 133 ❏
- ❏ Applying Psychology, p. 131 ❏   p. 135 ❏   p. 140 ❏
- ❏ Process Diagram, p. 141
- ❏ What a Psychologist Sees, p. 148
- ❏ Stop: Answer the Concept Checks before you go on:
  p. 139 ❏   p. 146 ❏   p. 150 ❏

End of chapter

- ❏ Review the Summary and Key Terms.
- ❏ Answer the Critical and Creative Thinking Questions.
- ❏ Complete the Self-Test and check your answers.

Consciousness, Sleep, and Dreaming

LEARNING OBJECTIVES

1. **Explain** the difference between controlled and automatic processes.
2. **Describe** the effects of sleep deprivation and disruption of circadian rhythms.
3. **Review** the stages of sleep.
4. **Compare** and **contrast** the theories of why we sleep and dream.
5. **Summarize** the types of sleep disorders.

illiam James, the first American psychologist, likened **consciousness** to a stream that's constantly present, constantly moving and changing, and yet always the same. Like liquid, it meanders and flows, sometimes where the person wills it and sometimes not. Through the process of selective attention (Chapter 4), we can influence our consciousness by deliberately attending to or providing focused attention on something or someone. For example, right now, you are awake and concentrating on the words on this page. At times, however, your control may weaken, and your stream of consciousness may drift back to thoughts of the old hag or fat demons, or forward to a laptop or cellphone you want to buy, or to a hot classmate.

In addition to meandering and flowing, your stream of consciousness also varies in depth. Consciousness is not an either/or phenomenon. Instead, it exists along a continuum. As you can see in **Figure 5.1**, this continuum extends from high awareness and sharp, focused alertness—such as when you learned how to drive a car—at one extreme, to middle levels of awareness, which require minimal attention, to no awareness and coma at the other extreme.

Other than awake, two common states of consciousness are sleep and dreaming. You may think of yourself as being unconscious while you sleep, but that's not the case. Rather, you are in an **altered state of consciousness (ASC)**.

To understand sleep and dreaming, we need to first explore **circadian rhythms**. Most organisms have adapted to our planet's daily cycle of light and dark by developing a pattern of behaviour and bodily functions that wax and wane over each 24-hour period. Our activity, alertness, core body temperature, moods, learning efficiency, blood pressure, metabolism, and pulse rate all follow these circadian rhythms (Leglise, 2008; Oishi et al., 2007; Sack et al., 2007). Usually, these processes reach their peak at some point during the day and their low point at night (**Figure 5.2**).

When our circadian rhythms are disrupted, as often happens during shift work, sleep deprivation, and long international flights, it impairs thinking and behaviour. Increased fatigue, decreased concentration, sleep disorders, and other health problems are all a consequence of circadian rhythm disturbances (James et al., 2007; Lader, 2007; Salvatore et al., 2008). Shift workers are often affected, as are those employees who work on rotating work schedules. Studies have shown that shift work and the resultant sleep deprivation can lead to decreased concentration, greater errors, and impaired productivity—as well as more accidents (Dembe et al., 2006; Papadelis et al., 2007; Yegneswaran & Shapiro, 2007). When the drowsy shift worker has a clerical position, they are unlikely to harm others by falling asleep on the job. In other areas, such as the transportation industry, a sleepy worker can have disastrous consequences. For example, a tired, napping Air Canada co-pilot woke suddenly and wrongly believed his plane was on a collision course with another aircraft. He pushed the plane sharply downward and the sudden dip injured 14 passengers and two crew members (FAIR, 2011).

With 30 percent of Canadian workers reporting some type of shift work (Statistics Canada, 2005a), sleep deprivation is a significant concern for many. What can be done to help? One way to reduce the negative effects of a rotating work schedule is by rolling into the next work schedule clockwise—that is, moving from days to evenings to night shifts. This requires less of an adjustment than doing it the other way around—probably because it's easier to go to bed later when a schedule changes than to go to bed earlier.

> **consciousness** An organism's awareness of its own self and surroundings (Damasio, 1999).

> **altered states of consciousness (ASC)** Mental states found generally during sleep, dreaming, psychoactive drug use, and hypnosis.

> **circadian [ser-KAY-dee-an] rhythms** Biological, biochemical, and behavioural changes that occur in living organisms on a 24-hour cycle (in Latin, *circa* means "about," and *dies* means "day").

Visualizing

Consciousness • Figure 5.1

Where Does Consciousness Reside?

One of the oldest philosophical debates is the *mind-body* issue. Is the "mind" (consciousness and other mental functions) fundamentally different from "matter" (the body)? How can a mind influence a physical body and vice versa? Most neurophysiologists today believe the mind *is* the brain and *consciousness* involves an activation and integration of several parts of the brain. But two aspects of consciousness, *awareness* and *arousal*, seem to rely on specific areas. Awareness generally involves the *cerebral cortex*, particularly the frontal lobes. Arousal generally results from *brain-stem* activation (Revonsuo, 2006; Thomson, 2007; Zillmer et al., 2008).

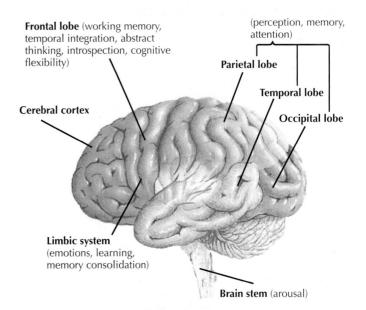

Frontal lobe (working memory, temporal integration, abstract thinking, introspection, cognitive flexibility)

(perception, memory, attention)

Parietal lobe

Temporal lobe

Occipital lobe

Cerebral cortex

Limbic system (emotions, learning, memory consolidation)

Brain stem (arousal)

LEVELS OF AWARENESS

Consciousness can exist on many levels of awareness, from high awareness to low awareness.

High Awareness

Middle Awareness

Low Awareness

Xavier Marchant/iStockphoto

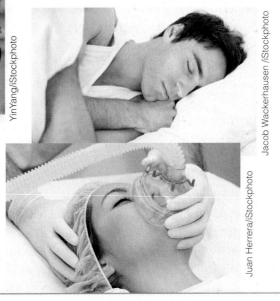
YinYang/iStockphoto
Jacob Wackerhausen /iStockphoto
Juan Herrera/iStockphoto

CONTROLLED PROCESSES

Require focused, maximum attention (e.g., studying for an exam, learning to drive a car)

AUTOMATIC PROCESSES

Require minimal attention (e.g., walking to class while talking on a cellphone, listening to your instructor while daydreaming)

SUBCONSCIOUS

Below conscious awareness (e.g., sleeping, dreaming)

NO AWARENESS

Biologically based lowest level of awareness (e.g., head injuries, anaesthesia, coma)

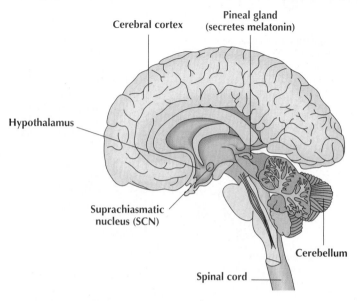

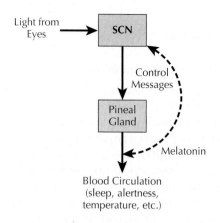

a. Circadian rhythms are regulated by a part of the hypothalamus called the *suprachiasmatic nucleus* (SCN).

b. The SCN receives information about light and darkness from the eyes and then sends control messages to the pineal gland, which releases *melatonin*—a hormone that influences sleep, alertness, and body temperature. Like other feedback loops in the body, the level of melatonin in the blood is detected by the SCN, which then can modify the output of the pineal to maintain the optimal level.

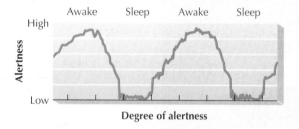

c. and d. Note how our degree of alertness and core body temperature rise and fall in similar ways.

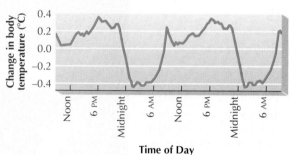

Productivity and safety also increase when shifts are rotated once every three weeks versus once per week. Taking naps has also been shown to improve alertness, learning, and performance (Debarnot et al., 2011; Faraut et al., 2011; Korman et al., 2007; Tremaine et al., 2010; Wamsley et al., 2010), as have longer breaks between work shifts, allowing the worker more time to rest and recover (Soares et al., 2012).

Like shift work, flying across several time zones can also disrupt circadian rhythms. Symptoms of jet lag include fatigue, gastrointestinal problems, and irritability. Jet lag is also correlated with decreased alertness, decreased mental agility, reduced efficiency, and a worsening of symptoms of psychiatric disorders (Dawson, 2004; Kyriacou & Hastings, 2010; Leglise, 2008; Morgenthaler et al., 2007; Reid et al., 2011; Sack et al., 2007). Jet lag generally tends to be worse when we fly eastward because our bodies find it more difficult to go to bed earlier—as in Eastern time zones, than going to bed later—as in Western time zones.

Researchers have learned that, like disrupted circadian cycles, sleep deprivation poses several hazards. These include reduced cognitive and motor performance, irritability and other mood alterations, decreased self-esteem, and elevated levels of the stress hormone cortisol (Dembe et al., 2006; Mirescu et al., 2006; Papadelis et al., 2007; Sack et al., 2007; Yegneswaran & Shapiro, 2007). Sleep deprivation has also been shown to trigger hallucinations and psychosis in some situations (Freeman et al., 2009; Orzeł-Gryglewska, 2010; Sharma & Mazmanian, 2003).

What about long-term sleep deprivation? How does that affect us? Exploring the scientific effects of severe sleep loss is limited by both ethical and practical concerns. For example, many cultures have historically used chronic sleep deprivation as a form of torture. In a modern research setting, ancient torture techniques are generally not reviewed favourably by research ethics boards. For similar reasons, including variables in research that

Applying Psychology

✔ THE PLANNER

A Wake-Up Call: Are You Sleep Deprived?

Take the following test to determine whether you are sleep deprived.

Part 1 Set up a small mirror next to the text. Using your non-dominant hand, try to trace the black star pictured here while watching your hand in the mirror. The task is difficult, and sleep-deprived people typically make many errors. If you are not sleep deprived, it may be difficult to trace the star, but you'll probably do it more accurately.

Part 2 Give yourself one point each time you answer yes to the following questions:

Do you often fall asleep . . .
watching TV?
during boring shows or lectures or in warm rooms?
after heavy meals or after a small amount of alcohol?
while relaxing after dinner?
within five minutes of getting into bed?

In the morning, do you generally . . .
need an alarm clock to wake up at the right time?
struggle to get out of bed?
hit the snooze bar several times before getting up?

During the day, do you . . .
feel tired, irritable, and stressed out?
have trouble concentrating and remembering?
feel mentally sluggish when it comes to critical thinking, problem solving, and creativity?
feel drowsy while driving?
have dark circles around your eyes?

If you answered yes to three or more items, you probably are not getting enough sleep.

Renowned sleep researcher and founder of the Stanford University Center for Human Sleep Research Dr. William C. Dement has stated that traditional-age college and university students need around eight hours of sleep per night (Dement, 1997). When was the last time you had that amount of sleep at night?

Source: "Sleep for Success!" Maas, James and Robbins, Rebecca, AuthorHouse 2011.

Think Critically

1. What factors might contribute to sleep deprivation in young adults?
2. How might melatonin secretion be related to jet lag and shift work?

---

have known negative health consequences (such as sleep deprivation) are also more ethically challenging for researchers. On a practical level, chronically sleep-deprived research participants often fall into repeated *microsleeps*. These tiny sleep bouts last only seconds at a time but can influence research findings. Sleep-deprived participants are also subject to stress effects, which have their own negative consequences. These must be separated from the effects of the sleep deprivation variables in order to obtain valid results.

Research with animals has revealed some startling findings about how essential sleep is. When rats are totally sleep deprived, they die on average after 19 days. Letting the animals sleep prevents their death (Rechtschaffen & Bergmann, 2002).

Human research has shown that after 17 to 19 hours without sleep, test performance, reaction time, and accuracy on attention, memory, and other cognitive tasks is actually worse than for those with a blood alcohol concentration (BAC) of 0.05 (Arned et al., 2005; Elmenhorst et al., 2009; Falleti et al., 2003)! After longer periods without sleep, performance reached levels equivalent to having a BAC of 1.0 (Williamson & Feyer, 2000). As a comparison, in Canada it is a criminal offence to drive with a BAC over 0.08. For new drivers this limit is 0.00.

An accumulating total of lost sleep is called a **sleep debt** and the consequences for students are wide ranging

For an interesting discussion on this topic, scan to download the author's podcast.

and include decreased school performance; reduced vigilance, attention, and concentration; and impairments to physical health. According to Dement (1997), feeling drowsy is the last step before falling asleep, not the first indication of tiredness. He has also gone on record declaring a large sleep debt will make you stupid (Dement & Vaughan, 1999).

Stages of Sleep: How Scientists Study Sleep

Surveys and interviews provide only limited information about the nature of sleep, and so researchers in sleep laboratories use a number of sophisticated instruments to study the physiological changes that occur during sleep.

Imagine that you are a participant in a sleep experiment. When you arrive at the sleep lab, you are assigned one of several—usually sparse—bedrooms. The researcher then hooks you up to various physiological recording devices (**Figure 5.3a**). You will need a night or two to "adjust" to the equipment (read: get lousy sleep) before the researchers can begin to monitor your typical night's sleep. As you fall asleep, you first enter a relaxed *presleep* state. As you continue relaxing, your brain's electrical activity slows. Over the next hour or so, you move through four distinct stages of sleep (stages 1 through 4), each progressively deeper (**Figure 5.3b**). Then the sequence reverses itself. Although you don't necessarily go through all sleep stages in this sequence during the night, people usually complete about four to five cycles of light to deep sleep and back, with each complete cycle lasting about 90 minutes.

REM and NREM sleep

Figure 5.3c also shows an interesting phenomenon that occurs at the end of the first sleep cycle (and subsequent cycles). You reverse back through stages 3 and 2. Scalp recordings of cortical activity then abruptly display a pattern of small-amplitude, fast-wave activity, similar to the activity of an awake, relaxed person. Your breathing and pulse rates become faster and more irregular than during stages 3 and 4, and your genitals likely show signs of arousal. Yet your musculature is deeply relaxed and unresponsive. Because of these contradictory qualities, this stage is sometimes referred to as *paradoxical sleep*.

During this stage of paradoxical sleep, rapid eye movements occur under closed eyelids. Researchers therefore also refer to this same sleep stage as **rapid-eye-movement (REM) sleep**. When awakened from REM sleep, people generally wake refreshed and almost always report dreaming. Because REM sleep is so different from the other periods of sleep, stages 1 through 4 are often collectively referred to as **non-rapid-eye-movement (NREM) sleep**. REM sleep is observed in many species. You may even have witnessed it in a family pet (**Figure 5.4**). Dreaming can also occur during NREM sleep but it's less frequent (Chellappa, 2011; Wamsley et al., 2007). It is usually more difficult to awaken people from stages 3 or 4 than from other sleep stages, and they often wake feeling groggy.

rapid-eye-movement (REM) sleep Stage of sleep marked by rapid eye movements, high-frequency brain waves, paralysis of large muscles, and dreaming.

non-rapid-eye-movement (NREM) sleep Stages 1 to 4 of sleep.

Scientists believe that REM sleep is important for learning and consolidating new memories (Marshall & Born, 2007; Massicotte-Marquez et al., 2008; Silvestri & Root, 2008). Evidence of the importance of REM sleep for complex brain functions comes from the research findings that show that the net amount of REM sleep increases after periods of stress or intense learning and that fetuses, infants, and young children—the age ranges where the greatest amounts of learning and adaptation take place—spend a large percentage of their sleep time in this stage. In addition, REM sleep occurs only in higher-order mammals and is absent in non-mammals, such as reptiles (Rechtschaffen & Siegel, 2000). Finally, when deprived of REM sleep, most people "catch up" later by spending more time than usual in this stage, underlining its inherent importance (Dement & Vaughan, 1999). As you will see, however, the exact function of sleep and its various stages is still a bit of a mystery.

NREM sleep may be even more important to our biological functioning than REM sleep. When people are temporarily deprived of total sleep, they spend more time in NREM sleep during their first uninterrupted night of sleep, as if they are making up for the time they missed (Borbely, 1982). Only after our need for NREM sleep has been satisfied each night do we begin to devote time to REM sleep. Further, studies show that adults who sleep five or fewer hours each night (*short sleepers*) spend less time in REM sleep than do those who sleep nine or more hours (*long sleepers*). Similarly, infants get much more sleep and have a higher percentage of REM sleep (about 40 percent of total daily sleep during the first six months of life)

Visualizing

The scientific study of sleep and dreaming • Figure 5.3

a. Sleep research participants wear electrodes on their heads and bodies to measure the brain's and body's behavioural and physiological responses during the sleep cycle. *An electroencephalogram* (EEG) records neural activity in the outer layers of the cortex by means of small electrodes placed on the scalp. Other electrodes measure muscle activity and eye movements.

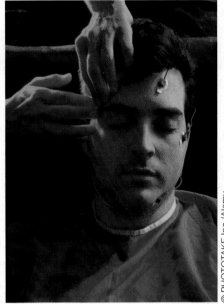

© PHOTOTAKE Inc./Alamy

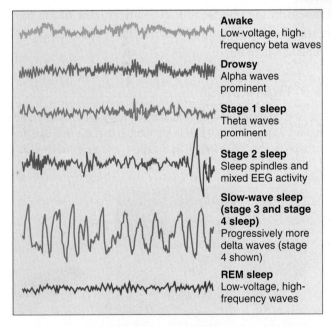

Awake
Low-voltage, high-frequency beta waves

Drowsy
Alpha waves prominent

Stage 1 sleep
Theta waves prominent

Stage 2 sleep
Sleep spindles and mixed EEG activity

Slow-wave sleep (stage 3 and stage 4 sleep)
Progressively more delta waves (stage 4 shown)

REM sleep
Low-voltage, high-frequency waves

b. The stages of sleep are defined by telltale changes in cortical activity and are indicated by the jagged lines. The short, compact brain waves of wakefulness gradually lengthen as people drift into stages 1 to 4.

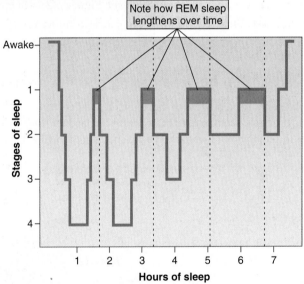

Note how REM sleep lengthens over time

c. During stage 2 sleep, if awakened the sleeper will often deny sleeping. You have probably encountered this yourself when you try to turn off the TV and your companion, who has had his or her eyes closed, sleeping on the couch next to you, then protests loudly. By the end of stage 4, a change in body position generally occurs and heart rate, blood pressure, and respiratory rates all decrease. The sleeper then reverses back through stages 3 and 2 before entering the first REM period of the night. If you sleep 8 hours, you'll typically go through approximately four or five sleep cycles (as shown by the vertical dotted lines). Although the brain and body are giving many signs of active arousal during REM sleep, the major muscle groups are deeply relaxed and temporarily paralyzed. Note how the length of the REM period increases as the night progresses and the lengths of stage 3 and 4 sleep diminish considerably.

Dorling Kindersley/Getty Images

Neo Vision/Getty Images

Observing REM sleep in cats • Figure 5.4

During NREM sleep, a cat will often sleep in an upright "sphinx" position. With the onset of REM sleep the cat rolls over on its side. Can you explain why? What might be the evolutionary adaptive function of this sleep behaviour?

than do adults (about 20 percent of total daily sleep at age 19, declining to about 14 percent in old age) (**Figure 5.5**).

Another developmental change that occurs as we age involves the suprachiasmatic nucleus (see Figure 5.2)—our biological clock. Puberty modifies this clock in many ways, but the change most relevant here is it causes sleep onset

to be delayed. Teenagers do not feel like sleeping until much later at night and do not want to wake early in the morning. Delayed sleep phase is not unique to pubertal development in humans. It has been observed in many mammalian species, including rhesus monkeys, degus (a small carnivorous rodent), rats, and mice (Hagenauer et al., 2009). As we age, the time at which we start to feel tired gets earlier in the evening, as does our wakeup time the next morning. This explains why your grandparents are often up and about when you have only been in bed a few hours and provides some insights into why you feel so tired in that 8:30 a.m. class. Incidentally, you are not alone; 60 to 70 percent of Canadian adolescents report that their sleepiest time of the day is between 8 and 10 a.m. (Canadian Institute of Health Research & Institute of Population and Public Health, 2002). In the interests of your grades, driver safety, and your overall mood, sleep researchers recommend you avoid those early classes, opting instead to take lectures later in the day or in the evening (Hagenauer et al., 2009; Kirby et al., 2011; Wahlstrom, 2002).

The relationship between aging and the sleep cycle • Figure 5.5

Have you ever noticed how much babies sleep and how little sleep older people seem to need? Our biological need for sleep changes throughout our lifetimes. The pie charts in this figure

show the relative amounts of REM sleep (dark blue), NREM sleep (medium blue), and awake time (light blue) that the average person experiences as an infant, as an adult, and as an older person.

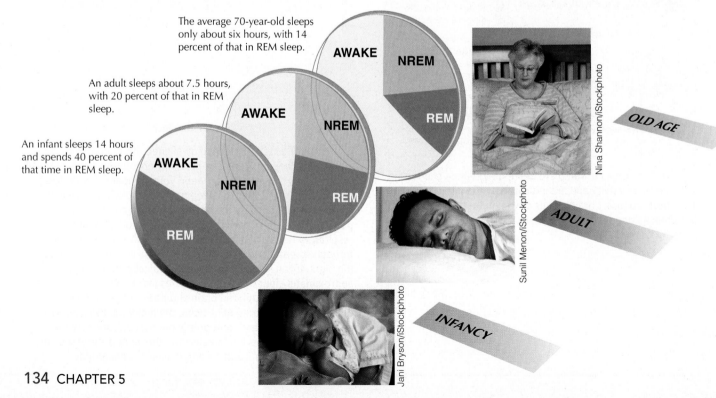

The average 70-year-old sleeps only about six hours, with 14 percent of that in REM sleep.

An adult sleeps about 7.5 hours, with 20 percent of that in REM sleep.

An infant sleeps 14 hours and spends 40 percent of that time in REM sleep.

AWAKE
NREM
REM

OLD AGE

ADULT

INFANCY

Nina Shannon/iStockphoto

Sunil Menon/iStockphoto

Jani Bryson/iStockphoto

Applying Psychology

Common Myths about Sleep and Dreams

Stream of Consciousness by Jason Zuckerman. Reproduced with permission.

Myth: *Everyone needs eight hours of sleep a night to maintain sound mental and physical health*. Although most of us average 7.6 hours of sleep a night, some people get by on an incredible 15 to 30 minutes. Others may need as much as 11 hours (Colrain, 2011; Daan, 2011; Doghramji, 2000; Maas et al., 1999).

Myth: *Dreams have special or symbolic meaning*. Many people mistakenly believe dreams can foretell the future, reflect unconscious desires, have secret meaning, can reveal the truth, or contain special messages, but scientific research finds little or no support for these beliefs (Blum, 2011; Carey, 2009; Domhoff, 2010; Hobson et al., 2011; Lilienfeld et al., 2010; Morewedge & Norton, 2009).

Myth: *Some people never dream*. In rare cases, adults with certain brain injuries or disorders do not dream (Solms, 1997). But otherwise, virtually all adults regularly dream. Even people who firmly believe they never dream do report dreams if they are repeatedly awakened during an overnight study in a sleep laboratory. Children also dream regularly. For example, between ages 3 and 8, they dream during approximately 20 to 28 percent of their sleep time (Foulkes, 1993, 1999). Apparently, almost everyone dreams, but some people don't remember their dreams.

Myth: *Dreams last only a few seconds and only occur in REM sleep*. Research shows that some dreams seem to occur in "real time." For example, a dream that seemed to last 20 minutes probably did last approximately 20 minutes (Dement & Wolpert, 1958). Dreams also occur in NREM sleep.

Myth: *When genital arousal occurs during sleep, it means the sleeper is having a sexual dream*. When sleepers are awakened during this time, they are no more likely to report sexual dreams than at other times.

Myth: *Most people dream only in black and white, and blind people don't dream*. People frequently report seeing colour in their dreams. Those who are blind do dream but report visual images only if they lost their sight after age 7 (Lilienfeld et al., 2010).

Myth: *Dreaming of dying can be fatal*. This is a good opportunity to exercise your critical thinking skills. Where did this myth come from? Although many people have personally experienced and recounted a fatal dream, how would we scientifically prove or disprove this belief?

Why do we sleep? What is the purpose of sleep? Why ever did it evolve? To date scientists are not sure why we sleep and the function it serves. There are two prominent theories about why we sleep. The **evolutionary/circadian theory** emphasizes the relationship between sleep and basic circadian rhythms. Sleep keeps animals still and safe when predators are active and allows them to conserve energy when not foraging or finding mates. Evidence for this theory comes from observations of the different sleep patterns seen across species (Siegel, 2008) (**Figure 5.6**).

In contrast, the **repair/restoration theory** stresses that sleep helps us recuperate physically, emotionally, and intellectually from daily activities that deplete our reserves (Maas, 1999; Payne, 2011).

Which theory is correct? Researchers do not currently know. Neither may be correct or it may be that both are correct—that sleep initially served to conserve energy and keep us out of trouble, but over time it co-evolved to allow for repair and restoration.

Dreaming: The nightly picture show

What do you think is the number one dream theme of Canadian university students? If you guessed being chased, you are correct. If you guessed a sexual experience, you are not far off, that was number two on the list, and falling was number three (Nielsen et al., 2003). Other

evolutionary/circadian theory As part of circadian rhythms, sleep evolved to conserve energy, and protect from predators.

repair/restoration theory A theory proposing that we sleep because it serves a recuperative function, allowing organisms to repair or replenish key cognitive and physiological factors.

Average daily hours of sleep for different mammals • Figure 5.6

According to the evolutionary/circadian theory, differences in diet and number of predators affect different species' sleep habits. Animals that sleep the longest are the least threatened by predators and can easily find food, while animals that must constantly forage or have many predators sleep the least.

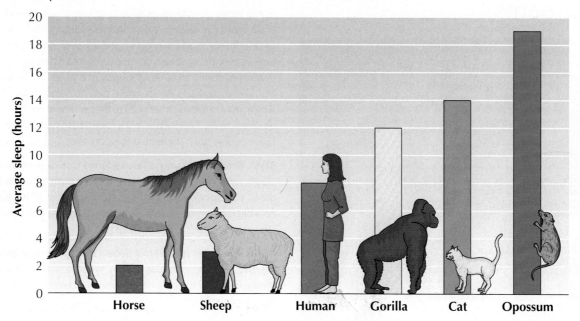

dream researchers have identified five top dream themes for female students: being chased, sexual experiences, falling, school, and arriving somewhere late (DeCicco, 2007). Interestingly, in follow-up research, sexual imagery in dreams was not reported by male university students (Dale & DeCicco, 2011). These researchers reasoned that the male students who participated in their study were just not comfortable reporting their sexy dreams. What do you think?

Dreams fascinate and entertain us. They also help and inspire; Mary Shelley wrote *Frankenstein* based on a dream she had (D'Amato, 2009), and the Beatles hit *Yesterday* came to Paul McCartney in a dream (Querna, 2006). Is this the purpose of dreams? The question of why we dream—and whether dreams carry special meaning or information—has fascinated and perplexed psychologists at least as much as the question of why we sleep. Currently there are three theories of why we dream.

The *activation-synthesis* hypothesis suggests that dreams are a by-product of random stimulation of neurons during REM sleep (Hobson, 1999, 2005, 2009; Hobson et al., 2003). Alan Hobson and Robert McCarley (1977) proposed that specific neurons in the brainstem fire spontaneously during REM sleep, and these signals are transmitted via the thalamus to the cortex. The cortex then struggles to "synthesize" or make sense out of this random stimulation by manufacturing coherent patterns or dreams. Dreams,

then, according to this theory, represent random neural brain stem activity that the cortex attempts to apply meaning to. This is not to say that dreams are meaningless. Hobson (1988, 2005) suggests that even if dreams begin with essentially random brain activity, your individual personality, motivations, memories, and life experiences, stored in your cortex, guide how your brain constructs the dream. This makes sense when we consider how personal our dreams are; we generally dream of friends, family, and personal events—products of our own experiences, stored in our own brains.

A second theory as to why we dream is the *cognitive view*. In this perspective dreams are simply another type of information processing. That is, our dreams help us to periodically sift and sort our daily experiences and thoughts. During sleep the brain shuts out sensory input so that it can process, consolidate, and assimilate information. This theory is supported by the research findings that REM sleep increases following stress and intense learning periods, and the strong similarities between dream content and waking thoughts, fears, and concerns (Domhoff, 2005, 2007; Erlacher & Schredl, 2004). For example, people working in the restaurant industry often have stressful dreams about work after a particularly busy shift.

Both theories of why we dream have proponents and critics, and neither theory has been fully researched.

One of the oldest and most scientifically controversial explanations for why we dream is Freud's *psychoanalytic view*. Freud proposed that unacceptable desires, which are normally repressed, rise into consciousness during dreaming. We avoid anxiety, Freud believed, by disguising our forbidden, unconscious needs (what Freud called the dream's latent content) as symbols (the manifest content or the actual storyline of the dream). For example, a journey is supposed to symbolize death; horseback riding and dancing would symbolize sexual intercourse; and a gun might represent a penis. What do you think might represent a vagina? (We discuss Freud's theory further in Chapter 12.)

Most current sleep research does not support Freud's view (Domhoff, 2004; Dufresne, 2007). Critics also argue that Freud's theory is highly subjective and that the symbols can be interpreted according to the particular view or training of the psychoanalyst providing the dream analysis.

Sleep Disorders

Mental health professionals divide sleep disorders into two major diagnostic categories: dyssomnias, which describe problems sleeping, and parasomnias, which describe abnormal sleep disturbances.

dyssomnias
Problems in the amount, timing, and quality of sleep, including insomnia, sleep apnea, and narcolepsy.

The most common **dyssomnias** is *insomnia*. Although it's normal to have trouble sleeping from time to time, as many as 1 in 10 people has persistent difficulty falling asleep, staying asleep, or waking too early. Most people report some form of clinical insomnia at some point in their life (Pearson, Johnson, & Nahin, 2006; Riemann & Voderholzer, 2003; Wilson & Nutt, 2008). A telltale sign of insomnia is feeling poorly rested and tired the next day. Most people with serious insomnia have other medical or psychological disorders, such as depression, anxiety disorders, or addiction. These often co-occur with the insomnia (Riemann & Voderholzer, 2003; Taylor, Lichstein, & Durrence, 2003).

Insomnia can be caused by a variety of factors, but most often it is related to anxiety, stress, and emotional problems (Pigeon, 2010; Roane & Taylor, 2008). It can also be caused by some medications, recreational drugs such as alcohol, and health problems (Bamer et al., 2008; Ogeil et al., 2011).

Despite advertising claims, non-prescription over-the-counter medications for insomnia generally don't work (Randall et al., 2008). Prescription tranquilizers and barbiturates, conversely, do help people sleep, but they interfere with the normal sleep cycle and thereby affect sleep quality. In the short term, drugs, such as Ambien, Xanax, and Imovane, seem to be helpful in treating sleep problems related to anxiety and acute, stressful situations; however, chronic use can cause dependency (Leonard, 2003; McKim, 2002). Because of this, sleeping pills are intended only for occasional short-term use, and chronic users can become dependent on them to fall asleep. The hormone melatonin has been shown to be useful in relieving mild insomnia. It appears to work by shifting the biological clock earlier, making it easier to fall asleep (Pevet & Challet, 2011; Rahman et al., 2009). Caution should be taken when using melatonin as it can interact with alcohol and other insomnia medications (Shatkin & Janssen, 2012).

Psychological interventions, such as relaxation training and cognitive-behavioural therapy (see Chapter 14), can also be helpful for people with insomnia (Constantino et al., 2007; Smith et al., 2005). Research has shown these types of non-drug treatments are just as effective as medication and have greater long lasting benefits (Bélanger et al., 2012; Okajima et al., 2011). You can use similar techniques in your own life if you experience transient disordered sleep:

- When you're having difficulty falling sleep, don't keep checking the clock and worrying about your loss of sleep.
- Remove all TVs, stereos, and books from the bedroom, and limit use of the room to just sleep.
- Work off tension and stress through exercise (but not too close to bedtime).
- Avoid stimulants, such as caffeine and nicotine.
- Avoid late meals and heavy drinking.
- Follow the same presleep routine every evening. It might include listening to music, writing in a diary, relaxing, or meditating, and try to go to bed at around the same time each night.
- Use progressive muscle relaxation. Alternately tense and relax various muscle groups, focusing on one muscle group at a time.
- Practise yoga or deep breathing, or take a warm bath to help you relax.

Narcolepsy is another serious dyssomnia, characterized by sudden and irresistible sleep bouts that occur during normal waking hours. Narcolepsy afflicts about 1 person in 2,000 and generally runs in families (Billiard, 2007; Pedrazzoli et al., 2007; Siegel, 2000). During a narcoleptic attack, REM-like sleep suddenly intrudes into the waking state of consciousness. Victims may experience sudden,

Narcoleptic dogs • Figure 5.7

William Dement and his colleagues at the Stanford Center for Narcolepsy have bred a group of narcoleptic dogs that have greatly increased our understanding of the genetics of this disorder. Research on these specially bred dogs have found degenerated neurons in certain areas of the brain (Siegel, 2000). Whether human narcolepsy results from similar degeneration is a question for future research, but human narcolepsy seems to be caused by a deficiency in hypocretin-1, a type of peptide (protein-based) hormone (Mignot, 2010; Nishino et al., 2000). Dement's research demonstrated how the excitement of seeing food caused his narcoleptic dogs to collapse into sleep.

Marcelo Maia/Getty Images

incapacitating attacks of muscle weakness or paralysis (known as cataplexy). They may fall asleep while walking, talking, during sex (after sex is normal), or driving a car. Symptoms usually appear when the person is between 10 and 20 years old, and once the sleep attacks develop, they continue throughout life. Although long naps each day and stimulant or antidepressant drugs may help reduce the frequency of narcoleptic attacks, researchers are only just beginning to understand the causes and develop possible cures (**Figure 5.7**). Sleep paralysis is often associated with narcolepsy. This is where the person remains awake but the body experiences a short bout of REM-induced paralysis. Sleep paralysis can also occur in people without narcolepsy, as discussed in the chapter opening vignette.

Perhaps the most serious dyssomnia is sleep apnea. People with sleep apnea have either irregular breathing, or occasional periods where they stop breathing for between 10 seconds and 1 minute or longer during sleep. They then wake up gasping for breath—often quite loudly. When they breathe during sleep, they often snore. Although people with sleep apnea are often unaware of it, the repeated awakenings result in insomnia and leave the person feeling tired and sleepy during the day. Sleep apnea

seems to result from blocked upper airway passages or from the brain ceasing to send signals to the diaphragm, thus causing breathing to stop. This disorder can lead to high blood pressure, stroke, and heart attack (Billiard, 2007; Hartenbaum et al., 2006; McNicholas & Javaheri, 2007; National Sleep Foundation, 2007).

Treatment for sleep apnea depends partly on its severity. If the problem occurs only when a person sleeps on his or her back, sewing tennis balls to the back of a pyjama top may encourage the person to sleep on his or her side. This, of course, would not work if you don't wear pyjamas. Because obstruction of the breathing passages can be related to obesity and heavy alcohol use (Christensen, 2000), losing weight and restricting alcohol are often recommended. For others, surgery, dental appliances that reposition the tongue, or machines that provide a stream of air to keep the airway open may be the answer (**Figure 5.8**).

Recent findings suggest that snoring alone (without the breathing stoppage characteristic of sleep apnea) can lead to heart disease (Stone & Redline, 2006). Although occasional mild snoring remains somewhat normal, chronic snoring is a potential "warning sign that should prompt people to seek help" (Christensen, 2000, p. 172; Lee et al., 2008).

The second major category of sleep disorders, **parasomnias**, includes abnormal sleep disturbances, such as nightmares and *night terrors* (**Figure 5.9**).

Sleepwalking, which can accompany night terrors, usually occurs during NREM sleep early in the sleep bout (recall that large muscles are paralyzed during REM sleep). Some sleep walkers wake during their travels and return to bed, while family members wake others. It is not unusual for sleepwalkers to wander outside and injure themselves (Abdul Ahad et al., 2010; Schenck et al., 1989). In a famous and tragic case of sleepwalking, Canadian Ken Parks drove to the home of his wife's parents, killed his mother-in-law, and seriously injured his father-in-law while sleepwalking. In his 1987 trial, Parks' lawyer argued he was not criminally liable because he was in fact asleep. Medical testimony supported the sleepwalking defence and his case was acquitted by the jury (Broughton et al., 1994).

Sleep talking can occur during any stage of sleep but is most common during NREM sleep. It can consist of single indistinct words or long, articulate sentences. It is even possible to engage some sleep talkers in a limited conversation.

> **parasomnias** Abnormal disturbances occurring during sleep, including nightmares, night terrors, sleepwalking, and sleep talking.

Treatments for sleep apnea • Figure 5.8

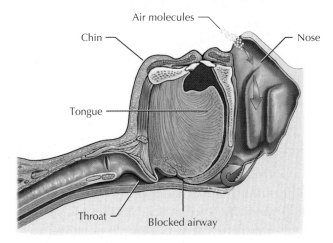

Air molecules
Chin
Nose
Tongue
Throat
Blocked airway

a. During sleep apnea, airways are blocked, causing breathing to be severely restricted. To treat this disorder, researchers and doctors have created equipment to promote respiration.

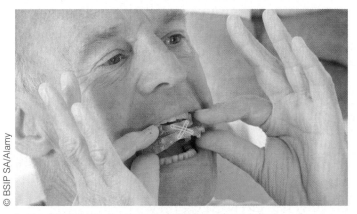

© BSIP SA/Alamy

b. For some patients, there is help from dental devices that reposition the tongue and open the airway.

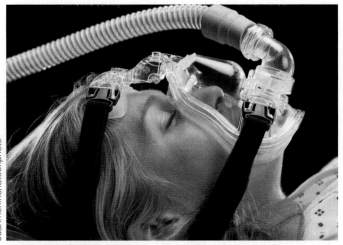

Juanmonino/iStockphoto

c. Another treatment for sleep apnea is a machine that provides a steady supply of air to keep the airway open.

Nightmares or night terrors? • Figure 5.9

Nightmares, or bad dreams, occur toward the end of the sleep cycle, usually during REM sleep. More frightening are night terrors, which occur early in the cycle, usually during NREM sleep stages 3 or 4. Night terrors are very common in childhood and are not indicative of emotional disturbances or psychological disorders. They typically present with the sleeper suddenly sitting bolt upright, screaming and sweating, walking around, or talking incoherently. The sleeper may also be difficult to awaken. The parent who is woken by the screaming or crying usually calms the child and helps him or her settle back to sleep. In the morning the child usually has no memory of the event.

© Bubbles Photolibrary/Alamy

Nightmares, night terrors, sleepwalking, and sleep talking are all more common among young children, but can also occur to a lesser extent in adults, usually during times of stress or major life events (Billiard, 2007; Hobson & Silvestri, 2009). Patience and soothing reassurance at the time of the sleep disruption are usually the most effective treatments for both children and adults.

CONCEPT CHECK STOP

1. **What** are the different levels of consciousness?
2. **Where** is the circadian clock and what does it do?
3. **Explain** the current theories about why we sleep and dream.
4. **How** do dyssomnias and parasomnias differ?

Psychoactive Drugs: Chemically Altered States

LEARNING OBJECTIVES

1. **Explain** the difference between physical dependence and addiction.

2. **Summarize** the differences among the four major types of psychoactive drugs.

3. **Compare** how the different psychoactive drugs affect the nervous system.

Psychoactive drugs influence the nervous system in a variety of ways. Alcohol, for example, has a diffuse effect on neural membranes throughout the nervous system. Most psychoactive drugs, however, act in a more specific way: by either enhancing or mimicking a particular neurotransmitter's effect (an **agonistic drug** action) or blocking or inhibiting it (an **antagonistic drug** action) (see **Figure 5.10**).

In North America the most popular psychoactive drugs are caffeine, tobacco, and ethyl

> **psychoactive drugs** Chemicals that alter perception, conscious awareness, or mood.
>
> **agonistic drug** A drug that mimics or enhances the activity of neurotransmitters.
>
> **antagonistic drug** A drug that blocks or inhibits the activity of neurotransmitters.

alcohol. Caffeine is the most widely used and is found in hot beverages, soft drinks, and energy drinks (see *Applying Psychology: Deja Brew*). Because these drugs are legal, do you think they are somehow better or safer than illegal drugs, such as Ecstasy, marijuana, and heroin? What about prescription drugs, such as antidepressants, or over-the-counter drugs, such as Aspirin and antacids? Because a pharmacist dispenses these drugs, are they "good" as opposed to "bad" drugs?

Most neuroscientists and biopsychologists believe that all drugs, regardless of their legal

Applying Psychology

Deja Brew: Energy Drinks Do Caffeine Differently

Since the introduction of Red Bull in North America in 1997, the energy drink market has grown exponentially. These soft drinks contain many different ingredients, such as vitamins and herbs, but their central ingredient is usually caffeine. Of the hundreds of different brands marketed in North America, the caffeine content can range from 50 mg to 500 mg per container (Reissig et al., 2009). Before 2011 most of these drinks were classified as natural health products, allowing them to make certain health claims, such as reducing drowsiness. In 2011 Health Canada amended the regulations, and now these beverages are classified as foods, meaning nutrition facts must be provided on the label. Other changes made at the time limited the maximum amount of caffeine to 100 mg per 250 mL and required warning labels stating that pregnant or breastfeeding women should not consume the drinks. Labels must also contain a warning that energy drinks shouldn't be mixed with alcohol (Health Canada, 2011a).

Although side effects from drinking energy drinks are possible (electrolyte disturbances, nausea, vomiting, and an irregular heartbeat), moderate and responsible use by adults is generally considered to be safe (Health Canada, 2006a; Health Canada, 2011a). Research has shown energy drinks may have some

beneficial effects, such as improving cognitive performance (Howard & Marczinski, 2010; Sünram-Lea et al., 2012). As with any psychoactive substance, the problem with energy drinks seems to occur not when they are *used*, but when they are *abused*, such as when they are mixed with alcohol or consumed in large quantities.

Energy drinks have been aggressively marketed, especially to young men, some of whom think they have performance-enhancing effects (Reissig et al., 2009). Energy drinks are very different from sports drinks, such as Gatorade or Powerade, which rehydrate and provide sugars and electrolytes needed by the body. Energy drinks are not recommended for fluid replacement as their caffeine content can actually mask the signs of dehydration (Health Canada, 2011a).

© Richard Levine/Alamy

How agonistic and antagonistic drugs produce their psychoactive effect
• Figure 5.10

Most psychoactive drugs produce their mood-, energy-, and perception-altering effects by interacting with neurotransmitter systems. They can alter synthesis, storage, and release of neurotransmitters (step **1**). They can also alter the binding effect of neurotransmitters on the receiving site of the receptor neuron (step **2**).

After neurotransmitters diffuse across the synapse, the sending neuron normally deactivates the unbound or excess neurotransmitter (step **3**). However, when agonistic drugs block this process, excess neurotransmitter remains in the synapse, which prolongs the psychoactive drug's effects.

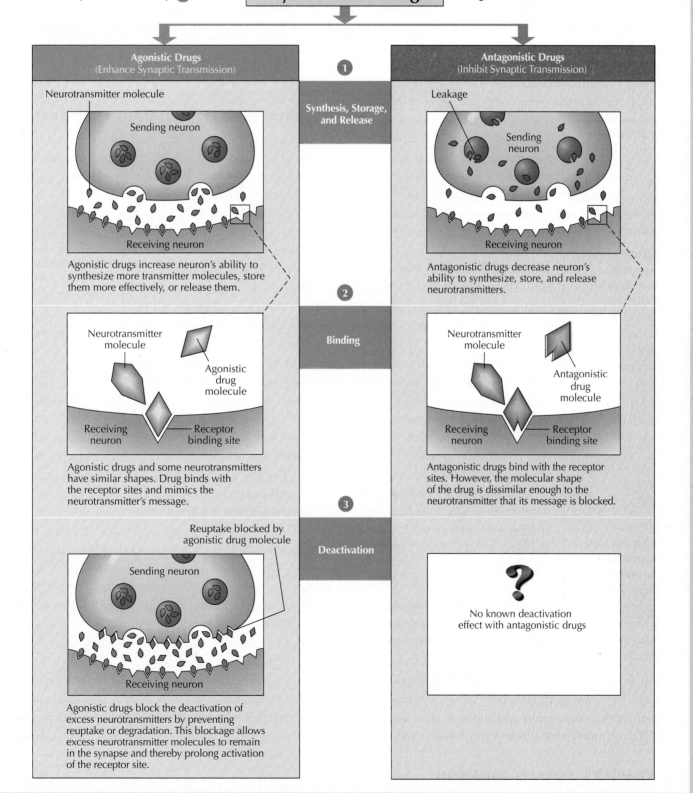

Psychoactive Drugs

Agonistic Drugs (Enhance Synaptic Transmission)

Antagonistic Drugs (Inhibit Synaptic Transmission)

1 Synthesis, Storage, and Release

Neurotransmitter molecule

Sending neuron

Receiving neuron

Agonistic drugs increase neuron's ability to synthesize more transmitter molecules, store them more effectively, or release them.

Leakage

Sending neuron

Receiving neuron

Antagonistic drugs decrease neuron's ability to synthesize, store, and release neurotransmitters.

2 Binding

Neurotransmitter molecule

Agonistic drug molecule

Receiving neuron

Receptor binding site

Agonistic drugs and some neurotransmitters have similar shapes. Drug binds with the receptor sites and mimics the neurotransmitter's message.

Neurotransmitter molecule

Antagonistic drug molecule

Receiving neuron

Receptor binding site

Antagonistic drugs bind with the receptor sites. However, the molecular shape of the drug is dissimilar enough to the neurotransmitter that its message is blocked.

3 Deactivation

Reuptake blocked by agonistic drug molecule

Sending neuron

Receiving neuron

Agonistic drugs block the deactivation of excess neurotransmitters by preventing reuptake or degradation. This blockage allows excess neurotransmitter molecules to remain in the synapse and thereby prolong activation of the receptor site.

?

No known deactivation effect with antagonistic drugs

status, have good and bad uses. For example, the illegal drug Ecstasy (or MDMA, which stands for 3-4-methylene-dioxymethamphetamine) has potential uses in helping treat post-traumatic stress disorder (Mithoefer et al., 2011), and marijuana has many therapeutic applications in a variety of medical settings (see Köfalvi, 2008, for a review). Conversely, legal drugs, such as tobacco, can be very harmful to our health, and other legal drugs can be harmful to the safety of others (such as when alcohol is consumed before a person drives). So in general, it is not a useful dichotomy to lump illegal drugs into a "bad" drugs category and legal drugs into a "good" drugs category. A better way to think about psychoactive drugs is to appreciate that psychoactive substances can be both harmful and beneficial and that a drug's legal status can be unrelated to its usefulness. This distinction, along with how drug *use* differs from drug *abuse* and how chemical alterations in consciousness affect us, are important topics in psychology.

Is drug abuse the same as drug addiction? The term **drug abuse** generally refers to drug taking that is greater than simple recreational *use*, continues despite adverse consequences, and is necessary for feelings of continued well-being. **Addiction** is a broad term referring to a condition in which a person has an overwhelming commitment to their drug of choice that supplants all other activities. Addicted individuals feel compelled to use a specific drug to the detriment of all other aspects of their life, such as work, family, and school (Alexander, 1997 Clay et al., 2008).

Some researchers use the term **physical dependence** to refer to changes in physical or bodily processes that make a drug necessary for daily functioning. Physical dependence may be evident when the drug is withheld and the user undergoes **withdrawal** reactions, which are the unpleasant symptoms associated with drug cessation, such as discomfort and cravings. After repeated use of a drug, many of the body's physiological processes

> **drug abuse** Drug use that is necessary for feelings of continued well-being; use continues despite adverse consequences.
>
> **addiction** A broad term referring to a condition in which a person has an overwhelming commitment to the drug of choice that supplants all other activities.
>
> **physical dependence** Changes in physical or bodily processes that make the drug necessary for daily functioning.
>
> **withdrawal** Characteristic signs that appear in a person when a drug is discontinued after prolonged use.

adjust, requiring more and more of the drug, producing a decreased sensitivity called **tolerance**.

Tolerance leads some users to escalate their drug use and to experiment with other drugs in an attempt to re-create the original pleasurable altered state. Sometimes, using one drug increases tolerance for another. This is known as **cross-tolerance**. For example, cross-tolerance is seen among the hallucinogens—LSD, mescaline, and psilocybin.

> **tolerance** A state reached when the physiological reaction to the drug decreases, such that increasing doses are necessary for the same effect.

Psychoactive Drugs: Four Categories

Psychologists typically divide psychoactive drugs into four broad categories: depressants, stimulants, opiates, and hallucinogens. **Table 5.1** provides examples of each and describes their effects.

Depressants act on the central nervous system to suppress or slow bodily processes and to reduce overall responsiveness.

Alcohol's effects are determined primarily by the amount that reaches the brain (**Figure 5.11**). Because the liver breaks down alcohol at the rate of about 30 mL per hour, the number of drinks and the speed of consumption are both very important. Men's bodies are more efficient at breaking down alcohol than are women's bodies: even after accounting for differences in size and muscle-to-fat ratio, women have a higher blood alcohol level than men following equal doses of alcohol. Because alcohol is legal, widely available, and commonly used as a recreational drug, a number of urban myths surround it (**Figure 5.12**).

> **depressants** Drugs that slow or depress nervous system activity.
>
> **stimulants** Drugs that speed up nervous system activity.

While depressants suppress central nervous system activity, **stimulants** increase its overall activity and responsiveness. One of the more commonly used legal stimulants is nicotine, which despite its legal status causes serious health problems. Cigarette smoking is the most preventable cause of lung cancer, accounting for 85 percent of all new Canadian cases of this cancer (Canadian Cancer Society, 2012). It has also been implicated in a variety of other cancers and in cardiovascular disease. The use of tobacco kills about 45,000 Canadians a year. That's more than the total number of deaths from AIDS, car accidents, suicide, murder, fires, and accidental poisonings combined (Canadian

Effects of the major psychoactive drugs   Table 5.1

	Category	Desired Effects	Excessive Use or Overdose Effects
	**Depressants (downers)** [slow nervous system activity]		
	Alcohol, barbiturates, anxiolytics, also known as antianxiety drugs or tranquilizers (Xanax), Rohypnol (roofies), Ketamine (special K), GHB	Tension reduction, euphoria, disinhibition, drowsiness, muscle relaxation, contentment	Anxiety, nausea, disorientation, impaired reflexes and motor functioning, amnesia, loss of consciousness, shallow respiration, convulsions, coma, death
	**Stimulants (uppers)** [speed up nervous system activity]		
	Cocaine, amphetamine, methamphetamine (crystal meth), MDMA (Ecstasy)	Exhilaration, euphoria, high physical and mental energy, reduced appetite, perceptions of power, sociability	Irritability, anxiety, sleeplessness, paranoia, hallucinations, psychosis, elevated blood pressure and body temperature, convulsions, death
	Caffeine	Increased alertness	Insomnia, restlessness, increased pulse rate, mild delirium, ringing in the ears, rapid heartbeat
	Nicotine	Relaxation, increased alertness, sociability, reduced appetite	Irritability, raised blood pressure, stomach pains, vomiting, dizziness, cancer, heart disease, emphysema
	**Opiates (narcotics)** [have sleep-inducing and pain-relieving properties]		
	Morphine, heroin, opium, codeine, Oxycodone	Euphoria, well-being, pain relief, sleep	Nausea, vomiting, constipation, shallow respiration, convulsions, coma, death
	**Hallucinogens (psychedelics)** [alter consciousness and distort mood and perception]		
	LSD (lysergic acid diethylamide), mescaline (extract from the peyote cactus), psilocybin (magic mushrooms), *Salvia divinorum**	Heightened aesthetic responses, euphoria, mild delusions, hallucinations, distorted perceptions and sensations	Panic, nausea, headaches, longer and more extreme delusions, hallucinations, perceptual distortions ("bad trips"), psychosis * long-term effects of excessive *Salvia* use are currently unknown
	Marijuana	Relaxation, mild euphoria, increased appetite	Perceptual and sensory distortions, hallucinations, fatigue, lack of motivation, impaired memory

Lung Association, 2008, 2011). Nicotine's effects (relaxation, increased alertness, diminished appetite) are so reinforcing that some people continue to smoke even after having a cancerous tumour removed. Psychology's own Sigmund Freud was one such person, continuing to smoke his trademark cigars even after diagnosis and more than 30 surgeries for oral cancer and bone cancer of the jaw.

Opiates (or narcotics) are either derived from the opium poppy (opium, morphine, and heroin) or synthetically produced (Demerol, Oxycodone). They are used to relieve severe pain (Kuhn et al., 2003; Watson et al., 2010), and

opiates Drugs derived from opium or synthetically derived and molecularly similar to opium that relieve pain and induce sleep.

Alcohol's effect on the body and behaviour • Figure 5.11

Number of drinks[a] in two hours	Blood alcohol content (%)[b]	General effect[c]
(2)	0.05	Relaxed state; increased sociability
(3)	0.08	Everyday stress lessened
(4)	0.10	Movements and speech become clumsy
(7)	0.20	Very drunk; loud and difficult to understand; emotions unstable
(12)	0.40	Difficult to wake up; incapable of voluntary action
(15)	0.50	Coma and/or death

[a]A drink is 335 mL (one bottle) of beer; a 125 mL (4-ounce) glass of wine; or a 37 mL (1.25-ounce) shot of spirits (there are approximately 20 shots in a 750 mL bottle of spirits).

[b]In Canada, the legal blood alcohol level for drinking and driving is below 0.08.

[c]There is considerable variation among people.

Zefa/SuperStock

Science and myths about alcohol consumption: Studies have shown none of these are true • Figure 5.12

- Alcohol increases sexual desire.
- Alcohol helps you sleep.
- Alcohol kills brain cells.
- It's easier to get drunk at high altitudes.
- Switching among different types of alcohol is more likely to lead to drunkenness.
- Drinking coffee or taking a cold shower are great ways to sober up after heavy drinking.
- Alcohol warms the body.
- You can't become an alcoholic if you only drink beer.
- Alcohol's primary effect is as a stimulant.
- People only experience impaired judgment after drinking if they show obvious signs of intoxication.

charovalenzuela/iStockphoto

are structurally similar to the brain's natural endorphins (Chapter 2), which decrease pain and elevate mood. Endorphins indirectly activate dopamine pathways in the brain and these pathways modulate reward. Both cocaine and amphetamines also interact with dopamine (and norepinephrine) systems. It is activation of dopamine pathways that accounts for the pleasurable and rewarding effects of these drugs (Di Chiara & Bassareo, 2007; Ersche, 2011). Incidentally, doing most anything we expect to find pleasurable also activates dopamine pathways (Bressan et al., Sharot et al., 2009) (**Figure 5.13**).

Heroin first got its name from the German word for "heroic," because when heroin was first commercially introduced by Bayer and Co. in 1898, it was hailed as a drug with incredible potential. Not only was it highly effective in treating the coughing, chest pain, and discomfort associated with pneumonia and tuberculosis—two leading causes of death at that time—but it also provided relief for severe pain (Alexander, 1997; Harris, 2012). Because of these tremendous benefits, and a lack of effective alternatives, it was widely prescribed. With its widespread use came the realization of its addictive properties.

Morphine, heroin, and many of the synthetic opiates are addictive because, after repeated flooding with these opiates, the brain eventually reduces the production of its own endorphins. If the user later attempts to stop, the brain lacks both the synthetic and the naturally occurring opiate chemicals, and withdrawal occurs. When opiates are used medically to relieve pain, they are generally not habit-forming (Ballantyne & Shin, 2008), although this can happen. However, when repeatedly taken in other circumstances, such as for self-medication to dull the anguish of a marginalized life or dampen emotional pain, they can be extremely addictive (Alexander, 1997; Fields, 2007; Levinthal, 2008).

How psychoactive drugs interact with dopamine pathways in the brain • Figure 5.13

Psychoactive drugs, such as cocaine and the opiates, interact with a dopamine pathway in the brain that runs from the midbrain through the medial forebrain bundle to the nucleus accumbens and then onward to the cortex.

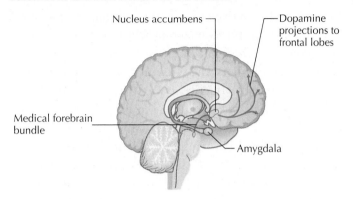

Nucleus accumbens
Dopamine projections to frontal lobes
Medical forebrain bundle
Amygdala

In the 2011 *Ontario Student Drug Use and Health Survey* (**Figure 5.14**), 14 percent of Ontario students in grades 7 to 12 report using opiate pain relievers, such as Tylenol 3, Oxycodone (OxyContin, a prescription synthetic opiate painkiller), and Percocet, for non-medical purposes (Paglia-Boak et al., 2011). Of this group, 63 percent report obtaining the drugs from home.

Because of its addictive properties and potential for abuse, OxyContin (a type of Oxycodone) was removed by Health Canada in March 2012 from the list of drugs doctors can prescribe. It has also been removed from the Health Canada program that pays for prescription drugs for First Nations people (CBC News, 2012). The replacement drug, OxyNeo, is believed (but not proven) to be more difficult to manipulate for abuse, as it forms a gel when in contact with water, and the pill has a much harder coating, making it difficult to crush.

One of the most intriguing alterations of consciousness comes from **hallucinogens**, drugs that produce sensory or perceptual distortions, including visual, auditory, and kinesthetic hallucinations. Some cultures use hallucinogens for spiritual purposes or as a way to experience "other realities." In Western societies, most people use hallucinogens for their reported "mind-expanding" potential.

> **hallucinogens**
> Drugs that alter consciousness and distort mood and perceptions.

Hallucinogens are commonly referred to as psychedelics (from the Greek for "mind manifesting"). They include mescaline (derived from the peyote cactus), psilocybin (derived from mushrooms), phencyclidine (synthetically derived), LSD (lysergic acid diethylamide, derived from

Psychoactive drug use among Ontario middle- and high-school students • Figure 5.14

The *Ontario Student Drug Use and Health Survey*, conducted by the Centre for Addiction and Mental Health, began in 1977 and is a self-administered, anonymous survey of drug use, mental health, physical activity, and risk behaviour of approximately 6,200 students in grades 7 to 12. The 2011 drug-use results are shown here. By far the most commonly used drug is alcohol, followed by cannabis, and then non-medical use of opioid pain relievers. Source: Paglia-Boak et al. (2011).

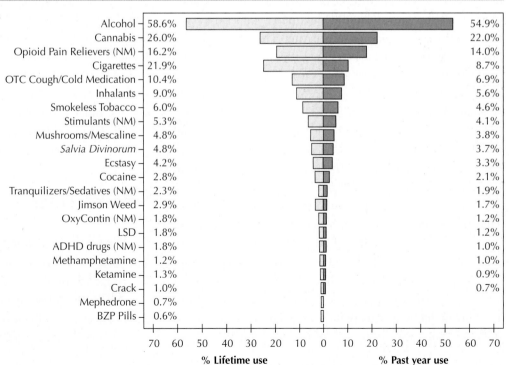

Drug	% Lifetime use	% Past year use
Alcohol	58.6%	54.9%
Cannabis	26.0%	22.0%
Opioid Pain Relievers (NM)	16.2%	14.0%
Cigarettes	21.9%	8.7%
OTC Cough/Cold Medication	10.4%	6.9%
Inhalants	9.0%	5.6%
Smokeless Tobacco	6.0%	4.6%
Stimulants (NM)	5.3%	4.1%
Mushrooms/Mescaline	4.8%	3.8%
Salvia Divinorum	4.8%	3.7%
Ecstasy	4.2%	3.3%
Cocaine	2.8%	2.1%
Tranquilizers/Sedatives (NM)	2.3%	1.9%
Jimson Weed	2.9%	1.7%
OxyContin (NM)	1.8%	1.2%
LSD	1.8%	1.2%
ADHD drugs (NM)	1.8%	1.0%
Methamphetamine	1.2%	1.0%
Ketamine	1.3%	0.9%
Crack	1.0%	0.7%
Mephedrone	0.7%	
BZP Pills	0.6%	

Psychoactive Drugs: Chemically Altered States **145**

ergot, a rye mould) and *Salvia* (*Salvia divinorum*, a herbaceous perennial of the mint family).

LSD, or acid, is a synthetic substance that produces dramatic alterations in sensation and perception. These alterations tend to primarily be visual, such as kaleidoscope-like images, vivid colours, and fantastic pictures. Generally when on a "trip," users are aware that their altered perceptions are not real.

LSD was first synthesized in 1943 by the Swiss chemist Albert Hofmann, who also took the first LSD trip after accidentally licking some of the drug off his finger. LSD is a serotonin agonist and is usually not considered to be addictive, but it can still be a dangerous drug. Bad LSD trips, while uncommon, can be terrifying and may lead to accidents, deaths, or suicide. Flashbacks may unpredictably recur long after the initial ingestion (Abadinsky, 2008).

LSD use by high school and university students has been increasing (Connolly, 2000; Hedges & Burchfield, 2006; Yacoubian, Green, & Peters, 2003; Young et al., 2011). Such psychoactive drugs as Rohypnol (the date-rape drug) and MDMA (Ecstasy) are also increasing in popularity, especially at all-night rave parties (DeMaria, 2012; Frei, 2010). Other "club drugs," such as GHB (gamma-hydroxybutyrate), Ketamine (Special K), and methamphetamine (crystal meth), are also now more common (Abadinsky, 2008; Weaver & Scholl, 2008).

Although these drugs can produce desirable effects (e.g., Ecstasy's feeling of great empathy, warmth, and connectedness with others), club drugs can be harmful. For example, they affect the motor coordination, perceptual skills, and reaction time necessary for safe driving. Their use may also lead to risky sexual behaviours. As with all illegal drugs, no quality control laws protect buyers from unscrupulous practices. Sellers can substitute or cut the drugs with unknown, cheaper, and possibly even more dangerous substances. Some drugs, such as Rohypnol, are odourless, colourless, and tasteless, and they can easily be added to beverages without a person's knowledge (Fernández et al., 2005; National Institute on Drug Abuse, 2005). It is for this reason they have been used to incapacitate victims of sexual assault. That being said, by far the most common drug involved in sexual assaults is not GHB or Rohypnol; it's actually alcohol (ElSohly & Salamone, 1999). Alcohol lowers inhibitions and impairs judgment, which can be a dangerous combination for both the potential perpetrator and the potential victim.

Marijuana is also classified as a hallucinogen, even though it has some properties of a depressant (it induces drowsiness and lethargy) and some of an opiate (it acts as a weak painkiller). In low doses, marijuana produces mild euphoria; moderate doses lead to an intensification of sensory experiences and the illusion that time is passing slowly. High doses may produce hallucinations, delusions, and distortions of body image (Kölfalvi, 2008; Ksir, Hart, & Ray, 2008). The active ingredient in marijuana (cannabis) is THC, or tetrahydrocannabinol, which binds to receptors abundant throughout the brain.

Many researchers and clinicians have found marijuana to be extremely effective in the treatment of glaucoma (an eye disease), in alleviating the nausea and vomiting associated with chemotherapy, and with other health problems, such as chronic pain and the general wasting seen in advanced AIDS (Darmani & Crim, 2005; Fogarty et al., 2007; Health Canada, 2006b, 2010c; Kölfalvi, 2008).

Medical use of marijuana is legal in Canada. Health Canada grants access to marijuana for patients suffering from the conditions listed above and for other diseases and disorders. It maintains its own supply of both dried marijuana and marijuana seeds via a contract with Prairie Plant Systems. A packet of 30 seeds costs $20 (plus tax) and the dried product costs patients $5/g (Health Canada, 2010b).

As mentioned, psychoactive drugs can be helpful, but they can also be harmful. This is often unrelated to their legal status or their recreational use. While it is somewhat normal to experiment as a young adult, excessive use at the expense of other areas of life, such as friends, family, work, play, and school, signals a problem that needs to be addressed. The excessive drug use may be a visible sign but not necessarily the cause of the problem (Alexander, 1997; Le Moal, 2009). When people are overwhelmingly involved with drugs (legal or illegal), their life history and current situation might provide powerful insights into their addiction. Indeed, this might explain why many of Canada's at-risk youth are far more likely than stable teenagers to be involved with illegal psychoactive drugs (Pearce et al., 2008).

CONCEPT CHECK

1. **What** are the four types of psychoactive drugs?
2. **What** are the differences between physical dependence and addiction? What are the differences between drug use and abuse?
3. **How** do psychoactive drugs affect nervous system functioning?

Altering Consciousness through Meditation and Hypnosis

LEARNING OBJECTIVES

1. **Summarize** some major forms of meditation.

2. **Explain** some of the uses of hypnosis and some of the myths about hypnosis.

s we have seen, such factors as sleep, dreaming, and psychoactive drug use can create altered states of consciousness. Changes in consciousness can also be achieved by means of meditation and hypnosis.

Meditation: Quiet the Mind

Suddenly, with a roar like that of a waterfall, I felt a stream of liquid light entering my brain through the spinal cord. I experienced a rocking sensation and then felt myself slipping out of my body, entirely enveloped in a halo of light. I felt the point of consciousness that was myself growing wider, surrounded by waves of light. (Krishna, 1999, pp. 4–5)

This is how spiritual leader Gopi Krishna described his experience with **meditation**. Although most people in the beginning stages of meditation report a simpler, mellow type of relaxation followed by a mild euphoria, some advanced meditators report experiences of profound rapture and joy or strong hallucinations.

> **meditation**
> A group of techniques designed to refocus attention, block out all distractions, and produce an altered state of consciousness.

Meditation is a technique that is used to alter consciousness. It usually involves a person sitting or relaxing comfortably in a location he or she finds peaceful and calming. In general, meditation refocuses a person's attention from outward sources to inward ones. There are a number of different types of meditation. In *concentrative meditation* the person clears his or her mind of all stressful thoughts and then focuses on a single object, idea, or thought. In *mindfulness meditation* the meditator widens his or her attention and becomes aware of all the activities and sounds that surrounds them. Thoughts are fluid and ideas move and change. In *movement meditation* the person moves his or her body in fluid, gentle ways to heighten their meditative focus. Yoga and tai chi are forms of movement meditation. *Spiritual meditation* involves incorporating prayer with meditation as a form of communication with a deity.

Meditation has been shown to have many beneficial effects that improve psychological health and well-being (Kilpatrick et al., 2011). People who meditate regularly report less stress and anxiety and are less affected by daily troubles and tensions (Matousek et al., 2011; Mohan et al., 2011). Regular meditation is also associated with reduced pain, lower alcohol consumption, less insomnia, and improved attention (Garland, 2011; Grant et al., 2011; Ong & Sholtes, 2010; Prakash et al., 2010). Some people who meditate experience a sense of timelessness and mild euphoria (Harrison, 2005) (see *What a Psychologist Sees*).

A concept related to meditation that has been gaining research interest is **mindfulness**. When a person is mindful, they are in a state somewhat opposite to daydreaming. The person is in a state of active, open, and focused attention and can observe their thoughts in a non-judgmental way. They are open to different views and perspectives, but their mind is quiet and limber. There are many examples of mindfulness in everyday experiences. Here are a few: fully attending to the textures and tastes of food at meal times; listening carefully and attentively to the voice of someone speaking; focusing on simple daily tasks, such as closing a door or getting dressed. Many of these tasks we perform automatically and are often somewhat detached from. Mindfulness training reminds us to experience everything as much as possible. Being mindful has a number of beneficial effects. It promotes effective emotional regulation and decreased reactivity, and fosters relationship satisfaction and possibly empathy and compassion (see Davis & Hayes, 2011, for a review). Mindfulness is increasingly being used as a therapeutic tool in psychotherapy (Segal et al., 2010).

> **mindfulness**
> A moment-to-moment non-judgmental awareness of one's experience.

Hypnosis: Myths and Practical Uses

Relax.... Your eyelids are so very heavy.... Your muscles are becoming more and more relaxed.... Your breathing is becoming deeper and deeper.... Relax.... Your eyes are closing.... Let go.... Relax.

What a Psychologist Sees

THE PLANNER

Meditation and the Brain

Researchers have found that a wider area of the brain responds to sensory stimuli during meditation, suggesting that meditation enhances the coordination between the brain hemispheres (see graphic: more blue means greater cortical involvement) (Kilpatrick et al., 2011; Lyubimov, 1992). One study has also found that meditation increases the density of grey matter in several brain areas involved in learning and memory processes, perspective taking, and emotional regulation (Holzel et al., 2011). ▼

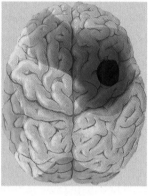

Top view of head

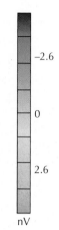

Before meditation   During meditation   nV

−2.6

0

2.6

Tetra Images/Getty Image

▲ Some types of meditation, such as tai chi and hatha yoga, involve body movements and postures, while in other techniques the meditator remains motionless, chanting or focusing on a single point.

Research has verified that meditation can produce dramatic changes in basic physiological processes, including heart rate, oxygen consumption, sweat gland activity, and brain activity. Meditation has also been somewhat successful in reducing pain, anxiety, and stress and lowering blood pressure (Carlson et al., 2007; Evans et al., 2008; Harrison, 2005). Studies have even implied that meditation can change the body's parasympathetic response (Sathyaprabha et al., 2008; Young & Taylor, 1998) and increase structural support for the sensory, decision-making, and attention-processing centres of the brain (Lazar et al., 2005; Slagter et al., 2007). It seems that during meditation, the part of the brain that is responsible for both sympathetic and parasympathetic responses, the hypothalamus, diminishes the sympathetic response and increases the parasympathetic response. Decreasing input to the fight-or-flight response pathways allows for deep rest, slower respiration, and increased and more coordinated use of the brain's two hemispheres. At the same time, meditation engages the frontal lobes, which contain the seat of many of our executive functions, such as problem solving, decision making, and reason (Cheng et al., 2010).

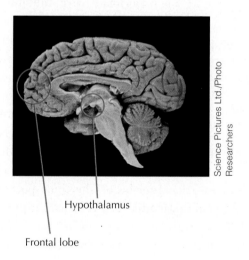

Science Pictures Ltd./Photo Researchers

Hypothalamus

Frontal lobe

Hypnotists use suggestions like these to begin a **hypnosis** session. Once hypnotized, some people can be convinced that they are standing at the edge of the ocean listening to the sound of the waves and feeling the ocean mist on their

> **hypnosis**
> A trancelike state of heightened suggestibility, deep relaxation, and intense focus.

faces. Invited to eat a delicious apple that is actually an onion, the hypnotized person may relish the flavour. Told they are watching a very funny or sad movie, hypnotized people may begin to laugh or cry at their self-created visions.

Hypnosis myths and empirical facts   Table 5.2

Myth	Fact
Remember the past: *Hypnosis can help people remember their early childhood experiences.*	Age-regressed adults behave like adults playacting as children and not how children would actually behave (Lilienfeld et al., 2010; Nash, 1987).
Forced hypnosis: *People can be involuntarily hypnotized or hypnotically "brainwashed."*	Hypnosis requires a willing, conscious choice to relinquish control of one's consciousness to someone else. The best potential subjects are those who are able to focus attention, are open to new experiences, and are capable of imaginative involvement or fantasy (Carvalho et al., 2008; Hutchinson-Phillips, Gow, & Jamieson, 2007; Wickramasekera, 2008).
Unethical behaviour: *Hypnosis can make people behave immorally or take dangerous risks against their will.*	Hypnotized people retain awareness and control of their behaviour, and they can refuse to comply with the hypnotist's suggestions (Kirsch & Braffman, 2001; Kirsh, Mazzoni, & Montgomery, 2006).
Faking: *Hypnosis participants are faking it, playing along with the hypnotist.*	There are conflicting research positions about hypnosis. Although many participants are not consciously faking hypnosis, some researchers believe the effects result from a blend of conformity, relaxation, obedience, suggestion, and role-playing (Fassler et al., 2008; Lynn, 2007; Orne, 2006). Other theorists believe that hypnotic effects result from a special altered state of consciousness (Bob, 2008; Naisch, 2007; Bowers & Woody, 1996; Hilgard, 1978, 1992). A group of "unified" theorists suggests that hypnosis is a combination of both relaxation/role-playing and a unique altered state of consciousness.
Superhuman strength: *Hypnotized people can perform acts of superhuman strength.*	When unhypnotized people are simply asked to try their hardest on tests of physical strength, they generally can do anything that a hypnotized person can (Orne, 2006).
Exceptional memory: *Hypnotized people can recall things they otherwise could not.*	Hypnosis does not enhance memory, and in some cases it actually makes it more difficult to differentiate fact from fantasy. It can also make people feel more confident about their memories even when they are incorrect (Mazzoni et al., 2010).

Michael Newman/PhotoEdit

Time & Life Pictures/Getty Images

Since the eighteenth century, entertainers, charlatans, and quacks have used (and abused) hypnosis (**Table 5.2**); but physicians, dentists, and therapists have also long employed it as a respected clinical tool.

A number of features characterize the hypnotic state (Jamieson & Hasegawa, 2007; Jensen et al., 2008; Nash & Barnier, 2008):

- narrowed, highly focused attention (ability to tune out competing sensory stimuli)
- increased use of imagination and hallucinations
- a passive and receptive attitude
- decreased responsiveness to pain
- heightened suggestibility or a willingness to respond to proposed changes in perception ("This onion is an apple") (Kosslyn & Thompson, 2000).

In psychotherapy, hypnosis can help patients relax, remember some events (which must be cautiously interpreted), and reduce anxiety. It has also been used with modest success in the treatment of phobias and in helping people to lose weight, stop smoking, and improve study habits

(Amundson & Nuttgens, 2008; Golden, 2006; Manning, 2007). Hypnosis is also occasionally used in surgery and for the treatment of chronic pain and severe burns (Jensen et al., 2008; Nash & Barnier, 2008). It has found its best use, however, in such areas as dentistry and childbirth, in which patients often have a high degree of anxiety, fear, and misinformation. Because tension and anxiety strongly affect pain, hypnosis, along with any technique that helps the patient relax, is generally medically useful.

CONCEPT CHECK

1. **What** are some major features of meditation?

2. **Who** might benefit from hypnosis?

3. **Why** can't people be hypnotized against their will?

Summary

1 Consciousness, Sleep, and Dreaming 128

- **Consciousness**, an organism's awareness of its own self and surroundings, exists along a continuum, from high awareness to no awareness and coma. Sleep is an **altered state of consciousness**.

- Controlled processes demand focused attention and generally interfere with other ongoing activities. Automatic processes require minimal attention and generally do not interfere with other ongoing activities.

- Many physiological functions follow 24-hour circadian rhythms. Disruptions in circadian rhythms, such as shift work, international travel, and sleep deprivation, cause increased fatigue, cognitive and mood disruptions, and other health problems but not hallucinations and psychosis.

Consciousness • Figure 5.1

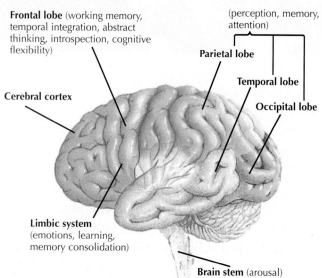

Frontal lobe (working memory, temporal integration, abstract thinking, introspection, cognitive flexibility)

Cerebral cortex

(perception, memory, attention)

Parietal lobe

Temporal lobe

Occipital lobe

Limbic system (emotions, learning, memory consolidation)

Brain stem (arousal)

- The electroencephalogram (EEG) detects and records electrical changes in the neurons of the cerebral cortex. People progress through four distinct stages of **non-rapid-eye-movement (NREM) sleep**, with periods of **rapid-eye-movement (REM) sleep** occurring at the end of each sleep cycle. Both REM and NREM sleep are important for our biological functioning.

- The **evolutionary/circadian theory** proposes that sleep evolved to conserve energy and as protection from predators. The **repair/restoration theory** suggests that sleep helps us recuperate from the day's events. Three major theories for why we dream are the activation-synthesis hypothesis, the information-processing view, and Freud's psychoanalytic view.

- **Dyssomnias** are problems in the amount, timing, and quality of sleep; they include insomnia, sleep apnea, and narcolepsy. **Parasomnias** are abnormal disturbances occurring during sleep; they include nightmares, night terrors, sleepwalking, and sleep talking. Although drugs are the most common method of treating sleep disorders, research has shown that cognitive-behaviour therapy is effective at treating some sleep problems.

2 Psychoactive Drugs: Chemically Altered States 140

- **Psychoactive drugs** influence the nervous system in a variety of ways. Alcohol affects neural membranes throughout the entire nervous system. Most psychoactive drugs act in a more specific way, by either enhancing or mimicking a particular neurotransmitter's effect (an **agonistic drug** action) or inhibiting it (an **antagonistic drug** action). Drugs can interfere with neurotransmission at any of four stages: production or synthesis, storage and release, binding, or removal.

How agonistic and antagonistic drugs produce their psychoactive effect • Figure 5.10

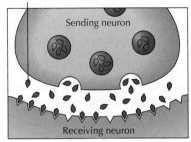

Neurotransmitter molecule

Sending neuron

Receiving neuron

- The term **drug abuse** refers to drug-taking behaviour that is greater than simple recreational use, continues despite adverse consequences, and is necessary for continued well-being. **Addiction** is a condition in which a person feels an overwhelming commitment to a drug that supplants all other activities. A related term is **physical dependence**, which refers to biological changes in the person that make a drug necessary for minimum daily functioning. Repeated use of a drug can produce decreased sensitivity, or **tolerance**. Sometimes, the use of one drug increases tolerance for another (**cross-tolerance**).

- Psychologists divide psychoactive drugs into four categories: **depressants** (such as alcohol, barbiturates, Rohypnol, and ketamine), **stimulants** (such as caffeine, nicotine, cocaine, amphetamine, methamphetamine, and Ecstasy), **opiates** (such as morphine, heroin, and Oxycodone), and **hallucinogens** (such as marijuana and LSD). Almost all psychoactive drugs—legal or illegal—have beneficial effects but can also cause health problems when abused.

3 Altering Consciousness through Meditation and Hypnosis 147

- The term **meditation** refers to techniques designed to refocus attention, block out distractions, and produce an altered state of consciousness. Some followers believe that meditation offers a more enlightened form of consciousness, and researchers have verified that it can produce changes in basic physiological processes.

- **Hypnosis** is a mild trancelike state of heightened suggestibility, deep relaxation, and intense focus. Although a number of myths surround its use and effectiveness, it is still used in some medical settings. In psychotherapy, hypnosis can help patients relax, remember certain events, and reduce anxiety. It can also be used to help with other circumstances, such as efforts to quit smoking, lose weight, overcome phobias, cope with dentistry, and endure labour.

What a Psychologist Sees: Meditation and the Brain

Top view of head

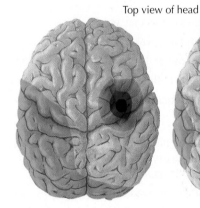 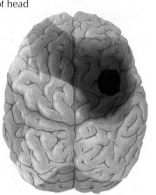

Before meditation   During meditation

Key Terms

Critical and Creative Thinking Questions

1. Do you believe that people have an unconscious mind? If so, how might it affect thoughts, feelings, and behaviour?

2. Which of the three main theories of dreaming do you most agree with, and why?

3. The medical use of marijuana is legal in Canada, while recreational use is illegal. What factors do you think contribute to a drug's legal or illegal status? What drugs do you think should be illegal, and what drugs do you think should be legal? What factors contribute to your decision?

4. How much of your week do you spend sleep deprived? After what you have read in this chapter, identify five things you can do to increase the amount of sleep you get.

5. Driving when sleep deprived can be as dangerous as driving after drinking alcohol. In light of this, should driving while sleep deprived be outlawed? What might a device designed to detect sleep deprivation in people look like, and what physiological systems would it need to detect and measure?

6. Why might hypnosis help treat people who suffer from chronic pain?

7. You have read about two theories that attempt to explain why sleep evolved. Another way to think about sleep and consciousness is to ask, why did being awake evolve? What might be the answer to this question?

8. Date-rape drugs, such as Rohypnol, have received considerable media attention; however, another drug is used far more often by both the perpetrators and the victims of sexual assault. What is the name of this drug and why has it been implicated in these types of crimes? (See Appendix A for the name of this drug.)

Self-Test

(Check your answers in Appendix A.)

1. Consciousness is defined in this text as _____.
   a. ordinary and extraordinary wakefulness
   b. an organism's awareness of its own self and surroundings
   c. mental representations of the world in the here and now
   d. any mental state that requires thinking and processing of sensory stimuli

2. For the past four days, Lisa has been either sleeping and dreaming, or using various psychoactive substances. Which of the following statements applies to Lisa?
   a. She needs to be enrolled in a substance abuse program.
   b. She has been in serious danger of permanently altering her circadian rhythms.
   c. She has recently been in a state of altered consciousness.
   d. She has been lacking any conscious awareness.

3. Mental activities that require focused attention are called _____.
   a. thinking processes   c. alert states of consciousness
   b. controlled processes   d. conscious awareness

4. Automatic processes require _____ attention.
   a. focused   c. minimal
   b. unconscious   d. delta wave

5. Circadian rhythms are _____.
   a. patterns that repeat themselves on a twice-daily schedule
   b. physical and mental changes associated with the cycle of the moon
   c. rhythmic processes in your brain
   d. biological and other changes that occur on a 24-hour cycle

6. Driving home late one night, you find yourself struggling to stay awake and think you may have fallen asleep for a couple of seconds. What name is given to this shift in your brain activity?
   a. a microsleep   c. a sleep spindle
   b. unconscious sleep   d. delta wave shift

7. On the following diagram, identify the main areas of the brain that control circadian rhythms.
   a. hypothalamus   c. suprachiasmatic nucleus
   b. pineal gland

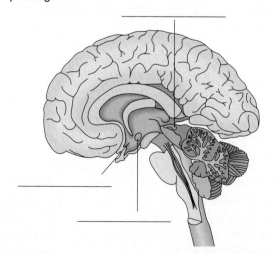

8. In the past week, Jessica has slept only three to four hours a night because of studying for exams and working. What name is given to this type of accumulation of lost sleep?
   a. short sleep bouts   c. sleep deprivation
   b. sleep spindles   d. sleep debt

9. A(n) _____ displays neural changes tracked by means of small electrodes on the scalp. This research tool is called _____.

   a. an EKG   c. an EEG recording

   b. a PET scan   d. an EMG

10. The sleep stage marked by irregular breathing, eye movements, high-frequency brain waves, and dreaming is called _____ sleep.

   a. beta   c. REM

   b. hypnologic   d. transitional

11. Which of the following people is clearly experiencing insomnia?

   a. Ian frequently cannot fall asleep the night before a final exam.

   b. Enzo regularly sleeps less than eight hours per night.

   c. Adam persistently has difficulty falling or staying asleep.

   d. All of these people are clearly experiencing insomnia.

12. Losing weight, restricting alcohol, having surgery, using dental appliances, and using tennis balls are all recommended treatments for _____, a dyssomnia.

   a. insomnia   c. nightmares

   b. parasomnia   d. sleep apnea

13. Psychoactive drugs _____.

   a. change conscious awareness, mood, or perception

   b. are addictive, mind altering, and dangerous to your health

   c. are illegal unless prescribed by a medical doctor

   d. all of these options

14. Jonathan has used LSD quite regularly for many years and has more recently started using mescaline. He finds that he can consume significant quantities of mescaline without getting much of an effect. Which of the following terms most accurately describes what Jonathan has developed?

   a. drug abuse   c. cross-tolerance

   b. tolerance   d. physical dependence

15. Match the four major categories of psychoactive drugs with the correct photo:

   a. depressants, photo _____   c. opiates, photo _____

   b. stimulants, photo _____   d. hallucinogens, photo _____

16. Which of the following is *not* a depressant?

   a. anxiolytics   c. nicotine

   b. alcohol   d. GHB

17. Psilocybin and *Salvia* are both _____.

   a. opiates   c. depressants

   b. hallucinogens   d. stimulants

18. Altered states of consciousness can be achieved in which of the following ways?

   a. during sleep and dreaming

   b. via psychoactive chemicals

   c. through hypnosis and meditation

   d. all of these options

19. _____ is a group of techniques designed to refocus attention and produce an altered state of consciousness.

   a. Hypnosis   c. Parapsychology

   b. Scientology   d. Meditation

20. _____ is an altered state of heightened suggestibility characterized by deep relaxation and intense focus.

   a. Meditation   c. Hypnosis

   b. Amphetamine psychosis   d. Daydreaming

THE PLANNER ✓

Review your Chapter Planner on the chapter opener and check off your completed work.

Self-Test 153

Learning

Phil Esposito is a Canadian-born Hockey Hall of Famer who played 18 seasons in the National Hockey League. "Espo" was famous for his superstitious game-day behaviour. He always drove through the same toll booth on his way to the game, always wore the same black turtleneck under his hockey sweater, and always laid out his clothes and equipment in exactly the same order in the locker room. Where did these habits come from? It seems when he'd behaved in these ways in previous games, he'd been the team's top scorer. For example, one evening, because he was nursing a sore throat, he put a turtleneck on under his hockey sweater. He scored three goals in that game. From then on, Esposito wore the same black turtleneck in every game! In other words, he had learned to behave in these ways. Lots of professional athletes have similar "superstitious" routines that they perform before important games. In fact, superstitious behaviours are not limited to athletes; some of your friends may have similar routines that they perform before exams or other important events. Superstitious behaviours are the result of learning.

When we think of learning, we usually think of what we learn in school, such as math and reading, or of skills we acquire, such as riding a bike or playing the piano. Psychologists define learning more broadly, as *a relatively permanent change in behaviour or mental processes because of practice or experience*. This relative permanence applies not only to useful behaviours (using a spoon or writing great novels) but also to superstitious behaviours like Phil Esposito's wearing the same black turtleneck in every hockey game. And the same principles of learning also apply to bad habits, such as procrastination, and to negative behaviours like bullying and victimization. In this chapter, we discuss several types of conditioning, the most basic form of learning. Then we look at social-cognitive learning and the biological factors involved in learning. Finally, we explore how learning theories and concepts touch everyday life.

B. Bennett/Getty Images

CHAPTER OUTLINE

CHAPTER PLANNER

- ❏ Study the picture and read the opening story.
- ❏ Scan the Learning Objectives in each section:
  p. 156 ❏   p. 161 ❏   p. 167 ❏   p. 170 ❏   p. 173 ❏

Analyze key features

- ❏ Process Diagram, p. 157
- ❏ Study Organizer, p. 163
- ❏ What a Psychologist Sees, p. 164
- ❏ Psychological Science, p. 166
- ❏ Applying Psychology, p. 174
- ❏ Visualizing, p. 175
- ❏ Stop: Answer the Concept Checks before you go on:
  p. 160 ❏   p. 166 ❏   p. 170 ❏   p. 173 ❏   p. 177 ❏

End of chapter

- ❏ Review the Summary and Key Terms.
- ❏ Answer the Critical and Creative Thinking Questions.
- ❏ Complete the Self-Test and check your answers.

Classical Conditioning

LEARNING OBJECTIVES

1. **Describe** how a neutral stimulus can become a conditioned stimulus by being paired with an unconditioned stimulus.

2. **Explain** how stimulus generalization and discrimination affect learning.

3. **Describe** the processes of extinction and spontaneous recovery.

4. **Identify** an example of higher-order conditioning.

One of the earliest forms of learning to be studied scientifically was conditioning. We discuss classical conditioning, made famous by Pavlov's dogs, in this section and a different form of conditioning, known as operant conditioning, in the next section.

The Beginnings of Classical Conditioning

Why does your mouth water when you see a large slice of chocolate cake or a hot pizza? The answer to this question was accidentally discovered in the laboratory of Russian physiologist Ivan Pavlov (1849–1936). Pavlov's early work focused on the role of saliva in digestion, and one of his experiments involved measuring salivary responses in dogs by using a tube attached to the dogs' salivary glands.

One of Pavlov's students noticed that many dogs began salivating at the sight of the food or the food dish, the smell of the food, or even the sight of the person who delivered the food long before receiving the actual food. This "unscheduled" salivation was intriguing. Pavlov recognized that an involuntary reflex (salivation) that occurred before the appropriate stimulus (food) was presented could not be inborn and biological. It had to have been acquired through experience—through **learning**.

learning A relatively permanent change in behaviour or mental processes because of practice or experience.

Excited by their accidental discovery, Pavlov and his students conducted several experiments. Their most basic method involved sounding a tone on a tuning fork just before food was placed in the dogs' mouths. After several pairings of tone and food, the dogs would salivate on hearing the tone, even without receiving food. Pavlov and others went on to show that many things can become conditioned stimuli for salivation if they are paired with food: the ticking of a metronome, a buzzer, a light, and even the sight of a circle or triangle drawn on a card.

The type of learning that Pavlov described came to be known as **classical conditioning** (**Figure 6.1**). To understand classical conditioning, you first need to realize that **conditioning** is just another word for learning. You also need to know that some responses are inborn and don't require conditioning. For example, the inborn salivation reflex consists of an **unconditioned stimulus (UCS)** and an **unconditioned response (UCR)**. That is, the UCS (food) elicits the UCR (salivation) without previous conditioning (learning).

classical conditioning Learning that occurs when a neutral stimulus (NS) is paired (associated) with an unconditioned stimulus (UCS) to elicit a conditioned response (CR).

conditioning The process of learning associations between environmental stimuli and behavioural responses.

Before conditioning occurs, a **neutral stimulus (NS)** does not naturally elicit a relevant or consistent response. For example, as shown in Figure 6.1, Pavlov's dogs did not naturally salivate when a tone sounded. Similarly, as the figure shows, the sight of a cardboard box (neutral stimulus) doesn't naturally make a person hungry for a slice of pizza.

Pavlov's discovery was that learning occurs when a neutral stimulus, such as a tone (or the cardboard box), is paired repeatedly with an unconditioned stimulus (food, or the smell of pizza in the cardboard box). The neutral stimulus (tone or the cardboard box) then becomes a **conditioned stimulus (CS)**, which elicits a **conditioned response (CR)**—salivation.

What does a salivating dog have to do with your life? Classical conditioning is the most fundamental way that all animals, including humans, learn many new responses, emotions, and attitudes. Your love for your parents (or boyfriend or girlfriend), your drooling at the sight of

Pavlov's classical conditioning • Figure 6.1

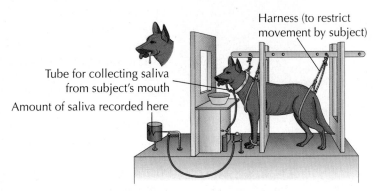

Harness (to restrict movement by subject)

Tube for collecting saliva from subject's mouth

Amount of saliva recorded here

	Pavlov's example	Modern-day example
1 **Before conditioning** The neutral stimulus (NS) produces no relevant response. The unconditioned (unlearned) *stimulus* (UCS) elicits the unconditioned *response* (UCR).	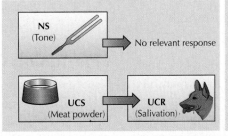	
2 **During conditioning** The neutral stimulus (NS) is repeatedly paired with the unconditioned (unlearned) *stimulus* (UCS) to produce the unconditioned *response* (UCR).	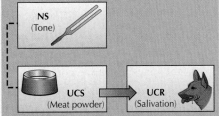	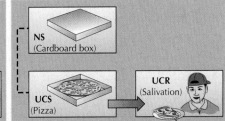
3 **After conditioning** The neutral stimulus (NS) has become a conditioned (learned) stimulus (CS). This CS now produces a conditioned (learned) *response* (CR), which is usually similar to the previously unconditioned (unlearned) response (UCR).	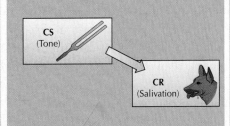	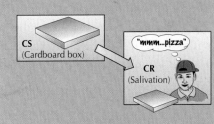
Summary An originally neutral stimulus (NS) becomes a conditioned stimulus (CS), which elicits a conditioned response (CR).	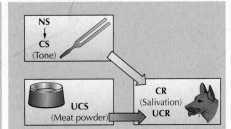	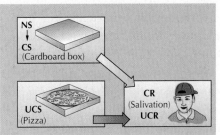

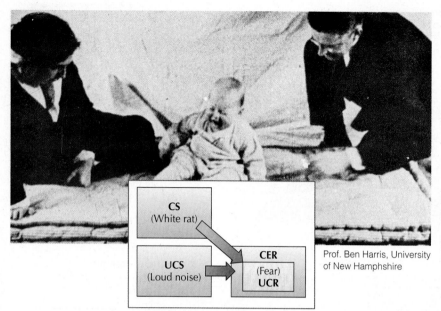

Conditioning and the case of Little Albert • Figure 6.2

In the famous "Little Albert" study, a healthy 11-month-old child was first allowed to play with a white laboratory rat. Like most infants, Albert was curious and reached for the rat, showing no fear. Watson used the fact that infants are naturally frightened (UCR) by loud noises (UCS). Watson stood behind Albert and put the rat (NS) near him. When the infant reached for the rat, Watson banged a steel bar with a hammer. The loud noise frightened Albert and made him cry. The white rat (NS) was paired with the loud noise (UCS) only seven times before the white rat alone produced a *conditioned emotional response* (CER) in Albert: fear of the rat.

Prof. Ben Harris, University of New Hamphshire

chocolate cake or pizza, and even negative reactions, such as the hatred and racism that some people display, are largely the result of classical conditioning.

In a famous experiment, John Watson and Rosalie Rayner (1920) demonstrated that fear could also be classically conditioned (**Figure 6.2**).

Watson and Rayner's experiment could not be performed today because it violates several of the Canadian Psychological Association's ethical principles for psychological research (Chapter 1). Moreover, Watson and Rayner ended their experiment without *extinguishing* (removing) Albert's fear, although they knew that his fear could endure for a long period. Watson and Rayner also have been criticized because they did not measure Albert's fear objectively. Their subjective evaluation raises doubt about the degree of fear they conditioned (Paul & Blumenthal, 1989).

Despite such criticisms, John Watson made important and lasting contributions to psychology. Unlike other psychologists of his time, Watson emphasized the study of strictly observable behaviours, and he founded the school of *behaviourism*, which explains behaviour as a result of observable stimuli and observable responses.

Watson's study of Little Albert has had legendary significance for many psychologists. Watson showed us that many of our likes, dislikes, prejudices, and fears are **conditioned emotional responses**—classically conditioned emotional responses to previously neutral stimuli. Watson's research in producing Little Albert's fears also led to powerful clinical tools for eliminating extreme, irrational fears known as *phobias* (Chapter 13).

Fine-Tuning Classical Conditioning

Now that you have an understanding of the key concepts of classical conditioning, we can discuss six important principles of classical conditioning: stimulus generalization, stimulus discrimination, extinction, spontaneous recovery, reconditioning, and higher-order conditioning (**Figure 6.3**).

Stimulus generalization occurs when a stimulus that is similar to the original conditioned stimulus triggers the same conditioned response. The more the stimulus resembles the conditioned stimulus, the stronger the conditioned response (Hovland, 1937). For example, after first conditioning dogs to salivate at the sound of low-pitched tones, Pavlov later demonstrated that the dogs would also salivate in response to higher-pitched tones. Similarly, after conditioning, "Little Albert," the infant in Watson and Rayner's experiment, showed a fear response not only to rats but also to a rabbit, a dog, and even a bearded Santa Claus mask.

Eventually, through the process of **stimulus discrimination** (a term that refers to a learned response to a specific stimulus but not to other similar stimuli), Albert presumably learned to recognize differences between rats and other stimuli. As a result, he probably overcame his fear of Santa Claus, even if he remained afraid of white rats. Similarly, Pavlov's dogs learned to distinguish between the tone that signalled food and those that did not.

Most behaviours that are learned through classical conditioning can be weakened or suppressed through **extinction**. Extinction occurs when the unconditioned stimulus (UCS) is repeatedly withheld whenever the conditioned stimulus (CS) is presented. This gradually

Six principles of classical conditioning • Figure 6.3

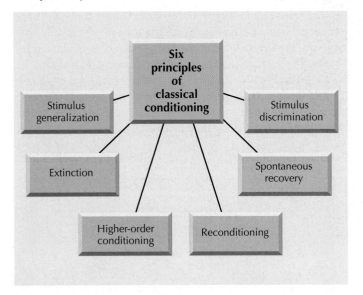

"I don't care if she is a tape dispenser. I love her."

Which of the six basic principles of classical conditioning explain(s) this cartoon?

weakens the previous association. When Pavlov repeatedly sounded the tone without presenting food, the dogs' salivation response gradually declined. Similarly, if you have a classically conditioned fear of cats and later start to work as a veterinary assistant, your fear will gradually diminish.

However, extinction is not unlearning. A conditioned behaviour becomes *extinct* when the response rate decreases, and the person no longer responds to the conditioned stimulus. This does not mean that a person or animal has "erased" the learned connection between the stimulus and the response (Bouton, 1994). In fact, if the stimulus is reintroduced, the conditioning is much faster the second time. Furthermore, Pavlov found that if he allowed several hours to pass after the extinction procedure and then presented the tone again, the salivation would spontaneously reappear (**Figure 6.4**). This reappearance of a conditioned response after extinction, referred to as **spontaneous recovery**, helps explain why you might suddenly feel excited at seeing a former girlfriend or boyfriend, even though years have passed (and extinction has occurred).

Extinction and spontaneous recovery • Figure 6.4

The more often the UCS is withheld when the CS is presented, the lower an individual's response rate to the UCS, until extinction occurs.

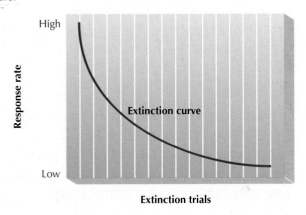

But an extinguished response may spontaneously reappear, which can trigger a rush of feelings and emotions as though the UCS were present.

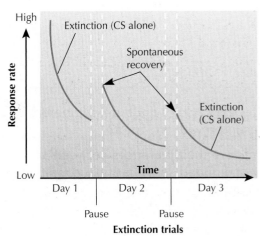

Higher-order conditioning • Figure 6.5

Children are not born salivating upon seeing the McDonald's Golden Arches. So why do they beg their parents to stop at McDonald's after simply seeing a billboard for the restaurant? It is because of higher-order conditioning, which occurs when a neutral stimulus (NS) becomes a conditioned stimulus (CS) through repeated pairings with a previously conditioned stimulus (CS). If you wanted to demonstrate higher-order conditioning in Pavlov's dogs, you would first condition the

dogs to salivate in response to the sound of the tone **(a)**. Then you would pair a flash of light with the tone **(b)**. Eventually, the dogs would salivate in response to the flash of light alone **(c)**. Similarly, children first learn to pair McDonald's restaurants with food and later learn that two Golden Arches are a symbol for McDonald's. Their salivation and begging to eat at the restaurant on seeing the arches are a classic case of higher-order conditioning (and successful advertising).

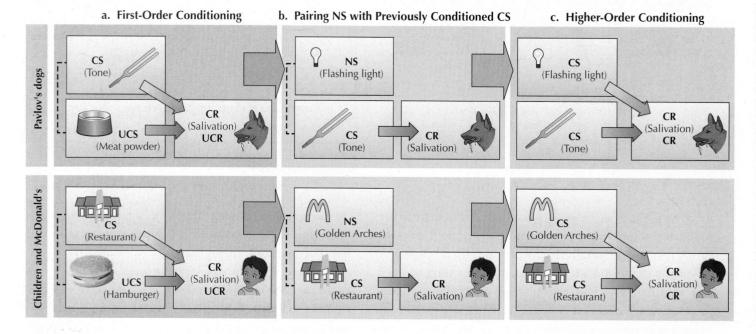

It also explains why couples who've recently broken up sometimes misinterpret a sudden flare-up of feelings and return to unhappy relationships. Furthermore, if a conditioned stimulus is reintroduced after extinction, the conditioning occurs much faster the second time around—a phenomenon known as **reconditioning**. Both spontaneous recovery and reconditioning help underscore why it can be so difficult for us to break bad habits (such as eating too many nachos) or internalize new beliefs (such as egalitarian racial beliefs). The phenomenon of **higher-order conditioning** (**Figure 6.5**) further expands and complicates our learned habits and associations.

CONCEPT CHECK

1. **Why** did Pavlov's dogs salivate before being presented with any food?

2. **What** are the differences between an unconditioned stimulus and a conditioned stimulus?

3. **How** does an unconditioned response differ from a conditioned response?

4. **When** does stimulus generalization occur?

5. **Under** what conditions might you expect to see extinction and spontaneous recovery?

Operant Conditioning

LEARNING OBJECTIVES

1. **Explain** how reinforcement and punishment influence behaviour.

2. **Describe** Thorndike's and Skinner's contributions to research on operant conditioning.

3. **Identify** examples of primary and secondary reinforcers.

4. **Explain** how different schedules of reinforcement affect behaviour.

5. **Describe** the negative side effects of punishment.

Consequences are the heart of **operant conditioning**. In classical conditioning, consequences are irrelevant—Pavlov's dogs were still allowed to eat whether they salivated or not. But in operant conditioning, the organism performs a behaviour (an *operant*, as in "operation") that produces either reinforcement or punishment. **Reinforcement** strengthens the response, making it more likely to recur. **Punishment** weakens the response, making it less likely to recur.

Classical and operant conditioning also differ in another important way. In classical conditioning, the organism's response is generally passive and involuntary. In operant conditioning, the organism's response is generally active and voluntary. The learner "operates" on the environment and produces consequences that influence whether the behaviour will be repeated. For example, if your friends smile and laugh when you tell a joke, you are likely to joke more with them. If they frown, groan, or ridicule you, you are likely to joke less.

> **operant conditioning** Learning in which voluntary responses are controlled by their consequences (also known as instrumental or Skinnerian conditioning).
>
> **reinforcement** A consequence that strengthens a response, making the response more likely to occur again.
>
> **punishment** A consequence that weakens a response, making the response less likely to occur again.

The Beginnings of Operant Conditioning

Edward Thorndike (1874–1949), a pioneer of operant conditioning, determined that the frequency of a behaviour is modified by its consequences. He developed the **law of effect** (Thorndike, 1911), a first step in understanding how consequences can modify active, voluntary behaviours (**Figure 6.6**).

> **law of effect** Thorndike's rule that the probability of an action being repeated is strengthened when followed by a pleasant or satisfying consequence.

B. F. Skinner (1904–1990) extended Thorndike's law of effect to more complex behaviours. He emphasized that reinforcement and punishment always occur after the behaviour of interest has occurred. In addition, Skinner cautioned that the only way to know how we have influenced someone's behaviour is to check whether the behaviour increases or decreases.

Sometimes, he noted, we think we're reinforcing or we think we're punishing when we may actually be doing the opposite. For example, a teacher may think she is encouraging shy students to talk by praising them each time they speak up in class. But what if shy students are embarrassed by this attention? If so, as Canadian researcher Mary Ann Evans (2010) has pointed out, teachers may actually decrease the number of times the students talk in class.

Reinforcement: Strengthening a Response

Reinforcers, which strengthen a response, can be grouped into two types: primary and secondary. *Primary reinforcers* satisfy an intrinsic, unlearned biological need (food, water, sex). *Secondary reinforcers* are not intrinsic; the value of these reinforcers (money, praise, attention) is learned.

For an interesting discussion on this topic, scan to download the author's podcast.

Thorndike box • Figure 6.6

In one famous experiment, Thorndike put a cat inside a specially built puzzle box. When the cat stepped on a pedal inside the box (at first, through trial and error), the door opened and the cat could get out to eat. With each additional success, the cat's actions became more purposeful, and it soon learned to open the door immediately (from Thorndike, 1898).

How reinforcement strengthens and increases behaviours Table 6.1		
Primary reinforcers	**Positive reinforcement** *adds to* (+) *and strengthens behaviour*	**Negative reinforcement** *takes away* (–) *and strengthens behaviour*
Satisfy an unlearned biological need	You hug your baby and he smiles at you. The "addition" of his smile strengthens the likelihood that you will hug him again.	Your baby is crying, so you hug him and he stops crying. The "removal" of crying strengthens the likelihood that you will hug him again.
	You do a favour for a friend and she buys you lunch in return.	You take an Aspirin for your headache, which takes away the pain.
Secondary reinforcers Value is learned, not intrinsic	You increase profits and receive $200 as a bonus.	After high sales, your boss says you won't have to work on weekends.
	You study hard and receive a good grade on your psychology exam.	Your professor says you won't have to take the final exam because you did so well on your in-class tests.

Thus, when we were babies, we most likely found milk (a primary reinforcer) much more reinforcing than a $100 bill. By the time we reached adolescence, however, we most likely had learned to prefer the money (a secondary reinforcer).

Reinforcers can produce **positive reinforcement** or **negative reinforcement**, depending on whether certain stimuli are added or taken away (see **Table 6.1**). It may be easy to confuse negative reinforcement with punishment; however, the two concepts are actually completely opposite. Reinforcement (whether positive or negative) always strengthens a behaviour, whereas punishment weakens a behaviour. If the terminology seems confusing, it may help to think of positive and negative reinforcement in the mathematical sense, that is, in terms of something being added (+) or taken away (–) rather than in terms of good and bad.

Sometimes we use high-frequency behaviour to reinforce low-frequency responses: making yourself study before going to the movies is a good example. In this case, you are using what is called the **Premack principle**, named after psychologist David Premack. Recognizing that you love to go to movies, you intuitively tie your less-desirable low-frequency activities (making yourself study) to your high-frequency behaviour (going to the movies), thereby positively reinforcing the completion of the less desirable, low-frequency behaviour.

Just as you saw in our discussion of classical conditioning, *extinction* can also occur in operant conditioning. In both classical and operant conditioning, removing the original source of learning causes extinction to occur. In classical conditioning, presenting the CS without the UCS eventu-

ally leads to extinction of the CR. In operant conditioning, if we remove the reinforcer that follows the response, the animal will eventually stop producing the response. How easy it is to extinguish a response depends on the rate with which we have been reinforcing that response.

What are the best circumstances for using reinforcement? It depends on the desired outcome. To make this decision, you need to understand various **schedules of reinforcement** (Terry, 2009): the rate or interval at which responses are reinforced. Although numerous schedules of reinforcement are possible, the most important distinction is whether they are continuous or partial. When Skinner was training his animals, he found that learning was most rapid if the response was reinforced every time it occurred—a procedure called **continuous reinforcement**.

As you have probably noticed, real life seldom provides continuous reinforcement. Yet your behaviour persists because your efforts are occasionally rewarded. Most everyday behaviour is rewarded on a **partial** (or **intermittent**) **schedule of reinforcement**, which involves reinforcing only some responses, not all (Miltenberger, 2011).

Once a task is well learned, it is important to move to a partial schedule of reinforcement. Why? Because under partial schedules, behaviour is more resistant to extinction. Four partial schedules of reinforcement may be used: **fixed ratio (FR)**, **variable ratio (VR)**, **fixed interval (FI)**, and **variable interval (VI)**. The type of partial schedule selected depends on the type of behaviour being studied and on the speed of learning desired. A fixed ratio leads to the highest overall response rate, but each of the

		Definition	Response Rates	Examples	
Ratio schedules (response based)	**Fixed ratio (FR)**	Reinforcement occurs after a predetermined set of responses; the ratio (number or amount) is fixed	Produces a high rate of response, but a brief drop-off or pause in responding just after reinforcement	A car wash employee receives $10 for every three cars washed. In a laboratory, a rat receives a food pellet every time it presses the bar seven times	
	Variable ratio (VR)	Reinforcement occurs unpredictably; the ratio (number or amount) varies	High response rates, no pause after reinforcement, and very resistant to extinction	Slot machines pay out after an average number of responses (maybe every 10 times), but any one machine may pay out on the first response, then seventh, then the twentieth	
Interval schedules (time based)	**Fixed interval (FI)**	Reinforcement occurs after a predetermined time has elapsed; the interval (time) is fixed	Responses tend to increase as the time for the reinforcer nears, but drop off after reinforcement and during interval	You get a monthly paycheque. A rat's behaviour is reinforced with a food pellet the first time it presses a bar after a period of 20 seconds has elapsed.	
	Variable interval (VI)	Reinforcement occurs unpredictably; the interval (time) varies	Relatively low response rates, but they are steady because the receiver cannot predict when reward will come	In a class with pop quizzes, you study at a slow but steady rate because you can't anticipate the next quiz. A rat's behaviour is reinforced with a food pellet for a response after an unpredictable interval of time	

four types of partial schedules has different advantages and disadvantages (see **Study Organizer 6.1**).

Partial reinforcement is described further in *What a Psychologist Sees: Partial Reinforcement Keeps 'Em Coming Back*. Each of the four schedules of partial reinforcement is important for *maintaining* behaviour. But how would you teach someone to play the piano or to speak a foreign language? For new and complex behaviours, such as these, which aren't likely to occur naturally, **shaping** is an especially valuable tool. Skinner believed that shaping explains a variety of abilities that we each possess, from eating with a fork, to playing a musical instrument, to driving a car with a stick shift. Parents, athletic coaches, teachers, and animal trainers all use shaping techniques, which involve reinforcing successively closer and closer approximations to the desired response (**Figure 6.7**).

> **shaping** The reinforcement of successively closer and closer approximations to the desired response.

Punishment: Weakening a Response

In contrast to reinforcement, punishment *decreases* the strength of a response. As with reinforcement, punishment also has two forms: positive and negative (Miltenberger, 2011; Skinner, 1953).

How does she do it? • Figure 6.7

Momoko, a female monkey, is famous in Japan for her water-skiing, deep-sea diving, and other amazing abilities. Her trainers used the successive steps of shaping to teach her these skills. First, they reinforced Momoko (with a small food treat) for standing or sitting on the water ski. Then they reinforced her each time she put her hands on the pole. Next, they slowly dragged the water ski on dry land and reinforced her for staying upright and holding the pole. Then they took Momoko to a shallow and calm part of the ocean and reinforced her for staying upright and holding the pole as the ski moved in the water. Finally, they took her into the deep part of the ocean.

Kaku Kurita/
Gamma-Rapho
via Getty Images

What a Psychologist Sees

Partial Reinforcement Keeps 'Em Coming Back

Age Fotostock/Superstock

Blend Images/iStockphoto

Have you noticed that people spend long hours pushing buttons and pulling levers on slot machines in hopes of winning the jackpot? This compulsion to keep gambling in spite of significant losses is evidence of the strong resistance to extinction with partial (or intermittent) schedules of reinforcement. Machines in Ontario casinos and racetracks, for example, have payout rates of at least 85 percent—that is, for every dollar spent, a player "wins" $0.85. These are average payouts based on hundreds of thousands of games (Ontario Lottery and Gaming Corporation, 2009). Different machines are programmed in different ways. Some meet the percentage by giving very large but infrequent payouts to a few lucky winners. Others give frequent smaller payouts to many players. In either case, people are reinforced just often enough to keep them coming back, always hoping the partial reinforcement will lead to more. The same expectations lead people to go on buying lottery tickets even though the odds of winning are very low.

This type of partial reinforcement also helps parents maintain children's positive behaviours, such as tooth brushing and bed making. After the child has initially learned these behaviours with continuous reinforcement, occasional, partial reinforcement is the most efficient way to maintain the behaviour. (Chart adapted from Skinner, 1961.)

How punishment weakens and decreases behaviours Table 6.2

Positive punishment *adds stimulus (+) and weakens the behaviour*	Negative punishment *takes stimulus away (–) and weakens the behaviour*
You must run four extra laps in your gym class because you were late.	You're excluded from participating in gym class because you were late.
A parent adds chores following a child's poor report card.	A parent takes away a teen's cellphone following a poor report card.
Your boss chews you out about your performance.	Your boss reduces your pay after a poor performance.

Positive punishment is the addition (+) of a stimulus that decreases (or weakens) the likelihood of the response occurring again. **Negative punishment** is the taking away (–) of a reinforcing stimulus, which decreases (or weakens) the likelihood of the response occurring again Table 6.2). (To check your understanding of the principles of reinforcement and punishment, see **Figure 6.8**.)

Punishment is a tricky business, and it isn't always intentional. Any process that adds or takes away something and causes a behaviour to decrease is punishment. Thus, if parents ignore all the A grades on their child's report card ("taking away" encouraging comments) and ask repeated questions about the B and C grades, they may unintentionally be punishing the child's excellent grade achievement and weakening the likelihood of future A grades. Similarly, dog owners who yell at or spank their dogs for finally coming to them ("adding" negative verbal or physical consequences) after being called several times are actually punishing the desired behaviour: coming when called.

Punishment plays an unavoidable role in our social world. Dangerous criminals must be stopped and possibly removed from society. Parents must stop their teenagers from drinking and driving. Teachers must stop disruptive students in the classroom and bullies on the playground. Yet punishment can be problematic (Borrego et al., 2007; Leary et al., 2008; Loxton et al., 2008).

To be effective, punishment should be immediate and consistent. However, in the real world, this is extremely

The Skinner box application • Figure 6.8

To test his behavioural theories, Skinner used an animal, usually a pigeon or a rat, and an apparatus that has come to be called a *Skinner box*. In Skinner's basic experimental design, an animal, such as a rat, received a food pellet each time it pushed a lever, and the number of responses was recorded. Note in this drawing that an electric grid on the cage floor could be used to deliver small electric shocks.

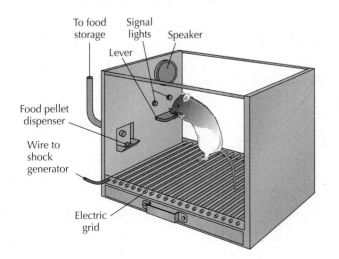

Test Yourself Is this positive reinforcement, negative reinforcement, positive punishment, or negative punishment? Fill in the name of the appropriate learning principle in the spaces provided in each box.

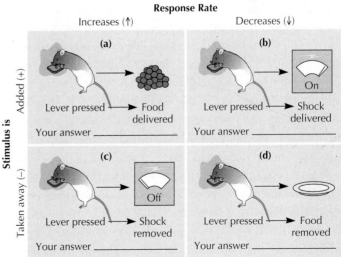

Answers: (a) positive reinforcement, (b) positive punishment, (c) negative reinforcement, (d) negative punishment

The Side Effects of Punishment

1. **Increased aggression.** Because punishment often produces a decrease in undesired behaviour, at least for the moment, the person administering the punishment is actually rewarded for applying punishment. Thus, a vicious circle may be established in which both the punisher and the recipient are reinforced for inappropriate behaviour: the punisher for punishing and the recipient for being fearful and submissive. This side effect partially explains the escalation of violence in family abuse and bullying (Anderson et al., 2008; Dodge et al., 2008; Fang & Corso, 2007). In addition to fear and submissiveness, the recipient may become depressed or respond with his or her own form of aggression.

2. **Passive aggressiveness.** For the recipient, punishment may lead to frustration, anger, and, eventually, aggression. But most of us have learned from experience that retaliatory aggression toward a punisher (especially one who is bigger and more powerful) is usually followed by more punishment. We therefore tend to control our impulse toward open aggression and instead resort to more subtle techniques, such as showing up late or forgetting to run an errand for someone. This is known as passive aggressiveness.

3. **Avoidance behaviour.** No one likes to be punished, and so we naturally try to avoid the punisher. Suppose every time you came home, a parent or spouse started to yell at you. You would delay going home or would find another place to go.

4. **Modelling.** Have you ever seen a parent spank or hit a child for hitting another child? The punishing parent may unintentionally serve as a model for the same behaviour the parent is attempting to stop—hitting.

Joel Sartore/National Geographic Stock

5. **Temporary suppression.** Do you notice that car drivers quickly slow down when they see a police car but quickly resume their previous speed once the police officer is out of sight? Punishment does not extinguish the behaviour but suppresses it only temporarily during the presence of the punishing person or circumstances.

6. **Learned helplessness.** Why do some people stay in abusive relationships? Research shows that people who repeatedly fail in their attempts to control their environment acquire a general sense of powerlessness or *learned helplessness* (Seligman, 1975) and may make no further attempts to escape even if it becomes possible (Bargai et al., 2007; Diaz-Berciano et al., 2008). (Learned helplessness is discussed in Chapter 13 as one explanation for depression.)

Think Critically

1. Why do you think drivers quickly slow down when they see a police car, and then quickly resume their previous speed once the police officer is out of sight?
2. Given all the problems associated with punishment, why is it so often used?

---

hard to do. Police officers cannot stop all drivers every time they speed. To make matters worse, when punishment is not immediate, the delay can cause the behaviour to be reinforced on a partial schedule, which makes it highly resistant to extinction. Think about gambling. It should be a punishing situation—gamblers usually lose far more than they win. However, the fact that they occasionally win keeps gamblers hanging in there.

Even if punishment immediately follows the misbehaviour, the recipient may learn what *not* to do but may not necessarily learn what he or she *should* do. It's much more effective to teach someone by giving clear examples of correct behaviour than by simply punishing the incorrect behaviour. Finally, punishment can have serious side effects.

CONCEPT CHECK STOP

1. **What** is the difference between negative reinforcement and punishment?

2. **What** are the law of effect and the Premack principle?

3. **Why** does a fixed ratio lead to the highest rate of response, compared with other schedules of reinforcement?

4. **When** is shaping most useful in learning?

Cognitive-Social Learning

LEARNING OBJECTIVES

1. **Explain** how insight and latent learning differ from the principles of classical and operant conditioning.

2. **Summarize** the evidence that animals (including humans) form internal cognitive maps.

3. **Identify** Bandura's necessary conditions for observational learning.

Both operant learning and classical conditioning involve learning associations between a stimulus and an observable behaviour. Although some behaviourists believe that almost all learning can be explained in such stimulus–response terms, other psychologists feel that there is more to learning than can be explained solely by operant and classical conditioning. **Cognitive-social theory** (also called cognitive-social learning or cognitive-behavioural theory) incorporates the general concepts of conditioning, but rather than relying on a simple S–R (stimulus and response) model, this theory emphasizes the interpretation or thinking that occurs within the organism: S–O–R (stimulus–organism–response). According to this view, people have attitudes, beliefs, expectations, motivations, and emotions that affect their learning. Furthermore, both human and non-human animals are social creatures that are capable of learning new behaviours through observation and imitation of others. We begin with a look at the *cognitive* part of cognitive-social theory, followed by an examination of the *social* aspects of learning.

> **cognitive-social theory** A perspective that emphasizes the roles of thinking and social learning in behaviour.

Insight and Latent Learning: Where Are the Reinforcers?

Early behaviourists likened the mind to a "black box" whose workings could not be observed directly. German psychologist Wolfgang Köhler wanted to look inside the box. He believed that there was more to learning—especially learning to solve a complex problem—than responding to stimuli in a trial-and-error fashion. In one of a series of experiments, he placed a banana just outside the reach of a caged chimpanzee (**Figure 6.9**). To reach the banana, the chimp had to use a stick to extend its reach. Köhler noticed that the chimp did not solve this problem in a random trial-and-error fashion but, instead,

Is this insight? • Figure 6.9

Grande, one of Köhler's chimps, has just solved the problem of how to get the banana. (Also, the thoughtful chimp in the foreground is engaged in observational learning, our next topic.)

American Philosophical Society

insight Sudden understanding of a problem that implies the solution.

seemed to sit and think about the situation for a while. Then, in a flash of **insight**, the chimp picked up the stick and manoeuvred the banana to within its grasp (Köhler, 1925).

Another of Köhler's chimps, an intelligent fellow named Sultan, was put in a similar situation. This time two sticks were available to him, and the banana was placed even farther away, too far to reach with a single stick. Sultan seemingly lost interest in the banana, but he continued to play with the sticks. When he later discovered that the two sticks could be interlocked, he instantly used the now longer stick to pull the banana within reach. Köhler designated this type of learning **insight learning** because some internal mental event that he could describe only as "insight" went on between the presentation of the banana and the use of the stick to retrieve it.

Like Köhler, Edward C. Tolman (1898–1956) believed that previous researchers underestimated animals' cognitive processes and cognitive learning. He noted that, when allowed to roam aimlessly in an experimental maze with no food reward at the end, rats seemed to develop a **cognitive map** or mental representation of the maze.

To test the idea of cognitive learning, Tolman allowed one group of rats to aimlessly explore a maze with no reinforcement. A second group was reinforced with food whenever they reached the end of the maze. The third group was not rewarded during the first 10 days of the trial, but starting on day 11 they found food at the end of the maze. As expected from simple operant conditioning, the first and third groups were slow to learn the maze, whereas the second group, which had reinforcement, showed fast, steady improvement. However, when the third group started receiving reinforcement (on the 11th day), their learning quickly caught up to the group that had been reinforced every time (Tolman & Honzik, 1930). This showed that the non-reinforced rats had been building cognitive maps of the area during their aimless wandering and that their **latent learning** only showed up

latent learning Hidden learning that exists without behavioural signs.

when there was a reason to display it (the food reward).

Cognitive maps and latent learning are not limited to rats. For example, a chipmunk will pay little attention to a new log in its territory (after initially checking it for food). When a predator comes along, however, the chipmunk heads directly for and hides beneath the log. Recent research provides additional evidence of

Is this learning? • Figure 6.10

This child often rides through her neighbourhood for fun, without a specific destination. Could she tell her mom where the nearest mailbox is located? What type of learning is this?

latent learning and the existence of internal cognitive maps in both human and non-human animals (Gómez-Laplaza & Gerlai, 2010; Lahav & Mioduser, 2008; Lew, 2011) **(Figure 6.10)**.

Observational Learning: What We See Is What We Do

In addition to classical and operant conditioning and cognitive processes (such as insight and latent learning), we also learn many things through **observational learning**. From birth to death, observational learning is very important to our biological, psychological, and social survival (the *biopsychosocial model*). Watching others helps us avoid dangerous stimuli in our environment, teaches us how to think and feel, and shows us how to act and interact socially.

observational learning The learning of new behaviour or information by watching and imitating others (also known as social learning or modelling).

Some of the most compelling examples of observational learning come from the work of Canadian-born psychologist Albert Bandura and his colleagues (Bandura, 2003; Bandura, Ross, & Ross, 1961; Bandura & Walters, 1963).

In several experiments conducted by Bandura and his colleagues, children watched an adult kick, punch, and shout at an inflated Bobo doll. Later, children who had seen the aggressive adult were much more aggressive with the Bobo doll than were those who had not seen the aggression. In other words, "monkey see, monkey

Bandura's classic Bobo doll studies • Figure 6.11

Bandura's "Bobo doll" study is considered a classic in psychology. It showed that children will imitate models they observe. Why is this new or important? Are there circumstances in which observational learning (for example, from television) could have positive effects?

With permission of Albert Bandura

do" (**Figure 6.11**). Bandura found that various characteristics of the adult model influenced whether children imitated the behaviour, including whether the model had been rewarded or punished for the aggressive behaviour (Figure 6.11). If the model had been rewarded for the behaviour, the children were more likely to imitate the behaviour, a phenomenon known as *vicarious reinforcement*.

In the same way, if the model had been reprimanded or received other negative consequences for the aggressive behaviour, children were less likely to imitate it, a phenomenon referred to as *vicarious punishment*.

According to Bandura, observational learning requires at least four separate processes: attention, retention, motor reproduction, and reinforcement (**Figure 6.12**).

Four key factors in observational learning • Figure 6.12

1. ATTENTION

Observational learning requires attention. This is why teachers insist on having students watch their demonstrations.

2. RETENTION

To learn new behaviours, we need to carefully note and remember the model's directions and demonstrations.

3. REPRODUCTION

Observational learning cannot occur if we lack the motivation or motor skills necessary to imitate the model.

4. REINFORCEMENT

We are more likely to repeat a modelled behaviour if the model is reinforced for the behaviour (vicarious reinforcement).

1. **Why** were Köhler's studies on insight in chimpanzees important?
2. **What** is a cognitive map?
3. **Why** was Bandura's work on the modelling of aggressiveness important?

The Biology of Learning

LEARNING OBJECTIVES

1. **Explain** how an animal's environment can affect learning and behaviour.
2. **Identify** an example of biological preparedness.
3. **Describe** how instinctive drift constrains learning.

So far in this chapter, we have considered how external forces—from reinforcing events to our observations of others—affect learning. But we also know that for changes in behaviour to persist over time, lasting biological changes must occur within the organism. In this section, we will examine neurological and evolutionary influences on learning.

Neuroscience and Learning: The Adaptive Brain

As Canadian psychologists Joe-Guillaume Pelletier and Denis Paré (2004) have suggested, each time we learn something, either consciously or unconsciously, that experience creates new synaptic connections and alterations in a wide network of brain structures, including the cortex, cerebellum, hypothalamus, thalamus, and amygdala (see also May et al., 2007; Möhler et al., 2008; Romero et al., 2008).

Evidence that experience changes brain structure first emerged in the 1960s from studies of animals raised in enriched versus deprived environments. Compared with rats raised in a stimulus-poor environment, those raised in a colourful, stimulating "rat Disneyland" had a thicker cortex, increased nerve growth factor (NGF), more fully developed synapses, more dendritic branching, and improved performance on many tests of learning (Harati et al., 2011; Lores-Arnaiz et al., 2007; Pham et al., 2002; Rosenzweig & Bennett, 1996).

Admittedly, it is a big leap from rats to humans, but research suggests that the human brain also responds to environmental conditions (**Figure 6.13**). For example, older adults who are exposed to stimulating environments generally perform better on intellectual and perceptual tasks than those who are in restricted environments (Daffner, 2010; Merrill & Small, 2011; Schaie, 1994, 2008).

Mirror Neurons and Imitation

Recent research has identified another neurological influence on learning processes, particularly imitation. By using fMRIs and other brain-imaging techniques (Chapter 1), researchers have identified specific mirror neurons believed to be responsible for human empathy and imitation (Ahlsén, 2008; Baird et al., 2011; Fogassi et al., 2005; Hurley, 2008; Jacob, 2008). These neurons are found in several key areas of the brain, and they help us identify with what others are feeling and to imitate their actions. When we see another person in pain, one reason we empathize and "share their pain" is that our mirror neurons are firing. Similarly, if we watch others smile, our mirror neurons make it harder for us to frown.

Mirror neurons were first discovered by neuroscientists who implanted wires in the brains of monkeys

For humans and non-human animals alike, environmental conditions play an important role in enabling learning. How might a classroom rich with stimulating toys, games, and books foster intellectual development in young children?

to monitor areas involved in planning and carrying out movement (Ferrari et al., 2005; Rizzolatti et al., 2002; Rizzolatti et al., 2006; Rizzolatti & Fabbri-Destro, 2009). When these monkeys moved and grasped an object, specific neurons fired, but they also fired when the monkeys simply observed another monkey performing the same or similar tasks.

Mirror neurons in humans also fire when we perform a movement or watch someone else perform it. Have you noticed how spectators at an athletic event sometimes slight-

ly move their arms or legs in synchrony with the athletes, or how newborns tend to imitate adults' facial expressions **Figure 6.14**)? Mirror neurons may be the underlying biological mechanism for this imitation and for an infant's copying of the lip and tongue movements necessary for speech. They also might help explain the emotional deficits of children and adults with autism or schizophrenia, who often misunderstand the verbal and non-verbal cues of others (Arbib & Mundhenk, 2005; Dapretto et al., 2006; Kana et al., 2011; Martineau et al., 2008).

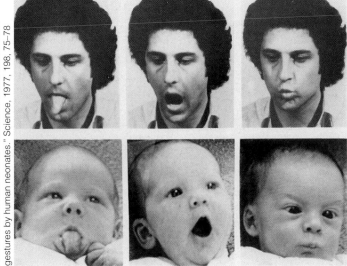

Infant imitation • Figure 6.14

In a series of classic studies, Andrew Meltzoff and M. Keith Moore (1977, 1985, 1994) found that newborns could imitate such facial movements as tongue protrusion, mouth opening, and lip pursing. Could such imitation reflect the action of mirror neurons?

Evolution and Learning: Biological Preparedness and Instinctive Drift

Humans and other animals are born with various innate reflexes and instincts. Although these biological tendencies help ensure evolutionary survival, they are inherently inflexible. Only through learning are we able to react to important environmental cues—such as spoken words and written symbols—that our innate reflexes and instincts do not address. Thus, from an evolutionary perspective, learning is an adaptation that enables organisms to survive and prosper in a constantly changing world or, more simply, to profit from experience.

Because animals can be operantly conditioned to perform a variety of novel behaviours (like water-skiing), learning theorists initially believed that the fundamental laws of conditioning would apply to almost all species and all behaviours. However, researchers have identified several biological constraints that limit the generality of conditioning principles. These include biological preparedness and instinctive drift.

Years ago, a young woman named Rebecca unsuspectingly bit into a Butterfinger candy bar filled with small, wiggling maggots. Horrified, she ran gagging and screaming to the bathroom. Many years later, Rebecca still feels nauseated when she sees a Butterfinger candy bar (but, fortunately, she doesn't feel similarly nauseated by the sight of her boyfriend, who bought her the candy).

Rebecca's graphic (and true!) story illustrates an important evolutionary process. When a food or drink is associated with nausea or vomiting, that particular food or drink can become a conditioned stimulus (CS) that triggers a conditioned **taste aversion**. Like other classically conditioned responses, taste aversions develop involuntarily (**Figure 6.15**).

Can you see why this automatic response would be adaptive? If our ancestral relatives became ill after eating a new plant, it would increase their chances for survival if they immediately developed an aversion to that plant but not to other family members who might have been present at the time. Similarly, people tend to develop *phobias* of snakes, darkness, spiders, and heights more easily than of guns, knives, and electrical outlets presumably because the former were present in the ancestral environment, while the latter were not. We apparently inherit an innate (built-in) readiness to form associations between certain stimuli and responses known as **biological preparedness**.

> **biological preparedness** Innate (built-in) readiness to form associations between certain stimuli and responses.

Laboratory experiments have provided general support for both taste aversion and biological preparedness. For example, John Garcia and Robert Koelling (1966) produced taste aversion in lab rats by pairing flavoured water (NS) and a drug

© Wildlife/Alamy

Taste aversion in the wild • Figure 6.15

In applied research, Garcia and his colleagues used classical conditioning to teach coyotes not to eat sheep (Gustavson & Garcia, 1974). The researchers began by lacing freshly killed sheep with a chemical that caused extreme nausea and vomiting in the coyotes that ate the tainted meat. The conditioning worked so well that the coyotes would run away from the mere sight and smell of sheep. This taste aversion developed involuntarily. This research has since been applied many times in the wild and in the laboratory with coyotes and other animals (Aubert & Dantzer, 2005; Domjan, 2005; Workman & Reader, 2008).

(UCS) that produced gastrointestinal distress and nausea (UCR). After being conditioned and then recovering from the illness, the rats refused to drink the flavoured water (CS) because of the conditioned taste aversion. Remarkably, however, Garcia discovered that only certain neutral stimuli could produce the nausea. Pairings of a noise (NS) or a shock (NS) with the nausea-producing drug (UCS) produced no taste aversion. Garcia suggested that when we are sick to our stomachs, we have a natural, evolutionary tendency to attribute it to food or drink. Being biologically prepared to quickly associate nausea with food or drink is adaptive because it helps us avoid that or similar food or drink in the future (Domjan, 2005; Garcia, 2003; Kardong, 2008).

Just as Garcia couldn't produce noise-nausea associations, other researchers have found that an animal's natural behaviour pattern can interfere with operant conditioning. For example, Keller Breland and Marian Breland (1961) tried to teach a chicken to play baseball. Through shaping and reinforcement, the chicken first learned to pull a loop that activated a swinging bat and then learned to actually hit the ball. But instead of running to first base, it would chase the ball as if it were food. Regardless of the lack of reinforcement for chasing the ball, the chicken's natural behaviour took precedence. This biological constraint is known as **instinctive drift**.

> **instinctive drift**
> The tendency of some conditioned responses to shift (or drift) back toward innate response patterns.

CONCEPT CHECK

1. **What** changes occur in rats' brains when they are raised in an enriched (versus a deprived) environment?

2. **Why** is taste aversion evolutionarily adaptive?

3. **Why** don't the fundamental laws of conditioning apply to all species and all behaviours?

Conditioning and Learning in Everyday Life

LEARNING OBJECTIVES

1. **Explain** how classical conditioning applies to prejudice, marketing, medical treatments, and phobias.

2. **Explain** the role of operant conditioning in prejudice, biofeedback, and superstition.

3. **Describe** how cognitive-social learning applies to prejudice and to media influences on behaviour.

 n this section, we discuss several everyday applications for classical conditioning, operant conditioning, and cognitive-social learning.

Classical Conditioning: From Prejudice to Phobias

One common—and very negative—instance of classical conditioning is prejudice. In a classic study in the 1930s, Kenneth Clark and Mamie P. Clark (1939) found that given a choice, both black and white children preferred white dolls to black dolls. In fact, both groups of children responded that the white doll was good and that the black doll was bad. The Clarks reasoned that the children had learned to associate negative qualities with darker skin and positive qualities with lighter skin. Such learned associations may in part explain racism and prejudice today.

Classical conditioning is also a primary tool for marketing and advertising professionals, filmmakers and musicians, medical practitioners, psychotherapists, and politicians who want to influence our purchases, emotions, health behaviour, motivations, and votes.

Instances of classical conditioning are also found in the medical field. For example, for alcoholic patients, some hospitals pair the smell and taste of alcohol with a nausea-producing drug. Afterward, just the smell or taste of alcohol makes the person sick. Some patients, although not all, have found this treatment successful (Chapter 14).

Applying Psychology

Classical Conditioning as a Marketing Tool

Jodi Cobb/National Geographic Stock

Marketers have mastered numerous classical conditioning principles. For example, TV commercials, magazine ads, and business promotions often pair a company's products or logo (the neutral stimulus/NS) with pleasant images, such as attractive models and celebrities (the conditioned stimulus/CS), which, through higher-order conditioning, automatically trigger favourable responses (the conditioned response/CR). Advertisers hope that after repeated viewings, the previously neutral stimulus (the company's products or logo) will become a conditioned stimulus that elicits a favourable response (CR)—we buy the advertised products. Researchers caution that these ads also help produce visual stimuli that trigger conditioned responses, such as urges to smoke, overeat, and drink alcohol (Kazdin, 2008; Martin et al., 2002; Tirodkar & Jain, 2003; Wakefield et al., 2003).

To appreciate the influences of classical conditioning on your own life, try this:

- Look through a popular magazine and find several advertisements. What images are used as the unconditioned stimulus (UCS) or conditioned stimulus (CS)? Note how you react to these images.

- While watching a movie or a favourite TV show, note what sounds and images are used as conditioned stimuli (CS).

(Hint: certain types of music are used to set the stage for happy stories, sad events, and fearful situations.) What are your conditioned emotional responses (CERs)?

Think Critically

1. In what way is the ad pictured here an application of psychology?
2. Can you think of other situations in which sounds and images are used as conditioned stimuli?

Conditioned emotional responses
• Figure 6.16

Classically conditioned emotional responses can explain the development of extreme fears, such as the fear of riding in elevators.

© Pierre Perrin/Zoko/Sygma/Corbis

Finally, researchers have found that classically conditioned emotional responses explain most everyday fears and even most *phobias*, which are exaggerated and irrational fears of a specific object or situation (**Figure 6.16**) (Cai et al., 2006; Field, 2006; Schweckendiek et al., 2011; Stein & Matsunga, 2006). The good news is that extreme fears—for example, of heights, spiders, or public places—can be effectively treated with *behaviour therapy* (Chapter 14).

Operant Conditioning: Prejudice, Biofeedback, and Superstition

Just as people can learn prejudice through classical conditioning, we also can learn prejudice through operant conditioning. Demeaning and bullying others gains attention and sometimes approval from others. Indeed, as Canadian researchers Debra Pepler and Wendy Craig (Hawkins, Pepler, & Craig, 2001) have noted, the reactions of others can encourage (or discourage) bullying and victimization (we discuss bullying further in Chapter 15). Positive reactions by others can positively

Visualizing

Operant conditioning in everyday life • Figure 6.17

a. Prejudice and Discrimination

What reinforcement might these boys receive for teasing this girl? Can you see how operant conditioning, beginning at an early age, can promote unkind or prejudiced behaviour?

Image Source/Getty Images

b. Biofeedback

In biofeedback, internal bodily processes (such as blood pressure, muscle tension, or neural activity) are electrically recorded and reported back to the patient. This information helps the person gain control over processes that are normally involuntary. Researchers have successfully used biofeedback (usually in conjunction with other techniques, such as behaviour modification) to treat hypertension, anxiety, epilepsy, urinary incontinence, cognitive functioning, chronic pain, and headache (Andrasik, 2006; Bohm-Starke et al., 2007; Hammond, 2007; Kazdin, 2008; Moss, 2004; Stokes & Lappin, 2010; Wheat & Larkin, 2010).

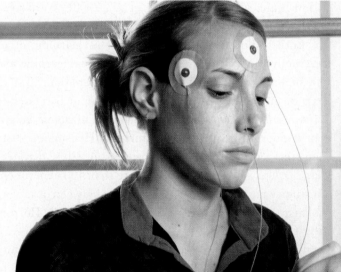

Flirt/SuperStock

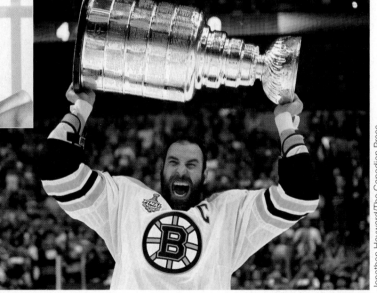

Jonathan Hayward/The Canadian Press

c. Superstition

Like Skinner's pigeons, we humans also believe in many superstitions that may have developed from accidental reinforcement: from wearing "something old" during one's wedding, to knocking on wood for good fortune, to not shaving during the Stanley Cup Playoffs.

reinforce prejudice and discrimination and may increase the instigator's self-esteem, at the expense of the victim (Fein & Spencer, 1997; Rigby, 2008; Kassin et al., 2008; Salmivalli et al., 2011) (**Figure 6.17a**). People also may have a single negative (punishing) experience with a specific member of a group, which they then generalize and apply to all members of the group—an example of stimulus generalization.

But what explains behaviour that is extreme, such as the vandalism and rioting that followed the Vancouver Canucks' loss in the 2011 Stanley Cup final game? Why would people do anything that they know could bring a major fine or even imprisonment? Punishment does weaken and suppress behaviour, but as mentioned before, to be effective it must be consistent and immediate. Unfortunately, it seldom is. Instead, when a person gets away with one or more crimes, that criminal behaviour is put on a partial (intermittent) schedule of reinforcement, making it more likely to be repeated and to become more resistant to extinction.

Biofeedback is another example of operant conditioning in action (**Figure 6.17b**). Something is added (feedback) that increases the likelihood that the behaviour will be repeated—positive reinforcement. The biofeedback itself is a secondary reinforcer because of the learned value of the relief from pain or other aversive stimuli (primary reinforcer). Finally, biofeedback involves shaping. A person using biofeedback watches a monitor screen (or other instrument) that provides graphs or numbers indicating some bodily state. Like a mirror, the biofeedback reflects back the results of the various strategies that the participant uses to gain control. Through trial and error, the participant gets progressively better at making the desired changes.

Even accidental reinforcement can exert a powerful effect, sometimes causing superstitious behaviour (**Figure 6.17c**). In a fascinating experiment, B. F. Skinner (1948, 1992) set the feeding mechanism in the cages of eight pigeons to release food once every 15 seconds. No matter what the birds did, they were reinforced at 15-second intervals. Six of the pigeons acquired behaviours that they repeated over and over, even though the behaviours were not necessary to receive the food. For example, one pigeon kept turning in counter-clockwise circles, and another kept making jerking movements with its head. Why did this happen?

Although Skinner was not using the food to reinforce any particular behaviour, the pigeons associated the food with whatever behaviour they were engaged in when the food was originally dropped into the cage.

Cognitive-Social Learning: We See, We Do?

We use cognitive-social learning in many ways in our everyday lives, yet two of the most powerful areas of learning are frequently overlooked: prejudice and media influences. Prejudice and other negative attitudes can be learned through observing others, particularly those whom we admire. For example, a 7-year-old in Winnipeg went to school with a swastika drawn on her arm. Her teacher scrubbed it off, but her mother helped her redraw it the next day. Child and Family Services investigated and found that her parents were involved in white supremacist activities, that she had watched skinhead videos with them, and that her home, where she lived with her 2-year-old brother, contained neo-Nazi symbols and flags (CBC News, 2009a). What kinds of attitudes might be learned through such modelling?

The media also propagate some forms of prejudice. When children watch television, go to the movies, and read books and magazines that portray minorities and women in demeaning or stereotypical roles, they learn to expect these behaviours and to accept them as "natural." Exposure of this kind initiates and reinforces the learning of prejudice (Dill & Thill, 2007; Kassin et al., 2008; Neto & Furnham, 2005; Berenbaum et al., 2008). We discuss prejudice further in Chapter 15.

Both children and adults may be learning other destructive behaviours through observational learning and the media. Correlational evidence from more than 50 studies indicates that observing violent behaviour is related to later desensitization and the performance of violent behaviour (Anderson et al., 2008; Bushman & Huesmann, 2010; Comstock & Scharrer, 2006; Coyne et al., 2004; Kronenberger et al., 2005). In addition, more than 100 experimental studies have also shown a causal link between observing violence and later performing it (Primavera & Herron, 1996). Moreover, the findings of a classic study that investigated the impact of the introduction of television into a Canadian community in the 1970s are telling: prior to the development of the Internet, and before cablevision and satellite television were widely available, there were few media models in this community. This "natural experiment" revealed that the introduction of a single television station (where there had previously been no television service) was associated with increases in both sex-typed attitudes and aggressive behaviour in the child residents of the community (Joy, Kimball, & Zabrack, 1986; Kimball, 1986).

Researchers are just beginning to study how video games (and virtual reality games) affect behaviour (**Figure 6.18**). For example, studies have found that students who play more violent video games in junior high and high school also engage in more aggressive behaviours (Anderson et al., 2007; Anderson et al., 2010; Bushman & Huesmann, 2010;

Video games and aggression • Figure 6.18

Researchers hypothesize that video games are more likely to model aggressive behaviour because, unlike TV and other media, they are interactive and engrossing, and require the player to identify with the aggressor. What forms of learning might be involved in this phenomenon?

Ariana Cubillos/AP/The Canadian Press

Carnagey, Anderson, & Bartholow, 2007; Gentile et al., 2004; Wei, 2007). Playing violent video games is associated with increases in aggressive behaviour, aggressive thoughts, aggressive emotions, and physiological arousal (Anderson, Carnagey, et al., 2004). Furthermore, playing violent video games has been found to desensitize players to real-life violence, which may then make them less likely to help others in distress (Anderson, 2004; Anderson et al., 2007; Anderson et al., 2010; Bushman & Anderson, 2009; Carnagey, Anderson, & Bushman, 2007; Gentile et al., 2004). How long these consequences last is unclear. Although it is likely that they dissipate as the effects of the game wear off, the implications for children who consume a steady diet of such violence remain to be examined (Carnagey, Anderson, & Bushman, 2007). We discuss the issue of media and video game violence and aggressive behaviour further in Chapter 15.

CONCEPT CHECK STOP

1. **In what ways** do classical conditioning, operant conditioning, and cognitive-social learning all contribute to prejudice?

2. **How** can "accidental reinforcement" affect behaviour?

3. **Why** might violent video games foster aggressiveness?

Summary

✓ THE PLANNER

1 Classical Conditioning 156

- **Learning** is a relatively permanent change in behaviour or mental processes as a result of practice or experience. Pavlov discovered a fundamental form of **conditioning** (learning) called **classical conditioning**, in which a **neutral stimulus** becomes associated with an **unconditioned stimulus** to elicit a **conditioned response**. In the "Little Albert" experiment, Watson and Rayner demonstrated how many of our likes, dislikes, prejudices, and fears are **conditioned emotional responses**.

Conditioning and the case of Little Albert • Figure 6.2

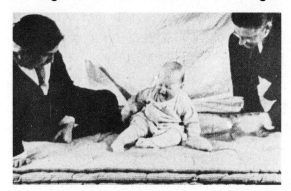

- **Stimulus generalization** occurs when an event similar to the originally **conditioned stimulus** triggers the same conditioned response. With experience, animals learn to distinguish between an original conditioned stimulus and similar stimuli—**stimulus discrimination**. Most learned behaviours can be weakened through extinction. **Extinction** is a gradual weakening or suppression of a previously conditioned response. However, if a conditioned stimulus is reintroduced after extinction, an extinguished response may spontaneously recover.

2 Operant Conditioning 161

- In **operant conditioning**, an organism performs a behaviour that produces either reinforcement or punishment. **Reinforcement** strengthens the response, while **punishment** weakens the response.

- Thorndike proposed the **law of effect**, a first step in understanding how consequences can modify voluntary behaviours. Skinner extended Thorndike's law of effect to more complex behaviours.

- Reinforcers can be either primary or secondary, and reinforcement can be either positive or negative. Reinforcement always strengthens a response. **Positive reinforcement** strengthens behaviour by adding positive consequences. **Negative reinforcement** strengthens behaviour through the removal of unpleasant stimulation.

- **Schedules of reinforcement** are the rate or interval at which responses are reinforced. Most behaviour is rewarded on one of four partial schedules of reinforcement: **fixed ratio**, **variable ratio**, **fixed interval**, or **variable interval**.

- Organisms learn complex behaviours through **shaping**, in which reinforcement is delivered for successive approximations of the desired response.

- Punishment weakens the response. To be effective, punishment must be immediate and consistent. Even

How reinforcement strengthens and increases behaviours • Table 6.1

then, the recipient may learn only what not to do. Punishment can have serious side effects: increased aggression, avoidance behaviour, passive aggressiveness, and learned helplessness.

3 Cognitive-Social Learning 167

- **Cognitive-social theory** emphasizes cognitive and social aspects of learning. Köhler discovered that animals sometimes learn through sudden **insight,** rather than through trial and error. Tolman provided evidence of **latent learning** and internal **cognitive maps**.

- Bandura's research found that children who watched an adult behave aggressively toward an inflated Bobo doll were later more aggressive than those who had not seen the aggression. According to Bandura, **observational learning** requires attention, retention, motor reproduction, and reinforcement. Children's behaviour can be influenced by their observations of the consequences of the model's behaviour (vicarious reinforcement and vicarious punishment).

Is this insight?
• Figure 6.9

4 The Biology of Learning 170

- Learning creates structural changes in the brain. Early evidence for such changes came from research on animals raised in enriched versus deprived environments.

- Learning is an evolutionary adaptation that enables organisms to survive and prosper in a constantly changing world. Researchers have identified biological constraints that limit the generality of conditioning principles: **biological preparedness** and **instinctive drift**.

Taste aversion in the wild • Figure 6.15

5 Conditioning and Learning in Everyday Life 173

- Classical conditioning is a primary tool for advertisers and others who want to manipulate beliefs, emotions, or behaviour by pairing a company's product with pleasant images. Classical conditioning is also used in medicine. It is also involved in the development and treatment of phobias.

- Operant conditioning plays a role in the development of prejudice, as the reactions of others can encourage (or discourage) demeaning behaviour. Operant conditioning also underlies **biofeedback**. Even accidental reinforcement can cause superstitious behaviour.

- Cognitive-social learning plays a role in many areas of everyday life through modelling and observational learning, including the development of prejudice and media influences on our behaviour.

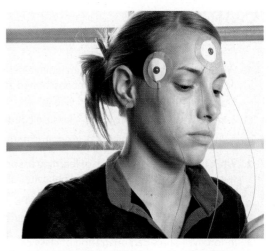

Operant conditioning in everyday life
• Figure 6.17

Key Terms

- biofeedback p. 176
- biological preparedness p. 172
- classical conditioning p. 156
- cognitive map p. 168
- cognitive-social theory p. 167
- conditioned emotional responses p. 158
- conditioned response (CR) p. 156
- conditioned stimulus (CS) p. 156
- conditioning p. 156
- continuous reinforcement p. 162
- extinction p. 158
- fixed interval (FI) p. 162
- fixed ratio (FR) p. 162
- higher-order conditioning p. 160

- insight p. 168
- insight learning p. 168
- instinctive drift p. 173
- latent learning p. 168
- law of effect p. 161
- learning p. 156
- negative punishment p. 165
- negative reinforcement p. 162
- neutral stimulus (NS) p. 156
- observational learning p. 168
- operant conditioning p. 161
- partial (or intermittent) schedule of reinforcement p. 162
- positive punishment p. 165
- positive reinforcement p. 162

- Premack principle p. 162
- punishment p. 161
- reconditioning p. 160
- reinforcement p. 161
- schedules of reinforcement p. 162
- shaping p. 163
- spontaneous recovery p. 159
- stimulus discrimination p. 158
- stimulus generalization p. 158
- taste aversion p. 172
- unconditioned response (UCR) p. 156
- unconditioned stimulus (UCS) p. 156
- variable interval (VI) p. 162
- variable ratio (VR) p. 162

Critical and Creative Thinking Questions

1. How might Watson and Rayner, who conducted the famous "Little Albert" study, have designed a more ethical study of conditioned emotional responses? Think in terms of the four ethical principles outlined by the Canadian Psychological Association (Chapter 1).

2. What are some examples of ways in which you have benefited from observational learning in your life? Are there instances in which observational learning has worked to your disadvantage?

3. Have you ever experienced a conditioned taste aversion? What principles of learning described in this chapter could be used to help remove a taste aversion?

4. Classical conditioning involves involuntary learning. Considering this, is it ethical for politicians and advertisers to use classical conditioning to influence our thoughts and behaviour? Why or why not?

5. Consider the effects of classical conditioning in your own life. Can you think of conditioned stimuli (CS) that elicit conditioned responses (CR) in you?

6. What are some things you use as positive reinforcers? How do you reward yourself after studying hard, completing a paper, exercising, and so on? Do you use the Premack principle?

Self-Test

(Check your answers in Appendix A.)

1. What form of conditioning occurs when a neutral stimulus becomes associated with an unconditioned stimulus (UCS) to elicit a conditioned response (CR)?

   a. reflexive conditioning   c. classical conditioning

   b. instinctive conditioning d. operant conditioning

2. What do we call the process of learning associations between environmental stimuli and behavioural responses?

   a. maturation   c. conditioning

   b. contiguity learning   d. latent learning

3. In John Watson's demonstration of classical conditioning with Little Albert, what was the unconditioned stimulus?

   a. symptoms of fear   c. a bath towel

   b. a rat   d. a loud noise

4. Which of the following is an example of classical conditioning in everyday life?

   a. treating alcoholism with a drug that causes nausea when alcohol is consumed

   b. the use of seductive women to sell cars to men

   c. politicians associating themselves with families, babies, and the Canadian flag

   d. all of these options

5. Extinction _____.

   a. is a gradual weakening or suppression of a previously conditioned behaviour

   b. occurs when a CS is repeatedly presented without the UCS

   c. is a weakening of the association between the CS and the UCS

   d. all of these options

6. A neutral stimulus (NS) is paired with a previously conditioned stimulus (CS) and thereby becomes a conditioned stimulus (CS) itself. What do we call this kind of learning?

   a. operant conditioning

   b. classical conditioning

   c. higher-order conditioning

   d. secondary conditioning

7. What is the term for learning in which voluntary responses are controlled by their consequences?

   a. self-control   c. operant conditioning

   b. classical conditioning d. higher-order conditioning

8. Match the illustration with the correct label:

   a. Thorndike box: law of effect, photo __2__

   b. Skinner box: reinforcement, photo __1__

   1.

   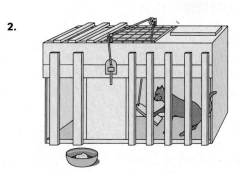

   2.

   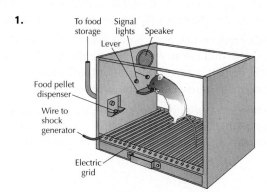

9. The addition of a(n) _____ stimulus results in *positive reinforcement*; whereas the subtraction of a(n) _____ stimulus results in *negative reinforcement*.

   a. desirable; painful or unpleasant

   b. primary; secondary

   c. operant; classical

   d. higher order; lower order

10. How did the chimpanzee in Köhler's *insight* experiment behave?

   a. It used trial-and-error to reach a banana placed just out of reach.

   b. It turned its back on the banana out of frustration.

   c. It sat for a while, then used a stick to bring the banana within reach.

   d. It didn't like bananas.

11. Learning new behaviour or information by watching others is known as _____.

    a. social learning
    b. observational learning
    c. modelling
    d. all of the above

12. Garcia and colleagues taught coyotes to avoid sheep by pairing a nausea-inducing drug with freshly killed sheep that was then eaten by the coyotes. This is an example of which of the following?

    a. classical conditioning
    b. operant conditioning
    c. positive punishment
    d. negative punishment

13. Mamie had an electromyography (EMG) done. When tension rises, a computer says, "That's too high." When it drops to normal or lower levels, it says, "That's very good." What is Mamie using to decrease her tension headaches?

    a. primary reinforcement
    b. computerized reinforcement
    c. biofeedback
    d. electromyography monitoring

14. According to the chapter, what is the consequence of exposure to media portrayals of demeaning and stereotypical roles for minorities and women?

    a. It increases critical thinking about minorities and women.
    b. It initiates and reinforces the learning of prejudice.
    c. It increases empathy for minorities and women.
    d. It decreases a child's stereotypical gender-role behaviour.

15. Which of the following increases modelling effects of violent video games?

    a. Videos are interactive.
    b. Videos are engrossing to the player.
    c. Video players identify with the aggressor in the game.
    d. All of these options.

16. Which of the following is an example of stimulus generalization?

    a. responding to the conditioned stimulus, but not to other stimuli that closely resemble it
    b. working hard at school to get a financial reward from your dad
    c. responding to other stimuli that closely resemble the conditioned stimulus
    d. getting out of bed at 3 a.m. to turn on the air conditioner because you cannot sleep

17. The Premack principle is best demonstrated by which of the following?

    a. Johnny does his best in school to get the new bike his parents promised him.
    b. Bianca stays away from people who remind her of her ex-boyfriend, to avoid thinking about him.
    c. Jimmy schedules studying time with a girl he likes in the hope that she will become attracted to him.
    d. Lisa does 2 hours of intense studying before allowing herself to watch her favourite TV show.

18. Which of the following best describes an *unconditioned stimulus*?

    a. forgetting a previously strong association between two stimuli
    b. a previously conditioned stimulus that no longer elicits a response
    c. a stimulus you respond to without having to learn its association with another stimulus
    d. trying to show a favourable reaction to a stimulus, regardless of what you think of it

19. After seeing his older brother throw rocks at a nasty dog, Vinny throws some of his toys at it too. Vinny's behaviour is best explained by which of the following?

    a. classical conditioning
    b. operant conditioning
    c. observational learning
    d. insight learning

20. Which researcher discovered that behaviours rewarded with something desirable are likely to be repeated? This is what type of conditioning?

    a. Skinner; operant conditioning
    b. Pavlov; classical conditioning
    c. Pavlov; operant conditioning
    d. Thorndike; operant conditioning

THE PLANNER ✓

Review your Chapter Planner on the chapter opener and check off your completed work.

Memory

When Henry Molaison was 27 years old, portions of his temporal lobes and limbic system were removed to treat severe epilepsy. The surgery was successful—that is, his seizures could now be controlled, but something was clearly wrong with his memory. Two years after the surgery, he still believed he was 27. He had to be repeatedly reminded of events that had occurred after his surgery. More than 50 years later, Henry could not recognize the people who cared for his daily needs or the features of his own room. He would read the same magazines over and over again and laugh at the same old jokes he had been told dozens of times before. Right into his 80s, he still saw himself as a young man and did not recognize a photograph of his own face (Corkin, 2002).

For more than three decades, Dr. Brenda Milner of the Montreal Neurological Institute worked with and studied Henry. Dr. Milner showed that while Henry could not remember things from one day from the next, on some of the tasks she administered his performance improved significantly. This occurred even though Henry had no memory of any prior exposure to the task.

Henry Molaison died at the age of 82 in December 2008. For most of his life he was recognized as the most important patient in the history of neuroscience. As a case study, he helped researchers and the medical community understand the biological basis of human learning and memory. Two generations of psychology students before you learned about this man, who was known to us only as H.M.

In December 2009, Henry Molaison's brain was sectioned into 2,401 paper-thin slices (see photo) and it now resides at the University of California, San Diego.

The Brain Observatory

CHAPTER OUTLINE

CHAPTER PLANNER ✓

- ❏ Study the picture and read the opening story.
- ❏ Scan the Learning Objectives in each section:
  p. 184 ❏   p. 194 ❏   p. 198 ❏   p. 202 ❏
- ❏ Read the text and study all visuals.
  Answer any questions.

Analyze key features

- ❏ Process Diagram, p. 184 ❏   p. 188 ❏   p. 199 ❏
- ❏ Applying Psychology, p. 186 ❏   p. 193 ❏   p. 202 ❏
- ❏ What a Psychologist Sees, p. 187
- ❏ Study Organizer, p. 189
- ❏ Visualizing, p. 192
- ❏ Psychological Science, p. 196 ❏   p. 200 ❏
- ❏ Stop: Answer the Concept Checks before you go on:
  p. 194 ❏   p. 198 ❏   p. 201 ❏   p. 205 ❏

End of chapter

- ❏ Review the Summary and Key Terms.
- ❏ Answer the Critical and Creative Thinking Questions.
- ❏ Complete the Self-Test and check your answers.

The Nature of Memory

LEARNING OBJECTIVES

1. **Review** the principles of the two major memory models.

2. **Describe** the different purposes of sensory memory, short-term memory, and long-term memory.

3. **Understand** the relationship between short-term memory and working memory.

4. **Identify** ways of extending the duration and capacity of short-term memory.

5. **Describe** the various types of long-term memory.

6. **Explain** how organization, elaborative rehearsal, and retrieval cues improve long-term memory.

Memory allows us to profit from our experiences and to adjust to ever-changing environments. Without memory we would not learn from past events or adapt to future situations. Consider Henry Molaison for a second as you read this paragraph; it is memory that makes the present meaningful and the future understandable. Yet our memories are also highly fallible. Although some people think of **memory** as a gigantic library or an automatic event recorder, our memories are never perfect records of events. Instead, memory is a *constructive and re-creative process* through which we actively organize and shape information. Memory is

> **memory** An internal record or representation of some prior event or experience.

malleable. As you might expect, the belief that memory is accurate and precise often leads to serious errors and biases, which we'll discuss throughout this chapter.

How Does Memory Work?

Over the years, psychologists have developed numerous models (or abstract representations) of how memory might operate. As emerging research has provided insights into memory, older models have largely been abandoned. In this first section, we briefly discuss the two approaches that have the most empirical evidence and have withstood research scrutiny: the information-processing model and the three-stage model. As you will see, these two

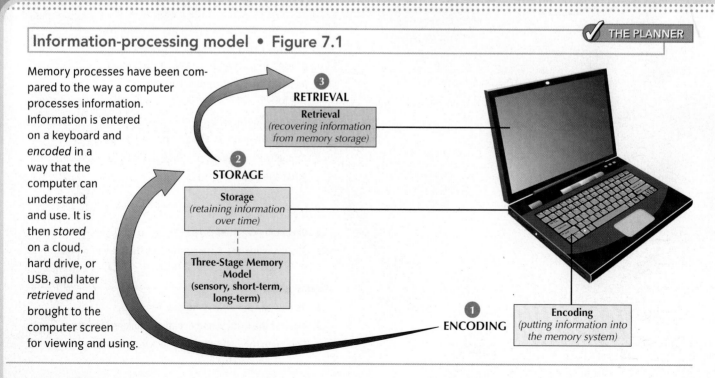

PROCESS DIAGRAM

Information-processing model • Figure 7.1

✔ THE PLANNER

Memory processes have been compared to the way a computer processes information. Information is entered on a keyboard and *encoded* in a way that the computer can understand and use. It is then *stored* on a cloud, hard drive, or USB, and later *retrieved* and brought to the computer screen for viewing and using.

③ RETRIEVAL
Retrieval *(recovering information from memory storage)*

② STORAGE
Storage *(retaining information over time)*

Three-Stage Memory Model *(sensory, short-term, long-term)*

① ENCODING
Encoding *(putting information into the memory system)*

models actually mesh together nicely to provide a more comprehensive understanding of memory.

Information-processing model

According to the **information-processing model**, the barrage of information that we encounter every day goes through three basic levels of processing: **encoding**, **storage**, and **retrieval** (**Figure 7.1**).

> **encoding** Processing information into the memory system.
>
> **storage** Retaining information over time.
>
> **retrieval** Recovering information from memory storage.

With this information-processing model of memory, the brain encodes sensory information, such as sounds or visual images, into a neural code that it can understand and use; stores the information for later use; and retrieves information by searching for the appropriate stored "files" and bringing them back into short-term memory where they can be worked with. These operations are analogous to incoming information being typed on a keyboard and translated into computer language, stored on a drive or cloud, and retrieved when brought to the computer screen to be viewed.

Before we encode anything, the information has to first get in. This occurs when we pay attention to something. Attention is the focused awareness we direct at some object or event while tuning out most everything else. When you attend to something, you impose a filter on your surroundings that allows only a portion of it into conscious awareness. Attention can be selective or divided. Divided attention usually results in "attentional multitasking," which means neither task gets your full and focused attention. This is one reason why driving and texting is so dangerous. In order to do both, your brain must momentarily switch attention between driving and then texting (Wilson & Stimpson, 2010). Between 2001 and 2007, 16,000 American road fatalities were attributed to people texting while driving (Wilson & Stimpson, 2010). Similarly, cellphone use while driving also involves divided attention (and increased risk of a crash), even when using a hands-free device (Collet et al., 2010; Kemker et al., 2009; Strayer et al., 2006). Because of this increased risk of injury or death, many provinces have outlawed driving while using a cellphone (Hands-Free Info, 2012). Despite this, many people continue to text and use a cellphone while driving, even with passengers, including children, in their vehicles (Harrison, 2011).

With selective or focused attention we tend to process the information at a much deeper level, and with deeper-level processing comes an enhanced memory of the event or object (Craik & Tulving, 1975). This is good to remember when you are preparing for a midterm or final exam. Simply reading over the text in a distracting environment will not result in good memory of its contents.

The three-stage model

Since the late 1960s, one of the most widely used models in memory research is called the **three-stage memory model** (Atkinson & Shiffrin, 1968). According to this model, memory comprises three different storage "boxes," or memory stages (sensory, short-term, and long-term), that each hold and process information in a specific way. Each stage has a different purpose, duration, and capacity, and specific terms are used to describe when information is moving between the stages (**Figure 7.2**).

The three-stage memory model • Figure 7.2

Each "box" represents a separate memory system that differs in function, duration, and capacity. When information is not transferred from sensory memory or short-term memory, it is assumed to be lost. Information stored in long-term memory can be retrieved and sent back to short-term memory for use.

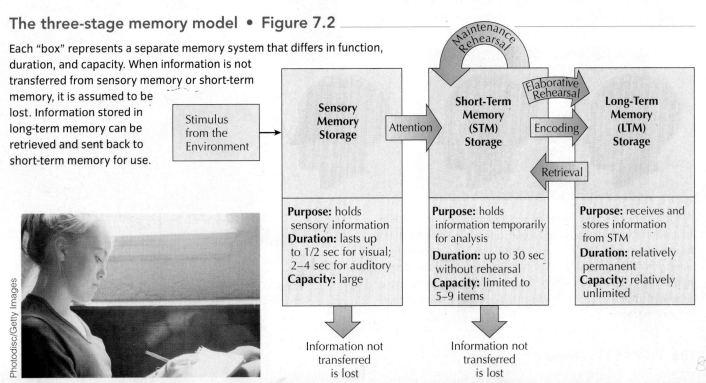

Photodisc/Getty Images

Stimulus from the Environment

Sensory Memory Storage
Attention
Short-Term Memory (STM) Storage
Encoding
Long-Term Memory (LTM) Storage

Maintenance Rehearsal
Elaborative Rehearsal
Retrieval

Purpose: holds sensory information
Duration: lasts up to 1/2 sec for visual; 2–4 sec for auditory
Capacity: large

Purpose: holds information temporarily for analysis
Duration: up to 30 sec without rehearsal
Capacity: limited to 5–9 items

Purpose: receives and stores information from STM
Duration: relatively permanent
Capacity: relatively unlimited

Information not transferred is lost

Information not transferred is lost

Sensory Memory: First Impressions

Everything we see, hear, touch, taste, and smell first enters our sensory memory. Information remains in **sensory memory** momentarily; if we attend to this new information, it is then transferred to the next stage of memory. For visual information, known as *iconic memory*, the visual image (icon) lasts around a half of a second (**Figure 7.3**). Auditory information (what we hear) is held in sensory memory for about the same time, but a weaker "echo," or *echoic memory*, of this auditory information can last up to four seconds (Lu, Williamson, & Kaufman, 1992; Neisser, 1967). Both iconic and sensory memory are demonstrated in *Applying Psychology: Demonstrating Iconic and Echoic Memory*.

> **sensory memory**
> The first memory stage that holds sensory information and has a relatively large capacity but a duration of only a few seconds.

How do researchers test sensory memory?
• Figure 7.3

In an early study of sensory memory, George Sperling (1960) flashed an arrangement of letters, like these, for 1/20 of a second. When told to recall the total arrangement in free recall, most people, he found, could recall only four or five letters. But when instructed to report just the top, middle, or bottom row, depending on whether they heard a randomly presented high, medium, or low tone after seeing the matrix, people reported almost all the letters correctly. It seems that all 12 letters are held in sensory memory right after they are viewed, but only those that are immediately attended to are noted and processed.

K	Z	R	A
Q	B	T	P
S	G	N	Y

Applying Psychology

 THE PLANNER

Demonstrating Iconic and Echoic Memory

As mentioned, visual and auditory information remains in sensory memory for a short time. For a simple demonstration of the duration of visual, or *iconic memory*, wave a lit sparkler when it is dark outside. Because the image, or icon, lingers for a fraction of a second after the sparkler is moved, you see the light as a continuous stream rather than a trail of individual points.

NuStock/iStockphoto

Auditory, or *echoic memory*, works similarly. Think back to a time when someone asked you a question while you were deeply absorbed in a task. Did you say "What?" and then immediately found you could answer them before they repeated the statement? Now you know why. You responded to the weaker "echo" (echoic memory) of auditory information reverberating in your sensory memory.

Mediaphotos/iStockphoto

Think Critically

1. What do you think would happen if we did not possess iconic or echoic memory?
2. What might happen if visual or auditory sensations lingered not for seconds but for minutes?

Early researchers believed that sensory memory had an unlimited capacity. However, later research suggested that sensory memory does have limits and that stored images are fuzzier than once thought (Goldstein, 2008; Grondin et al., 2004).

Short-Term Memory: "Working With" Memory

The second stage of memory processing, **short-term memory (STM)**, temporarily stores and processes sensory stimuli that has been attended to. Whatever you are thinking about right now is in your short-term memory. If the information is meaningful, STM organizes and sends it along to relatively permanent storage, called long-term memory (LTM). Otherwise, it decays and is lost. STM can also access stored memories from LTM.

short-term memory (STM) This second memory stage temporarily stores encoded sensory information and decides whether to send it on to long-term memory (LTM). Its capacity is limited to five to nine items, and its duration is about 30 seconds.

The *capacity* of STM is limited to seven items (plus or minus two) and its *duration* lasts about 30 seconds (Best, 1999; Kareev, 2000; Mathy & Feldman, 2012). To extend the *capacity* of STM, you might use a memory technique called **chunking** (Boucher & Dienes, 2003; Miller, 1956). Have you noticed that credit card, social insurance, and telephone numbers are all grouped into three or four units separated by spaces? This is because it's easier to remember numbers in "chunks" rather than as a long string of single digits. Different types of information can also be chunked, as shown in *What a Psychologist Sees: Chunking and Elite Athletes*.

chunking The act of grouping separate pieces of information into a single unit (or chunk).

You can extend the *duration* of your STM almost indefinitely by consciously repeating the information, a process called **maintenance rehearsal**. You are using maintenance rehearsal when you look up a phone number and say it over and over again in your head until you dial the number. We sometimes use

maintenance rehearsal Repeating information to keep it active and reverberating in short-term memory.

What a Psychologist Sees

Chunking and Elite Athletes

What do you see when you look at this playing field? To the novice spectator, a soccer game in progress can look like a random scattering of players. To an elite athlete playing the game, the players form meaningful patterns—classic arrangements they have seen before. Seeing a game in this way allows the experienced athlete more cognitive space to think about other things, such as rapidly reacting to the next play. Just as you group the letters of this sentence into meaningful words and remember them long enough to understand the meaning of the entire sentence, elite team sport athletes group players into patterns (or chunks) to quickly evaluate game dynamics.

Pascale Beroujon/Lonely Planet/Getty Images

maintenance rehearsal when we are trying to remember people's names when being introduced to a group. By repeating the name of each person a few times we try to keep it active in STM. As you are probably aware, once you stop maintenance rehearsal the information is often forgotten.

"Working with" memory Short-term memory is more than just a passive, temporary "holding area." Most current researchers (Baddeley, 1992; Baddeley & Jarrold, 2007; Jonides et al., 2008) realize that active processing of information occurs in STM. Because short-term memory is dynamic, and its contents are constantly being cognitively massaged, we can think of STM as **working memory**. Ongoing research in this area suggests working memory has three parts (**Figure 7.4**).

Components of working memory • Figure 7.4

 THE PLANNER

Central executive: Coordinates attention and the actions of the other two components
Visuospatial sketchpad: Temporarily holds and manipulates visual images
Phonological loop: Rehearsal of information to maintain in STM

The *central executive* supervises and coordinates two subsystems, the *phonological rehearsal loop* and the *visuospatial sketchpad*, while also sending and retrieving information to and from LTM. Picture yourself as a food server in a busy restaurant, and a couple has just given you a complicated food order.

Central executive
(Coordinates material phonologically and visuospatially along with long-term memory)

When you mentally rehearse the food order (the phonological loop) and combine it with a mental picture of the layout of plates on the customers' table (the visuospatial sketchpad), you're using your central executive.

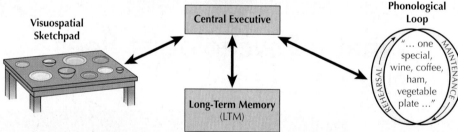

The *visuospatial sketchpad* holds and manipulates visual images and spatial information (Baddeley & Jarrold, 2007; Lehnert & Zimmer, 2008). Again, imagine yourself as the food server who's delivering the food to the same customers. Using your mind's visuospatial sketchpad, you can mentally visualize where to fit all the entrees, side dishes, and dinnerware on their table.

Visuospatial sketchpad
(Mentally imagines visual and spatial material)

The working memory's *phonological rehearsal loop* holds and manipulates verbal (phonological) information (Dasi et al., 2008; Jonides et al., 2008). Your phonological loop allows you to subvocally repeat all your customers' specific requests while you write a brief description on your order pad.

Phonological loop
(Rehearses through speech, words, numbers)

Long-Term Memory: Giving Context to the Present

Think back to the opening story of Henry Molaison. Although his surgery was successful in stopping his severe seizures, it also destroyed the mechanism that transfers information from short-term to long-term memory. That was why he could not remember the people he saw every day and didn't recognize photos of his own aging face.

Once information is transferred from STM, it is encoded and integrated with other information in **long-term memory (LTM)**. LTM serves as a storehouse of information that must be kept for long periods. When we need the information—perhaps to remember something—it is sent back to STM for our use. Compared with sensory memory and STM, LTM has relatively unlimited *capacity* and *duration* (Klatzky, 1984).

How do we store the vast amount of information that we collect over our lifetime? Several types of LTM exist (see **Study Organizer 7.1**). The two major systems are explicit/declarative memory and implicit/nondeclarative memory.

Explicit/declarative memory refers to intentional learning or conscious knowledge. If asked to remember your cellphone number or your mother's name, you can state (declare) the answers directly (explicitly). Explicit/declarative memory can be further subdivided into two parts. *Semantic* memory is memory for general knowledge, rules, public events, facts, and specific information. It is our mental encyclopedia.

In contrast, *episodic* memory is like a mental journal into which personal experiences are written. This subsystem records the major events (episodes) in our lives. Some of our episodic memories are short lived, such as where you had coffee this morning, while others can last a lifetime, such as remembering your first elementary school crush or first passionate kiss.

> **long-term memory (LTM)** This third memory stage stores information for long periods. Its capacity is limitless; its duration is relatively permanent.

> **explicit/declarative memory** The subsystem within long-term memory that consciously stores facts, information, and personal life experiences.

STUDY ORGANIZER 7.1 Types of Long-Term Memory ✓ THE PLANNER

Long-term memory (LTM) is divided and subdivided into various types of memory.

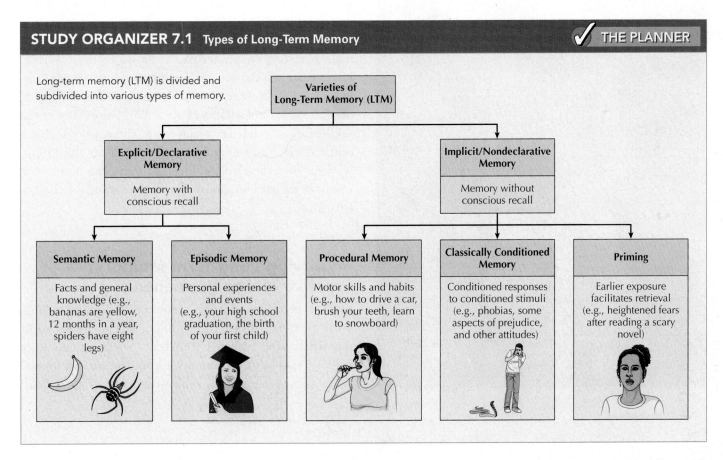

Varieties of Long-Term Memory (LTM)

Explicit/Declarative Memory — Memory with conscious recall

Implicit/Nondeclarative Memory — Memory without conscious recall

Semantic Memory — Facts and general knowledge (e.g., bananas are yellow, 12 months in a year, spiders have eight legs)

Episodic Memory — Personal experiences and events (e.g., your high school graduation, the birth of your first child)

Procedural Memory — Motor skills and habits (e.g., how to drive a car, brush your teeth, learn to snowboard)

Classically Conditioned Memory — Conditioned responses to conditioned stimuli (e.g., phobias, some aspects of prejudice, and other attitudes)

Priming — Earlier exposure facilitates retrieval (e.g., heightened fears after reading a scary novel)

Have you ever wondered why most preschoolers can remember events that happened to them in the previous few months, yet most adults can recall almost nothing of those years before age 3? Not that you would want to, but why don't we remember our own birth? Research suggests that for us to encode these early events and recall them much later, the frontal lobes—along with other neural structures—need to be sufficiently mature

What do babies remember? • Figure 7.5

As adults we lack the ability to look back into our childhood and remember important early milestones like learning to walk or drink from a cup. In fact, memories of events before age 3 or 4 are scant at best. One explanation for this infantile amnesia is that a young child's brain is not neurologically mature enough to form long-lasting episodic memories that can be recalled as adults. Based on what you have learned about the brain in Chapter 2, what brain regions involved in memory—other than the frontal lobes—do you think might still be maturing during early childhood?

Scott Dunlap/iStockphoto

(Leichtman, 2006; Morris, 2007; Prigatano & Gray, 2008; Suzuki & Amaral, 2004; Wang, 2008). Moreover, Canadian research has shown it's not just adults who can't remember. Older children are also unable to recall their earliest memories (Peterson, Warren, & Short, 2011) (**Figure 7.5**).

Implicit/nondeclarative memory refers to non-conscious learning or the acquiring of knowledge unintentionally. Try telling someone else how you tie shoelaces without demonstrating the actual behaviour. Because your memory of this skill is non-conscious and hard to describe (declare) in words, this type of memory is sometimes referred to as *nondeclarative*.

> **implicit/ nondeclarative memory** The subsystem within long-term memory that consists of non-conscious procedural skills, simple classically conditioned responses (Chapter 6), and priming.

Implicit/nondeclarative memory consists of *procedural* motor skills like skateboarding, as well as *classically conditioned memory* responses, such as fears and phobias or taste aversions. Imagine how you would feel about chocolate chip cookies after eating one filled with bug larva? Those conditioned emotional responses, such as nausea and disgust, that arise from subsequent encounters with chocolate chip cookies are a type of implicit memory.

Implicit/nondeclarative memory also includes *priming*, where prior exposure to a stimulus facilitates or inhibits (primes) the processing of new information (Amir et al., 2008; Becker, 2008; Tulving, 2000; Tulving & Schacter, 1990; Woollams et al., 2008). For example, you might feel a little edgy being home alone after seeing a scary movie, and watching a romantic movie might kindle your own romantic feelings. Priming can occur even when we do not consciously remember being exposed to the prime.

Improving Long-Term Memory: Practice Makes Permanent

Several processes can be employed to improve long-term memory. These include organization, rehearsal or repetition, and effective retrieval. Some people have made a sport out of memory recall and attend annual competitions to test their skills with others (**Figure 7.6**).

Could you beat The Memory Master?
• Figure 7.6

This is Wang Feng, memory grand master and winner of the 2010 and 2011 World Memory Championships. To claim this prestigious title, he achieved some remarkable feats of memory: He accurately recalled 500 random digits in less than 15 minutes after only 5 minutes of memorization time; and he accurately memorized 1,196 playing cards in just one hour (World Memory Sports Council, n.d.). Wang Feng wasn't born with any special memory ability. He believes anyone can improve their memory through training (CRI English, 2012). Research supports this claim (Carretti et al., 2007; Jausovec & Jausovec, 2012; Langdon & Corbett, 2012; Ranganath et al., 2011). To read more about the World Memory Championships, and perhaps become a competitor, visit www.worldmemorychampionships.com.

Seth Coleman

Organization To successfully encode information for LTM, we need to *organize* material into hierarchies. This involves arranging a number of related items into broad categories that are further divided and subdivided. (This organization strategy for LTM is similar to the strategy of chunking material in STM.) Many textbooks are laid out by using organization principles in the hope of improving long-term retention of the contents. Grouping small subsets of ideas together as subheadings under larger main headings, and within diagrams, tables, and so on, helps to make the material in the text more understandable and memorable.

Admittedly, organization takes time and effort. But you'll be happy to know that a little memory organization and filing is done automatically while you sleep (Mograss et al., 2008; Siccoli et al., 2008). Unfortunately, despite claims to the contrary, research shows that we can't recruit our sleeping hours to memorize new material, such as a foreign language.

Rehearsal Like organization, *rehearsal* also improves encoding for both STM and LTM. If you need to hold information in STM for longer than 30 seconds, you can simply keep repeating it (maintenance rehearsal). But storage in LTM requires *deeper levels of processing* called **elaborative rehearsal** (**Figure 7.7a**).

The immediate goal of elaborative rehearsal is to *understand the information better* and not to simply memorize it. Understanding is one of the best ways to encode new information into long-term memory.

> **elaborative rehearsal** The process of linking new information to previously stored material.

Studying for a psychology exam nicely illustrates both shallow and deep level processing. Simply reading over the chapter and perhaps highlighting important points represents shallow-level processing. This is because while you are reading the material, and it is passing through STM, it is not being encoded into LTM. Encoding into LTM is essential for you to be able to recall the material on the exam. Deep-level processing requires actually working with the material, such as taking study notes, designing concept charts, and writing questions that can be answered with content from the textbook. This form of elaborative rehearsal encodes the material at a much deeper level and cements (at least some of it) into LTM for later recall on the exam. It is no surprise then that deep-level processing is a better predictor of exam success than actual time spent studying (Eley, 1992; Meyer et al., 1990; Ward & Walker, 2008).

For an interesting discussion on this topic, scan to download the author's podcast.

Retrieval Finally, effective *retrieval* is critical to improving long-term memory. There are two types of **retrieval cues**. *Specific cues* require you only to recognize the correct response. *General cues* require you to recall previously learned material by searching through all possible matches in LTM—a much more difficult task (**Figure 7.7b** and **Figure 7.7c**).

> **retrieval cue** A clue or prompt that helps stimulate recall and retrieval of a stored piece of information from long-term memory.

Visualizing

Rehearsal and retrieval • Figure 7.7

a. Elaborative rehearsal

To improve elaborative rehearsal, you can expand (or elaborate on) the information to try to understand it better, actively explore and question new information, and search for meaningfulness. For example, a student might compare what she reads in an anthropology or history textbook with what she knows about world geography. Can you see how this might deepen her understanding and memory for the subject? (See *Applying Psychology: Mnemonic Devices*.)

Ted Tamburo/National Geographic Stock

Antonio M. Rosario/Photographer's Choice/Getty Images

b. Recall versus recognition memory

Can you *recall* from memory the names of the eight planets in our solar system? Why is it so much easier to *recognize* the names if you're provided with the first three letters of each planet's name: Mer-, Ven-, Ear-, Mar-, Jup-, Sat-, Ura-, Nep-? *Recall*, like an essay question, requires you to retrieve previously learned material with only general (often vague), nonspecific cues. In contrast, *recognition* tasks, as in a multiple-choice question, offer specific cues that only require you to identify (recognize) the correct response.

c. Longevity and recognition memory

Both name recognition and picture recognition for high school classmates remain high even many years after graduation, whereas recall memory would be expected to drop significantly over time.

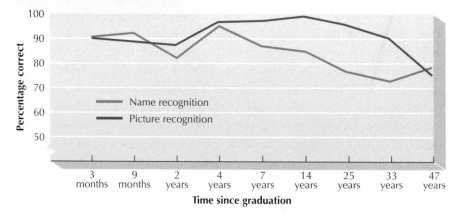

Applying Psychology

Mnemonic Devices

The SQ4R method discussed in Chapter 1 is an example of elaborative rehearsal. Another strategy that has proven useful in improving memory recall is the use of **mnemonic devices** to encode items in a special way.

Three popular mnemonic techniques are listed here.

a. Method of loci Greek and Roman orators developed the *method of loci* to keep track of the many parts of their long speeches. Orators would imagine the parts of their speeches attached to places in a familiar courtyard. For example, if an opening point in a speech was the concept of *justice*, they might visualize a courtroom placed in the first corner of their garden. As they mentally walked around their garden during their speech, they would encounter each of the points to be made. The method of loci is most effective when instead of a courtyard or garden, a person uses the sexiest, most edgy, or most disgusting image they can conjure (Worthen, 2006). For example, to easily memorize the seven critical thinking guidelines in Chapter 1, mentally attach each one of them to parts of a road kill, the naked body of a favourite celebrity, or a rat-infested home (students are usually very good at the visualizing component of this memory strategy). ▼

b. Peg words To use the *peg-word* mnemonic, you first need to memorize a set of 10 images that you can use as "pegs" on which to hang ideas. For example, if you learn 10 items that rhyme with the numbers they stand for, you can then use the images as pegs to hold the items of any list. Try it with the correct order of appearance of famous historical figures in psychology:

One is a bun: Imagine Wilhem Wundt eating a sticky bun.

Two is a shoe: Imagine William James walking in red high-heeled shoes.

Three is a tree: Imagine Sigmund Freud swinging from a tree.

Four is a door: Imagine John B. Watson breaking through a door.

Five is a hive: Imagine B. F. Skinner with a beehive hairstyle.

Six is a licks: Imagine Carl Rogers licking an ice cream.

c. Acronyms To use the acronym method, create a new code word from the first letters of the items you want to remember. For example, to recall the Big Five personality traits (see Chapter 12) simply take the first letters of each trait and make a new word out of it: openness, conscientiousness, extroversion, agreeableness, neuroticism = OCEAN. ▼

Reniw-Imagery/iStockphoto

Think Critically

1. Practise what you have learned: Use the method of loci to remember the types of long-term memory described in the Study Organizer.
2. Use the peg-word method to remember the five theories of forgetting in Figure 7.11 later in the chapter.

Whether cues require recall or only recognition is not all that matters. Imagine that while apartment hunting, you walk into a stranger's kitchen and are greeted with the unmistakable smells of dinner being prepared. Instantly, the aroma transports you to the kitchen you grew up in, where you spent many childhood afternoons doing your homework. You find yourself suddenly thinking of the mental shortcuts your Mom taught you to help you learn your multiplication tables. You hadn't thought about these little tricks for years, but somehow a whiff of homemade cooking brought them back to you. Why?

encoding specificity principle Retrieval of information is improved when the conditions of recovery are similar to the conditions that existed when the information was first encoded.

In this imagined episode, you have stumbled on the **encoding specificity principle**, which states that retrieval of information will be better if conditions of recall are similar to conditions when encoded (Amir et al., 2008; Becker, 2008; Tulving & Thompson, 1973; Woollams et al., 2008). One important contextual cue for retrieval is *location*. In a clever, now classic study, Godden and Baddeley (1975) had underwater divers learn a list of 40 words either on land or underwater. The divers had better recall for lists that they had encoded underwater if they were also underwater at the time of retrieval; similarly, lists that were encoded above water were better recalled above water.

People also remember information better if their moods during learning and retrieval match (Kenealy, 1997; Nouchi & Hyodo, 2007). This phenomenon, called *mood congruence*, occurs because a given mood tends to evoke memories that are consistent with that mood.

When you're sad (or happy or angry), you're more likely to remember events and circumstances from other times when you were also sad (or happy or angry).

Finally, as generations of coffee-devouring university students have discovered, if you learn something while under the influence of a drug, such as caffeine, you will remember it a little more easily when you take that drug again than during other times (Ahmadi et al., 2007; Baddeley, 1998; Zarrindast et al., 2005; Zarrindast et al., 2007). This is called *state-dependent retrieval*.

CONCEPT CHECK STOP

1. **What** happens to information after it leaves sensory memory?

2. **What** is working memory?

3. **What** is the difference between recognition and recall?

4. **How** do contextual cues, such as location, mood, and physiological state, affect memory retrieval?

Biological Bases of Memory

LEARNING OBJECTIVES

1. **Describe** two kinds of biological changes that occur when we learn something new.

2. **Identify** the primary brain areas involved in memory.

3. **Explain** how injury and disease can affect memory.

Many biological changes occur when we learn something new. Among them are neuronal and synaptic changes. In this section we will discuss these changes, along with the research surrounding where memories are located in the brain and what might cause memory loss.

Neuronal and Synaptic Changes in Memory

We know that learning and new experiences modify the brain's neural architecture (Chapters 2 and 6). As you learn to snowboard, for example, repeated practice builds specific neural pathways in your brain that make it easier

and easier for you to get down the mountain without falling over and breaking your neck. Research has shown this **long-term potentiation (LTP)** happens in at least two ways.

First, as early research with rats raised in enriched environments showed (Rosenzweig et al., 1972; Chapter 6), repeated stimulation of a synapse strengthened the synapse by causing the dendrites to grow more spines. Spines are knobby outcroppings on dendrites, and more of them means more synapses, more receptor sites, and more sensitivity. The neuron is said to be more sensitive because the action potential can

long-term potentiation (LTP) Long-lasting increase in neural excitability caused by repeated neural input. Believed to be the biological basis of learning and memory.

now affect a greater number of downstream neurons. In addition, when rats are given LTP-enhancing drugs they learn and remember a maze better than rats that did not get the drug (Ballard et al., 2009; Xue et al., 2009).

Second, learning affects a particular neuron's ability to release its neurotransmitters. This has been shown in research with *Aplysia*, a rather beautiful sea slug that can be classically conditioned to reflexively withdraw its gill when squirted with water. This change in *Aplysia* is mediated by an increase in neurotransmitter release at specific synapses (**Figure 7.8**).

Further evidence comes from research with genetically engineered "smart mice," which have extra neural receptors for a neurotransmitter named NMDA (N-methyl-d-aspartate). These mice performed significantly better on memory tasks than did normal mice (Tang et al., 2001; Tsien, 2000). Evidence of long-term potentiation (LTP) has also been documented in humans (Berger et al., 2008; Tecchio et al., 2008).

How does a sea slug learn and remember?
• Figure 7.8

After repeated squirting with water, followed by a mild shock, the sea slug *Aplysia* releases more neurotransmitters at certain synapses. These synapses then become more efficient at transmitting signals that allow the slug to withdraw its gill when squirted. Why might this ability be evolutionarily advantageous?

© Daniel L. Geiger/SNAP/Alamy

Hormonal Changes and Memory

Emotional arousal often leads to stronger memories. When stressed or excited, we naturally produce fight-or-flight hormones, such as epinephrine and cortisol (Chapter 3), that arouse and energize the body to deal with the threat. These hormones in turn affect the amygdala, a brain structure involved in emotion (Chapter 2), which then signals the hippocampus and cerebral cortex. The activation of these brain regions is essential for laying down strong memories of the event. They're important in situations of threat, as remembering what happened will enhance survival for the organism should the situation present itself again. Research has shown that direct injections of epinephrine or cortisol or electrical stimulation of the amygdala increases the encoding and storage of new information (Hamilton & Gotlib, 2008; Jackson, 2008; van Stegeren, 2008). Moreover, newer animal research has shown that a region of the amygdala can influence representations in the cortex, and this may be the mechanism by which long-term memories are strengthened (Chavez et al., 2009; McReynolds et al., 2010). Too much stress is not good, however, as increased levels of cortisol has been shown to interfere with memory formation (Al'absi et al., 2002; Heffelfinger & Newcomer, 2001; McAllister-Williams & Rugg, 2002).

The powerful effect of hormones on memory is evident in *flashbulb memories*—vivid images of circumstances associated with surprising or strongly emotional events (Brown & Kulik, 1977). In such situations, we secrete fight-or-flight hormones when the event occurs, which make the memory more durable, and then by replaying the scary event over and over again in our minds, the memory is strengthened. You probably can recall a number of your own flashbulb memories, such as being in a car crash at the moment of impact or experiencing some other very frightening or disturbing event. Flashbulb memories feel very intense and vivid, but despite their intensity, they are not as accurate as you might think (Cubelli & Della Sala, 2008; Talarico & Rubin, 2007). Even memories that seem crystal clear are subject to errors; while we tend to remember the emotion and generalities of the event, many of the details are actually lost.

It's All in Your Head: Where Are Memories Located?

Early memory researchers believed that memory was localized, or stored in a particular discrete brain area. We now know that there is no single memory storehouse in the brain and that memories are housed in a vast network

Brain and Memory Formation

Damage to any one of these areas can affect the encoding, storage, and retrieval of memories.

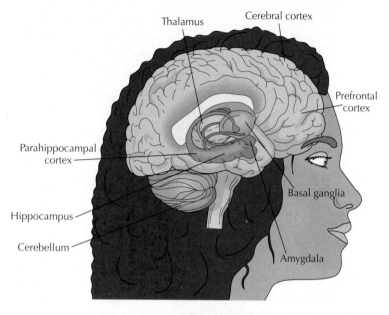

Amygdala	Emotion and memory (Gerber et al., 2008; Hamilton & Gotlib, 2008; van Stegeren, 2008)
Basal ganglia and cerebellum	Creation and storage of the basic memory trace and implicit (nondeclarative) memories (such as skills, habits, and simple classically conditioned responses) (Chiricozzi et al., 2008; Gluck, 2008; Thompson, 2005)
Hippocampal formation (hippocampus and surrounding area)	Memory recognition; implicit, explicit, spatial, episodic memory; declarative long-term memory; sequences of events (Hamilton & Gotlib, 2008; Yoo et al., 2007)
Thalamus	Formation of new memories and spatial and working memory (Hart & Kraut, 2007; Hofer et al., 2007; Ponzi, 2008)
Cortex	Encoding of explicit (declarative) memories; storage of episodic and semantic memories; skill learning; working memory (Davidson et al., 2008; Dougal et al., 2007; Thompson, 2005)

Think Critically

1. What effect might damage to the amygdala have on a person's interpersonal relationships?
2. What effect do you think damage to the thalamus might have on a person's day-to-day functioning?

of associations located throughout the brain. Memory is more of a process than an anatomical structure.

Today, research techniques have advanced such that we can experimentally induce and measure memory-related brain changes as they occur. For example, James Brewer and his colleagues (1998) used functional magnetic resonance imaging (fMRI) to locate areas of the brain responsible for encoding memories of pictures. They showed 96 pictures of indoor and outdoor scenes to participants while scanning their brains, and then later tested participants' ability to recall the pictures. Brewer and his colleagues identified the *right prefrontal cortex* and the *parahippocampal cortex* as being the most active during the encoding of the pictures. These are only two of several brain regions involved in memory storage.

Injury, Disease, and Memory Loss

Traumatic brain injury (TBI) occurs when an external force injures the brain. Damage caused by compression, twisting, penetration, and distortion of the brain inside the skull all can cause serious and oftentimes permanent damage to the brain. TBIs are a major cause of death and injury for young adults in Canada and elsewhere (Hyder et al., 2007; SMARTRISK, 2009). They are usually caused by falls, car crashes, and misadventure (Corrigan et al., 2010).

Loss of memory as a result of brain injury or trauma is called *amnesia*. Two major types of amnesia are **retrograde amnesia** and **anterograde amnesia** (**Figure 7.9**). Retrograde amnesia for events that occurred just before an injury is believed to be caused by a failure of consolidation. After LTP has occurred, it takes a bit of time for the neural changes to become stable. If

Two types of amnesia • Figure 7.9

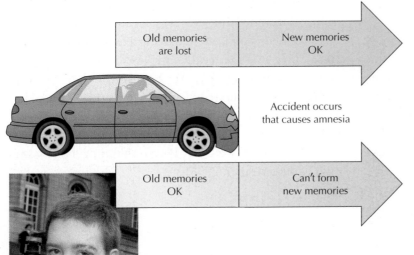

a. In *retrograde amnesia*, the person loses memories of events that occurred just before the accident yet has no trouble remembering things that happened afterward (old, "retro" memories are lost).

Accident occurs that causes amnesia

Old memories are lost	New memories OK

Old memories OK	Can't form new memories

b. In *anterograde amnesia*, the person cannot form new memories for events that occur after the accident. Anterograde amnesia also may result from a surgical injury (as in the case of Henry Molaison) or from diseases, such as chronic alcoholism.

Michel Euler/AP Photo

Bodyguard Trevor Rees-Jones, the sole survivor of the car accident that killed Diana, Princess of Wales; Dodi Al-Fayed; and Henri Paul, experienced both anterograde and retrograde amnesia caused by his serious head injuries. He reports having no memory after getting into the black Mercedes and no memory of the accident or what happened soon after.

the injury occurs during this time, the recent memories can be erased (Gaskin et al., 2009). In most cases retrograde amnesia is temporary and patients slowly recover over time (Parsons & Otto, 2010). Anterograde amnesia is most commonly caused by surgical damage, or disease. Unfortunately, anterograde amnesia is usually permanent, but patients often show surprising abilities to learn and remember implicit/nondeclarative tasks (such as procedural motor skills). This type of memory was somewhat preserved for Henry Molaison.

Like traumatic brain injuries, disease can damage the physiology of the brain and nervous system and thereby affect memory

Alzheimer's disease (AD) Degenerative brain disease characterized by progressive mental deterioration and pathological memory loss.

processes. For example, **Alzheimer's disease (AD)** is a degenerative brain disease characterized by progressive mental deterioration; it occurs most commonly in later life (**Figure 7.10**). The most noticeable early symptoms are minor

disturbances in memory, which become progressively worse until in the final stages, the person fails to recognize

The effect of Alzheimer's disease on the brain • Figure 7.10

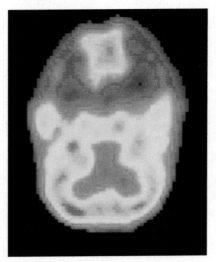

Science Source/Photo Researchers

a. Healthy brain Note the large amount of red and yellow (signs of lots of brain activity) in the positron emission tomography (PET) scan of the normal brain.

b. Brain of a patient with Alzheimer's disease The reduced activity in the brain of a person with Alzheimer's disease. The loss is most significant in the temporal and parietal lobes, which indicates that these areas are particularly important for storing memories.

loved ones, cannot take care of himself or herself, and needs nursing care around the clock. The person ultimately dies from the advancing disease.

Alzheimer's does not attack all types of memory equally. A hallmark of the disease is an extreme decline in explicit/declarative memory (Haley, 2005; Libon et al., 2007). People with AD fail to recall facts, information, and personal life experiences, yet they still retain some implicit/nondeclarative memories, such as simple classically conditioned responses and procedural tasks, like brushing their teeth and hair.

What causes this disease? Brain autopsies of people with AD show unusual tangles (structures formed from dead and dying cell bodies) and plaques (structures formed from dead and dying axons and dendrites). Hereditary AD generally strikes between the ages of 45 and 55. Some experts believe that the cause of Alzheimer's is primarily genetic, but others think that genetic makeup may make some people more susceptible to environmental influences (Diamond & Amso, 2008; Ertekin-Taner, 2007; Persson et al., 2008; Vickers et al., 2000; Weiner, 2008).

CONCEPT CHECK   STOP

1. **Why** would rats raised in enriched environments develop different neuronal connections than littermates raised in impoverished environments?

2. **How** are hormones involved in memory formation?

3. **What** is the difference between retrograde and anterograde amnesia?

Forgetting

LEARNING OBJECTIVES

1. **Describe** Ebbinghaus' research on learning and forgetting.

2. **Outline** the five key theories of why we forget.

3. **Explain** the factors that contribute to forgetting.

sychologists have developed several theories to explain forgetting and have identified a number of factors that can interfere with the process of forming new memories and retaining old ones.

Theories of Forgetting

If you couldn't forget, your mind would be filled with meaningless data, such as every snack you've ever had in your life, or every outfit you have ever worn. Similarly, think of the incredible pain you would continually endure if memories of life's tragedies did not fade with time? The ability to forget is essential to the proper functioning of memory. Our annoyance with forgetting occurs when we forget things we did not intend to forget. These are the times when forgetting is an inconvenience, and we might fail to recognize how adaptive and useful it really is.

Five major theories attempt to explain why forgetting occurs (**Figure 7.11**): decay, interference, encoding failure, retrieval failure, and motivated forgetting. Each theory focuses on a different stage of the memory process or a particular type of problem in processing neural information.

Errors in Remembering

Since Ebbinghaus' original research (see *Psychological Science: How Quickly We Forget*), scientists have discovered numerous factors that contribute to inaccurate remembering. Five of the most important are the misinformation effect, the serial position effect, source amnesia, the sleeper effect, and spacing of practice.

Why we forget: Five key theories • Figure 7.11

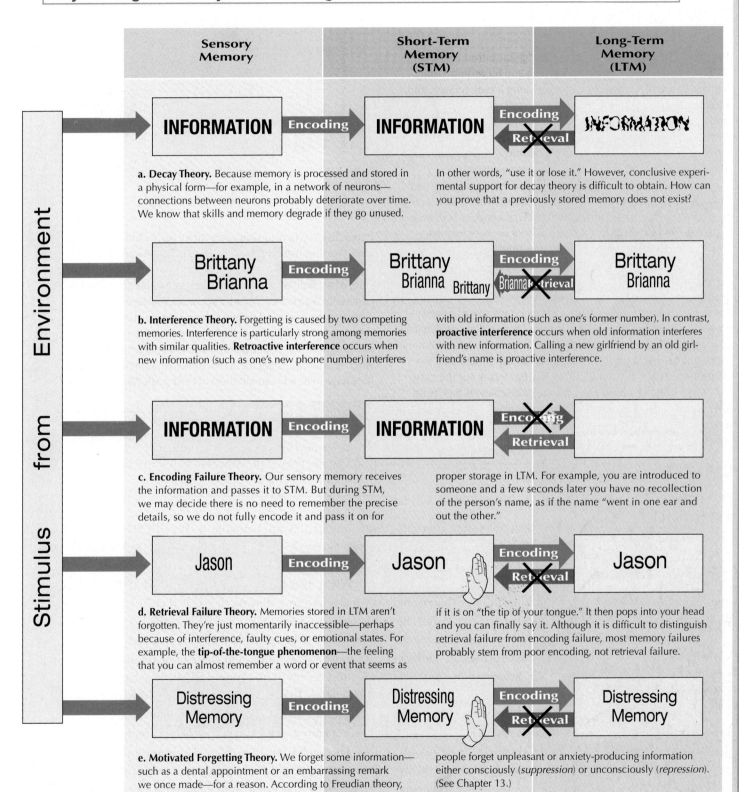

| | Sensory Memory | Short-Term Memory (STM) | Long-Term Memory (LTM) |

a. Decay Theory. Because memory is processed and stored in a physical form—for example, in a network of neurons—connections between neurons probably deteriorate over time. We know that skills and memory degrade if they go unused. In other words, "use it or lose it." However, conclusive experimental support for decay theory is difficult to obtain. How can you prove that a previously stored memory does not exist?

b. Interference Theory. Forgetting is caused by two competing memories. Interference is particularly strong among memories with similar qualities. **Retroactive interference** occurs when new information (such as one's new phone number) interferes with old information (such as one's former number). In contrast, **proactive interference** occurs when old information interferes with new information. Calling a new girlfriend by an old girlfriend's name is proactive interference.

c. Encoding Failure Theory. Our sensory memory receives the information and passes it to STM. But during STM, we may decide there is no need to remember the precise details, so we do not fully encode it and pass it on for proper storage in LTM. For example, you are introduced to someone and a few seconds later you have no recollection of the person's name, as if the name "went in one ear and out the other."

d. Retrieval Failure Theory. Memories stored in LTM aren't forgotten. They're just momentarily inaccessible—perhaps because of interference, faulty cues, or emotional states. For example, the **tip-of-the-tongue phenomenon**—the feeling that you can almost remember a word or event that seems as if it is on "the tip of your tongue." It then pops into your head and you can finally say it. Although it is difficult to distinguish retrieval failure from encoding failure, most memory failures probably stem from poor encoding, not retrieval failure.

e. Motivated Forgetting Theory. We forget some information—such as a dental appointment or an embarrassing remark we once made—for a reason. According to Freudian theory, people forget unpleasant or anxiety-producing information either consciously (*suppression*) or unconsciously (*repression*). (See Chapter 13.)

Psychological Science

How Quickly We Forget

About 120 years ago Hermann Ebbinghaus introduced the first experimental study on learning and forgetting. Using himself as a subject, he calculated how long it took to learn and remember a list of three-letter *nonsense syllables*, such as *SIB* and *RAL*. He then found that just one hour after learning a list perfectly, he remembered only 44 percent of the syllables. A day later, he recalled 35 percent, and a week later, only 21 percent. This figure shows his now famous "forgetting curve."

Depressing as these findings (or the fact that Ebbinghaus had little else to do with his days) may seem, keep in mind that meaningful material is much more memorable than meaningless nonsense syllables. Even so, we all forget some of what we have learned.

On a more positive note, after some time passed and he believed he had forgotten the list, Ebbinghaus found that *relearning* a previously learned list took less time than the initial learning did. This research suggests that we retain some memory for things that we have learned, even when we seem to have forgotten them completely. This is one of the challenges to decay theory, which you have just read about (Figure 7.11). If a memory trace has been lost through disuse, relearning should take the same amount of time as initial learning, but this is not the case.

Most research based on Ebbinghaus' discoveries has found that there is an ideal time to practise something you have learned. Practising too soon is a waste of time, and if you practise too late, you will already have forgotten what you learned. The ideal time

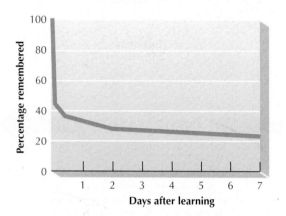

to practise is when you are about to forget. Polish psychologist Piotr Wozniak used this insight to create a software program called SuperMemo. The program can be used to predict the future state of an individual's memory and help the person schedule reviews of learned information at the optimal time. So far the program has been applied mainly to language learning, helping users retain huge amounts of vocabulary. But Wozniak hopes that some day programs like SuperMemo will tell people when to wake and when to exercise, help them remember what they read and whom they have met, and remind them of their goals (Wolf, 2008).

Think Critically

1. How do you think Ebbinghaus' findings might be applied to learning to play a musical instrument?
2. Can you think of any disadvantage of depending on a program like SuperMemo?

Many people who haven't taken first-year psychology classes believe that when they are recalling an event, they're remembering it as if it were a video instant replay. However, as you know, our memories are re-creative and malleable, and therefore highly fallible, filled with personal constructions and amendments that we create during encoding and storage. Research on the **misinformation effect** shows that information that occurs after an event may further alter and revise those constructions. Experimenters have created false memories in subjects by showing them doctored photos of themselves taking a fictitious hot-air balloon ride or by asking subjects to simply imagine an event, such as having a nurse remove a skin sample from their finger. In these and similar cases, a large number of subjects later believed that misleading information was correct and that fictitious

misinformation effect Distortion of a memory by misleading post-event information.

or imagined events actually occurred (Allan & Gabbert, 2008; Garry & Gerrie, 2005; Mazzoni & Memon, 2003; Mazzoni & Vannucci, 2007; Pérez-Mata & Diges, 2007).

When research participants are given lists of words to learn and are allowed to recall them in any order they choose, they remember the words at the beginning (*primacy effect:* STM is less crowded with information, so the words are more memorable) and the end of the list (*recency effect:* the most recent items put into STM and so are more memorable) better than those in the middle, which are quite often forgotten (Azizian & Polich, 2007; Healy et al., 2008). This effect is known as the **serial position effect**.

The serial position effect has some interesting real-life implications. For example, a potential employer's memory for you might be enhanced if you are either the first or the last candidate interviewed.

Each day we read, hear, and process an enormous amount of information, and it's easy to confuse who said

Culture and memory • Figure 7.12

In many societies, important information is passed down by telling related stories that are woven together to create rich oral traditions. As a result, children growing up in these cultures have better memories for the information that is relayed to them through stories than do children not raised in these cultures. Can you think of other ways in which culture might influence memory?

what to whom, where, and in what context. Forgetting the true source of a memory is known as **source amnesia** (Kleider et al., 2008; Leichtman, 2006; Mitchell et al., 2005), and it has happened to all of us. While you know what city is Canada's capital, you probably don't remember where and when you learned it.

When we first hear something from an unreliable source, we tend to disregard the information in favour of a more reliable source. However, as the source of the information is forgotten (source amnesia), the unreliable information is less likely to be discounted. This is called the **sleeper effect** (Appel & Richter, 2007; Kumkale & Albarracín, 2004; Nabi et al., 2007).

The sleeper effect can be a significant problem when reliable and unreliable information are mixed—for example, when advertisements are disguised to look like more objective reports or newspaper articles. Can you see how, after a time, we may forget the actual source and no longer discount the information in the ad?

If we try to memorize too much information at once (as when students stay up and pull an all-nighter cramming before an exam), we learn and remember less than when study sessions are divided up (Donovan & Radosevich, 1999). *Distributed practice* refers to spacing your learning periods, with rest periods between sessions. Cramming is an example of *massed practice* because the time spent learning is massed into a single long, unbroken bout.

Finally, as illustrated in **Figure 7.12**, cultural factors can play a role in how well people remember what they have learned.

CONCEPT CHECK

1. **How** does previous learning affect relearning?
2. **What** is the difference between proactive and retroactive interference?
3. **Why** do we sometimes fall prey to those who offer erroneous information, even when we know it is suspect?
4. **Which** is more effective: distributed practice or massed practice?

Memory Distortions

LEARNING OBJECTIVES

1. **Explain** why our memories sometimes become distorted.

2. **Describe** the dangers of relying on eyewitness testimony.

3. **Summarize** the controversy surrounding repressed memories.

One of my first memories would date, if it were true, from my second year. I can still see, most clearly, the following scene, in which I believed until I was about fifteen. I was sitting in my pram, which my nurse was pushing in the Champs-Elysees, when a man tried to kidnap me. I was held in by the strap fastened round me while my nurse bravely tried to stand between the thief and me. She received various scratches, and I can still see vaguely those on her face. Then a crowd gathered, a policeman with a short cloak and a white baton came up, and the man took to his heels. I can still see the whole scene, and can even place it near the tube station. When I was about fifteen, my parents received a letter from my former nurse saying that she had been converted to the Salvation Army. She wanted to confess her past faults, and in particular to return the watch she had been given as a reward on this occasion. She had made up the whole story, faking the scratches. I, therefore, must have heard, as a child, the account of this story, which my parents believed, and projected it into the past in the form of a visual memory, which was a memory of a memory, but false. (Piaget, 1962, pp. 187–188)

Applying Psychology

 THE PLANNER

A Memory Test

Carefully read all the words in the columns below.

Bed	Drowse
Awake	Nurse
Tired	Sick
Dream	Lawyer
Wake	Medicine
Snooze	Health
Snore	Hospital
Rest	Dentist
Blanket	Physician
Doze	Patient
Slumber	Stethoscope
Nap	Curse
Peace	Clinic
Yawn	Surgeon

Now cover the list and write down all the words you remember. Number of correctly recalled words:

21 to 28 words = excellent memory

16 to 20 words = better than most

12 to 15 words = average

8 to 11 words = below average

7 or fewer words = you might need a nap

How did you do? Do you have a good or excellent memory? Did you recall seeing the words *sleep* and *doctor*? Look back over the list. These words are not there. However, more than 65 percent of students commonly report seeing these words in this type of list. Why? Memory is not a faithful replication of an event; it is a *constructive* and *re-creative process*. We actively shape and build on information as it is encoded and retrieved. Because *sleep* and *doctor* fit nicely and logically into the list, it is easy for us to conclude on recall that they were there all along.

Think Critically

1. Look back at the two memory test lists. Did you remember the words *bed* and *surgeon*? If so explain why based on what you have learned in this chapter.
2. As societies make technological advancements, what do you predict might happen to human memory abilities? Why?

This is a self-reported childhood memory of Jean Piaget, a brilliant and world-famous cognitive and developmental psychologist (we discuss Piaget in Chapter 9). Why did Piaget create such a strange and elaborate memory for something that never happened?

We shape, rearrange, and distort our memories for several reasons. One of the most common is our need for logic and consistency. When we're initially forming new memories or sorting through the old ones, we fill in missing pieces, make "corrections," and rearrange information to make it logical, smooth, and consistent with our previous experiences and knowledge of the world. If Piaget's beloved and loyal nurse said someone attempted to kidnap him, it was only logical for the boy to "remember" the event as she said it had happened.

We also shape and construct our memories for the sake of efficiency. We summarize, augment, and tie new information in with related memories in LTM. Similarly, when we need to retrieve the stored information, we leave out seemingly unimportant elements or misremember the details. Often this is done without our conscious awareness and we therefore believe the recreated memory is an accurate account of the event.

Despite all their problems and biases, however, our memories are as accurate as they need to be and serve us well in most situations. From an evolutionary perspective, our memories evolved to encode, store, and retrieve key survival information. Memory and remembering did not need to be perfect, but good enough for survival and reproduction. In the ancestral environment of the early humans, we did not need to remember the precise details of a psychology text, the faces and names of potential clients, or where we left our house keys. So, when we encounter this type of information today, our memory and the accurate remembering of events might seem to be less than optimal.

"I Saw It with My Own Eyes": Memory and Eyewitness Testimony

When memory errors involve the criminal justice system, they can lead to wrongful judgements of guilt or innocence and occasionally life-or-death decisions. In 1992 the small Saskatchewan community of Martensville was rocked by allegations of horrific child sexual abuse, animal mutilation, and satanic rituals in a home daycare run by Ron and Lynda Sterling. Along with the Sterlings, seven other people were charged with 180 sex-related offences against the children in their care. Ultimately, the Sterlings were tried and acquitted on all charges. After a thorough investigation it was discovered that the methods of police investigation—namely, using leading questions when interviewing the daycare children—caused the initial unfounded allegations. The Province of Saskatchewan ultimately paid out $1.3 million in compensation to those wrongly accused, and the fallout from the charges were still present some 14 years later ("Martensville Saga Ends," 2006).

In the past, one of the best forms of trial evidence a lawyer could have was an *eyewitness* "I was there; I saw it with my own eyes." Unfortunately, research has identified several problems with eyewitness testimony (Loftus, 2000, 2001, 2007; Ran, 2007; Rubinstein, 2008; Sharps et al., 2007; Yarmey, 2004). A number of researchers have demonstrated that it is relatively easy to influence eyewitness accounts and to create false memories (Allan & Gabbert, 2008; Howes, 2007; Loftus & Cahill, 2007; Pérez-Mata & Diges, 2007). It was the creation of false memories in the daycare children by police leading questions that led to the initial and wrongful arrest of Ron and Lynda Sterling (CBC News, 2003).

In a now classic study of false memory generation and the misinformation effect, research participants watched a film of a car driving through the countryside. Later, those who were asked to estimate how fast the car was going when it passed the barn (actually nonexistent) were six times as likely to report that they had seen a barn in the film as participants who hadn't been asked about a barn (Loftus, 1982). False memories can be created for almost any event, including events that are quite impossible (**Figure 7.13**).

Problems with eyewitness recollections are so well established and legally important that judges now allow expert testimony on the unreliability of eyewitness reports, and routinely instruct jurors on its limits (Durham & Dane, 1999; Ramirez et al., 1996; Loftus, 2010). Sadly, even with instructions from the judge, sometimes jurors simply just do not understand the instructions to disregard specific elements of the eyewitness testimony, and they make erroneous decisions (McAuliff & Groscup, 2009; Sheehan, 2011). If you serve as a member of a jury or listen to accounts of crimes in the news, remind yourself of the problems surrounding eyewitness testimony. Also keep in mind that research participants in eyewitness studies generally report their inaccurate memories with great self-assurance and strong personal conviction (Migueles & Garcia-Bajos, 1999).

Bugs Bunny and the rest of the Disneyland crew • Figure 7.13

Research participants who had been to Disneyland were told they were going to be part of a team to evaluate an advertising campaign for the theme park. Half the participants either saw a cardboard cutout of Bugs Bunny or heard a Disneyland advertisement featuring Bugs Bunny. The other half heard the advertising campaign, but it made no mention of the rabbit. More than a third of the "Bugs" group later recalled meeting him at Disneyland and shaking his hand (or paw, to be completely accurate). By contrast fewer than 8 percent of the "no Bugs" group said they had met Bugs at Disneyland (Braun et al., 2002). This is a irrefutable illustration of the ease with which false memories can be created— Bugs Bunny would never be seen at Disneyland, let alone shaking hands with people there. He is a Warner Brothers character.

Pascal Le Segretain/Getty Images   Ric Francis/AP Photo

Eyewitnesses to an actual crime may similarly identify—with equally high confidence—an innocent person as the perpetrator (**Figure 7.14**).

Our strength of personal conviction in the accuracy of our memories and events we have experienced is powerful. Consider this personal account: When Elizabeth was 14 years old, her mother drowned in their backyard pool. As she grew older, the details surrounding her mother's death became increasingly vague for Elizabeth. Decades later, a relative told Elizabeth that she had been the one to find her mother's body. Despite her initial shock, the memories soon slowly started coming back to her.

> *I could see myself, a thin, dark-haired girl, looking into the flickering blue-and-white pool. My mother, dressed in her nightgown, is floating face down. I start screaming. I remember the police cars,*

their lights flashing, and the stretcher with the clean, white blanket tucked in around the edges of the body. The memory had been there all along, but I just couldn't reach it. (Loftus & Ketcham, 1994, p. 45)

This is the true story of Elizabeth Loftus, who today is a well-known psychologist and influential memory researcher (her studies have been mentioned a number of times in this chapter). Elizabeth's recovery of these gruesome childhood memories, although painful, initially brought great relief. It also seemed to explain why she had always been so fascinated by the topic of memory.

Then, years later her brother called to say there had been a mistake! The relative who told Elizabeth that she had been the one to discover her mother's body later remembered—and other relatives confirmed—that it had actually been Aunt Pearl and not Elizabeth Loftus. Loftus, a world-renowned expert on memory distortions, had

Eyewitness testimony helped convict these Canadians • Figure 7.14

What do David Milgaard (left), Donald Marshall Jr. (right), and Thomas Sophonow (not pictured) have in common? They were all wrongfully convicted of sexual assault, murder, or both in Canadian courts, and in each case eyewitness testimony contributed to their convictions. These men spent years in prison before their convictions were eventually overturned once DNA testing or newer, more reliable evidence became available. Recall that witnessing or being the victim of a violent crime is an extremely emotional event, and emotional events tend to make stronger flashbulb memories, and not weaker ones. What memory distortions do you think might have contributed to the witnesses' errors in these cases?

Rick Eglinton/GetStock.com

Elizabeth Loftus: Memory researcher and victim of false memories • Figure 7.15

Jodi Hilton/POOL/AP Photo

unknowingly created her own false memory based on misinformation she had subsequently heard (**Figure 7.15**).

Repressed Memories

Creating false memories may be somewhat common, but can we actually recover true memories from childhood that are buried? **Repression**, which is mentioned earlier as a potential factor in motivated forgetting, is the supposed unconscious coping mechanism by which we prevent anxiety-provoking thoughts from reaching consciousness. According to some research, repressed memories are actively and consciously "forgotten" in an effort to avoid the pain of their retrieval (Anderson, Ochsner, et al., 2004).

Others suggest that some memories are so painful that they exist only in an unconscious corner of the brain, making them inaccessible to the individual (Karon & Widener, 1998). In these cases, therapy would be necessary to unlock the hidden memories (Davies, 1996).

This is a complex and controversial topic in psychology. No one doubts that some memories are forgotten and later recovered. What is questioned, however, is the concept of *repressed memories* of painful experiences (especially of childhood sexual abuse) and their storage in the unconscious mind (Goodman et al., 2003; Kihlstrom, 2004; Loftus & Cahill, 2007).

Critics of repressed memories suggest that most people who have witnessed or experienced a violent crime, or who are adult survivors of childhood sexual abuse, have intense, persistent memories. They have trouble forgetting the terrible memories, not remembering they happened in the first place. Some critics also wonder whether therapists sometimes inadvertently create false memories in their clients during therapy. Some worry that if a clinician even suggests the possibility of abuse, the client's own constructive memory processes may lead them to cre-

ate a false memory. The client might start to incorporate portrayals of abuse from movies and books into their own memory, forgetting their original sources and eventually coming to see them as true, reliable, and real.

This is not to say that all psychotherapy clients who recover memories of sexual abuse (or other painful incidents) have invented those memories. Indeed, the repressed memory debate has grown increasingly bitter, and research on both sides is hotly contested. The stakes are high because some civil lawsuits and criminal prosecutions of sexual abuse have been based on recovered memories of childhood sexual abuse. As researchers continue exploring the mechanisms underlying memory systems, we must be careful not to chastise or condemn people who report recovering memories of abuse. In the same spirit, we must also protect the innocent from wrongful accusations that come from false memories. We look forward to a time when we can justly balance the interests and reputation of the victim with those of the accused.

CONCEPT CHECK	

1. **How** can our desire for logic, consistency, and efficiency actually thwart accurate memory processes?

2. **Why** might Elizabeth Loftus have formed a false memory about her mother's death?

Summary

1 The Nature of Memory 184

- **Memory** is an internal representation of some prior event or experience. The two major perspectives on memory are the **information-processing model**—information enters memory in three stages: **encoding**, **storage**, and **retrieval**; and the three-stage memory model—information is stored and processed in **sensory memory**, **short-term memory (STM)**, and **long-term memory (LTM)**.

- Information remains in sensory memory very briefly. Visual information is stored as an iconic memory and auditory information is stored as an echoic memory.

- **Chunking** and **maintenance rehearsal** improve STM's duration and capacity. Researchers now think of STM as a three-part **working memory**.

- LTM is an almost unlimited storehouse of information that is kept for long periods. The two major types of LTM are **explicit/declarative memory** and **implicit/nondeclarative memory**. Organization and **elaborative rehearsal** improve encoding for LTM. **Retrieval cues** help stimulate retrieval of information from LTM. According to the **encoding specificity principle**, retrieval is improved when conditions of recovery are similar to encoding conditions.

- **Mnemonic devices** help us remember lists and facts. Three popular mnemonic techniques are method of loci, the peg-word mnemonic, and the method of acronyms.

Visualizing: Rehearsal and retrieval • Figure 7.7

2 Biological Bases of Memory 194

- Learning modifies the brain's neural architecture through **long-term potentiation (LTP)**, strengthening particular synapses and affecting neurons' ability to release their neurotransmitters.

- Stress hormones affect the amygdala, which activates brain areas that are important for memory storage. Heightened arousal increases the encoding and storage of new information. Secretion of fight-or-flight hormones can contribute to flashbulb memories.

- Research using advanced techniques has indicated that several brain regions are involved in memory storage.

- Traumatic brain injuries and disease, such as **Alzheimer's disease (AD)**, can cause memory loss. Two major types of amnesia are **retrograde** and **anterograde**.

The effect of Alzheimer's disease on the brain • Figure 7.10

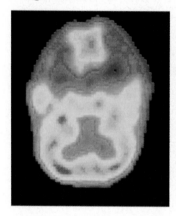

3 Forgetting 198

- Researchers have proposed that we forget information through decay, **retroactive** and **proactive interference**, encoding failure, retrieval failure, and motivated forgetting.

- Early research by Ebbinghaus showed that we tend to forget newly learned information quickly but that we relearn the information more readily the second time.

- Five factors that contribute to forgetting are the **misinformation effect**, the **serial position effect** (primacy and recency effects), **source amnesia**, the **sleeper effect**, and spacing of practice (distributed versus massed practice).

Psychological Science: How Quickly We Forget

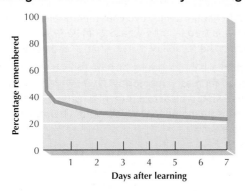

- Problems with eyewitness recollections are well established.

- Memory **repression** (especially of childhood sexual abuse) is a complex and controversial topic in memory research. Critics note that most people who have witnessed or experienced a violent or traumatic event have intense, persistent memories. They also worry that if a clinician suggests the possibility of abuse, the client's *constructive memory processes* may lead them to create a false memory of being abused. Researchers continue to explore this aspect of memory.

Elizabeth Loftus: Memory researcher and victim of false memories • Figure 7.15

4 Memory Distortions   202

- People shape, rearrange, and distort memories to create logical, consistent, and efficient thought processes. Despite all their problems and biases, our memories are normally quite accurate and usually serve us well.

- When memory errors involve the criminal justice system, they can have serious legal and social consequences.

Key Terms

- Alzheimer's disease (AD) p. 197
- anterograde amnesia p. 196
- chunking p. 187
- elaborative rehearsal p. 191
- encoding p. 185
- encoding specificity principle p. 194
- explicit/declarative memory p. 189
- implicit/nondeclarative memory p. 190
- information-processing model p. 185
- long-term memory (LTM) p. 189

- long-term potentiation (LTP) p. 194
- maintenance rehearsal p. 187
- memory p. 184
- misinformation effect p. 200
- mnemonic devices p. 193
- proactive interference p. 199
- repression p. 205
- retrieval p. 185
- retrieval cue p. 191
- retroactive interference p. 199

- retrograde amnesia p. 196
- sensory memory p. 186
- serial position effect p. 200
- short-term memory (STM) p. 187
- sleeper effect p. 201
- source amnesia p. 201
- storage p. 185
- three-stage memory model p. 185
- tip-of-the-tongue phenomenon p. 199
- working memory p. 188

Critical and Creative Thinking Questions

1. If you were forced to lose one type of memory—sensory, short-term, or long-term—which would you select? Why?

2. Why might students do better on a test if they take it in the same seat and classroom where they originally studied the material?

3. What might be the evolutionary advantage of heightened emotional arousal when a memory is being formed?

4. How might the serial position effect impact a person's ability to remember the names of a group of people when introduced at a party or other social gathering?

5. Why might advertisers of shoddy services or poor-quality products benefit from consumers "channel surfing" among news programs, talk shows, and infomercials?

6. As an eyewitness to a crime, how could you use the information in this chapter to improve your memory for specific details? If you were a juror, what would you say to the other jurors about the reliability of eyewitness testimony?

7. Do you think scientific inquiry has the tools to test for the presence of repressed memories? If you were a memory researcher what type of experiment would you design to evaluate this phenomenon? What might a behaviourist say about repression?

Self-Test

(Check your answers in Appendix A.)

1. Label these terms on the following figure. In the information-processing model of memory that compares memory to a computer, (a) _____ would happen at the keyboard, (b) _____ on the screen, and (c) _____ on the hard drive.

    a. _____

    b. _____

    c. _____

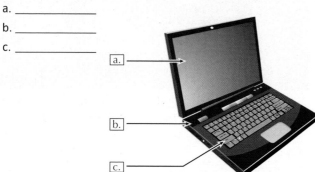

2. Label the three-stage memory model in the correct sequence on the following figure.

    a. _____

    b. _____

    c. _____

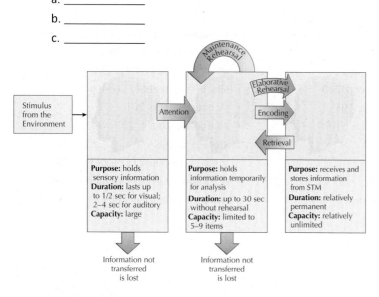

Purpose: holds sensory information	**Purpose:** holds information temporarily for analysis	**Purpose:** receives and stores information from STM
Duration: lasts up to 1/2 sec for visual; 2–4 sec for auditory	**Duration:** up to 30 sec without rehearsal	**Duration:** relatively permanent
Capacity: large	**Capacity:** limited to 5–9 items	**Capacity:** relatively unlimited

Information not transferred is lost   Information not transferred is lost

3. The following descriptions are characteristic of _____: information lasts only a few seconds or less, and it has a relatively large (but not unlimited) storage capacity.

    a. perceptual processes   c. working memory

    b. short-term storage   d. sensory memory

4. _____ is the process of grouping separate pieces of information into a single unit.

    a. Chunking   c. Method of loci

    b. Distributed practice   d. Peg method

5. The two major systems of long-term memory are _____.

    a. _____   b. _____

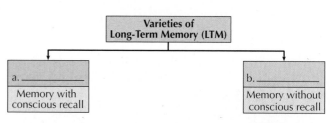

6. In answering this question, the correct multiple-choice option may serve as a _____ for recalling accurate information from your long-term memory.

    a. specificity code   c. retrieval cue

    b. priming pump   d. flashbulb stimulus

7. Although he had known how to skate since he was a young boy, Rian recently skated for the first time in many years. To his surprise, he did great and skated as he had as a child. What type of memory is Rian using in this situation?

    a. episodic (explicit/declarative)

    b. long-term memory

    c. motor memory

    d. procedural (implicit/nondeclarative)

8. Which type of memory ability is Mia using when she happily recalls her 13th birthday party?

a. procedural (implicit/nondeclarative)

b. episodic (explicit/declarative)

c. motor memory

d. flashbulb stimulus

9. The encoding specificity principle says that information retrieval is improved when _____.

a. both maintenance and elaborative rehearsal are used

b. reverberating circuits consolidate information

c. conditions of recovery are similar to encoding conditions

d. long-term potentiation is accessed

10. What is the name for the long-lasting increase in neural excitability caused by repeated neural input, which is believed to be the biological basis of learning and memory?

a. maintenance rehearsal

b. adrenaline activation

c. long-term potentiation

d. the reverberating response

11. A progressive mental deterioration characterized by severe memory loss that occurs most commonly old in age is called _____.

a. retrieval loss

b. prefrontal cortex deterioration

c. Alzheimer's disease

d. age-related amnesia

12. Label the two types of amnesia on the following.

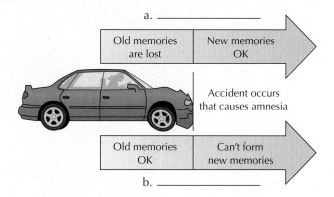

a. _____

Old memories are lost | New memories OK

Accident occurs that causes amnesia

Old memories OK | Can't form new memories

b. _____

13. Which of the following brain structures has not been implicated in memory formation?

a. pons

b. hippocampus

c. cerebral cortex

d. basal ganglia and cerebellum

14. List the five major theories of forgetting:

a. _____

b. _____

c. _____

d. _____

e. _____

15. Distributed practice is a learning technique in which _____.

a. subjects are distributed across equally sized study groups

b. learning periods alternate with non-learning rest periods

c. learning decays faster than it can be distributed

d. several students study together, distributing various subjects according to their individual strengths

16. Jill easily recalls knowing that her neighbour is an engineer, but she cannot remember exactly where she learned this information; she thinks it could be from another neighbour, her mother, or the woman at the post office. What is Jill experiencing?

a. the sleeper effect   c. sleeper amnesia

b. source amnesia   d. repressed source

17. Researchers have demonstrated that it is _____ to create false memories.

a. relatively easy   c. rarely possible

b. moderately difficult   d. possible

18. _____ is a common mechanism by which anxiety-provoking thoughts or events are prevented from reaching consciousness.

a. Suppression   c. Serial position

b. Flashback   d. Repression

19. _____ devices improve memory by encoding items in a special way.

a. Eidetic imagery   c. Reverberating circuit

b. Mnemonic   d. ECS

20. Jessica meets Paulo, Shari, Yani, Cody, and Hugh at a party and remembers them by realizing that the first letters of their names spell the word PSYCH. Which memory technique is Jessica using?

a. peg words   c. acronyms

b. mnemonic   d. method of loci

THE PLANNER ✓

Review your Chapter Planner on the chapter opener and check off your completed work.

Thinking, Language, and Intelligence

On February 14, 2010, Alexandre Bilodeau from Rosemère, Quebec, became the first Canadian athlete to win an Olympic gold medal on Canadian soil. Bilodeau took first place in the men's moguls skiing competition at the winter games in Vancouver. Executing a perfect backflip while skiing the course in one of the fastest times in the event, Bilodeau scored the highest points in the competition. Do you think that this feat reflects merely athletic skill and daring, or does it also speak to Bilodeau's intelligence?

When we think of intelligence, many of us think of Nobel Prize winners, great inventors, or chess champions. But success as an Olympic skier also requires intelligence—perhaps of a different kind than people generally associate with being "smart." Skiing enthusiasts admire the creativity and style that makes Bilodeau a world-class moguls competitor.

throughout this textbook because psychology is "the scientific study of behaviour and *mental processes*" (Chapter 1). For example, the chapters on sensation and perception (Chapter 4), consciousness (Chapter 5), learning (Chapter 6), and memory (Chapter 7) all focus on cognition.

In this chapter, we emphasize thinking, language, and intelligence. As you will discover, each is a complex phenomenon that is affected by numerous factors.

The three topics of this chapter—thinking, language, and intelligence—are often studied together under the broader umbrella of cognition: the mental activities involved in acquiring, storing, retrieving, and using knowledge. In a real sense, we discuss cognition

CHAPTER OUTLINE

CHAPTER PLANNER ✓

- ❏ Study the picture and read the opening story.
- ❏ Scan the Learning Objectives in each section:
  p. 212 ❏   p. 218 ❏   p. 223 ❏   p. 229 ❏
- ❏ Read the text and study all visuals. Answer any questions.

Analyze key features

- ❏ Process Diagram, p. 214
- ❏ Applying Psychology, p. 216
- ❏ Study Organizer, p. 220
- ❏ Psychological Science, p. 221 ❏   p. 228 ❏   p. 233 ❏
- ❏ Visualizing, p. 227
- ❏ What a Psychologist Sees, p. 231
- ❏ Stop: Answer the Concept Checks before you go on:
  p. 217 ❏   p. 223 ❏   p. 228 ❏   p. 234 ❏

End of chapter

- ❏ Review the Summary and Key Terms.
- ❏ Answer the Critical and Creative Thinking Questions.
- ❏ Complete the Self-Test and check your answers.

Jae C. Hong/AP Photo/The Canadian Press

Thinking

LEARNING OBJECTIVES

1. **Explain** the role of the prefrontal cortex in thinking.
2. **Describe** how mental images, concepts, and prototypes enable thinking.
3. **Identify** the three steps involved in problem solving.
4. **Summarize** how biases and heuristics can hamper problem solving.
5. **Explain** Sternberg and Lubart's investment theory of creativity.

T hinking, language, and intelligence are closely related facets of **cognition**. Every time you take information and mentally act on it, you are thinking. Our thought processes are distributed throughout our brains in networks of neurons. However, they are also localized. For example, during problem solving or decision-making, our brains are active in the **prefrontal cortex**. This region associates complex ideas; makes plans; forms, initiates, and allocates attention; and supports multitasking. The prefrontal cortex also links to other areas of the brain, such as the limbic system (Chapter 2), to synthesize information from several senses (Banich & Compton, 2011; Heyder et al., 2004; Sacchetti et al., 2007).

> **cognition** The mental activities involved in acquiring, storing, retrieving, and using knowledge.

Cognitive Building Blocks

Imagine yourself lying relaxed on the warm, gritty sand of a tropical ocean beach. Do you see palm trees swaying in the wind? Can you smell the sea and taste the dried salt on your lips? Can you hear children playing in the surf? What you've just created is a **mental image** (**Figure 8.1**), a mental representation of a previously stored sensory experience that includes visual, auditory, olfactory, tactile, motor, and gustatory imagery (McKellar, 1972).

We all have a mental space in which we visualize and manipulate our sensory images (Moulton & Kosslyn, 2011; Schifferstein & Hilscher, 2010). Interestingly, using mental imagery activates many of the same brain regions that are used for the actual experience itself. For example, visualizing an event or scene activates the occipital lobes, whereas thinking about a fearful event arouses the amygdala (Bensafi et al., 2007; Shin et al., 2010).

In addition to creating mental images, our thinking also involves forming **concepts**, or mental representations of a group or category. We form concepts by grouping together objects, events, activities, or ideas that share

similar characteristics (Smith, 1995). Concepts can be concrete (*car, concert*) or abstract (*intelligence, pornography*). They are essential to thinking and communication because they simplify and organize information. Normally, when you see a new object or encounter a new situation, you relate it to the concepts you've already formed, and you categorize it according to where it fits. For example, if you see a metal box with four wheels being driven on the highway, you know it's a car, even if you've never seen that particular model before.

Mental imagery • Figure 8.1

Some of our most creative and inspired moments come when we're forming and manipulating mental images. This mountain climber is probably visualizing her next move, and her ability to do so is critical to her success.

Scott Hailstone/iStockphoto

Night and DayImages/iStockphoto

Volodymyr Goinyk/iStockphoto

a. Most of us have a *prototype* for a bird that captures the essence of "birdness" and that allows us to quickly classify flying animals correctly.

b. When we encounter an example that doesn't quite fit our prototype, we need time to review our artificial concept. Because the penguin doesn't fly, it's harder to classify than a robin.

Some birds are "birdier" than others • Figure 8.2 _____

Some of our concepts are artificial, that is, created from logical rules or definitions. The concept of *triangle* is a good example. Triangles are defined as geometric forms with three sides and three angles. Any geometric form that contains these features would be included in the concept of triangle, and if any feature were missing, we would not classify the form as a triangle. Such concepts are called *artificial* (or *formal*) because the rules for inclusion are sharply defined.

Artificial concepts are often found in science and other academic disciplines. In everyday life, however, we seldom use precise, artificial definitions. When we see birds in the sky, we don't think *warm-blooded animals that fly, have wings, and lay eggs*—an artificial concept. Instead, we use *natural concepts*, or **prototypes**, which are based on a personal "best example" or typical representative of that concept (Rosch, 1973) (**Figure 8.2**).

Some of our concepts also develop when we create **hierarchies**, that is, grouping specific concepts as subcategories within broader concepts. In the hierarchy depicted in **Figure 8.3** note how the top (*superordinate*) category of *animal* is very broad and includes many members, the mid-level categories of *bird* and *dog* are more specific but still rather general, and the lowest (*subordinate*) categories of *parakeet* and *cocker spaniel* are the most specific.

When we first learn something, we rely primarily on the middle or basic-level concepts (Rosch, 1978). Thus, children tend to learn *bird* or *dog* before they learn superordinate concepts like *animal* or subordinate concepts like *parakeet* or *cocker spaniel*. Even as adults, when shown a picture of a parakeet, we classify it as a *bird* first.

Problem Solving

Several years ago in Los Angeles, a 3.5-metre-high tractor-trailer got stuck under a bridge that was a few centimetres too low. After hours of towing, tugging, and pushing, the police and transportation workers were stumped. Then a young boy happened by and asked, "Why don't you let some air out of the tires?" It was a simple, creative suggestion—and it worked.

Our lives are filled with problems, some simple, some difficult. In most cases, **problem solving** requires moving from a given state (the problem) to a goal state (the solution), a process that usually involves three steps (Bourne, Dominowski, & Loftus, 1979) (**Figure 8.4**).

A concept hierarchy • Figure 8.3 _____

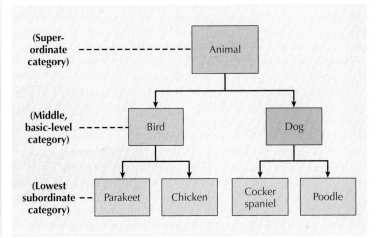

Three steps to the goal • Figure 8.4

❶ PREPARATION

Imagine that you are determined to find a new home close to work. There are at least three separate components to successful preparation.

1. *Identifying given facts.* Decide what are your most basic, non-negotiable limits and desires.

Must be able to walk to work.

I prefer a house to a large apartment building.

2. *Separating relevant from irrelevant facts.* What are your negotiable items? What do you consider irrelevant and easily compromised?

A fireplace would be a plus.

Must allow cats.

3. *Defining the ultimate goal.*

❷ PRODUCTION

During the *production step*, the problem solver produces possible solutions, called *hypotheses*. Two major approaches to generating hypotheses are *algorithms* and *heuristics*.

Algorithm:

Answers every ad.

An **algorithm** is a logical, step-by-step procedure (well suited for computers) that will always produce the solution. (For example, an algorithm for solving the problem 2 × 4 is 2 + 2 + 2 + 2.) For complex problems, algorithms may take a long time.

A **heuristic** is a simple rule or shortcut that does not guarantee a solution. Heuristics include working backward from the solution (a known condition) and *creating subgoals*, stepping-stones to the original goal.

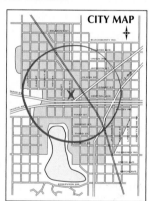

CITY MAP

Heuristic:

Works backward—start by drawing a 1.5 kilometre radius around work to narrow search.

> **algorithm** A logical, step-by-step procedure that, if followed correctly, will eventually solve the problem.
>
> **heuristic** A simple rule or shortcut for problem solving that does not guarantee a solution but does narrow the alternatives.

❸ EVALUATION

1. Did your hypotheses (possible solutions) solve the problem? If not, then you must return to the production stage and produce more possible solutions.

2. Take action. Once you've identified the right home, sign the lease and start packing.

Barriers to Problem Solving

We all encounter barriers to solving problems. We stick to problem-solving strategies (**mental sets**) that worked in the past, rather than trying solutions that are new and possibly more effective (**Figure 8.5**). Or we may fail to let our inventive instincts run free, thinking of objects as functioning only in their prescribed, customary way—a phenomenon called **functional fixedness** (**Figure 8.6**).

Other barriers to effective problem solving stem from our tendency to ignore important information. Have you ever found yourself agreeing with friends who support your environmental opinions while discounting conflicting opinions? This inclination to seek confirmation of our existing beliefs and to overlook contradictory evidence is known as the **confirmation bias** (Jonas et al., 2008; Kerschreiter et al., 2008; Nickerson, 1998; Reich, 2004).

British researcher Peter Wason (1968) was the first to demonstrate the confirmation bias. He asked participants to generate a list of numbers that conformed to the same rule that applied to this set of numbers:

2   4   6

Hypothesizing that the rule was "numbers increasing by two," most participants generated sets such as (4, 6, 8) or (1, 3, 5). Each time, Wason assured them that their sets of numbers conformed to the rule, but that the rule "numbers increasing by two" was incorrect. The problem was that the participants were searching only for

"Repurposing" as art • Figure 8.6 _____

Some people look at a pile of garbage and see only trash. Others see possibility. This photo shows how an artist recycled old hubcaps. Have you ever "repurposed" a discarded object, such as an old LP record for use as a wall decoration or even a bowl? If so, you have overcome *functional fixedness*.

information that confirmed their hypothesis. Proposing a series such as (1, 3, 4) would have led them to reject their initial hypothesis and discover the correct rule, which was actually "numbers in increasing order of size."

Cognitive psychologists Amos Tversky and Daniel Kahneman found that heuristics, as handy as they can be, can lead us to ignore relevant information (Kahneman, 2003; Tversky & Kahneman, 1974, 1993). When we use the **availability heuristic**, we judge the likelihood of an event based on how easily recalled (or "available") other instances of the event are (Buontempo & Brockner, 2008; Caruso, 2008; Oppenheimer, 2004). For example, shortly after the September 11, 2001, terrorist attacks, one study found that the average American believed he or she had a 20.5 percent chance of being hurt in a terrorist attack within a year (Lerner et al., 2003). Can you see how intense media coverage of the attacks created this erroneously high perception of risk?

Tversky and Kahneman also demonstrated that a second heuristic, called the **representativeness heuristic,** can sometimes also hinder problem solving. Using this heuristic, we estimate the probability of something based on how well the circumstances match (or "represent") our prototype (Fisk et al., 2006; Greene & Ellis, 2008). For example, if John is six feet, five inches tall, we may guess that he is a member of Canada's Olympic basketball team

The nine-dot problem • Figure 8.5 _____

Draw no more than four lines that run through all nine dots on this page without lifting your pencil from the paper. (The solution is provided at the end of this chapter, before the chapter summary.)

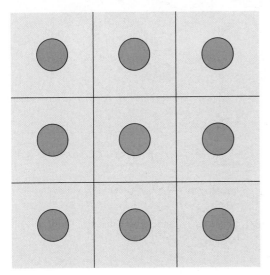

rather than, say, a physician. But in this case, the representative heuristic ignores *base rate information*—the probability of a characteristic occurring in the general population. In Canada, physicians outnumber members of the Olympic basketball team by more than 3,000 to 1. So despite his height, John is much more likely to be a physician.

Creativity: Finding Unique Solutions

What makes a person creative? Conceptions of creativity are subject to cultural relevance and to whether a solution or performance is considered useful at the time. In general,

creativity The ability to produce valued outcomes in a novel way.

three characteristics are associated with **creativity**: originality, fluency, and flexibility. Thomas Edison's invention of the light bulb offers a prime example of each of these characteristics (**Table 8.1**).

Most tests of creativity focus on **divergent thinking**, a type of thinking in which many possibilities are developed from a single starting point (Baer, 1994). For example, in the Unusual Uses Test, people are asked to think of as many uses as possible for an object (such as "How many ways can you use a brick?"). In the Anagrams Test, people are asked to reorder the letters in a word to make as many new words as possible.

A classic example of divergent thinking is the decision of Xiang Yu, a Chinese general in the third century B.C., to crush his troops' cooking pots and burn their ships. You might think that no general in his right mind would make such a decision, but Xiang Yu explained that his purpose was to focus the troops on moving forward, as they had no hope of retreating. His divergent thinking was rewarded with victory on the battlefield.

One prominent theory of creativity is Robert J. Sternberg and Todd Lubart's **investment theory** (1992,

Applying Psychology

Are You Creative?

Everyone exhibits a certain amount of creativity in some aspects of life. Even when doing ordinary tasks, such as planning an afternoon of errands, you are being somewhat creative. Similarly, if you've ever tightened a screw with a penny or used a telephone book on a chair as a booster seat for a child, you've found creative solutions to problems.

Would you like to test your own creativity?

- Find 10 coins and arrange them in the configuration shown here. By moving only 2 coins, form two rows that each contains 6 coins. (The solution is provided at the end of this chapter, before the chapter summary.)

- In five minutes, see how many words you can make by using the letters in the word *hippopotamus*.

- In five minutes, list all the things you can do with a paper clip.

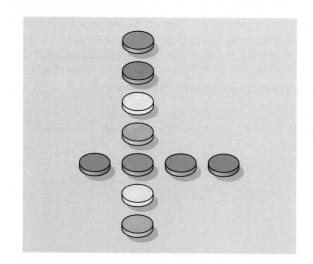

Think Critically

1. How did you do? If you had trouble with any of these tasks, can you use the list of resources of creative people in Table 8.2 to identify the resources you lack? Is there anything you could do to increase your share of these resources?
2. Creativity is usually associated with art, poetry, and the like. Can you think of other areas in which creativity is highly valued?

Three elements of creative thinking Table 8.1

	Explanations	Thomas Edison Examples
Originality	Seeing unique or different solutions to a problem	After noting that when electricity passes through a conductor, it produces a glowing red or white heat, Edison imagined using this light for practical uses.
Fluency	Generating a large number of possible solutions	Edison tried literally hundreds of different materials to find one that would heat to the point of glowing white without burning up.
Flexibility	Shifting with ease from one type of problem-solving strategy to another	When he couldn't find a long-lasting material, Edison tried heating it in a vacuum—thereby creating the first light bulb.

U.S. National Parks Service

1996; Sternberg, 2009b). According to this theory, creative people tend to "buy low" in the realm of ideas, championing ideas that others dismiss (much like a bold entrepreneur might invest in low-priced, unpopular stocks, believing that their value will rise). Once their creative ideas are highly valued, they "sell high" and move on to another unpopular but promising idea.

Investment theory also suggests that creativity requires the coming together of six interrelated resources (Sternberg, 2009b). These resources are summarized in **Table 8.2**. One way to improve your personal creativity is to study this list and then strengthen those areas in which you think you need improvement.

Matt Sayles/AP Photo/The Canadian Press

Resources of creative people Table 8.2

Intellectual Ability	Enough intelligence to see problems in a new light
Knowledge	Sufficient basic knowledge of the problem to effectively evaluate possible solutions
Thinking Style	Novel ideas and ability to distinguish between the worthy and worthless
Personality	Willingness to grow and change, take risks, and work to overcome obstacles
Motivation	Sufficient motivation to accomplish the task and more internal than external motivation
Environment	An environment that supports creativity

Which resources best explain Ryan Gosling's phenomenal success?

CONCEPT CHECK STOP

1. **What** is the difference between artificial and natural concepts?

2. **Why** are heuristics sometimes more appropriate for problem solving than are algorithms? When might the reverse be true?

3. **What** is an example of the availability heuristic?

Language

LEARNING OBJECTIVES

1. **Identify** the building blocks of language.
2. **Describe** the prominent theories of how language and thought interact.
3. **Describe** the major stages of language development.
4. **Review** the evidence that non-human animals may be able to learn and use language.

anguage allows us to communicate our thoughts, ideas, and feelings. It also enables us to mentally manipulate symbols, thereby expanding our thinking. To produce language, we first build words by using **phonemes** and **morphemes**. Then we string words into sentences by using rules of **grammar** (*syntax* and *semantics*) (**Figure 8.7**).

> **language** A form of communication that uses sounds and symbols combined according to specified rules.
>
> **phoneme [FO-neem]** The smallest basic unit of speech or sound (the English language has about 40 phonemes).

Language and Thought: A Complex Interaction

Does the fact that you speak English instead of Spanish—or Chinese instead of Swahili— determine how you reason, think, and perceive the world? Linguist Benjamin Whorf (1956) believed so. As evidence for his **linguistic relativity hypothesis**, Whorf offered a now classic example: because the Inuit have many words for snow (*apikak* for "first snow falling," *pukak* for "snow for drinking water," and so on), they can perceive and think about snow differently from English speakers, who have only one word—*snow*.

Although intriguing, Whorf's hypothesis has not fared well. He apparently exaggerated the number of Inuit words for snow (Pullum, 1991) and ignored the fact that English speakers have a number of terms to describe various forms of snow, such as *powder, hard-packed, granular, slush,* and so on. Other research has directly

> **morpheme [MOR-feem]** The smallest meaningful unit of language, formed from a combination of phonemes.
>
> **grammar** The rules that specify how phonemes, morphemes, words, and phrases should be combined to express thoughts; these rules include syntax and semantics.

Building blocks of language
• **Figure 8.7** _____

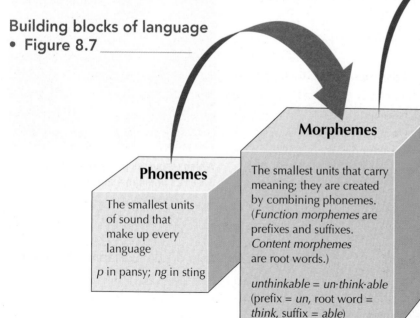

Grammar

A system of rules (syntax and semantics) used to generate acceptable language that enables us to communicate with and understand others.

They were in my psychology class.
versus
They was in my psychology class.

Syntax	**Semantics**
A system of rules for putting words in order	A system of using words to create meaning
I am happy. versus *Happy I am.*	*I went out on a limb for you.* versus *Humans have several limbs.*

Morphemes

The smallest units that carry meaning; they are created by combining phonemes. (*Function morphemes* are prefixes and suffixes. *Content morphemes* are root words.)

unthinkable = un·think·able (prefix = *un*, root word = *think*, suffix = *able*)

Phonemes

The smallest units of sound that make up every language

p in pansy; *ng* in sting

Brand X Pictures

Arina Ermilova/iStockphoto

Early non-verbal communication • Figure 8.8

Even before they begin to communicate verbally, infants use non-verbal signals to "speak" to others. Infants as young as 3½ months express basic emotions, such as interest, joy, disgust, anger, and sadness (Lewis, 2008). Children who are born blind and deaf exhibit the same emotional expressions as children who can see and hear, supporting the contention that these expressions are universal and innate. What emotions are each of these infants expressing?

contradicted Whorf's theory. For example, Eleanor Rosch (1973) found that although people of the Dani tribe in New Guinea possess only two colour names—one indicating cool, dark colours, and the other describing warm, bright colours—they discriminate among multiple hues as well as English speakers do.

Whorf apparently was mistaken in his belief that language determines thought. But there is no doubt that language *influences* thought (Hoff, 2009). People who speak both Chinese and English report that the language they're currently using affects their sense of self (Matsumoto & Juang, 2008). When using Chinese, they tend to conform to Chinese cultural norms; when speaking English, they tend to adopt Western norms.

Our words also influence the thinking of those who hear them. That's why companies avoid *firing* employees; instead, employees are *let go* or *non-renewed*. Similarly, military forces use such terms as *pre-emptive strike* to cover the fact that they attacked first and *tactical redeployment* to refer to a retreat. And research has shown that consumers who receive a *rebate* are less likely to spend the money than those who receive a *bonus* (Epley, 2008).

Language Development: From Crying to Talking

From birth, a child communicates through facial expressions, eye contact, and body gestures (**Figure 8.8**). Babies who are only hours old begin to "teach" their caregivers when and how they want to be held, fed, and handled.

For an interesting discussion on this topic, scan to download the author's podcast.

Eventually, children also communicate verbally, progressing through several distinct stages of language acquisition. These stages are summarized in **Study Organizer 8.1**. By age 5, most children have mastered basic grammar, and as Jeremy Anglin (1993) of the University of Waterloo reports, by age 6 they have a vocabulary of about 10,000 words. In fact, between the ages of 18 months and 6 years, they've learned, on average, six new words a day! Past this point, vocabulary and grammar gradually improve throughout life.

Some theorists argue that the capability to acquire and use language is innate in humans. Noam Chomsky (1968, 1980) has argued for this nativist position, proposing that children are "prewired" with a set of cognitive and neurological abilities, labelled a **language acquisition device (LAD)**. This set of abilities enables children to analyze language and infer the basic rules of grammar. This mechanism needs only exposure to speech to unlock its potential. As evidence for this nativist position, Chomsky observed that children everywhere progress through the same stages of language development at about the same ages. He also noted that babbling is the same in all languages and that babies who are deaf initially babble just like hearing babies. Steven Pinker, an internationally acclaimed Canadian psychologist at Harvard University, agrees strongly with the nativist position (Pinker, 2007; Pinker & Jackendoff, 2005). Pinker elaborated this view in his 1994 New York Times best-seller, *The Language Instinct*.

Nurturists, on the other hand, argue that the nativist position doesn't fully explain individual differences in language development. They hold that children learn language through

Developmental Stage	Age	Language Features	Example
Prelinguistic stage	Birth to ~12 months	Crying (reflexive in newborns; soon, crying becomes more purposeful)	hunger cry anger cry pain cry
	2 to 3 months	*Cooing* (vowel-like sounds)	"ooooh" "aaaah"
	4 to 6 months	*Babbling* (consonants added)	"bahbahbah" "dahdahdah"
Linguistic stage	~12 months	Babbling begins to resemble language of the child's home. Child seems to understand that sounds relate to meaning.	
		At first, speech is limited to one-word utterances.	"Mama" "juice" "Daddy" "up"
		Expressive ability more than doubles once the child begins to join words into short phrases.	"Daddy, milk" "no night-night!"
	~2 years	Child sometimes *overextends* (using words to include objects that do not fit the word's meaning).	all men = "Daddy" all furry animals = doggy
	~2 years to ~5 years	Child links several words to create short but intelligible sentences. This speech is called *telegraphic speech* because (like telegrams) it omits nonessential connecting words.	"Me want cookie." "Grandma go bye-bye?"
		Vocabulary increases at a phenomenal rate. Child acquires a wide variety of rules for grammar.	adding -*ed* for past tense adding -*s* to form plurals
		Child sometimes *overregularizes* (applying the basic rules of grammar even to cases that are exceptions to the rule).	"I goed to the zoo." "I brushed my tooths."

stock CD

Anita Patterson-Peppers/iStockphoto

kate_sept2004/iStockphoto

a complex system of rewards, punishments, and imitation. For example, parents smile and encourage any vocalizations from a very young infant. Later, they respond even more enthusiastically when the infant babbles "Mama" or "Dada." In this way, parents unknowingly use *shaping* and *reinforcement* (Chapter 6) to help babies learn language (**Figure 8.9**).

Bilingualism and French Immersion

More than 6.6 million Canadians have a first language other than English or French (Statistics Canada, 2012c). Yet most children from such families readily acquire one of Canada's two official languages in addition to the heritage language spoken at home. Exposure to two languages does not present an unusually difficult challenge to young children. Moreover, as noted by York University psychologist Ellen Bialystok (2007, 2011), bilingualism may be associated with gains in some areas of cognition. Furthermore, Fred Genesee of McGill University reported that bilingualism may also increase children's appreciation of both linguistic groups and their cultures (Genesee & Ganadara, 1999). Bilingualism, therefore, may be viewed as both a cognitive and a social asset to many children. Indeed, the value of

Nature or nurture? • Figure 8.9

Both sides of the nature-versus-nurture issue have had staunch supporters. However, most psychologists nowadays believe that language acquisition is a combination of both biology (nature) and environment (nurture) (Hoff, 2009; Plomin, De Fries, & Fulker, 2007). Can you see how both might contribute to this child's pretend phone conversation?

Jin Yong /iStockphoto

Psychological Science

Baby Sign Language

Many babies and toddlers—beginning as young as 9 months of age—can learn to communicate by using a modified form of sign language, sometimes called baby sign language. Symbolic gestures for basic ideas, such as *more, milk,* and *love* enhance parents' and caregivers' interactions with children who cannot yet talk. Many parents find that signing with their infant or toddler gives them a fascinating window into the baby's mind—and can eliminate a lot of frustration for both them and the baby! Some researchers believe that teaching babies to sign helps foster better language comprehension and can speed up the process of learning to talk (Goodwyn, Acredolo, & Brown, 2000). In recent years, baby signing has become hugely popular in both Canada and the United States (Baby Signs Canada, 2006; CBC News Online, 2004).

It is important to realize that baby signing is not the same as actual sign languages, such as American Sign Language. Sign languages, like spoken languages, have large vocabularies and possess grammar. Baby signing, in contrast, consists of isolated signs that may or may not be based on words from sign languages. Moreover, these baby signs are never combined into actual sentences.

Given the popularity of baby sign language, a team of Canadian investigators at the University of Ottawa and the University of Waterloo (Johnston, Durieux-Smith, & Bloom, 2005) reviewed the available research on its effects. They found that there have actually not been very many studies of baby sign language. Moreover, many of the studies that have been conducted lacked adequate experimental control procedures, making their findings difficult to interpret. In short, much more research is needed in this area. Nevertheless, whether baby signing actually accelerates language development or not, its use provides for increased parent–child interactions, which can never be a bad thing for children's development.

Think Critically

1. Would you teach your own child baby sign language? Why or why not?
2. How could signing be combined with a child's early attempts to talk in order to enhance language development?

---

bilingualism extends beyond childhood: Toronto researchers Fergus Craik, Ellen Bialystok, and Morris Freedman (2010) recently reported exciting findings that bilingualism can actually delay the onset of Alzheimer's disease (AD) later in life (AD is discussed in Chapter 7) by promoting cognitive reserves in bilingual (or multilingual) individuals.

An approach to bilingualism that is uniquely Canadian is the popular French immersion programs offered across the country. In these programs, children who speak English receive much of their school instruction in French. French immersion programs were initially developed in the 1960s by a group of English-speaking parents in a suburb of Montreal (Genesee & Gandara, 1999). Since then, French immersion programs have become popular across the country (**Figure 8.10**). In 2011, almost 353,000 students

were enrolled in such programs in Canada (Canadian Parents for French, 2012).

French immersion programs take various forms. *Early immersion* begins in the lower elementary school grades, while *middle immersion* begins in grades 4 or 5, and *late immersion* begins at the end of elementary school or the beginning of high school (Canadian Council on Learning, 2007). Students who have participated in such programs usually have excellent French comprehension and high levels of speaking and writing abilities in French.

The majority of children in French immersion are in Quebec and eastern Canada. Many other English-speaking children across the country participate in core French programs, which offer up to one hour of instruction in French each day (Dicks & Kristmanson, 2008). In 2011, more than

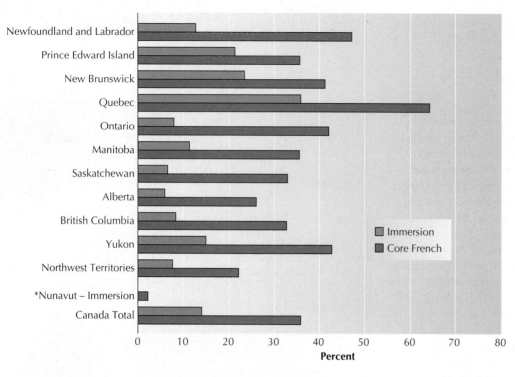

Percentage of students enrolled in French immersion and core French programs in 2011 • Figure 8.10 _____

Why do you think participation in French immersion is highest in Quebec? What might explain the high participation in both immersion and core French programs in the Atlantic provinces?

35 percent of Canadian children in junior kindergarten through grade 12 were enrolled in core French instruction (Canadian Parents for French, 2012c). In general, research finds that the more exposure to French, whether through core French instruction, immersion, exchange programs, and so on, the better the students' proficiency (Genesee, 1987).

Can Humans Talk to Non-Human Animals?

Without question, non-human animals communicate, sending warnings, signalling sexual interest, sharing locations of food sources, and so on. But can non-human animals master the complexity of human language? Since the 1930s, many language studies have attempted to answer this question by probing the language abilities of chimpanzees and gorillas (e.g., Barner et al., 2008; Fields et al., 2007; Savage-Rumbaugh, 1990; Segerdahl, Fields, & Savage-Rumbaugh, 2006).

One of the most successful early studies was conducted by Beatrice and Allen Gardner (1969), who recognized chimpanzees' manual dexterity and ability to imitate gestures. The Gardners used American Sign Language (ASL) with a chimp named Washoe. By the time Washoe was 4 years old, she had learned 132 signs and was able to combine them into simple sentences, such as "Hurry, gimme toothbrush" and "Please tickle more." The famous gorilla Koko also uses ASL to communicate; she reportedly uses more than 1,000 signs (**Figure 8.11**).

In another well-known study, a chimp named Lana learned to use symbols on a computer to get things she wanted, such as food, a drink, a tickle from her trainers, and her curtains opened (Rumbaugh et al., 1974) (**Figure 8.12**).

Dolphins are also the subject of interesting language research. Communication with dolphins is done by means of hand signals or audible commands transmitted through an underwater speaker system. In one typical study, trainers gave dolphins commands made up of two- to five-word sentences, such as "Big ball—square—return," which meant that they should go get the big ball, put it in the floating

Signing • Figure 8.11 _____

According to her teacher, Penny Patterson, Koko uses ASL to converse with others, talk to herself, joke, express preferences, and even lie (Linden, 1993; Patterson, 2002).

square, and return to the trainer (Herman et al., 1984). By varying the syntax (for example, the order of the words) and specific content of the commands, the researchers showed that dolphins are sensitive to these aspects of language.

Psychologists disagree on how to interpret these findings about apes and dolphins. Most psychologists believe that non-human animals do communicate but that their ideas are severely limited. Critics claim that apes and dolphins are unable to convey subtle meanings, use language creatively, or communicate at an abstract level (Jackendoff, 2003; Siegala & Varley, 2008).

Others claim that these animals do not truly understand language but have simply been operantly conditioned (Chapter 6) to imitate symbols to receive rewards (Savage-Rumbaugh, 1990; Terrace, 1979). Finally, other critics argue that data regarding animal language have not always been well documented (Lieberman, 1998; Willingham, 2001; Wynne, 2007).

Proponents of animal language respond that apes can use language creatively and have even "coined" (created) some words of their own. For example, Koko signed "finger bracelet" to describe a ring and "eye hat" to describe a mask (Patterson & Linden, 1981). Proponents also argue that, as demonstrated by the dolphin studies, animals can be taught to understand basic rules of sentence structure.

Still, the gap between human and non-human animals' language is considerable. Current evidence suggests that, at best, non-human animal language is less complex, is less creative, and has fewer rules than any language used by humans.

Michael Nichols/National Geographic Stock

Computer-aided communication • Figure 8.12

Apes lack the necessary anatomical structures to vocalize the way humans do. For this reason, language research with chimps and gorillas has focused on teaching the animals to use sign language or to "speak" by pointing to symbols on a keyboard. Do you think this amounts to using language the same way as humans do?

CONCEPT CHECK STOP

1. **What** are phonemes, morphemes, and grammar?

2. **Outline** the stages of language acquisition through which children pass.

3. **Why** do some psychologists believe that language is an innate ability, whereas others believe that it is learned through reinforcement and imitation?

4. **What** are some differences between human and non-human animal language?

Intelligence

LEARNING OBJECTIVES

1. **Review** the debate about single versus multiple intelligences.

2. **Identify** the similarities and differences between two commonly used IQ tests.

3. **Explain** why standardization, reliability, and validity are all essential to scientifically acceptable IQ tests.

Many people equate intelligence with "book smarts." For others, what is intelligent depends on the characteristics and skills that are valued in a particular social group or culture (Berry et al., 2011; Hunt, 2011; Sternberg, 2009a). For example, the Mandarin word that corresponds most closely to the word *intelligence* is a character meaning "good brain

intelligence The global capacity to think rationally, act purposefully, and deal effectively with the environment.

and talented" (Matsumoto, 2000). The word is associated with such traits as imitation, effort, and social responsibility (Keats, 1982).

Even Western psychologists debate the definition of intelligence. In this discussion, we rely on a formal definition developed by psychologist David Wechsler (pronounced "WEX-ler") (1944, 1977). Wechsler defined **intelligence** as the global capacity to think rationally, act purposefully, and deal effectively with the environment.

Do We Have One or Many Intelligences?

One of the central debates in research on intelligence concerns whether intelligence is a single ability or a collection of many specific abilities.

In the 1920s, British psychologist Charles Spearman first observed that high scores on separate tests of mental abilities tend to correlate with one another. Spearman (1923) thus proposed that intelligence is a single factor, which he termed **general intelligence** (**g**). He believed that g underlies all intellectual behaviour, including reasoning, solving problems, and performing well in all areas of cognition. Spearman's work laid the foundation for today's standardized intelligence tests (Goldstein, 2008; Johnson, Bouchard, et al., 2004).

About a decade later, L. L. Thurstone (1938) proposed seven primary mental abilities: verbal comprehension, word fluency, numerical fluency, spatial visualization, associative memory, perceptual speed, and reasoning. J. P. Guilford (1967) later expanded this number, proposing that as many as 120 factors were involved in the structure of intelligence.

Around the same time, Raymond Cattell (1963, 1971) re-analyzed Thurstone's data and argued against the idea of multiple intelligences. He believed that two subtypes of g exist—fluid intelligence and crystallized intelligence:

- **Fluid intelligence** (**gf**) refers to innate, inherited reasoning abilities, memory, and speed of information processing. Fluid intelligence is relatively independent of education and experience, and like other biological capacities it declines with age (Bugg et al., 2006; Daniels et al., 2006; Rozencwajg et al., 2005; Whitbourne & Whitbourne, 2011).
- **Crystallized intelligence** (**gc**) refers to the store or accumulation of knowledge and skills gained through experience and education (Hunt, 2011; Sternberg, 2009a). Crystallized intelligence tends to increase over the lifespan (Whitbourne & Whitbourne, 2011).

Today the concept of g as a measure of "academic smarts" has considerable support. However, many contemporary cognitive theorists believe that intelligence is not a single general factor but a collection of many separate specific abilities.

One of these cognitive theorists, Howard Gardner, believes that people have a number of kinds of intelligences. The fact that people with brain damage often lose some intellectual abilities while retaining others suggests to Gardner that different intelligences are located in separate areas throughout the brain. According to Gardner's (1983, 1999, 2008) **theory of multiple intelligences**, people have different profiles of intelligence because they are stronger in some areas than others (**Table 8.3**). They also use their intelligences differently to learn new material, perform tasks, and solve problems.

Robert Sternberg's **triarchic theory of successful intelligence** also involves multiple abilities. As discussed in **Table 8.4**, Sternberg proposed three separate, learned aspects of intelligence: (1) *analytic*, (2) *creative*, and (3) *practical* (Sternberg, 1985, 2007, 2009c).

Sternberg (1985, 1999, 2009c) emphasizes the process underlying thinking rather than just the product. He also stresses the importance of applying mental abilities to real-world situations rather than testing mental abilities in isolation (e.g., Sternberg, 2005, 2009d; Sternberg & Hedlund, 2002). Sternberg (1998, 2009c) introduced the term *successful intelligence* to describe the ability to adapt to, shape, and select environments in order to accomplish personal and societal goals.

Measuring Intelligence

As you've just seen, intelligence is difficult to define, and there is debate over whether it is one or multiple abilities. Despite this uncertainty, many college and university admissions offices, scholarship committees, and employers use scores from intelligence tests (or similar types of tests) as a significant part of their selection criteria. How well do these tests predict student and employee success? Different IQ tests approach the measurement of intelligence from different perspectives. However, most have been designed to predict grades in school. Let's look at some of the most commonly used IQ tests.

The **Stanford-Binet Intelligence Scale** is loosely based on the first IQ tests developed in France around the turn of the twentieth century by Alfred Binet. Lewis Terman (1916) developed the Stanford-Binet at Stanford University to test the intellectual ability of American children from ages 3 to 16. The test is revised periodically—most recently in 2003 (Roid, 2003). The test is administered individually and consists of such tasks as copying geometric designs, identifying similarities, and repeating number sequences.

Gardner's multiple intelligences and possible careers   Table 8.3

Linguistic: language, such as speaking, reading a book, writing a story	**Careers:** novelist, journalist, teacher
Spatial: mental maps, such as figuring out how to pack multiple presents in a box or how to draw a floor plan	**Careers:** engineer, architect, pilot
Bodily/kinesthetic: body movement, such as dancing, gymnastics, or figure skating	**Careers:** athlete, dancer, ski instructor
Intrapersonal: understanding oneself, such as setting achievable goals or recognizing self-defeating emotions	**Careers:** increased success in almost all careers
Logical/mathematical: problem solving or scientific analysis, such as following a logical proof or solving a mathematical problem	**Careers:** mathematician, scientist, engineer
Musical: musical skills, such as singing or playing a musical instrument	**Careers:** singer, musician, composer
Interpersonal: social skills, such as managing diverse groups of people	**Careers:** salesperson, manager, therapist, teacher
Naturalistic: attuned to nature, such as noticing seasonal patterns or using environmentally safe products	**Careers:** biologist, naturalist
(Possible) Spiritual/existential: attuned to meaning of life and death and other conditions of life	**Careers:** philosopher, theologian

Source: Adapted from Gardner, 1983, 1999.

Who is intelligent? What kinds of intelligence do television host George Stroumboulopoulos, Olympic gold medal mogul skier Alexandre Bilodeau, and novelist Margaret Atwood demonstrate?

Sternberg's triarchic theory of successful intelligence   Table 8.4

	Analytical Intelligence	**Creative Intelligence**	**Practical Intelligence**
Sample Skills	Good at analysis, evaluation, judgement, and comparison skills	Good at invention, coping with novelty, and imagination skills	Good at application, implementation, execution, and utilization skills
Sample Methods of Assessment	These skills are assessed by intelligence or scholastic aptitude tests. Questions ask about the meanings of words based on context and how to solve number-series problems.	These skills are assessed in many ways, including completing open-ended tasks, writing a short story, drawing a piece of art, or solving a scientific problem requiring insight.	Although these skills are more difficult to assess, they can be measured by asking for solutions to practical and personal problems.

In the original version of the Stanford-Binet, results were expressed in terms of a mental age. For example, if a 7-year-old's score equalled that of an average 8-year-old,

intelligence quotient (IQ) An individual's mental age divided by his or her chronological age and multiplied by 100.

the child was considered to have a mental age of 8. To determine the child's **intelligence quotient (IQ)**, mental age was divided by the child's chronological age (actual age in years) and multiplied by 100 (IQ = MA/CA × 100). Thus, a 7-year-old with a mental age of 8 would have an IQ of 8/7 × 100, or 114. (Figure 8.14 describes another widely used intelligence test.)

Today, most intelligence test scores no longer use the original formula comparing mental age to chronological age, but instead compare a person's score to a national sample of people of similar age (**Figure 8.13**). Nevertheless, the term *IQ* remains as a shorthand expression for intelligence test scores.

What makes a good test? How are the tests developed by Binet and Wechsler (**Figure 8.14**) any better than those published in popular magazines and found on Internet websites? To be scientifically acceptable, all psychological tests must fulfill three basic requirements:

- **Standardization.** Intelligence tests (as well as person-

standardization The establishment of the norms and uniform procedures for giving and scoring a test.

ality, aptitude, achievement, and most other tests) must be standardized in two ways. First, every test must have norms, or average scores, developed by giving the test to a large representative sample of

people (a diverse group of people who resemble those for whom the test is intended). Second, testing procedures must be standardized; that is, all test takers must be given the same instructions, questions, and time limits, and all test administrators must follow the same objective score standards.

- **Reliability.** To be trustworthy, a test must be consistent, or reliable, across time and situations. Reliability is usually determined by retesting subjects to see whether their test scores change significantly (Gregory, 2011). Retesting can be done via the **test-retest method**, in

reliability A measure of the consistency and stability of test scores when a test is re-administered.

which participants' scores on two separate administrations of the same test are compared, or via the **split-half method**, which involves splitting a test into two equivalent parts (e.g., odd and even questions) and determining the degree of similarity between the two halves.

- **Validity.** Validity is the ability of a test to measure what it is designed to measure. The most important type of valid-ity is **criterion-related valid-ity**, or the accuracy with which test scores can be used to pre-

validity The ability of a test to measure what it was designed to measure.

dict another variable of interest (known as the crite-rion). Criterion-related validity is expressed as the *correlation* (Chapter 1) between the test score and the criterion. If two variables are highly correlated, then one variable can be used to predict the other. Thus, if a test is valid, its scores will be useful in predict-ing people's behaviour or performance in some other specified situation. A good example of this is the use of intelligence test scores to predict grades at school.

Can you see why a test that is standardized and reliable, but not valid, would be worthless? For example, a scale to measure weight is easy to standardize (the instruc-tions specify exactly how to stand on the scale and accurately measure your weight), and it is usually reliable (similar weight is obtained for the same in-dividual on each retest). But it certainly would not be valid as a measure of intelligence.

Frequency distribution of IQ scores
- **Figure 8.13**

Sixty-eight percent of children score within one standard deviation (15 points) above or below the average, which is 100 points. About 16 percent score above 115, and about 16 percent score below 85.

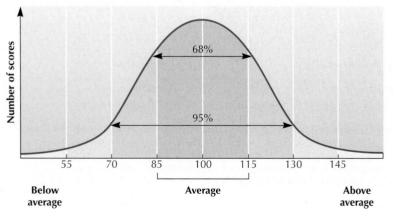

Visualizing

A modern intelligence test • Figure 8.14

The most widely used intelligence test, the Wechsler Adult Intelligence Scale (WAIS), was developed by David Wechsler in the mid-twentieth century. The test is currently in its fourth edition (WAIS-IV). Wechsler later created a similar test for school-age children, the Wechsler Intelligence Scale for Children (shown below), also now in its fourth edition (WISC-IV), and one for preschool children, the Wechsler Preschool and Primary Scale of Intelligence (WPPSI-III).

Like the Stanford-Binet, Wechsler's tests yield an overall intelligence score. The most recent versions of both the Stanford-Binet and the Wechsler tests also provide scores for a number of more specific intellectual abilities (Becker, 2003). The Wechsler scales provide separate scores for *Verbal Reasoning* (such as vocabulary and knowledge of general information), *Perceptual Reasoning* (such as arranging blocks to match a given pattern and indicating what's missing from a picture), *Working Memory* (such as short-term memory and mental arithmetic), and *Processing Speed* (such as pairing symbols with numbers and scanning for symbols in a list).

Verbal Comprehension

Information
How many wings does a bird have?
How many nickels make a dime?
What is pepper?

Vocabulary
What is a_____? What does_____ mean?
Hammer
Protect
Epidemic

Perceptual Reasoning

Block Design
Copy this design with blocks.

Picture Completion
What is missing from this ambulance?

Working Memory

Arithmetic
Sam had three pieces of candy, and Joe gave him four more. How many pieces of candy did Sam have altogether?
If two apples cost $0.15, what will be the cost of a dozen apples?

Digit Span
Repeat the following numbers:
4 1 7
7 1 9 5 4 8 2

Processing Speed

Coding
Write the appropriate number above each symbol.

1	2	3	4	5							
☀	✳	❋	❋	❋	❋	☀	❋	✳	❋	☀	❋

Psychological Science

Emotional Intelligence (EI): How Important Are "Emotional Smarts"?

Most people have heard of IQ, the intelligence quotient, but what about **EI—emotional intelligence**? According to Daniel Goleman (1995, 2000) *emotional intelligence* involves knowing and managing your emotions, empathizing with others, and maintaining satisfying relationships. In other words, an emotionally intelligent person successfully combines the three components of emotions (cognitive, physiological, and behavioural).

Goleman suggested that having a high EI explains why people of modest IQ may often be more successful than people with much higher IQ scores. He proposed that traditional measures of human intelligence ignore a crucial range of abilities that characterize people who excel in real life: self-awareness, impulse control, persistence, zeal and self-motivation, empathy, and social deftness.

Research suggests that EI may be positively related to relations with others, performance on the job and at school, and health and psychological well-being (Mayer et al., 2008).

Nancy Ney/Digital Vision/Getty Images

Proponents of EI have suggested, therefore, that medical schools and other professional training programs should make training in EI a core ingredient in their curriculum (see Parker et al., 2009). Moreover, some evidence suggests that the abilities that are involved in EI may be positively related to children's social and academic success in school (Mayer et al., 2008). Advocates suggest that parents and educators can help children develop EI through encouraging them to identify their emotions and helping them understand how their feelings are connected to their actions and how emotions can be changed (Alegre, 2011; Brackett et al., 2011; Furnham, 2009).

A number of researchers are more skeptical. They point out that the various components of EI are difficult to identify and measure, and they suggest a cautious approach when trying to make use of measures of EI in the clinic or workplace (Fiori & Antonakis, 2011; Furnham, 2009; Mayer et al., 2008; Petrides, 2011; van Heck & den Oudsten, 2008). Others are unconvinced of the effectiveness of school-based EI training programs. The abilities involved in EI may indeed be related to school success (Mayer et al.,2008), but as Canadian researchers James Parker, Donald Safloske, and Laura Wood (Parker et al., 2009) note, there is actually not much empirical evidence concerning the effectiveness of training children in EI at school.

EI is a controversial concept, but most researchers are pleased that the subject of emotion is being taken seriously. Research in this area has flourished in recent years, and it will increase our understanding of emotion and perhaps even reveal the ultimate value of the notion of emotional intelligence.

Think Critically

1. Do you think you have high or low emotional intelligence? Why?
2. What value might EI have for a person's functioning in everyday life?

CONCEPT CHECK STOP

1. **What** is the difference between Gardner's and Sternberg's theories of intelligence?

2. **What** is meant by *standardization, reliability,* and *validity*? Why are these important?

3. **What** are some modern intelligence tests, and how do they define intelligence?

4. **What** is emotional intelligence?

The Intelligence Controversy

LEARNING OBJECTIVES

1. **Explain** why extremes in intelligence provide support for the validity of IQ testing.
2. **Review** research on how brain functioning is related to intelligence.
3. **Describe** how genetics and environment interact to shape intelligence.
4. **Summarize** the debate over ethnicity and intelligence.

Psychologists have long debated two important questions related to intelligence: What causes some people to be more intelligent than others, and what factors—environmental or hereditary—influence an individual's intelligence? A related question is whether IQ tests are culturally biased. These questions, and the controversies surrounding them, are discussed in this section.

Extremes in Intelligence: Intellectual Disability and Giftedness

One of the best methods for judging the validity of a test is to compare people who score at the extremes. Despite the uncertainties discussed in the previous section, intelligence tests provide one of the major criteria for assessing mental ability at the extremes—specifically, for diagnosing **intellectual disability** and **giftedness**.

The clinical label *intellectually disabled* (also referred to as *mentally retarded*) is applied when someone is significantly below average in intellectual functioning and has significant deficits in adaptive functioning (such as communicating, living independently, social or occupational functioning, or maintaining safety and health) (American Psychiatric Association, 2000; Phares, 2008).

Fewer than 3 percent of people are classified as having an intellectual disability. Of this group, 85 percent have only a mild intellectual disability and many become self-supporting, integrated members of society. Furthermore, people can score low on some measures of intelligence and still be average or even gifted in others.

> **savant syndrome**
> A condition in which a person who has an intellectual disability exhibits exceptional skill or brilliance in some limited field.

The most dramatic examples are people with **savant syndrome** (**Figure 8.15**).

Some forms of intellectual disability, such as Down syndrome, fragile-X syndrome, and phenylketonuria (PKU), stem from genetic or chromosomal abnormalities. Other causes are environmental, including prenatal exposure to excessive alcohol and other drugs, extreme deprivation or neglect in early life, and brain damage from accidents. However, in many other cases, there is no known cause of the intellectual disability.

At the other end of the intelligence spectrum are people with especially high IQs (typically defined as 135 or above or being in the top 1 or 2 percent). Have you ever wondered what happens to people with such superior intellectual abilities?

In 1921, Lewis Terman identified 1,500 gifted children with IQs of 140 or higher. He then tracked their progress through adulthood. His study of these gifted children—affectionately nicknamed the "Termites"—put to rest many myths and stereotypes about gifted people. As children, they not only received excellent grades but were also found to be socially well adjusted. By adulthood, the number who had

An unusual form of intelligence • Figure 8.15

Although people with *savant syndrome* score very low on IQ tests (usually between 40 and 70), they demonstrate exceptional skills or brilliance in specific areas, such as rapid calculation, art, memory, or musical ability (Bor et al., 2007; Iavarone, 2007; Miller, 2005; Pring et al., 2008). Brittany Maier has autism and severe visual impairment; she's also a gifted composer and pianist who performs publicly and has recorded a CD. Her musical repertoire includes more than 15,000 songs.

Timothy Fadek/© Polaris 222 Images

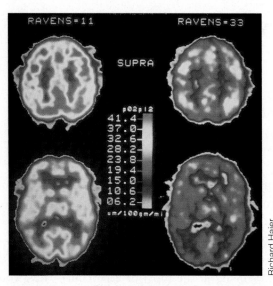

Richard Haier

Do intelligent brains work more efficiently?
• Figure 8.16

When given problem-solving tasks, people of low intelligence (PET scans on the left) show more activity (red and yellow indicate more brain activity) in relevant brain areas than people of higher intelligence (PET scans on right).

become research scientists, engineers, physicians, lawyers, or professors, or who were highly successful in business or other fields was many times the number a random group would have provided (Leslie, 2000; Terman, 1954). Those who were most successful tended to have extraordinary motivation, and they also had someone at home or school who was especially encouraging (Goleman, 1980). In other ways, however, many Termites were similar to their peers of average intelligence. Their rates of alcoholism, divorce, and suicide were close to the national rates (Leslie, 2000), and some of them were even quite unsuccessful. Thus, a high IQ is no guarantee of success in every endeavour; it offers only more intellectual opportunities.

The Brain's Influence on Intelligence

A basic tenet of neuroscience is that all mental activity (including intelligence) results from neural activity in the brain. Most recent research on the biology of intelligence has focused on brain functioning. One such aspect of brain function is speed of processing. People who score highest on intelligence tests also respond more quickly on tasks involving perceptual judgements (Bowling & Mackenzie, 1996; Deary & Stough, 1996, 1997; Posthuma, de Geus, et al., 2001; Posthuma, Neale, et al., 2001). Moreover, a recent review of the research conducted by Leah Sheppard and Philip Vernon (2008) of the University of Western Ontario found that across 172 studies conducted over the past 50 years, intelligence has been consistently related to the speed with which people process information.

Other research using positron emission tomography (PET) to measure brain activity (Chapter 1) reveals that the areas of the brain involved in problem solving show less activity in people of high intelligence than in people of lower intelligence when they are given the same problem-solving tasks (**Figure 8.16**) (Jung & Haier, 2007; Neubauer et al., 2004). Apparently, intelligent brains work smarter, or more efficiently, than do less-intelligent brains.

Does size matter? Intuitively, it would seem to make sense that bigger brains would be smarter—after all, humans have larger brains than less-intelligent species, such as dogs. (Some animals, such as whales and dolphins, have larger brains than humans, but human brains are still larger relative to our body size.) In fact, brain-imaging studies have found a correlation between brain size (adjusted for body size) and intelligence (Christensen et al., 2008; Deary et al., 2007; Ivanovic et al., 2004). However, other studies have failed to fully support the size-intelligence correlation (Gignac & Vernon, 2003; Wickett et al., 2000). Indeed, studies of Albert Einstein's brain found that it was not larger or heavier than normal (Witelson, Kigar, & Harvey, 1999). In fact, some of Einstein's brain areas were actually smaller than average. Nevertheless, the area responsible for processing mathematical and spatial information was 15 percent larger than average.

Genetic and Environmental Influences on Intelligence

Similarities in intelligence between family members are due to a combination of hereditary (shared genetic material) and environmental factors (similar living arrangements and experiences). Researchers who are interested in the role of heredity in intelligence often focus on *twin* studies. Recall from Chapter 2 that one of the most popular ways to study the relative effects of heredity versus the environment is to use identical (monozygotic) twins because they share 100 percent of their genetic material. Such studies have found significant hereditary influences for intelligence (see *What a Psychologist Sees: Family Studies of Intelligence*), personality, and psychopathology (Blonigen et al., 2008; Johnson et al., 2007; Plomin, DeFries, & Faulkner, 2007; Sternberg, 2008, 2012).

The long-running Minnesota Study of Twins, an investigation of identical twins raised in different homes and reunited only as adults (Bouchard, 1994, 1999; Bouchard et al., 1998; Johnson et al., 2007), found that genetic factors appear to play a surprisingly large role in the IQ scores of identical twins.

What a Psychologist Sees

Family Studies of Intelligence

Why are some people intellectually gifted while others struggle? As twin studies demonstrate, genetics play an important role. In **Figure 8.17**, note the higher correlations between identical twins' IQ scores compared with the correlations between all other pairs (Bouchard & McGue, 1981; Bouchard et al., 1998; McGue et al., 1993). Although heredity equips each person with innate intellectual capabilities, the environment significantly influences whether a person will reach his or her full intellectual potential (Dickens & Flynn, 2001; Sangwan, 2001). For example, early malnutrition can retard a child's brain development, which in turn affects the child's curiosity, responsiveness to the environment, and motivation for learning—all of which can lower the child's IQ. The reverse is also true: an enriching early environment can set the stage for intellectual growth.

Correlations in IQ scores • Figure 8.17

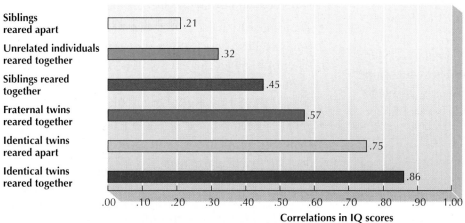

jjmm888/iStockphoto

However, such results are not conclusive. Even when twins are adopted into different homes, adoption agencies tend to use similar criteria when choosing adoptive parents. Therefore, the homes of these "reared apart" twins were actually quite similar. In addition, identical twins also shared the same nine-month prenatal environment, which also might have influenced their brain development and intelligence (White, Andreasen, & Nopoulos, 2002).

Ethnicity and Intelligence: Are IQ Tests Culturally Biased?

How would you answer the following questions?

1. A symphony is to a composer as a book is to a(n) _____. (a) musician; (b) editor; (c) novel; (d) author
2. If you throw a pair of dice and they land showing 7 on top, what is on the bottom? (a) snake eyes; (b) box cars; (c) little Joes; (d) 11

Can you see how the content and answers to these questions might reflect cultural bias? People from some backgrounds will find the first question easier. Other groups will more easily answer the second. Which of these two questions do you think is most likely to appear on standard IQ tests?

One of the most hotly debated and controversial issues in psychology involves differences in intelligence test scores between ethnic groups and what these differences really mean. The issue has been of particular concern for American researchers, where many studies have found that middle-income Caucasians outperform other groups, such as Blacks, Hispanics, and Aboriginal people in terms of the average scores of these groups on IQ tests (Dolan, 1999; Loehlin, 2000; Salois, 1999), although the differences have narrowed in recent years (Dickens & Flynn, 2006).

In considering such differences, it is important to realize that the ranges of scores on IQ tests for different ethnic groups are completely overlapping. There is much more variability in IQ scores within groups (for example, among Caucasian children or among Black American children) than there are differences between groups (Suzuki & Valencia, 1997). There is no way, therefore, to predict anything about a child's abilities simply from knowing his or her ethnic background.

What could account for such inter-group discrepancies? Some have argued that if heredity is important for individual differences in IQ, it may also be important for differences between ethnic groups (Herrnstein & Murray, 1994; Rushton & Jensen, 2005). Indeed, in 1969, Arthur Jensen began a heated debate when he argued that genetic factors are "strongly implicated" as the cause of ethnic differences in intelligence scores. Later, Richard J. Herrnstein and Charles Murray's book *The Bell Curve: Intelligence and Class Structure in American Life* reignited this debate in 1994; in the book, the authors claimed that Black Americans score below average in IQ because of their "genetic heritage."

Most developmental psychologists have not been persuaded by the arguments underlying this genetic position (Dickens & Flynn, 2001; Sternberg, Grigorenko, & Kidd, 2005). Various environmental differences between groups could underlie group differences in IQ scores. Psychologists have responded to these claims with several important points:

- Lack of cultural exposure to the concepts required on IQ tests can result in lowered test performance. Therefore, the tests may not be an accurate measure of true capability—they may be culturally biased (Manly et al., 2004; Naglieri & Ronning, 2000; Sternberg, 2004; Sternberg et al., 2005).

- Group differences in IQ may have more to do with socio-economic differences than with ethnicity. Minority children are disproportionately more likely to be living in poverty (Duncan & Magnuson, 2005). Moreover, the consequences of living in poverty—poor nutrition, poor medical care, lack of educational resources, psychological and emotional stress—have well-documented negative effects on children's intellectual development (Duncan & Brooks-Gunn, 1997, 2000; Sattler & Hoge, 2006; Solan & Mozlin, 2001).

- Differences in IQ scores may also reflect motivational and language factors. In some minority groups, a child who excels in school may be ridiculed for trying to be different from his or her classmates. Similarly, children from some groups may see little value in trying hard on a test or may even view such effort as negative, being associated with competitiveness (Sattler, 1988). Moreover, if children's own language and dialect do not match their education system or the IQ

tests they take, they are obviously at a disadvantage (Cathers-Schiffman & Thompson, 2007; Sternberg, 2007; Sternberg & Grigorenko, 2008; Sattler & Hoge, 2006).

- Members of every ethnic group can be found who have scores at all levels of the IQ scale. The distributions of IQ scores of different groups overlap considerably, and IQ scores and intelligence have their greatest relevance in terms of individuals, rather than groups (Garcia & Stafford, 2000; Myerson et al., 1998; Reifman, 2000). Indeed, many individual ethnic minority group members receive higher IQ scores than many individual Caucasians.

- Traditional IQ tests do not measure many of our multiple intelligences. Rather, they tend to focus in particular on school-related abilities (Manly et al., 2004; Naglieri & Ronning, 2000; Rutter, 2007; Sternberg, 2007, 2012; Sternberg & Grigorenko, 2008).

- People's performance on an IQ test may reflect, to some degree, their expectations of how well they will do. In particular, negative stereotypes about minority groups, referred to as **stereotype threat**, can significantly reduce the test scores of people in stereotyped groups (Keller & Bless, 2008; Owens & Massey, 2011; Schmader et al., 2008; Steele, 2003).

> **stereotype threat** Negative stereotypes about minority groups that cause some members to doubt their abilities.

- Intelligence (as measured by IQ tests) is not a fixed trait. Around the world, IQ scores have increased over the last half century, and this well-established phenomenon is known as the **Flynn effect**, in honour of New Zealand researcher James Flynn. Because these increases have occurred in a relatively short time, the cause or causes cannot be due to genetics or heredity. Other possible factors include improved nutrition, better public education, more proficient test-taking skills, and rising levels of education for a greater percentage of the world's population (Flynn, 1987, 2006, 2007; Mingroni, 2004).

The ongoing debate over the nature of intelligence and its measurement highlights the complexities of studying *cognition*. In this chapter, we've explored three cognitive processes: thinking, language, and intelligence. As you've seen, all three processes are greatly affected by numerous interacting factors.

Psychological Science

Stereotype Threat: Potential Pitfall for Minorities?

In the first study of stereotype threat, Claude Steele and Joshua Aronson (1995) asked black and white Stanford University students to solve a series of challenging problems similar to those on the Graduate Record Exam (GRE), a standardized academic test used for graduate school admissions. In one condition, participants were told that the questions were a "performance exam" that supposedly measured intellectual abilities. In a second condition, they were told that the questions were simply part of a "laboratory task." Results showed that the black students performed more poorly when they viewed the problems as a performance exam than as a laboratory task. This effect was not seen in the white students' performance, which was the same under both conditions.

Subsequent research showed that this effect, which Steele labelled stereotype threat, undermines performance in two ways (**Figure 8.18**). First, it raises anxiety as members of stereotyped groups worry that they will fulfill their group's negative stereotype. This anxiety, in turn, can hinder students' performance on tests, possibly through reducing the amount of working memory (Chapter 7) available as they work on the test (Schmader, 2010; Schmader & Johns, 2003). Second, stereotype threat can also interfere with academic performance through the ways students cope with the threat it poses to their self-esteem. Some people cope with stereotype threat by *"disidentifying,"* telling themselves they don't care about the test scores (Cadinu et al., 2005; Major et al., 1998; Marsh et al., 2005). Disidentifying can be short-lived, as when a student discounts the importance of a poor exam score. However, it can also contribute to a general disidentifying with academics over time. Unfortunately, this attitude lessens motivation, decreasing performance (Figure 8.18).

Stereotype threat affects the test performance of many social groups, including black Americans, women, Aboriginal people, Hispanic Americans, people with low incomes, seniors, and even white male athletes (e.g., Bates, 2007; Cadinu et al., 2005; Ford et al., 2004; Keller & Bless, 2008; Klein et al., 2007; Steele, 2003; Steele, James, & Barnett, 2002). This research helps explain some group differences in intelligence and achievement tests. As such, it underscores why relying solely on such tests to make critical decisions affecting individual lives—for example, in hiring, college or university admissions, or clinical application—is unwarranted and possibly even unethical.

Larry Downing/Landov/Reuters

Barack Obama's election as U.S. president versus the stereotype threat: Shortly after the election of Barack Obama as the first black president in the United States, some researchers noticed a positive effect on African Americans' academic performance, a phenomenon aptly labelled the "Obama effect" (Marx, Ko, & Friedman, 2009).

Think Critically

1. Have you, or someone you know, experienced "stereotype threat"? If so, did it negatively affect your performance?
2. Apart from intelligence and achievement tests, what do you think might be some other areas where stereotype threat could affect performance?

Stereotype threat • Figure 8.18

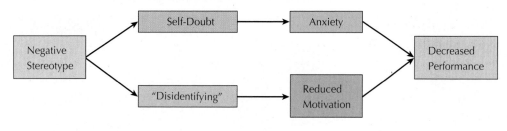

Stereotype threat can undermine test performance in two ways: (1) the anxiety that results from self-doubt can decrease test performance and (2) the reduced motivation associated with "disidentifying" as a way to protect self-esteem can negatively affect performance.

Solution to the Nine-Dot Problem
People find this puzzle difficult because they see the arrangement of dots as a square—a mental set that limits possible solutions.

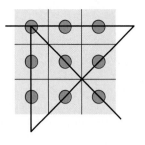

Solution to the Coin Problem
Stack one coin on top of the middle coin so that it shares both the row and the column.

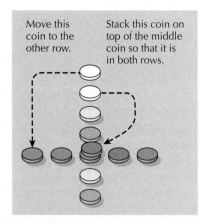

Move this coin to the other row.

Stack this coin on top of the middle coin so that it is in both rows.

CONCEPT CHECK 🛑 STOP

1. **Why** might more-intelligent people show less activity in cognitive-processing areas of the brain than less-intelligent people?

2. **How** have twin studies improved researchers' understanding of intelligence?

3. **What** is stereotype threat, and why does it occur?

Summary

✓ THE PLANNER

1 Thinking 212

- Thinking is a central aspect of **cognition.** Thought processes are distributed throughout the brain in neural networks. Mental images, **concepts** (both artificial and natural), and **hierarchies** aid our thought processes.

- Problem solving usually involves three steps: preparation, production, and evaluation. **Algorithms** and **heuristics** help us produce solutions.

- Barriers to problem solving include **mental sets, functional fixedness, confirmation bias, availability heuristic,** and **representativeness heuristic.**

- **Creativity** is the ability to produce valued outcomes in a novel way. Tests of creativity usually focus on **divergent thinking.** One prominent theory of creativity is **investment theory.**

Mental imagery • Figure 8.1

2 Language 218

- **Language** enables us to communicate and also supports thinking. To produce language, we use **phonemes, morphemes, and grammar** (syntax and semantics).

- According to Whorf's **linguistic relativity hypothesis,** language determines thought. Generally, Whorf's hypothesis is not supported. However, language does strongly influence thought.

- Children communicate non-verbally from birth. Their verbal communication proceeds in stages: prelinguistic (crying, cooing, babbling) and linguistic (single utterances, telegraphic speech, and acquisition of rules of grammar).

- According to Chomsky, humans are "prewired" with a **language acquisition device** that enables language development. Nurturists hold that children learn language through rewards, punishments, and imitation. Most psychologists hold an intermediate view.

Psychological Science: Baby Sign Language

- Many children in Canada and elsewhere learn more than one language quite easily. French immersion programs of various forms have been instituted in schools across Canada. The programs have been quite successful in developing French-language abilities in English-speaking children.

- Research with apes and dolphins suggests that these animals can learn and use basic rules of language. However, non-human animal language is less complex, less creative, and not as rule-laden as human language.

3 Intelligence 223

- There is considerable debate over the meaning of **intelligence.** Here it is defined as the global capacity to think rationally, act purposefully, and deal effectively with the environment.

- Spearman proposed that intelligence is a single factor, which he termed **general intelligence** (g). Thurstone and Guilford argued that intelligence included distinct abilities. Cattell proposed two subtypes of g: **fluid intelligence** and **crystallized intelligence**. Many contemporary cognitive theorists, including Gardner and Sternberg, believe that intelligence is a collection of many separate specific abilities.

- Early intelligence tests involved computing a person's mental age to arrive at an **intelligence quotient (IQ)**. Today, the most widely used intelligence tests are the **Stanford-Binet Intelligence Scale**, the Wechsler Adult Intelligence Scale (WAIS), and the Wechsler Intelligence Scale for Children (WISC).

- To be scientifically acceptable, all psychological tests must fulfill three basic requirements: **standardization, reliability,** and **validity.**

- **Emotional intelligence** involves knowing and managing your emotions, empathizing with others, and maintaining satisfying relationships.

4 The Intelligence Controversy 229

- Intelligence tests provide one of the major criteria for assessing **intellectual disability** and **giftedness**. Intellectual disability exists on a continuum. In **savant syndrome**, a person who has an intellectual disability is exceptional in some limited field. Studies of people who are intellectually gifted have found that they had more intellectual opportunities and tended to excel professionally. However, a high IQ is no guarantee of success in every endeavour.

- Most recent research on the biology of intelligence has focused on brain functioning, not size. Research indicates that intelligent people's brains respond especially quickly and efficiently.

- Both hereditary and environmental factors contribute to intelligence. Researchers interested in the role of heredity on intelligence often focus on identical twins. Twin studies have found that genetics play an important role in intelligence. However, the environment significantly influences whether a person will reach his or her full intellectual potential.

- Claims that genetic factors underlie ethnic differences in intelligence have caused heated debate and have received intense scrutiny. Among other arguments, some psychologists argue that IQ tests may be culturally biased; that **stereotype threat** can significantly reduce test scores of people in stereotyped groups; that socio-economic factors may heavily influence intellectual development; and that traditional IQ tests do not measure many of our multiple intelligences.

What a Psychologist Sees: Family Studies of Intelligence

Frequency distribution of IQ scores • Figure 8.13

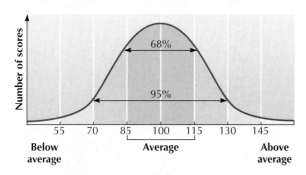

Key Terms

- algorithm p. 214
- availability heuristic p. 215
- cognition p. 212
- concepts p. 212
- confirmation bias p. 215
- creativity p. 216
- criterion-related validity p. 226
- crystallized intelligence (*gc*) p. 224
- divergent thinking p. 216
- emotional intelligence (EI) p. 228
- fluid intelligence (*gf*) p. 224
- Flynn effect p. 232
- functional fixedness p. 215
- general intelligence (*g*) p. 224
- giftedness p. 229

- grammar p. 218
- heuristic p. 214
- hierarchies p. 213
- intellectual disability p. 229
- intelligence p. 223
- intelligence quotient (IQ) p. 226
- investment theory p. 216
- language p. 218
- language acquisition device (LAD) p. 219
- linguistic relativity hypothesis p. 218
- mental image p. 212
- mental sets p. 215
- morpheme p. 218
- phoneme p. 218

- prefrontal cortex p. 212
- problem solving p. 213
- prototypes p. 213
- reliability p. 226
- representativeness heuristic p. 215
- savant syndrome p. 229
- split-half method p. 226
- standardization p. 226
- Stanford-Binet Intelligence Scale p. 224
- stereotype threat p. 232
- test-retest method p. 226
- theory of multiple intelligences p. 224
- triarchic theory of successful intelligence p. 224
- validity p. 226

Critical and Creative Thinking Questions

1. During problem solving, do you use primarily algorithms or heuristics? What are the advantages of each?

2. Would you like to be more creative? Can you do anything to acquire more of the resources of creative people?

3. Do you believe that we are born with an innate "language acquisition device," or is language development a function of our environments?

4. Do you think apes and dolphins have true language? Why or why not?

5. Physicians, teachers, musicians, politicians, and people in many other occupations may become more successful with age and can continue working well into old age. Which kind of general intelligence might explain this phenomenon?

6. If Gardner's and Sternberg's theories of multiple intelligences are correct, what are the implications for intelligence testing and for education?

7. What are some areas in which you feel you have higher intelligence? How do these fit with either Sternberg's or Gardner's theories of intelligence?

8. Have you listened to the speech of 2- to 3-year- old children? What sorts of language errors do they make?

9. Jerry Levy and Mark Newman, twins separated at birth, first met as adults at a firefighters' convention. What factors might explain why they both became firefighters? Does the brothers' choosing the same uncommon profession seem like a case of "telepathy"? How might *confirmation bias* contribute to this perception?

Self-Test

(Check your answers in Appendix A.)

1. What term is used for the mental activities involved in acquiring, storing, retrieving, and using knowledge?

   a. perception   c. consciousness

   b. cognition   d. awareness

2. Which of the following refer to mental representations of previously stored sensory experiences?

   a. illusions   c. mental images

   b. psychoses   d. mental propositions

3. Label the three stages of problem solving on the figure.

a. _____

b. _____

c. _____

4. Which term describes a simple rule or shortcut that does not guarantee a solution but that can be useful in problem solving?
   a. an algorithm
   c. a problem-solving set
   b. a heuristic
   d. brainstorming

5. Sarah and Richard mailed out 100 invitations to their wedding. They then took the number of replies they received and multiplied them by the price per plate provided by the caterer, to arrive at the cost of the reception dinner. What type of problem-solving strategy did they use?
   a. an algorithm
   c. a heuristic
   b. a hierarchy
   d. a prototype

6. When the fan belt broke on her car, Chantal pulled a pair of nylons out of her shopping bag and told Pierre: "We can use these to fix it!" Pierre couldn't imagine how you could use nylons for anything other than wearing. Which of the following describes Pierre's "problem"?
   a. the representativeness heuristic   c. functional fixedness
   b. the availability heuristic   d. confirmation bias

7. Dahlia sees an attractive man in the coffee shop and assumes he is a model at the nearby agency, when in fact he is a dentist with an office nearby. What is Dahlia demonstrating?
   a. the availability heuristic
   b. creativity
   c. the representativeness heuristic
   d. functional fixedness

8. What is the name for our ability to produce valuable outcomes in a novel way?
   a. problem solving
   c. functional flexibility
   b. incubation
   d. creativity

9. What is the term for the set of rules that specifies how phonemes, morphemes, words, and phrases should be combined to express meaningful thoughts?
   a. syntax
   c. semantics
   b. pragmatics
   d. grammar

10. List the three building blocks of language in order.

11. According to Chomsky, what is the innate mechanism that enables a child to analyze language?
    a. telegraphic understanding device (TUD)
    b. language acquisition device (LAD)
    c. language and grammar translator (LGT)
    d. overgeneralized neural net (ONN)

12. Three-year-old Nika told her older sister that she and mommy "goed to the store." What is this an example of?
    a. telegraphic speech
    c. babbling
    b. overregularizing
    d. overextending

13. The definition of *intelligence* stated in your textbook stresses the global capacity to do which of the following?
    a. perform in school and on the job
    b. read, write, and make computations

    c. perform verbally and physically
    d. think rationally, act purposefully, and deal effectively with the environment

14. The IQ test sample in the figure below is from which intelligence scale?
    a. Wechsler Intelligence Scale for Children
    b. Wechsler Adult Intelligence Scale
    c. Stanford-Binet Intelligence Scale
    d. Binet-Terman Intelligence Scale

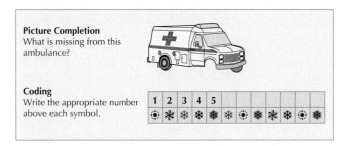

Picture Completion
What is missing from this ambulance?

Coding
Write the appropriate number above each symbol.

15. What do psychologists call the development of standard procedures for administering and scoring a test?
    a. norming
    c. procedural protocol
    b. standardization
    d. normalization

16. What term is used for people with an intellectual disability who demonstrate exceptional ability in specific areas?
    a. savants
    c. mildly retarded
    b. idiot geniuses
    d. connoisseurs

17. How is speed of response correlated with IQ scores?
    a. negatively
    c. highly
    b. positively
    d. there is no correlation between the two

18. Stereotype threat can affect the performance of which of the following groups?
    a. women
    c. seniors
    b. white male athletes
    d. all of these options

19. Jian helps his father in his auto repair shop and can fix many different types of vehicles, although he has never been formally trained in automotive repair. Which type of intelligence does Jian demonstrate?
    a. Sternberg's analytical intelligence
    b. Sternberg's practical intelligence
    c. Gardner's naturalistic intelligence
    d. Goleman's emotional intelligence

20. Dr. Hitchcock administered an intelligence test to a number of children throughout the Atlantic provinces. One year later he administered the test again to these same students and found similar results. What does this test seem to have?
    a. validity
    c. reliability
    b. standardization
    d. a good split-half method

THE PLANNER

Review your Chapter Planner on the chapter opener and check off your completed work.

Lifespan Development I: Physical and Cognitive Development

If you have ever spent time at a daycare centre, you were probably struck by the sight of many exuberant children laughing, shrieking, and jostling for attention from those entrusted with their care. Yet amid this barely controlled chaos, babies learn to crawl, toddlers learn not to bite one another, and preschoolers learn their ABCs. Day by day, every child grows a little stronger, a little more independent.

Over a lifetime, every person undergoes many physical changes. These changes are most striking in early childhood because they happen so rapidly and are so visible. But everyone is in a state of constant change and development throughout his or her entire life. The typical person will be many different people in his or her lifetime—infant, child, teenager, adult, and senior.

Would you like to know more about yourself at each of these ages? In the next two chapters, we will explore research in developmental psychology. We will begin this chapter by studying how developmental psychologists conduct their research. Then we will look at changes in our physical and cognitive development from conception to death. In Chapter 10, we will examine important aspects of our social, moral, and personality development across the lifespan. To emphasize that development is an ongoing, lifelong process, throughout the next two chapters we will trace physical, cognitive, social, moral, and personality development— one at a time—from conception to death. This topical approach will allow us to see how development affects an individual over the entire lifespan.

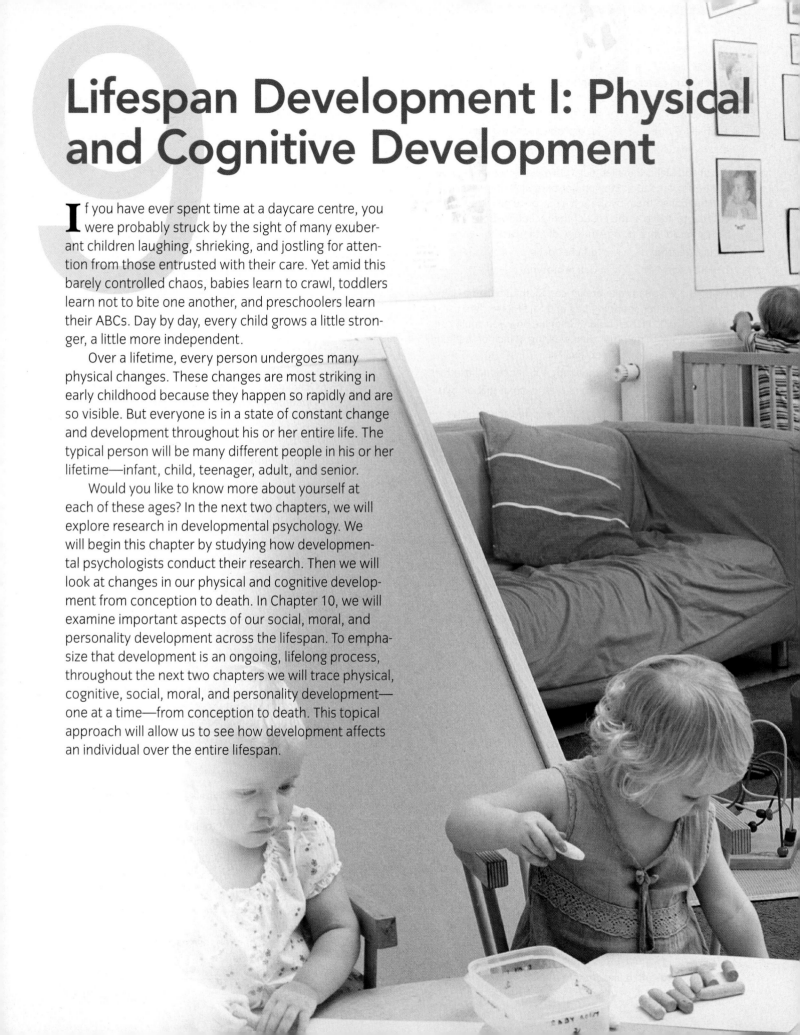

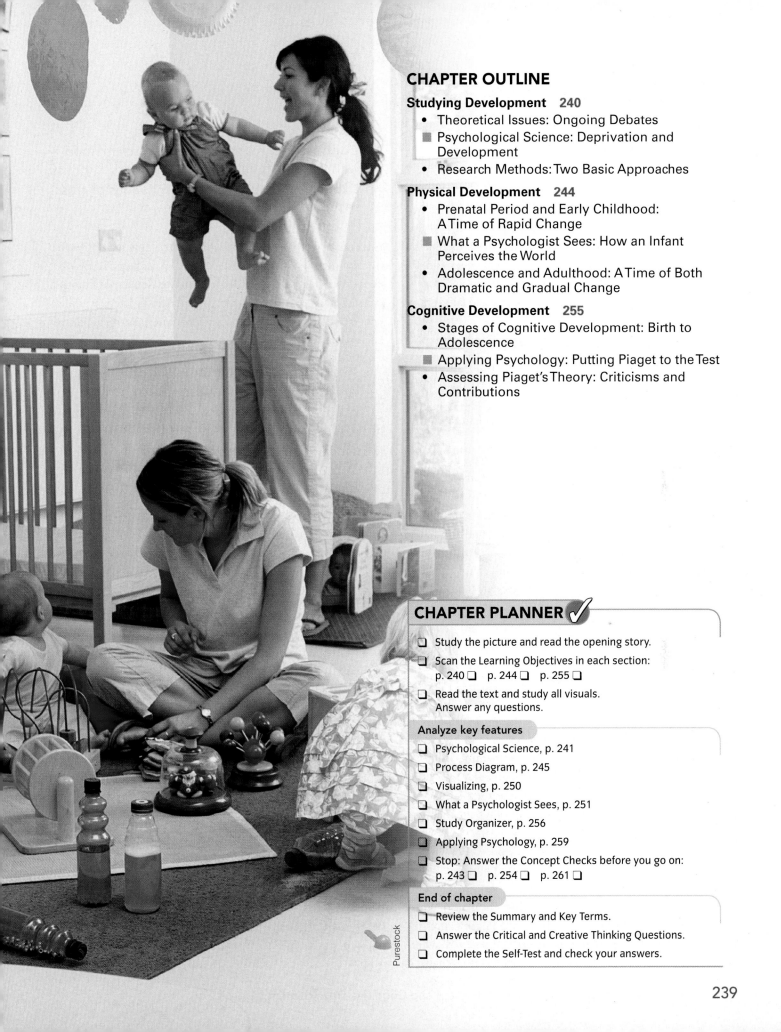

CHAPTER OUTLINE

Studying Development 240

- Theoretical Issues: Ongoing Debates
- ■ Psychological Science: Deprivation and Development
- Research Methods: Two Basic Approaches

Physical Development 244

- Prenatal Period and Early Childhood: A Time of Rapid Change
- ■ What a Psychologist Sees: How an Infant Perceives the World
- Adolescence and Adulthood: A Time of Both Dramatic and Gradual Change

Cognitive Development 255

- Stages of Cognitive Development: Birth to Adolescence
- ■ Applying Psychology: Putting Piaget to the Test
- Assessing Piaget's Theory: Criticisms and Contributions

CHAPTER PLANNER ✓

- ❑ Study the picture and read the opening story.
- ❑ Scan the Learning Objectives in each section:
  p. 240 ❑ p. 244 ❑ p. 255 ❑
- ❑ Read the text and study all visuals. Answer any questions.

Analyze key features

- ❑ Psychological Science, p. 241
- ❑ Process Diagram, p. 245
- ❑ Visualizing, p. 250
- ❑ What a Psychologist Sees, p. 251
- ❑ Study Organizer, p. 256
- ❑ Applying Psychology, p. 259
- ❑ Stop: Answer the Concept Checks before you go on:
  p. 243 ❑ p. 254 ❑ p. 261 ❑

End of chapter

- ❑ Review the Summary and Key Terms.
- ❑ Answer the Critical and Creative Thinking Questions.
- ❑ Complete the Self-Test and check your answers.

Purestock

Studying Development

LEARNING OBJECTIVES

1. **Summarize** the three most important issues or questions in developmental psychology.
2. **Define** *maturation* and *critical periods*.
3. **Contrast** the cross-sectional research method with the longitudinal research method.
4. **Explain** the advantages and limitations of cross-sectional and longitudinal research.

 e begin our study of human development by focusing on some key theoretical issues and debates. We then discuss two basic research methods and their advantages and disadvantages.

Theoretical Issues: Ongoing Debates

Three of the most important debates or questions in **developmental psychology** have been about nature versus nurture, continuity versus stages, and stability versus change.

> **developmental psychology** The study of age-related changes in behaviour and mental processes from conception to death.

Nature or nurture The issue of "nature versus nurture" has been with us since the beginning of psychology (Chapter 1). Even the ancient Greeks had the same debate—Plato argued that humans are born with innate knowledge and abilities, while Aristotle held that learning occurs through the five senses. Some early philosophers, the best known of whom is John Locke, proposed that at birth our minds are a *tabula rasa*, a Latin expression meaning a "blank slate" (think of a blank computer screen with nothing written on it), and that the environment determines what messages are written on that slate (Crain, 2011).

According to the *nature* side of the issue, human development is governed largely by genetically predetermined signals in a process known as **maturation**. Just as a flower unfolds in accord with its genetic blueprint, we humans crawl before we walk, walk before we run, and so on. Where the environment plays a role, it may be during optimal points in time during this maturation process. Such points in time are referred to as **critical periods**, when an organism is especially sensitive

> **maturation** Development governed by automatic genetically predetermined signals.
>
> **critical period** A time of special sensitivity to specific experiences that shape the capacity for future development.

to certain experiences that shape the capacity for future development. (*Psychological Science: Deprivation and Development* describes the story of a girl who was deprived of human contact during the period from toddlerhood to early adolescence and the serious negative consequences of the lack of such social input from the environment as she matured.)

On the other side of the nature versus nurture issue, an extreme *nurturist* position would hold that development is completely the result of the environment in which a child grows up, much as the philosopher John Locke proposed. According to the nurture view, development involves learning through personal experience and observation of others, a process that occurs continually throughout development, rather than at specific critical points in time.

Continuity or stages Is development a continuous process, or does it take place in stages? Continuity proponents believe that development is continuous, with new abilities, skills, and knowledge being gradually added at a relatively uniform pace. The continuity model would suggest, for example, that an adult's thinking and intelligence differ from those of a child in terms of quantity or amount. That is, adults simply have more math and verbal skills than do children. Stage theorists, on the other hand, believe that development takes place in steps, alternating between periods of abrupt, rapid change and periods of relatively little change (**Figure 9.1**). In this chapter, we discuss one well-known stage theory: Piaget's theory of cognitive development. In Chapter 10, we discuss two additional stage theories: Erikson's psychosocial theory of personality development and Kohlberg's theory of moral development.

Stability or change Have you generally maintained your personal characteristics as you matured from toddler to adult (*stability*)? Or do your current characteristics bear little resemblance to those you displayed as a young child (*change*)? Psychologists who emphasize stability in development hold that measurements of characteristics or abilities (e.g., personality traits, intelligence) taken during

Psychological Science

Deprivation and Development

Patricia McDonough/The Image Bank/Getty Images

What happens if a child is deprived of important stimulation during critical periods of development? Consider the story of Genie, the so-called wild child. From the time she was 20 months old until authorities rescued her at age 13, Genie was locked alone in a tiny, windowless room. By day, she sat naked, tied to a chair with nothing to do and no one to talk to. At night, she was put in a kind of straitjacket and "caged" in a covered crib. Genie's abusive father forbade anyone to speak to her for those 13 years. If Genie made any noise, her father beat her while he barked and growled like a dog.

Genie's tale is a heartbreaking account of the lasting scars from a disastrous childhood. In the years after her rescue, Genie spent thousands of hours receiving special training, and by age 19 she could use public transportation and was adapting well to her foster home and special classes at school (Rymer, 1993). Genie was far from normal, however. Her intelligence scores were still close to the cut-off for mental retardation. Her language, too, was virtually nonexistent. And although linguists and psychologists worked with Genie for many years, she never progressed beyond sentences such as "Genie go" (Curtiss, 1977; Rymer, 1993). To make matters worse, she was also subjected to a series of foster home placements, one of which was abusive. At last report, Genie was living in a home for adults with developmental disabilities (Rymer, 1993).

Think Critically

1. Does Genie's case prove that there is a critical period for language development? Why or why not?
2. Does Genie's case support either the nurture argument or the nature explanation of human development? Why or why not?

Continuous development and development in stages • Figure 9.1

Continuous development is a gradual process that involves the addition of new abilities and skills at a uniform rate. Development in stages alternates between periods of abrupt change and periods of little change, much like climbing stairs. (Adapted from Comer et al., 2012, Figure 3-1, p. 68.)

Infancy   Adulthood

Infancy   Adulthood

a. Continuous development

b. Development in stages

childhood can be important predictors of those characteristics and abilities in adolescence and adulthood. Of course, psychologists who emphasize change disagree.

Which sides of these three issues are more correct? In fact, most psychologists do not take a hard line either way. Rather, they prefer an **interactionist perspective**. For example, in the nature versus nurture debate, psychologists generally agree that development is the result of both the individual's unique genetic predisposition *and* individual experiences in the environment (Hartwell, 2008; Hudziak, 2008; Rutter, 2007). More recently, the interactionist position has evolved into the *biopsychosocial model* mentioned throughout this text. According to this model, biological factors (genetics, brain functions, and biochemistry), psychological influences (learning, thinking, emotion, personality, and motivation), and social forces (family, school, culture, ethnicity, social class, and politics) all affect and are affected by one another.

Like the nature versus nurture debate, the debates about continuity versus stages and stability versus change are also not matters of "either-or." How development takes place depends on what aspect of development we're considering. Physical development and motor skills, for example, are believed to be primarily continuous in nature (with some exceptions, such as physical changes at puberty), whereas cognitive skills are often described as developing in discrete stages. Similarly, some traits and abilities appear to be stable, whereas others change greatly across the lifespan.

Research Methods: Two Basic Approaches

How do we go about studying changes that take place as people develop and differences that exist at different ages? Two major methods are frequently used, each with its own advantages as well as its own shortcomings. One common approach is the **cross-sectional method**. This method examines individuals of various ages (e.g., 20, 40, 60, and 80 years old) at the same point in time and gives information about *age differences*. The other approach is the **longitudinal method**. Using this approach, researchers follow a group of same-aged individuals over a period of time in order to gain information about *age changes* (**Figure 9.2**).

Imagine that you are a developmental psychologist interested in studying how intelligence changes with age in adults. Which method would you choose: cross-sectional or

> **cross-sectional method** Research design that compares individuals of various ages at one point in time to provide information about age differences.
>
> **longitudinal method** Research design that follows a group of same-aged individuals over a period of time to provide information about age changes.

Cross-sectional versus longitudinal research • Figure 9.2 _____

Note that cross-sectional research uses different participants and is interested in age-related *differences*, whereas longitudinal research studies the same participants over time to find age-related *changes*.

CROSS-SECTIONAL RESEARCH

Different participants of various ages are compared at one point in time to determine age-related *differences*.

Group One
20-year-old participants

Group Two
40-year-old participants

Group Three
60-year-old participants

Research done in 2014

LONGITUDINAL RESEARCH

The **same** participants are studied at various ages to determine age-related *changes*.

Study One
Participants are 20 years old
Research done in 2014

Study Two
Same participants are now 40 years old
Research done in 2034

Study Three
Same participants are now 60 years old
Research done in 2054

Which results are "true"? • Figure 9.3

Cross-sectional studies have shown that reasoning and intelligence reach their peak in early adulthood and then gradually decline. In contrast, longitudinal studies have found that a marked decline does not begin until about age 60. (Adapted from Schaie, 1994, with permission.)

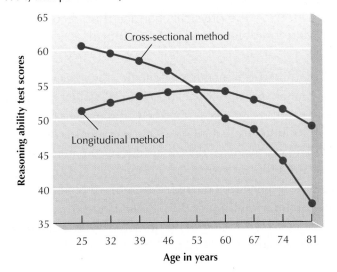

longitudinal? Before you decide, take a look at the different research findings shown in **Figure 9.3**.

Why do the two methods show such different results? Researchers suggest that the different results may reflect a central problem with cross-sectional studies. Cross-sectional studies have the potential to confuse genuine age differences with **cohort effects**, differences that result from specific histories of the age group studied (Goodwin, 2011). As Figure 9.3 shows, the 81-year-olds measured by the cross-sectional method have lower IQ scores than do the 25-year-olds. But is this due to aging or to environmental differences between the groups, such as less formal education or poorer nutrition? The different age groups, referred to as *cohorts*, grew up in different historical periods. Each group, therefore, may differ from each other group not just in terms of age but also in terms of life experiences. With the cross-sectional method, age effects and cohort effects are often hopelessly entangled.

Longitudinal studies, on the other hand, because they follow the same group of participants over time, allow researchers to be fairly confident that changes seen across age do indeed reflect genuine age differences. Nevertheless, longitudinal studies also have their limits. Following participants over time can be quite expensive in terms of time and money. In addition, participants may drop out of the study or move away during the test period. As a consequence, the researcher may end up with a self-selected sample that differs from the group that began the study—perhaps a more motivated group or a less-mobile sample of participants.

As you can see in **Table 9.1** each method of research has its own strengths and weaknesses. Keep these differences in mind when you read the findings of developmental research in this chapter and in the popular media.

Advantages and disadvantages of cross-sectional and longitudinal research design Table 9.1		
	Cross-sectional	**Longitudinal**
Advantages	Gives information about age differences Quick Less expensive Typically larger sample	Gives information about age changes Increased reliability More in-depth information per participant
Disadvantages	Age effects are difficult to separate from cohort effects Restricted generalizability (measures behaviours at only one point in time)	More expensive Time consuming Restricted generalizability (typically smaller sample and some participants may drop out over time)

CONCEPT CHECK STOP

1. **What** is developmental psychology?

2. **What** are the three major questions in developmental psychology?

3. **Which** kind of study provides the most in-depth information: cross-sectional or longitudinal?

Physical Development

LEARNING OBJECTIVES

1. **Describe** the three phases of prenatal physical development.
2. **Identify** some important teratogens and their effects on prenatal development.
3. **Summarize** physical development during early childhood.
4. **Describe** the physical changes that occur during adolescence and adulthood.

 n this section, we will explore the fascinating processes of physical development from conception through childhood, adolescence, and adulthood.

Prenatal Period and Early Childhood: A Time of Rapid Change

The early years of development are characterized by rapid and unparalleled change. In fact, if you had continued to develop at the same rapid rate that marked your first two years of life, you would weigh several thousand kilograms and be more than four metres tall as an adult! Thankfully, physical development slows; yet it is important to note that change continues until the very moment of death. Let's look at some of the major physical changes that occur throughout the lifespan.

Prenatal development begins at conception, when an ovum from the mother unites with a sperm from the father (**Figure 9.4**), producing a single cell barely 0.1 millimetres in diameter—smaller than the period at the end of this sentence. This new cell, called a **zygote**, then begins a process of rapid cell division that results in a multimillion-celled infant some nine months later.

The vast changes that occur during the nine months of a full-term pregnancy are usually divided into three stages: the **germinal period**, the **embryonic period**, and the **fetal period** (**Figure 9.5**). Prenatal growth, as well as growth during the first few years after birth, is **cephalocaudal** (head to toe), with the head and upper body developing before the lower body.

During pregnancy, the **placenta** (the vascular life-support organ that unites the fetus to the mother's uterus) serves as the link for food and excretion of wastes. It also screens out some, but not all, harmful substances. Environmental hazards, such as radiation or toxic waste; drugs; and diseases such as rubella (German measles), can cross the placental barrier. These influences generally have their most devastating effects during the first two to three months of pregnancy, making this a critical period in development.

Conception • Figure 9.4

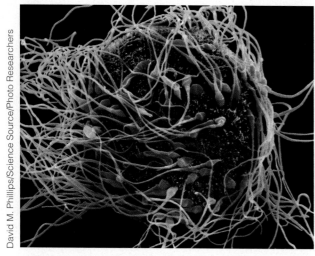

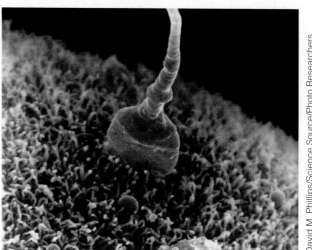

a. Note the large number of sperm surrounding the ovum (egg).

b. Although a joint effort is required to break through the outer coating, only one sperm will actually fertilize the egg.

Prenatal development • Figure 9.5

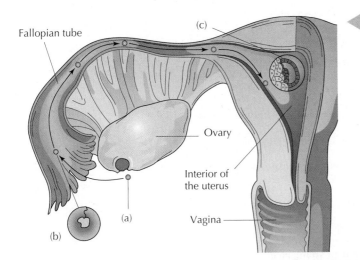

Fallopian tube

(c)

Ovary

Interior of
the uterus

Vagina

(a)

(b)

1 **Germinal period**: From ovulation to implantation, the first two weeks. After discharge from either the left or right ovary (a), the ovum travels to the opening of the Fallopian tube.

If fertilization occurs (b), it normally takes place in the first third of the Fallopian tube. The fertilized ovum is referred to as a *zygote*.

When the zygote reaches the uterus, it implants itself in the wall of the uterus (c) and begins to grow tendril-like structures that intertwine with the rich supply of blood vessels located there. After implantation, the organism is known as an embryo.

germinal period The first stage of prenatal development, which begins with conception and ends with *implantation* in the uterus (the first two weeks).

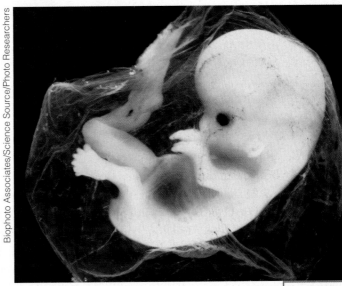

Biophoto Associates/Science Source/Photo Researchers

Petit Format/Science Source/Photo Researchers

2 **Embryonic period**: This stage lasts from implantation to eight weeks. At eight weeks, the major organ systems have become well differentiated. Note that at this stage, the head grows at a faster rate than other parts of the body.

embryonic period The second stage of prenatal development, which begins after uterine implantation and lasts through the eighth week.

3 **Fetal period**: This is the period from the end of the second month until birth. At four months, all the body parts and organs have been established. The fetal stage is primarily a time for increased growth and "fine detailing."

fetal period The third and final stage of prenatal development (eight weeks to birth), which is characterized by rapid weight gain in the fetus and the fine detailing of bodily organs and systems.

Sample environmental conditions that can endanger the child Table 9.2	
Maternal factors	**Possible effects on embryo, fetus, newborn, or young child**
Malnutrition	Low birth weight, malformations, less developed brain, greater vulnerability to disease
Stress exposure	Hyperactivity, irritability, feeding and sleep difficulties
Teratogens	**Possible effects on embryo, fetus, newborn, or young child**
Aspirin	In large quantities, miscarriage, bleeding, newborn respiratory problems
Thalidomide	Deformed limbs, sensory deficits, defects in internal organs, death
Cocaine/crack, heroin	Intellectual disability, growth retardation, premature birth, irritableness in the newborn, withdrawal symptoms after birth
Alcohol	Brain and heart damage, growth retardation, intellectual disability, fetal alcohol syndrome (FAS)
Tobacco smoking	Low birth weight, prematurity, increased risk of SIDS, risk of behavioural and cognitive problems
Diseases	**Possible effects on embryo, fetus, newborn, or young child**
Rubella (German measles)	Intellectual disability, eye damage, deafness, heart defects
Herpes	Intellectual disability, eye damage, death
HIV	Congenital malformations; can result in AIDS in the infant

Source: Adapted from Younger, Adler, & Vasta (2012).

The pregnant mother plays a primary role in prenatal development because her health can directly influence the child she is carrying (**Table 9.2**). Almost everything she ingests can cross the placental barrier. However, the father also plays a role (other than just fertilization). Environmentally, if the father smokes, this may pollute the air the mother breathes, and genetically, the father may transmit heritable diseases. In addition, research suggests that a number of drugs, various gases, lead, pesticides, and industrial chemicals have the potential to damage sperm (Baker & Nieuwenhuijsen, 2008; Ferretti et al., 2006; Levy et al., 2011).

Perhaps the most important—and generally avoidable—danger to the fetus comes from drugs, both legal and illegal, ingested by the mother. Cigarette smoke and alcohol are good examples of **teratogens**, environmental agents that cause damage during prenatal development.

Although the number of women who smoke while pregnant is on the decline, almost 10 percent of Canadian women continue to smoke through their pregnancies (Health Canada, 2007). Mothers who smoke during pregnancy have significantly higher rates of premature births, low-birth-weight infants, and fetal deaths (Cowperthwaite et al., 2007; Gabbe et al., 2007; Huijbregts et al., 2006). Moreover, the risk of sudden infant death syndrome

(SIDS) is elevated in babies exposed prenatally to cigarette smoke (Dietz et al., 2010: Mitchell & Milerad, 2006). Children whose mothers smoked while pregnant also show a higher incidence of behavioural abnormalities and cognitive problems (Abadinsky, 2008; Breslau et al., 2005; Fryer et al., 2008; Howell et al., 2008; Hyde & DeLamater, 2008). To reduce such risks, the Public Health Agency of Canada (2008) advises expectant mothers to quit smoking completely—the sooner the better. Indeed, recent Canadian guidelines strongly advise mothers who smoke to discuss methods of smoking cessation with their physician and to implement them as soon into the pregnancy as possible (Osadchy, Kazmin, & Koren, 2009).

Alcohol also readily crosses the placenta, can affect fetal development, and can result in a neurotoxic syndrome called **fetal alcohol syndrome (FAS)** (**Figure 9.6**). Although the number of mothers who drink alcohol while pregnant is also on the decline, 6 to 10 percent of Canadian mothers report consuming some alcohol during their pregnancy (Public Health Agency of Canada, 2009; Thanh & Jonsson, 2010). Between one and three out of a thousand babies in Canada and the United States are born with FAS (Chudley et al., 2005). Many others exposed prenatally to alcohol display some, although not all, of the features of

Fetal alcohol syndrome • Figure 9.6

Prenatal exposure to alcohol can cause facial abnormalities and stunted growth. But the most disabling features of FAS are neurobehavioural problems, ranging from hyperactivity and learning disabilities to intellectual disability, depression, and psychoses (Pellegrino & Pellegrino, 2008; Sanders & Buck, 2010; Sowell et al., 2008; Wass, 2008). Prenatal alcohol exposure is the leading cause of intellectual disability among Canadian children (Public Health Agency of Canada, 2006).

David H. Wells/Corbis

FAS (National Organization on Fetal Alcohol Syndrome, 2008). Such children are said to have *fetal alcohol spectrum disorder* (*FASD*) (Chudley et al., 2005; Public Health Agency of Canada, 2007). FASD is more common than FAS, occurring in about 10 in 1,000 births (Carson et al., 2010; Streissguth & Connor, 2001). Indeed, an estimated 300,000 Canadians of all ages live with some negative effects of prenatal alcohol exposure (Public Health Agency of Canada, 2007).

The large majority of Canadians are aware that alcohol use is harmful to the fetus; however, many are unsure whether there is a "safe" amount (Public Health Agency of Canada, 2006). The answer to this question is not clear-cut. The Public Health Agency of Canada (2007) advises that there is no known safe amount and no known safe time to drink alcohol during pregnancy. The Canadian Paediatric Society (2009) likewise cautions that the more alcohol consumed while pregnant, the greater the risk, and advises that it is best to have none.

For many years, researchers have been aware of the harmful effects alcohol and tobacco can have on the developing fetus. In fact, for some time, Canadian health authorities have been attempting to educate the public, through the use of advertising in public places, pamphlets in doctors' offices and pharmacies, warnings on cigarette packages (see **Figure 9.7**), and so on.

In 2006, the Public Health Agency of Canada reported the results of a nationwide survey in which 3,633 respondents (2,724 women and 909 men) were asked to name the important things women can do to increase the likelihood of having a healthy baby. As **Table 9.3** shows, the top three answers, mentioned by more than half the respondents, included getting proper nutrition, stopping/cutting down on alcohol use, and stopping/cutting down on smoking while pregnant.

Smoking and prenatal development • Figure 9.7

Do you think the Canadian public is aware of the risks that alcohol and tobacco pose to the fetus? If someone asked you what you should or should not do to have a healthy baby, how would you respond? Would you mention avoiding alcohol and cigarettes? What else would you mention? (See Table 9.3.)

Health Canada. Licensed under Health Canada copyright.

WARNING

TOBACCO SMOKE HURTS BABIES

Tobacco use during pregnancy increases the risk of preterm birth. Babies born preterm are at an increased risk of infant death, illness and disability.

Health Canada

Top 10 ways to increase the likelihood of having a healthy baby as mentioned by respondents in a Canada-wide survey   Table 9.3

	Total (%)	Women (%)	Men (%)
Eat well/good nutrition/vitamins	86	87	80
Cut down/stop alcohol use	52	51	54
Cut down/stop smoking	51	49	55
Increase/maintain exercise/physical activity	38	41	30
Visit doctor/health professional	18	20	10
Cut down/stop drug use (marijuana, crack, heroin, etc.)	17	17	14
Get rest/sleep	9	10	8
Avoid stress	6	6	3
Take prenatal class	4	4	3
Lifestyle/healthy living	3	3	4

Source: Public Health Agency of Canada (2006).

Is the message getting across? What do you think health authorities could do to make their message more widely known?

Like the prenatal period, early childhood is also a time of rapid physical development. Although Shakespeare described newborns as capable of only "mewling and puking in the nurse's arms," they are actually capable of much more. Let's explore three key areas of change in early childhood: brain, motor, and sensory and perceptual development.

Brain development The brain and other parts of the nervous system grow faster than any other part of the body during both prenatal development and the first two years of life. At birth, a healthy newborn's brain is one-fourth its full adult size, and it will grow to about 75 percent of its adult weight and size by the age of 2. At age 6, the child's brain is 90 percent of its full adult weight (**Figure 9.8**).

The rapid brain growth of infancy and early childhood slows down in later childhood. Further brain development

Body proportions • Figure 9.8

As noted earlier in the chapter, a large part of human development results from the orderly sequence of genetically designed biological processes called maturation. Notice how our body proportions change as we grow older. At birth, an infant's head is one-fourth its total body's size, whereas in adulthood, the head is one-eighth.

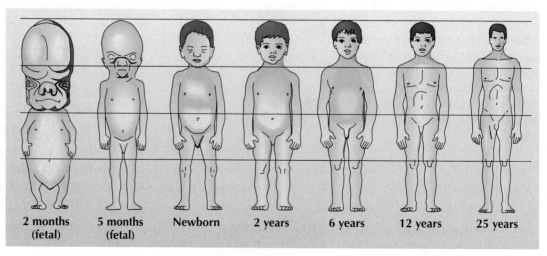

| 2 months (fetal) | 5 months (fetal) | Newborn | 2 years | 6 years | 12 years | 25 years |

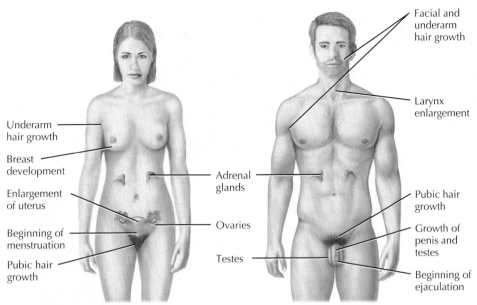

Secondary sex characteristics • Figure 9.14

Complex physical changes in puberty primarily result from hormones secreted from the ovaries and testes, the hypothalamus and the pituitary gland in the brain, and the adrenal glands on top of the kidneys.

found that almost two-thirds felt relief that their periods had stopped, and more than half did not experience hot flashes (Brim, 1999). When psychological problems do arise, they may in part reflect the social devaluation of aging women, not the physiological process of menopause. Given that in Western society women are highly valued for their youth and beauty, such a biological process as aging can be difficult for some women. Women in cultures that have a negative view of aging tend to experience more anxiety and depression during menopause (Mingo et al., 2000; Sampselle et al., 2002; Winterich, 2003).

For men, youthfulness is less important and the physical changes of middle age are less obvious. Beginning in middle adulthood, men experience a gradual decline in

Use it or lose it? • Figure 9.15

Contrary to the unfortunate (and untrue) stereotype that "You can't teach an old dog new tricks," our cognitive abilities generally grow and improve throughout our lifespan.

Willie B. Thomas/iStockphoto

the production of sperm and testosterone (the dominant male hormone), although they remain capable of reproduction into their eighties or nineties. Physical changes, such as unexpected weight gain, decline in sexual responsiveness, loss of muscle strength, and greying or loss of hair, may lead some men (and women as well) to feel depressed and to question their life progress. They often see these alterations as a biological signal of aging and mortality. Such gradual physical and psychological changes in men are known as the **male climacteric**.

After middle age, most physical changes in development are gradual and occur in the heart and arteries and in the sensory receptors. For example, cardiac output (the volume of blood pumped by the heart each minute) decreases, whereas blood pressure increases because of the thickening and stiffening of arterial walls. Visual acuity and depth perception decline, hearing acuity lessens (especially for high-frequency sounds), and smell sensitivity decreases (Chung, 2006; Snyder & Alain, 2008; Whitbourne, 2011).

Television, magazines, movies, and advertisements generally portray aging as a time of balding and greying hair, sagging parts, poor vision, hearing loss, and, of course, no sex life. Such negative portrayals contribute to our society's widespread **ageism**—prejudice or discrimination based on physical age. However, as advertising companies pursue the revenue of the huge population of aging baby boomers, a shift has occurred toward a more accurate portrayal of aging as a time of vigour, interest, and productivity (**Figure 9.15** and **Figure 9.16**).

What about memory problems and inherited genetic tendencies toward Alzheimer's disease and other serious

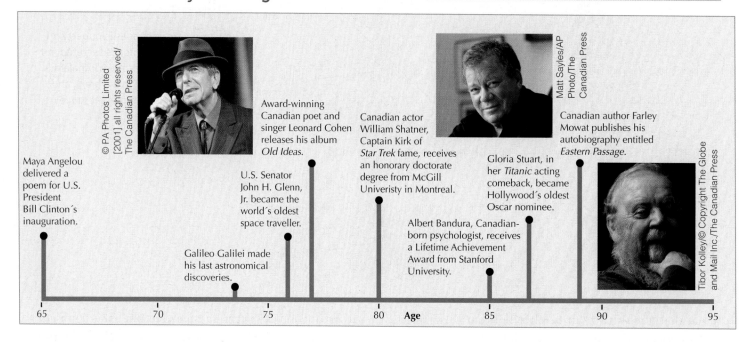

Maya Angelou delivered a poem for U.S. President Bill Clinton's inauguration.

Award-winning Canadian poet and singer Leonard Cohen releases his album *Old Ideas*.

U.S. Senator John H. Glenn, Jr. became the world's oldest space traveller.

Galileo Galilei made his last astronomical discoveries.

Canadian actor William Shatner, Captain Kirk of *Star Trek* fame, receives an honorary doctorate degree from McGill Univeristy in Montreal.

Albert Bandura, Canadian-born psychologist, receives a Lifetime Achievement Award from Stanford University.

Gloria Stuart, in her *Titanic* acting comeback, became Hollywood's oldest Oscar nominee.

Canadian author Farley Mowat publishes his autobiography entitled *Eastern Passage*.

65   70   75   80   **Age**   85   90   95

diseases of old age? The public and most researchers have long thought that aging is accompanied by widespread death of neurons in the brain. Although this decline does happen with degenerative disorders, such as Alzheimer's disease, this is no longer believed to be a part of normal aging (Chapter 2). It is also important to remember that age-related memory problems are not on a continuum with Alzheimer's disease (Wilson et al., 2000). That is, normal forgetfulness does not mean that serious dementia is around the corner.

Aging does seem to take its toll on the speed of information processing (Chapter 7). Decreased speed of processing may reflect problems with encoding (putting information into long-term storage) and retrieval (getting information out of storage). If memory is like a filing system, older people may have more filing cabinets, and it may take them longer to initially file and later retrieve information. Although mental speed declines with age, general information processing and memory ability are largely unaffected by the aging process (Lachman, 2004; Whitbourne, 2011).

What causes us to age and die? If we set aside contributions from **secondary aging** (changes resulting from disease, disuse, or neglect), we are left to consider **primary aging** (gradual, inevitable age-related changes in physical and mental processes). There are two main theories that explain primary aging and death: programmed theory and damage theory (Cristofalo, 1996; Medina, 1996; Wallace, 1997).

According to the **programmed theory**, aging is genetically controlled. Once the ovum is fertilized, the program

for aging and death is set and begins to run. Researcher Leonard Hayflick (1977, 1996) found that human cells seem to have a built-in lifespan. He observed that after doubling about 50 times, laboratory-cultured cells ceased to divide—they reached the *Hayflick limit*. The other explanation of primary aging is **damage theory**, which proposes that an accumulation of damage to cells and organs over the years ultimately causes death.

Whether aging is genetically controlled or caused by accumulated damage over the years, scientists generally agree that humans appear to have a maximum lifespan of about 110 to 120 years. Although we can try to control secondary aging in an attempt to reach that maximum, so far we have no means to postpone primary aging.

CONCEPT CHECK   STOP

1. **What** role does the placenta play in prenatal development?

2. **What** are some important teratogens and what are their potential effects?

3. **What** are some important milestones in motor development in early childhood?

4. **How** does the developmental concept of adolescence differ between cultures?

5. **What** physical changes occur during middle age and late adulthood?

Cognitive Development

LEARNING OBJECTIVES

1. **Explain** the role of schemas, assimilation, and accommodation in cognitive development.

2. **Describe** the major characteristics of Piaget's four stages of cognitive development.

3. **Discuss** two critiques of Piaget's theory.

he following fan letter was written to Shari Lewis (1963), a children's television performer, about her puppet Lamb Chop:

Dear Shari:

All my friends say Lamb Chop isn't really a little girl that talks. She is just a puppet you made out of a sock. I don't care even if it's true. I like the way Lamb Chop talks. If I send you one of my socks will you teach it how to talk and send it back?

Randi

Randi's understanding of fantasy and reality is certainly different from an adult's. Just as a child's body and physical abilities change, his or her way of knowing and perceiving the world also grows and changes. This seems intuitively obvious, but early psychologists—with one exception—focused on physical, emotional, language, and personality development. The one major exception was Swiss psychologist Jean Piaget (pronounced Pee-ah-ZHAY).

Piaget demonstrated that a child's intellect is fundamentally different from an adult's. He showed that an infant begins at a cognitively "primitive" level and that intellectual growth progresses in distinct stages, motivated by an innate need to know. Piaget's theory, developed in the 1920s and 1930s, has proven so comprehensive and insightful that it remains an important force in the cognitive area of developmental psychology today.

To appreciate Piaget's contributions, we need to consider three major concepts: schemas, assimilation, and accommodation. **Schemas** are the most basic units of intellect. They act as patterns of thought or action that organize our interactions with the environment. They serve as mental frameworks, similar to an architect's drawings or a builder's blueprints, that we use to understand our world.

> **schemas** Cognitive structures or patterns consisting of a number of organized ideas that grow and differentiate with experience.

In the first few weeks of life, for example, infants have several primitive schemas that are based on their innate reflexes, such as sucking and grasping. These schemas are primarily motor and may be little more than stimulus-and-response mechanisms—the nipple is presented, and the baby sucks. Soon, other schemas emerge. Over time, the infant develops a more detailed schema for eating solid food, a different schema for the concepts of *mother* and *father*, and so on. Schemas, our tools for learning about the world, expand and change throughout our lives. For example, music lovers who were previously accustomed to LP records and cassette tapes have had to develop schemas for burning CDs and downloading MP3s.

Assimilation and accommodation are the two major processes by which schemas grow and change over time. **Assimilation** is the process of absorbing new information into existing schemas. For instance, infants use their sucking schema not only in sucking nipples but also in sucking blankets and fingers. In fact, as you may have observed, putting objects into their mouths and assimilating them into the sucking schema is one way young infants learn about their environment. Likewise, some toddlers may assimilate all male adults into their schema *dada,* using this word to refer to all men and not just their fathers. In short, assimilation involves using the schemas we already have to understand the world around us.

> **assimilation** In Piaget's theory, the process of absorbing new information into existing schemas.

Accommodation occurs when new information cannot easily be assimilated into existing schemas. New schemas must be developed (or old schemas are changed) to better fit with the new information. An infant's first attempt to eat solid food with a spoon is a good example. When the spoon first enters her mouth, she attempts to assimilate it by using the previously successful sucking schema—shaping the lips and tongue around the spoon as if it were a nipple. After repeated attempts, she accommodates by adjusting her lips and tongue in a way that moves the food off the spoon and into her mouth. Similarly, a preschooler who

> **accommodation** In Piaget's theory, the process of adjusting old schemas or developing new ones to better fit with new information.

Sensorimotor stage (birth to age 2)

Limits
• Beginning of stage lacks object permanence (understanding that things continue to exist even when not seen, heard, or felt)

Abilities
• Uses senses and motor skills to explore and develop cognitively

Example
• Children at this stage like to play with their food.

Paul Hakimata/iStockphoto

Preoperational stage (ages 2 to 7)

Limits
• Cannot perform "operations" (lacks reversibility)
• Intuitive thinking versus logical reasoning
• Egocentric thinking (inability to consider another's point of view)
• Animistic thinking (believing all things are living)

Abilities
• Has significant language and thinks symbolically

Example
• Children at this stage often believe the moon follows them.

Igor Demchenkov/iStockphoto

Concrete operational stage (ages 7 to 11)

Limits
• Cannot think abstractly and hypothetically
• Thinking tied to concrete, tangible objects and events

Abilities
• Can perform "operations" on concrete objects
• Understands conservation (realizing that changes in shape or appearance can be reversed)
• Less egocentric
• Can think logically about concrete objects and events

Example
• Children at this stage begin to question the existence of Santa.

Hill Street Studios/Blend Images/Getty Images

Formal operational stage (age 11 and over)

Limits
• Adolescent egocentrism at the beginning of this stage, with related problems of the personal fable and imaginary audience

Abilities
• Can think abstractly and hypothetically

Example
• Children at this stage show great concern for physical appearance.

Roy Melnychuk/Taxi/Getty Images

sees a kangaroo at the zoo may refer to it as a "doggie," assimilating it into his understanding of dogs as creatures with four legs and a tail. Over time, as he understands more about the characteristics of dogs, he is forced to acknowledge that this new creature is not a dog. He must develop new schemas to account for his new knowledge that there are four-legged animals that are not dogs.

Stages of Cognitive Development: Birth to Adolescence

According to Piaget, all children go through approximately the same four stages of cognitive development, regardless of the culture in which they live (**Study Organizer 9.1**). Stages cannot be skipped because skills acquired at earlier stages are essential for mastery at later stages. Let's take a closer look at these four stages: sensorimotor, preoperational, concrete operational, and formal operational.

Sensorimotor stage During the **sensorimotor stage**, which lasts from birth until

sensorimotor stage Piaget's first stage (birth to approximately age 2) in which schemas are developed through sensory and motor activities.

preoperational stage Piaget's second stage (roughly ages 2 to 7 years), which is characterized by the ability to employ significant language and to think symbolically, although the child lacks operations (reversible mental processes) and thinking is egocentric and animistic.

significant language acquisition (about age 2), children explore the world and develop their schemas primarily through their senses and motor activities—hence the term *sensorimotor*. One important concept that infants acquire during the sensorimotor stage is **object permanence**, the understanding that objects continue to exist even when they cannot be seen, heard, or touched (**Figure 9.17**). Peekaboo becomes fabulously exciting for infants when they attain an understanding of object permanence. Because they know you are still there even though you are hidden, their anticipation is delightfully rewarded when you pop back into their sight.

Preoperational stage During the **preoperational stage** (roughly ages 2 to 7), language advances significantly, and the child begins to think symbolically—using symbols, such as words and images, to represent concepts. Symbolic play (i.e., make believe) becomes important during this stage. Three other qualities characterize this stage.

Concepts Are Not Yet Operational. Piaget labelled this period "preoperational" because

Object permanence • Figure 9.17

At birth and for the next three or four months, children lack object permanence. They seem not to realize that objects continue to exist even when they cannot see, hear, or touch them—out of sight is truly out of mind. Why do you suppose this happens?

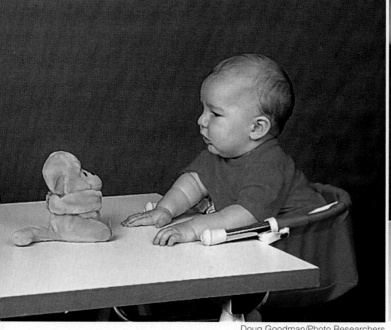
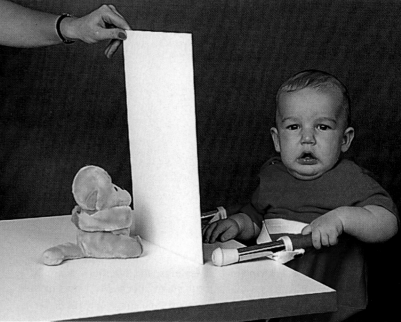

Doug Goodman/Photo Researchers

Doug Goodman/Photo Researchers

the child lacks **operations**, or reversible mental processes. For instance, if a preoperational boy who has a brother is asked, "Do you have a brother?" he will easily respond, "Yes." However, when asked, "Does your brother have a brother?" he will likely answer, "No!" To understand that his brother has a brother, he would have to be able to reverse the concept of "having a brother." In addition, thinking is very *intuitive*—with little use of reasoning and logic (e.g., believing the sun follows them while they're taking a walk).

Thinking Is Egocentric. Children's thinking in the preoperational stage is characterized by **egocentrism**. That is, they show limited ability to distinguish between their own perspective and that of someone else. Egocentrism is not the same as selfishness. The preschooler who moves in front of you to get a better view of the TV or repeatedly asks questions while you are talking on the telephone is not being selfish. She is displaying her egocentric thought processes. Preoperational children naïvely assume that others see, hear, feel, and think exactly as they do. Consider the following telephone conversation between a 3-year-old, who is at home, and her mother, who is at work:

Mother: *Emma is that you?*

Emma: (Nods silently.)

Mother: *Emma, is Daddy there?*
         May I speak to him?

Emma: (Twice nods silently.)

Animism • Figure 9.18

Children in the preoperational stage believe that many non-living objects have motives, feelings, and intentions. A preschooler who says that the sun shines 'because it wants to' or 'because it is happy' is showing such animism in his or her thinking.

Egocentric preoperational children fail to realize that the phone caller cannot see their nodding head. Charming as this is, preoperational children's egocentrism also sometimes leads them to believe that their "bad thoughts" caused their sibling or parent to get sick or that their misbehaviour caused their parents' marital problems. Because they think the world centres on them, they often cannot separate reality from what goes on inside their own heads.

Thinking Is Animistic. Children in the preoperational stage believe that objects, such as the sun, trees, clouds, and bars of soap, have motives, feelings, and intentions (for example, "dark clouds are angry" and "a piece of paper will be hurt if cut") (**Figure 9.18**). **Animism** refers to the belief that all things are alive (or animated). Our earlier example of Randi's letter asking puppeteer Shari Lewis to teach her sock to talk like Lamb Chop is also an example of animistic thinking. Indeed, researchers at the University of Calgary have found that children even ascribe living characteristics to robots (Beran, Ramirez-Serrano, Kuzyk, Fior, & Nugent, 2011).

Can preoperational children be taught how to use operations and to avoid egocentric and animistic thinking? Although some researchers have reported success in accelerating the preoperational stage, Piaget did not believe in pushing children ahead of their own developmental schedules. He believed that children should grow at their own pace, with minimal adult interference (Elkind, 2007). In fact, Piaget thought that Americans were particularly guilty of pushing their children, calling American childhood the "Great American Kid Race."

Concrete operational stage Following the preoperational stage, at approximately age 7, children enter the **concrete operational stage**. During this stage, many important thinking skills emerge. Unlike in the preoperational stage, concrete operational children can perform operations on concrete objects. Because they understand the concept of reversibility, they recognize that certain physical attributes (such as volume) remain unchanged when the outward appearance of an object is altered, a process known as **conservation**.

> **concrete operational stage** Piaget's third stage (roughly ages 7 to 11) in which the child can perform mental operations on concrete objects and understand reversibility and conservation, although abstract thinking is not yet present.

Applying Psychology

Putting Piaget to the Test

If you have access to children in the preoperational or concrete operational stages, try some of the following experiments, used by researchers to test Piaget's various forms of conservation. The equipment is easily obtained, and you will find the children's responses fascinating. Keep in mind that this should be done as a game. The child should never feel that he or she is failing a test or making a mistake.

Type of Conservation Task (Average age at which concept is grasped)	Your task as experimenter . . .	Child is asked . . .
Length (ages 6–7)	**Step 1** Centre two sticks of equal length. Child agrees that they are of equal length. **Step 2** Move one stick.	**Step 3** *"Which stick is longer?"* Preoperational child will say that one of the sticks is longer. Child in concrete stage will say that they are both the same length.
Substance amount (ages 6–7)	**Step 1** Centre two identical clay balls. Child acknowledges that the two have equal amounts of clay. **Step 2** Flatten one of the balls.	**Step 3** *"Do the two pieces have the same amount of clay?"* Preoperational child will say that the flat piece has more clay. Child in concrete stage will say that the two pieces have the same amount of clay.
Area (ages 8–10)	**Step 1** Centre two identical sheets of cardboard with wooden blocks placed on them in identical positions. Child acknowledges that the same amount of space is left open on each piece of cardboard. **Step 2** Scatter the blocks on one piece of the cardboard.	**Step 3** *"Do the two pieces of cardboard have the same amount of open space?"* Preoperational child will say that the cardboard with scattered blocks has less open space. Child in concrete stage will say that both pieces have the same amount of open space.

For an interesting discussion on this topic, scan to download the author's podcast.

Think Critically

1. Based on their responses, are the children you tested in the preoperational or concrete stage?
2. If you repeat the same tests with each child, do their answers change? Why or why not?

Formal operational stage The final stage in Piaget's theory is the **formal operational stage**, which typically begins around age 11. In this stage, children begin to

formal operational stage Piaget's fourth stage (around age 11 and beyond), which is characterized by abstract and hypothetical thinking.

be able to extend their operations beyond concrete objects, applying them to abstract concepts as well. Such new forms of reasoning allow them to master the abstract thinking involved in such academic subjects as algebra and physics, thinking that would not be possible at earlier stages. Children at the formal operational stage also become capable of hypothetical thinking ("What if?"), which allows systematic formulation and testing of concepts.

For example, before filling out applications for part-time jobs, adolescents may think about possible conflicts with school and friends, the number of hours they want to work, and the kind of work for which they are qualified. Formal operational thinking also allows the adolescent to construct a well-reasoned argument based on hypothetical concepts and logical processes.

Consider the following argument:

1. If you hit a glass with a feather, the glass will break.
2. You hit the glass with a feather.

What is the logical conclusion? The correct answer, "The glass will break," is contrary to fact and direct experience. As a result, the child in the concrete operational stage would have difficulty with this task. In contrast, the formal operational thinker understands that this problem is about abstractions that need not correspond to the real world.

Along with the benefits of this cognitive style come several problems. Adolescents in the early stages of the formal operational period demonstrate a type of egocentrism different from that of the preoperational child. Although adolescents recognize that others have unique thoughts and perspectives, they often fail to differentiate between what they are thinking and what others are thinking. This adolescent egocentrism has two characteristics that may affect social interactions, as well as problem solving:

• *Personal fable.* Because of their unique form of egocentrism, adolescents may conclude that they alone are having insights or difficulties and that no one else could understand or sympathize. Psychologist David Elkind (1967, 2007) described this as the formation of a **personal fable**, an adolescent's intense investment in his or her own thoughts and feelings and a belief that these

gaspr13/iStockphoto

The personal fable • Figure 9.19

Thanks to advances in brain imaging, scientists now know that the prefrontal cortex of the adolescent's brain is one of the later areas to develop (Giedd, 2008; Steinberg, 2008). How might this relatively slow development of the part of the brain responsible for higher processes, such as planning ahead and controlling emotions, provide a biological basis for the personal fable and for risk taking during adolescence?

thoughts are unique. For example, one young woman remembered being very upset in middle school when her mother tried to comfort her over the loss of an important relationship. "I felt like she couldn't possibly know how it felt—no one could. I couldn't believe that anyone had ever suffered like this or that things would ever get better."

Several forms of risk taking, such as engaging in sexual intercourse without contraception, driving dangerously, and experimenting with drugs, seem to arise from the personal fable (Aalsma et al., 2006; Alberts, Elkind, & Ginsburg, 2007; Omori & Ingersoll, 2005). Adolescents have a sense of uniqueness, invulnerability, and immortality. They recognize the dangers of these activities but think the rules don't apply to them (**Figure 9.19**).

• *Imaginary audience.* Adolescents also tend to believe that they are the centre of others' thoughts and attentions, instead of considering that everyone is equally wrapped up in his or her own concerns and plans. In other words, adolescents feel that all eyes are focused on their behaviours. Elkind (1967, 2007) aptly described this as an **imaginary audience**. This new form of egocentrism may explain what seems like extreme forms of self-consciousness and concern for physical appearance ("Everyone knows I don't know the answer;" or "They're all noticing this awful haircut").

Thankfully, these two forms of adolescent egocentrism tend to decrease during later stages of the formal operational period.

Assessing Piaget's Theory: Criticisms and Contributions

As influential as Piaget's account of cognitive development has been, it has received significant criticisms. Let's look briefly at two major areas of concern: underestimated abilities and underestimated genetic and cultural influences.

Research shows that Piaget may have underestimated young children's cognitive development (**Figure 9.20**). For example, researchers report that very young infants have a basic concept of how objects move, have at least some awareness that objects continue to exist even when screened from view, and can recognize speech sounds (Baillargeon et al., 2011; Charles, 2007).

Non-egocentric responses may also appear early in life. For example, some newborn babies cry "empathically" in response to the cry of another baby (Diego & Jones, 2007; Hoffman, 2008). Also, preschoolers will adapt their speech by using shorter, simpler expressions when talking to 2-year-olds than when talking to adults, suggesting some understanding of the perspective of the listener.

Piaget's model, like other stage theories, has also been criticized for not sufficiently taking into account hereditary and cultural differences (Cole & Gajdamaschko, 2007; Matusov & Hayes, 2000; Maynard & Greenfield, 2003). When Piaget developed his theory, hereditary influences on cognitive abilities were not well understood, but there has been an explosion of information in this field in recent years. In addition, formal education and specific cultural experiences can also significantly affect cognitive development. Consider the following example from a researcher attempting to test the formal operational skills of a farmer in Liberia (Scribner, 1977):

> *Researcher:* All Kpelle men are rice farmers. Mr. Smith is not a rice farmer. Is he a Kpelle man?
>
> *Kpelle farmer:* I don't know the man. I have not laid eyes on the man myself.

Instead of reasoning in the "logical" way of Piaget's formal operational stage, the Kpelle farmer reasoned according to his specific cultural and educational training, which

Are preoperational children always egocentric? • Figure 9.20 _____

Some toddlers and preschoolers clearly demonstrate empathy for other people. How does this ability to take others' perspective contradict Piaget's beliefs about egocentrism in very young children?

apparently emphasized personal knowledge. Not knowing Mr. Smith, the Kpelle farmer did not feel qualified to comment on him. Thus, Piaget's theory may have underestimated the effect of culture on a person's cognitive functioning.

Despite criticisms, Piaget's contributions to psychology are enormous. As one scholar put it, "assessing the impact of Piaget on developmental psychology is like assessing the impact of Shakespeare on English literature or Aristotle on philosophy—impossible" (Beilin, 1992, p. 191).

CONCEPT CHECK | STOP

1. **Under** what circumstances does accommodation occur?

2. **How** do egocentrism and animism limit children's thinking during the preoperational stage?

3. **What** are some important differences between the concrete operational and preoperational stages?

4. **How** might the personal fable explain risky behaviour among adolescents?

5. **What** are some criticisms of Piaget's theory?

Summary

1 Studying Development 240

- **Developmental psychology** is the study of age-related changes in behaviour and mental processes from conception to death. Development is an ongoing, lifelong process.

- The three most important debates or questions in human development are about nature versus nurture (including studies of **maturation** and **critical periods**), continuity versus stages, and stability versus change. For each question, most psychologists prefer an interactionist perspective.

- Developmental psychologists use two research methods: the **cross-sectional method** and the **longitudinal method**. Although both have valuable attributes, each also has disadvantages. Cross-sectional studies can confuse true developmental effects with **cohort effects,** while longitudinal studies are expensive and time-consuming, and their results are restricted in generalizability.

Continuous development and development in stages • Figure 9.1

a. Continuous development   b. Development in stages

2 Physical Development 244

- The early years of development are characterized by rapid change. Prenatal development begins at conception and is divided into three stages: the **germinal period**, the **embryonic period**, and the **fetal period**. During pregnancy, the **placenta** serves as the link for food and the excretion of wastes, and it screens out some harmful substances. However, some environmental hazards (**teratogens**), such as alcohol and nicotine, can cross the placental barrier and endanger prenatal development.

- Early childhood is also a time of rapid physical development, including brain, motor, and sensory and perceptual development.

Milestones in development • Figure 9.10

- During **adolescence**, both boys and girls undergo dramatic changes in appearance and physical capacity. **Puberty** is the period of adolescence when a person becomes capable of reproduction. The clearest and most dramatic physical sign of puberty is the **growth spurt**, characterized by rapid increases in height, weight, and skeletal growth and by significant changes in reproductive structures and sexual characteristics.

- During adulthood, most individuals experience only minor physical changes until middle age. Around age 45–55, women experience **menopause**, the cessation of the menstrual cycle. At the same time, men experience a gradual decline in the production of sperm and testosterone, as well as other physical changes, known as the **male climacteric**.

- After middle age, most physical changes in development are gradual and occur in the heart and arteries and in the sensory receptors. Most researchers, as well as the public in general, have long thought that aging is accompanied by widespread death of neurons in the brain. Although this decline does happen with degenerative disorders, such as Alzheimer's disease, this is no longer believed to be a part of normal aging. Although mental speed declines with age, general information processing and much of memory ability is largely unaffected by the aging process. There are two main theories explaining primary aging and death—**programmed theory** and **damage theory**.

Are preoperational children always egocentric?
• Figure 9.20

3 Cognitive Development   255

- In the 1920s and 1930s, Jean Piaget conducted ground-breaking work on children's cognitive development. Piaget's theory remains a major force in the cognitive area of developmental psychology today.

- Three major concepts are central to Piaget's theory: **schemas**, **assimilation**, and **accommodation**. According to Piaget, all children progress through four stages of cognitive development: the **sensorimotor stage**, the **preoperational stage**, the **concrete operational stage**, and the **formal operational stage**. As they progress through these stages, children acquire progressively more sophisticated ways of thinking.

- Piaget's account of cognitive development has been enormously influential, but it has also been criticized. In particular, research shows that Piaget may have underestimated the cognitive abilities of infants and young children. He may also have underestimated genetic and cultural influences on cognitive development.

Key Terms

- accommodation p. 255
- adolescence p. 252
- ageism p. 253
- animism p. 258
- assimilation p. 255
- cephalocaudal p. 244
- cohort effects p. 243
- concrete operational stage p. 258
- conservation p. 258
- critical period p. 240
- cross-sectional method p. 242
- damage theory p. 254
- developmental psychology p. 240
- egocentrism p. 258

- embryonic period p. 245
- fetal alcohol syndrome (FAS) p. 246
- fetal period p. 245
- formal operational stage p. 260
- germinal period p. 245
- growth spurt p. 252
- imaginary audience p. 260
- interactionist perspective p. 242
- longitudinal method p. 242
- male climacteric p. 253
- maturation p. 240
- menarche p. 252
- menopause p. 252
- object permanence p. 257

- operations p. 258
- personal fable p. 260
- placenta p. 244
- preoperational stage p. 257
- primary aging p. 254
- programmed theory p. 254
- puberty p. 252
- schema p. 255
- secondary aging p. 254
- sensorimotor stage p. 257
- spermarche p. 252
- teratogen p. 246
- zygote p. 244

Critical and Creative Thinking Questions

1. Do you have characteristics that seem to have been more influenced either by nature or by nurture? What might be some ways to study how nature and nurture influence development?

2. With what you have learned about the advantages and disadvantages of cross-sectional and longitudinal methods of study, think up some situations where one method might be preferable over the other.

3. If a mother knowingly ingests a quantity of alcohol that causes her child to develop fetal alcohol syndrome (FAS), is she guilty of child abuse? Why or why not?

4. From an evolutionary perspective, why might babies prefer looking at more complex patterns and at faces, rather than at simple patterns?

5. Based on what you have learned about development during late adulthood, do you think that this period is necessarily a time of physical and mental decline?

6. Piaget's theory states that all children progress through all of the stages of cognitive development in order and without skipping any. Do you agree with this? Do you know of any children whose development would seem to contradict this notion?

7. Consider Piaget's concepts of assimilation and accommodation. Think of some examples of these processes in your own thinking. Are there times when one of these processes is better than the other?

8. Can you remember having thoughts consistent with the personal fable when you were an adolescent? Could such thoughts have contributed to risky behaviour on your part?

Self-Test

(Check your answers in Appendix A.)

1. What term is used to describe the study of age-related changes in behaviour and mental processes from conception to death?

   a. psychodevelopment

   b. neo-gerontology

   c. developmental psychology

   d. longitudinal psychology

2. Which of the following is governed by automatic, genetically predetermined signals?

   a. growth   c. maturation

   b. natural progression   d. tabula rasa

3. Label the two basic types of research studies in the figure below:

   a. _____

   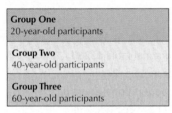

Group One 20-year-old participants	
Group Two 40-year-old participants	Research done in 2014
Group Three 60-year-old participants	

   b. _____

   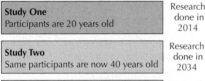

Study One Participants are 20 years old	Research done in 2014
Study Two Same participants are now 40 years old	Research done in 2034
Study Three Same participants are now 60 years old	Research done in 2054

4. What is the first stage of prenatal development, which begins with conception and ends with implantation in the uterus?

   a. embryosis   c. critical period

   b. zygote stage   d. germinal period

5. At birth, an infant's head is _____ its body's size, whereas in adulthood, the head is _____ its body's size.

   a. 1/3; 1/4   c. 1/4; 1/10

   b. 1/3; 1/10   d. 1/4; 1/8

   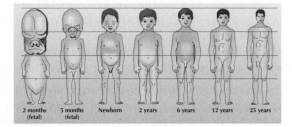

   2 months (fetal)   5 months (fetal)   Newborn   2 years   6 years   12 years   25 years

6. Which of the following is not true regarding infant sensory and perceptual development?

   a. Infants' vision is almost 20/20 shortly after birth.

   b. A newborn's sense of pain is highly developed at birth.

   c. Breast-fed infants can recognize, and prefer, their own mother's breast milk by smell.

   d. Newborns show a preference for stories their mother read to them while in the womb.

7. Which of the following is the clearest and most physical sign of puberty, characterized by rapid increases in height, weight, and skeletal development?

   a. menses

   b. spermarche

   c. a growth spurt

   d. age of fertility

8. What do we call it when employers are reluctant to hire 50- to 60-year-old workers because of a generalized belief that they are sickly and will take too much time off?

   a. discrimination

   b. prejudice

   c. ageism

   d. all of these options

9. What is the term for changes in physical and mental processes throughout adulthood that are gradual, inevitable, and age related?

   a. ageism

   b. primary aging

   c. programmed theory

   d. secondary aging

10. Who was one of the first scientists to demonstrate that a child's intellect is fundamentally different from that of an adult?

    a. Fantz

    b. Bandura

    c. Piaget

    d. Shatner

11. _____ occurs when existing schemas are used to interpret new information, whereas _____ involves changing and adapting the schemas.

    a. Adaptation; accommodation

    b. Adaptation; reversibility

    c. Egocentrism; post-schematization

    d. Assimilation; accommodation

12. Label the four stages of Piaget's cognitive development model on the table below.

Piaget's four stages of cognitive development

a. _____

b. _____

c. _____

d. _____

13. What phenomenon do the photos below illustrate?

a. the lack of sensory permanence

b. the lack of perceptual constancy

c. the lack of perceptual permanence

d. the lack of object permanence

14. The ability to think abstractly or hypothetically occurs in which of Piaget's stages?

a. egocentric   c. formal operational

b. postoperational   d. concrete operational

15. Extreme forms of self-consciousness and concerns for physical appearance are common in adolescents. What is the term David Elkind used for this early formal operational characteristic?

a. the personal fable

b. adolescent apprehension

c. the imaginary audience

d. the egocentric fable

16. What is one major criticism of Piaget's theory?

a. Few of his findings have been replicated in subsequent studies.

b. He placed far too much emphasis on the role of genetic influences in development.

c. He ignored cognitive development in adolescents.

d. He underestimated the cognitive abilities of infants and young children.

17. Which of the following is characteristic of children at the preoperational stage?

a. realizing that changes in shape or appearance can be reversed

b. being able to think in mildly abstract ways

c. being able to use symbols in their thinking

d. believing that they're at the centre of others' thoughts and attentions

18. Four-year-old Johnny believes that others think, feel, and perceive things the same way as he does. What is the name for this way of thinking?

a. animism   c. selfishness

b. egocentrism   d. the personal fable

19. Which of the following is characteristic of Piaget's concrete operational stage?

a. reversibility   c. animism

b. abstract thinking   d. lack of object permanence

20. Alex is a teenager who feels unique and invulnerable. This perspective likely contributes to his tendency to engage in risky behaviours. What is the term for this type of thinking?

a. the personal fable   c. secondary aging

b. the imaginary audience   d. sensation seeking

THE PLANNER ✓

Review your Chapter Planner on the chapter opener and check off your completed work.

Lifespan Development II: Social and Personality Development

Imagine that you are standing on a bridge over a railroad track when you see that a runaway train is about to kill five people. Coincidentally, you are standing next to a switching mechanism, and you realize that by simply throwing a switch, you can divert the train onto a spur, allowing the five to survive. But here is the catch: diverting the train will condemn one person, who is standing on the spur, to death. What would you do? Would you allow one person to die in order to save five others? Would your answer be different if that person were your mother, father, or some other much-loved person? What might lead different people to make different decisions?

It's unlikely that you will ever have to make such a gruesome choice. Yet everyone encounters moral dilemmas from time to time. Should you remind the cable company that they forgot to disconnect the cable after you discontinued the service? Should you give spare change to a friendly panhandler in your neighbourhood? Likewise, every one of us has personal relationships and particular character traits that colour our decisions. How we approach moral dilemmas—as well as many other events and circumstances throughout our lives—reflects several key facets of our personal growth: our social, moral, and personality development. In this chapter, we'll look at these aspects of development. We'll also examine how sex, gender, and culture influence our development. Finally, we'll explore several key developmental challenges during adulthood.

CHAPTER OUTLINE

CHAPTER PLANNER ✓

- ☐ Study the picture and read the opening story.
- ☐ Scan the Learning Objectives in each section:
  p. 268 ☐   p. 278 ☐   p. 283 ☐
- ☐ Read the text and study all visuals.
  Answer any questions.

Analyze key features

- ☐ What a Psychologist Sees, p. 269
- ☐ Study Organizer, p. 271
- ☐ Psychological Sciences, p. 272 ☐   p. 286 ☐   p. 289 ☐
- ☐ Process Diagram, p. 274 ☐   p. 277 ☐
- ☐ Visualizing, p. 279
- ☐ Applying Psychology, p. 284
- ☐ Stop: Answer the Concept Checks before you go on:
  p. 278 ☐   p. 282 ☐   p. 289 ☐

End of chapter

- ☐ Review the Summary and Key Terms.
- ☐ Answer the Critical and Creative Thinking Questions.
- ☐ Complete the Self-Test and check your answers.

© Oleksiy Mark/iStockphoto

Social, Moral, and Personality Development

LEARNING OBJECTIVES

1. **Describe** the three types of attachment identified by Mary Ainsworth.

2. **Explain** how attachment influences social development.

3. **Summarize** the central characteristics of Kohlberg's theory of moral development.

4. **Identify** Erikson's eight stages of psychosocial development.

In addition to physical and cognitive development (Chapter 9), developmental psychologists study social, moral, and personality development by looking at how social forces and individual differences affect development over the lifespan. Poet John Donne wrote, "No man is an island, entire of itself." In this section, we focus on three major facets of development that shed light on how we affect one another: attachment, Kohlberg's stages of moral development, and Erikson's psychosocial stages.

Social Development: The Importance of Attachment

An infant arrives in the world with a multitude of behaviours that encourage a strong bond of **attachment** with primary caregivers. This bond provides a sense of security in which the infant can explore the physical and social environment.

> **attachment** A strong affectional bond with primary caregivers that endures over time.

Perhaps the most prominent theorist in the study of attachment was British psychiatrist John Bowlby. Bowlby (1969, 1989, 2000) proposed that newborn infants are biologically equipped with behaviours, such as crying, clinging, and smiling, that draw the caregiver close and seem designed to keep her nearby. As infants develop, they are also increasingly able to seek proximity with the caregiver on their own accord, through "following" behaviours, such as crawling and walking after their caregiver. Konrad Lorenz's (1937) early studies of **imprinting** in geese further support the notion of inborn following behaviours that seem designed to keep young members of the species in close proximity to their mother (**Figure 10.1**). Infant-caregiver attachment in humans develops gradually over the first year of

life, such that by about 8 months of age most infants show an attachment relationship to their primary caregiver and possibly to one or two other special people in their lives (Cassidy, 2008; Marvin & Britner, 2008). Attachment is discussed in more detail in *What a Psychologist Sees: Attachment: The Power of Touch.*

Is attachment designed only to keep the infant close to his or her caregiver, or does it serve a broader function? Perhaps the best answer to this question comes from studies of infants who have failed to form an attachment. Research shows that infants raised in highly impersonal surroundings (such as in understaffed institutions that are not able to provide the stimulation and love of a regular caregiver) or under abusive conditions suffer from a number of serious problems. They seldom cry, coo, or babble; they become rigid when picked up; and

Imprinting • Figure 10.1

Konrad Lorenz's studies on *imprinting* demonstrated that baby geese attach to, and then follow, the first large moving object they see during a certain critical period shortly after hatching. In fact, in the example shown in the photo, the baby geese imprinted on Lorenz himself! What might be the advantages of this instinctual pattern of behaviour?

Nina Leen/Time Life Pictures/Getty Images, Inc.

What a Psychologist Sees

Attachment: The Power of Touch

In a classic experiment involving infant rhesus monkeys, Harry Harlow and Robert Zimmerman (1959) investigated the variables that might affect attachment. They created two types of wire-framed surrogate (substitute) "mother" monkeys: one covered by soft terry cloth and one left uncovered (**a.**). The infant monkeys were fed by either the cloth or the wire mother, but they otherwise had access to both mothers. The researchers found that monkeys "reared" by a cloth mother clung frequently to the soft material of their surrogate mother and developed greater emotional security and curiosity than did monkeys assigned to the wire mother.

In later research (Harlow & Harlow, 1966), monkey babies were exposed to rejection. Some of the "mothers" contained metal spikes that would suddenly protrude from the cloth covering and push the babies away; others had air jets that would sometimes blow the babies away. Nevertheless, the infant monkeys waited until the rejection was over and then clung to the cloth mothers as tightly as before. From these and related findings, Harlow concluded that **contact comfort**, the pleasurable tactile sensations provided by a soft and cuddly "mother," is a powerful contributor to attachment.

Several studies suggest that contact comfort between human infants and mothers is similarly important. For example, touching and massaging premature infants produces significant physical and emotional benefits (Field et al., 2010; Guzzetta et al., 2009; McGrath, 2009). Mothers around the world tend to kiss, nuzzle, nurse, comfort, clean, and respond to their children with lots of physical contact (**b.**).

Although almost all research on attachment and contact comfort has focused on mothers and infants, recent research shows that similar results can also apply to fathers and other loving caregivers (**c.**) (Berlin et al., 2008; Grossmann et al., 2008; Lamb & Lewis, 2010).

a.

Nina Leen/Time & Life Pictures/Getty Images

b.

© Simon Jarratt/Corbis

c.

Jodi Cobb/National Geographic Stock

they develop few language skills. They also tend to form shallow or anxious relationships with others. Some appear forlorn, withdrawn, and uninterested in their caretakers, whereas others seem insatiable in their need for affection (Dozier & Rutter, 2008). Finally, they also may show intellectual, physical, and perceptual deficits; increased susceptibility to infection; and bizarre "rocking" and isolation behaviours. In some extreme cases, some infants have even died from lack of attachment (Bowlby, 1973, 1982, 2000; Combrink-Graham & McKenna, 2006; Dozier & Rutter, 2008; Nelson et al., 2007; Spitz & Wolf, 1946).

Most children, of course, are never exposed to such extreme conditions of neglect or abuse. Nevertheless, Mary Ainsworth (1967; Ainsworth et al., 1978), a world-renowned developmental psychologist who was educated at the University of Toronto, found that there can be significant differences among infants in terms of the quality of their attachment relationships with their mothers. Moreover, these differences in the quality of attachment can affect long-term behaviours. Ainsworth developed a method called the **strange situation procedure** to assess infant-mother attachment. Using this procedure, she observed how infants responded to the presence or absence of their mother and to a stranger. Ainsworth found that children could be divided into three groups: securely attached, anxious/avoidant, and anxious/ambivalent (**Figure 10.2**).

Ainsworth found that infants with a secure attachment style had caregivers who were sensitive and responsive to their signals of distress, happiness, and fatigue (Ainsworth, 1967; Ainsworth et al., 1978; Belsky & Fearon, 2008; Weinfield et al., 2008). Anxious/avoidant infants had caregivers who were aloof and distant, while anxious/ambivalent infants had inconsistent caregivers who alternated between strong affection and indifference. Follow-up studies have found that, over time, securely attached children, compared to their anxious/avoidant and anxious/ambivalent counterparts, are the most sociable, emotionally aware, enthusiastic, cooperative, persistent, curious, and competent (Booth-Laforce & Kerns, 2009; Kerns, 2008; Sroufe et al., 2005; Thompson, 2008; Thompson & Meyer, 2007; Weinfield et al., 2008).

Parenting Styles: Their Effect on Development

How much of our personality comes from the way our parents treat us as we are growing up? Researchers since as far back as the 1920s have studied the effects of different methods of child rearing on children's behaviour, development, and mental health. Studies done by Diana Baumrind (1980, 1991, 1995) found that parenting styles could be reliably divided into three broad patterns: *permissive, authoritarian*, and *authoritative*, which could be identified by their degree of *control/demandingness* and *warmth/responsiveness* (**Study Organizer 10.1**).

Types of attachment • Figure 10.2

Ainsworth's research identified three different types of attachment.

Securely attached (65 percent). When exposed to the stranger, the infant seeks closeness and contact with the mother, uses the mother as a safe base from which to explore (**a.**), shows moderate distress on separation from the mother, and is relieved and happy when the mother returns (**b.**).

Anxious/avoidant (20 percent). Although distressed by the strange situation, the infant avoids the mother, does not seek closeness or contact with her, treats her much like a stranger, and rarely cries when she leaves the room.

Anxious/ambivalent (15 percent). The infant becomes very upset when the mother leaves the room. When she returns, the infant displays ambivalent (mixed) feelings toward her, seeking close contact, while at the same time squirming angrily to get away.

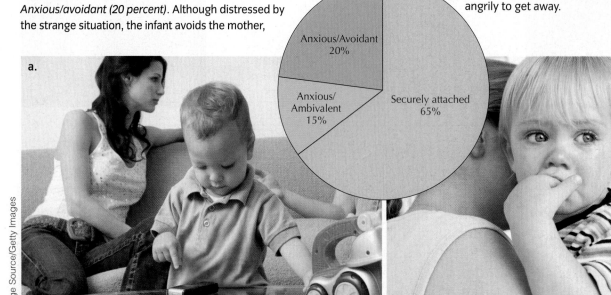

Anxious/Avoidant 20%

Anxious/Ambivalent 15%

Securely attached 65%

Image Source/Getty Images

Bananastock/AGE Fototstock

Parenting Style	Description	Example	Effect on Children
Permissive-neglectful (permissive-indifferent) (low control, low warmth)	Parents make few demands, with little structure or monitoring, and show little interest or emotional support; may be actively rejecting.	"I don't care about you—or what you do."	Children tend to have poor social skills and poor self-control (being overly demanding and disobedient). Have an increased tendency to be rebellious and antisocial.
Permissive-indulgent (low control, high warmth)	Parents set few limits or demands but are highly involved and emotionally connected.	"I care about you—and you're free to do what you like!"	Children often fail to learn respect for others and tend to be impulsive, immature, and out of control.
Authoritarian (high control, low warmth)	Parents are rigid and punitive while also being low on warmth and responsiveness.	"I don't care what you want. Just do it my way, or else!"	Children tend to be easily upset, moody, some are aggressive but some are timid, and often fail to learn good communication skills.
Authoritative (high control, high warmth)	Parents generally set and enforce firm limits while also being highly involved, tender, and emotionally supportive.	"I really care about you, but there are rules and you need to be responsible."	Children tend to be self-reliant, self-controlled, high achieving, and well adjusted; also seem more content, goal oriented, friendly, and socially competent.

Sources: Coplan, Arbeau, & Armer (2008); Martin & Fabes (2009); Parke & Clarke-Stewart (2011); Younger, Adler, & Vasta (2012).

Siblings and Peers

In Canada, the United States, and Europe, approximately 80 percent of children have siblings. For many children, their relationships with siblings will be the longest-lasting relationships they ever have (Dunn, 2007; Howe et al., 2011). Siblings spend more time in one another's company than with parents or even peers and come to know one another well (Dunn 2007). Such proximity can have both positive and negative ramifications: it can result in mutual caring and support, but it can also result in conflict (**Figure 10.3**). Indeed, as Canadian researchers Nina Howe, Hildy Ross, and Holly Recchia (2011) point out, quarrels and disagreements among siblings are a normal part of their relationships and may even be useful in teaching children conflict-resolution skills.

The presence of siblings can have valuable cognitive benefits for children. Sibling interactions are a frequent context for sharing of emotions, as well as for teasing and tricks. It is not surprising, therefore, that through such interactions children can learn about other people's thoughts and feelings, and how these can differ from their own

Sibling cooperation and conflict • Figure 10.3 _____

Both cooperation and conflict are frequent components of sibling interaction. What possible benefits might there be from both positive and negative sibling interactions?

Attachment across the Lifespan

Murat Sarica/iStockphoto

Nina Vaclavova/iStockphoto

If you've been around young children, you've probably noticed how they share toys and discoveries with their parent and seem much happier when the parent is nearby. You may also have thought how sweet it is when infants and parents share baby talk with each other. But have you noticed that similar behaviours often occur between adults in romantic relationships?

Intrigued by these parallels, researchers have studied the relationship between an infant's attachment to a parent and an adult's love for a romantic partner (Feeney, 2008; Zeifman & Hazan, 2008). In a classic study, Cindy Hazan and Phillip Shaver (1987, 1994) discovered that adults who report having had an anxious/avoidant pattern in infancy often find it hard to trust others and to self-disclose, and they rarely report finding "true love." In short, it seems they block intimacy by being emotionally distant. Those who report having been anxious/ambivalent as infants tend to be obsessed with their romantic partners as adults, fearing their intense love will not be reciprocated. As a result, they may smother intimacy by being possessive and emotionally demanding. Fortunately, adults who report having been securely attached as infants easily become close to others, expect intimate relationships to endure, and perceive others as trustworthy. As you may expect, the securely attached lover has intimacy patterns that foster long-term

relationships and is the most desired partner by most adults (Lele, 2008; Mikulincer & Goodman, 2006; Vorria et al., 2007).

Can attachment style in adults be changed? Canadian psychologist Sue Johnson (2008, 2011) has developed a therapy for couples, which uses the attachment perspective to understand negative patterns of interaction and guide couples into less distressed and more secure relationships. Her internationally renowned *emotionally focused therapy* (EFT) argues that habitual ways of dealing with attachment needs and fears often define adult love relationships. EFT attempts to foster feelings of security as a means to improve intimate relationships in couples.

As you consider the suggested relationship between attachment in infancy and adult romantic love, remember that it is always risky to infer causation from correlation. Accordingly, the relationship between romantic love and infant attachment could have several alternative explanations. Also, be aware that early attachment experiences may predict the future, but they do not determine it. Throughout life, we can learn new social skills and different attitudes toward relationships.

Think Critically

1. What factors other than just early infant attachment might account for our romantic love styles as adults?
2. How do you think an anxious/ambivalent attachment style might affect an individual's relationships later in life? What about an anxious/avoidant style?

(Dunn, 2007), important information for learning to understand the perspectives of others. Older siblings can also be effective teachers of younger siblings (Howe & Recchia, 2008); they can also serve as models of both positive and

negative social behaviours, as well as gender-role behaviour (McHale et al., 2001, 2003; Rust et al., 2000).

Most children have experiences not only with siblings but with other children as well. Experiences with peers can begin

Bartosz Hadyniak/ iStockphoto

Peer relationships • Figure 10.4

The most important peer relationship is that of friendship. What characteristics of friends can you see in this photo?

For an interesting discussion on this topic, scan to download the author's podcast.

as early as infancy but become especially important in the elementary school and high school years. As children grow older, they spend more and more time with peers and relatively less time with adults, including their parents (Ellis et al, 1981).

One very important peer relationship is friendship—an enduring relationship characterized by loyalty, intimacy, and mutual affection. The most important thing that attracts children to friendship relationships with one another is similarity (Bukowski, Motzoi, & Meyer, 2009). Elementary school children are more likely to choose as friends peers who are similar to them in a variety of ways, including age (Berndt, 1988), gender (Rose & Smith, 2009), ethnicity and race (Graham et al., 2009), and especially interests and behaviours (Rubin et al., 2006; Ryan, 2001): children become friends because they enjoy the same sorts of things (**Figure 10.4**).

As is true for relationships with siblings, friends can provide support for one another and can serve as models of behaviour, both positive and negative. Indeed, having even just one close friend provides children with important social support and can serve as a buffer against being picked on by others (Vitaro et al., 2009).

Moral Development: Kohlberg's Stages

Developing a sense of right and wrong, or morality, is a part of psychological development. Consider the following situation in terms of what you would do.

In Europe, a woman was near death from a special kind of cancer. There was one drug that doctors thought might save her. It was a form of ra-dium that a druggist in the same town had recently discovered. The drug was expensive to make, but the druggist was charging 10 times what the drug cost him to make. He paid $200 for the radium and charged $2,000 for a small dose of the drug. The sick woman's husband, Heinz, went to everyone he knew to borrow the money, but he could gather together only about $1,000, half of what it cost. He told the druggist that his wife was dying and asked him to sell it cheaper or let him pay later. But the druggist said, "No, I discovered the drug, and I'm going to make money from it." So Heinz got desperate and broke into the man's store to steal the drug for his wife. (Kohlberg, 1964, pp. 18–19)

Was Heinz right to steal the drug? What do you consider moral behaviour? Is morality "in the eye of the beholder," or are there universal truths and principles? Whatever your answer, your ability to think, reason, and respond to Heinz's dilemma demonstrates another type of development that is very important to psychology: morality.

One of the most influential researchers in moral development was Lawrence Kohlberg (1927–1987). He presented what he called "moral stories," such as the Heinz dilemma, to people of all ages, and on the basis of his findings, he developed a model of moral development (1964, 1984).

What is the right answer to Heinz's dilemma? Kohlberg was interested not in whether participants judged Heinz to be right or wrong but in the reasons they gave for their decisions. On the basis of participants' responses, Kohlberg proposed three broad levels in the evolution of moral reasoning—preconventional, conventional, and postconventional—with each level being composed of two distinct stages. Individuals at each stage and level may or may not support Heinz's stealing of the drug, but their reasoning changes from level to level. **Figure 10.5** describes each of the three levels and the two stages that make up each level.

Kohlberg believed that, like Piaget's stages of cognitive development (Chapter 9), his stages of moral development are universal and invariant. That is, they supposedly exist in all cultures, and everyone goes through each of the stages in a predictable fashion. The age trends tend to be rather broad.

Preconventional level (Stages 1 and 2: Birth to adolescence)

At the **preconventional level**, moral judgement is self-centred. What is right is what you can get away with or what is personally satisfying. Moral understanding is based on rewards, punishments, and the exchange of favours. This level is called "preconventional" because children have not yet accepted society's (conventional) rule-making processes.

preconventional level Kohlberg's first level of moral development in which morality is based on rewards, punishment, and the exchange of favours.

PROCESS DIAGRAM

Kohlberg's stages of moral development • Figure 10.5

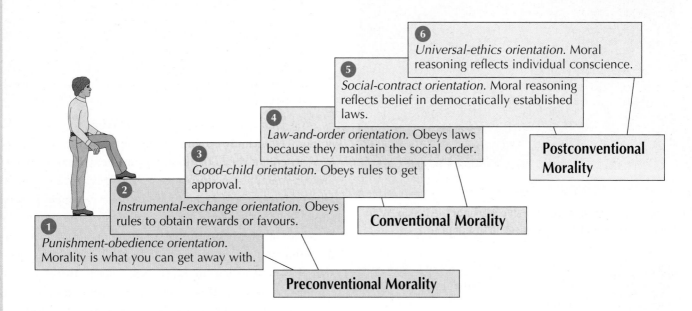

6 *Universal-ethics orientation.* Moral reasoning reflects individual conscience.

5 *Social-contract orientation.* Moral reasoning reflects belief in democratically established laws.

Postconventional Morality

4 *Law-and-order orientation.* Obeys laws because they maintain the social order.

3 *Good-child orientation.* Obeys rules to get approval.

Conventional Morality

2 *Instrumental-exchange orientation.* Obeys rules to obtain rewards or favours.

1 *Punishment-obedience orientation.* Morality is what you can get away with.

Preconventional Morality

Preconventional level (Stages 1 and 2—birth to adolescence) Moral judgement is *self-centred*. What is right is what one can get away with, or what is personally satisfying. Moral understanding is based on rewards, punishments, and the exchange of favours.

1  Focus is on self-interest—obedience to authority and avoidance of punishment. Because children at this stage have difficulty considering another's point of view, they also ignore people's intentions.

2 Children become aware of others' perspectives, but their morality is based on reciprocity—an equal exchange of favours.

Conventional level (Stages 3 and 4—adolescence and young adulthood) Moral reasoning is *other-centred*. Conventional societal rules are accepted because they help ensure the social order.

3  Primary moral concern is being nice and gaining approval. The person judges others by their intentions—"His heart was in the right place."

4  Morality is based on a larger perspective—societal laws. Understands that if everyone violated laws, even with good intentions, there would be chaos.

Postconventional level (Stages 5 and 6—adulthood) Moral judgements are based on *personal standards for right and wrong*. Morality is also defined in terms of abstract principles and values that apply to all situations and societies.

5 Appreciates the underlying purposes served by laws. Societal laws are obeyed because of the "social contract," but they can be morally disobeyed if they fail to express the will of the majority or fail to maximize social welfare.

6 "Right" is determined by universal ethical principles (e.g., non-violence, human dignity, freedom) that all religions or moral authorities might view as compelling or fair. These principles apply whether or not they conform to existing laws.

Sources: Adapted from Kohlberg, L. "Stage and Sequence: The Cognitive Developmental Approach to Socialization." In D. A. Goslin, *The Handbook of Socialization Theory and Research*. Chicago, IL: Rand McNally, 1969. p. 376 (Table 6.2).

- *Stage 1 (punishment and obedience orientation)*. Children at this stage focus on self-interest: obedience to authority and avoidance of punishment. Because they also have difficulty considering another's point of view, they also ignore people's intentions in their moral judgements.
- *Stage 2 (instrumental-exchange orientation)*. During this stage, children become aware of others' perspectives, but their morality is based on reciprocity: an equal exchange of favours. "I'll share my lunch with you because if I ever forget mine you'll share yours with me."

Tom Hanson/The Canadian Press

Postconventional moral reasoning
• **Figure 10.6**

Would you travel hundreds of kilometres to participate in a political demonstration? Would you be willing to be arrested for violating the law to express your moral convictions? How would Kohlberg's theory explain such actions?

conventional level Kohlberg's second level of moral development in which moral judgements are based on compliance with the rules and values of society.

Conventional level (Stages 3 and 4: Adolescence and young adulthood) At the conventional level, moral reasoning advances from being self-centred to other-centred. The individual personally accepts conventional societal rules because they help ensure social order.

- *Stage 3 ("good child" orientation)*. At Stage 3, the primary moral concern is with being nice and gaining approval. People are also judged by their intentions and motives ("His heart was in the right place").
- *Stage 4 (law-and-order orientation)*. During this stage, the individual takes into account a larger perspective: societal laws. Stage 4 individuals understand that if everyone violated laws, even with good intentions, there would be chaos. Thus, doing your duty and respecting law and order are highly valued.

Postconventional level (Stages 5 and 6: adulthood)

postconventional level Kohlberg's highest level of moral development in which individuals develop personal standards for right and wrong and they define morality in terms of abstract principles and values that apply to all situations and societies.

At the postconventional level, individuals develop personal standards for right and wrong. They also define morality in terms of abstract principles and values that apply to all situations and societies. A 20-year-old who judges the "discovery" and settlement of North America by Europeans as immoral because it involved the theft of land from native peoples is thinking in postconventional terms.

- *Stage 5 (social-contract orientation)*. Individuals at Stage 5 appreciate the underlying purposes served by laws. When laws are consistent with interests of the majority, they are obeyed because of the "social contract."

However, laws can be morally disobeyed if they fail to express the will of the majority or fail to maximize social welfare (**Figure 10.6**).

- *Stage 6 (universal ethics orientation)*. At this stage, "right" is determined by universal ethical principles (e.g., non-violence, human dignity, freedom) that all religions or moral authorities might view as compelling or fair. These principles apply, whether or not they conform to existing laws. Few individuals actually achieve Stage 6 (about 1 or 2 percent of those tested worldwide), and Kohlberg found it difficult to separate stages 5 and 6. So, in time, he combined the two last stages (Kohlberg, 1981).

Assessing Kohlberg's theory Kohlberg has been credited with enormous insights and contributions, but his theories have also been the focus of three major areas of criticism:

- *Moral reasoning versus behaviour.* Are people who achieve higher stages on Kohlberg's scale really more moral than others, or do they just "talk a good game"? Some studies show a positive correlation between higher stages of reasoning and higher levels of moral behaviour (Borba, 2001; Rest et al., 1999), but others have found that situational factors are better predictors

Morality gap? • Figure 10.7

What makes people who normally behave ethically willing to steal intellectual property, such as music or software?

"I swear I wasn't looking at smut—I was just stealing music."

© Alex Gregory/Conde Nast Publications/www.cartoonbank.com

of moral behaviour (**Figure 10.7**) (Bandura, 1986, 1991, 2008; Kaplan, 2006; Satcher, 2007; Slováčková & Slováček, 2007). For example, research participants are more likely to steal when they are told the money comes from a large company rather than from individuals (Greenberg, 2002). And both men and women will tell more sexual lies during casual relationships than during close relationships (Williams, 2001).

- *Possible gender bias*. Researcher Carol Gilligan (1977, 1990, 1993) criticized Kohlberg's model because on his scale, women tend to be classified at a lower level of moral reasoning than men. Gilligan suggested that this difference occurred because Kohlberg's theory emphasizes values more often held by men, such as rationality and independence, while de-emphasizing common female values, such as concern for others and belonging. Most follow-up studies of Gilligan's theory, however, have found few, if any, gender differences in level or type of moral reasoning. Indeed, Lawrence Walker (1991, 2006) of the University of British Columbia surveyed 80 studies using Kohlberg's methods in which gender differences could be reported. Walker found no gender differences in 86 percent of these studies! Of the remaining studies, females scored higher in 6 percent, and males scored higher in 9 percent.

- *Cultural differences*. Cross-cultural studies confirm that children from a variety of cultures generally follow Kohlberg's model and progress sequentially from his first level, the *preconventional*, to his second, the *conventional* (Rest et al., 1999; Snarey, 1985, 1995). At the same time, some critics have argued that Kohlberg's moral

dilemmas may not adequately address certain moral issues and concepts found in other cultures (Miller, 2006). For example, cross-cultural comparisons of responses to Heinz's moral dilemma show that Europeans and North Americans tend to consider whether they like or identify with the victim in questions of morality. In contrast, Hindu Indians consider social responsibility and personal concerns to be separate issues (Miller & Bersoff, 1998). Researchers suggest that the difference reflects the Hindus' broader sense of social responsibility. In other cultures, the conflict between what is right for the individual and what is right for society is not ideally resolved by choosing one over the other (as is required in Kohlberg's hypothetical dilemmas). Instead, the most appropriate solution is thought to be reconciling the two interests by arriving at a compromise solution (Dien, 1982; Killen & Hart, 1999; Miller & Bersoff, 1998).

Personality Development: Erikson's Psychosocial Theory

Like Piaget and Kohlberg, Erik Erikson (1902–1994) developed a stage theory of development. He identified eight **psychosocial stages** of social development (**Figure 10.8**), each marked by a "psychosocial" crisis or conflict related to a specific developmental task. The name given to each stage reflects the specific crisis encountered at that stage

> **psychosocial stages** In Erikson's theory, the eight developmental stages, each involving a crisis that must be successfully resolved.

and the two possible outcomes. For example, the crisis faced by most young adults is *intimacy versus isolation*. This age group's developmental task is developing deep, meaningful relationships with others. Those who don't meet this developmental challenge risk social isolation. Similarly, the crisis faced by adolescents is *identity versus role confusion*. During a period of serious questioning, intense soul-searching, and the trying on various roles, many adolescents develop a coherent sense of self and their role in society. Failure to resolve this **identity crisis** may be related to a lack of a stable identity, delinquency, and difficulty in maintaining close personal relationships in later life. Erikson believed that the more successfully we overcome each psychosocial crisis, the better chance we have to develop in a healthy manner (Erikson, 1950).

Many psychologists agree with Erikson's general idea that psychosocial crises contribute to personality development (Berzoff, 2008; Markstrom & Marshall, 2007; Torges,

Erikson's eight stages of psychosocial development • Figure 10.8

Stage 1

Trust versus mistrust (birth–age 1)

Infants learn to trust or mistrust their caregivers and the world based on whether or not their needs—such as food, affection, safety—are met.

Stage 2

Autonomy versus shame and doubt (ages 1–3)

Toddlers start to assert their sense of independence (*autonomy*). If caregivers encourage this self-sufficiency, the toddler will learn to be independent versus developing feelings of *shame* and *doubt*.

Stage 3

Initiative versus guilt (ages 3–6)

Preschoolers learn to initiate activities and develop self-confidence (*initiative*) and a sense of social responsibility. If not, they feel irresponsible, anxious, and *guilty*.

Stage 4

Industry versus inferiority (ages 6–12)

Elementary-school-age children who succeed in learning new, productive life skills develop a sense of pride and competence (*industry*). Those who fail to develop these skills feel inadequate and unproductive (*inferior*).

Ana Abejon/iStockphoto

kali9/iStockphoto

Jo Unruh/iStockphoto

Wojciech Gajda/iStockphoto

Stage 5

Identity versus role confusion (ages 12–20)

Adolescents develop a coherent and stable self-definition (*identity*) by exploring many roles and deciding who or what they want to be in terms of career, attitudes, and so on. Failure to resolve this *identity crisis* may lead to apathy, withdrawal, and *role confusion*.

Stage 6

Intimacy versus isolation (young adulthood)

Young adults form lasting, meaningful relationships, which help them develop a sense of connectednesss and *intimacy* with others, especially partners in romance and love. If not, they may become psychologically *isolated*.

Stage 7

Generativity versus stagnation (middle adulthood)

The challenge for middle-aged adults is to be nurturant of the younger generation (*generativity*). Failing to meet this challenge can lead to self-indulgence and a sense of *stagnation* and self-absorption.

Stage 8

Ego integrity versus despair (late adulthood)

During this stage, older adults reflect on their past. If this reflection reveals a life well spent, the person experiences self-acceptance and satisfaction (*ego integrity*). If not, he or she experiences regret, deep dissatisfaction, and a feeling that it is now too late to make changes (*despair*).

Ariel Duhon/iStockphoto

Nicolas Hansen/iStockphoto

Zurijeta/iStockphoto

Jacob Wackerhausen/iStockphoto

Stewart, & Duncan, 2008). However, some critics argue that his theory oversimplifies development. Others observe that the eight stages and the direction of their resolution do not apply equally to all groups. For example, in some cultures, *autonomy* is highly preferable to *shame and doubt*, but in others, the preferred resolution might be *dependence* or *merging relations* (Matsumoto & Juang, 2008). Despite their limits, Erikson's stages have greatly contributed to the study of North American and European psychosocial development. By suggesting that development continues past adolescence, Erikson's theory has encouraged further research into the development of personality across the lifespan.

CONCEPT CHECK STOP

1. **How** do the securely attached, anxious/avoidant, and anxious/ambivalent attachment styles of children differ?
2. **Why** was Kohlberg interested in the reasoning behind people's answers to the Heinz dilemma?
3. **What** criticisms have been levelled at Kohlberg's theory of moral development?
4. **What** are some cross-cultural limitations to Erikson's psychosocial theory?

How Sex, Gender, and Culture Affect Development

LEARNING OBJECTIVES

1. **Identify** biological sex differences in physical development.
2. **Describe** how gender differences are related to cognitive, personality, and social development.
3. **Explain** how individualistic versus collectivistic cultures shape personality development.

Imagine for a moment what your life would be like if you were a member of the other sex. Would you think differently? Would you be more or less sociable and outgoing? Would your career plans or friendship patterns change? Most people believe that whether we are male or female has a strong impact on many facets of development. But why is that? Why is it that the first question most people ask after a baby is born is, "Is it a girl or a boy?"

Sex and Gender Influences on Development

In this section, we will explore how our development is affected by **sex** (a biological characteristic determined at the moment of conception) and by **gender** (psychological and sociocultural meanings added to our biological sex) and **gender roles** (societal expectations that accompany biological sex).

Sex differences Physical anatomy is the most obvious biological sex difference between men and women (**Figure 10.9**). Men and wom-

sex Biological maleness and femaleness including chromosomal sex.

gender Psychological and sociocultural meanings added to biological maleness or femaleness.

gender roles Societal expectations for normal and appropriate male and female behaviour.

en also differ in secondary sex characteristics, such as facial hair and breast growth; signs of reproductive capability, such as menstruation and ejaculation of sperm; and physical responses to middle age or the end of reproduction, such as *menopause* and the *male climateric*. The brains of men and women also show several functional and structural differences. These result partly from the influence of prenatal sex hormones on the developing fetal brain.

Gender differences In addition to biological sex differences, scientists have found numerous gender differences, which affect our cognitive, social, and personality development.

For example, on average females tend to score higher on tests of verbal skills, whereas males score higher on tests of visuospatial abilities and some aspects of math (Halpern, 2012; Kimura, 2004; Priess & Hyde, 2010). These differences in cognitive ability may to some extent reflect biological factors, including structural differences in the cerebral hemispheres, sex hormones, or the degree of hemispheric specialization. However, male-female differences

Visualizing

Major physical differences between the sexes • Figure 10.9

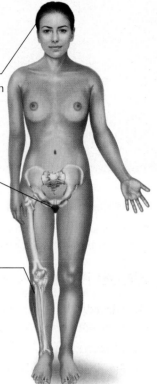

Body Size and Shape
The average man is 35 pounds heavier, has less body fat, and is 5 inches taller than the average woman. Men tend to have broader shoulders, slimmer hips and slightly longer legs in proportion to their height.

Brain
On average, men's brains are heavier and larger than women's (primarily because men have larger bodies). Women have larger speech and communication neural regions than men. The corpus callosum, the bridge joining the two halves of the brain, is larger in women. This size difference is interpreted by some to mean that women can more easily integrate information from the two halves of the brain and more easily perform more than one task simultaneously.

Sex Hormones
Although both men and women produce the sex hormones testosterone and estrogen, men have far more testosterone than women, and women have far more estrogen. Across the month, men have relatively constant levels of sex hormones, whereas women show cyclic sex hormone production that regulates the menstrual cycle.

Muscular System
Until puberty, boys and girls are well matched in physical strength and ability. Once hormones kick in, the average man has more muscle mass and greater upper body strength than the average woman.

kristian sekulic/iStockphoto

in verbal abilities and math scores have declined in recent years, suggesting that the origins of these male-female differences may not be solely biological (Halpern, 2012).

Like cognitive ability, aggressive behaviour also differs between the sexes. Boys are more likely to engage in mock fighting and rough-and-tumble play, and as adolescents and adults, they are more likely to commit violent crimes (Bjorklund & Pellegrini, 2011; Campbell & Muncer, 2008; Ostrov & Keating, 2004). Girls, on the other hand, are more likely to engage in more indirect and relational forms of aggression, such as spreading rumours and ignoring or excluding someone. Indeed, research shows that girls tend to perceive such relational forms of aggression as more hurtful than do boys (Rose & Smith, 2009). Gender differences in the types of aggression that children use have been noted as early as the preschool years (Ostrov & Crick, 2007; Ostrov & Keating, 2004), increase throughout elementary school, and tend to peak by high-school age (Crick et al., 2007; Murray-Close et al., 2007; Rose & Smith, 2009).

Some research has found that biological factors play an important role in male-female differences in aggression—a nativist position. Several studies have linked the masculinizing hormone testosterone to aggressive behaviour (Hermans et al., 2008; Popma et al., 2007; Trainor et al. 2004). Indeed, exposure to testosterone during the

Rockstar/AP Photo

Modelling gendered behaviour • Figure 10.10

Some computer and video games include a great deal of violence and are often criticized for modelling and encouraging violence. In a game called *Bully*, shown here, the main character ultimately takes on bullies rather than becoming one. The game includes plenty of fighting, but it also claims to show that actions have consequences. Do you think such an approach might encourage or discourage violent behaviour?

prenatal period has been found to underlie a number of "male" characteristics, including rough-and-tumble play, aggressiveness, and increased spatial abilities (Auyeung et al., 2009; Saucier & Ehresman, 2010; Wallen, 2005). In addition, studies of identical twins have found that genetic factors account for a considerable portion of aggressive behaviour (Dodge et al., 2008; Rhee & Waldman, 2011). We discuss these and other factors related to aggression further in Chapter 15.

Other research has underscored the importance of nurture. This research suggests that male-female differences in aggressiveness may result from environmental experiences with social dominance and pressures that encourage "sex appropriate" behaviours and skills (Rowe et al., 2004) **(Figure 10.10)**. **Table 10.1** summarizes the gender differences between men and women.

Gender-role development By age 2, children are aware of gender roles. They recognize that boys "should" be strong, independent, aggressive, dominant, and achieving, whereas girls "should" be soft, dependent, passive, emotional, and "naturally" interested in children (Halim

Research-supported sex and gender differences Table 10.1

Behaviour	More often shown by men	More often shown by women
Sexual	• Begin masturbating sooner in life cycle and have higher overall occurrence rates • Start sexual life earlier and have first orgasm through masturbation • Are more likely to recognize their own sexual arousal • Experience more orgasm consistency in their sexual relations	• Begin masturbating later in life cycle and have lower overall occurrence rates • Start sexual life later and have first orgasm from partner stimulation • Are less likely to recognize their own sexual arousal • Experience less orgasm consistency in their sexual relations
Touching	• Are touched, kissed, and cuddled less by parents • Exchange less physical contact with other men and respond more negatively to being touched • Are more likely to initiate both casual and intimate touch with sexual partner	• Are touched, kissed, and cuddled more by parents • Exchange more physical contact with other women and respond more positively to being touched • Are less likely to initiate either casual or intimate touch with sexual partner
Friendship	• Prefer to interact in large groups of friends and express friendship by shared activities	• Prefer to interact in small groups of friends and express friendship by shared communication about self
Personality	• Are more self-confident of future success • Tend to attribute success to internal factors and failures to external factors • Achievement is task oriented; motives are mastery and competition • Tend to be more self-validating • Have higher self-esteem	• Are less self-confident of future success • Tend to attribute success to external factors and failures to internal factors • Achievement is socially directed with emphasis on self-improvement; have higher work motives • Tend to be more dependent on others for validation • Have lower self-esteem

Sources: Crooks & Baur (2011); Hyde & DeLamater (2011); Harter (2006); King (2012); Masters & Johnson (1961, 1966, 1970); Matlin (2012); Rose & Rudolph (2006); Rose & Smith (2009).

& Ruble, 2010; Poulin-Dubois & Serbin, 2006; Renzetti et al., 2006). Indeed, Canadian researchers Diane Poulin-Dubois and Lisa Serbin (2006) have found that by age 2, toddlers also show knowledge of the typical activities of men and women. The existence of similar gender roles in many cultures suggests that biology may play a role. However, most research emphasizes two major theories of gender role development: social learning and cognitive developmental.

Social learning theorists emphasize the importance of the immediate situation and observable behaviours on gender-role development. They suggest that girls learn how to be "feminine" and boys learn how to be "masculine" in two major ways: (1) they receive rewards or punishments for specific gender-role behaviours, and (2) they watch and imitate the behaviour of others, particularly the same-sex parent (Bussey & Bandura, 2004; Fredricks & Eccles, 2005; Kulik, 2005; Leaper & Friedman, 2007). A boy who puts on his father's tie or baseball cap wins big, indulgent smiles from his parents. But what would happen if he put on his mother's nightgown or lipstick? Parents, teachers, and friends generally reward or punish behaviours according to traditional gender-role expectations (Basow, 2010; Brody & Hall, 2010; Rose & Rudolph, 2006). However, they are much more accepting if girls deviate from traditional roles than if boys do so. Thus, a child "socially learns" what it means to be male or female.

The media have greatly expanded the variety of models available to children. In particular, television communicates a great deal about gender roles and behaviour. Analyses of the contents of programs and commercials reveal that TV has tended to portray characters in very traditional gender roles (Collins, 2011; Leaper & Friedman, 2007). This is especially the case for children's cartoons (Leaper et al., 2002; England et al., 2011), as well as music videos, video games, and even teen magazines (Ruble et al., 2006; Wallis, 2011).

Cognitive developmental theorists, on the other hand, while agreeing that social learning is part of gender-role development, argue that the process is much more than simply a passive process of receiving rewards or punishments and modelling others. Instead, cognitive developmentalists argue that children actively observe, interpret, and judge the world around them (Brannon, 2011; Halim & Ruble, 2010; Ruble et al., 2006). As children process information about the world, they also create internal rules governing correct behaviours for boys versus girls. On the basis of these rules, they form **gender schemas** (mental images)

© Romell/Masterfile

Developing gender schemas • Figure 10.11

How would social learning theory and cognitive developmental theory explain why children tend to choose stereotypically "appropriate" toys?

of how they should act (**Figure 10.11**). Such gender schemas prompt the child to pay greater attention to information relevant to his or her own gender and also influence the child's choice of activities (Halim & Ruble, 2010; Martin et al., 2002).

Cultural Influences on Development

Our development is rooted in the concept of **self**—how we define and understand ourselves (Harter, 2008). Yet the very concept of *self* reflects our culture. In **individualistic cultures**, the needs and goals of the individual are emphasized over the needs and goals of the group. When asked to complete the statement "I am . . . ," people from individualistic cultures tend to respond with personality traits ("I am shy"; "I am outgoing") or their occupation ("I am a teacher"; "I am a student").

In **collectivistic cultures**, however, the opposite is true. The person is defined and understood primarily by looking at his or her place in the social unit (Laungani,

> **individualistic cultures** Cultures in which the needs and goals of the individual are emphasized over the needs and goals of the group.
>
> **collectivistic cultures** Cultures in which the needs and goals of the group are emphasized over the needs and goals of the individual.

A worldwide ranking of cultures Table 10.2

Individualistic cultures	Intermediate cultures	Collectivistic cultures
United States	Israel	Hong Kong
Australia	Spain	Chile
Great Britain	India	Singapore
Canada	Argentina	Thailand
Netherlands	Japan	West Africa region
New Zealand	Iran	El Salvador
Italy	Jamaica	Taiwan
Belgium	Arab region	South Korea
Denmark	Brazil	Peru
France	Turkey	Costa Rica
Sweden	Uruguay	Indonesia
Ireland	Greece	Pakistan
Norway	Philippines	Colombia
Switzerland	Mexico	Venezuela

Greg Smith/AP Photo

Keren Su/China Span/Getty Images

How might these two groups differ in their physical, socioemotional, cognitive, moral, and personality development?

2007; Matsumoto & Juang, 2008; McCrae, 2004). Relatedness, connectedness, and interdependence are valued, as opposed to separateness, independence, and individualism. When asked to complete the statement "I am . . . ," people from collectivistic cultures tend to mention their families or nationality ("I am a daughter"; "I am Chinese").

If you are North American or Western European, you are more likely to be individualistic than collectivistic (**Table 10.2**). And you may find the concept of a self that is defined in terms of others almost contradictory. A core selfhood probably seems intuitively obvious to you. Recognizing that more than 70 percent of the world's population lives in collectivistic cultures, however, may improve your cultural sensitivity and prevent misunderstandings (Singelis et al., 1995). For example, North Americans generally define sincerity as behaving in accordance with their inner feelings, whereas Japanese see it as behaviour that conforms to a person's role expectations (carrying out one's duties) (Yamada, 1997). Can you see how Japanese behaviour might appear insincere to a North American and vice versa?

We can see the influence of culture on the development of the self even in infancy. Infant sleeping arrangements are a good example. Starting very early in life, most infants in North American Caucasian families sleep alone in their own beds (often in their own rooms) (Goldberg & Keller, 2007). Asked about the reason for this practice, a significant number of parents report that sleeping alone trains children to be independent, a characteristic valued by individualistic cultures. This is not the case, however, in many other cultures, where co-sleeping of infants with parents is common (Germo et al, 2007; Goldberg & Keller, 2007; McKenna & Volpe, 2007).

CONCEPT CHECK STOP

1. **What** is the difference between sex and gender?

2. **How** do people develop gender roles?

3. **How** is the concept of "self" different in individualistic versus collectivistic cultures?

Developmental Challenges through Adulthood

LEARNING OBJECTIVES

1. **Describe** the factors that ensure realistic expectations for marriage and long-term committed relationships.

2. **Explain** the factors that affect life satisfaction during the adult working years and retirement.

3. **Describe** the three basic concepts about death and dying that people learn to understand through the course of development.

I n this section, we will explore three of the most important developmental tasks that people face during adulthood: developing a loving, committed relationship with another person; finding rewarding work and a satisfying retirement; and coping with death and dying.

Committed Relationships: Overcoming Unrealistic Expectations

One of the most important tasks faced during adulthood is that of establishing some kind of continuing, loving, sexual relationship with another person. Yet navigating such partnerships is often very challenging. For example, about 38 percent of marriages in Canada end in divorce (Wu & Schimmele, 2009), with serious implications for both adults and children. Most divorces occur early in a marriage: the rate of divorce in Canada is highest three to four years into a marriage and then decreases slowly for each additional year (Statistics Canada, 2005). Following divorce, both spouses generally experience emotional as well as practical difficulties and are at high risk for depression and physical health problems. Often these problems were present even before the marital disruption.

About 30 percent of Canadian children under age 16 have experienced the effects of divorce (Wu & Schimmele, 2009). Post-divorce experiences can be difficult for children. Many children whose parents have recently divorced experience emotional, behavioural, and/or academic problems (Amato, 2006; Pruett & Barker, 2009). However, after a two- to three-year initial period of difficulty, most adapt to their new situations and do not experience lasting distress (Emery, 2004; Wu & Schimmele, 2009). Nevertheless, for some children the negative effects may be longer lasting, with approximately 20 to 25 percent remaining at risk for a variety of socioemotional and behaviour problems (Emery, 2004; Pruett & Barker, 2009).

A number of factors contribute to how well children cope with the effects of divorce. These include the age and sex of the child (Hetherington, 2006; Pruett & Barker, 2009), and whether conflict continues between the divorcing parents (Amato, 2006; Hetherington, 2006). In addition, in all but a very few cases, continued contact with their non-custodial parent (usually their father) has been found beneficial to children's adjustment (Amato & Dorius, 2010; Juby et al., 2007). Almost half of divorced Canadian dads maintain regular contact with their children, seeing them on a weekly or biweekly basis, while another 32 percent maintain some contact, albeit on a less regular basis (Juby et al., 2007). Moreover, recent Canadian data show that fathers who establish close connections with their children shortly after the divorce are likely to remain closely involved with their children, both emotionally and financially, as their children grow up (Juby et al., 2007).

It can be discouraging to think that 38 percent of Canadian marriages end in divorce. However, it is important to realize that this figure also reveals that more than 60 percent of Canadian marriages do not end in divorce! Realistic expectations are a key ingredient in successful relationships (Gottman & Levenson, 2002; Waller & McLanahan, 2005). Yet many people harbour unrealistic expectations about marriage and the roles of husband and wife, opening the door to marital problems (see *Applying Psychology: Are Your Relationship Expectations Realistic?*)

Work and Retirement: How They Affect Us

Throughout most of our adult lives, work defines us in fundamental ways. It affects our friendships and family, our health, where we live, and even our leisure activities, and it affects both males and females. Indeed, in Canada, there are currently almost as many women in the workforce as men (Marshall, 2006). Choosing an

Applying Psychology

Are Your Relationship Expectations Realistic?

To evaluate your own expectations, answer the following questions about traits and factors common to happy marriages and committed long-term relationships (Amato, 2007; Gottman & Levenson, 2002; Gottman & Notarius, 2000; Marks et al., 2008; Rauer, 2007):

1. Established "love maps"

Yes ❑ No ❑ *Do you believe that emotional closeness "naturally" develops when two people have the right chemistry?*

In successful relationships, both partners are willing to share their feelings and life goals. This sharing leads to detailed "love maps" of each other's inner emotional life and the creation of shared meaning in the relationship.

2. Shared power and mutual support

Yes ❑ No ❑ *Have you unconsciously accepted the imbalance of power promoted by many TV sitcoms, or are you willing to fully share power and to respect your partner's point of view, even if you disagree?*

The old ideas of husbands as "head of household" and wives as the "little women" who secretly wield the true power may help create unrealistic expectations for marriage.

3. Conflict management

Yes ❑ No ❑ *Do you expect to "change" your partner or to be able to resolve all your problems?*

Successful couples work hard (through negotiation and accommodation) to solve their solvable conflicts, to accept their unsolvable ones, and to know the difference.

4. Similarity

Yes ❑ No ❑ *Do you believe that "opposites attract?"*

Although we all know couples who are very different but are still happy, similarity (in values, beliefs, religion, and so on)

Mark Hatfield/iStockphoto

is one of the best predictors of long-lasting relationships (Chapter 15).

5. Supportive social environment

Yes ❑ No ❑ *Do you believe that "love conquers all"?*

Unfortunately, several environmental factors can overpower or slowly erode even the strongest love. These include age (younger couples have higher divorce rates), money and employment (divorce is higher among the poor and unemployed), parents' marriages (divorce is higher for children of divorced parents), length of courtship (longer is better), and premarital pregnancy (no pregnancy is better, and waiting a while after marriage is even better).

6. Positive emphasis

Yes ❑ No ❑ *Do you believe that an intimate relationship is a place where you can indulge your bad moods and openly criticize one another?*

Think again. Positive emotions, positive mood, and positive behaviour toward one's partner are vitally important to a lasting, happy relationship.

---

occupation is one of the most important decisions in a person's life, and the task is becoming ever more complex. The *National Occupational Classification*, a government publication, currently lists more than 30,000 Canadian job titles (Human Resources and Social Development Canada, 2007). According to psychologist John Holland's **personality-job fit theory**, a match (or "good fit") between our individual personalities and our career choices is a major factor in determining job success and satisfaction. Holland's *self-directed search* questionnaire scores each person

on six personality types and then matches their individual interests and abilities to the job demands of various occupations (Holland, 1985, 1994; see also Brkich et al., 2002; Kieffer et al., 2004; Spokane et al., 2000; Tett & Murphy, 2002) (**Table 10.3**).

Work and career are a big part of adult life and self-identity, but the large majority of men and women in Canada and the United States choose to retire sometime in their sixties (Whitbourne & Whitbourne, 2011). What helps people successfully navigate this important life change?

Are you in the right job?   Table 10.3

Personality characteristics	Holland personality type	Matching/congruent occupation
Shy, genuine, persistent, stable, conforming, practical	1. *Realistic:* Prefers physical activities that require skill, strength, and coordination	Mechanic, drill press operator, assembly-line worker, farmer
Analytical, original, curious, independent	2. *Investigative:* Prefers activities that involve thinking, organizing, and understanding	Biologist, economist, mathematician, news reporter
Sociable, friendly, cooperative, understanding	3. *Social:* Prefers activities that involve helping and developing others	Social worker, counsellor, teacher, clinical psychologist
Conforming, efficient, practical, unimaginative, inflexible	4. *Conventional:* Prefers rule-regulated, orderly, and unambiguous activities	Accountant, bank teller, file clerk, corporate manager
Imaginative, disorderly, idealistic, emotional, impractical	5. *Artistic:* Prefers ambiguous and unsystematic activities that allow creative expression	Painter, musician, writer, interior decorator
Self-confident, ambitious, energetic, domineering	6. *Enterprising:* Prefers verbal activities with opportunities to influence others and attain power	Lawyer, real estate agent, public relations specialist, small business manager

Charles Rex Arbogast/AP Photo/The Canadian Press

Jeff McIntosh/The Canadian Press

Kevin Winter/Getty Images for AMA

Source: Adapted and reproduced by special permission of the publisher, Psychological Assessment Resources, Inc., 16204 North Florida Avenue, Lutz, Florida 33549, from the Self-Directed Search by John L. Holland, Ph.D., copyright 1985, 1987, 1994. Further reproduction is prohibited without permission from PAR, Inc.

---

activity theory of aging Successful aging is fostered by a full and active commitment to life.

disengagement theory Successful aging is characterized by mutual withdrawal between the aging person and society.

socioemotional selectivity theory A natural decline in social contact as older adults become more selective with their time.

According to the **activity theory of aging**, successful aging appears to be most strongly related to good health, control over one's life, social support, and participation in community services and social activities (Warr et al., 2004; Yeh & Lo, 2004) (**Figure 10.12**).

The activity theory of aging has largely displaced the older notion that successful aging entails a natural and graceful withdrawal from life (see Depp et al., 2012; Whitebourne & Whitbourne, 2011, for a discussion). This **disengagement theory** has been seriously questioned and largely abandoned; we mention it because of its historical relevance and because of its connection to an influential modern theory, **socioemotional selectivity theory**.

Satisfaction after retirement • Figure 10.12

Active involvement is a key ingredient to a fulfilling old age.

Mark Bowden/iStockphoto

Developmental Challenges through Adulthood 285

Psychological Science

Myths of Development

A number of popular beliefs about age-related crises are not supported by research. The popular idea of a midlife crisis began largely as a result of Gail Sheehy's national best-seller *Passages* (1976). Sheehy drew on the theories of Daniel Levinson (1977, 1996) and psychiatrist Roger Gould (1975), as well as her own interviews. She popularized the idea that almost everyone experiences a "predictable crisis" at about age 35 for women and 40 for men. Middle age often is a time of re-examining values and lifetime goals. However, Sheehy's book led many people to automatically expect a midlife crisis with drastic changes in personality and behaviour. Research suggests that a severe reaction or crisis may actually be quite rare and not typical of what most people experience during middle age (Lachman, 2004; Lilienfeld et al., 2010).

Many people also believe that when the last child leaves home, most parents experience an *empty nest syndrome*: a painful separation and time of depression for the mother, the father, or both parents. Again, research suggests that the empty nest syndrome may be an exaggeration of the pain experienced by a few individuals and an effort to downplay positive reactions (Clay, 2003; Lilienfeld et al., 2010). Recent Canadian data indicate that only a small proportion of parents experience a negative reaction to their children's leaving home (Mitchell & Lovegreen, 2009). For example, one major benefit of the empty nest is an increase in marital satisfaction (Gorchoff et al., 2008). Data from Statistics Canada's *General Social Survey* and the *National Population Health Survey* indicate that many Canadian couples whose children have grown up and left home actually report higher levels of marital satisfaction and sexual activity than do those with adult children still living at home (Chalmers & Milan, 2005; Fraser et al., 2004).

Hammondovi/iStockphoto

Of course, moving out of their parents' home does not imply that grown children have no further contact with their parents; most continue to maintain relationships with their parents. As one mother said, "The empty nest is surrounded by telephone wires" (Troll et al., 1979). Moreover, as children move out and establish their own relationships, the role played by their parents often expands to include that of grandparent. The majority of older Canadians have grandchildren, and, for some the role of grandparent is central in their lives (Rosenthal & Gladstone, 2000).

Think Critically

1. Have you heard people saying that someone you know is "having a midlife crisis"? If so, do you think the crisis is genuine?
2. If your last child "left the nest," how do you think you would react?

This perspective helps explain the predictable decline in social contact that almost everyone experiences as they move into their older years (Carstensen et al., 2011; Charles & Carstensen, 2007; Stanley & Isaacowitz, 2012) (**Figure 10.13**). According to this theory, we don't naturally withdraw from society in our later years—we just

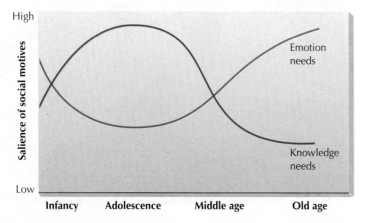

Socioemotional selectivity • Figure 10.13 ____

During infancy, emotional connection is essential to our survival. During childhood, adolescence, and early adulthood, information gathering is critical and the need for emotional connection declines relative to knowledge needs. During late adulthood, emotional satisfaction is again more important—we tend to invest our time in those who can be counted on in times of need.

Cultures differ in their views of older people
• Figure 10.14

Aboriginals generally revere and respect the elder members of their community. How might viewing old age as an honour and a blessing—rather than a dreaded process—affect the experience of aging?

John Eastcott and Yva Momatiuk/National Geographic Stock

become more selective with our time. We deliberately decrease our total number of social contacts in favour of familiar people who provide emotionally meaningful interactions.

As you've seen, there are losses and stresses associated with the aging process—although much less than most people think. Perhaps the greatest challenge for older adults, at least in Canada and the United States, is the ageism they may encounter. In societies that value older people as wise elders or keepers of valued traditions (**Figure 10.14**), the stress of aging is much less than in societies that view them as mentally slow and socially useless. In cultures such as those in Canada and the United States in which youth, speed, and progress are strongly emphasized, a loss or decline in any of these qualities may be deeply feared and denied (Powell, 1998).

Death and Dying:
Our Final Developmental Crisis

One unavoidable part of life is death. In this section, we will look at developmental changes in how people understand and prepare for their own deaths and for the deaths of loved others.

As adults, we understand death in terms of three basic concepts: (1) *permanence*—once a living thing dies, it cannot be brought back to life; (2) *universality*—all living things eventually die; and (3) *non-functionality*—all living functions, including thought, movement, and vital signs, end at death.

Research has shown that permanence, the notion that death cannot be reversed, is the first and most easily understood concept (**Figure 10.15**). Understanding of universality comes slightly later, and by the age of 7, most children have mastered non-functionality and have an adult-like understanding of death.

Although parents may fear that discussing death with children and adolescents will make them unduly anxious, those who are offered open, honest discussions of death have an easier time accepting it (Corr et al., 2009; Kastenbaum, 2012).

The same is true for adults—in fact, avoiding thoughts and discussion of death and associating aging with death can contribute to ageism (Atchley, 1997).

How do children understand death?
• Figure 10.15

Preschoolers seem to accept the fact that the dead person cannot get up again, perhaps because of their experiences with dead butterflies and beetles found while playing outside (Furman, 1990). Later, they begin to understand all that death entails and that they, too, will someday die.

Franky De Meyer/iStockphoto

Developmental Challenges through Adulthood **287**

Moreover, the better we understand death and the more wisely we approach it, the more fully we can live. Since the late 1990s, right-to-die and death-with-dignity advocates have brought death out into the open, and mental health professionals have suggested that understanding the psychological processes of death and dying may play a significant role in good adjustment. Cultures around the world interpret and respond to death in widely different ways: "Funerals are the occasion for avoiding people or holding parties, for fighting or having sexual orgies, for weeping or laughter, in a thousand combinations" (Metcalf & Huntington, 1991) (**Figure 10.16**).

Confronting our own death is the last major crisis we face in life. What is it like? Is there a "best" way to prepare to die? Is there such a thing as a "good" death? After spending hundreds of hours at the bedsides of the terminally ill, Elisabeth Kübler-Ross developed her stage theory of the psychological processes surrounding death (1983, 1997, 1999). She proposed that most people go through five sequential stages when facing death:

- *Denial* of the terminal condition ("This can't be true; it's a mistake!")
- *Anger* ("Why me? It isn't fair!")
- *Bargaining* ("God, if you let me live, I'll dedicate my life to you!")
- *Depression* ("I'm losing everyone and everything I hold dear.")
- *Acceptance* ("I know that death is inevitable and my time is near.")

Critics of the stage theory of dying stress that the five-stage sequence has not been scientifically validated and that each person's death is a unique experience (Kastenbaum, 2012; Konigsberg, 2011). Others worry that popularizing such a stage theory will cause more avoidance of or stereotyping of those who are dying (e.g., "He's just in the anger stage right now") (Friedman & James, 2008; Lilienfeld et al., 2010). In fact, some research has questioned the notion that all people facing death pass through these stages in the sequence specified by Kübler-Ross: some people skip stages, while others pass through the stages in a different sequence (Lilienfeld et al., 2010). Kübler-Ross (1983, 1997, 1999) agrees that not all people go through the same stages in the same way and regrets that anyone would use her theory as a model for a "good" death.

In spite of the potential abuses, Kübler-Ross' theory has provided valuable insights and spurred research into a long-neglected topic. **Thanatology**, the study of death and dying, has become a major topic in human development. Thanks in part to thanatology research, the dying are being helped to die with dignity by the **hospice** movement, which has created special facilities and trained staff and volunteers to provide loving support for the terminally ill and their families (McGrath, 2002; Parker-Oliver, 2002). Canadian health service providers have been among the leaders in the hospice movement in North America. Canadians have also been at the forefront in providing hospice care for homeless and marginalized individuals (McNeil & Guirguis-Younger, 2012).

Culture influences our response to death • Figure 10.16

In October 2006, a dairy truck driver took over a one-room Amish schoolhouse in Pennsylvania, killed and gravely injured several young girls, and then shot himself. Instead of responding in rage, his Amish neighbours attended his funeral. Amish leaders urged forgiveness for the killer and called for a fund to aid his wife and three children. Rather than creating an on-site memorial, the schoolhouse was torn down and replaced by a pasture. What do you think of this response? The fact that many people were offended, shocked, or simply surprised by the Amish reaction illustrates how strongly culture affects our emotion, beliefs, and values.

Mel Evans/AP Photo

Psychological Science

Should Physician-Assisted Suicide Be Decriminalized?

In 1992, Sue Rodriguez, a Victoria, British Columbia, woman with Lou Gehrig's disease, a degenerative and fatal disease of the central nervous system, petitioned Parliament and the Supreme Court of Canada to legalize physician-assisted suicide. Her petition was ultimately denied. Two years later, however, she took her own life with the help of an anonymous doctor (CBC News, 2009b). More recently, Bloc Québécois MP Francine Lalonde introduced a bill in Parliament to legalize euthanasia and physician-assisted suicide. The bill had a rough ride, however, and was defeated three times (Lewis, 2009). Physician-assisted suicide is a criminal offence in Canada, punishable by up to 14 years in prison, and many Canadians have serious questions about whether it should be legalized.

Is it morally wrong for doctors to assist patients who wish to end their lives in order to terminate their suffering? Although the answer depends on many factors, including personal ethics and religious beliefs, the majority of doctors are not in favour. In a survey of more than 2,000 Canadian physicians, 57 percent reported that they would not be willing to participate in an assisted suicide, even if it were legal (Kinsella & Verhoef, 1999). Patients, however, appear to hold a different view. The Canadian National Palliative Care Survey reported that of 379 terminally ill cancer patients, 63 percent believed that physician-assisted suicide should be legalized (Wilson et al., 2007). Interestingly, 40 percent of respondents in both surveys—whether physicians or patients—reported that they would consider making such a request for themselves. The debate over assisted suicide continues. In March 2012, the Quebec National Assembly's *Dying with Dignity* commission published a report that includes discussion of assisted suicide, and in June 2012, a British Columbia Supreme Court judge ruled that Canada's law against assisted suicide is unconstitutional. As argued in a recent editorial in the *Canadian Medical Association Journal* (Flegel & Fletcher, 2012), it appears time for a public discussion in Canada on the topic of assisted suicide.

Chuck Stoody/The Canadian Press

Sue Rodriguez, who petitioned the Supreme Court of Canada to legalize physician-assisted suicide, ultimately took her own life in 1994 with the help of an anonymous physician.

Think Critically
1. In cases of debilitating illness, where recovery is impossible and patients are suffering grievously, should doctors be allowed to end a patient's suffering?
2. Does it make a difference if the patient requests the doctor's help? What about someone who is too ill to communicate his or her desires?

CONCEPT CHECK STOP

1. **Why** do people develop unrealistic expectations about marriage?
2. **What** is the socioemotional selectivity theory?
3. **What** are the stages of Kübler-Ross' theory of the psychological processes surrounding death?

Summary

1 Social, Moral, and Personality Development 268

• Konrad Lorenz's studies of **imprinting** support the nativist view of **attachment**. Harlow and Zimmerman's research with monkeys raised by cloth or wire "mothers" supports the nurturist view and indicates that **contact comfort** is an important contributor to attachment. Most infants are securely attached to their caregivers, but some exhibit either an anxious/avoidant or an anxious/ambivalent attachment style. These styles may carry over into adult relationships.

Types of attachment • Figure 10.2

• Parenting styles may be divided on the basis of degree of *control/demandingness* and *warmth/responsiveness* into three categories: authoritative, authoritarian, and permissive (either permissive-indulgent or permissive-neglectful).

• The majority of Canadian children have siblings. Sibling relationships can be a source of support and of conflict. Children are attracted to peers who are similar to them in terms of age, sex, ethnicity and race, and interests and behaviours. As with siblings, friends are sources of support and can serve as models of behaviour.

• Kohlberg proposed three levels in the development of moral reasoning: the **preconventional level** (Stages 1 and 2), the **conventional level** (Stages 3 and 4), and the **postconventional level** (Stages 5 and 6). According to Kohlberg, Stage 4 is the highest level attained by most individuals.

• Erikson identified eight **psychosocial stages** of development, each marked by a crisis related to a specific developmental task. Although some critics argue that Erikson's theory oversimplifies development, many psychologists agree with Erikson's general idea that psychosocial crises do contribute to personality development.

2 How Sex, Gender, and Culture Affect Development 278

• In addition to biological **sex** differences, scientists have found numerous **gender** differences relevant to cognitive, social, and personality development (for example, in cognitive ability and aggressive behaviour) and have proposed both biological and environmental explanations for these differences. Most research emphasizes two major theories of **gender-role** development: social learning and cognitive developmental.

Developing gender schemas • Figure 10.11

• Our culture shapes how we define and understand ourselves. In **individualistic cultures**, the needs and goals of the individual are emphasized; in **collectivistic cultures**, the person is defined and understood primarily by looking at his or her place in the social unit.

3 Developmental Challenges through Adulthood 283

• Having unrealistic expectations about marriage can open the door to marital problems. Developing realistic expectations is critical to a happy marriage.

• Choosing an occupation is an important and complex decision. According to Holland's **personality-job fit theory**, a match between personality and career choice is a major factor in determining job success and satisfaction.

- The **activity theory of aging** proposes that successful aging depends on having control over one's life, having social support, and participating in community services and social activities. **Disengagement theory** is an older approach to aging that has been largely abandoned. According to the **socioemotional selectivity theory**, people don't naturally withdraw from society in late adulthood but deliberately decrease the total number of their social contacts in favour of familiar people who provide emotionally meaningful interactions.

- Adults understand death in terms of three basic concepts: permanence, universality, and non-functionality. Children most easily understand the concept of permanence; understanding of universality and non-functionality come later. For children, adolescents, and adults, understanding the psychological processes of death and dying are important to good adjustment. Kübler-Ross proposed that most people go through five sequential stages when facing death: denial, anger, bargaining, depression, and acceptance. But she has emphasized that her theory should not be interpreted as a model for a "good" death.

Satisfaction after retirement • Figure 10.12

Key Terms

- activity theory of aging p. 285
- attachment p. 268
- collectivistic cultures p. 281
- contact comfort p. 269
- conventional level p. 275
- disengagement theory p. 285
- gender p. 278
- gender roles p. 278

- gender schemas p. 281
- hospice p. 288
- identity crisis p. 276
- imprinting p. 268
- individualistic cultures p. 281
- personality-job fit theory p. 284
- postconventional level p. 275
- preconventional level p. 273

- psychosocial stages p. 276
- self p. 281
- sex p. 278
- socioemotional selectivity theory p. 285
- strange situation procedure p. 270
- thanatology p. 288

Critical and Creative Thinking Questions

1. Were Harlow and his colleagues acting ethically when they separated young rhesus monkeys from their mothers and raised them with either a wire or cloth "mother"? Why or why not?

2. What are some of the similarities between sibling relationships and peer relationships? What do you think are some likely differences? In what ways do siblings and peers contribute to children's development?

3. Think of some current world events. Can you find examples of individuals reasoning at Kohlberg's postconventional level of moral development? Do you think it is possible for world leaders to be guided by a universal ethics orientation (Stage 6) and at the same time be effective leaders of their country?

4. According to Erikson's psychosocial theory, what developmental crisis is characteristic of your stage of life? What must you resolve in order to successfully move on to the next stage? Are there any earlier crises that you feel you may not have completely resolved successfully?

5. Research points to male-female differences in verbal and spatial abilities. Do the abilities of your male and female friends agree with or contradict these findings? How could the environment in which a child is raised influence the development of these abilities?

6. The media recently reported that a pair of Toronto parents had decided not to reveal the sex of their newborn baby because of their desire to raise the baby as "gender-less." Do you think someone could be raised without a gender? Is the development of gender solely the result of how people treat a child?

7. According to Holland's personality-job fit theory, what occupations might be a good match for your personality?

8. Would you like to know ahead of time that you were dying? Or would you prefer to die suddenly with no warning? Briefly explain your choice.

9. Do you think all people would pass through Elizabeth Kübler-Ross' stages of dying, if given sufficient time? What could be some problems with assuming that all people should pass through this sequence of stages?

Self-Test

(Check your answers in Appendix A.)

1. What term is used by developmental psychologists for a strong affectional bond with special others that endures over time?

   a. bonding   c. attachment

   b. love   d. intimacy

2. In Ainsworth's studies on infant attachment, which group of infants sought their mothers' comfort yet also squirmed to get away when the mother returned to the room?

   a. anxious/ambivalent

   b. anxious/avoidant

   c. securely attached

   d. dependently attached

3. Which parenting style is characterized by the combination of low control and high warmth?

   a. authoritative

   b. authoritarian

   c. permissive-indulgent

   d. permissive-neglectful

4. Kohlberg believed his stages of moral development to be which of the following?

   a. universal and invariant

   b. culturally bound, but invariable within a culture

   c. universal, but variable within each culture

   d. culturally bound and variable

5. Which level of moral development involves accepting and complying with the rules and values of society?

   a. preconventional

   b. unconventional

   c. conventional

   d. postconventional

6. After listening to the dilemma of Heinz and the druggist, an individual responds that Heinz should steal the drug, because the value of human life is far more important than obeying the law. This answer is consistent with which of Kohlberg's levels of moral development?

   a. preconventional

   b. postconventional

   c. unconventional

   d. conventional

7. According to Erikson, humans progress through eight stages of psychosocial development. Provide the correct labels for the "successful" completion of the first four stages as shown below.

Stage 1 _____

Stage 2 _____

Stage 3 _____

Stage 4 _____

8. Provide the correct labels for the "successful" completion of the last four stages of Erikson's psychosocial development as shown below.

Stage 5 _____

Stage 6 _____

Stage 7 _____

Stage 8 _____

Applying Psychology

Overcoming Test Anxiety

If you do become overly aroused on exam day, you may want to take a class in study skills or test anxiety. You can also try these basic study tips:

Step 1: *Prepare in advance.* The single most important cure for test anxiety is advance preparation and *hard work*. If you are well prepared, you will feel calmer and more in control.

- Read your textbook by using the SQ4R (survey, question, read, recite, review, and write) method (see Chapter 1).

- Practise good time management and distribute your study time; don't cram the night before.

- Actively listen during lectures and take detailed summarizing notes.

- Review the strategies for memory improvement (Chapter 7).

Step 2: *Learn to cope with the anxiety.* Performance is best at a moderate level of arousal, so a few butterflies before and during exams are okay and to be expected. However, too much anxiety can interfere with concentration and ruin your performance. To achieve the right amount of arousal, try these methods:

- Replace anxiety with relaxed feelings. Practise deep breathing, which activates the parasympathetic nervous system (Chapter 2).

- Exercise regularly. This is a great stress reliever that also promotes deeper and more restful sleep.

Commercial Eye/Iconica/Getty Images

- Desensitize yourself to the test situation (Chapter 14): Start by creating a 10-step test-taking hierarchy beginning with the least anxiety-arousing image (perhaps the day your instructor first mentions an upcoming exam) and ending with actually taking the exam. Then picture yourself completing each stage, from first to last, while maintaining a calm, relaxed state. If you become anxious at any stage, stay there, repeating your relaxation technique until the anxiety diminishes.

- If your anxiety persists, talk to your doctor. There are a number of therapeutic interventions that have been shown to reduce anxiety.

Don Smetzer/PhotoEdit

Social and cognitive aspects of motivation • Figure 11.4

How might the attributions, goals, and expectations of these learners affect their motivation to master a new language? Would you answer the same way if it were traditional-aged college or university students in a math, geography, or physics course? What say the government *required* a person to take a particular course, how do you think this might influence their level of motivation?

Motivation and the Biopsychosocial Model

As in many areas of psychology, the best explanation is often the one that includes biological, social, and cognitive factors (the *biopsychosocial model*). As mentioned earlier, motivation is no exception. One researcher who recognized this three-way interaction was Abraham Maslow (1954, 1970, 1999). Maslow believed that we all have numerous needs that compete for fulfillment but that some needs are just more

Maslow's hierarchy of needs • Figure 11.5

As a humanistic psychologist, Maslow believed that we all have a compelling need to move up the hierarchy—to grow, belong, improve ourselves, and ultimately become self-actualized (Chapters 12 and 14).

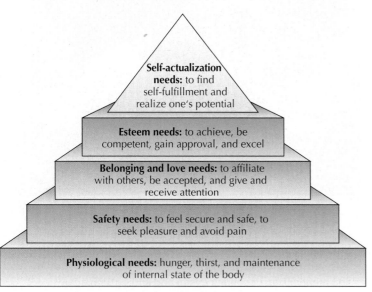

Bypassing basic needs • Figure 11.6

What higher-level needs do these women seem to be trying to fulfill? Does it appear that their lower-level needs have been met? Is it possible to only partially satisfy lower-level needs and still pursue higher-level needs? What about the simultaneous pursuit of both higher- and lower-level needs?

James A. Sugar/National Geographic Stock

---

hierarchy of needs Maslow's theory of motivation that some needs (such as physiological and safety needs) must be met before higher needs (such as belonging and self-actualization).

important than others. For example, your need for food and housing is generally more important than your need for good grades. Maslow's **hierarchy of needs** prioritizes our needs; survival needs are at the bottom (needs that must be met before others), and social and intellectual needs are at the top (**Figure 11.5**).

Maslow's hierarchy of needs seems intuitively correct—a starving person would be motivated to find food before seeking love and friendship. Once lower-level needs are satisfied, higher-order needs, such as self-esteem and self-fulfillment, become more important. This prioritizing, along with the concept of *self-actualization* (Chapter 12) are important contributions to the study of motivation (Frick, 2000; Harper et al., 2003). But critics argue that parts of Maslow's theory are poorly researched and biased toward Western individualism. They also note that people sometimes seek to satisfy higher-level needs even when their lower-level needs have not been met (Cullen

& Gotell, 2002; Hanley & Abell, 2002; Neher, 1991), effectively completely inverting the hierarchy triangle. For example, in some countries, people live in war zones with little food, poor shelter, and ongoing risk of injury and disease, yet these people still seek the higher needs of strong social ties and self-esteem. Before the arrival of Europeans, Indigenous peoples of the Pacific Northwest Coast would host elaborate potlatches and give away abundant survival items, such as food and blankets—often at great cost—in return for earned prestige ("Potlatch," 2011) (**Figure 11.6**).

CONCEPT CHECK

1. **Which** theory of motivation lends greatest support for the biopsychosocial model? Why?
2. **What** four factors are associated with sensation seeking?
3. **What** criticisms have been made of Maslow's hierarchy of needs theory?

Motivated Behaviours

LEARNING OBJECTIVES

1. **Describe** how internal and external factors regulate hunger and eating and how they influence eating disorders.
2. **Summarize** what happens to the human body during sexual arousal.
3. **Discuss** the evidence that suggests biology and genes are the dominant cause of sexual orientation.
4. **Explain** why some people are more highly achievement motivated than others.
5. **Explain** why providing extrinsic rewards can undermine intrinsic motivation.

Why do people put themselves in dangerous situations? Why do salmon swim upstream to spawn? Why do people surf the Internet when they should be working on an assignment? Behaviour results from many motives. For example, we discuss the need for sleep in Chapter 5, and we look at aggression, altruism, and interpersonal attraction in Chapter 15. Here, we will focus on two basic motivations that are essential for species survival: eating and sex. We then discuss a motivation that is distinctly human: the motivation to achieve.

The Motivation to Eat: More than Sustenance

What motivates hunger? Is it seeing someone else eating? Or is it your growling stomach? Or is it the sight of a juicy hamburger or the smell of a freshly baked cinnamon roll?

The stomach Early hunger researchers believed that it was the stomach that directly controlled hunger; when it was empty the contractions sent hunger signals to the brain. Today, we know that it's much more complicated than that; stomach contractions often accompany hunger, but they don't cause it, and sensory input from the stomach is not essential for feeling hungry. Dieters learn this the hard way when they realize they cannot trick their stomachs into feeling full by drinking copious amounts of water. In fact, humans and non-human animals without stomachs continue to experience feelings of hunger (Bergh et al., 2003; Wangensteen & Carlson, 1931).

A connection *does* exist, however, between the stomach and feeling hungry. Receptors in the stomach and intestines detect levels of nutrients, and specialized pressure receptors in the stomach walls signal feelings of emptiness or satiety (fullness or satiation). The stomach and other parts of the gastrointestinal tract also release chemical signals that play a role in hunger (Donini, Savina, & Cannella, 2003; Näslund & Hellstrom, 2007; Nogueiras & Tschöp, 2005).

Biochemistry Like the stomach, the brain and other parts of the body produce and are affected by numerous neurotransmitters, hormones (e.g., insulin), enzymes, and other chemicals (e.g., glucose) that affect hunger and satiety (e.g., Arumugam et al., 2008; Cummings, 2006; Wardlaw & Hampl, 2007). It is not the case that any one chemical completely controls our hunger and eating. Research in this area is complex because of the large number of known (and unknown) bodily chemicals that influence eating, and the interactions among them. One substance worth noting, however, is leptin, which seems to be important in long-term hunger physiology. This protein is released by fat cells as they grow larger. When receptors in the brain detect high leptin levels, the brain sends a signal that ultimately inhibits eating (Farooqi & O'Rahilly, 2009). Obese animals (including humans) may be insensitive to the effects of leptin, resulting in a delay in the signal to stop eating and concomitant weight gain (Altintas et al., 2012).

The brain In addition to its chemical signals, particular brain structures also influence hunger and eating. Primary among them is the hypothalamus, which regulates many motivated behaviours, including eating and drinking.

Early research suggested that one area of the hypothalamus, the lateral hypothalamus (LH), stimulates eating, while another area, the ventromedial hypothalamus (VMH), creates feelings of satiation, signalling the animal to stop eating. Humans who develop tumours in the VMH dramatically increase their food intake and become markedly heavier (Xu et al., 2010). When the VMH area was lesioned (destroyed) in rats, researchers found that the rats overate to the point of extreme obesity

How the hypothalamus affects eating • Figure 11.7 _____

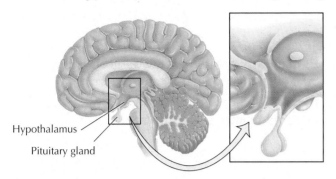

Olivier Voisin/Science Source/Photo Researchers

a. This diagram shows a section of a rat's brain, locating the ventromedial hypothalamus (VMH) and the lateral hypothalamus (LH). Notice that the rather complicated names are really just "neural landmarks." *Lateral means* "away from midline." *Ventromedial* means "toward the underside of the brain (ventro) and toward the midline (medial)."

Hypothalamus

Pituitary gland

b. After the ventromedial area of the hypothalamus of the rat on top was destroyed, its body weight increased. A rat of normal weight is shown below it for comparison.

(**Figure 11.7**). In contrast, when the LH area was destroyed, a starving animal would refuse to eat.

Subsequent research, however, showed that the LH and VMH areas are not simply on-off switches, and they influence eating in more complicated way, such as through interactions with insulin (Berthoud & Münzberg, 2011; Shiraishi et al., 2011). For example, the VMH seems to be important for modulating blood insulin levels (insulin helps the body utilize glucose). Damage to the VMH can increase insulin levels (Duparc et al., 2011), which ultimately causes fat cells to store more glucose and get larger. Because these animals store energy from glucose as fat faster than animals without VMH lesions, the signal of satiety (elevated blood glucose levels) doesn't occur, and the animal keeps eating (Benarroch, 2010; Chao et al., 2012).

Today, researchers know that while the hypothalamus plays an important role in hunger and eating, it is not the brain's "eating centre" as was once thought. In fact, eating, like virtually all complex behaviours, is influenced by environmental factors, numerous brain regions, and multiple neural pathways that run throughout the brain and body (Berthoud, 2002; Berthoud & Morrison, 2008; Smith et al., 2011).

Psychosocial factors The internal biological motivations for hunger we've discussed this far are powerful. But psychosocial factors—for example, spotting a dessert tray in a restaurant, or seeing a pizza commercial or even simply noticing that it's lunchtime—can be equally important triggers for hunger and eating.

How much we eat is determined by many psychosocial factors. When food is presented as a buffet, we tend to

eat more (Brondel et al., 2009; Wansink & Payne, 2008). We also eat more when meals are eaten with familiar and friendly people, but we eat less with unfamiliar diners (Wansink, 2004). Women tend to choose lower-calorie meals in the presence of men. Interestingly, caloric intake by men is not affected by the presence of either men or women (Young et al., 2009). We also become conditioned to eat certain foods at certain locations, such as popcorn at movies, and hotdogs and beer at hockey games (Delormier et al., 2009; Sheth et al., 1991).

Another important psychosocial influence on when, what, where, and why we eat is cultural conditioning. North Americans, for example, have their main meal of the day at dinnertime, whereas for people in Spain and South America, lunch is usually the main meal (Dummies.com, 2012; Leffel, 2004). Exactly what we eat is also influenced by culture; have you ever eaten ostrich, dog, horsemeat, or seal heart? If you are a typical urban Canadian, these might sound distasteful to you, yet these are common foods in many cultures. Most Hindus would feel a similar distaste at the thought of eating meat from a cow.

Eating disorders As you can see, hunger and eating are motivated by a variety of biological, psychological, and social factors, and these same biopsychosocial forces also play a role in three serious eating disorders: obesity, anorexia nervosa, and bulimia nervosa.

Obesity has reached epidemic proportions in Canada and many developed nations. Approximately one quarter of Canadians and more than one third of Americans meet the current criteria for clinical obesity (Shields et al., 2011).

A fattening environment • Figure 11.8

For many North Americans, controlling weight is a particularly difficult task. We typically don't get enough exercise, and we've become accustomed to large portions ("supersized" fries, "Big Gulp" drinks) and their appeal to good value. We are also used to high-fat meals (poutine, Wendy's "Baconator," and the KFC "Double Down" sandwich) and high-fat condiments (gravy, hollandaise, and mayonnaise) (Carels et al., 2008; Herman & Polivy, 2008; Fisher & Kral, 2008). We've learned that we should eat three meals a day (whether we're hungry or not); that "tasty" food requires lots of salt, sugar, and fat; and that food is an essential part of *all* social gatherings. Can you see how our everyday situations, such as in the workplace scene shown here or a fast-food advertisement, might foster overeating and obesity?

Christian Thomas/Getty Images

Lauri Patterson/iStockphoto

These rates are even higher among Aboriginal people (Health Canada, 2012). Each year, millions of dollars are spent treating serious and life-threatening medical problems related to obesity, such as diabetes, heart disease, and hypertension (Anis et al., 2010; Withrow & Alter, 2011), and consumers spend millions more on largely ineffective weight-loss products and services (National Eating Disorders Association, 2005; Smolak, 1996; Worldometers, n.d.).

Given our culture's preference for thinness (Cochran, 2009; Bonafini & Pozzilli, 2011), why are so many Canadians and Americans overweight? The simple answer is we take in more food calories than we expend through exercise and daily activity. However, we all know some people who seem to be able to eat anything they want and still not gain weight. This may be a result of their ability to burn calories more effectively, a higher metabolic rate, or other factors, such as moving more often and faster than most people.

Adoption and twin studies indicate that genes also play a significant role. Heritability estimates for obesity range between 30 and 75 percent (Fernández et al., 2008; Haworth et al., 2008; Lee et al., 2008; Lee et al., 2010; Schmidt, 2004). Identifying the genes that contribute to obesity is the subject of ongoing research. To date, scientists have isolated about 600 genes that contribute in some way to obesity in humans (Johansson et al., 2012; Nirmala et al., 2008; Poirier et al., 2006; Rankinen et al., 2006). For many, though, obesity is heavily influenced by social and environmental factors (**Figure 11.8**). It's difficult to regulate the amount of food consumed when portion size and fat content are more extreme than levels recommended for maintaining a healthy weight.

Evolutionary psychologists have suggested overeating occurs as a natural consequence of our ancestral past, when food availability was patchy and unpredictable. Back then, overeating when food was abundant (such as after an animal kill) would lead to fat storage for times when resources were scarce. There would be a survival advantage for such a behaviour. Today, in many cultures where food is abundant all the time, the built-in survival mechanism to feast during times of plenty has resulted in chronic overeating (de Graaf, 2006; de Ridder & van den Bos, 2006).

As obesity has reached epidemic proportions, a similar rise has occurred in the rates of two other eating disorders: **anorexia nervosa** and **bulimia nervosa** (Swanson et al., 2011). Both disorders are serious and chronic conditions

anorexia nervosa
An eating disorder characterized by a pathological drive to be thin, excessive food restriction, extreme weight loss, and a distorted body image.

bulimia nervosa
An eating disorder characterized by the consumption of large quantities of food (bingeing) followed by vomiting, extreme exercise, or laxative use (purging) to prevent weight gain.

Distorted body image • Figure 11.9

In anorexia nervosa, body image is severely distorted such that patients do not see themselves to be as thin as they really are. Many people with anorexia nervosa not only refuse to eat but also take up extreme exercise regimens—hours of cycling or running or constant walking to stay thin. One of the more famous victims of anorexia nervosa was French actress and model Isabelle Caro, who died in 2010. Caro made headlines in 2007 when she participated in an Italian advertising campaign to raise awareness about anorexia nervosa. At the time of the campaign, she said she weighed about 27 kg (59 lb.). She was 28 years old when she died and had battled the disease for 15 years ("Isabelle Caro dies," 2010).

Ernesto Ruscio/Getty Images

that generally require some form of psychological and medical intervention.

A significant percentage of women, across all socioeconomic strata, in Western industrialized countries show some signs of an eating disorder, and 1.7 percent meet the clinical criteria for anorexia nervosa or bulimia nervosa (Statistics Canada, 2004). Men also develop eating disorders, and while the incidence is lower (Raevuori et al., 2008; Jacobi et al., 2004), eating disorder rates in men are increasing (Cain et al., 2011; Lavender et al., 2010; Striegel-Moore et al., 2009). Sadly, many treatment programs are not set up to accommodate men, and resources for them are often lacking (Gadalla, 2009).

Anorexia nervosa is characterized by an overwhelming fear of gaining weight, a distorted body image, a need for control, and the use of dangerous weight-loss strategies. The resulting extreme malnutrition often leads to emaciation, osteoporosis, bone fractures, interruption of menstruation, and the loss of neural tissue. A significant percentage of individuals with anorexia nervosa ultimately die from the disorder (Kaye, 2008; Wentz et al., 2007; Werth et al., 2003) (**Figure 11.9**).

Treatment for anorexia depends on its severity. If extreme weight loss has occurred, the patient might need to be hospitalized. Counselling has been shown to be useful, and therapy can take many forms: one-on-one with a psychologist, family therapy, or as part of a residential care program (Fairburn et al., 2009; Peterson et al., 2009; Schmidt et al., 2007). The overall goal of therapy is to help the patient develop a healthier body image, and healthy emotional expression, restore a healthy weight,

and develop good eating habits (Watson et al., 2011; Wilfley et al., 2011).

Bulimia nervosa is an eating disorder characterized by alternating bouts of gorging food followed by vomiting or laxative use to rid the body of the calories. Intensive exercise is also common. Bulimia can co-occur with anorexia, but it can also present independently. Unlike anorexia, bulimia is exemplified by weight fluctuations within or above the normal range, which can make the illness easier to hide. The vomiting associated with bulimia nervosa causes dental damage, severe damage to the throat and stomach, heart problems, metabolic deficiencies, and serious digestive disorders. Research suggests bulimia is more common than anorexia, with approximately 1.5 percent women and 0.5 percent men affected (Hudson et al., 2007). Treatment for bulimia nervosa is similar to treatments for patients with anorexia: improve self-image and foster healthy eating behaviours (Zweig & Leahy, 2012).

An eating disorder related to bulimia is binge eating disorder (BED). It is characterized by bouts of binging but without the subsequent purging or fasting behaviour (Chambers, 2009). Unlike people with bulimia, those with BED tend to be obese (Blaine, 2009). Some excellent websites, such as the National Eating Disorder Information Centre (www.nedec.ca), can offer assistance to people struggling with an eating disorder.

There are many suspected causes of anorexia nervosa and bulimia nervosa but no known causes. Some theories focus on physical causes, such as hypothalamic disorders, low levels of various neurotransmitters, and genetic or hormonal disorders. Other theories emphasize psychosocial

The pressure to be thin has many influences • Figure 11.10

Steve Granitz/WireImage/Getty Images

a. Can you explain why popular movie and television stars' extreme thinness may contribute to eating disorders in the general public? What about advertisers? Do they share some responsibility in creating eating disorders by often portraying women as flawless?

b. The drive to be thin is instilled into young girls from an early age. If a real woman standing 173 cm (5′ 7″) tall had the measurements of Barbie, she would have an 81 cm (32 in.) bust, a 40.5 cm (16 in.) waist, and 73.75 cm (29 in.) hips (Norton et al., 1996).

© Christian Charisius/Reuters/Corbis

factors, such as a need for perfection or control, being teased about body weight, destructive thought patterns, underling anxiety, depression, dysfunctional families, distorted body image, and sexual abuse (e.g., Behar, 2007; Fairburn et al., 2008; Kaye, 2008; Sachdev et al., 2008).

Sociocultural perceptions and stereotypes about weight and eating also play important roles in eating disorders (Eddy et al., 2007; Fairburn et al., 2008; Herman & Polivy, 2008). For example, in Western culture the ongoing obsession with images of thinness and youth has been blamed for the increase in eating disorders like anorexia nervosa (Bell & Dittmar, 2011; National Eating Disorders Association, 2004). Moreover, the use of computer programs, such as Photoshop, to modify the image of a face or a body to be "flawless" creates magazine covers and advertisements portraying a kind of perfection in beauty ideals. These images are often so heavily modified they bear no resemblance to real bodies and faces and therefore represent impossible beauty role models (Glamour, 2012; Goldberg, 2009). Failing to appreciate the artificiality of these perfect images can affect self-esteem as some women (and men)

strive unsuccessfully to attain the unattainable (Dittmar, 2009; Grabe et al., 2008; Smeesters et al., 2010).

Although social pressures for thinness certainly contribute to eating disorders (**Figure 11.10**), anorexia nervosa has also been found in non-industrialized areas, like the Caribbean island of Curacao (Hoek et al., 2005). On that island, being overweight is socially acceptable, and the average woman is considerably heavier than the average woman in North America. However, some women there still have anorexia nervosa. This research suggests that both sociocultural and biological factors help contribute to the development of eating disorders.

The Motivation to Have Sex: Both Recreation and Procreation

Obviously, there is a strong motivation to have sex: it's essential for the survival of ours and many other species, and, for most, it's also extremely pleasurable. While sex evolved for reproductive purposes, it serves multiple other functions, such as intimacy, pleasure, communication, and passion. Most of the sex we have in our lives is for recreational and enjoyment purposes and not simply to procreate. Said more simply, even if a person has just one sex partner in his or her entire life, most of the sex they will have will be for pleasure and not simply to make babies. Acknowledging this role for human sexual behaviour is an important component of the scientific discipline of sexuality (also known as sexology) (Benagiano & Mori, 2009).

For an interesting discussion on this topic, scan to download the author's podcast.

Alfred Kinsey (1894–1956) conducted some of the earliest descriptive studies investigating human sexuality. Using in-depth face-to-face interviews, he quizzed people about their sex lives and past sexual experiences (Bullough, 1998; Weber, 2010). His research, while highly controversial at the time, profoundly influenced North American social values. After Kinsey came William Masters and Virginia Johnson (1966). This married team were the first to conduct laboratory studies on what happens to the human body during sexual activity. Somewhat daring, even by today's standards, they achieved this by watching people having sex. By attaching recording devices to the genitalia of male and female volunteers and filming their physical responses

while engaging in partnered sex or masturbating, Masters and Johnson could monitor people as they moved from non-aroused to orgasm and back to non-aroused. They labelled the bodily changes during this series of events the **human sexual response cycle**.

The cycle has four stages (**Figure 11.11**):

Excitement This stage can last from minutes to hours and involves the beginning of arousal. Heart rate and respiration rate both increase. Increased blood flow to the genitals causes swelling, penile and clitoral erection, and vaginal lubrication in women. In both men and women, the nipples may become erect.

Plateau Arousal continues. In men, the penis becomes more engorged and erect and the testicles swell and pull upward closer to the body. In women, the clitoris retracts under the clitoral hood, the vaginal opening tightens, and the uterus rises slightly. The uterine movement causes the upper two-thirds of the vagina to balloon. With the heightened arousal, both sexes may feel that orgasm is imminent.

> **human sexual response cycle**
> Masters and Johnson's influential description of the four physiological stages of sexual arousal: excitement, plateau, orgasm, and resolution.

Masters and Johnson's human sexual response cycle • Figure 11.11

The cycle has four stages that often differ between men and women. *Note that sexual expression is extremely diverse and this general description does not account for all the individual variation seen in our species.*

a. After orgasm men generally enter a refractory period. This can last from a few seconds to an entire day, depending on the age of the man. As men age, their refractory periods increase.

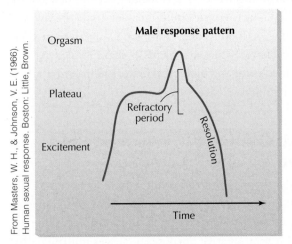

b. Sexual response in women is a little more variable and tends to follow one or more of three basic patterns.

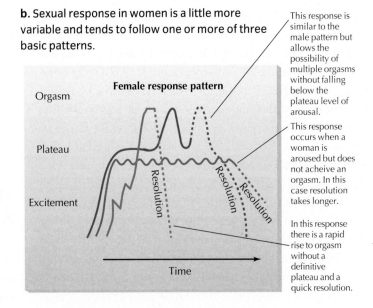

This response is similar to the male pattern but allows the possibility of multiple orgasms without falling below the plateau level of arousal.

This response occurs when a woman is aroused but does not acheive an orgasm. In this case resolution takes longer.

In this response there is a rapid rise to orgasm without a definitive plateau and a quick resolution.

Orgasm This stage involves an intense and pleasurable release of sexual tension. It is usually experienced as a brief sequence of muscle contractions in the genital area, but the sensation may radiate out to other parts of the body. In men, orgasm is associated with ejaculation—the discharge of semen from the penis. Some women also report the release of fluid at orgasm (Korda, Goldstein, & Sommer, 2010). The nature and origin of this fluid is the topic of ongoing research (Colson, 2010).

Resolution During this stage, physiological responses gradually return to baseline. Men usually enter a *refractory period* after an orgasm, during which time further excitement to orgasm is unlikely. Some women (and a few men), however, are capable of multiple orgasms in fairly rapid succession. Because of this, it is in this stage of the human sexual response that men and women are most different from each other.

When it comes to sexual behaviour, research has shown that while men and women are very similar, there are some notable differences. Compared with women, men begin masturbating earlier in life, and they have higher overall lifetime masturbation rates (Robbins, 2011). They are usually younger when they start having sex (Alan Guttmacher Institute, 2002) and orgasm more consistently during partnered sex (Conley et al., 2011; Wallen & Lloyd, 2011). They are also more likely to initiate sex, or accept offers for casual sex (Clark & Hatfield, 1989). Evolutionary psychologists and others attribute this sex difference in part to an evolved adaptation (Chapter 2) in which males were more likely to produce offspring by being sexually "ever ready." Their abundant production of copious quantities of sperm throughout adulthood is consistent with this explanation. Ancestral women, conversely, had to be more careful. With just one ovum (egg) per month in which to pass on her genes, they evolved to be choosier about sex partners (Ellis, 1992). This is not to say our early ancestors actually "thought" this through. They just lived their life. What evolved was a preference, or urge, to copulate more or less (Small, 1992).

Sexual orientation Of course, an essential part of any person's sexuality is the direction of their sexual attraction. For hundreds of years scientists and scholars have wondered what causes some people to be gay.

What is missing from this age-old question is the assumption that heterosexuality needs no explanation. Therefore, a better question to ask is, What causes **sexual orientation**? To date, the direct or indirect causes are not well understood. However, most current studies suggest that genetics and biology play the dominant role (Bailey, Dunne, & Martin, 2000; Byne, 2007; Ellis et al., 2008; Gooren, 2006; Zucker, 2008).

> **sexual orientation**
> The direction of a person's sexual attraction toward persons of the same sex (homosexual, gay, or lesbian) the other sex, (heterosexual), or both sexes (bisexual).

Studies with identical (monozygotic) and fraternal (dizygotic) twins and adopted siblings found that if one identical twin was gay, 48 to 65 percent of the time so was the second twin (Hyde, 2005; Kirk et al., 2000). If the cause were totally genetic, the percentage would be 100, so clearly other factors are at play. The rate was 26 to 30 percent for fraternal twins and 6 to 11 percent for brothers and sisters who were adopted. Estimates of exclusive homosexuality in the general population are much lower than this, at around 2 to 3 percent (Savin-Williams, 2009).

Research with rats and sheep and other animal species suggests that prenatal sex hormone levels (primarily the androgens, such as testosterone) affect fetal brain development and sexual orientation (Bagermihl, 1999; Roselli & Stormshak, 2010). For example, the preference of rats for male or female sex partners can be altered by modifying their androgen levels during different stages of development (Bakker et al., 1993; Dominguez-Salazar et al., 2002; Hosokawa & Chiba, 2010). It is not ethically possible to do comparable experiments in humans. However, sometimes babies are born with hormonal disorders that mimic this type of experiment for us. In cases like this, women who were born with one of these disorders where she was exposed to high levels of androgens *in utero* are more likely to experience lesbian attractions (Bao & Swaab, 2011; Berenbaum & Beltz, 2011). The exact mechanism by which sex hormones (and other factors) have their effect on our sexual orientation is still a long way from being understood, though it is an active area of research.

Gay families On July 20, 2005, Canada became the fourth country to legalize same-sex marriage with the enactment of the *Civil Marriage Act*. This act redefined marriage from "the lawful union of a man and woman to the exclusion of all others" to "the lawful union of two persons to the exclusion of all others." A number of polls and surveys have consistently shown that the majority of Canadians support the right of gay men and lesbians to marry (Angus Reid Public Opinion, 2009; Matthews, 2005).

According to the 2011 census, Canada had 64,575 same-sex couple families, of which 21,015 (32.5 percent) were married. Between 2006 and 2011, the number of same-sex married couples has nearly tripled, and the number of same-sex common-law couples has risen by 15 percent. Same-sex couples in Canada were a little more likely to be male; this was the case for both married and common-law couples. About 9 percent of people in same-sex cohabiting relationships had children (defined as 24 years and under) living in the home (**Figure 11.12**). This was far more common for women (16.5 percent) than for men (3.4 percent) (Statistics Canada, 2012d). Some of these children are from prior heterosexual relationships, and some are either adopted or conceived by using assisted reproductive technologies. Because gay sex is not procreative sex, the children born in same-sex relationships are not accidentally conceived and are wanted and planned for.

Psychologists and others have been interested in investigating how children raised in same-sex families compare with children raised in opposite-sex families. The results of more than two dozen studies addressing this topic are clear. Children of same-sex families do not differ from those of opposite-sex families on a variety of dimensions, including general well-being, adjustment, self-esteem, gender roles, sexual identity, sexual orientation, psychiatric evaluations, behaviour problems, self-concept, moral judgement, school adjustment, and social relationships; see Patterson (2009) for a review. Research has shown the most crucial ingredient in raising well-adjusted children appears to be the presence of at least one supportive and accepting caregiver (Deci & Ryan, 2008; Farr et al., 2010; Strickland, 1995).

Achievement: The Need for Success

Do you wonder what motivates Olympic athletes to work so hard just for one shot at a gold medal? Or what about someone like Thomas Edison, who patented more

Dispelling myths with empirical research • Figure 11.12

Research has investigated and dispelled some long-held myths about homosexuality (Bergstrom-Lynch, 2008; Boysen & Vogel, 2007; LeVay, 2003). Here are a few of the findings: Being raised by gay or lesbian (or cross-dressing) parents does not make a person gay. Nor is it true that gay men and lesbians were seduced as children by adults of their own sex. Sons do not become gay because of domineering mothers or weak fathers, and daughters do not become lesbians because their fathers were their primary role models. Finally, having unfruitful or unhappy heterosexual experiences does not "make" a person gay or lesbian.

Sunday's Child Photography

than 1,000 inventions? What drives some people to high achievement?

The key to understanding what motivates high-achieving individuals lies in what psychologist Henry Murray (1938) identified as a high need for achievement (nAch), or **achievement motivation**.

Several traits distinguish people who have high achievement motivation (McClelland, 1958, 1987, 1993; Quintanilla, 2007; Senko et al., 2008):

> **achievement motivation** A desire to excel, especially when in competition with others.

• *Preference for moderately difficult tasks.* People high in nAch avoid tasks that are too easy because they offer little challenge or satisfaction. They also avoid extremely difficult tasks because the probability of success is too low.

- *Competitiveness.* High-achievement-oriented people are more attracted to careers and tasks that involve competition and an opportunity to excel.
- *Preference for clear goals with competent feedback.* High-achievement-oriented people tend to prefer tasks with a clear outcome and situations in which they can receive feedback on their performance. They also prefer criticism from a harsh but competent evaluator to that which comes from one who is friendlier but less competent.
- *Responsibility.* People with high nAch prefer being personally responsible for a project so that they can feel satisfied when the task is well done.
- *Persistence.* High-achievement-oriented people are more likely to persist at a task when it becomes difficult (Sideridis & Kaplan, 2011). In one older study, 47 percent of high nAch individuals persisted on an "unsolvable task" until time was called, compared with only 2 percent of people with low nAch (French & Thomas 1958).
- *More accomplished.* People who have high nAch scores do better than others on exams, earn better grades in school, and excel in their chosen professions.

Achievement orientation appears to be largely learned in early childhood, primarily through interactions with parents, teachers, and the culture in which a person is raised (**Figure 11.13**).

Intrinsic versus Extrinsic Motivation: Which Is Better?

Should parents give their children money for getting good grades? Do pay raises improve work performance? Some psychologists and others are concerned about the

extrinsic motivation Motivation based on obvious external rewards or threats of punishment.

intrinsic motivation Motivation resulting from personal enjoyment of a task or activity.

practice of giving external, or extrinsic, rewards to motivate and increase desirable behaviour (e.g., Deci & Moller, 2005; Markle, 2007; Prabhu et al., 2008; Reeve, 2005). They're concerned that providing such **extrinsic motivation** will significantly influence the individual's personal, **intrinsic motivation**. Participation in sports and hobbies, like swimming or playing Halo or

Future high achiever? • Figure 11.13

Highly motivated children tend to have parents who encourage independence and frequently reward successes (e.g. Katz et al., 2011; Maehr & Urdan, 2000). Cultural values also affect achievement needs (Lubinski & Benbow, 2000). Events and themes in children's literature, for example, often contain subtle messages about what the culture values. In North American and Western European cultures, many children's stories are about persistence and the value of hard work.

Courtesy of Claire Vanston

Mass Effect, is usually intrinsically motivated—we like to do it. Going to work is primarily extrinsically motivated—we do it for the paycheque. As you might expect intrinsic/extrinsic motivation is closely related to the *incentive theory of motivation* we discussed earlier in the chapter, in which people are driven to attain some goal or reward.

Some research has shown that people who are given extrinsic rewards (money, praise, or other incentives) for an intrinsically satisfying activity, such as watching TV, playing cards, or engaging in sex, often lose enjoyment and interest and may decrease the time spent on the activity (Hennessey & Amabile, 1998; Kohn, 2000; Moneta & Siu, 2002). One of the earliest experiments to demonstrate this effect was conducted with preschool children who liked to draw (Lepper, Greene, & Nisbett, 1973). Researchers found that children who were given paper and markers and promised a reward for their drawings were subsequently less interested in drawing than children who

Extrinsic versus intrinsic rewards • Figure 11.14

Not all extrinsic motivation is bad, however (Banko, 2008; Konheim-Kalkstein & van den Broek, 2008; Moneta & Siu, 2002). Extrinsic rewards are motivating if they are used to inform a person of superior performance or as a special "no strings attached" treat (Deci, 1995). In fact, rewards may intensify the desire to do well again. Thus, getting a raise or an Olympic gold medal can inform us and provide valuable feedback about great performance, which may increase enjoyment. But if rewards are used to control behaviour—for example, when parents give children money or privileges as an incentive for good grades—they reduce intrinsic motivation (Eisenberger & Armeli, 1997; Eisenberger & Rhoades, 2002; Houlfort, 2006).

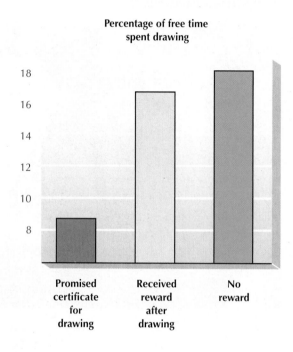

Percentage of free time spent drawing

- Promised certificate for drawing
- Received reward after drawing
- No reward

Courtesy of Claire Vanston

were not given a reward or who were given an unexpected reward when they were done (**Figure 11.14**). Since this early research was conducted, somewhat of a scientific debate has arisen regarding the relationship between extrinsic rewards and levels of intrinsic satisfaction. Some research findings are in agreement: extrinsic rewards do decrease intrinsic motivation (Deci et al., 1999; Warneken & Tomasell, 2008); while others report conflicting findings (Bright & Penrod, 2009; Fang & Gerhart, 2012; Hagger & Chatzisarantis, 2011). Interestingly, one recent brain-imaging study found evidence supporting the original 1973 research by Lepper and associates; when the task involves extrinsic rewards (in this case, money), brain regions involved in subjective task value were less active (Murayama et al., 2010).

CONCEPT CHECK

1. **What** are the biological, psychological, and social factors that can motivate hunger and eating?

2. **What** are the four stages of the human sexual response?

3. **How** are men and woman different in their sexual behaviour?

4. **What** traits characterize people with high achievement motivation?

5. **What** impact can using extrinsic motivation to reward behaviour have?

6. **How** do you think employees could be motivated so they don't think of work as "just a job"?

7. **What** type of motivation spurs the Tough Mudders, discussed in the opening vignette?

Components and Theories of Emotion

LEARNING OBJECTIVES

1. **Describe** the physiological, cognitive, and behavioural components of emotion.

2. **Outline** the four major theories of emotion.

3. **Explain** the cultural similarities and differences in emotion.

4. **Review** the problems with relying on polygraph testing as a "lie detector."

Three Components of Emotion: Much More than Just Feelings

 motions play an essential role in our lives. They colour our memories, dreams, and perceptions. When disordered, they increase psychological problems and influence our key relationships. But what really are emotions, and how are they different from our subjective feelings? To answer this question, psychologists define and study **emotion** in three basic components: physiological, cognitive, and behavioural.

> **emotion** A state of physiological arousal and tendency toward action involving changes in behaviour, cognitions, facial expressions, and subjective feelings.

The physiological (arousal) component Internal physical changes occur in our bodies whenever we experience an emotion. Imagine walking alone on a dark street when someone appears from behind a parked vehicle and starts running toward you. How would you respond? Like most people, you would probably interpret the situation as threatening and would either run or prepare to confront the stranger. Your predominant emotion, fear, would involve several physiological reactions: increased breathing, heart rate, and blood pressure; perspiration; and goose bumps (also known as piloerection).

Our emotional and related physiological reactions result from important interactions between several areas of the brain, most particularly the *cerebral cortex* and the *limbic system* (Langenecker et al., 2005; LeDoux, 2002; Panksepp, 2005). As we discussed in Chapter 2, the cerebral cortex serves as the body's ultimate control and information-processing centre and includes the ability to recognize and regulate emotions. Recall how Phineas Gage (Chapter 1) could no longer regulate his emotions after his encounter with the iron rod? The tool severely damaged his frontal lobes.

The limbic system is also essential to our emotions. Electrical stimulation of specific parts of this brain region can produce an automatic rage that turns a docile cat into a hissing, slashing animal. Stimulating adjacent areas can cause the same animal to purr and lick your fingers (Natarajan & Caramaschi, 2010; Siegel, 2004). These dramatic changes in behaviour occur in the absence of provocation and disappear the moment the stimulus is removed.

Several studies have shown that one area of the limbic system, the *amygdala*, plays a key role in emotion—especially fear. This structure sends signals to other areas of the brain, causing increased heart rate and all the other physiological reactions related to fear. Individuals with damage to their amydgala do not easily learn fear responses (Angrilli et al., 1996; Angrilli et al., 2008; Cristinzio et al., 2010; Coppens et al., 2010;), and many cannot recognize facial expressions of fear (Adolphs et al., 2005; Berntson et al., 2007; LeDoux & Phelps, 2008).

The amygdala has a direct connection with the *thalamus* (our brain's sensory switchboard) and this allows almost instantaneous processing of incoming fear-related stimuli (Carretié et al., 2009; Doron & Ledoux, 2000; Maren et al., 2001). This can result in emotional arousal without immediate conscious awareness. That is, we react with fear before we know we are frightened. For example, have you ever rapidly recoiled thinking you have just seen a spider, but a split second later realize it is just lint or fluff? According to psychologist Joseph LeDoux (1996a, 2002, 2007), when sensory inputs arrive in the thalamus, it sends simultaneous separate messages up to the cortex (which "thinks" about the stimulus) and to the amygdala (which immediately activates the body's alarm system). The amygdala triggers a behavioural reaction before the cortex has time to "think about" what has happened.

As important as the brain is to emotion, it is the *autonomic nervous system* (ANS, Chapter 2) that produces the obvious signs of arousal. These largely automatic responses result from interconnections between the ANS and the various glands and muscles of the body (**Figure 11.15**).

The autonomic nervous system • Figure 11.15

During emotional arousal, the sympathetic branch of the autonomic nervous system prepares the individual (both human and non-human animals) for fight or flight. The hormones epinephrine and norepinephrine keep the nervous system under sympathetic control until the emergency is over. The parasympathetic branch returns the body to a non-aroused state (remember homeostasis?), which is where it remains for most of the time. If sympathetic arousal is so good at mobilizing an organism to fight or flee, why do you think we need a parasympathetic system?

John Dominis/Time & Life Pictures/Getty Images

Sympathetic		Parasympathetic
Pupils dilated	**Eyes**	Pupils constricted
Dry	**Mouth**	Salivating
Goose bumps (pilo-erection), perspiration	**Skin**	No goose bumps
Respiration increased	**Lungs**	Respiration normal
Increased rate	**Heart**	Decreased rate
Increased epinephrine and norepinephrine	**Adrenal glands**	Decreased epinephrine and norepinephrine
Decreased motility	**Digestion**	Increased motility

The cognitive (thinking) component Our thoughts, values, and expectations help determine the type and intensity of our emotional responses. Consequently, emotional reactions are very individual: what you experience as intensely pleasurable may be boring, annoying, or aversive to another. To study the cognitive (thought) component of emotions, psychologists typically use self-report techniques, such as paper-and-pencil tests, surveys, and interviews. However, people are sometimes unable or unwilling to accurately describe (or remember) their emotional states. For these reasons, our cognitions about our own and others' emotions are difficult to measure scientifically. This is why many researchers supplement participants' reports of their emotional experiences with methods that assess emotional experience indirectly (for example, by measuring physiological responses or behaviour).

The behavioural (expressive) component We wear our emotions on our body. Think about anger—we clench our teeth when we are angry, ball our fists, often our face reddens and our eyes narrow. Emotional expression is a powerful form of communication, and while our bodily posture changes to reflect our emotions, facial expressions may be our most important form of emotional communication. Researchers have developed sensitive techniques to measure facial expressions of emotion and to differentiate honest expressions from fake ones. Perhaps most interesting is the distinctive difference between the *social smile* and the *Duchenne smile* (named after French anatomist Duchenne de Boulogne, who first described it in 1862) (**Figure 11.16**). In a false, social smile, our voluntary cheek muscles are pulled back, but our eyes are unsmiling. Smiles of real pleasure (Duchenne smiles), conversely, use the muscles not only around the cheeks but also around the eyes. Most people have experienced this difference. When you are having your picture taken and the flash takes just a moment too long to activate, what was a Duchenne smile on your face morphs into a social smile. All of a sudden, it takes effort to prop up the sides of your mouth into a smile.

The Duchenne smile illustrates the importance of non-verbal means of communicating emotion. We all know that people communicate in ways other than speaking or writing. However, few people recognize the full importance of non-verbal signals. Imagine yourself as an interviewer with two equally qualified applicants, both of whom are well spoken. Your first job applicant greets you with a big smile, full eye contact, a firm handshake, and an erect, open posture. The second applicant doesn't smile, looks down, offers a weak handshake, and slouches. Whom do you think you will hire? Our dependence on non-verbal

The Duchenne smile: Which smile looks happier and more sincere? • Figure 11.16

People who show a Duchenne smile (**a.**) elicit more positive responses from strangers and enjoy better interpersonal relationships and personal adjustment than those who use social smiles (**b.**) (Bernstein et al., 2010; Keltner et al., 1999; Prkachin & Silverman, 2002; Reed et al.).

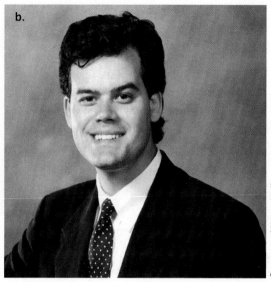

communication, particularly facial expressions, is illustrated by the popularity of "smileys," and other emoticon symbols, in our email and text messages. We seem to need to "add" these emotions to our written words because the letters alone do not seem to capture the essence of our feelings.

Four Major Theories of Emotion

Where do emotions come from? Researchers generally agree on the three components of emotion (physiological, cognitive, and behavioural), but there is less agreement on *how* we become emotional. The four major theories in this area are the James-Lange, the Cannon-Bard, the facial-feedback, and Schachter's two-factor. Each theory has its supporters and critics, and each has flaws, but as shown in **Figure 11.17** (on the next page), they all emphasize different sequences or aspects of the same three elements of emotion.

According to the **James-Lange theory** (originated by psychologist William James and later expanded on by physiologist Carl Lange), emotions depend on feedback from our physiological arousal and behavioural expression (**Figure 11.17a**). In other words, as James wrote: "We feel sorry *because* we cry, angry *because* we strike, afraid *because* we

tremble" (James, 1890). In short, emotions are the *result* of physiological arousal. Without arousal or expression, there is no emotion. This theory of emotion is consistent with our earlier discussion where perception of environmental events (spider) produce physiological arousal and behavioural change before the information is processed in the cortex (lint or fluff).

In contrast, the **Cannon-Bard theory** holds that all emotions are physiologically similar and that arousal, cognitions, and expression all occur simultaneously. Important in this theory is the belief that arousal is not a necessary or even major factor in emotion. Walter Cannon (1927) and Philip Bard (1934) proposed that the thalamus sends simultaneous messages to both the ANS and the cerebral cortex (**Figure 11.17b**). Messages to the cortex produce the cognitive experience of emotion (such as feelings of fear), whereas messages to the autonomic nervous system produce physiological arousal and behavioural expressions (such as increased heart rate, running, and widening eyes).

Cannon supported his position with several experiments in which animals were surgically prevented from experiencing physiological arousal. His results showed these animals still exhibited emotion-like behaviours, such as growling and defensive postures (Cannon, Lewis, & Britton, 1927).

Four major theories of emotion • Figure 11.17

James-Lange: Emotion occurs after the body is aroused.

Cannon-Baird: Arousal and emotion occur simultaneously.

Facial-Feedback: Emotion is influenced by sensory feedback from facial muscles.

Schachter's Two-Factor: Both physiological arousal and cognitive labels determine the emotion experienced.

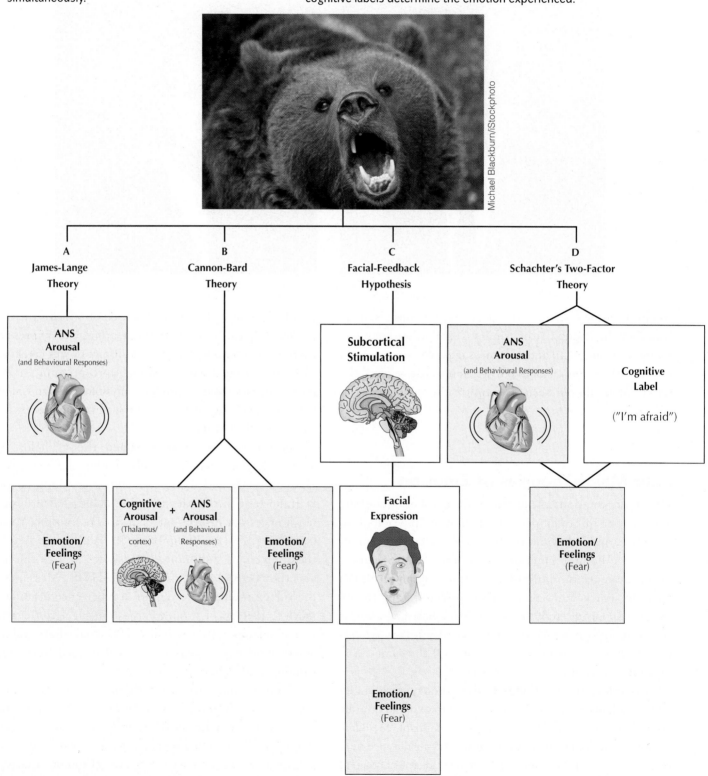

Michael Blackburn/iStockphoto

A
James-Lange Theory

ANS Arousal
(and Behavioural Responses)

Emotion/ Feelings
(Fear)

B
Cannon-Bard Theory

Cognitive Arousal + **ANS Arousal**
(Thalamus/ cortex) (and Behavioural Responses)

Emotion/ Feelings
(Fear)

C
Facial-Feedback Hypothesis

Subcortical Stimulation

Facial Expression

Emotion/ Feelings
(Fear)

D
Schachter's Two-Factor Theory

ANS Arousal
(and Behavioural Responses)

Cognitive Label
("I'm afraid")

Emotion/ Feelings
(Fear)

Testing the facial-feedback hypothesis • Figure 11.18

Hold a pen or pencil between your teeth with your mouth open. Spend about 30 seconds in this position. How do you feel? According to research, pleasant feelings are more likely when teeth are showing than when they are not. *Source:* Adapted from Blaesi & Wilson (2010), and Strack et al. (1988).

The third major theory of emotion was derived from Charles Darwin's (1872) theory, which states that muscular activity can either strengthen or lessen the experience of emotion. According to the **facial-feedback hypothesis** (**Figure 11.17c**), facial changes not only correlate with and intensify emotions but also cause or reinforce the very emotions themselves (Adelmann & Zajonc, 1989; Ceschi & Scherer, 2001; Prkachin, 2005; Sigall & Johnson, 2006). Contractions of the various facial muscles send specific messages to the brain, identifying each of the basic emotions (**Figure 11.18**).

One way to test the facial-feedback hypothesis is to see if paralysis of some facial muscles influences emotionality. It seems it does. A recent study involving recipients of Botox (Chapter 2) found that people who cannot frown because of cosmetic Botox injections report feeling happier and less anxious than those who received other cosmetic treatments (Lewis & Bowler, 2009). Other research with Botox has found that blocking the muscles involved in frowning actually inhibits our ability to perceive and interpret negative emotions (Neal & Chartrand, 2011), and in some cases, it can influence our emotional experiences (Davis et al., 2010). Future research will be necessary to clarify the effects of Botox on emotional interpretation and expression (**Figure 11.19**).

Interestingly, watching another's facial expressions causes an automatic, reciprocal change in our own facial muscles (Dimberg & Thunberg, 1998). When people are exposed to pictures of angry faces, for example, the eyebrow muscles involved in frowning are activated. This

Wrinkles and emotions • Figure 11.19

While facial wrinkles convey information about age, they also provide clues about how we are feeling: a wrinkled nose can convey disgust, a frown can convey anger, worry or concern. The wrinkles we develop as we age are based then on a lifetime of wearing our emotions on our face. What do you think the human world would be like if we could not express emotions with our faces?

Visualizing

Schachter's two-factor theory of emotion • Figure 11.20

In Schachter and Singer's classic study (1962), participants were given injections of epinephrine and were all told it was a type of vitamin (called *Suproxin*). One group of participants was correctly informed about the effects of the epinephrine (hand tremors, excitement, and heart palpitations). A second group was misinformed and told to expect itching, numbness, and headache. A third group was deceived and not told anything about the effects of the epinephrine.

Following the injection, each participant was placed in a room with a confederate (an assistant who was part of the expe-riment but who pretended to be a fellow volunteer) who acted either happy or angry.

The results showed that participants who received an epinephrine injection but were *not* given a proper explanation for their physiological arousal (the misinformed and deceived groups) tended to look to the situation for an explanation. Thus, those placed with a happy confederate reported being happy, whereas those with an angry confederate reported anger. In contrast, participants in the correctly informed group who knew their physiological arousal was the result of the needle were immune to the effects of the arousal manipulation and their emotions were generally unaffected by the confederate.

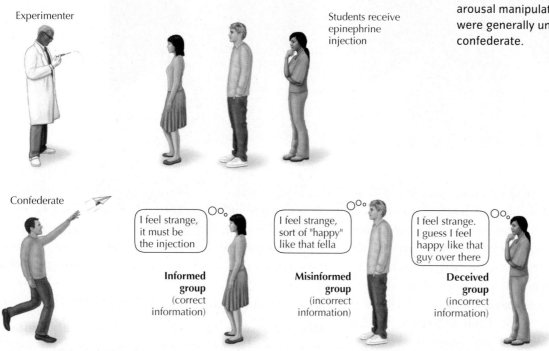

Experimenter

Students receive epinephrine injection

Confederate

I feel strange, it must be the injection

Informed group
(correct information)

I feel strange, sort of "happy" like that fella

Misinformed group
(incorrect information)

I feel strange. I guess I feel happy like that guy over there

Deceived group
(incorrect information)

automatic matching response can occur even without the participant's attention or conscious awareness (Cheng & Chartrand, 2003; Dimberg et al., 2000; Heyes, 2011).

Finally, according to psychologist Stanley **Schachter's two-factor theory** (**Figure 11.20**), emotions have two parts (or factors): physiological and cognitive. The cognitive factor is necessary to evaluate what in the situation has caused the physiological arousal. In other words, it is physical arousal and the cognitive label of the arousal that produces the subjective experience of emotion. If we cry at a wedding, we interpret our emotion as happiness, but if we cry at a funeral, we label our emotion sadness.

Which theory is correct? As said, each has its benefits and limitations for our understanding of emotion. For example, the James-Lange theory fails to acknowledge that physical arousal can occur without emotional experi-ence (e.g., when we work out). This theory also requires a distinctly different pattern of arousal for each emotion. Otherwise, how do we know whether we are sad, happy, disgusted, or mad? Although brain-imaging studies do show subtle differences among basic emotions (Levenson, 1992, 2007; Werner et al., 2007), most people are not aware of these slight variations. Thus, there must be other explanations for why we experience emotion.

Does emotional arousal increase feelings of sexual attraction? • Figure 11.21

In a classic study, psychologists at the University of British Columbia had an attractive female researcher interview young men after they had just walked across the scary Capilano Suspension Bridge in North Vancouver, B.C. (Dutton & Aron, 1974). Men who had just crossed the scary bridge (experimental group) were more inclined to telephone the researcher for further contact than were men who had just crossed a non-scary bridge (control group). Could the men in the experimental group have misinterpreted their high levels of emotional arousal as sexual attraction to the researcher?

Jim Lo Scalzo/U.S. News & World Report/GetStock.com

The Cannon-Bard theory (that the cortex and autonomic nervous system receive simultaneous messages from the thalamus) has received some experimental support. People with spinal cord damage still experience emotions, often more intensely than before their injuries (Nicotra et al., 2006; Schopp et al., 2007). Other research, however, shows that instead of the thalamus, it is the limbic system, hypothalamus, and prefrontal cortex that are activated during emotional experiences (LeDoux, 2007; Zillmer et al., 2008).

Research on the facial-feedback hypothesis has found that facial feedback does seem to contribute somewhat to the intensity of our subjective emotions and overall moods (Davis et al., 2010; Lewis & Bowler, 2009; Neal & Chartrand, 2011). Thus, if you want to change a bad mood or intensify a particularly good emotion, adopt the appropriate facial expression. In other words, "fake it 'til you make it."

Finally, Schachter's two-factor theory emphasizes the importance of cognitive labels in emotions, but research suggests some neural pathways involved in emotion bypass the cortex and go directly to the limbic system, and we are not always accurate when labelling our emotions (see **Figure 11.21**). This and other evidence suggest that emotion can take place without conscious cognitive processes and is not simply a label of arousal (Dimberg et al., 2000; LeDoux, 1996b, 2002; Mineka & Ohman, 2002).

Culture, Evolution, and Emotion

All people, no matter where they live in the world, have feelings and emotions. Where do they come from? Did they evolve from millennia past, or are they shaped by the culture in which we are raised? The answer to this question seems to be that both evolution and culture shape and influence our emotions.

Given the seemingly vast array of emotions within Canadian culture (and elsewhere), it may surprise you to learn that in general, emotion researchers believe that all our feelings can be condensed into 7 to 11 basic universal emotions: fear, anger, disgust, surprise, joy, contempt, sadness, and perhaps also interest, anticipation, acceptance, and shame (Ekman, 1994, 1999; Izard, 1977, 1992; Plutchik, 1962; Tomkins, 1962). These researchers hold that other emotions, such as love and

Trait Theories

LEARNING OBJECTIVES

1. **Explain** how early trait theorists approached the study of personality.

2. **Identify** the "Big Five" personality traits.

3. **Summarize** the major critiques of trait theory.

Personality describes you as a person, how you are different from other people, and what patterns of behaviour are typical of you. You might qualify as an "extrovert," for example, if you are talkative and outgoing most of the time. Or you might be considered "conscientious" if you are responsible and self-disciplined most of the time.

The terms we use to describe other people (and ourselves) are called **traits**. Trait theorists are interested in discovering which traits best describe people and in measuring the degree of variation in traits within individuals and among people.

> **personality**
> Relatively stable and enduring patterns of thoughts, feelings, and actions.
>
> **trait** A relatively stable and consistent characteristic that can be used to describe someone.

Early Trait Theorists: Allport, Cattell, and Eysenck

An early study of dictionary terms found almost 4,500 words that described personality traits (Allport & Odbert, 1936). Faced with this enormous list, Gordon Allport (1937) believed that the best way to understand personality was to arrange a person's unique personality traits into a hierarchy, with the most pervasive or important traits at the top.

Later psychologists reduced the list of possible personality traits by using a statistical technique called **factor analysis**, in which large arrays of data are grouped into more basic units (factors). Raymond Cattell (1950, 1965, 1990) condensed the list of traits to between 30 and 35 basic characteristics. Hans Eysenck (1967, 1982, 1990) reduced the list even further: He described personality as a relationship among three basic types of traits: extroversion-introversion (E), neuroticism (N), and psychoticism (P).

The Five-Factor Model: Five Basic Personality Traits

Factor analysis was also used to develop the most promising modern trait theory, the **five-factor model (FFM)** (Costa & McCrae, 2011; McCrae & Costa, 1990, 1999; McCrae & Sutin, 2007).

Combining previous research findings and the long list of possible personality traits, researchers discovered that five traits came up repeatedly, even when different tests were used (Funder & Fast, 2010). These five major dimensions of personality are often dubbed the **Big Five**. As a handy way to remember the five factors, the first letters of each factor spell the word ocean:

> **five-factor model (FFM)** The trait theory that explains personality in terms of the "Big Five" dimensions of openness, conscientiousness, extroversion, agreeableness, and neuroticism.

O *Openness.* People who score high in this factor are original, imaginative, curious, open to new ideas, artistic, and interested in cultural pursuits. Low scorers tend to be conventional, down-to-earth, narrower in their interests, and not artistic. Interestingly, critical thinkers tend to score higher than others on this factor (Clifford et al., 2004).

C *Conscientiousness.* This factor ranges from responsible, self-disciplined, organized, and achieving at the high end to irresponsible, careless, impulsive, lazy, and undependable at the other.

E *Extroversion.* This factor contrasts people who are sociable, outgoing, talkative, fun loving, and affectionate at the high end with introverted individuals who tend to be withdrawn, quiet, passive, and reserved at the low end.

A *Agreeableness.* Individuals who score high on this factor are good-natured, warm, gentle, cooperative, trusting, and helpful, whereas low scorers are irritable, argumentative, ruthless, suspicious, uncooperative, and vindictive.

N *Neuroticism* (or emotional stability). People who score high on neuroticism are emotionally unstable and prone to insecurity, anxiety, guilt, worry, and moodiness. People at the other end are emotionally stable, calm, even-tempered, easygoing, and relaxed. (See *Applying Psychology: Love and the Big Five on the next page*.)

Personality and your career • Figure 12.1

Are some people better suited for certain jobs than others? According to psychologist John Holland's *personality–job fit* theory, a match (or "good fit") between our individual personality and our career choice is a major factor in determining job satisfaction (Holland, 1985, 1994). Research shows that a good fit between personality and occupation helps increase subjective feelings of well-being, job success, and job satisfaction. In other words, people tend to be happier and like their work when they're well matched to their jobs (Donohue, 2006; Gottfredson & Duffy, 2008; Kieffer et al., 2004).

Damir Cudic/iStockphoto

Edward Mallia/iStockphoto

Rich Legg/iStockphoto

Dan Barnes/iStockphoto

Applying Psychology

Love and the Big Five

Using the figure below, plot your personality profile by placing a dot on each line to indicate your degree of openness, conscientiousness, and so on. Do the same for a current, previous, or prospective boyfriend or girlfriend.

Now look at the two mate preferences lists. David Buss and his colleagues (1989, 2003) surveyed more than 10,000 men and women from 37 countries and found a surprising level of agreement in the characteristics that men and women value in a mate. Moreover, most of the Big Five personality traits are found at the top of the list. Both men and women prefer dependability (conscientiousness), emotional stability (low neuroticism), pleasing disposition (agreeableness), and sociability (extroversion) to the alternatives. These findings may reflect an evolutionary advantage for people who are open, conscientious, extroverted, agreeable, and free of neuroses. (We discuss the topics of attraction and love in more detail in Chapter 15.)

Big Five Traits	Low Scorers	High Scorers
1 **O**penness	Down-to-earth Uncreative Conventional Uncurious	Imaginative Creative Original Curious
2 **C**onscientiousness	Negligent Lazy Disorganized Late	Conscientious Hard-working Well-organized Punctual
3 **E**xtroversion	Loner Quiet Passive Reserved	Joiner Talkative Active Affectionate
4 **A**greeableness	Suspicious Critical Ruthless Irritable	Trusting Lenient Soft-hearted Good-natured
5 **N**euroticism	Calm Even-tempered Comfortable Unemotional	Worried Temperamental Self-conscious Emotional

Mate preferences around the world

In the two lists below, note how the top four desired traits are the same for both men and women, as well as how closely their desired traits match those of the five-factor model (FFM).

♂ What Men Want in a Mate	♀ What Women Want in a Mate
1. Mutual attraction—love	1. Mutual attraction—love
2. Dependable character	2. Dependable character
3. Emotional stability and maturity	3. Emotional stability and maturity
4. Pleasing disposition	4. Pleasing disposition
5. Good health	5. Education and intelligence
6. Education and intelligence	6. Sociability
7. Sociability	7. Good health
8. Desire for home and children	8. Desire for home and children
9. Refinement, neatness	9. Ambition and industriousness
10. Good looks	10. Refinement, neatness

Source: Buss, D. M., et al. (1990). International preferences in selecting mates. *Journal of Cross-Cultural Psychology, 21,* 5–47, Sage Publications, Inc.

Think Critically

1. How do your personality traits compare with those of your boyfriend or girlfriend?
2. If your scores are noticeably different, what might explain the differences?

Evaluating Trait Theories

The five-factor model is the first to achieve the major goal of trait theory—to describe and organize personality characteristics by using the fewest number of traits. Some critics argue, however, that the great variation seen in personalities cannot be accounted for by simply five traits and that the Big Five model fails to offer causal explanations for these traits (Friedman & Schustack, 2006; Funder, 2001; Funder & Fast, 2010; Sollod et al., 2009).

Critics maintain that, in general, trait theories are good at describing personality, but they have difficulty explaining why people develop these traits (Funder & Fast, 2010) or why personality traits differ across cultures. For example, trait theories do not explain why people in cultures that are geographically close tend to have similar personalities or why Europeans and North Americans tend to be higher in extroversion and openness to experience and lower in agreeableness than people in Asian and African cultures (Allik & McCrae, 2004).

In addition, some critics have faulted trait theories for their lack of specificity. Although trait theorists have documented a high level of personality stability after age 30 (Funder & Fast, 2010) (**Figure 12.2**), they haven't identified which characteristics last a lifetime and which are most likely to change.

Finally, trait theorists have been criticized for ignoring the importance of situational and environmental effects on personality. In one example, psychologists Fred Rogosch and Dante Cicchetti (Cicchetti, 2010; Rogosch & Cicchetti, 2004) found that abused and neglected children scored significantly lower in the traits of openness to experience, conscientiousness, and agreeableness and higher in the trait of neuroticism than did children who were not

Personality change over time • Figure 12.2

Have you noticed how Madonna's public image and behaviour have changed over time? Cross-cultural research has found that neuroticism, extroversion, and openness to experience tend to decline from adolescence to adulthood, whereas agreeableness and conscientiousness increase (McCrae, Costa, Hrebícková et al., 2004). How would you explain these changes? Do you think they're good or bad?

Gill Allen/Associated Press

Jennifer Graylock/Associated Press

maltreated. Unfortunately, these maladaptive personality traits create significant liabilities that may trouble these children throughout their lifetimes.

CONCEPT CHECK STOP

1. **What** is the purpose of factor analysis?
2. **What** dimensions of personality are central to the five-factor model?
3. **What** are some weaknesses of trait theory?

Psychoanalytic/Psychodynamic Theories

LEARNING OBJECTIVES

1. **Identify** Freud's most basic and controversial contributions to the study of personality.

2. **Explain** how Adler's, Jung's, and Horney's theories differ from Freud's views.

3. **Explore** the major criticisms of Freud's psychoanalytic theories.

In contrast to trait theories that describe personality as it exists, psychoanalytic (or psychodynamic) theories of personality attempt to explain individual differences by examining how unconscious mental forces interplay with thoughts, feelings, and actions. The originator of psychoanalytic theory is Sigmund Freud. We will examine Freud's theories in some detail and then briefly discuss the contributions made by three of his most influential followers.

Freud's Psychoanalytic Theory: The Power of the Unconscious

Who is the best-known figure in the field of psychology? Most people immediately name

conscious Freud's term for thoughts or motives that a person is currently aware of or is remembering.

preconscious Freud's term for thoughts, motives, or memories that exist just beneath the surface of awareness and that can be easily brought to mind.

unconscious Freud's term for thoughts, motives, or memories blocked from normal awareness but that still exert great influence.

Sigmund Freud, whose theories have been applied not only to psychology but also to anthropology, sociology, religion, medicine, art, and literature. Working from about 1890 until he died in 1939, Freud developed a theory of personality that has been one of the most influential—and most controversial—theories in all of science (Dufresne, 2007; Dumont, 2010; Heller, 2005). Let's examine some of Freud's most basic and most debated concepts.

Levels of consciousness Freud called the mind the "psyche" and asserted that it contains three **levels of consciousness**, or awareness: the **conscious**, the **preconscious**, and the **unconscious** (**Figure 12.3**).

Freud believed that most psychological disorders originate from repressed memories

Freud's three levels of consciousness
• Figure 12.3

Freud compared people's conscious awareness—thoughts, feelings, and actions that we are actively aware of—to the tip of an iceberg, open to easy inspection. Beneath the conscious realm, and the water's surface, is the larger preconscious. It includes mental activities that we can access without much extra effort. The large, deeply submerged base of the iceberg is like the unconscious mind, hidden from personal inspection. According to Freud, the unconscious stores our primitive, instinctual motives and anxiety-laden memories and emotions, which are prevented from entering the conscious mind.

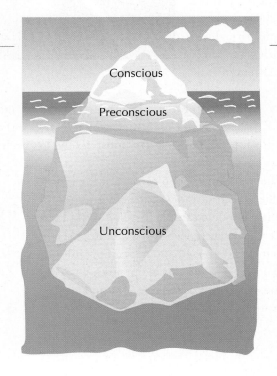

Conscious

Preconscious

Unconscious

Freudian slips • Figure 12.4

Freud believed that a small slip of the tongue (known as a "Freudian slip") can reflect unconscious feelings that we normally keep hidden.

"Good morning, beheaded—uh, I mean beloved."

© Dana Fradon/Condé Nast Publications/www.cartoonbank.com.

Freud's personality structure • Figure 12.5

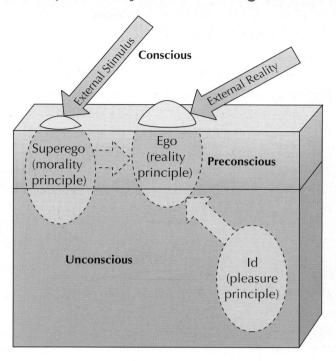

and instincts (sexual and aggressive) that are hidden in the unconscious (**Figure 12.4**). To treat these disorders, Freud developed *psychoanalysis* (Chapter 14).

Personality structures   In addition to proposing that the mind functions at three levels of consciousness, Freud also argued that personality was composed of three mental structures: the *id*, the *ego*, and the *superego* (**Figure 12.5**).

According to Freud, the **id** is made up of innate, biological instincts and urges. It is immature, impulsive, and irrational. The id is also totally unconscious and serves as the reservoir of mental energy. When its primitive drives build up, the id seeks immediate gratification to relieve the tension—a concept known as the **pleasure principle**.

As a child grows older, the second personality structure—the **ego**—develops. The ego is responsible for planning, problem solving, reasoning, and controlling the potentially destructive energy of the id. In Freud's system, the ego corresponds to the **self**—our conscious identity of ourselves as persons.

One of the ego's tasks is to channel and release the id's energy in ways that are compatible with the external world. Thus, the ego is responsible for delaying gratification until it is practical or appropriate. Contrary

to the id's pleasure principle, the ego operates according to the **reality principle** because it can understand and deal with objects and events in the "real world."

The final personality structure to develop is the **superego**, a set of ethical standards or rules for behaviour. The superego develops from internalized parental and societal standards. It constantly strives for perfection and is therefore as unrealistic as the id. Some Freudian followers have suggested that the superego operates according to the **morality principle** because violating its rules results in feelings of guilt.

What happens when the ego fails to satisfy both the id and the superego? Anxiety and/or guilt can slip into conscious awareness. Because these emotions are uncomfortable, people attempt to avoid them by using **defence mechanisms**. For example, an alcoholic who uses his paycheque to buy drinks (a message from the id) may feel very guilty (a response from the superego). He may reduce this conflict by telling himself that he deserves a drink because he works so hard. This is an example of the defence mechanism **rationalization**.

> **defence mechanisms** In Freudian theory, the ego's protective method of reducing anxiety by self-deception and the distortion of reality.

Defence Mechanism	Description	Example
Repression	Preventing painful or unacceptable thoughts from entering consciousness	Forgetting the details of your parent's painful death
Regression	Responding to a threatening situation in a way appropriate to an earlier age or level of development	Throwing a temper tantrum when a friend doesn't want to do what you'd like
Denial	Protecting yourself from an unpleasant reality by refusing to perceive it	Alcoholics refusing to admit their addiction
Projection	Transferring unacceptable thoughts, motives, or impulses to others	Becoming unreasonably jealous of your mate while denying your own attraction to others
Reaction formation	Refusing to acknowledge unacceptable urges, thoughts, or feelings by exaggerating the opposite state	Promoting a petition against adults-only bookstores even though you are secretly aroused by pornography
Sublimation	Redirecting unmet desires or unacceptable impulses into acceptable activities	Rechannelling unacceptable desires into school, work, art, sports, or hobbies (e.g., joining a wrestling team, taking an art class to paint nude models)
Rationalization	Substituting socially acceptable reasons for unacceptable ones	Justifying cheating on an exam by saying "everyone else does it"
Intellectualization	Ignoring the emotional aspects of a painful experience by focusing on abstract thoughts, words, or ideas	Emotionless discussion of your divorce while ignoring the underlying pain
Displacement	Redirecting impulses toward a less threatening person or object	Yelling at a co-worker after being criticized by your boss

Although Freud described many kinds of defence mechanisms (**Study Organizer 12.1**), he believed that repression was the most basic. **Repression** is the mechanism by which the ego prevents the most unacceptable, anxiety-provoking thoughts from entering consciousness (**Figure 12.6**).

The concept of defence mechanisms has generally withstood the test of time, and it is an accepted part

Is it bad to use defence mechanisms?
• Figure 12.6 _____

Although defence mechanisms do distort reality, some misrepresentation seems to be necessary for our psychological well-being (Marshall & Brown, 2008; Wenger & Fowers, 2008). During a gruesome surgery, for example, physicians and nurses may **intellectualize** the procedure as an unconscious way of dealing with their personal anxieties. Can you see how focusing on highly objective technical aspects of the situation might help these people avoid becoming emotionally overwhelmed by the potentially tragic circumstances they often encounter?

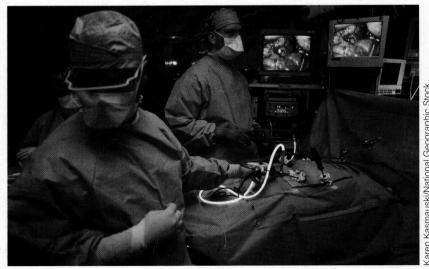

Karen Kasmauski/National Geographic Stock

Freud's five psychosexual stages of development • Figure 12.7

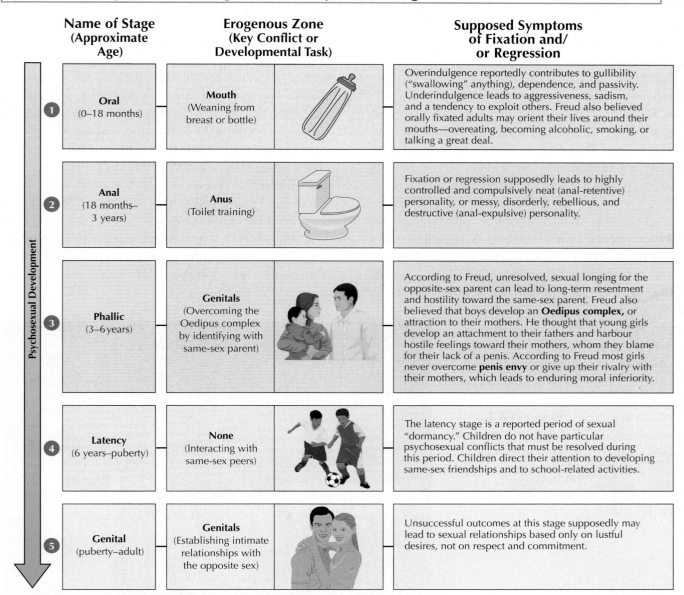

Name of Stage (Approximate Age)	Erogenous Zone (Key Conflict or Developmental Task)		Supposed Symptoms of Fixation and/ or Regression
① **Oral** (0–18 months)	**Mouth** (Weaning from breast or bottle)		Overindulgence reportedly contributes to gullibility ("swallowing" anything), dependence, and passivity. Underindulgence leads to aggressiveness, sadism, and a tendency to exploit others. Freud also believed orally fixated adults may orient their lives around their mouths—overeating, becoming alcoholic, smoking, or talking a great deal.
② **Anal** (18 months– 3 years)	**Anus** (Toilet training)		Fixation or regression supposedly leads to highly controlled and compulsively neat (anal-retentive) personality, or messy, disorderly, rebellious, and destructive (anal-expulsive) personality.
③ **Phallic** (3–6 years)	**Genitals** (Overcoming the Oedipus complex by identifying with same-sex parent)		According to Freud, unresolved, sexual longing for the opposite-sex parent can lead to long-term resentment and hostility toward the same-sex parent. Freud also believed that boys develop an **Oedipus complex,** or attraction to their mothers. He thought that young girls develop an attachment to their fathers and harbour hostile feelings toward their mothers, whom they blame for their lack of a penis. According to Freud most girls never overcome **penis envy** or give up their rivalry with their mothers, which leads to enduring moral inferiority.
④ **Latency** (6 years–puberty)	**None** (Interacting with same-sex peers)		The latency stage is a reported period of sexual "dormancy." Children do not have particular psychosexual conflicts that must be resolved during this period. Children direct their attention to developing same-sex friendships and to school-related activities.
⑤ **Genital** (puberty–adult)	**Genitals** (Establishing intimate relationships with the opposite sex)		Unsuccessful outcomes at this stage supposedly may lead to sexual relationships based only on lustful desires, not on respect and commitment.

Psychosexual Development

---

psychosexual stages In Freudian theory, the five developmental periods (oral, anal, phallic, latency, and genital) during which particular kinds of pleasures must be gratified if personality development is to proceed normally.

of modern psychology. However, this is not the case for Freud's theory of psychosexual stages of development.

According to Freud, strong biological urges residing within the id push all children through five universal **psychosexual stages** (**Figure 12.7**). The term *psychosexual* reflects Freud's belief that children experience pleasure-related,

sexual feelings from birth (although in different forms from those of adolescents or adults). These urges are expressed through different areas of the body (*erogenous zones*) as the child develops.

Freud held that if a child's needs are not met or if they are overindulged at one particular psychosexual stage, the child may become *fixated*, and a part of his or her personality will remain stuck at that stage. Furthermore, when under stress, individuals may return (or *regress*) to a stage at which earlier needs were frustrated or overly gratified (Wolitzky, 2011).

Neo-Freudian/Psychodynamic Theories: Revising Freud's Ideas

Several of Freud's initial followers split away from his ideas and developed theories of their own. Three of the most influential of these **neo-Freudians** were Alfred Adler, Carl Jung, and Karen Horney.

Alfred Adler (1870–1937) was the first to leave Freud's inner circle. Rather than viewing behaviour as motivated by unconscious forces, Adler believed that it is purposeful and goal-directed. According to Adler's **individual psychology**, we are motivated by our goals in life—especially our goals of obtaining security and overcoming feelings of inferiority.

Adler held that almost everyone suffers from an **inferiority complex**, or deep feelings of inadequacy and incompetence that arise from our feelings of helplessness as infants. According to Adler, these early feelings result in a "will-to-power" that can take one of two paths. It can either cause children to strive to develop superiority over others through dominance, aggression, or expressions of envy, or—more positively—it can cause children to develop their full potential and creativity and to gain mastery and control in their lives (Adler, 1964, 1998) (**Figure 12.8**).

Another early Freud follower turned dissenter, Carl Jung (pronounced YOONG), developed **analytical psychology**. Like Freud, Jung (1875–1961) emphasized unconscious processes, but he believed that the unconscious contains positive and spiritual motives, as well as sexual and aggressive forces.

Jung also believed that we have two forms of unconscious mind: the *personal unconscious* and the *collective unconscious*. The personal unconscious is created from our individual experiences, whereas the *collective unconscious* is identical in each person and is inherited (Jung, 1946, 1959, 1969). The collective unconscious consists of primitive images and patterns of thought, feeling, and behaviour that Jung called **archetypes** (**Figure 12.9**).

Because of archetypal patterns in the collective unconscious, we perceive and react in certain predictable ways. One set of archetypes refers to gender roles (Chapter 10). Jung claimed that both males and females have patterns for feminine aspects of personality (*anima*) and masculine aspects of personality (*animus*), which allow us to express both masculine and feminine personality traits and to understand the opposite sex.

An upside to feelings of inferiority? • Figure 12.8

Adler suggested that the will-to-power could be positively expressed through social interest—identifying with others and cooperating with them for the social good. Can you explain how these volunteers might be fulfilling their will-to-power interest?

Sam Abell/National Geographic Stock

Archetypes in literature and film • Figure 12.9

According to Jung, the collective unconscious is the ancestral memory of the human race, which explains the similarities in religion, art, symbolism, and stories and literature across cultures. Gordon Flett (2007) of York University in Toronto points out that the appeal of many popular films is partly because they include characters who represent several of the archetypes found in our collective unconscious. These often include a hero, a mother figure, a wise old man, a trickster, and so on. The character Aragorn, from the *Lord of the Rings*, is a good example of the hero archetype (Flett, 2007). Can you think of other such archetypal symbols in films you've seen or stories you've read?

Pierre Vinet/New Line Productions/The Canadian Press

Like Adler and Jung, psychoanalyst Karen Horney (pronounced HORN-eye) was an influential follower of Freud who later came to reject major aspects of Freudian theory. She is remembered most for having developed a creative blend of Freudian, Adlerian, and Jungian theory, with added concepts of her own (Horney, 1939, 1945) (**Figure 12.10**).

Horney is also known for her theories of personality development. She believed that adult personality is shaped by the child's relationship with his or her parents—not by fixation at a stage of psychosexual development, as Freud argued. Horney believed that a child whose needs were not met by nurturing parents would experience extreme feelings of helplessness and insecurity. How people respond to this basic anxiety greatly determines emotional health.

According to Horney, everyone searches for security in one of three ways: We can move toward people (by seeking affection and acceptance from others); we can move away from people (by striving for independence, privacy, and self-reliance); or we can move against people (by trying to gain control and power over others). Emotional health requires a balance among these three styles.

Karen Horney (1885–1952) • Figure 12.10

Horney argued that most of Freud's ideas about female personality reflected male biases and misunderstanding. She contended, for example, that Freud's concept of penis envy reflected women's feelings of cultural inferiority, not biological inferiority—*power envy*, not penis envy.

© Bettman/Corbis

Evaluating Psychoanalytic Theories: Criticisms and Enduring Influence

In this section, we look at major criticisms of Freud's psychoanalytic theory. In addition, we discuss the reasons why Freud's theory has had enormous influence in the field of psychology.

Today there are few Freudian purists. Instead, modern psychodynamic theorists and psychoanalysts use empirical methods and research findings to reformulate and refine traditional Freudian thinking (Knekt et al., 2008; Shaver & Mikulincer, 2005; Tryon, 2008; Westen, 1998; Wolitzky, 2011).

But wrong as he was on many counts, Freud still ranks as one of the giants of psychology (Flett, 2007; Heller, 2005; Wolitzky, 2011). Furthermore, Freud's impact on Western intellectual history cannot be overstated. He attempted to explain dreams, religion, social groupings, family dynamics, neurosis, psychosis, humour, the arts, and literature.

It's easy to criticize Freud if you forget that he began his work at the start of the twentieth century and lacked the benefit of modern research findings and technology. Indeed, we can only imagine how our current theories will look 100 years from now. Right or wrong, Freud has a lasting place among the pioneers in psychology (**Table 12.1**).

Evaluating psychoanalytic theories Table 12.1		
Criticisms	• *Difficult to test.* From a scientific perspective, a major problem with psychoanalytic theory is that most of its concepts—such as the id or unconscious conflicts—cannot be empirically tested. • *Overemphasizes biology and unconscious forces.* Modern psychologists believe that Freud did not give sufficient attention to learning and culture in shaping behaviour. • *Inadequate empirical support.* Freud based his theories almost exclusively on the subjective case histories of his adult patients. Moreover, his patients represented a small and selective sample of humanity: upper-class women in Vienna (Freud's home), who had serious adjustment problems.	• *Sexism.* Many psychologists (beginning with Karen Horney) argue that Freud's theories are derogatory toward women. • *Lack of cross-cultural support.* The Freudian concepts that ought to be most easily supported empirically—the biological determinants of personality—are generally not borne out by cross-cultural studies.
Enduring influences	• The emphasis on the unconscious and its influence on behaviour. • The conflict among the id, ego, and superego and the resulting defence mechanisms.	• Encouraging open talk about sex in Victorian times. • The development of psychoanalysis, an influential form of therapy. • The sheer magnitude of Freud's theory.

CONCEPT CHECK STOP

1. **How** do the conscious, preconscious, and unconscious shape personality, in Freud's view?

2. **What** is the collective unconscious?

3. **What** is an example of sexism in Freud's psychoanalytic theory?

Humanistic Theories

LEARNING OBJECTIVES

1. **Explain** the importance of the self in Rogers' theory of personality.

2. **Describe** how Maslow's hierarchy of needs affects personality.

3. **Identify** three criticisms of humanistic theories.

Humanistic theories of personality emphasize each person's internal feelings, thoughts, and sense of basic worth. Humanists believe that people are naturally good (or, at worst, neutral), and that our personality and behaviour depend on how we perceive and interpret the world. Indeed, as noted by Jeanne Watson of the University of Toronto and Leslie Greenberg of York University in Toronto, the humanistic approach emphasizes our drive toward self-fulfillment and growth, our capacity for self-reflection, and our ability to make choices in our lives (Watson & Greenberg, 1996; Watson, Goldman, & Greenberg, 2011). Two of the most prominent humanistic psychologists were Carl Rogers and Abraham Maslow.

Rogers' Theory: The Importance of the Self

To psychologist Carl Rogers (1902–1987), the most important component of personality is the *self*—what a person comes to identify as "I" or "me." Today, Rogerians (followers of Rogers) use the term **self-concept** to refer to all the information and beliefs you have regarding your own nature, unique qualities, and typical behaviours.

> **self-concept** Rogers' term for all the information and beliefs that individuals have about their own nature, qualities, and behaviour.

What a Psychologist Sees

Congruence, Mental Health, and Self-Esteem

According to Carl Rogers, mental health and adjustment are related to the degree of congruence (accord or agreement) between a person's self-concept and life experiences. Rogers argued that self-esteem—how we feel about ourselves—is particularly dependent on this congruence. Can you see how an artistic child would likely have higher self-esteem if her family valued art highly than if they did not?

Masterfile

Congruence

Experience

Self-concept

Well-adjusted individual
Considerable overlap between self-concept and experience

Incongruence

Self-concept   Experience

Poorly adjusted individual
Little overlap between self-concept and experience

Rogers was very concerned with the match between a person's self-concept and his or her actual experiences with life. He believed that poor mental health and maladjustment developed from a mismatch, or incongruence, between the self-concept and actual life experiences.

Rogers argued that mental health, congruence, and self-esteem are part of our innate, biological capacities. In this view, all individuals naturally approach and value experiences and people that enhance their growth and fulfillment and avoid those that do not. Therefore, Rogers believed that we should trust our feelings to guide us toward mental health and happiness. (See *What a Psychologist Sees* on the previous page.)

If this is so, then why do some people have low self-esteem and poor mental health? Rogers believed that these outcomes generally result from early childhood experiences with parents and other significant adults who make their love conditional. That is, children learn that their acceptance is conditional on behaving in certain ways and expressing only certain feelings.

If children learn over time that their negative feelings and behaviours (which we all have) are unacceptable and unlovable, their self-concept and self-esteem may become distorted. They may always doubt the love and approval of others because others don't know "the real person hiding inside."

To help children develop to their fullest potential, adults need to create an atmosphere of **unconditional positive regard**—a setting in which children realize that they will be accepted no matter what they say or do.

Some people mistakenly believe that unconditional positive regard means that we should allow people to do whatever they please. But humanistic theorists separate the value of the person from his or her behaviours. They accept the person's positive nature while discouraging destructive or hostile behaviours. Humanistic psychologists believe in guiding children to control their behaviour so that they can develop a healthy self-concept and healthy relationships with others (**Figure 12.11**).

unconditional positive regard Rogers' term for positive behaviour toward a person without attaching any requirements or prerequisites.

Mark Bowden/iStockphoto

Conditional love? • Figure 12.11

If a child is angry and hits her younger brother, some parents might punish the child or deny her anger, saying, "Nice children don't hit their brothers; they love them!" To gain parental approval, the child then has to deny her true feelings of anger, but inside she secretly suspects she is not a "nice girl" because she did hit her brother and (at that moment) did not love him. How might repeated incidents of this type have a lasting effect on someone's self-esteem? What would be a more appropriate response to the child's behaviour where a parent indicates that it is the behaviour, not the child, that is unacceptable?

Maslow's Theory: In Pursuit of Self-Actualization

Like Rogers, Abraham Maslow believed that there is a basic goodness to human nature and a natural tendency toward **self-actualization**. He saw personality as the quest to fulfill basic physiological needs (including safety, belonging and love, and esteem) and then move upward toward the highest level of self-actualization.

According to Maslow, self-actualization is the inborn drive to develop all our talents and capacities. It involves understanding our own potential, accepting ourselves and others as unique individuals, and taking a problem-centred approach to life situations (Maslow, 1970). Self-actualization is an ongoing process of growth rather than an end product or accomplishment.

Maslow believed that only a few, rare individuals, such as Albert Einstein or Mohandas Gandhi, become fully self-actualized. However, he saw self-actualization as part of every person's basic hierarchy of needs. (See Chapter 11 for more information on Maslow's theory.)

Evaluating Humanistic Theories: Three Major Criticisms

Humanistic psychology was extremely popular during the 1960s and 1970s. It was seen as a refreshing new perspective on personality after the negative determinism of the psychoanalytic approach and the mechanical nature of learning theories (Chapter 6). Although this early popularity has declined, many humanistic ideas have been incorporated into approaches to counselling and psychotherapy (Chapter 14).

At the same time, humanistic theories have also been criticized (e.g., Funder, 2001). Three of the most important criticisms are the following:

1. *Naïve assumptions*. Critics suggest that the humanistic perspective is unrealistic, romantic, and even naïve concerning human nature (**Figure 12.12**).
2. *Poor testability and inadequate evidence*. As is the case with many psychoanalytic terms and concepts, humanistic concepts (such as unconditional positive regard and self-actualization) are difficult to define operationally and to test scientifically.

Are all people as inherently good as they say?
• Figure 12.12

Humankind's continuing history of murders, warfare, and other acts of aggression suggests otherwise.

David Pluth/National Geographic Stock

3. *Narrowness*. Like trait theories, humanistic theories have been criticized for merely describing personality rather than explaining it. For example, where does the motivation for self-actualization come from? To say that it is an "inborn drive" doesn't satisfy those who favour using experimental research and hard data to learn about personality.

CONCEPT CHECK

1. **How** are self-concept and self-esteem linked in Rogers' theory?
2. **What** is self-actualization?
3. **What** criticism of humanistic theories is also a weakness of trait theories?

Social-Cognitive Theories

LEARNING OBJECTIVES

1. **Explain** Bandura's concepts of self-efficacy and reciprocal determinism and how they affect personality.

2. **Describe** the role that Rotter's concept of locus of control plays in personality.

3. **Summarize** the attractions and criticisms of the social-cognitive perspective on personality.

 ccording to the social-cognitive perspective, each of us has a unique personality because we have individual histories of interactions with the environment (social) and because we think (cognitive) about the world and interpret what happens to us. Two of the most influential social-cognitive theorists are Albert Bandura and Julian Rotter.

Bandura's and Rotter's Approaches: Social Learning Plus Cognitive Processes

Canadian-born Albert Bandura (also discussed in Chapter 6) has played a major role in reintroducing thought processes into personality theory. Cognition is central to his concept of **self-efficacy** (Bandura, 1997, 2000, 2006, 2008, 2011).

> **self-efficacy**
> Bandura's term for the learned belief that you are capable of producing desired results, such as mastering new skills and achieving personal goals.

According to Bandura, if you have a strong sense of self-efficacy, you believe you can generally succeed, regardless of past failures and current obstacles. Your feelings of self-efficacy will in turn affect which challenges you choose to accept and the effort you expend in reaching goals. However, Bandura emphasized that the perception of self-efficacy is always specific to the situation—it does not necessarily carry across situations. For example, self-defence training significantly improves women's belief that they could escape from or disable a potential assailant, but it does not lead them to feel more capable in all areas of their lives (Weitlauf et al., 2001). Finally, according to Bandura's concept of **reciprocal determinism**, self-efficacy beliefs will affect how others respond to you, influencing your chances for success (**Figure 12.13**). Thus, a cognition ("I can succeed") will affect behaviours ("I will work hard and ask for a promotion"), which in turn will affect the environment ("My employer recognized my efforts and promoted me").

> **reciprocal determinism**
> Bandura's belief that cognitions, behaviours, and the environment interact to produce personality.

Julian Rotter's theory is similar to Bandura's in that it suggests that learning experiences create **cognitive expectancies** that guide behaviour and influence the environment (Rotter, 1954, 1990). According to Rotter, your behaviour or personality is determined by (1) what you *expect* to happen following a specific action and (2) the *reinforcement value* attached to specific outcomes—that is, the degree to which you prefer one reinforcer to another.

Albert Bandura's theory of reciprocal determinism • Figure 12.13

According to Bandura, thoughts (or cognitions), behaviour, and the environment all interact to produce personality.

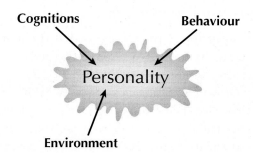

Locus of control and achievement
• Figure 12.14 _____

Research links possession of an internal locus of control with higher achievement and better mental health (Burns, 2008; Jones, 2008; Ruthig et al., 2007). What might this connection imply for human survival?

"We're encouraging people to become involved in their own rescue."

To understand your personality and behaviour, Rotter would want to know your expectancies and what you see as the source of life's rewards and punishments. To gain this information, Rotter would use personality tests that measure your internal versus external **locus of control** (Chapter 3). Rotter's tests ask people to respond to such statements as "People get ahead in this world primarily by luck and connections rather than by hard work and perseverance," and "When someone doesn't like you, there is little you can do about it." As you may suspect, people with an external locus of control think that environment and external forces have primary control over their lives, whereas people with an internal locus of control think that they can control events in their lives through their own efforts (**Figure 12.14**).

Evaluating Social-Cognitive Theory: The Pluses and Minuses

The social-cognitive perspective holds several attractions. First, it emphasizes how the environment affects and is affected by individuals. Second, it offers testable, objective hypotheses and operationally defined terms, and it relies on empirical data for its basic principles. However, critics note that social-cognitive theory ignores the unconscious and emotional aspects of personality (Mischel et al., 2008; Westen, 1998). For example, certain early experiences might have prompted a person to develop an external locus of control.

CONCEPT CHECK STOP

1. **Why** might self-efficacy beliefs affect actual achievement, according to Bandura?

2. **What** might be an advantage and a disadvantage of having either an external or internal locus of control?

Biological Theories

LEARNING OBJECTIVES

1. **Summarize** the roles that brain structures and neurochemistry play in personality.
2. **Describe** how researchers study genetic influences on personality.
3. **Describe** how the biopsychosocial model integrates different theories of personality.

In this section, we explore how inherited biological factors influence our personalities. We conclude with a discussion of how all theories of personality ultimately interact within the *biopsychosocial model*.

Three Major Contributors to Personality: The Brain, Neurochemistry, and Genetics

Modern biological research suggests that certain brain areas may contribute to some personality traits. For instance, increased electroencephalographic (EEG) activity in the left frontal lobes of the brain is associated with sociability (or extroversion), whereas greater EEG activity in the right frontal lobes is associated with shyness and introversion (Fox & Reeb-Sutherland, 2010; Tellegen, 1985). Indeed, Canadian researchers Kenneth Rubin and Robert Coplan point out that greater activity in the right frontal lobes is evident even in children who are shy (Rubin et al., 2009). Moreover, shy adults, when presented with faces of strangers, show greater activation of the area of the brain known as the amygdala (Chapter 2) than do non-shy adults (Beaton et al., 2008).

A major issue with research on brain structures and personality, however, is the difficulty in identifying which structures are uniquely connected with particular personality traits. Neurochemistry may offer more precise information on how biology influences personality (Kagan & Fox, 2006). For example, sensation seeking (Chapter 11) has consistently been linked with levels of monoamine oxidase (MAO), an enzyme that regulates levels of neurotransmitters, such as dopamine (Lee, 2011; Zuckerman, 1994, 2004). Dopamine also seems to be correlated with novelty-seeking and extroversion (Dalley et al., 2007; Lang et al., 2007; Linnett et al., 2011; Nemoda et al., 2011).

How can neurochemistry have such effects? Studies suggest that high-sensation seekers and extroverts tend to experience less physical arousal from the same stimulus than do introverts (Lissek & Powers, 2003). Extroverts' low arousal apparently motivates them to seek out situations that will increase their arousal. Moreover, it is believed that a higher arousal threshold is genetically transmitted. In other words, some personality traits, such as sensation-seeking and extroversion, may be inherited.

Finally, psychologists have recently recognized that genetic factors also have an important influence on personality. This relatively new area, called **behavioural genetics**, attempts to determine the extent to which behavioural differences among people are the result of genetics as opposed to environment (Chapter 2).

For example, researchers often study similarities in personality between identical twins and fraternal twins. Findings from such studies generally report a relatively high correlation between identical twins on certain personality traits. Indeed, genetic factors appear to contribute about 40 to 50 percent of personality (Bouchard, 1997, 2004; Eysenck, 1967, 1990; McCrae, Costa, Martin, et al., 2004; Plomin, 1990; Weiss et al., 2008). Moreover, a genetic contribution to personality has been found across cultures, comparing samples from Canada, Germany, and Japan (Jang et al., 2006).

In addition to twin studies, researchers have compared the personalities of parents with those of their biological children and their adopted children. Studies of extroversion and neuroticism have found that parents' traits correlate moderately with those of their biological children and hardly at all with those of their adopted children (Bouchard, 1997; McCrae et al., 2000).

At the same time, researchers are careful not to overemphasize genetic influences on personality (Deckers, 2005; Funder, 2001; Sollod et al., 2009). Some researchers believe that the importance of the *nonshared environment* (aspects of the environment that differ from one individual to another, even within a family) has been overlooked (Saudino, 1997). Others fear that research on "genetic determinism"—do our genes determine who we are?—could be misused to "prove" that an ethnic or a racial group is inferior, that male dominance is natural, or that social progress is impossible. In short, they worry that an emphasis on genetic determinants of personality and behaviour might lead people to

Multiple Influences on Personality

Taylor S. Kennedy/National Geographic Stock

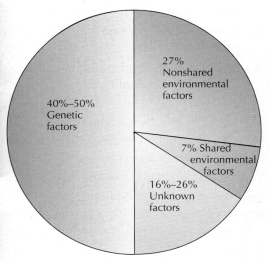

40%–50% Genetic factors

27% Nonshared environmental factors

7% Shared environmental factors

16%–26% Unknown factors

Source: Bouchard, 1997, 2004; Eysenck, 1967, 1990; Jang et al., 2006; McCrae, Costa, Martin, et al., 2004; Plomin, 1990; Weiss et al. 2008.

What gives an individual certain personality characteristics, such as shyness or conscientiousness or aggressiveness? As shown in this figure, research indicates that four major factors overlap to influence personality. These include genetic (inherited) factors; nonshared environmental factors, or how each individual's genetic factors react and adjust to his or her particular environment; shared environmental factors, including parental patterns and shared family experiences; and unknown factors (which may include error, problems with testing, or unidentified factors).

For example, Hans Eysenck (1990) proposed that certain traits (like introversion and extroversion) may reflect inherited patterns of cortical arousal, as well as social learning, cognitive processes, and the environment. Can you see how someone with an introverted personality (and therefore a higher level of cortical arousal) might try to avoid excessive stimulation by seeking friends and jobs with low stimulation levels? Eysenck's view exemplifies how trait, biological, and social-cognitive theories can be combined to provide better insight into personality—the *biopsychosocial model*.

Think Critically

1. Can you identify one key inherited influence and one major environmental influence on your personality?
2. What kinds of jobs would an individual with an extroverted personality be most likely to choose?

see themselves as merely "victims" of their genes. Clearly, studying the role of genetics on personality has produced exciting and controversial results. However, more research is necessary before a cohesive biological theory of personality can be constructed.

The Biopsychosocial Model: Pulling the Perspectives Together

No one personality theory explains everything we need to know about personality or the rich diversity seen across our species. Each theory offers different insights into how a person develops the distinctive set of characteristics we call "personality." This is why instead of adhering to any one theory, many psychologists favour the biopsychosocial approach, or the idea that several factors—biological, psychological, and social—overlap in their contributions to personality (Mischel et al., 2008).

CONCEPT CHECK STOP

1. **What** evidence suggests that particular brain areas contribute to some personality traits?
2. **Why** is the biopsychosocial model important to research on personality?
3. **How** can traits like sensation seeking and extroversion be related to neurochemistry?

Personality Assessment

LEARNING OBJECTIVES

1. **Identify** the major methods that psychologists use to assess personality, and explore the benefits and limitations of each.

2. **Summarize** the major features of objective personality tests.

3. **Explain** why psychologists use projective tests to assess personality.

Numerous methods have been used over the decades to assess personality. Modern personality assessments are used by clinical and counselling psychologists, psychiatrists, and others to diagnose psychotherapy patients and to assess their progress in therapy. Personality assessment is also used for educational and vocational counselling and to aid businesses in making hiring decisions. Personality assessments can be grouped into a few broad categories: interviews, observations, objective personality tests, and projective personality tests. An older and no longer used method of assessing personality is described in **Figure 12.15**.

Interviews and Observation

We all use informal "interviews" to get to know other people. When first meeting someone, we often ask about his or her job, academic interests, family, hobbies, and so on. Psychologists also use interviews. Unstructured interviews are often used for job and college or university selection, as well as for diagnosing psychological problems. In an unstructured format, interviewers get impressions and pursue hunches or let the interviewee expand on information that promises to disclose unique personality characteristics. In contrast, when using structured interviews, the interviewer asks specific questions that allow the interviewee's responses to be evaluated more objectively (and compared with the responses of others).

In addition to using interviews, psychologists also assess personality by directly observing behaviour. The psychologist looks for examples of specific behaviours and follows a careful set of evaluation guidelines. During an interview, for example, a psychologist usually takes careful note of the individual's behaviour, including activity level, attention span, impulsivity, and so on (Hunsley & Lee, 2010). In addition, an individual might be observed in a more "natural" setting. For instance, a psychologist might arrange to observe a troubled client's interactions with his or her family. Does the person become agitated by the presence of certain family members and not others? Does he or she become passive and withdrawn when asked a direct question? Through careful observation, the psychologist can gain valuable insights into the individual's personality, as well into the dynamics of his or her family (**Figure 12.16**).

Objective Personality Tests

Objective personality tests are standardized questionnaires that require written responses (usually using a multiple-choice or true-false format). These tests are considered objective because each item includes a limited number of possible responses. In many cases, they can be administered to a large number of people relatively quickly, and the tests can be evaluated in a standardized fashion. Objective tests are the most widely used method of assessing personality.

> **objective personality tests** Standardized questionnaires that require written responses, usually to multiple-choice or true-false questions.

Some objective tests measure one specific personality trait, such as sensation seeking (Chapter 11) or locus of control. However, psychologists in clinical, counselling, and industrial settings often wish to

Personality and bumps on the head? • Figure 12.15

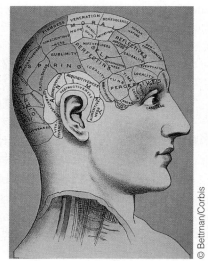

In the 1800s, if you wanted to have your personality assessed, you would go to a phrenologist, who would determine your personality by measuring bumps on your skull and by comparing the measurements with a chart that associated different areas of the skull with particular traits, such as *sublimity* (the ability to squelch natural impulses, especially sexual) and *ideality* (the ability to live by high ideals). What traits might be measured if we still believed in phrenology today?

© Bettman/Corbis

Behavioural observation • Figure 12.16

How might careful observation help a psychologist better understand a troubled individual's personality and family dynamics?

assess a range of personality traits. To do so, they generally use multitrait (or *multiphasic*) inventories.

One of the most widely studied and clinically used multitrait tests is the **Minnesota Multiphasic Personality Inventory (MMPI)**—or its revision, the MMPI-2 (Butcher, 2000, 2011; Butcher & Perry, 2008). This test consists of 567 statements that participants respond to as *true* or *false* (or *cannot say*). The following are examples of the kinds of statements found on the MMPI:

> My stomach frequently bothers me.
> I have enemies who really wish to harm me.
> I sometimes hear things that other people can't hear.
> I would like to be a mechanic.
> I have never indulged in any unusual sex practices.

Did you notice that some of these questions are about very unusual, abnormal behaviour? Although the full MMPI includes many "normal" questions, the test is designed primarily to help clinical and counselling psychologists diagnose psychological disorders. MMPI test items are grouped into 10 clinical scales, each assessing symptoms associated with a particular psychological disorder (**Table 12.2**). There are also a number of validity scales designed to reflect the extent to which respondents (1) distort their answers (for example, to fake psychological disturbances or to appear more psychologically healthy than they really are), (2) do not understand the items, and (3) are being uncooperative.

Another well-known and well-researched test that also focuses on psychological disorders is the Dimensional Assessment of Personality Pathology, developed by John Livesley and colleagues at the University of British Columbia. This measure assesses 18 personality traits, such as anxiety, suspiciousness, oppositionality, and so on (Livesley & Jackson, 2002). There are many other objective personality measures that are less focused on psychological disorders. Some good examples include the NEO Personality Inventory-Revised (Costa & McRae, 1992), which assesses the dimensions comprising the five-factor model (discussed earlier in this chapter), and the Jackson Personality Inventory-Revised (Jackson, 1997), developed by Douglas N. Jackson at the University of Western Ontario.

One personality test with which you may be familiar is the Myers-Briggs Type Indicator (MBTI). This measure assesses four dimensions derived from Carl Jung's theory of personality: extroversion-introversion

Subscales of the MMPI-2 Table 12.2

Clinical Scales	Typical Interpretations of High Scores	Validity Scales	Typical Interpretations of High Scores
1. Hypochondriasis	Numerous physical complaints	1. L (lie)	Denies common problems, projects a "saintly" or false picture
2. Depression	Seriously depressed and pessimistic	2. F (confusion)	Answers are contradictory
3. Hysteria	Suggestible, immature, self-centred, demanding	3. K (defensiveness)	Minimizes social and emotional complaints
4. Psychopathic deviate	Rebellious, nonconformist	4. ? (cannot say)	Many items left unanswered
5. Masculinity-femininity	Interests like those of other sex		
6. Paranoia	Suspicious and resentful of others		
7. Psychasthenia	Fearful, agitated, brooding		
8. Schizophrenia	Withdrawn, reclusive, bizarre thinking		
9. Hypomania	Distractible, impulsive, dramatic		
10. Social introversion	Shy, introverted, self-effacing		

(EI), sensing-intuition (SI), thinking-feeling (TF), and judging-perceiving (JP). The MBTI has gained huge popularity among the general public and has been used in assessments as varied as career counselling, the hiring of executives, and even assigning roommates in college residences (Flett, 2007). Despite its huge popularity, the MBTI has also received considerable criticism. As Gordon Flett (2007) of York University in Toronto points out, serious questions have been raised about its test-retest reliability (i.e., whether an individual will obtain the same pattern of scores when taking the test a second time) and its validity for psychological assessments (see also Pittenger, 2005).

Projective Personality Tests

Unlike objective tests, **projective tests** use ambiguous, unstructured stimuli, such as drawings or inkblots, that can be perceived in many ways. As the name implies, projective tests are thought to allow the individual to project his or her own unconscious conflicts,

> **projective tests**
> Psychological tests that use ambiguous stimuli, such as inkblots or drawings, onto which the test taker is believed to project his or her unconscious thoughts and conflicts.

psychological defences, motives, and personality traits onto the test stimuli (Lilienfeld et al., 2010). Because respondents may be unable (or unwilling) to express their true feelings if asked directly, the ambiguous stimuli are said to provide an indirect "psychological X-ray" of the respondents' important unconscious processes (Hogan, 2006). Two of the most widely used projective tests are the **Rorschach Inkblot Test** and the **Thematic Apperception Test (TAT)** (**Figure 12.17**). The Rorschach test is one of the most popularly known tests in psychology (although the actual stimuli have remained confidential for decades). The test has found its way into television shows and films, where scenes of psychologists interacting with their clients frequently involve an assessment with a Rorschach-like test. Indeed, the test even took on the role of a film character in the 2009 film *Watchmen* (based on the DC comic book series), which featured a character named Rorschach who wears a mask that consists of an inkblot that constantly changes shape (Lilienfeld et al., 2010).

Visualizing

✓ THE PLANNER

Projective tests • Figure 12.17

Responses to projective tests reportedly reflect unconscious parts of the personality that "project" onto the stimuli.

For an interesting discussion on this topic, scan to download the author's podcast.

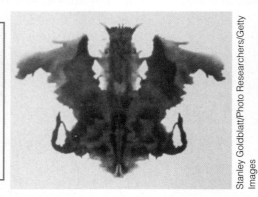

Stanley Goldblatt/Photo Researchers/Getty Images

a. The Rorschach Inkblot Test was introduced in 1921 by Swiss psychiatrist Hermann Rorschach. With this technique, individuals are shown 10 inkblots similar to this example, one at a time. They are asked to report what figures or objects they see in each inkblot.

b. Created by personality researcher Henry Murray in 1938, the Thematic Apperception Test (TAT) consists of a series of ambiguous black-and-white pictures, similar to this drawing, that are shown to the test taker, who is asked to create a story related to each. Can you think of two different stories that someone might create for this picture? How might a psychologist interpret these stories?

Are Personality Measurements Accurate?

Let's evaluate the strengths and the challenges of each of the four methods of personality assessment: interviews, observation, objective tests, and projective tests.

Interviews and observations Interviews and observations can provide valuable insights into personality, but they can be time-consuming and expensive. Furthermore, as University of Ottawa psychologists John Hunsley and Catherine Lee (2010) point out, it is important for psychologists to be sensitive to a variety of cultural variables, including ethnic, sociocultural, and spiritual factors, that could affect the interview. This is especially important in Canada, as our society becomes increasingly multicultural (Hunsley & Lee, 2010). Indeed, as Canadian psychologists Robert Hoge (Sattler & Hoge, 2006) and Alastair Younger (Younger et al., 2012) note, aspects of the interaction between the psychologist and the client—including pauses, prompts, and interruptions, as well as non-verbal communication such as nodding, eye contact, and so on—can convey different meanings to people from different cultural backgrounds, which could influence the interview process. Notwithstanding these concerns, both structured and unstructured interviews are widely used methods of assessment, particularly by clinical and counselling psychologists assessing psychological problems (see Chapters 13 and 14).

Observations can add valuable information to an assessment. Nevertheless, they often involve unnatural settings (e.g., in the psychologist's office), which can influence the validity of the information gathered (Hunsley & Lee, 2010). Observations conducted in more natural settings, such as the individual's home, may perhaps provide a more valid assessment. However, it is important to note that such observations can be time-consuming and may provide only a small picture of the individual's overall behaviour. Finally, as we saw in Chapter 1, the very presence of an observer can alter the behaviour being studied, whether in the psychologist's office or in a natural setting.

Objective tests Objective personality tests provide specific, objective information about a broad range of personality traits in a relatively short period. However, they are also the subject of several major criticisms:

1. *Deliberate deception and social desirability bias.* Some items on personality inventories are easy to "see through," so respondents may intentionally, or unintentionally, fake particular personality traits. In addition, some respondents want to look good and may answer questions in ways that they perceive to be *socially desirable* (Funder & Fast, 2010). (The validity scales of the MMPI-2 were deliberately designed to help prevent these problems.)

2. *Diagnostic difficulties.* When inventories are used for diagnosis, overlapping items sometimes make it difficult to pinpoint a diagnosis. In addition, clients with severe disorders sometimes score within the normal range, and normal clients sometimes score within the elevated range (Gregory, 2011; Weiner, 2008).

3. *Possible cultural bias.* Some critics think that the standards for "normalcy" on objective tests may fail to recognize the impact of culture. This can especially be a problem when a test is translated into another language. Although an item may be an accurate translation, this does not mean that it necessarily conveys the same meaning to an individual from another cultural background.

Projective tests Projective tests are extremely time-consuming to administer and interpret. Psychologists who make extensive use of these tests, nevertheless, argue that because there are no right or wrong answers to such tests, test takers may be less likely to deliberately fake their responses (Flett, 2007). Also, because projective tests are unstructured, respondents may be more willing to talk honestly about sensitive topics. Critics however, have questioned the *reliability* (Are the results consistent?) and *validity* (Does the test measure what it's designed to measure?) of projective tests (Garb et al., 2005; Gacono et al., 2008; Lilienfeld et al., 2010). (We discussed the topics of reliability and validity in our discussion of IQ tests in Chapter 8.)

What would the effects be if the stimuli used in projective tests became widely known? Would this influence the responses given by people taking the test? In June 2009, an emergency room physician in Moose Jaw, Saskatchewan, upset many psychologists around the world by posting all 10 Rorschach images on the Wikipedia website. Shortly thereafter, another individual posted the most common responses given for each image (CBC News, 2009b; Kyle, 2009). Critics claimed that publicizing the test and responses likely invalidates it for future use, by influencing how people will respond to the images. What do you think? Could revealing the content and common answers make the test less valid as a measure of personality?

As you can see, each of the four methods of personality assessment has its limits. Psychologists typically combine the results from various methods to create a full picture of an individual's personality.

CONCEPT CHECK STOP

1. **How** do structured and unstructured interviews differ?

2. **Why** are objective personality tests, like the MMPI, used so widely?

3. **Why** might people respond more openly on projective tests than on other kinds of personality tests?

Summary

 THE PLANNER

1 Trait Theories 326

- Psychologists define **personality** as an individual's relatively stable and enduring patterns of thoughts, feelings, and actions.

- Allport believed that the best way to understand personality was to arrange a person's unique personality **traits** into a hierarchy. Cattell and Eysenck later reduced the list of possible personality traits by using **factor analysis**.

- According to the **five-factor model (FFM)**, the five major dimensions of personality are openness, conscientiousness, extroversion, agreeableness, and neuroticism (OCEAN).

Applying Psychology: Love and the Big Five

Big Five Traits

1	**O**penness
2	**C**onscientiousness
3	**E**xtroversion
4	**A**greeableness
5	**N**euroticism

2 Psychoanalytic/Psychodynamic Theories 330

- Freud, the originator of psychodynamic theory, believed that the mind contained three levels of consciousness: the **conscious**, the **preconscious**, and the **unconscious**. He believed that most psychological disorders originate from unconscious memories and instincts. Freud also proposed that personality was composed of the **id**, the **ego**, and the **superego**. When the ego fails to satisfy both the id and the superego, anxiety slips into conscious awareness, which triggers **defence mechanisms**. Freud outlined a sequence of five **psychosexual stages**: oral, anal, phallic, latency, and genital, through which we pass as our personality develops.

Is it bad to use defence mechanisms? • Figure 12.6

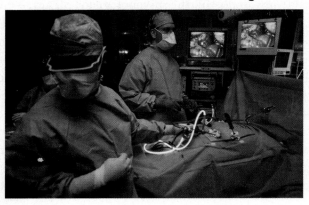

- Neo-Freudians, such as Adler, Jung, and Horney, were influential followers of Freud who later came to reject significant aspects of Freudian theory and develop their own approaches. Today, few Freudian purists remain, but Freud's impact on psychology and on Western intellectual history cannot be overstated.

3 Humanistic Theories 337

- According to Rogers, mental health and self-esteem are related to the degree of congruence between our **self-concept** and life experiences. He argued that poor mental health results when young children do not receive **unconditional positive regard** from caregivers.

- Maslow saw personality as the quest to fulfill basic physiological needs and to move toward the highest level of **self-actualization**.

What a Psychologist Sees: Congruence, Mental Health, and Self-Esteem

4 Social-Cognitive Theories 340

- Cognition is central to Bandura's concept of **self-efficacy**. According to Bandura, our feelings of self-efficacy affect the challenges we choose to accept and the effort we expend in reaching goals. His concept of **reciprocal determinism** holds that self-efficacy beliefs can also affect how others respond to us.

- Rotter's theory suggests that learning experiences create cognitive expectancies that guide behaviour and influence the environment. Rotter proposed that having an internal versus external **locus of control** affects personality and achievement.

Albert Bandura's theory of reciprocal determinism • Figure 12.13

5 Biological Theories 342

- There is evidence that certain areas of the brain may contribute to personality. However, neurochemistry seems to offer more precise data on how biology influences personality. Research in behavioural genetics indicates that genetic factors may also strongly influence personality.

- Instead of adhering to any one theory of personality, many psychologists believe in the biopsychosocial approach—the idea that several factors overlap in their contributions to personality.

Psychological Science: Multiple Influences on Personality

6 Personality Assessment 344

- In an unstructured interview format, interviewers get impressions, pursue hunches, and let the interviewee expand on information that promises to disclose personality characteristics. In structured interviews, the interviewer asks specific questions so that the interviewee's responses can be evaluated more objectively. Psychologists also assess personality by directly observing behaviour.

- **Objective personality tests** are widely used because they can be administered broadly and relatively quickly, and because they can be evaluated in a standardized fashion. To assess a range of personality traits, psychologists use multitrait inventories, such as the **MMPI**.

- **Projective tests** use ambiguous stimuli that can be perceived in many ways. Projective tests are thought to allow individuals to project their own unconscious conflicts, psychological defences, motives, and personality traits onto the test materials.

Projective tests • Figure 12.17

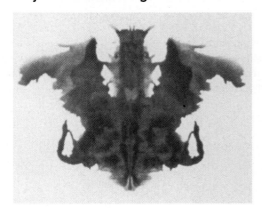

Key Terms

- analytical psychology p. 334
- archetypes p. 334
- behavioural genetics p. 342
- Big Five p. 326
- cognitive expectancies p. 340
- conscious p. 330
- defence mechanisms p. 331
- ego p. 331
- factor analysis p. 326
- five-factor model (FFM) p. 326
- id p. 331
- individual psychology p. 334
- inferiority complex p. 334
- intellectualization p. 332

- levels of consciousness p. 330
- locus of control p. 341
- Minnesota Multiphasic Personality Inventory (MMPI) p. 345
- morality principle p. 331
- neo-Freudians p. 334
- objective personality tests p. 344
- Oedipus complex p. 333
- penis envy p. 333
- personality p. 326
- pleasure principle p. 331
- preconscious p. 330
- projective tests p. 346
- psychosexual stages p. 333

- rationalization p. 331
- reality principle p. 331
- reciprocal determinism p. 340
- repression p. 332
- Rorschach Inkblot Test p. 346
- self p. 331
- self-actualization p. 339
- self-concept p. 337
- self-efficacy p. 340
- superego p. 331
- Thematic Apperception Test (TAT) p. 346
- traits p. 326
- unconditional positive regard p. 338
- unconscious p. 330

Critical and Creative Thinking Questions

1. How do you think you would score on each of the Big Five personality dimensions?

2. Think of Freud's defence mechanisms. Have you noticed any of these operating in your family members or friends?

3. If scientists have so many problems with Freud, why do you think his theories are still popular with the public? Should psychologists continue to discuss his theories (and include them in textbooks)? Why or why not?

4. In what ways is Adler's individual psychology more optimistic than Freud's theory?

5. What do you think of Rogers' notion of unconditional positive regard? How might parents discipline their children for

misbehaving yet still maintain unconditional positive regard toward them?

6. How do Bandura's and Rotter's social-cognitive theories differ from biological theories of personality?

7. Do you think that personality traits are consistent across time and situations?

8. Which method of personality assessment (interviews, behavioural observation, objective testing, or projective testing) do you think is likely to be most informative? Can you think of circumstances in which one type of assessment might be more effective than the others?

Self-Test

(Check your answers in Appendix A.)

1. A relatively stable and consistent characteristic that can be used to describe someone is known as _____.

   a. character
   b. a trait
   c. temperament
   d. personality

2. Label the list of personality traits in the five-factor model on the figure below.

Big Five Traits	Low Scorers	High Scorers
1 **O**penness	Down-to-earth Uncreative Conventional Uncurious	Imaginative Creative Original Curious
2 **C**onscientiousness	Negligent Lazy Disorganized Late	Conscientious Hard-working Well-organized Punctual
3 **E**xtroversion	Loner Quiet Passive Reserved	Joiner Talkative Active Affectionate
4 **A**greeableness	Suspicious Critical Ruthless Irritable	Trusting Lenient Soft-hearted Good-natured
5 **N**euroticism	Calm Even-tempered Comfortable Unemotional	Worried Temperamental Self-conscious Emotional

3. Label Freud's three levels of consciousness on the figure below.

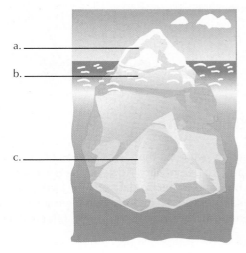

a. _____

b. _____

c. _____

4. According to Freud, what are the three mental structures that form personality?

a. unconscious, preconscious, and conscious

b. oral, anal, and phallic

c. Oedipus, Rorschach, and TAT

d. id, ego, and superego

5. While shopping, Jacqueline ran out of money and slipped some CDs from the record store into her bag. According to Freud, which part of her personality would likely produce feelings of guilt for this action?

a. the preconscious   c. the ego

b. the superego   d. the id

6. Used excessively, defence mechanisms can be dangerous because they _____.

a. hide true feelings   c. distort reality

b. become ineffective   d. become fixated

7. List Freud's psychosexual stages of development in the correct sequence.

8. Ten-year-old Bianca does not experience any psychosexual conflict that needs to be resolved. Instead, she spends her time interacting with her female friends and devotes herself to school activities. In which Freudian stage is Bianca?

a. genital stage   c. oral stage

b. latency stage   d. psychosexual stage

9. Which of the following were three of the most influential neo-Freudians?

a. Eysenck, Allport, and Cattell

b. Adler, Bandura, Rogers

c. Rotter, Rogers, and Maslow

d. Adler, Jung, and Horney

10. Many of Derrick's friends comment on how he shows qualities that seem stereotypically feminine (empathy, compassion, care). Jung would refer to this aspect of Derrick's personality as _____.

a. the animus   c. self-efficacy

b. the ego   d. the anima

11. Which of the following is *not* a criticism of Freud's psychoanalytic theory?

a. Most of his concepts are difficult to test.

b. Most of his data show a lack of cross-cultural support.

c. He underemphasized the role of biological determinants.

d. Some of his views were sexist.

12. Justifying cheating on an exam by telling yourself "If I don't pass this course, my parents will be stuck paying my tuition for another whole year!" is an example of the defence mechanism of _____.

a. denial   c. sublimation

b. rationalization   d. projection

13. Unconditional positive regard is a Rogerian term for _____.

a. accepting any and all behaviour as a positive manifestation of self-actualization

b. positive behaviour toward a person without attaching any qualifications

c. non-judgemental listening

d. the inborn drive to develop all our talents and capacities

14. Which personality theorist believed in the basic goodness of individuals and their natural tendency toward self-actualization?

a. Karen Horney   c. Abraham Maslow

b. Alfred Adler   d. Hans Eysenck

15. Bandura uses the term _____ to refer to an individual's belief about whether he or she can successfully engage in behaviours related to personal goals.

a. self-actualization   c. self-efficacy

b. self-esteem   d. self-congruence

16. Extroversion, neuroticism, and psychoticism are three types of personality traits identified by_____.

a. Karen Horney   c. Julian Rotter

b. Carl Rogers   d. Hans Eysenck

17. The study of the contribution of heredity to personality differences among people is referred to as _____.

a. the biobehavioural approach

b. the genetic-environmental perspective

c. behavioural genetics

d. the biopsychosocial model

18. Which of the following appear(s) to have the largest influence (40 to 50 percent) on personality?

a. nonshared environment   c. genetics

b. shared environments   d. unknown factors

19. Which of the following is the most widely researched and clinically used objective personality test?

a. Minnesota Multiphasic Personality Inventory

b. Jackson Personality Inventory-Revised

c. Thematic Apperception Test

d. NEO Personality Inventory-Revised

20. The Rorschach Inkblot Test is an example of _____.

a. a career inventory

b. a projective personality test

c. the most reliable and valid personality test

d. a culturally biased personality test

THE PLANNER ✓

Review your Chapter Planner on the chapter opener and check off your completed work.

Psychological Disorders

Mary's troubles first began in adolescence. She began to miss curfew, was frequently truant, and her grades declined sharply. Mary later became promiscuous and prostituted herself several times to get drug money. . . . She also quickly fell in love and overly idealized new friends. But when they quickly (and inevitably) disappointed her, she would angrily cast them aside. . . . Mary's problems, coupled with a preoccupation with inflicting pain on herself (by cutting and burning) and persistent thoughts of suicide, eventually led to her admittance to a psychiatric hospital, at age 26.

(Kring et al., 2010, pp. 354–355)

As an Air Canada ticket agent in Calgary during the early 1980s, Michele Misurelli was convinced that Communist agents were plotting against her. "I believed that some of the people I worked with were Communist spies who travelled from airport to airport trying to blow things up," recalls Misurelli, 31, whose own illness has now been largely controlled by antipsychotic drugs. She adds, "You take in information from all five senses properly, but you interpret it wrong. If someone followed me down a hallway, I thought they were going to kill me." Overwhelmed by paranoia, Misurelli finally resigned from Air Canada in June 1988 to evade the colleagues she believed were trying to kill her. "I thought," she says, "that I was thinking normally."

(Davison et al., 2010, p. 351)

Both Mary and Michele have severe psychological problems. Was there something in their early backgrounds that explains their later behaviours? Is there something medically wrong with them? What about less severe forms of abnormal behaviour?

In this chapter, we discuss how psychological disorders are identified, explained, and classified, and explore six major categories of psychological disorders. We also look at gender and cultural factors related to mental disorders.

CHAPTER OUTLINE

Rudyanto Wijaya/IStockphoto

CHAPTER PLANNER ✓

- ❏ Study the picture and read the opening story.
- ❏ Scan the Learning Objectives in each section:
  p. 354 ❏   p. 359 ❏   p. 363 ❏   p. 365 ❏   p. 371 ❏
  p. 375 ❏
- ❏ Read the text and study all visuals.
  Answer any questions.

Analyze key features:

- ❏ Visualizing, p. 355
- ❏ What a Psychologist Sees, p. 356 ❏   p. 364 ❏
- ❏ Study Organizer, p. 358
- ❏ Applying Psychology, p. 367
- ❏ Process Diagram, p. 370
- ❏ Stop: Answer the Concept Checks before you go on:
  p. 359 ❏   p. 362 ❏   p. 365 ❏   p. 370 ❏   p. 374 ❏
  p. 378 ❏

End of chapter:

- ❏ Review the Summary and Key Terms.
- ❏ Answer the Critical and Creative Thinking Questions.
- ❏ Complete the Self-Test and check your answers.

Studying Psychological Disorders

LEARNING OBJECTIVES

1. Describe the four criteria for identifying abnormal behaviour.

2. Review how views of abnormal behaviour have changed through history.

3. Explain how the *DSM-IV-TR* is used to classify psychological disorders.

Identifying Abnormal Behaviour: Four Basic Standards

 s the introductory cases show, mental disorders vary in type and severity from person to person. The behaviours of both Mary and Michele are clearly abnormal. However, many cases of abnormal behaviour are not so clear-cut. Rather than being two discrete categories, "normal" and "abnormal," **abnormal behaviour** lies along a continuum. At the end points, people can show unusually healthy or extremely disturbed behaviour.

Mental health professionals generally agree on four criteria for abnormal behaviour: statistical infrequency, disability or dysfunction, personal distress, and violation of norms (**Figure 13.1**). However, as we consider these criteria, remember that no single criterion is adequate for identifying all forms of abnormal behaviour.

> **abnormal behaviour** Patterns of emotion, thought, and action that are considered pathological (diseased or disordered) for one or more of these reasons: statistical infrequency, disability or dysfunction, personal distress, or violation of norms (Davison et al., 2010).

Explaining Abnormality: From Superstition to Science

What causes abnormal behaviour? Historically, evil spirits and witchcraft have been blamed (Goodwin, 2011; Millon, 2004; Petry, 2012). Stone Age people, for example, believed that abnormal behaviour stemmed from demonic possession; the "therapy" was to bore a hole in the skull so that the evil spirit could escape. During the European Middle Ages, troubled people were sometimes treated with exorcism in an effort to drive the Devil out through prayer, fasting, noise making, beating, and drinking terrible-tasting brews. During the fifteenth century, many believed that some individuals chose to consort with the Devil. Many of these supposed witches were tortured, imprisoned for life, or executed.

As the Middle Ages ended, special mental hospitals called *asylums* began to appear in Europe. Initially designed to provide quiet retreats from the world and to protect society (Coleborne & Mackinnon, 2011; Millon, 2004), the asylums unfortunately became overcrowded, inhumane prisons.

Improvement came in 1792 when Philippe Pinel, a French physician in charge of a Parisian asylum, insisted that asylum inmates—whose behaviour he believed to be caused by underlying physical illness—be unshackled and removed from their unlighted, unheated cells. Many inmates improved so dramatically that they could be released. Pinel's **medical model** eventually gave rise to the modern medical specialty of **psychiatry**.

Unfortunately, when we label people "mentally ill," we may create new problems. One of the most outspoken critics of the medical model is psychiatrist Thomas Szasz (1960, 2000, 2004). Szasz believes that the medical model encourages people to believe that they have no responsibility for their actions. He contends that mental illness is a myth used to label individuals who are peculiar or offensive to others (Breeding, 2011; Cresswell, 2008). Furthermore, labels can become self-perpetuating—that is, the person can begin to behave according to the diagnosed disorder.

Despite these potential dangers, the medical model—and the concept of mental illness—remains a founding principle of psychiatry. In contrast, psychology offers a multifaceted approach to explaining abnormal behaviour, as described in *What a Psychologist Sees: Seven Psychological Perspectives on Abnormal Behaviour.*

> **medical model** The perspective that diseases (including mental illness) have physical causes that can be diagnosed treated, and possibly cured.
>
> **psychiatry** The branch of medicine that deals with the diagnosis, treatment, and prevention of mental disorders.

Visualizing

The four criteria and a continuum of abnormal behaviour • Figure 13.1

Rather than fixed categories, both "abnormal" and "normal" behaviours exist along a continuum, and no single criterion is adequate for identifying all forms of abnormal behaviour (Hansell & Damour, 2008).

(Rare)   (Common)

Statistical Infrequency
(e.g., believing others are plotting against you)

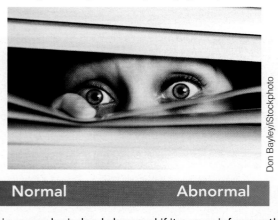

Don Bayley/iStockphoto

Normal   **Abnormal**

A behaviour may be judged abnormal if it occurs infrequently in a given population. *Statistical infrequency* alone does not determine what is normal—for example, no one would classify Albert Einstein's great intelligence or Wayne Gretzky's exceptional athletic ability as "abnormal."

(Low)   (High)

Disability or Dysfunction
(e.g., being unable to go to work because of alcohol abuse)

Cristian Lazzari/iStockphoto

Normal   **Abnormal**

People who have psychological disorders may be so disabled or *dysfunctional* that they are unable to get along with others, hold a job, eat properly, or clean themselves. Their ability to think clearly and make rational decisions also may be impaired.

(Low)   (High)

Personal Distress
(e.g., having thoughts of suicide)

Courtney Keating/iStockphoto

Normal   **Abnormal**

The *personal distress* criterion focuses on the individual's judgement of his or her level of functioning. Yet many people with psychological disorders deny they have a problem. Also, some serious psychological disorders (such as antisocial personality disorder) cause little or no emotional discomfort. The personal distress criterion by itself is not sufficient for identifying all forms of abnormal behaviour.

(Rare)   (Common)

Violation of Norms
(e.g., shouting at strangers)

Digital Vision/Photodisc/Getty Images

Normal   **Abnormal**

The fourth approach to identifying abnormal behaviour is *violation of norms*, or cultural rules that guide behaviour in particular situations. A major problem with this criterion, however, is that cultural diversity can affect what people consider a violation of norms.

What a Psychologist Sees

Seven Psychological Perspectives on Abnormal Behaviour

Each of the seven major perspectives in psychology (Chapter 1) emphasizes different factors believed to contribute to abnormal behaviour, but in practice they overlap. Consider the phenomenon of compulsive hoarding. Everyone makes an impulsive purchase occasionally, and most people are reluctant to discard some possessions that are of questionable value. But when the acquisition of and inability to discard worthless items becomes extreme, it can interfere with basic aspects of living,

such as cleaning, cooking, sleeping on a bed, and moving around one's home. This abnormal behaviour is associated with several psychological disorders, but it is most commonly found in people who have obsessive-compulsive disorder, or OCD (an anxiety disorder discussed later in this chapter). Can you imagine how each of the seven major perspectives might explain compulsive hoarding?

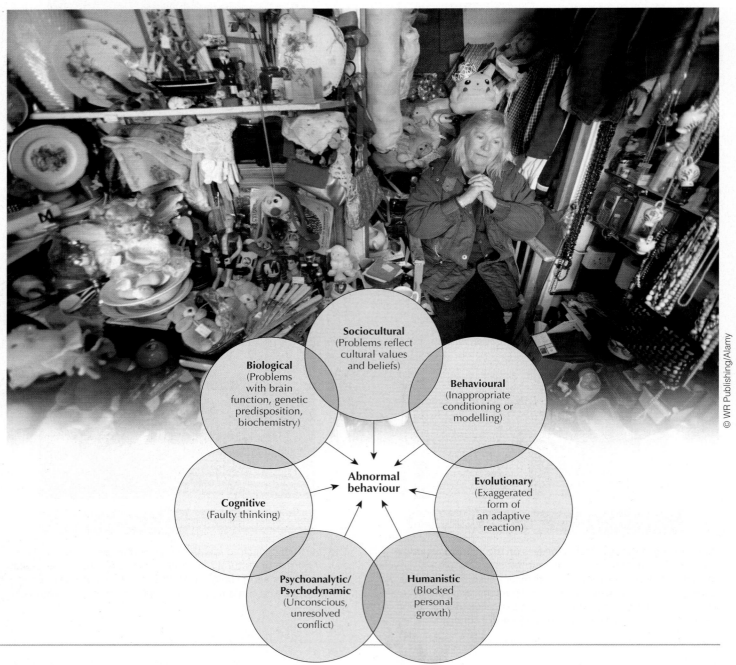

© WR Publishing/Alamy

Sociocultural (Problems reflect cultural values and beliefs)

Biological (Problems with brain function, genetic predisposition, biochemistry)

Behavioural (Inappropriate conditioning or modelling)

Cognitive (Faulty thinking)

Abnormal behaviour

Evolutionary (Exaggerated form of an adaptive reaction)

Psychoanalytic/ Psychodynamic (Unconscious, unresolved conflict)

Humanistic (Blocked personal growth)

Classifying Abnormal Behaviour: *The Diagnostic and Statistical Manual of Mental Disorders* (DSM-IV-TR)

Without a clear, reliable system for classifying the wide range of psychological disorders, scientific research on them would be almost impossible, and communication among mental health professionals would be difficult. Fortunately, mental health specialists share a uniform clas-

> **Diagnostic and Statistical Manual of Mental Disorders (DSM-IV-TR)** The classification system developed by the American Psychiatric Association used to describe abnormal behaviours; the *IV-TR* indicates that it is the text revision (*TR*) of the fourth major edition (*IV*).

sification system: the text revision of the fourth edition of the *Diagnostic and Statistical Manual of Mental Disorders* (DSM-IV-TR) (American Psychiatric Association, 2000). A more substantial revision, the *DSM-V*, is scheduled for publication in 2013.

Each revision of the *DSM* has expanded the list of disorders and changed the descriptions and categories to reflect both the latest in scientific research and the changes in the way abnormal behaviours are viewed within our social context (Blashfield et al., 2010; First & Tasman, 2004) (**Figure 13.2**). For example, consider the terms *neurosis* and *psychosis*. In previous *DSM* editions, the term *neurosis* reflected Freud's belief that all neurotic conditions arise from unconscious conflicts (Chapter 12). Now, conditions that were previously grouped under the heading *neurosis* have been formally redistributed as anxiety disorders, somatoform disorders, and dissociative disorders.

Unlike neurosis, the term *psychosis* is still listed in the *DSM-IV-TR* because it is useful for distinguishing the most severe mental disorders, such as schizophrenia and some mood disorders.

Understanding the DSM-IV-TR The *DSM-IV-TR* is organized according to five major dimensions called *axes*, which serve as guidelines for making decisions about symptoms. Axis I describes **state disorders** (the patient's current condition, or "state"), such as anxiety, substance abuse, and depression. Axis II describes **trait disorders** (enduring problems that seem to be an integral part of the self), including long-running personality disorders and intellectual disability (mental retardation).

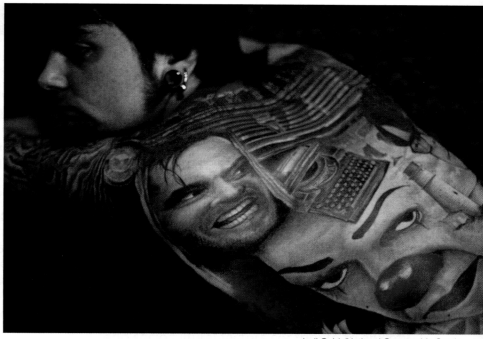

Jodi Cobb/National Geographic Stock

Is this man's behaviour abnormal? • Figure 13.2

Which criteria for abnormal behaviour do this man's piercings and tattoos meet? Which do they not? Can you think of any behaviour you exhibit that might be considered abnormal if your own cultural norms were not taken into account?

The other three axes are used to record important supplemental information. Medical conditions (Axis III) and psychosocial and environmental stressors (Axis IV) can contribute to moods and mental health problems. Finally, Axis V evaluates a person's overall level of functioning, on a scale from 1 (serious attempt at suicide) to 100 (happy and productive).

The *DSM-IV-TR* contains more than 200 diagnostic categories grouped into 17 subcategories (**Study Organizer 13.1**).

In this chapter, we focus on only the first 6 of the 17 categories shown in Study Organizer 13.1. Before we go on, note that the *DSM-IV-TR* classifies disorders, not people. Accordingly, we use such terms as *a person with schizophrenia*, rather than describing people as *schizophrenic*.

Evaluating the DSM-IV-TR The *DSM-IV-TR* has been praised for carefully and completely describing symptoms, standardizing diagnoses and treatments, facilitating communication, and serving as a valuable educational tool. Critics, however, suggest that it relies too heavily on the medical model and unfairly labels people

(Post-traumatic stress disorder [PTSD], another major anxiety disorder, was discussed in Chapter 3.) Although we discuss these disorders separately, people often have more than one anxiety disorder (Halgin & Whitbourne, 2008).

Generalized anxiety disorder

Generalized anxiety disorder affects twice as many women as it does men (Horwath & Gould, 2011). It is characterized by chronic, uncontrollable, and excessive fear and worry that lasts at least six months and that is not focused on any particular object or situation. As the name implies, the anxiety is *generalized* and *non-specific* or *free-floating*. Because of persistent muscle tension and autonomic fear reactions, people with this disorder may develop headaches, heart palpitations, dizziness, and insomnia, making it even harder to cope with normal daily activities.

Panic disorder

Sudden, but brief, attacks of intense apprehension that cause trembling, dizziness, and difficulty breathing are symptoms of **panic disorder**. Panic attacks generally happen after frightening experiences or prolonged stress (and sometimes even after exercise). Panic disorder is diagnosed when several apparently spontaneous panic attacks lead to a persistent concern about future attacks. A common complication of panic disorder is *agoraphobia*, which is discussed below (Cully & Stanley, 2008; Horwath & Gould, 2011).

Phobias

Phobias involve a strong, irrational fear and avoidance of objects or situations that are usually considered harmless (fear of elevators or fear of going to the dentist, for example). Although the person recognizes that the fear is irrational, the experience is still one of overwhelming anxiety, and a full-blown panic attack may follow. The *DSM-IV-TR* divides phobic disorders into three broad categories: agoraphobia, specific phobias, and social phobias.

People with *agoraphobia* restrict their normal activities because they fear having a panic attack in crowded, enclosed, or wide-open places where they would be unable to escape easily or to receive

For an interesting discussion on this topic, scan to download the author's podcast.

help. In severe cases, people with agoraphobia may even refuse to leave the safety of their homes.

A *specific phobia* is a fear of a specific object or situation, such as needles, heights, rats, or spiders. Claustrophobia (fear of closed spaces) and acrophobia (fear of heights) are the specific phobias most often treated by therapists. People with specific phobias generally recognize that their fears are excessive and unreasonable, but they are unable to control their anxiety and will go to great lengths to avoid the feared stimulus.

People with *social phobias* are irrationally fearful of embarrassing themselves in social situations. Fear of public speaking and of eating in public are the most common social phobias. The fear of public scrutiny and potential humiliation may become so pervasive that normal life is impossible (Acarturk et al., 2008; Alden & Regambal, 2011).

Obsessive-compulsive disorder

Obsessive-compulsive disorder (OCD) involves persistent, anxiety-provoking thoughts that will not go away (obsessions) and/or irresistible urges to perform repetitive, ritualistic behaviours (compulsions), which help relieve the anxiety created by the obsession. In adults, this disorder is equally common in men and women. However, it is more prevalent among boys when the onset is in childhood (American Psychiatric Association, 2000).

Common examples of obsessions are fear of germs, of being hurt or of hurting others, and troubling religious or sexual thoughts (**Figure 13.4**). Examples of compulsions are repeatedly checking, counting, cleaning, washing the body or parts of it, or putting things in a certain order.

Imagine what it would be like to worry so obsessively about germs that you compulsively wash your hands hundreds of times a day until they are raw and bleeding. Most sufferers of OCD realize that their actions are senseless. But when they try to stop the behaviour, they experience mounting anxiety, which is relieved only by giving in to the urges.

Causes of Anxiety Disorders

Why do people develop anxiety disorders? Research emphasizes psychological, biological, and sociocultural processes (the *biopsychosocial model*).

Obsessive-compulsive disorder • Figure 13.4

Canadian comedian, game-show host, and author of the book *Don't Touch Me*, Howie Mandel has OCD and an irrational fear of germs (*mysophobia*). He will not shake hands with anyone (including contestants on the game show he used to host, *Deal or No Deal*) because of his fear of contamination.

Paul Lapid/The Canadian Press

Psychological causes of anxiety disorders

Psychological contributions to anxiety disorders are primarily in the form of faulty cognitive processes and maladaptive learning.

Faulty Cognitions. People with anxiety disorders have certain cognitive (thinking) habits that make them prone to fear. They tend to be *hypervigilant*—they constantly scan their environment for signs of danger and ignore signs of safety. They also tend to magnify ordinary threats and failures and to be hypersensitive to others' opinions of them (**Figure 13.5**).

Maladaptive Learning. According to learning theorists, anxiety disorders generally result from maladaptive classical and operant conditioning, as well as from social learning (Chapter 6) (Cully & Stanley, 2008; Mineka & Oehlberg, 2008; Swartz, 2008). During classical conditioning, for example, a stimulus that is originally neutral (e.g., a harmless spider) becomes paired with a frightening event (a sudden panic attack) so that it becomes a conditioned stimulus that elicits anxiety. The person then begins to avoid spiders as a means of reducing anxiety (the operant conditioning process of negative reinforcement).

Most people with phobias, however, cannot remember a specific situation in which their fear was learned. Moreover, such frightening experiences do not always trigger the development of phobias. In other words, conditioning may not be the only explanation.

Social learning theorists propose that some phobias are the result of modelling and imitation. Parents who are fearful and overprotective, for example, may create family environments in which anxiety is easily learned. Phobias may also be learned vicariously (indirectly). In one study, rhesus monkeys viewed videos showing another

Faulty thinking patterns • Figure 13.5

People who suffer from social phobia are excessively concerned about others' evaluations, hypersensitive to any criticism, and obsessively worried about potential mistakes. This intense self-preoccupation leads these people to perpetually believe they have failed. What changes in thinking patterns might lessen this anxiety?

Image Source/Getty Images

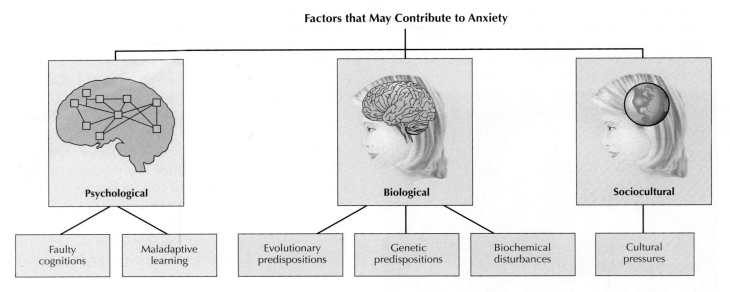

monkey apparently experiencing extreme fear of a toy snake, a toy rabbit, a toy crocodile, and flowers (Cook & Mineka, 1989). The "viewing" monkeys were later afraid of the snake and crocodile but not of the rabbit or flowers, suggesting that phobias have both learned and biological components.

Biological causes of anxiety disorders Some researchers believe that phobias reflect an evolutionary predisposition to fear things that were dangerous to our ancestors (Mineka & Oehlberg, 2008; Ohman & Mineka, 2001). Such "preparedness" (Seligman, 1971) to develop fears to certain stimuli might account for selective fears learned vicariously by rhesus monkeys in the study discussed previously.

Anxiety disorders may also have a biological basis. Some people with panic disorder seem to be genetically predisposed toward an overreaction of the autonomic nervous system, responding more readily than other people to anxiety-producing stimulation (Smoller et al., 2008). In addition, stress and arousal seem to play a role in panic attacks, and drugs, such as caffeine or nicotine, and even hyperventilation can trigger an attack, all suggesting a biochemical disturbance.

Sociocultural causes of anxiety disorders In addition to psychological and biological components, sociocultural factors can contribute to anxiety. The number of people diagnosed with anxiety disorders has risen sharply in the past 50 years, particularly in Western industrialized countries. Can you see how our increasingly fast-paced lives—along with our increased mobility, decreased job and financial security, and decreased family support—might contribute to anxiety? Unlike the dangers that humans may have faced in our evolutionary history, today's threats are less identifiable and immediate, which may lead some people to become hypervigilant and predisposed to anxiety disorders (**Figure 13.6**).

Anxiety disorders can have dramatically different forms in other cultures, further supporting the influence of sociocultural factors. For example, in a collectivist twist on anxiety, the Japanese have a type of social phobia called *taijin kyofusho* (TKS), which involves morbid dread of doing something to embarrass others. This disorder is quite different from the Western version of social phobia, which centres on a fear of criticism.

CONCEPT CHECK

1. **How** do generalized anxiety disorder and phobias differ?

2. **What** are examples of the faulty cognitions that characterize anxiety disorders?

Mood Disorders

LEARNING OBJECTIVES

1. **Explain** how major depressive disorder and bipolar disorder differ.

2. **Summarize** the research on the biological and psychological factors that contribute to mood disorders.

Understanding Mood Disorders: Major Depressive Disorder and Bipolar Disorder

 s the name implies, **mood disorders** (also known as affective disorders) are characterized by extreme disturbances in emotional states. There are two main types of mood disorders: major depressive disorder and bipolar disorder.

We all feel sad sometimes, especially following the loss of a job, end of a relationship, or death of a loved one. People suffering from **major depressive disorder**, however, may experience a lasting and continuously depressed mood without a clear trigger or precipitating event.

> **major depressive disorder** A long-lasting depressed mood that interferes with the ability to function, feel pleasure, or maintain interest in life.

People with clinical depression are so deeply sad and discouraged that they often have trouble sleeping, are likely to lose (or gain) weight, and may feel so fatigued that they cannot go to work or school or even comb their hair and brush their teeth. They may sleep both day and night, have problems concentrating, and feel so profoundly sad and guilty that they consider suicide. These feelings have no apparent cause and may be so severe that the individual loses contact with reality.

When depression is *unipolar*, the depressive episode eventually ends, and the person returns to a "normal" emotional level. People with **bipolar disorder**, however, rebound to the opposite state, known as *mania* (**Figure 13.7** and **Figure 13.8**).

> **bipolar disorder** Repeated episodes of mania (unreasonable elation and hyperactivity) and depression.

During a manic episode, the person is overly excited, extremely active, and easily distracted. The person exhibits unrealistically high self-esteem, an inflated sense of importance, or even delusions of grandeur. The person may not sleep for days at a time yet does not become fatigued. Thinking is speeded up and can change abruptly to new topics, showing "rapid flight of ideas." Speech is also rapid ("pressured speech"), and it is difficult for others to get a word in edgewise. Poor judgement is also common: a person may give away valuable possessions or go on wild spending sprees.

Bipolar disorder • Figure 13.8

Vancouver musician Matthew Good has been outspoken about his bipolar disorder. In fact, his album *Hospital Music* was inspired by his time in treatment (Davison et al., 2010). He was the keynote speaker at a 2009 Vancouver conference entitled "Workplace Mental Illness and the Family" (Canadian Mental Health Association, 2009).

Jason McLoughlin

Mood disorders • Figure 13.7

If major depressive disorders and bipolar disorders were depicted on a graph, they might look something like this.

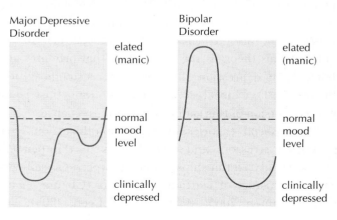

What a Psychologist Sees

A Psychologist's Struggle with Bipolar Disorder

In his early 40s, Dr. Norman Endler was at the pinnacle of his career. The eminent Canadian researcher was chair of the psychology department of York University in Toronto, was a clinical consultant to a major hospital, and was an international expert in the areas of anxiety, stress, and coping. His energy level seemed limitless, as he not only took care of his numerous professional responsibilities but also filled his days with many athletic, cultural, and family activities. He was always on the go. But then things began to change. What had once seemed easy became insurmountable. He became troubled by anxiety and self-doubt. His work and relationships began to suffer as he sank into a deep depression. Realizing the seriousness of his condition, he sought psychiatric help, where it was discovered that he had been experiencing the highs and lows of bipolar disorder. Dr. Endler wrote of his experiences, his symptoms, and the treatments he received, with the goal of de-stigmatizing mental illness and offering help to the public. His 1982 book, *Holiday of Darkness: A Psychologist's Personal Journey Out of His Depression*, chronicled his struggle and his eventual recovery, offering guidance and reassurance to those suffering from mood disorders.

York University

A manic episode may last a few days or a few months, and it generally ends abruptly. The ensuing depressive episode generally lasts three times as long as the manic episode. The lifetime risk for bipolar disorder among Canadians is low—about 2.4 percent (Public Health Agency of Canada, 2006b). However, it can be one of the most debilitating disorders (Carballo et al., 2008; Kinder et al., 2008; Klimes-Dougan et al., 2008; Public Health Agency of Canada, 2006b). Renowned Canadian psychologist Norman Endler's account of his personal struggle with bipolar depression is described in *What a Psychologist Sees: A Psychologist's Struggle with Bipolar Disorder*.

Explaining Mood Disorders: Biological and Psychosocial Factors

Biological factors appear to play a significant role in both major depression and bipolar disorder. Some research suggests that structural brain changes may contribute to these mood disorders (Almeida et al., 2003; Lyoo et al., 2004; Ravindran & Kennedy, 2007). Other research points to imbalances of the neurotransmitters serotonin, norepinephrine, and dopamine (Barton et al., 2008; Delgado, 2004; Lopez-Munoz & Alamo, 2011; Montgomery, 2008; Wiste et al., 2008). Indeed, University of Toronto researchers Lakshmi Ravindran and Sydney Kennedy (2007) note that drugs that alter the activity of these neurotransmitters also decrease the symptoms of depression. Such

drugs are referred to as *antidepressants*. (We discuss treatments for depression and other psychological disorders in Chapter 14.)

As Canadian researchers Hymie Anisman, Zul Merali, and John Stead (2008) point out, mood disorders may have an inherited component (see also Baldessarini & Hennen, 2004; Horiuchi et al., 2004; Sequeira et al., 2004). This suggestion is supported by twin studies showing that when one twin has a mood disorder, the chance that the other twin will also develop the illness is much higher for identical twins than for fraternal twins (Boardman et al., 2011; Elder & Mosack, 2011; Faraone, 2008). It is important to remember, however, that relatives generally have similar environments, as well as similar genes (Boardman et al., 2011).

Finally, the evolutionary perspective suggests that moderate depression may be a normal and healthy adaptive response to a very real loss (such as the death of a loved one). The depression helps us to step back and reassess our goals (Nesse, 2000; Nesse & Jackson, 2006; Nettle, 2011). Consistent with this theory is the observation that primates also show signs of depression when they suffer a significant loss (Suomi, 1991). Clinical, severe depression may just be an extreme version of this generally adaptive response.

Psychosocial theories of depression focus on environmental stressors and disturbances in the person's interpersonal relationships, thought processes, self-concept, and history of learned behaviours (Cheung et al., 2004; Hammen, 2005; Mathews & McLeod, 2005). The psychoanalytic explanation sees depression as anger turned inward against oneself when an important relationship or attachment is lost. The anger is assumed to result from feelings of rejection or withdrawal from rejection, especially when a loved one dies. The humanistic school says that depression results when a person demands perfection of himself or herself or when positive growth is blocked.

The **learned helplessness** theory of depression, developed by Martin Seligman (1975, 1994, 2007), maintains that when people (and other animals) are subjected to pain that they cannot escape, they develop a sense of helplessness or resignation and thereafter do not attempt to escape painful experiences. The perception of being unable to change things for the better leads to giving up. Learned helplessness may be particularly likely to trigger depression if the person attributes failure to causes that are internal ("my own weakness"), stable ("this weakness is long-standing and unchanging"), and global ("this weakness is a problem in many settings") (Alloy et al., 2011; Ball et al., 2008; Gotlieb & Abramson, 1999; Wise & Rosqvist, 2006).

Whatever the causes of depression, one of the major dangers associated with the condition is the increased risk of suicide. Because of the shame and secrecy associated with suicide, many fail to get or to give help. If you believe someone is contemplating suicide, there are some things you can do. Stay with the person if he or she is in any immediate danger. Encourage the person to talk to you rather than to withdraw. Show the person that you care, but try not to give false reassurances that "everything will be OK." Instead, you could openly ask if the person is feeling hopeless and suicidal. Do not be afraid to ask about suicide with people who are depressed or hopeless, fearing that you will just put ideas into their heads. The reality is that people who are left alone or who are told they can't be serious about suicide are more likely to attempt it.

If you do suspect someone is suicidal, it is vitally important that you do your best to help the person obtain counselling. Most cities have suicide-prevention centres with 24-hour hotlines or walk-in centres that provide emergency counselling. Hospital emergency rooms are also well equipped to deal with potentially suicidal people. In addition, it is valuable to inform the person's family doctor and to also share your suspicions with parents, friends, or others who can help in a suicidal crisis. To save a life, you may have to betray a secret when someone confides in you. (See *Applying Psychology: Finding a Therapist* in Chapter 14.)

CONCEPT CHECK

1. **What** are the key characteristics of major depressive disorder and bipolar disorder?

2. **How** might major depression be an exaggeration of an evolutionary adaptation?

Schizophrenia

LEARNING OBJECTIVES

1. **Describe** some common symptoms of schizophrenia.

2. **Compare** the traditional (four-group) system for classifying different types of schizophrenia with the (two-group) system that has recently emerged.

3. **Summarize** the biological and psychosocial factors that contribute to schizophrenia.

I magine that your daughter has just left for college and that you hear voices inside your head shouting, "You'll never see her again! You have been a bad mother! She'll die." Or what if you saw live animals in your refrigerator? These experiences have plagued Mrs. T for decades (Gershon & Rieder, 1993).

> **schizophrenia**
> A group of psychotic disorders involving major disturbances in perception, language, thought, emotion, and behaviour.

Mrs. T suffers from **schizophrenia** [skit-so-FREE-nee-uh], a disorder characterized by major disturbances in perception, language, thought, emotion, and behaviour. Schizophrenia is often so severe that it is considered a psychosis, meaning that the person is out of touch with reality. People with schizophrenia have serious problems caring for themselves, relating to others, and holding a job. In extreme cases, people with schizophrenia require institutional or custodial care.

Schizophrenia is one of the most widespread and devastating mental disorders. Approximately 1 out of every 100 people will develop schizophrenia in his or her lifetime, and approximately 30 percent of people admitted to psychiatric hospitals in Canada are diagnosed with this disorder (Public Health Agency of Canada, 2006b). Schizophrenia usually emerges between the late teens and the mid-30s. It seems to be equally prevalent in men and women, but it's generally more severe and strikes earlier in men than in women (Combs et al., 2008; Faraone, 2008; Gottesman, 1991; Lee et al., 2011; Mueser & Jeste, 2008).

Many people confuse schizophrenia with dissociative identity disorder, which is sometimes referred to as *split* or *multiple personality disorder*. Schizophrenia means "split mind," but when Eugen Bleuler coined the term in 1911, he was referring to the fragmenting of thought processes and emotions, not personalities (Neale et al., 1983). As we discuss later in this chapter, dissociative identity disorder is the rare condition of having more than one distinct personality.

Symptoms of Schizophrenia: Five Areas of Disturbance

Schizophrenia is a group of disorders characterized by a disturbance in one or more of the following areas: perception, language, thought, affect (emotions), and behaviour.

Perceptual symptoms The senses of people with schizophrenia may be either enhanced or blunted. That is, the filtering and selection processes that allow most people to concentrate on whatever they choose are impaired, and their sensory and perceptual experiences are jumbled and distorted (**Figure 13.9**). These disruptions may explain why people with schizophrenia experience **hallucinations**, which can occur in all the senses but are most commonly auditory (hearing voices and sounds).

On rare occasions, people with schizophrenia will hurt others in response to their distorted perceptions (see

hallucinations Imaginary sensory perceptions that occur without an external stimulus.

Perceptual distortions in schizophrenia • Figure 13.9

These pictures of a cat were painted by Louis Wain, an English artist who suffered from schizophrenia. Some psychologists believe that his paintings became more abstract as his schizophrenia progressed.

© Lebrecht Music and Arts Photo Library/Alamy

© Lebrecht Music and Arts Photo Library/Alamy

Applying Psychology). Unfortunately, these cases receive undue media attention and create exaggerated fears of "mental patients." In reality, a person with schizophrenia is more likely to be self-destructive and suicidal than violent toward others.

Language and thought disturbances For people with schizophrenia, words lose their usual meanings and associations, logic is impaired, and thoughts are disorganized and bizarre. When language and thought disturbances are mild, the individual jumps from topic to topic. With more severe disturbances, the person jumbles phrases and words together (into a *word salad*) or creates artificial words (*neologisms*). The most common—and frightening—thought disturbance experienced by people with schizophrenia is the lack of contact with reality (psychosis).

Delusions are also common in people with schizophrenia. We all experience exaggerated thoughts from time to time, such as thinking a friend is trying to avoid us. But the delusions of schizophrenia are extreme. For example, Michele (the former Air Canada ticket agent in the chapter opener) was completely convinced that others were plotting to kill her (a *delusion of persecution*). In *delusions of grandeur*, people believe that they are someone very important, perhaps Jesus Christ or the queen of England (**Figure 13.10**).

delusions Mistaken beliefs based on misrepresentations of reality.

Applying Psychology

✔ THE PLANNER

The Not Criminally Responsible Defence: Guilty of a Crime or Mentally Disordered?

On the night of July 30, 2008, 22-year-old Tim McLean was riding a Greyhound bus, heading home to Winnipeg after spending part of his summer working at a carnival. Seated at the rear of the bus, he fell asleep while listening to music near Portage la Prairie, Manitoba. According to reports, the passenger in the seat next to McLean suddenly pulled out a knife and, in front of horrified passengers, repeatedly stabbed McLean. With his knife, he then beheaded McLean, dismembered his body, and cannibalized some of the remains (McIntyre, 2009a).

At his trial seven months later, it was learned that the accused, Vincent Li, suffered from schizophrenia and had been hearing voices telling him that McLean was an evil presence who must be killed (Lett, 2009; McIntyre, 2009b). Li was found not criminally responsible on account of mental disorder (formerly called the insanity plea) and was committed to a psychiatric institution, where he will remain until he is no longer considered a danger.

Despite high-profile cases like this, it is important to keep in mind that the not criminally responsible defence is used very rarely and is successful only when individuals are severely disturbed. Individuals found not criminally responsible on account of mental disorder are typically held for long periods in a psychiatric institution (Davison et al., 2010).

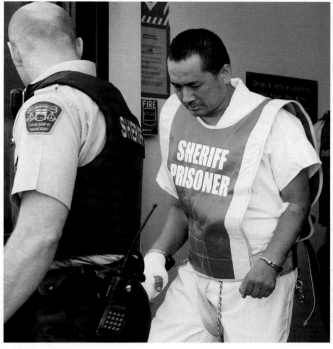

John Woods/The Canadian Press

Think Critically

1. If you had been on the jury at Vincent Li's trial, what would have been your verdict, and why?
2. Do you think the not criminally responsible defence lets guilty people off the hook?

Lefteris Pitarakis/Associated Press

The Jerusalem syndrome • Figure 13.10 _____

Every year, dozens of tourists to Jerusalem are hospitalized with symptoms of *Jerusalem syndrome*, in which they become obsessed with the significance of Jerusalem and engage in bizarre, deluded behaviour. For example, a person might come to believe that he or she is Jesus Christ, transform hotel linens into a long, white robe, and publicly recite Bible verses, a classic example of delusional thought disturbances.

In *delusions of reference*, unrelated events are given special significance, as when a person believes that a radio station is giving him or her a special message.

Affect (emotional) disturbances Changes in emotion usually occur in people with schizophrenia. In some cases, emotions are exaggerated and fluctuate rapidly. At other times, emotions become blunted. Some people with schizophrenia have *flattened affect*—almost no emotional response of any kind.

Behavioural disturbances Disturbances in behaviour may take the form of unusual actions that have special meaning. For example, one patient massaged his head repeatedly to "clear it" of unwanted thoughts. People with schizophrenia may become *cataleptic* and assume a nearly immobile stance for an extended period.

Types of Schizophrenia: Recent Methods of Classification

For many years, researchers divided schizophrenia into five subtypes: paranoid, catatonic, disorganized, undifferentiated, and residual (**Table 13.1**). Many critics point out, however, that this system does not differentiate in terms of prognosis, cause, or response to treatment, and that the undifferentiated type is merely a catchall for cases that are difficult to diagnose.

For these reasons, researchers have proposed an alternative classification system of two groups of symptoms:

1. *Positive symptoms* involve *additions* to or exaggerations of normal thought processes and behaviours, including bizarre delusions and hallucinations.
2. *Negative symptoms* involve the *loss* or absence of normal thought processes and behaviours, including impaired attention, limited or toneless speech, flattened affect (or blunted emotions), and social withdrawal.

Positive symptoms are more common when schizophrenia develops rapidly, whereas negative symptoms are more often found in slow-developing schizophrenia. Positive symptoms are associated with better adjustment before the onset and a better prognosis for recovery.

In addition to these two groups, the latest *DSM* suggests adding another dimension to reflect *disorganization of behaviour*. Symptoms in this category include rambling speech, erratic behaviour, and inappropriate affect (or feelings).

Causes of Schizophrenia: Nature and Nurture Theories

Because schizophrenia comes in many different forms, it probably has multiple biological and psychosocial bases (Walker et al., 2004). Let's look at biological contributions first.

Prenatal viral infections, birth complications, immune responses, maternal malnutrition, and advanced paternal age all may contribute to the development of schizophrenia (Ellman & Cannon, 2008; Markham & Koenig, 2011; Meyer et al., 2008; Tandon et al., 2008; Zuckerman & Weiner, 2005). However, most biological theories of schizophrenia focus on genetics, neurotransmitters, and brain abnormalities.

- *Genetics.* Although researchers are beginning to identify specific genes related to schizophrenia, most genetic studies have focused on twins and adoptions (Faraone, 2008; Riley & Kendler, 2011; Tandon et al., 2008). This research indicates that the risk for schizophrenia increases with genetic similarity; that is, people who share more genes with a person who has schizophrenia are more likely to develop the disorder (**Figure 13.11**).
- *Neurotransmitters.* Precisely how genetic inheritance produces schizophrenia is unclear. According to the **dopamine hypothesis**, overactivity of certain dopamine neurons in the brain causes schizophrenia (Lodge & Grace, 2011; Miyake et al., 2011; Seeman, 2011). This hypothesis is based on two observations. First, administering drugs

Subtypes of schizophrenia Table 13.1	
Paranoid	Major symptoms include delusions (of persecution or of self-importance) and auditory hallucinations (e.g., hearing voices).
Catatonic	Marked by motor disturbances such as immobility or wild, excited activity. May echo (repeat) the speech of others.
Disorganized	Characterized by disordered thoughts, speech that is difficult to follow, and flat or exaggerated emotions.
Undifferentiated	Displays symptoms of schizophrenia, but does not fit into any of the above subtypes.
Residual	Shows some symptoms of schizophrenia, but their intensity is low.

Genetics and schizophrenia • Figure 13.11

Your lifetime risk of developing schizophrenia depends, in part, on how closely you are genetically related to someone with schizophrenia.

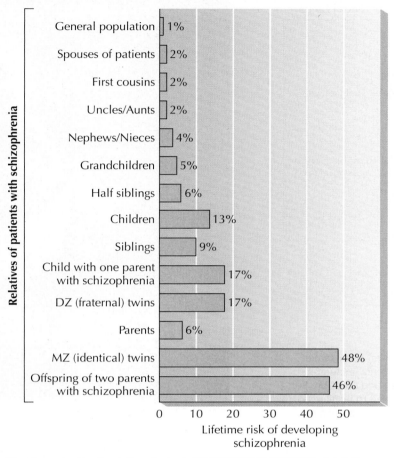

Relatives of patients with schizophrenia

- General population — 1%
- Spouses of patients — 2%
- First cousins — 2%
- Uncles/Aunts — 2%
- Nephews/Nieces — 4%
- Grandchildren — 5%
- Half siblings — 6%
- Children — 13%
- Siblings — 9%
- Child with one parent with schizophrenia — 17%
- DZ (fraternal) twins — 17%
- Parents — 6%
- MZ (identical) twins — 48%
- Offspring of two parents with schizophrenia — 46%

Lifetime risk of developing schizophrenia (0, 10, 20, 30, 40, 50)

'Genetics and schizophrenia' from the book, SCHIZOPHRENIA GENESIS by I. I. Gottesman. Copyright © 1991 by W. H. Freeman and Company. Reprinted by arrangement with Henry Holt and Company, LLC.

and schizophrenia itself, may also result from an overall loss of grey matter (neurons in the cerebral cortex) (Crespo-Facorro et al., 2007; Salgado-Pineda et al., 2011; White & Hilgetag, 2011).

Clearly, biological factors play a key role in schizophrenia. But even in identical twins—who share identical genes—if one twin has schizophrenia, the chance of the other also having schizophrenia is only 48 percent. Non-genetic factors must contribute the remaining percentage. Most psychologists believe that there are at least two possible psychosocial contributors.

According to the **diathesis-stress model** of schizophrenia, stress plays an essential role in triggering schizophrenic episodes in people with an inherited predisposition (or diathesis) toward the disease (see Figure 13.11) (Jones & Fernyhough, 2007; McGrath, 2011).

Some investigators suggest that communication disorders in family members may also be a predisposing factor for schizophrenia. Such disorders include using unintelligible speech, having fragmented communication, and frequently sending

Brain activity in schizophrenia sufferers • Figure 13.12

These positron emission tomography (PET) scans show variations in the brain activity of individuals without a disorder, people with major depressive disorder, and individuals with schizophrenia. Warmer colours (red, yellow) indicate increased activity.

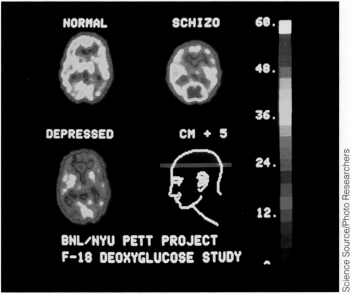

Science Source/Photo Researchers

that increase dopamine activity can produce (or worsen) some symptoms of schizophrenia, especially in people with a genetic predisposition to the disorder. Second, drugs that reduce dopamine activity in the brain reduce or eliminate some symptoms of schizophrenia.

- *Brain abnormalities.* The third major biological theory for schizophrenia involves abnormalities in brain function and structure. Researchers have found larger cerebral ventricles (fluid-filled spaces in the brain) in some people with schizophrenia (Fusar-Poli et al., 2011; Galderisi et al., 2008; Gaser et al., 2004). Also, some people with chronic schizophrenia have a lower level of activity in their frontal and temporal lobes—areas that are involved in language, attention, and memory (**Figure 13.12**). Damage in these regions might explain the thought and language disturbances that characterize schizophrenia. This lower level of brain activity,

The biopsychosocial model and schizophrenia • Figure 13.13

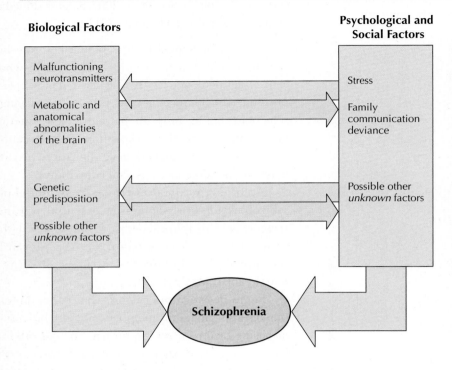

Biological Factors
- Malfunctioning neurotransmitters
- Metabolic and anatomical abnormalities of the brain
- Genetic predisposition
- Possible other *unknown* factors

Psychological and Social Factors
- Stress
- Family communication deviance
- Possible other *unknown* factors

Schizophrenia

In his portrayal of homeless musical prodigy Nathaniel Ayers, actor Jamie Foxx demonstrated several classic symptoms of schizophrenia, including disturbances in perception, language, thought, behaviour, and emotion. For Ayers, as with others with schizophrenia, no single factor led to his illness.
   Strong evidence links schizophrenia to biological, psychological, and social factors—the *biopsychosocial model*.

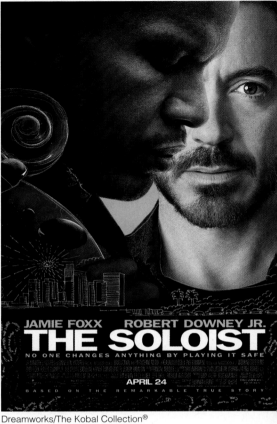

Dreamworks/The Kobal Collection®

severely contradictory messages to children. However, disturbed communication also characterizes the families of people with manic disorder and may actually be a reaction to a disturbed child rather than a cause of schizophrenia (Davison et al., 2010). Several studies have also shown greater rates of relapse and worsening of symptoms among hospitalized patients who went home to families that were critical and hostile toward them or overly involved in their lives emotionally (Hooley & Hiller, 2001; McFarlane, 2006).

How should we evaluate the different theories about the causes of schizophrenia? Critics of the dopamine hypothesis and the brain abnormalities theory argue that those theories fit only some cases of schizophrenia and that it is difficult to determine cause and effect. The issue

of cause and effect has also been hotly debated concerning the disturbed-communication theories, and the research is inconclusive. In summary, schizophrenia is most likely the result of a combination of known and unknown interacting factors (**Figure 13.13**).

CONCEPT CHECK

1. **How** do hallucinations and delusions differ?
2. **How** do the positive and negative symptoms of schizophrenia differ?
3. **What** is the diathesis-stress model of schizophrenia?

Other Disorders

LEARNING OBJECTIVES

1. **Explain** how substance abuse and substance dependence differ.

2. **Describe** the types of dissociative disorders.

3. **Identify** the major characteristics of personality disorders.

Substance-Related Disorders

The category of **substance-related disorders** is subdivided into two general groups: substance abuse and substance dependence.

When people are substance dependent, they often show a tolerance for the substance, requiring a greater dose to get the effect they're looking for. When they

> **substance-related disorders** Abuse of or dependence on a mood- or behaviour-altering drug.

stop using the substance, they may experience physical and psychological withdrawal symptoms (see Chapter 5). Their life often revolves around getting and using the substance, while other activities, such as family interactions, social ties, and employment activities, are cut back or even given up. And the person may continue to use the substance, even in the face of physical or psychological harm resulting from its use (Davison et al., 2010).

Substance abuse is less serious than substance dependence, although it too can interfere with people's lives. Substance abuse is often characterized by problems such as not taking care of one's obligations at home or at work. Moreover, people may repeatedly use the substance even in situations where it is dangerous to do so (e.g., driving while intoxicated). They may get in trouble with the law because of their use of the substance. And they may continue to use the substance, despite the social and relationship problems it causes (Davison et al., 2010) (**Figure 13.14**).

Some people can use alcohol and other drugs and not develop a problem. Unfortunately, researchers have not been able to definitively identify ahead of time those who can use drugs without developing problems and those who are likely to become abusers. Complicating diagnosis and treatment is the fact that substance-related disorders commonly coexist with other mental disorders, including anxiety disorders, mood disorders, schizophrenia, and personality disorders (Cornelius & Clark, 2008; Cosci & Fava, 2011; Thomas et al., 2008). This co-occurrence of disorders is called **comorbidity**.

Substance-related disorders affect even famous people • Figure 13.14 _____

Many of the famous, among them actress Lindsay Lohan and the late singer Amy Winehouse, have been made infamous because of their recurrent issues with substance-related disorders.

Dimitrios Kambouris/WireImage/Getty Images

What causes comorbidity? Perhaps the most influential hypothesis is **self-medication:** individuals drink or use drugs to reduce their painful and frightening symptoms (Bailey & Covell, 2011; Strahan et al., 2011). Indeed, approximately 1 in 10 Canadian adults with an anxiety disorder or a mood disorder shows evidence of substance dependence (Public Health Agency of Canada, 2006b). Regardless of the causes, however, it is critical that patients, family members, and clinicians recognize and deal with comorbidity if treatment is to be effective.

Dissociative Disorders: When the Personality Splits Apart

The most dramatic and controversial psychological disorders are **dissociative disorders**. There are several types of dissociative disorders, but all involve a splitting apart (a *dis*-association) of significant aspects of experience from memory or consciousness. Individuals dissociate from the core of their personality by failing to remember past experiences (*dissociative amnesia*) (**Figure 13.15**), by leaving home and wandering off (*dissociative fugue*), by losing their sense of reality and feeling estranged from the self (*depersonalization disorder*), or by developing completely separate personalities (*dissociative identity disorder*).

> **dissociative disorders** Amnesia, fugue, or multiple personalities resulting from avoidance of painful memories or situations.

Unlike most other psychological disorders, the primary cause of dissociative disorders appears to be environmental variables, with little or no genetic influence (Hulette et al., 2011; Sinason, 2011; Waller & Ross, 1997).

The most severe dissociative disorder is **dissociative identity disorder (DID)**—previously known as multiple personality disorder—in which two or more distinct personalities reportedly exist within the same person at different times. Each personality has unique memories, behaviours, and social relationships. Transition from one personality to another occurs suddenly and is often triggered by psychological stress. Usually, the original personality has no knowledge or awareness of the other personalities, but all the personalities may be aware of lost periods of time. The disorder is diagnosed more among women than among men. Women with DID also tend to have more identities, averaging 15 or more, compared with men, who average 8 (American Psychiatric Association, 2000).

Dissociation as an escape • Figure 13.15

The major force behind all dissociative disorders is the need to escape from anxiety. Imagine witnessing a loved one's death in a horrible car accident. Can you see how your mind might cope by blocking out all memory of the event?

DID is a controversial diagnosis. Some experts suggest that many cases are faked or result from false memories and an unconscious need to please the therapist (Kihlstrom, 2005; Lawrence, 2008; Pope et al., 2007; Stafford & Lynn, 2002). On the other side of the debate are psychologists who accept the validity of multiple personality and provide treatment guidelines (Brown, 2011; Chu, 2011; Dalenberg et al., 2007; Lipsanen et al., 2004; Spiegel & Maldonado, 1999).

Personality Disorders: Antisocial and Borderline

What would happen if the characteristics of a personality were so inflexible and maladaptive that they significantly impaired someone's ability to function? This is what happens with **personality disorders**. Several types of personality disorders are included in this category in the *DSM-IV-TR*, but here we will focus on antisocial personality disorder and borderline personality disorder.

> **personality disorders** Inflexible, maladaptive personality traits that cause significant impairment of social and occupational functioning.

Antisocial personality disorder **Antisocial personality disorder (APD)** (sometimes used interchangeably with the term *sociopathy*) is characterized by behaviour so far outside the ethical and legal standards of society that many consider it the most serious of all mental disorders. Unlike people with anxiety, mood disorders, and schizophrenia, those with this diagnosis feel little personal distress (and may not be motivated to change). Yet their maladaptive traits generally bring considerable harm and suffering to others. Although serial killers are often seen as classic examples of those with antisocial personality disorder (**Figure 13.16**), many people with APD harm people in less dramatic ways—for example, as ruthless businesspeople and crooked politicians.

The four hallmarks of antisocial personality disorder are egocentrism (preoccupation with oneself and insensitivity to the needs of others), lack of conscience, impulsive behaviour, and superficial charm (American Psychiatric Association, 2000).

Unlike most adults, individuals with antisocial personality disorder act impulsively, without giving thought to the consequences. They are usually poised when confronted with their destructive behaviour and feel contempt for anyone they are able to manipulate. They also change jobs and relationships suddenly, and they often have a history of truancy from school and of being expelled for destructive behaviour. People with antisocial personalities can be charming and persuasive, and they have remarkably good insight into the needs and weaknesses of other people.

Twin and adoption studies suggest a possible genetic predisposition to antisocial personality disorder (Bock & Goode, 1996; Rhee & Waldman, 2007). Biological contributions are also suggested by studies that have found

© HO/Reuters/Corbis

Convicted murderer Russell Williams
• Figure 13.16

In 2010, Russell Williams was convicted of the forcible confinement, sexual assault, and murder of two women in eastern Ontario and of the sexual assault of two other women. Williams had been a highly regarded colonel in the Canadian Forces and the base commander of CFB Trenton in Ontario. Many people were shocked that someone who appeared so polite, self-disciplined, and well-mannered could display such cruelty to his victims, photographing them as they lay dying (CBC News, 2010; McKeown & Rumak, 2010). Williams has not been officially diagnosed with antisocial personality disorder. However, such egocentrism and apparent lack of concern for the feelings of victims are primary characteristics of the disorder.

abnormally low autonomic activity during stress, right hemisphere abnormalities, reduced grey matter in the frontal lobes, and biochemical disturbances (Lyons-Ruth et al., 2007; Patrick & Verona, 2007; Scarpa & Raine, 2007; Ségin et al., 2007; Sundram et al., 2011).

Evidence also exists for environmental or psychological causes. Antisocial personality disorder is highly correlated with abusive parenting styles and inappropriate modelling (Barnow et al., 2007; De Oliveira-Souza et al., 2008; Grover et al., 2007; Lyons-Ruth et al., 2007). People with antisocial personality disorder often come from homes characterized by emotional deprivation, harsh and inconsistent disciplinary practices, and antisocial parental behaviour. Still other studies show a strong interaction between both heredity and environment (Dodge & Sherrill, 2007; Hudziak, 2008).

Borderline personality disorder

Borderline personality disorder (BPD) is among the most commonly diagnosed personality disorders (Ansell & Grilo, 2007; Bradley et al., 2007; Gunderson, 2011). The core features of this disorder are impulsivity and instability in mood, relationships, and self-image. Originally, the term implied that the person was on the borderline between neurosis and schizophrenia (Davison et al., 2010). The modern conceptualization no longer has this connotation, but BPD remains one of the most complex and debilitating of all the personality disorders.

Mary's story of chronic, lifelong dysfunction, described in the chapter opener, illustrates the serious problems associated with this disorder. People with borderline personality disorder experience extreme difficulties in relationships. They are subject to chronic feelings of depression, emptiness, and intense fear of abandonment, and engage in destructive, impulsive behaviours, such as sexual promiscuity, drinking, gambling, and eating sprees (Davison et al., 2010). They sometimes engage in self-mutilating behaviour (Chapman et al., 2008; Crowell et al., 2008; Links et al., 2008; Muehlenkamp et al., 2011). Suicide is also a risk (Leichsenring et al., 2011): indeed,

Montreal psychiatrist Joel Paris (2002) reports that close to 1 in 10 people with borderline personality disorder commits suicide.

People with BPD tend to see themselves and everyone else in absolute terms—perfect or worthless (Mondimore & Kelly, 2011). They constantly seek reassurance from others and may quickly erupt in anger at the slightest sign of disapproval. The disorder is also typically marked by a long history of broken friendships, divorces, and lost jobs.

People with borderline personality disorder frequently have a childhood history of neglect; emotional deprivation; and physical, sexual, or emotional abuse (Christopher et al., 2007; Distel et al., 2011; Gratz et al., 2011). Borderline personality disorder also tends to run in families, and some data suggest it is a result of impaired functioning of the brain's frontal lobes and limbic system, areas that regulate impulsive behaviours (Leichsenring et al., 2011; Tebartz van Elst et al., 2003).

Some therapists have had success treating BPD with drug therapy and behaviour therapy (Bohus et al., 2004; Markovitz, 2004), but people with BPD have intense loneliness and a chronic fear of abandonment (Davison et al., 2010). Unfortunately, given their troublesome personality traits, friends, lovers, and even family and therapists often do "abandon" them—creating a tragic self-fulfilling prophecy.

CONCEPT CHECK

1. **Why** does the presence of comorbid disorders complicate the diagnosis and treatment of substance-related disorders?

2. **Why** is the diagnosis of dissociative identity disorder considered controversial?

3. **How** do personality disorders differ from the other psychological disorders discussed in this chapter?

How Gender and Culture Affect Abnormal Behaviour

LEARNING OBJECTIVES

1. **Identify** the biological, psychological, and social factors that might explain gender differences in depression.

2. **Explain** why it is difficult to directly compare mental disorders across cultures.

3. **Explain** why recognizing the difference between culture-general and culture-bound disorders and symptoms can help prevent ethnocentrism in the diagnosis and treatment of psychological disorders.

Among the Ojibwa, Cree, and Montagnais-Naskapi First Nations in Canada, there is a disorder called *windigo*—or *wiitiko*—*psychosis*, which is characterized by delusions and cannibalistic impulses. Believing that they have been possessed by the spirit of a *windigo* (**Figure 13.17**), a cannibal

Windigo psychosis • Figure 13.17

In 1878, believing he was possessed by a *windigo* spirit, Swift Runner, a member of the Cree First Nation in central Alberta, murdered and cannibalized eight members of his family. Why do you think some disorders, such as *windigo* psychosis, are limited to a particular group or culture?

Glenbow Museum Archives

giant with a heart and entrails of ice, victims become severely depressed (Faddiman, 1997). As the malady begins, the individual typically experiences loss of appetite, diarrhea, vomiting, and insomnia, and he or she may see people turning into beavers and other edible animals.

In later stages, the victim becomes obsessed with cannibalistic thoughts and may even attack and kill loved ones to devour their flesh (Berreman, 1971), sometimes begging to be killed to end the obsession.

If you were a therapist, how would you treat this disorder? Does it fit neatly into any of the categories of psychological disorders that you have learned about? We began this chapter discussing the complexities and problems with defining, identifying, and classifying abnormal behaviour. Before we close, we need to add two additional confounding factors: sex and culture. In this section, we explore a few of the many ways in which men and women differ in how they experience abnormal behaviour. We also look at cultural variations in abnormal behaviour.

Sex Differences and Depression: Why Are Women More Prone to Depression?

In Canada, the United States, and other countries, the rate of severe depression for women is two to three times the rate for men (Nolen-Hoeksema et al., 2000; Public Health Agency of Canada, 2006b; Seedat et al., 2009).

Why is there such a disparity between the rates for men and women? Research explanations can be grouped under biological influences (hormones, biochemistry, and genetic predisposition), psychological processes (ruminative thought processes), and social factors (greater poverty, work-life conflicts, unhappy marriages, and sexual or

Depression in disguise? • Figure 13.18 _____

In our society, men are typically socialized to suppress their emotions and to show their distress by acting out (showing aggression), acting impulsively (driving recklessly and committing petty crimes), and engaging in substance abuse. How might such societal pressures lead us to underestimate male depression?

physical abuse) (Cooper et al., 2008; Jackson & Williams, 2006; Shear et al., 2007).

According to the *biopsychosocial model*, some women inherit a genetic or hormonal predisposition toward depression. This biological predisposition may combine with society's socialization processes to help reinforce behaviours—such as greater emotional expression, passivity, and dependence—that increase the chances for depression (Alloy et al., 1999; Nolen-Hoeksema et al., 2000). At the same time, males are socialized to suppress their emotions or at least not to report them. Focusing only on traditionally identified symptoms of depression (sadness, low energy, and feelings of helplessness) may cause us to overlook large numbers of depressed men, who may show their distress in other ways (e.g., aggression or substance abuse) (Fields & Cochran, 2011) (**Figure 13.18**).

Culture and Schizophrenia: Differences around the World

Peoples of different cultures experience mental disorders in a variety of ways. For example, the reported incidence of schizophrenia varies for different cultures around the world. It is unclear whether these differences result from actual differences in prevalence of the disorder or from differences in definition, diagnosis, or reporting (Berry et al., 2011; Butler et al., 2011; Papageorgiou et al., 2011).

The symptoms of schizophrenia also vary across cultures (Stompe et al., 2003), as do the particular stresses that may trigger its onset (**Figure 13.19**). In Western nations, the major symptom is auditory hallucinations (e.g., hearing voices). Interestingly, the perceived sources of these auditory hallucinations have changed with technological advances, with voices coming from the radio in the 1920s, from the television in the 1950s, from satellites in the 1960s, and from microwave ovens in the 1970s and 1980s (Brislin, 2000).

Finally, despite the advanced treatment facilities and methods in industrialized nations, the prognosis for people with schizophrenia is actually better in non-industrialized societies. This may be because the core symptoms of schizophrenia (poor rapport with others, incoherent speech, etc.) make it more difficult to survive in highly industrialized countries. In addition, in most industrialized nations, families and other support groups are less likely to feel responsible for relatives and friends with schizophrenia (Brislin, 2000; Lefley, 2000).

Avoiding Ethnocentrism

Most research on psychological disorders originates and is conducted primarily in Western cultures. Such a restricted sampling can limit our understanding of disorders in general and lead to an ethnocentric view of mental disorders.

Fortunately, cross-cultural researchers have devised ways to overcome these difficulties (Matsumoto & Juang,

David Alan Harvey/National Geographic Stock

© Benelux/Corbis

a. Some stressors are culturally specific, such as feeling possessed by evil forces or being the victim of witchcraft.

b. Other stressors are shared by many cultures, such as the death of a spouse or the unexpected loss of a job.

2008; Triandis, 2007). For example, Robert Nishimoto (1988) has found several **culture-general symptoms** that are useful in diagnosing disorders across cultures (**Table 13.2**).

In addition, Nishimoto found several **culture-bound symptoms**. For example, the Vietnamese Chinese reported "fullness in head," the Mexican respondents had "problems with [their] memory," and the Anglo-Americans reported "shortness of breath" and "headaches." Apparently, people learn to express their problems in ways that are acceptable to others in the same culture (Brislin, 1997, 2000; Butler et al., 2011; Dhikav et al., 2008; Iwata et al., 2011; Marques et al., 2011). This division between culture-general and culture-bound symptoms also helps us understand depression. Certain symptoms of depression (such as intense sadness, poor concentration, and low energy) seem to exist across all cultures (World Health Organization, 2007, 2008), but some are culture-bound. For example, feelings of guilt are found more often in North America and Europe. And in China, *somatization* (the conversion of depression into bodily complaints) occurs more frequently than it does in other parts of the world (Helms & Cook, 1999).

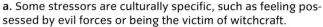

Twelve culture-general symptoms of mental health difficulties Table 13.2		
Nervous	Trouble sleeping	Low spirits
Weak all over	Personal worries	Restless
Feel apart, alone	Can't get along	Hot all over
Worry all the time	Can't do anything worthwhile	Nothing turns out right

Culture-bound disorders • Figure 13.20

Some disorders are fading as remote areas become more Westernized, whereas other disorders (such as anorexia nervosa) are spreading as other countries adopt Western values.

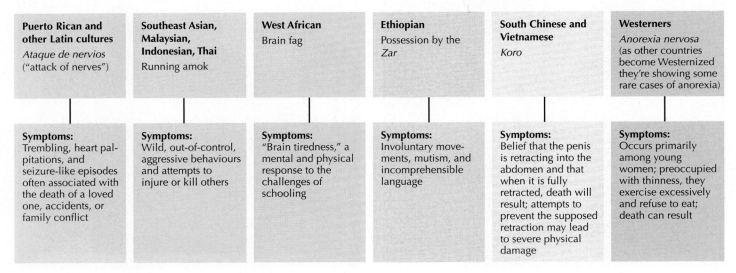

Puerto Rican and other Latin cultures	Southeast Asian, Malaysian, Indonesian, Thai	West African	Ethiopian	South Chinese and Vietnamese	Westerners
Ataque de nervios ("attack of nerves")	Running amok	Brain fag	Possession by the *Zar*	*Koro*	*Anorexia nervosa* (as other countries become Westernized they're showing some rare cases of anorexia)
Symptoms: Trembling, heart palpitations, and seizure-like episodes often associated with the death of a loved one, accidents, or family conflict	**Symptoms:** Wild, out-of-control, aggressive behaviours and attempts to injure or kill others	**Symptoms:** "Brain tiredness," a mental and physical response to the challenges of schooling	**Symptoms:** Involuntary movements, mutism, and incomprehensible language	**Symptoms:** Belief that the penis is retracting into the abdomen and that when it is fully retracted, death will result; attempts to prevent the supposed retraction may lead to severe physical damage	**Symptoms:** Occurs primarily among young women; preoccupied with thinness, they exercise excessively and refuse to eat; death can result

Sources: Barlow & Durand, 2009; Dhikav et al., 2008; Gaw, 2001; Kring et al., 2010; Laungani, 2007; Tolin et al., 2007.

Just as there are culture-bound and culture-general symptoms, researchers have found that mental disorders are themselves sometimes culturally bound (**Figure 13.20**). The earlier example of *windigo* psychosis, a disorder limited to certain Canadian First Nations groups, illustrates just such a case.

As you can see, culture has a strong effect on mental disorders. Studying the similarities and differences across cultures can lead to better diagnosis and understanding. It also helps mental health professionals who work with culturally diverse populations understand both cultural-general and cultural-bound symptoms.

CONCEPT CHECK STOP

1. **Why** might depression be frequently overlooked in men?

2. **How** does schizophrenia differ from one culture to another?

3. **What** are some examples of culture-bound disorders?

✓ THE PLANNER

Summary

1 Studying Psychological Disorders 354

- The criteria for **abnormal behaviour** include statistical infrequency, disability or dysfunction, personal distress, and violation of norms. None of these criteria alone is adequate for classifying abnormal behaviour.

- Superstitious explanations for abnormal behaviour were replaced by the **medical model**, which eventually gave rise to the modern specialty of **psychiatry**. In contrast to the medical model, psychology offers a multifaceted approach to explaining abnormal behaviour.

- The *Diagnostic and Statistical Manual of Mental Disorders*, fourth edition, text revision (*DSM-IV-TR*) is organized according to five major axes, which serve as guidelines for making decisions about symptoms.

What a Psychologist See: Seven Psychological Perspectives on Abnormal Behaviour

2 Anxiety Disorders 359

- Major **anxiety disorders** include **generalized anxiety disorder, panic disorder, phobias** (including agoraphobia, specific phobias, and social phobias), and **obsessive-compulsive disorder (OCD)**.

- Psychological (faulty cognitions and maladaptive learning), biological (evolutionary and genetic predispositions, biochemical disturbances), and sociocultural (cultural pressures toward hypervigilance) factors likely all contribute to anxiety.

Obsessive-compulsive disorder • Figure 13.4

3 Mood Disorders 363

- **Mood disorders** are characterized by extreme disturbances in emotional states. People suffering from **major depressive disorder** may experience a lasting depressed mood without a clear trigger. In contrast, people with **bipolar disorder** alternate between periods of depression and mania (hyperactivity and poor judgement).

- Biological factors play a significant role in mood disorders. Psychosocial theories of depression focus on environmental stressors and disturbances in interpersonal relationships, thought processes, self-concept, and learning history (including **learned helplessness**).

Mood disorders • Figure 13.7

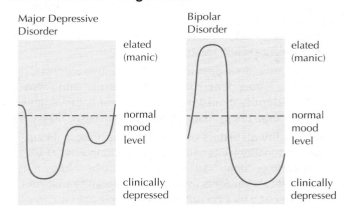

4 Schizophrenia 365

- **Schizophrenia** is a group of disorders, each characterized by a disturbance in perception (including **hallucinations**), language, thought (including **delusions**), emotions, and/or behaviour.

- In the past, researchers divided schizophrenia into multiple subtypes. More recently, researchers have proposed focusing instead on positive versus negative symptoms. *DSM-IV-TR* also suggests adding another dimension to reflect disorganization of behaviour.

- Most biological theories of schizophrenia focus on genetics, neurotransmitters, and brain abnormalities. Psychologists believe that there are also at least two possible psychosocial contributors: stress and communication disorders in families.

Brain activity in schizophrenia sufferers • Figure 13.12

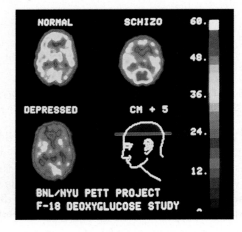

5 Other Disorders 371

- **Substance-related disorders** fall into two general groups: substance abuse and substance dependence. Substance-related disorders commonly coexist with other mental disorders (**comorbidity**), which complicates their diagnosis and treatment.

- **Dissociative disorders** include dissociative amnesia, dissociative fugue, depersonalization disorder, and **dissociative identity disorder (DID)**. Environmental variables appear to be the primary cause of dissociative disorders.

- **Personality disorders** occur when inflexible, maladaptive personality traits cause significant impairment of social and occupational functioning. The best-known personality disorder is **antisocial personality disorder**, characterized by egocentrism, lack of conscience, impul-

Other disorders • Figure 13.14

sive behaviour, and superficial charm. The most common personality disorder is **borderline personality disorder (BPD)**. Its core features are impulsivity and instability in mood, relationships, and self-image. Although some therapists have success with drug therapy and behaviour therapy, prognosis is not favourable.

6 How Gender and Culture Affect Abnormal Behaviour 375

- Men and women differ in how they experience and express abnormal behaviour. For example, in North America severe depression is much more common in women than in men. Biological, psychological, and social factors probably combine to explain this phenomenon.

- Peoples of different cultures experience mental disorders in a variety of ways. The reported incidence of schizophrenia varies within different cultures around the world, as do the disorder's symptoms, triggers, and prognosis.

- Some symptoms of psychological disorders, as well as some disorders themselves, are **culture-general**, whereas others are **culture-bound**.

Depression in disguise? • Figure 13.18

Key Terms

- abnormal behaviour p. 354
- antisocial personality disorder (APD) p. 373
- anxiety disorder p. 359
- bipolar disorder p. 363
- borderline personality disorder (BPD) p. 374
- comorbidity p. 371
- culture-bound symptoms p. 377
- culture-general symptoms p. 377
- delusions p. 366
- *Diagnostic and Statistical Manual of Mental Disorders (DSM-IV-TR)* p. 357
- diathesis-stress model p. 369
- dissociative disorders p. 372
- dissociative identity disorder (DID) p. 372
- dopamine hypothesis p. 368
- generalized anxiety disorder p. 360
- hallucinations p. 366
- learned helplessness p. 365
- major depressive disorder p. 363
- medical model p. 354
- mood disorders p. 363
- obsessive-compulsive disorder (OCD) p. 360
- panic disorder p. 360
- personality disorders p. 373
- phobias p. 360
- psychiatry p. 354
- schizophrenia p. 365
- self-medication p. 372
- state disorders p. 357
- substance-related disorders p. 371
- trait disorders p. 357

Critical and Creative Thinking Questions

1. Can you think of cases in which each of the four criteria for abnormal behaviour might *not* be suitable for classifying a person's behaviour as abnormal?

2. Do you think the not criminally responsible defence, as it is currently structured, should be abolished? Why or why not?

3. Why do you suppose that anxiety disorders are among the easiest to treat?

4. Most people have felt "depressed" from time to time. How would you distinguish between "normal" depression and a major depressive disorder?

5. Culture can have clear effects on mental disorders. How does culture influence the way you think about what is normal or abnormal?

6. What are some social and cultural reasons why women may talk about their depression or anxiety more easily than do men?

7. For many of the disorders discussed in this chapter, there is some evidence for a genetic predisposition. If someone has a family member with one of these disorders, does that mean he or she has a good chance of developing the same disorder? What else might contribute to the development of a disorder?

8. If a disorder appears to run in families, does that necessarily mean the disorder must be inherited?

Self-Test

(Check answers in Appendix A.)

1. *Abnormal behaviour* can be defined as _____.
   a. a statistically infrequent pattern of pathological emotion, thought, or action
   b. patterns of emotion, thought, and action that are considered pathological
   c. a pattern of pathological emotion, thought, or action that causes personal distress, or violates social norms
   d. all of these options

2. Which of the following is the branch of medicine that deals with the diagnosis, treatment, and prevention of mental disorders?
   a. psychological medicine   c. psychobiology
   b. psychiatry   d. psychodiagnostics

3. Label the five axes of the *Diagnostic and Statistical Manual of Mental Disorders (DSM-IV-TR)* on the figure below.

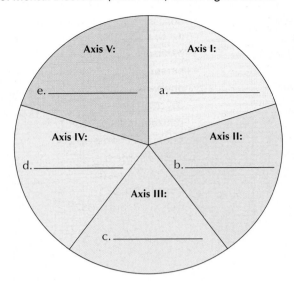

4. Anxiety disorders are _____.

a. characterized by unrealistic, irrational fear

b. the least frequent of the mental disorders

c. twice as common in men as in women

d. all of these options

5. Label the five major anxiety disorders on the figure below.

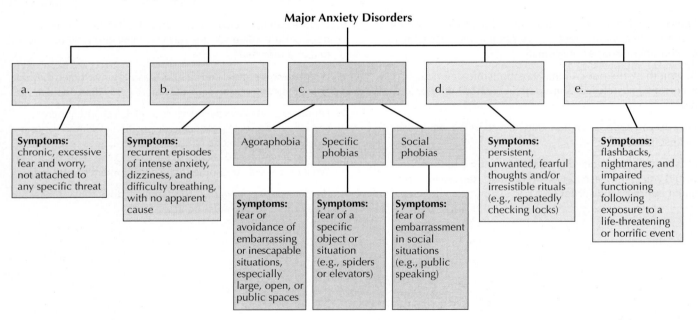

Major Anxiety Disorders

a. _____

b. _____

c. _____

d. _____

e. _____

| a. Symptoms: chronic, excessive fear and worry, not attached to any specific threat | b. Symptoms: recurrent episodes of intense anxiety, dizziness, and difficulty breathing, with no apparent cause | Agoraphobia | Specific phobias | Social phobias | d. Symptoms: persistent, unwanted, fearful thoughts and/or irresistible rituals (e.g., repeatedly checking locks) | e. Symptoms: flashbacks, nightmares, and impaired functioning following exposure to a life-threatening or horrific event |

Agoraphobia — Symptoms: fear or avoidance of embarrassing or inescapable situations, especially large, open, or public spaces

Specific phobias — Symptoms: fear of a specific object or situation (e.g., spiders or elevators)

Social phobias — Symptoms: fear of embarrassment in social situations (e.g., public speaking)

6. For the past nine months, Nura has been experiencing intense fear and worry that just won't go away. She's been having trouble sleeping and finds it hard to cope with her daily activities. What is the most likely label for her problems?

a. bipolar disorder

b. a phobic disorder

c. panic disorder

d. generalized anxiety disorder

7. What are the two main types of mood disorders?

a. major depression and bipolar disorder

b. mania and depression

c. generalized anxiety disorder and OCD

d. learned helplessness and suicide

8. Someone who experiences repeated episodes of mania, or alternates between mania and depression, has which of the following disorders?

a. disruption of circadian rhythms

b. bipolar disorder

c. manic-depressive personality disorder

d. post-traumatic stress disorder

9. When faced with a painful situation from which there is no escape, animals and people enter a state of helplessness and resignation. What is the term for this condition?

a. autonomic resignation

c. resigned helplessness

b. helpless resignation

d. learned helplessness

10. Which of the following is a psychotic disorder characterized by major disturbances in perception, language, thought, emotion, and behaviour?

a. schizophrenia

b. multiple personality disorder

c. antisocial personality disorder

d. neurotic psychosis

11. Perceptions for which there are no appropriate external stimuli are called _____, and the most common type among people suffering from schizophrenia is _____.

a. hallucinations; auditory

c. delusions; auditory

b. hallucinations; visual

d. delusions; visual

12. An individual is firmly convinced that he is Michael Jackson, even though he has never been a singer or a songwriter and is actually of Asian descent. What is this symptom called?

a. severe schizophrenia

c. a compulsion

b. a hallucination

d. a delusion

13. Label the five subtypes of schizophrenia.

14. The neurotransmitter that seems to be implicated in schizophrenia is

a. dopamine

c. norepinephrine

b. GABA

d. acetylcholine

15. A patient believes that people are secretly talking to him, sending him "special" important messages. What is the term for this symptom?

a. a delusion of grandeur

b. a delusion of persecution

c. a delusion of reference

d. a delusion of control

16. Failure to meet obligations may be indicative of alcohol or drug _____, whereas tolerance and withdrawal may be indicative of alcohol or drug _____.

a. use; abuse

c. abuse; abuse

b. abuse; dependence

d. dependence; abuse

17. Which disorder is an attempt to avoid painful memories or situations and is characterized by amnesia, fugue, or multiple personalities?

a. dissociative disorder

c. disoriented disorder

b. displacement disorder

d. identity disorder

18. Which of the following are characterized by inflexible, maladaptive personality traits that cause significant impairment of social and occupational functioning?

a. nearly all mental disorders

b. the psychotic and dissociative disorders

c. personality disorders

d. anxiety disorders

19. A patient who grew up in a severely abusive family reports serious difficulties in her relationships. She often feels "empty" and depressed, and she constantly worries about abandonment by others. What might be a likely diagnosis for these symptoms?

a. post-traumatic stress disorder

b. antisocial personality disorder

c. borderline personality disorder

d. dissociative identity disorder

20. Which of the following are examples of culture-general symptoms of mental health difficulties, useful in diagnosing disorders across cultures?

a. trouble sleeping

c. worry all the time

b. can't get along

d. all of the above

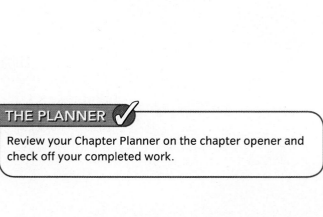

THE PLANNER ✓

Review your Chapter Planner on the chapter opener and check off your completed work.

Therapy

14

Since the beginning of the movie age, people who have mental illness and the treatment they receive have been the subject of some of Hollywood's most popular and influential films. But consider how people with mental illness are generally portrayed in the movies. They are either cruel, sociopathic criminals (Anthony Hopkins in *Silence of the Lambs*) or helpless, incompetent victims (Jack Nicholson in *One Flew Over the Cuckoo's Nest* and Natalie Portman in *Black Swan*). Although these portrayals may boost movie ticket sales, they also perpetuate harmful stereotypes (Kondo, 2008).

In this chapter, we offer a balanced, factual presentation of the latest research on psychotherapy and mental illness. As you will see, modern psychotherapy can be very effective and prevent much needless suffering, not only for people with serious psychological disorders but also for those seeking help with everyday problems in living.

In addition to psychologists, professionals involved in psychotherapy include psychiatrists, psychiatric nurses, social workers, counsellors, and clergy with training in pastoral counselling (Hunsley & Lee, 2010). Psychotherapy can take numerous forms. According to one expert (Kazdin, 1994), there may be more than 400 approaches to treatment. To organize our discussion, we have grouped treatments into three categories: insight therapies, behaviour therapies, and biomedical therapies. After exploring these approaches, we conclude with a discussion of issues that are common to all major forms of psychotherapy.

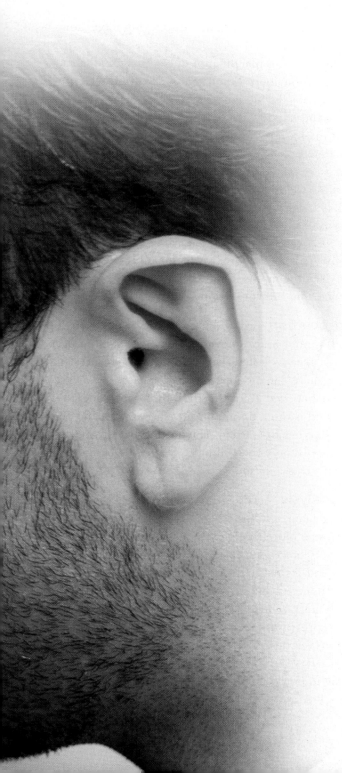

CHAPTER OUTLINE

CHAPTER PLANNER ✓

- ❑ Study the picture and read the opening story.
- ❑ Scan the Learning Objectives in each section:
  p. 386 ❑   p. 395 ❑   p. 398 ❑   p. 402 ❑
- ❑ Read the text and study all visuals. Answer any questions.

Analyze key features:

- ❑ Study Organizer, p. 387 ❑   p. 399 ❑
- ❑ Process Diagram, p. 389
- ❑ Applying Psychology, p. 393 ❑   p. 404 ❑
- ❑ Visualizing, p. 396
- ❑ What a Psychologist Sees, p. 400
- ❑ Psychological Science, p. 401
- ❑ Stop: Answer the Concept Checks before you go on:
  p. 394 ❑   p. 398 ❑   p. 402 ❑   p. 406 ❑

End of chapter:

- ❑ Review the Summary and Key Terms.
- ❑ Answer the Critical and Creative Thinking Questions.
- ❑ Complete the Self-Test and check your answers.

Endopack/iStockphoto

Insight Therapies

LEARNING OBJECTIVES

1. **Describe** the core treatment techniques in psychoanalysis and modern psychodynamic treatments.

2. **Explain** the principles underlying cognitive therapies.

3. **Summarize** the four key qualities of communication in Rogerian therapy.

4. **Identify** several benefits of group therapy.

W e begin our discussion of professional **psychotherapy** with traditional psychoanalysis and its modern counterpart: psychodynamic therapy. Then we explore *cognitive*, *humanistic*, *group*, and *family* therapies. Although these therapies differ significantly, they're often grouped together as **insight therapies** because they seek to increase clients' insight (or awareness) into their difficulties. The general goal is to help people gain greater control over and improve their thoughts, feelings, and behaviours. (See **Study Organizer 14.1**.)

> **psychotherapy**
> Techniques employed to improve psychological functioning and promote adjustment to life.

Psychoanalysis and Psychodynamic Therapies: Unlocking the Secrets of the Unconscious

In **psychoanalysis**, a person's *psyche* (or mind) is analyzed. In traditional psychoanalysis, the patient lies on a couch, with the psychoanalyst out of the patient's view. The process involves three to five 1-hour sessions per week over several years. Psychoanalysis is based on Sigmund Freud's central belief that abnormal behaviour is caused by unconscious conflicts among the three parts of the psyche: the id, ego, and super-ego (Chapter 12).

> **psychoanalysis**
> Freudian therapy designed to bring unconscious conflicts, which usually date back to early childhood experiences, into consciousness. Also refers to Freud's theoretical school of thought, which emphasizes unconscious processes.

During psychoanalysis, these conflicts are brought into consciousness. The patient comes to understand the reasons for his or her behaviour and realizes that the childhood conditions under which the conflicts developed no longer exist. Once this realization (or insight) occurs, the conflicts can be resolved and the patient can develop more adaptive behaviour patterns.

How can gaining insight into one's unconscious conflicts change behaviour? Freud explained that becoming aware of previously hidden conflicts permits a release of tension and anxiety called **catharsis**. He observed that when his patients relived a traumatic incident, the conflict seemed to lose its power to control the person's behaviour.

According to Freud, the ego has strong defence mechanisms that block unconscious thoughts from coming to awareness. Thus, to gain insight into the unconscious, the ego must be "tricked" into relaxing its guard. With that goal, psychoanalysts employ five major methods: free association, dream analysis, analyzing resistance, analyzing transference, and interpretation.

Free association According to Freud, when you let your mind wander and remove conscious censorship over thoughts—a process called **free association**—interesting and even bizarre connections seem to spring into awareness. Freud believed that the first thing to come to a patient's mind is often an important clue to what the person's ego is trying to conceal. Having the patient recline on a couch, with only the ceiling to look at, is believed to encourage free association.

Dream analysis According to Freud, defences are lowered during sleep, and forbidden desires and unconscious conflicts can be more freely expressed. Even while people are dreaming, however, the ego may recognize these feelings and conflicts as being unacceptable and frequently disguises them as images that have deeper symbolic meaning. Thus, according to Freudian theory, a therapist might interpret a dream of riding a horse or driving a car (the surface description or **manifest content** of the dream) as a desire for, or a concern about, sexual intercourse (the underlying meaning or **latent content** of the dream).

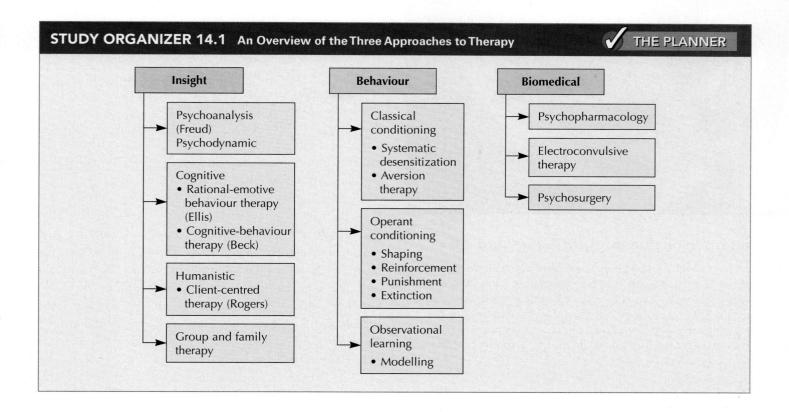

Insight	Behaviour	Biomedical
Psychoanalysis (Freud) Psychodynamic	Classical conditioning • Systematic desensitization • Aversion therapy	Psychopharmacology
Cognitive • Rational-emotive behaviour therapy (Ellis) • Cognitive-behaviour therapy (Beck)	Operant conditioning • Shaping • Reinforcement • Punishment • Extinction	Electroconvulsive therapy
Humanistic • Client-centred therapy (Rogers)	Observational learning • Modelling	Psychosurgery
Group and family therapy		

Analyzing resistance During free association or dream analysis, Freud found that patients often show **resistance**— the inability or unwillingness to discuss or reveal certain memories, thoughts, motives, or experiences. For example, patients may suddenly "forget" what they were saying or completely change the subject. It is the therapist's job to identify these cases of resistance and help patients face their problems and learn to deal with them realistically.

Analyzing transference During psychoanalysis, patients disclose intimate feelings and memories, and the relationship between the therapist and patient may become complex and emotionally charged. As a result, patients often unconsciously *transfer* (or apply) some of their unresolved emotions and attitudes from past relationships onto the therapist. The therapist uses this process of **transference** to help patients "relive" painful past relationships in a safe, therapeutic setting so that they can move on to healthier relationships.

Interpretation The core of all psychoanalytic therapy is **interpretation**. During free association, dream analysis, resistance, and transference, the analyst listens closely and tries to find patterns and hidden conflicts. At the right time, the therapist *interprets* (or explains) the underlying meanings to the client.

As you can see, most of psychoanalysis rests on the assumption that repressed memories and unconscious conflicts actually exist. But, as noted in chapters 7 and 12, this assumption is questioned by some modern scientists and has become the subject of a heated, ongoing debate. In addition to questioning the validity of repressed memories, critics also point to two other problems with psychoanalysis:

- *Limited applicability*. Critics argue that psychoanalysis seems to suit only a select group of highly motivated, articulate individuals with less severe disorders. Psychoanalysis is also time consuming and expensive, often lasting several years, with three to five sessions per week. Moreover, it seldom works well with severe mental disorders, such as schizophrenia, in which verbalization and rationality are significantly disrupted. Finally, critics suggest that spending years looking for unconscious conflicts from the past allows patients to escape from the responsibilities and problems of adult life.

- *Lack of scientific credibility*. The goals of psychoanalysis are explicitly stated—to bring unconscious conflicts to conscious awareness. But how do we know when this goal has been achieved? A serious problem with psychoanalysis is that its "insights" (and therefore its success)

© BEW Authors/Agefotostock

Interpersonal therapy (IPT) • Figure 14.1

Interpersonal therapy (IPT) is an influential, brief form of psychodynamic therapy. As the name implies, interpersonal therapy focuses almost exclusively on the client's current relationships. Its goal is to relieve immediate symptoms and to help the client learn better ways to solve future interpersonal problems. Why do you think many patients might prefer psychodynamic therapy to psychoanalysis?

cannot be proven or disproven. This shortcoming makes it impossible to test psychoanalysis as a theory, to see how well its claims hold up to scientific scrutiny.

Psychoanalysts acknowledge that it is impossible to scientifically document certain aspects of their therapy. However, there is evidence that psychoanalysis can be effective in treating some chronic mental disorders (Carey, 2008). Nevertheless, the problems associated with this form of treatment have led to the development of more streamlined forms of psychotherapy, collectively referred to as psychodynamic therapy.

In modern **psychodynamic therapy**, treatment is briefer, the patient is treated face to face (rather than reclining on a couch), and the therapist takes a more direc-

> **psychodynamic therapy**
> A modern form of psychoanalysis that emphasizes internal conflicts, motives, and unconscious forces.

tive approach (rather than waiting for unconscious memories and desires to be slowly uncovered). Also, as Canadian psychologists John Hunsley and Catherine Lee (2010) point out, contemporary psychodynamic therapists focus less on unconscious early childhood roots of problems and more on conscious processes and current problems. Such refinements have helped make psychoanalysis more available and more effective for an increasing number of people (Knekt et al., 2008; Lehto et al., 2008; Lerner, 2008) (**Figure 14.1**).

Cognitive Therapies: A Focus on Faulty Thoughts and Beliefs

Cognitive therapy assumes that faulty thought processes—beliefs that are irrational, that are overly demanding, or that fail to match reality—create problem behaviours and emotions (Davies, 2008; Dobson, 2012; Ellis & Ellis, 2011; Kellogg & Young, 2008).

> **cognitive therapy**
> Therapy that focuses on changing faulty thought processes and beliefs to treat problem behaviours.

Like psychoanalysts, cognitive therapists believe that exploring unexamined beliefs can produce insight into the reasons for disturbed behaviours. However, instead of believing that a change in behaviour occurs because of insight and catharsis, cognitive therapists believe that insight into negative self-talk (the unrealistic things a person tells himself or herself) is most important. As Canadian psychologist Keith Dobson (2012) notes, cognitive therapists help clients challenge their thoughts, change how they interpret events, and change maladaptive behaviours. This process is called **cognitive restructuring** (**Figure 14.2**).

In addition, whereas psychoanalysts focus primarily on childhood family relationships, cognitive therapists assume that a broad range of events and people—both inside and outside the family—influence beliefs. One of the best-known cognitive therapists was Albert Ellis (1913–2007), who developed an approach known as *rational-emotive therapy* (RET) (1961, 2003a, 2003b, 2004). Ellis called RET an A-B-C-D approach, referring to the four steps involved in creating and dealing with maladaptive thinking: A stands for an *activating event*, B for the person's *belief system*, C for the emotional and behavioural *consequences* that the person experiences, and D for *disputing* (or challenging) erroneous beliefs (**Figure 14.3**).

According to Ellis, when we demand certain "musts" ("I must get into graduate school") and "shoulds" ("He should love me") from ourselves and others, we create emotional distress and behavioural dysfunction (Ellis & Ellis, 2011).

Rational-emotive therapists believe that such unrealistic, unproductive self-talk generally goes unexamined unless the client is confronted directly. In therapy, Ellis would often argue with clients, cajoling and teasing them, sometimes in very blunt language. Once clients recognized their self-defeating thoughts, he would begin working with them on how to behave differently—to test out new beliefs and to learn better coping skills. Reflecting this increased attention to behavioural change, Ellis renamed his therapy **rational-emotive behaviour therapy (REBT)** (Crosby, 2003).

Cognitive restructuring • Figure 14.2

By changing the way a person interprets events, cognitive restructuring helps alter the person's behaviour.

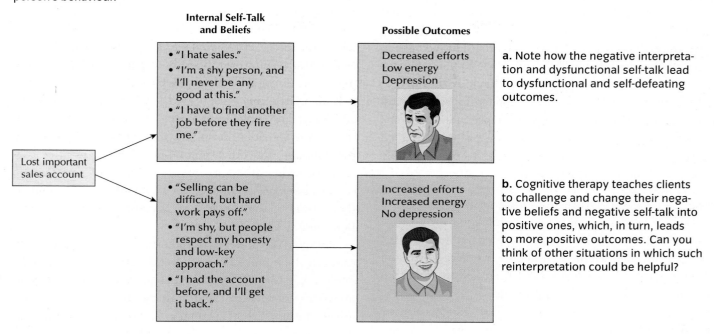

Internal Self-Talk and Beliefs

- "I hate sales."
- "I'm a shy person, and I'll never be any good at this."
- "I have to find another job before they fire me."

Lost important sales account

Possible Outcomes

Decreased efforts
Low energy
Depression

a. Note how the negative interpretation and dysfunctional self-talk lead to dysfunctional and self-defeating outcomes.

- "Selling can be difficult, but hard work pays off."
- "I'm shy, but people respect my honesty and low-key approach."
- "I had the account before, and I'll get it back."

Increased efforts
Increased energy
No depression

b. Cognitive therapy teaches clients to challenge and change their negative beliefs and negative self-talk into positive ones, which, in turn, leads to more positive outcomes. Can you think of other situations in which such reinterpretation could be helpful?

The development and treatment of irrational misconceptions • Figure 14.3

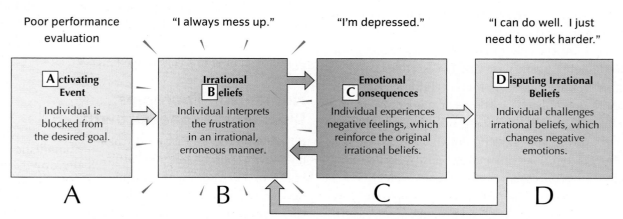

Poor performance evaluation

"I always mess up."

"I'm depressed."

"I can do well. I just need to work harder."

| **A**ctivating Event | **Irrational B**eliefs | **Emotional C**onsequences | **D**isputing Irrational Beliefs |
| Individual is blocked from the desired goal. | Individual interprets the frustration in an irrational, erroneous manner. | Individual experiences negative feelings, which reinforce the original irrational beliefs. | Individual challenges irrational beliefs, which changes negative emotions. |

A   B   C   D

According to Albert Ellis, our emotional reactions are produced by our interpretation of an event, not by the event itself. For example, if you receive a poor performance evaluation at work, you might directly attribute your bad mood to the negative feedback. Ellis would argue that the self-talk ("I always mess up") between the event and the feeling is what upset you. Furthermore, ruminating on all the other bad things in your life maintains your negative emotional state. Ellis' therapy emphasizes disputing, or challenging, these irrational beliefs, which, in turn, causes changes in maladaptive emotions—it breaks the vicious cycle.

PROCESS DIAGRAM

THE PLANNER

Another well-known cognitive therapist is Aaron Beck (1976, 2000; Clark & Beck, 2009). Like Ellis, Beck believes that psychological problems result from illogical thinking and negative self-talk. But Beck seeks to directly confront and change the behaviours associated with negative cognitions by providing clients with experiences, both inside and outside the therapy session, that will alter their self-talk in a favourable way—hence the term **cognitive-behaviour therapy**.

One of the most successful applications of Beck's theory has been in the treatment of depression. Beck has identified several maladaptive thinking patterns that he believes are associated with depression. Among the most important of these are the following:

- *Selective perception.* Depression-prone people tend to focus selectively on negative events while ignoring positive events. ("Why am I the only person alone at this party?")
- *Overgeneralization.* Depressed people overgeneralize and draw negative conclusions about their self-worth. ("I'm worthless because I failed that exam.")
- *Magnification.* Depressed people tend to exaggerate the importance of undesirable events or personal shortcomings, seeing them as catastrophic and unchangeable. ("She left me, and I'll never find someone like her again.")
- *All-or-nothing thinking.* Depressed people tend to see things in black-or-white categories—everything is either totally good or bad, right or wrong, a success or a failure. ("If I don't get straight-A grades, I'll never be able to get a good job.")

In Beck's cognitive-behaviour therapy, clients are first taught to recognize and keep track of their thoughts. Next, the therapist trains the client to develop ways to test these automatic thoughts against reality. If the client believes straight-A grades are necessary for a certain job, the therapist needs to find only one instance of this not being the case to refute the belief. Obviously, the therapist chooses the tests carefully so that they do not confirm the client's negative beliefs but lead instead to positive outcomes. This approach—identifying dysfunctional thoughts followed by active testing—helps depressed people discover that negative attitudes are largely a product of unrealistic or faulty thought processes (**Figure 14.4**).

At this point, Beck introduces the second phase of therapy—persuading the client to actively pursue pleasurable activities. Depressed individuals often lose motivation, even for experiences they used to find enjoyable. Taking an active rather than a passive role and reconnecting with enjoyable experiences help people to recover from depression.

Cognitive therapies, whether REBT or cognitive-behaviour therapy, are effective treatments for depression, anxiety disorders, chronic pain, anger management, addiction, and even some symptoms of schizophrenia and insomnia (Beck & Grant, 2008; Dienes et al., 2011; Dobson, 2012; Hofmann, 2011; Kalodner, 2011; Kellogg & Young, 2008; Thomas et al., 2011; Winterowd, Beck, & Greuner, 2003). Over the past 25 years, cognitive therapies have become quite popular in Canada. Training in cognitive therapy is a core component of clinical psychology programs in Canadian universities. Many Canadian hospitals, mental health clinics, and psychologists and other mental-health workers offer cognitive-behavioural interventions. More information on cognitive-behaviour therapy in Canada can be found at the website of the Canadian Association of Cognitive and Behavioural Therapies (2011).

Despite the popularity and efficacy of their approaches, both Beck and Ellis have been criticized for ignoring or denying the client's unconscious dynamics, overemphasizing rationality, and minimizing the importance of the client's past (Hammack, 2003). Other critics suggest that the success of cognitive therapies may be the result of their use of behavioural techniques, rather than because they change the underlying cognitive structure (Antony & Roemer, 2011; Follette & Callaghan, 2011; Miltenberger, 2011). Imagine that you sought treatment for depression and learned to construe events more positively and to curb your all-or-nothing thinking. Imagine that your therapist also helped you identify activities and behaviours that would promote greater fulfillment. If you found your depression lessening, would you attribute the improvement to your changing thought patterns or to changes in your overt behaviour?

Humanistic Therapies: Blocked Personal Growth

Humanistic therapy assumes that people with problems are suffering from a disruption of their normal growth potential and, hence, their self-concept (Chapter 12). When obstacles are removed, the individual is free to become the self-accepting, genuine person everyone is capable of being.

> **humanistic therapy** Therapy that seeks to maximize personal growth through affective restructuring (emotional readjustment).

One of the best-known humanistic therapists, Carl Rogers, developed an approach that encourages people to actualize their potential and to relate to others in

Tracking faulty thoughts • Figure 14.4

In cognitive-behaviour therapy, clients often record their thoughts in thought journals so that, together with the therapist, they can compare their thoughts with reality, detecting and correcting faulty thinking.

Name: _____Jordan Holley_____   Date: __October 11__

DYSFUNCTIONAL THOUGHT RECORD

Directions: When you notice your mood getting worse, ask yourself, **"What's going through my mind right now?"** and as soon as possible jot down the thought or mental image in the Automatic Thought Column.

DATE/TIME	SITUATION	AUTOMATIC THOUGHT(S)	EMOTION(S)	ALTERNATIVE RESPONSE	OUTCOME
	1. What actual event or stream of thoughts, or daydreams, or recollection led to the unpleasant emotion? 2. What (if any) distressing physical sensations did you have?	1. What thought(s) and/or image(s) went through your mind? 2. How much did you believe each one at the time?	1. What emotion(s) (sad, anxious, angry, etc.) did you feel at the time? 2. How intense (0–100%) was the emotion?	1. (optional) What cognitive distortion did you make (e.g., all-or-nothing thinking, mind-reading, catastrophizing)? 2. Use questions at the bottom to compose a response to the automatic thought(s). 3. How much do you believe each response?	1. How much do you now believe each automatic thought? 2. What emotion(s) do you feel now? How intense (0–100%) is the emotion? 3. What will you do? (or did you do?)
Oct. 10, 9 P.M.	My mom called last night. When I saw her number on the caller I.D., I felt my jaw clench and my heart rate go up.	She's going to nag me again to spend the whole Thanksgiving weekend there to make me feel guilty. I was 90% this was it, so I didn't pick up.	I felt angry and frustrated. Intensity = about 80%	Cognitive distortion was mind-reading or maybe all-or-nothing thinking. The evidence that the automatic thoughts were true is from my past talks with my mom. Maybe she was calling for another reason, not to make me feel guilty about Thanksgiving. The worst that could happen is that she'd make me feel guilty again... If so, I could refuse to feel that way. I could also say I didn't like the repeated pressure — it makes me guilty and sad. Maybe she'd understand and we'd break this pattern, or she'd stop nagging me so much. Now, I feel angry whenever she calls and often don't pick up the phone. If I changed my thinking, maybe I'll feel better about her calls, at least sometimes. So, I should work on not expecting the worst when she calls.	1. 50% 2. Now I feel more optimistic, anger is decreased to about 20% 3. Next time I will remind myself of the alternative response before picking up the phone.

Questions to help compose an alternative response:

1. What is the evidence that the automatic thought is true? Not true?
2. Is there an alternative explanation?
3. What's the worst that could happen? If it did happen, how could I cope? What's the best that could happen? What's the most realistic outcome?
4. What's the effect of my believing the automatic thought? What could be the effect of changing my thinking?
5. What should I do about it?
6. If _____ (friend's name) was in this situation and had this thought, what would I tell him/her?

digitalskillet/iStockphoto

Nurturing growth • Figure 14.5

Imagine how you feel when you are with someone who believes that you are a good person with unlimited potential, a person who believes that your "real self" is unique and valuable. These are the feelings that are nurtured in humanistic therapy.

genuine ways. His approach is referred to as **client-centred therapy** (also referred to as *person-centred therapy*). Using the term *client* rather than *patient* was significant to Rogers. He believed the label "patient" implied being sick or mentally ill rather than being responsible and competent. Treating people as clients demonstrates that *they* are the ones in charge of the therapy (Rogers, 1961, 1980). It also demonstrates the equality of the therapist-client relationship (**Figure 14.5**).

Client-centred therapy, like psychoanalysis and cognitive therapies, explores thoughts and feelings as a way for clients to obtain insight into the causes of their behaviours. For Rogerian therapists, however, the focus is on providing an accepting atmosphere and encouraging healthy emotional experiences. Clients are responsible for discovering their own maladaptive patterns.

Rogerian therapists create a therapeutic relationship by focusing on four important qualities of communication: *empathy*, *unconditional positive regard*, *genuineness*, and *active listening*.

1. *Empathy* is the sensitive understanding and sharing of another person's inner experience, putting yourself into another's shoes. Therapists pay attention to body language and listen for subtle cues to help them understand the emotional experiences of clients. To help clients explore their feelings, therapists use open-ended statements, such as "You found that upsetting," or "You haven't been able to decide what to do about this," rather than asking questions or offering explanations.

2. *Unconditional positive regard* is genuine caring for people because of their innate value as individuals. Because humanistic therapists believe human nature is positive and each person is unique, clients can be respected and valued without having to prove themselves worthy of the therapist's esteem. The therapist avoids judging the client and the client's actions. Humanistic therapists believe that when people receive unconditional caring from others, they become better able to value themselves in a similar way.

3. *Genuineness* (or *authenticity*) is being aware of our true inner thoughts and feelings, and sharing them honestly with others. When people are genuine, they are not artificial or defensive, nor do they play a particular role. When therapists are genuine with their clients, they believe their clients will, in turn, develop self-trust and honest self-expression.

4. *Active listening* involves reflecting, paraphrasing, and clarifying what the client says and means. To *reflect* is to hold a mirror in front of a person, enabling the person to see himself or herself. To *paraphrase* is to summarize in different words what the client is saying. To *clarify* is to check that both the speaker and the listener are on the same wavelength. By being an *active listener*, the therapist communicates that he or she is genuinely interested in what the client is saying (**Figure 14.6**). An excerpt from an actual client-centred therapy session can be found in *Applying Psychology: Client-Centred Therapy in Action*.

Supporters say that there is empirical evidence for the efficacy of client-centred therapy (Bohart & Watson, 2011; Kirschenbaum & Jourdan, 2005; Stiles et al., 2008). However, critics argue that such outcomes as self-actualization and self-awareness can be difficult to test scientifically. In addition, research on specific therapeutic techniques, such as "genuineness" and "positive regard," has had mixed results (Clark, 2007; Hodges & Biswas-Diener, 2007; Norcross & Wampold, 2011).

Group and Family Therapies: Healing Interpersonal Relationships

The therapies described so far involve sessions in which a client meets individually with a therapist. However, not all therapy involves the treatment of individual clients; group and family therapies treat several individuals simultaneously. During sessions, therapists often apply psychoanalytic, cognitive, or humanistic techniques.

Applying Psychology

Client-Centred Therapy in Action

This is an excerpt from an actual session. As you can see, humour and informality can be an important part of the therapeutic process.

THERAPIST (TH): What has it been like coming down to the emergency room today?

CLIENT (CL): Unsettling, to say the least. I feel very awkward here, sort of like I'm vulnerable. To be honest, I've had some horrible experiences with doctors. I don't like them.

TH: I see. Well, they scare the hell out of me, too (smiles, indicating the humour in his comment).

CL: (Chuckles) I thought you were a doctor.

TH: I am (pauses, smiles)—that's what's so scary.

CL: (smiles and laughs)

TH: Tell me a little more about some of your unpleasant experiences with doctors, because I want to make sure I'm not doing anything that is upsetting to you. I don't want that to happen.

CL: Well, that's very nice to hear. My last doctor didn't give a hoot about what I said, and he only spoke in huge words. (Shea, 1988, pp. 32–33)

Don Hammond/Design Pics/Agefotostock

Think Critically

1. What techniques of client-centred therapy are being used in this excerpt?
2. If you were the client in this case, would you find this exchange helpful?

Mark Bowden/iStockphoto

Active listening • Figure 14.6

Noticing a client's furrowed brow and downcast eyes while he is discussing his military experience, a clinician might respond, "It sounds as if you're angry with your situation and feeling pretty miserable right now." Can you see how this statement reflects the client's anger, paraphrases his complaint, and gives feedback to clarify the communication?

Family therapy • Figure 14.7

Many families initially come into therapy believing that one member is the cause of all their problems. However, family therapists generally find that this "identified patient" is a scapegoat for deeper disturbances. For example, instead of confronting their own problems with intimacy, a couple may focus all their attention and frustration on a delinquent child. How could changing the ways of interacting within the family system promote the health of individual family members and the family as a whole?

Group therapy In **group therapy**, people meet together to work toward therapeutic goals. Typically, a group of 8 to 10 people meets with a therapist on a regular basis to talk about problems in their lives.

> **group therapy**
> A form of therapy in which a number of people meet together to work toward therapeutic goals.

A variation on group therapy is the **self-help group**. Unlike other group therapy approaches, a professional does not guide these groups. They are simply groups of people who share a common problem (such as alcoholism, single parenthood, or breast cancer) and who meet to give support to and receive support from one another. Good examples of Canadian self-help groups include Alcoholics Anonymous, Narcotics Anonymous, and Debtors Anonymous.

Although clients don't receive the same level of individual attention in group therapies as is found in one-on-one therapies, there are advantages to group approaches (Brabender, 2011; Corey, 2012). Compared with one-on-one therapies, group therapies are less expensive and provide a broader base of social support. Moreover, group members can learn from one another's mistakes, share insights and coping strategies, and role-play social interactions together.

Therapists sometimes refer their patients to group therapy or self-help groups to supplement individual therapy. Research on self-help groups for alcoholism, obesity, and other disorders suggests that the groups can be very effective, either alone or in addition to individual psychotherapy (Brabender, 2011; McEvoy, 2007; Oei & Dingle, 2008; Silverman et al., 2008).

Family therapy Because a family or marriage is an intimate system of interdependent parts, the problem of any one individual unavoidably affects all the others, and therapy can help everyone involved (Dattilio & Nichols, 2011; Kaslow et al., 2011). The line between marital (or couples) therapy and family therapy is often blurred. Here, our discussion will focus on **family therapy**, in which the primary aim is to change maladaptive family interaction patterns (**Figure 14.7**). All members of the family attend therapy sessions, though at times the therapist may see family members individually or in twos or threes.

> **family therapy**
> Treatment to change maladaptive interaction patterns within a family.

Family therapy is also useful in treating a number of disorders and clinical problems. As we discussed in Chapter 13, patients with schizophrenia are more likely to relapse if their family members express emotions, attitudes, and behaviours that involve criticism, hostility, or emotional overinvolvement. Family therapy can help family members modify their behaviour toward the patient. Family therapy can also be a favourable setting for the treatment of adolescent eating disorders and substance abuse (Dakof, 2011; Lock et al., 2005; O'Farrell, 2011).

CONCEPT CHECK STOP

1. **How** does modern psychodynamic therapy differ from traditional psychoanalysis?
2. **What** are the four steps of Albert Ellis' RET?
3. **What** is the significance of the term *client-centred therapy*?
4. **When** might family therapy be more successful than individual psychotherapy?

Behaviour Therapies

LEARNING OBJECTIVES

1. **Identify** a key difference between these two classical conditioning techniques: systematic desensitization and aversion therapy.

2. **Explore** how operant conditioning can be used in therapy.

3. **Summarize** how modelling therapy works.

Sometimes having insight into a problem does not automatically solve it. In **behaviour therapy**, the focus is on the problem behaviour itself, rather than on any underlying causes.

> **behaviour therapy** A group of techniques based on learning principles that is used to change maladaptive behaviours.

Although the person's feelings and interpretations are not disregarded, they are just not emphasized. The therapist diagnoses the problem by listing the maladaptive behaviours that occur and the adaptive behaviours that are absent. The therapist then attempts to shift the balance of the two, drawing on the principles of classical conditioning, operant conditioning, and observational learning (Chapter 6).

Classical Conditioning Techniques

Behaviour therapists use the principles of classical conditioning to decrease maladaptive behaviours by creating new associations to replace the faulty ones. We will explore two techniques based on these principles: systematic desensitization and aversion therapy.

Systematic desensitization is a widely used behavioural approach for the treatment of phobias (Wolpe & Plaud, 1997). The theoretical premise behind this approach is that phobias are emotional responses that have been classically conditioned to certain environmental stimuli (Chapter 6). For example, the emotional response associated with a terrifying automobile accident may become conditioned to sitting in the driver's seat of a car (a previously neutral stimulus). The person then experiences terror simply upon sitting behind the wheel (Kowalski & Westen, 2011). According to the principles of classical conditioning, this fear should extinguish as the person drives without further accidents. However, because people with phobias learn to avoid the feared stimulus or situation, the conditioned emotional response never has the opportunity to be extinguished. Systematic desensitization is a therapy

For an interesting discussion on this topic, scan to download the author's podcast.

© Sidney Harris/ScienceCartoonsPlus.com

Virtual reality therapy • Figure 14.8

Rather than using mental imaging or actual physical experiences of a fearful situation, modern therapy can use the latest in computer technology—virtual reality headsets and data gloves. A Canadian researcher, Stéphane Bouchard of the Université du Québec en Outaouais, is among the leading researchers in the use of computer-generated environments to treat phobias. What kind of virtual experiences do you think a therapist might provide for a client with a fear of spiders?

© Syracuse Newspapers/D. Lassman/The Image Works

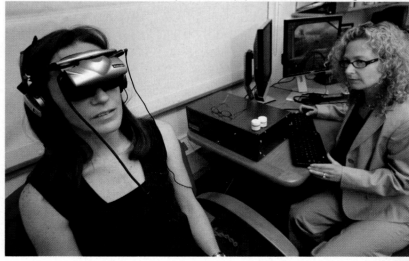

Visualizing

Systematic desensitization • Figure 14.9

To treat phobias, the client begins with relaxation training and the construction of a hierarchy, or ranked listing, of anxiety-arousing images or situations, starting first with an image that produces very little anxiety and escalating to those that arouse extreme anxiety. To extinguish a driving phobia, the patient begins with images of sitting behind the wheel of a nonmoving car and ends with driving on a busy expressway at night in the rain.

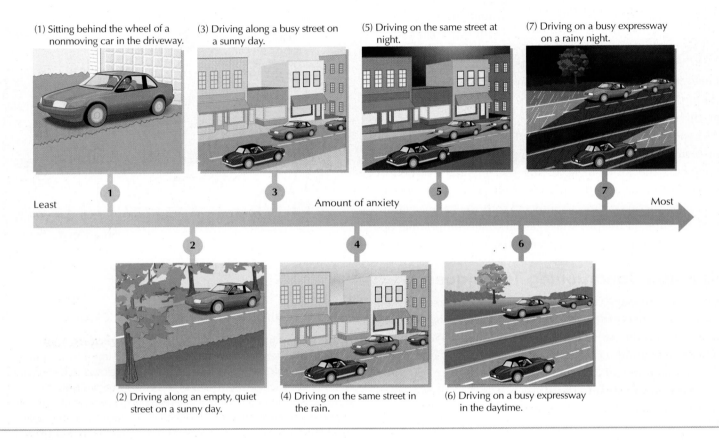

(1) Sitting behind the wheel of a nonmoving car in the driveway.

(3) Driving along a busy street on a sunny day.

(5) Driving on the same street at night.

(7) Driving on a busy expressway on a rainy night.

Least   Amount of anxiety   Most

(2) Driving along an empty, quiet street on a sunny day.

(4) Driving on the same street in the rain.

(6) Driving on a busy expressway in the daytime.

that exposes people to the fear-producing stimulus, allowing the conditioned emotional response to extinguish (Antony & Roemer, 2011). The therapy begins with relaxation training, followed by imagining or directly experiencing various versions of a feared object or situation while remaining deeply relaxed. Recently, some therapists have begun using advanced technologies to aid in the desensitization process (**Figure 14.8**).

Desensitization is a three-step process. First, the client is taught how to maintain a state of deep relaxation that is physiologically incompatible with an anxiety response. Next, the therapist and client construct a hierarchy, or ranked listing, of anxiety-arousing images (**Figure 14.9**). In the final step, the relaxed client mentally visualizes or physically experiences items in the hierarchy, starting at the bottom and working his or her way to the most anxiety-producing images at the top. If any image or situation begins to create a high degree of anxiety, the client stops momentarily and returns to a state of complete relaxation. Eventually, the fear response is extinguished.

Aversion therapy uses principles of classical conditioning to create anxiety rather than extinguish it (**Figure 14.10**). People who engage in excessive drinking, for example, build up a number of pleasurable associations. Because these pleasurable associations cannot always be prevented, aversion therapy provides negative associations to compete with the pleasurable ones (think back to the discussion of conditioned taste aversions in Chapter 6). Someone who wants to stop drinking, for example, could take a drug that causes nausea (e.g., disulfiram)

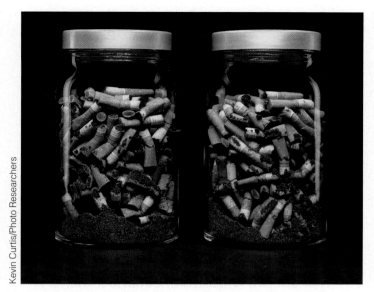

Making a nasty habit nastier • Figure 14.10

A person who wants to quit smoking could collect a jar full of (smelly) cigarette butts or smoke several cigarettes at once to create an aversion to smoking. Can you see how this aversion therapy uses classical conditioning?

whenever alcohol is consumed. When the new connection between alcohol and nausea has been classically conditioned, engaging in the once-desirable behaviour will cause an immediate negative response: Alcohol has now become a conditioned stimulus for nausea.

Aversion therapy is controversial. First, some researchers question whether it is ethical to hurt someone (even when the person has given permission). The treatment also has been criticized because it does not provide lasting relief (Seligman, 1994). One reason is that (in the case of the aversion therapy for alcoholism) people understand that the nausea is produced by the drug and do not generalize their learning to the alcohol.

Operant Conditioning Techniques

As we learned in Chapter 6, operant conditioning involves learning to associate a behaviour with its consequences. One operant conditioning technique for eventually bringing about a desired (or target) behaviour is **shaping**— providing reinforcement for successive approximations to the target behaviour. One of the most successful applications of shaping and reinforcement has been with developing language skills in children with autism. First, the child is rewarded for making any sounds, and later, for forming words and sentences.

Shaping can also help people acquire social skills and greater assertiveness (Antony & Roemer, 2011). If you are painfully shy, for example, a behaviour therapist might first ask you to role-play simply saying hello to someone you find attractive. Then you might practise behaviours that gradually lead you to suggest a date. During such role-playing, or *behaviour rehearsal*, the behaviour therapist would give you feedback and reinforcement.

Adaptive behaviours can also be taught or increased with techniques that provide immediate reinforcement in the form of tokens (Kazdin, 2008; Tarbox et al., 2006). For example, patients in an in-patient treatment facility might at first be given tokens (to be exchanged for primary rewards, such as food, treats, TV time, a private room, or outings) for merely attending group therapy sessions. Later they will be rewarded only for actually participating in the sessions. Eventually, the tokens can be discontinued when the patient receives the reinforcement of being helped by participation in the therapy sessions.

Some elementary school teachers effectively employ such reinforcement procedures, using behaviour checklists, gold stars, and other tokens as a means of encouraging positive classroom behaviours, such as student participation, neatness, cooperation, and so on.

Observational Learning Techniques

We all learn many things by observing others. Therapists use this principle in **modelling therapy**, in which clients are asked to observe and imitate appropriate models as they perform desired behaviours. For example, in a classic study, Canadian-born psychologist Albert Bandura (1969) asked clients with snake phobias to watch other (non-phobic) people handle snakes. After only two hours of exposure, more than 92 percent of the phobic observers allowed a snake to crawl over their hands, arms, and necks.

> **modelling therapy** A learning technique in which the subject watches and imitates models who demonstrate desirable behaviours.

Modelling is also part of social skills training and assertiveness training. Clients learn how to interview for a job by first watching the therapist role-play the part of the interviewee. The therapist models the appropriate language (assertively asking for a job), body posture, and so forth, and then asks the client to imitate the behaviour and play the same role. Over several sessions, the client gradually becomes desensitized to the anxiety of interviews and learns interview skills.

Evaluating Behaviour Therapies

Behaviour therapy has been effective in treating various problems, including phobias, obsessive-compulsive disorder (OCD), depression, eating disorders, autism, development disability, and delinquency (Antony & Roemer, 2011; Ekers et al., 2008; Miltenberger, 2011). Critics of behaviour therapy, however, raise important questions that fall into two major categories:

- *Generalizability*. What happens after the treatment stops? Critics argue that in the "real world," patients are not consistently reinforced, and their newly acquired behaviours may disappear. To deal with this possibility, behaviour therapists work to gradually shape clients toward rewards that are typical of life outside the clinic setting.

- *Ethics*. Critics contend that it can be unethical for one person to control another's behaviour. Behaviour therapists, however, argue that rewards and punishments already control our behaviours and that behaviour therapy actually increases a person's freedom by making these controls overt and by teaching people how to change their own behaviour.

CONCEPT CHECK 🛑 STOP

1. **What** three types of learning are used in behaviour therapy?
2. **How** can shaping be used to develop desired behaviours?
3. **What** are two criticisms of behaviour therapy?

Biomedical Therapies

LEARNING OBJECTIVES

1. **Identify** the major types of drugs used to treat psychological disorders.
2. **Explain** what happens in electroconvulsive therapy and psychosurgery.
3. **Describe** the risks associated with biomedical therapies.

Biomedical therapies are based on the premise that problem behaviours are caused, at least in part, by chemical imbalances or disordered nervous system functioning. A physician, rather than a psychologist, must prescribe biomedical therapies. Nevertheless, psychologists commonly work with patients receiving biomedical therapies and are frequently involved in research programs to evaluate the effectiveness of the therapy. In this section, we will discuss three aspects of biomedical therapies: *psychopharmacology*, *electroconvulsive therapy* (ECT), and *psychosurgery*.

> **biomedical therapy** The use of physiological interventions (drugs, electroconvulsive therapy, and psychosurgery) to reduce or alleviate symptoms of psychological disorders.

Psychopharmacology: Treating Psychological Disorders with Drugs

Since the 1950s, drug companies have developed an amazing variety of chemicals to treat abnormal behaviours (**Figure 14.11**). In some cases, discoveries from **psychopharmacology** have helped correct chemical imbalances. In other cases, drugs have been used to relieve or suppress the symptoms of psychological disturbances even when the underlying cause was not thought to be biological. Canadian researchers have been at the forefront of this field. The first North American research on the use of drugs to control the symptoms of psychosis was published in 1954 by Dr. Hans Lehmann of Montreal (Davison et al., 2010). Moreover, for the last 15 years, a nationwide network of researchers in hospitals and universities—the Canadian Network for Mood and Anxiety Treatments (CANMAT)—has promoted innovative research and education in pharmaceutical treatment of mental disorders (Canadian Network for Mood and Anxiety Treatments, 2009). As shown in **Study Organizer 14.2**, psychiatric drugs are classified into four major categories: antianxiety, antipsychotic, mood stabilizer, and antidepressant.

> **psychopharmacology** The study of drug effects on the brain and behaviour.

How Prozac and other SSRI antidepressants work • Figure 14.11

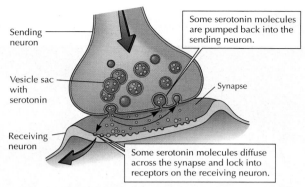

Sending neuron

Vesicle sac with serotonin

Receiving neuron

Some serotonin molecules are pumped back into the sending neuron.

Synapse

Some serotonin molecules diffuse across the synapse and lock into receptors on the receiving neuron.

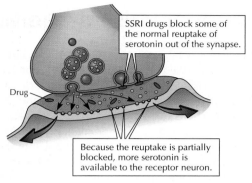

SSRI drugs block some of the normal reuptake of serotonin out of the synapse.

Drug

Because the reuptake is partially blocked, more serotonin is available to the receptor neuron.

a. Under normal conditions, a nerve impulse (or action potential) travels down the axon to the terminal buttons of a sending neuron. If the vesicle sac of this particular neuron contains the neurotransmitter serotonin, the action potential will trigger its release. Some of the serotonin will travel across the synapse and lock into the receptors on the receiving neuron. Excess serotonin within the synapse will be pumped back up into the sending neuron for storage (the "serotonin reuptake").

b. When selective serotonin reuptake inhibitors (SSRIs), such as Prozac, are taken to treat depression and other disorders, they block the normal reuptake of excess serotonin that lingers in the synaptic gap after being released from the sending neuron. This action leaves more serotonin molecules free to stimulate receptors on the receiving neuron, which enhances its mood-lifting effects.

STUDY ORGANIZER 14.2 Common Drug Treatments for Psychological Disorders ✓ THE PLANNER

Type of Drug	Description	Example (Trade Names)
Antianxiety drugs (used to produce relaxation, reduce anxiety, and decrease overarousal in the brain)	Also known as *anxiolytics* and "minor tranquilizers," these drugs lower the sympathetic activity of the brain—the crisis mode of operation—so that anxious responses are diminished or prevented and are replaced by feelings of tranquility and calmness.	Ativan, Restoril, Valium, Xanax
Antipsychotic drugs (used to diminish or eliminate hallucinations, delusions, withdrawal, and other symptoms of psychosis; also known as neuroleptics or major tranquilizers)	Also known as *neuroleptics*, these drugs are used to treat schizophrenia and other acute psychotic states. Unfortunately, these drugs are often referred to as "major tranquilizers," creating the mistaken impression that they invariably have a strong sedating effect. However, the main effect of antipsychotic drugs is to diminish or eliminate psychotic symptoms, including hallucinations, delusions, withdrawal, and apathy. Traditional antipsychotics work by decreasing activity at the dopamine receptors in the brain. A large majority of patients show marked improvement when treated with antipsychotic drugs.	Clozaril, Apo-Haloperidol, Navane, Prolixin, Risperdal, Seroquel
Mood-stabilizer drugs (used to treat the combination of manic episodes and depression characteristic of bipolar disorders)	These drugs, such as *lithium*, can help relieve manic episodes and depression for people who have bipolar disorder. Because lithium acts relatively slowly—it can take 3 or 4 weeks before it takes effect—its primary use is in preventing future episodes and helping to break the manic-depressive cycle.	Lithane, Lithmax, Tegretol
Antidepressant drugs (used to treat depression, some anxiety disorders, and certain eating disorders, such as bulimia)	These drugs are used primarily to treat people with depression. There are five types of antidepressant drugs: *tricyclics, monoamine oxidase inhibitors (MAOIs), selective serotonin reuptake inhibitors (SSRIs), serotonin and norepinephrine reuptake inhibitors (SNRIs),* and *atypical antidepressants.* Each class of drugs affects neurochemical pathways in the brain in slightly different ways, increasing or decreasing the availability of certain chemicals. SSRIs (such as *Paxil* and *Prozac*) are by far the most commonly prescribed antidepressants (see Figure 14.11). The atypical antidepressants are a miscellaneous group of drugs used for patients who fail to respond to the other drugs or for people who experience side effects when using other antidepressants.	Anafranil, Celexa, Cymbalta, Effexor, Elavil, Nardil, Parnate, Paxil, Prozac, Wellbutrin, Zoloft

What a Psychologist Sees

Electroconvulsive Therapy (ECT)

Electroconvulsive therapy may seem barbaric, but for some severely depressed people it is their only hope for lifting the depression. Unlike portrayals of ECT in such movies as *One Flew Over the Cuckoo's Nest* and *The Snake Pit*, patients show few, if any, visible reactions to the treatment, because patients are now given muscle-relaxant drugs that dramatically reduce muscle contractions during the seizure. Most ECT patients are also given an anaesthetic to block their memories of the treatment, but some patients still find the treatment extremely uncomfortable (Jain et al., 2008; Khalid et al., 2008).

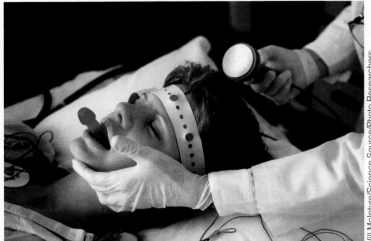

Will McIntyre/Science Source/Photo Researchers

Electroconvulsive Therapy and Psychosurgery

> **electroconvulsive therapy (ECT)** Biomedical therapy in which electrical current is passed through the brain.

In **electroconvulsive therapy (ECT)**, also known as electroshock therapy (EST), a moderate electrical current is passed through the brain between two electrodes placed on the outside of the head. The current triggers a widespread firing of neurons, resulting in a convulsion or seizure. The convulsions produce many changes in the central and peripheral nervous systems, including activation of the autonomic nervous system, increased secretion of various hormones and neurotransmitters, and changes in the blood-brain barrier.

During the early years of ECT, some patients received hundreds of treatments, but today most receive 12 or fewer treatments. Sometimes the electrical current is applied only to the right hemisphere, which causes less interference with verbal memories and left hemisphere functioning.

Modern ECT is used primarily on patients with severe depression who do not respond to antidepressant drugs or psychotherapy and on suicidal patients because it works much faster than antidepressant drugs (Birkenhäger et al., 2004; Kobeissi et al., 2011; Loo et al., 2011). In his account of his personal struggle with bipolar disorder (Chapter 13), Canadian psychologist Norman Endler (1982) provided a well-balanced discussion of the pros and cons of ECT, cogently describing its rapid and positive effects on his depression. (ECT is described further in *What a Psychologist Sees: Electroconvulsive Therapy (ECT)*.)

Although clinical studies of ECT conclude that it is effective for very severe depression, its use remains controversial because it triggers massive changes in the brain. ECT is also controversial because we do not fully understand why it works. Most likely it helps reestablish levels of neurotransmitters that control mood.

The most extreme, and least used, biomedical therapy is **psychosurgery**—brain surgery performed to reduce serious, debilitating psychological problems.

> **psychosurgery** Operative procedures on the brain designed to relieve severe mental symptoms that have not responded to other forms of treatment.

You may have heard of lobotomy, a form of psychosurgery that is no longer practised. This technique originated in 1936, when Portuguese neurologist Egaz Moniz first treated uncontrollable psychoses by cutting the nerve fibres between the frontal lobes (where association areas for monitoring and planning behaviour are found) and the thalamus and hypothalamus.

Although these surgeries did reduce emotional outbursts and aggressiveness, many patients were left with

What about Herbal Remedies?

Some recent research suggests that the herbal supplement St. John's wort may be an effective treatment for mild to moderate depression, with fewer side effects than traditional medications (Butterweck, 2003; Howland, 2010; Kasper et al., 2010; Lecrubier et al., 2002). However, other studies have found the drug to be ineffective for people with major depression (Hypericum Depression Trial Study Group, 2002). Herbal supplements, such as kava, valerian, and *gingko biloba*, also have been used in the treatment of anxiety, insomnia, and memory problems (e.g., Connor & Davidson, 2002; Parrott et al., 2004; Sarris & Byrne, 2011). Although many people assume that these products are safe because they are "natural," they can produce a number of potentially serious side effects. Since 2004, the Natural Health Products Directorate (NHPD) branch of Health Canada has regulated the quality, importing, labelling of, and claims that manufacturers can make about herbal supplements (Health Canada, 2011). However, because they are not considered drugs, natural remedies do not typically undergo the same rigorous research trials as do pharmaceuticals. For these reasons, researchers advise caution, more research, and a wait-and-see approach (Camfield et al., 2011; Crone & Gabriel, 2002; Swartz, 2008).

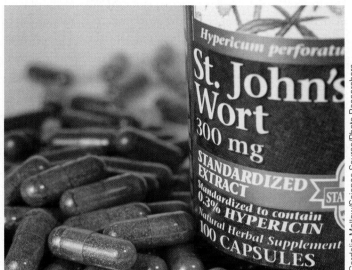

Cordelia Mollow/Science Source/Photo Researchers

Think Critically

1. Do you think the government should regulate herbal remedies in the same way as drugs?
2. Do you think these products should carry labels warning that they can produce potentially serious side effects?

---

permanent brain damage. In the mid-1950s, when antipsychotic drugs came into use, psychosurgery virtually stopped.

Evaluating Biomedical Therapies

Like all forms of therapy, biomedical therapies have both proponents and critics.

Pitfalls of psychopharmacology Drug therapy poses several potential problems. First, although drugs may relieve symptoms for some people, they seldom provide cures. We can easily treat an anxiety disorder with a drug, but the symptoms will often return when the medication stops. To cure the disorder, the patient also needs some form of psychotherapy. In addition, some patients may become physically dependent on the drugs. Also, researchers are still learning about the long-term effects and potential interactions of pharmacological interventions. Furthermore, psychiatric medications can cause a variety of side effects, ranging from mild fatigue to severe impairments in memory and movement.

A final potential problem with drug treatment is that its relative inexpensiveness and generally fast results have led to its overuse in some cases. One report found that antidepressants are prescribed roughly 50 percent of the time a patient walks into a psychiatrist's office (Olfson et al., 1998).

Despite the problems associated with them, psychotherapeutic drugs have led to revolutionary changes in mental health. Before the use of drugs, some patients were destined to spend a lifetime in psychiatric institutions. Today, most patients improve sufficiently to return to their homes and live successful lives if they continue to take their medications to prevent relapse. In *Psychological Science: What about Herbal Remedies?* we discuss the use of herbal remedies in treating depression and anxiety.

Challenges to ECT and psychosurgery As we mentioned, ECT is a controversial treatment for several reasons. However, problems with ECT may become less prominent thanks to **repetitive transcranial magnetic stimulation (rTMS)**, which delivers a brief (but powerful) electrical current through a coil of wire placed close to the head. Unlike ECT, which passes a strong electrical current directly through the brain, the rTMS coil creates a strong magnetic field that is applied to certain areas in the brain. When used to treat depression, the coil is usually placed over the prefrontal cortex, a region linked to deeper parts of the brain that regulate mood. Currently, the benefits of rTMS over ECT remain uncertain, but studies have shown marked improvement in depression, without the seizures or memory loss that accompany ECT (Hadley et al., 2011; Husain & Lisanby, 2011).

In contrast to pharmacological interventions or ECT, psychosurgery is largely viewed negatively as a treatment for psychological disorders. Because all forms of psychosurgery have potentially serious or fatal side effects and complications, some critics suggest that they should be banned altogether. Furthermore, the consequences are irreversible. For these reasons, psychosurgery is considered experimental and remains a highly controversial treatment of last resort.

CONCEPT CHECK

1. **When** are drug therapies used?
2. **How** does modern ECT differ from the therapy's early use?
3. **Why** is psychosurgery a rarely used and controversial treatment?

Therapy Essentials

LEARNING OBJECTIVES

1. **Summarize** the goals that are common to all major forms of psychotherapy.
2. **Describe** some key cross-cultural similarities and differences in therapy.
3. **Explain** why therapists need to be sensitive to gender issues that pertain to mental illness.
4. **Explore** some alternatives to long-term institutionalization for people with severe psychological disorders.

Earlier, we mentioned that there may be more than 400 forms of therapy. How would you choose one for yourself or someone you know? In this section, we help you to synthesize the material in this chapter and to put what you have learned about each of the major forms of therapy into a broader context.

Therapy Goals and Effectiveness

All major forms of therapy are designed to help the client in five specific areas (**Figure 14.12**).

Although most therapists work with clients in several of these areas, the emphasis varies according to the therapist's training (psychodynamic, cognitive, humanistic, behaviourist, or biomedical). Clinicians who regularly borrow freely from various theories are said to take an **eclectic approach**.

Does therapy work? After many years of controlled research and *meta-analysis* (a method of statistically combining and analyzing data from many studies), we have fairly clear evidence that it does. Forty to 80 percent of people who receive treatment are better off than those who do not. Furthermore, some short-term treatments can be as effective as long-term treatments (Dewan et al., 2011; Knekt et al., 2008; Lazar, 2010; Loewenthal & Winter, 2006; Stiles et al., 2008; Wachtel, 2011).

Some therapies are more effective than others for specific problems. For example, anxiety is most effectively treated by using cognitive therapy, phobias seem to respond best to systematic desensitization, and OCD can be significantly relieved with cognitive-behaviour therapy accompanied by medication. Most studies that have compared medication alone versus medication plus therapy have found the combination to be more effective (e.g., Doyle & Pollack, 2004).

Who are the people who benefit from psychotherapy? Data from the *National Population Health Survey* conducted by Statistics Canada reveal some interesting findings (Hunsley & Lee, 2010; Hunsley, Lee, & Aubry, 1999). The survey revealed that 2.2 percent of Canadians aged 12 and

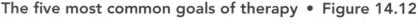

The five most common goals of therapy • Figure 14.12

Most therapies focus on one or more of these five goals. Can you identify which would be of most interest to a psychoanalyst, a cognitive therapist, a behaviour therapist, and a psychiatrist?

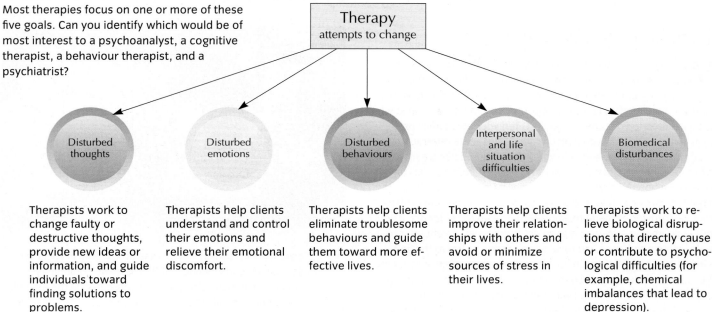

Therapy attempts to change

Disturbed thoughts
Therapists work to change faulty or destructive thoughts, provide new ideas or information, and guide individuals toward finding solutions to problems.

Disturbed emotions
Therapists help clients understand and control their emotions and relieve their emotional discomfort.

Disturbed behaviours
Therapists help clients eliminate troublesome behaviours and guide them toward more effective lives.

Interpersonal and life situation difficulties
Therapists help clients improve their relationships with others and avoid or minimize sources of stress in their lives.

Biomedical disturbances
Therapists work to relieve biological disruptions that directly cause or contribute to psychological difficulties (for example, chemical imbalances that lead to depression).

older had consulted with a psychologist in the past year. Twice as many women as men sought psychological help. Teenagers and adults between 30 and 50 years of age were most likely to consult a psychologist, as were those with higher education and higher income. Canadians living in urban settings were three times as likely as those in rural settings to consult a psychologist. Those seeking psychological help reported poorer health, higher stress levels, and more distress in their lives. They were also more likely to be using medication to deal with their distress. Despite the documented effectiveness of psychological interventions for many disorders, the study revealed that a large number of Canadians are not, in fact, receiving treatment. The authors conclude that the Canadian public would benefit from being made more aware of psychotherapeutic interventions and their effectiveness (Hunsley et al., 1999). In *Applying Psychology: Finding a Therapist*, we discuss four major groups of therapists that offer counselling and psychotherapy in Canada.

Cultural Issues in Therapy

The therapies described in this chapter are based on Western European and North American culture. Does this mean they are unique? Or do our psychotherapists do some of the same sorts of things that, say, an Aboriginal healer or shaman does? Are there similarities in therapies across cultures? Conversely, are there fundamental therapeutic differences among cultures?

When we look at therapies in all cultures, we find that they have certain key features in common (Laungani, 2007; Lee, 2002; Sue & Sue, 2012). Richard Brislin (2000) has summarized some of these features:

- *Naming the problem*. People often feel better just by knowing that others experience the same problem and that the therapist has had experience with their particular problem.
- *Qualities of the therapist*. Clients must feel that the therapist is caring, competent, approachable, and concerned with finding solutions to their problem.
- *Establishing credibility*. Word-of-mouth testimonials and status symbols (such as diplomas on the wall) establish the therapist's credibility. Among Aboriginal healers, in lieu of diplomas, credibility may be established by having served as an apprentice to a revered healer.
- *Placing the problem in a familiar framework*. If the client believes that evil spirits cause psychological disorders, the therapist will direct treatment toward eliminating these spirits. Similarly, if the client believes in the importance of early childhood experiences and the unconscious mind, a psychoanalytically based approach would likely be the treatment of choice.
- *Applying techniques to bring relief*. In all cultures, therapy involves action. Either the client or the therapist must do something. Moreover, what they do must fit the client's expectations—whether it is performing a ceremony to

Applying Psychology

Finding a Therapist

When stresses overwhelm our natural coping mechanisms, professional therapy can provide invaluable relief. But how do we find a good therapist for our specific needs? If you have the time (and the money) to explore options, search for a therapist who is best suited to your specific goals. Often your own family physician can provide you with a recommendation and a referral. However, if you are in a crisis—you have suicidal thoughts or are the victim of abuse—get help fast (see Chapter 13). Most communities have telephone hotlines that provide counselling on a 24-hour basis. In addition, most colleges and universities have counselling centres that can provide immediate, short-term therapy to students. If you are encouraging someone else to get therapy, you might offer to help locate a therapist and to accompany him or her to the first visit. If the person refuses help and the problem affects you, it may be a good idea to seek therapy yourself. You will gain insights and skills that will help you deal with the situation more effectively.

In Canada, a variety of therapists can offer counselling or psychological help, including psychologists, psychiatrists, social workers, and psychotherapists. Depending on your situation, goals, and preferences, a professional from one of these groups may be helpful for your needs:

- *Psychologists* most often have doctoral degrees in psychology and advanced training in the diagnosis and treatment of psychological disorders. Psychologists must be licensed by the province or territory in which they practise (see the Canadian Psychological Association's website at www.cpa.ca for a listing of all provincial and territorial licensing agencies).
- *Psychiatrists* are licensed medical doctors who also have advanced training in the diagnosis and treatment of psychological disorders. In addition to providing psychotherapy, psychiatrists frequently prescribe drugs to treat psychological disorders.

Brad Killer/iStockphoto

- *Social workers* usually have a master's degree in social work, with expertise in working with families and community agencies, and many also provide counselling. In the majority of provinces, social workers are licensed (see the Canadian Association of Social Workers website at www.casw-acts.ca).
- The terms *counsellor* or *psychotherapist* refer to professionals who, although not psychologists or psychiatrists, have advanced training (usually a master's degree) in counselling. In some provinces, counsellors and psychotherapists are licensed by the province. The Canadian Counselling and Psychotherapy Association website, www.ccpa-accp.ca, provides more information on the professions of counselling and psychotherapy.

Think Critically

1. If you were looking for a therapist, would you want the therapist's gender to be the same as yours, or wouldn't it matter? Why?
2. Some therapists treat clients online. Do you think this is a good idea? Why or why not?

---

expel demons or talking with the client about his or her thoughts and feelings.
- *A special time and place.* The fact that therapy occurs outside the client's everyday experiences seems to be an important feature of all therapies.

Although therapies across cultures share basic similarities, they also have important differences. In the traditional Western European and North American model, the emphasis is on the self and on independence and control over one's life—qualities that are highly valued in individualistic cultures. In collectivist cultures, however, the focus of therapy is on interdependence and accepting the realities of one's life (Sue & Sue, 2012) (**Figure 14.13**).

Not only does culture affect the types of therapy that are developed, but it also influences the perceptions of the therapist. What one culture considers abnormal behaviour may be quite common—and even healthy—in others. For this reason, recognizing cultural differences is very important for building trust between therapists and clients and for effecting behavioural change (Laungani, 2007; Sue & Sue, 2012; Tseng, 2004).

Gender and Therapy

Within our individualistic Western culture, men and women present different needs and problems to therapists. For example, compared with men, women are more

Emphasizing interdependence • Figure 14.13

In Japanese Naikan therapy, the patient sits quietly from 5:30 a.m. to 9:00 p.m. for seven days and is visited by an interviewer every 90 minutes. During this time, the patient reflects on his or her relationships with others, with the goals of discovering personal guilt for having been ungrateful and troublesome to others and developing gratitude toward those who have helped (Nakamura, 2006; Ozawa-de Silva, 2007; Ryback et al., 2001). How do these goals and methods differ from those of the therapies we have described in this chapter? Do you think this approach would work with Westerners? Why or why not?

comfortable and familiar with their emotions and have fewer negative attitudes toward therapy (Komiya et al., 2000). In contrast, as discussed in Chapter 13, men are more likely to suppress their emotions and to show their distress through being aggressive, acting impulsively, or engaging in substance abuse. Moreover, as noted above, Canadian women are more likely than men to seek psychological help (Hunsley & Lee, 2010).

Research has identified five major concerns related to gender and psychotherapy (Halbreich & Kahn, 2007; Hall, 2007; Hyde, 2007; Matlin, 2012; Russo & Tartaro, 2008).

1. *Rates of diagnosis and treatment of mental disorders*. Women are diagnosed and treated for mental illness at a much higher rate than men. Is this because women experience more mental health problems than men, or are they just more willing to admit their problems? Or perhaps the categories for illness may be biased against women. More research is needed to answer this question.
2. *Stresses of poverty*. Women are disproportionately more likely to be poor than are men. Poverty contributes to stress, which is an important contributor to many psychological disorders.

Paying attention to gender-specific needs • Figure 14.14

Therapists must be sensitive to possible connections between clients' problems and their gender. Rather than prescribing drugs to relieve depression in women, for example, it may be more appropriate for therapists to explore ways to relieve the stresses of multiple roles or poverty. Can you see how helping a single mother identify parenting resources, such as play groups, parent support groups, and high-quality child care, might be just as effective at relieving depression as prescribing drugs? In the case of men, can you see how relieving loneliness or depression might alleviate issues with alcohol abuse or aggression?

3. *Stresses of multiple roles*. Women today are mothers, wives, homemakers, professionals, wage earners, students, and so on, whereas men are less likely to occupy such multiple roles. The conflicting demands of their multiple roles often create special stresses (**Figure 14.14**).
4. *Stresses of aging*. Aging brings additional concerns for women than it brings for for men. Women, on average, live longer than men. Older women, primarily those with age-related dementia, account for more than 70 percent of those with chronic mental illnesses who live in nursing homes.
5. *Violence against women*. Sexual assault, incest, and sexual harassment—which are much more likely to happen to women than to men—may lead to depression, insomnia, post-traumatic stress disorders, eating disorders, and other problems.

Institutionalization

Despite Hollywood film portrayals, forced institutionalization of people with mental illness poses serious ethical problems and is generally reserved for only the most serious and life-threatening situations or when no reasonable, less restrictive alternative is available.

In emergencies, mental health professionals can authorize temporary commitment for 24 to 72 hours—time enough for laboratory tests to be performed to rule out medical illnesses that could be causing the symptoms.

The patient can also receive psychological testing, medication, and short-term therapy during this time.

Today, many provinces in Canada have a policy of **deinstitutionalization**—discharging patients from psychiatric hospitals as soon as possible and discouraging admissions (Davison et al., 2010). As an alternative to institutionalizing people in public psychiatric institutions, most clinicians suggest expanding and improving community care. They recommend that general hospitals be equipped with special psychiatric units where acutely ill patients can receive in-patient care. For less disturbed individuals and chronically ill patients, they recommend walk-in clinics, crisis intervention services, improved residential treatment facilities, and psychosocial and vocational rehabilitation. Public psychiatric institutions would be reserved for the most unmanageable patients.

CONCEPT CHECK   STOP

1. **What** is the evidence that therapy works?
2. **How** do individualistic and collectivistic cultures differ in their approaches to therapy?
3. **What** is deinstitutionalization?

THE PLANNER

Summary

1 Insight Therapies   386

- **Insight therapies** are forms of **psychotherapy** that seek to increase clients' insight into their difficulties.

- In **psychoanalysis,** the therapist seeks to identify the patient's unconscious conflicts and to help the patient resolve them through **catharsis**. In modern **psychodynamic therapy,** treatment is briefer and the therapist takes a more directive approach (and puts less emphasis on unconscious childhood memories) than in traditional psychoanalysis.

- **Cognitive therapy** seeks to help clients challenge faulty thought processes and adjust maladaptive behaviours. Ellis' **rational-emotive behaviour therapy (REBT)** and Beck's **cognitive-behaviour therapy** are important examples of cognitive therapy.

- **Humanistic therapy**, such as Rogers' **client-centred therapy**, seeks to maximize personal growth, encouraging people to actualize their potential and relate to others in genuine ways.

- In **group therapy,** multiple people meet together to work toward therapeutic goals. A variation is the **self-help group**, which is not guided by a professional. Therapists often refer their patients to group therapy and self-help groups to supplement individual therapy.

- In **family therapy**, the aim is to change maladaptive family interaction patterns. All members of the family attend therapy sessions, although at times the therapist may see family members individually or in twos or threes.

Active listening • Figure 14.6

2 Behaviour Therapies   395

- In **behaviour therapy,** the focus is on the problem behaviour itself, rather than on any underlying causes. The therapist uses learning principles to change behaviour.

- Classical conditioning techniques include **systematic desensitization** and **aversion therapy**.

- Operant conditioning techniques used to increase adaptive behaviours include shaping and reinforcement.

- In **modelling therapy,** clients observe and imitate others who are performing the desired behaviours.

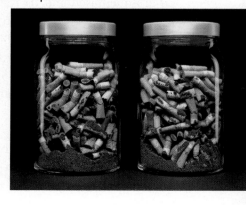
Making a nasty habit nastier • Figure 14.10

3 Biomedical Therapies 398

- **Biomedical therapies** are based on the premise that chemical imbalances or disturbed nervous system functioning contribute to problem behaviours.

- **Psychopharmacology** is the most common form of biomedical therapy. Major classes of drugs used to treat psychological disorders are **antianxiety drugs, antipsychotic drugs, mood-stabilizer drugs**, and **antidepressant drugs.**

- In **electroconvulsive therapy (ECT),** an electrical current is passed through the brain, stimulating convulsions that produce changes in the central and peripheral nervous systems. ECT is used primarily in cases of severe depression that do not respond to other treatments.

- The most extreme biomedical therapy is **psychosurgery.** Lobotomy, a well-known form of psychosurgery, is no longer used.

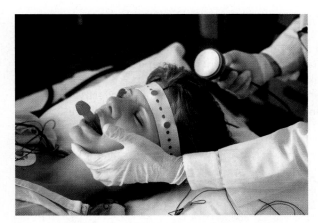

What a Psychologist Sees: Electroconvulsive Therapy (ECT)

4 Therapy Essentials 402

- All major forms of therapy are designed to address disturbed thoughts, disturbed emotions, disturbed behaviours, interpersonal and life situation difficulties, and biomedical disturbances. Research indicates that, overall, therapy does work.

- Therapies in all cultures have certain key features in common; however, important differences also exist among cultures. Therapists must recognize cultural differences to build trust with clients and effect behavioural change.

- Therapists must also be sensitive to possible gender issues in therapy.

- Forced institutionalization of people with mental illnesses is generally reserved for only the most serious and life-threatening situations. Many provinces have a policy of **deinstitutionalization**, and most clinicians suggest expanding and improving community care to ensure that people with mental health problems receive appropriate care.

Emphasizing interdependence • Figure 14.13

Key Terms

Critical and Creative Thinking Questions

1. You undoubtedly had certain beliefs about therapy before reading this chapter. Has studying the therapies described here altered your beliefs? Explain.

2. Which form of therapy do you personally find most appealing? Why?

3. What do you consider to be the most important similarities among the major forms of therapy described in this chapter? What are the most important differences?

4. Do you think dreams can really reveal unconscious conflicts and desires? Why would such desires or conflicts be more likely to emerge while we're sleeping than while we're awake?

5. Imagine that you were going to use a cognitive-behavioural intervention to change some aspect of your own thinking and behaviour. (Maybe you'd like to quit smoking or be more

organized or overcome your fear of riding in elevators.) How would you identify your faulty thinking? How could you change your thinking patterns and behaviour?

6. Cognitive therapists believe that negative thoughts or negative "self-talk" can lead to negative feelings. Have you ever noticed your own thoughts about a situation leading to negative emotions? Have you tried changing these thoughts? If so, did the change in thinking affect your feelings?

7. Client-centred therapy emphasizes techniques of empathy and active listening. Could these techniques be used outside the therapy situation? Could using empathy and active listening skills improve your relations with family and friends?

8. Why do you think some therapists use an eclectic approach? What could be the advantages and disadvantages of using different therapeutic techniques with different clients?

Self-Test

(Check your answers in Appendix A.)

1. Psychoanalysis, cognitive, humanistic, group, and family therapy are often grouped together as _____.
   a. insight therapies
   b. behaviour therapies
   c. humanistic and operant conditioning
   d. cognitive restructuring

2. The type of psychotherapy developed by Freud that seeks to bring unconscious conflicts into conscious awareness is referred to as _____.
   a. transference
   b. conscious restructuring
   c. psychoanalysis
   d. the "hot seat" technique

3. Which modern form of therapy emphasizes internal conflicts, motives, and unconscious forces?
   a. self-talk therapy
   b. belief-behaviour therapy
   c. psychodynamic therapy
   d. thought analysis

4. Jessica's therapist has been drawing attention to how her close friends and family members affect her overall well-being. What type of therapy is being used in this situation?
   a. cognitive restructuring
   b. interpersonal therapy (IPT)
   c. psychodynamic therapy
   d. interpretation

5. Antipsychotic medications are also sometimes called _____.
   a. benzodiazepines
   b. selective serotonin reuptake inhibitors (SSRIs)
   c. major tranquilizers
   d. monoamine oxidase (MAO) inhibitors

6. The following figure illustrates the process by which the therapist and client work to change dysfunctional ways of thinking. What is this process called?
   a. problem solving
   b. self-talk
   c. cognitive restructuring
   d. rational recovery

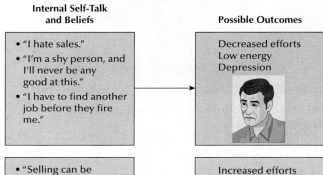

7. Beck practises _____, which attempts to change not only dysfunctional thoughts and beliefs but the associated behaviours as well.
   a. psycho-behaviour therapy
   b. cognitive-behaviour therapy
   c. thinking-acting therapy
   d. belief-behaviour therapy

8. _____ therapy seeks to maximize personal growth through affective restructuring.
   a. Cognitive-emotive
   b. Emotive
   c. Humanistic
   d. Actualization

9. In Rogerian therapy, the _____ is responsible for discovering maladaptive patterns.
   a. therapist
   b. analyst
   c. patient
   d. client

10. This type of group does not have a professional leader, and members assist each other in coping with a specific problem.
    a. self-help group
    b. encounter group
    c. peer group
    d. behaviour group

11. The main focus in behaviour therapy is to increase _____ and decrease _____.
    a. positive thoughts and feelings; negative thoughts and feelings
    b. adaptive behaviours; maladaptive behaviours
    c. coping resources; coping deficits
    d. all of these options

12. A therapist devises a treatment in which smokers receive a mild shock whenever they reach for a cigarette. What type of therapy is the therapist using?
    a. systematic desensitization
    b. virtual reality therapy
    c. operant conditioning
    d. aversion therapy

13. The three steps in systematic desensitization include all of the following except _____.
    a. learning to become deeply relaxed
    b. arranging anxiety-arousing stimuli into a hierarchy from least to worst arousing
    c. practising relaxation to anxiety-arousing stimuli, starting at the top of the hierarchy
    d. all of these options are included

14. Which form of therapy involves watching and imitating appropriate models who demonstrate desirable behaviours?
    a. shaping
    b. spectatoring
    c. modelling
    d. systematic desensitization

15. Label the four major categories of psychiatric drugs on the following table.

Common drug treatments for psychological disorders	
Type of drug	*Psychological disorder*
a. _____.	Anxiety disorders
b. _____.	Schizophrenia
c. _____.	Bipolar disorder
d. _____.	Depressive disorders

16. In Canada, both _____ and _____ usually have doctorate degrees, with advanced training in diagnosis of psychological disorders.
    a. social workers and counsellors
    b. social workers and psychotherapists
    c. psychiatrists and psychologists
    d. all of the above

17. In electroconvulsive therapy (ECT), _____.
    a. current is never applied to the left hemisphere
    b. convulsions activate the autonomic nervous system, stimulate hormone and neurotransmitter release, and change the blood-brain barrier
    c. electrical current passes through the brain for up to one minute
    d. most patients today receive hundreds of treatments because it is safer than in the past

18. Label the five most common goals of therapies on the following figure.

Therapy attempts to change

a._____   b._____   c._____   d._____   e._____

19. Transference refers to _____.
    a. the ways that selective serotonin reuptake inhibitors (SSRIs) affect chemical pathways in the brain
    b. the replacement of a conditioned fear response with relaxation in the process of systematic desensitization
    c. the process by which people apply some of their unresolved emotions and attitudes from past relationships onto the therapist
    d. the process by which the therapist models a behaviour and then gradually encourages the patient to engage in the same behaviour

20. Psychiatric professionals may authorize temporary commitment for assessment and treatment of a dangerous or incompetent individual for up to_____.
    a. 12 to 24 hours
    b. 24 to 72 hours
    c. 3 to 4 days
    d. 3 to 4 weeks

THE PLANNER ✓

Review your Chapter Planner on the chapter opener and check off your completed work.

Our Thoughts about Others

LEARNING OBJECTIVES

1. **Explain** how attributions and attitudes affect the way we perceive and judge others.

2. **Summarize** the three components of attitudes.

3. **Describe** cultural differences in how people explain behaviour.

Attribution: Explaining Behaviour

One critical aspect of **social psychology** is the search for reasons and explanations for our own and others' behaviour. It's natural to want to understand and explain why people behave as they do and why events occur as they do. Many social psychologists believe that developing logical **attributions** for people's behaviour makes us feel safer and more in control (Baumeister & Vohs, 2011; Chiou, 2007; Heider, 1958; Krueger, 2007). To do so, most people begin with the basic question of whether a given action stems mainly from the person's internal disposition or from the external situation.

> **social psychology** The study of how other people influence a person's thoughts, feelings, and actions.
>
> **attributions** Our explanations for the causes of our own and others' actions.

Mistaken attributions Making the correct choice between disposition and situation is central to accurately judging why people do what they do. Unfortunately, our attributions are frequently marred by two major errors: the fundamental attribution error and the self-serving bias. Let's explore each of these.

Our attributions as to the reasons for people's actions are generally accurate when we take into account situational influences on behaviour. However, given that people have enduring personality traits (Chapter 12) and a tendency to take cognitive shortcuts (Chapter 8), we more often choose *dispositional* attributions—that is, we blame the person rather than the circumstance. For example, suppose a new student joins your class and seems distant, cold, and uninterested in interaction. It is easy to conclude that she is unfriendly and maybe even stuck-up—a dispositional attribution. You might be surprised to find that in one-on-one interactions with familiar, close friends, she is actually much more outgoing and warm. In other words, her behaviour depends on the situation.

This bias toward personal, dispositional factors rather than situational factors in our explanations for others'

behaviour is so common that it is called the **fundamental attribution error (FAE)** (Arkes & Kajdasz, 2011; Gebauer et al., 2008; Kennedy, 2010; Tal-Or & Papirman, 2007).

Why do we so often jump to internal, personal dispositional explanations? Social psychologists suggest that one reason is that human personalities and behaviours are more *salient* (or noticeable) than situational factors, leading to the **saliency bias** (**Figure 15.1**).

> **fundamental attribution error (FAE)** The tendency to attribute people's behaviour to internal (dispositional) causes rather than external (situational) factors.

Saliency bias • Figure 15.1

How would you explain this situation? According to the saliency bias, we're likely to blame homeless individuals for their condition because human personalities and behaviours (dispositional factors) are more conspicuous and "salient" than are the situational factors that lead to poverty and homelessness. How would the *just-world phenomenon* explain this same situation?

Carol Thacker/iStock

In addition, we tend to focus on people and "blame the victim" because of our need to believe that the world is just and fair. This **just-world phenomenon** suggests that people generally deserve what they get, which allows us to feel safer in an uncontrollable world.

When judging others, we often blame the person rather than the situation. However, when explaining our own behaviour, we favour internal attributions for our successes and external attributions for our failures. This **self-serving bias** is motivated by a desire to maintain positive self-esteem and a good public image (Alloy et al., 2011; Krusemark et al., 2008; McClure et al., 2011; Shepperd et al., 2008). For example, students often take personal credit for doing well on an exam. If they fail the test, however, they tend to blame the instructor, the textbook, or the "tricky" questions.

Culture and attributional biases Both the fundamental attribution error and the self-serving bias may depend in part on cultural factors (Kudo & Numazaki, 2003; Matsumoto, 2000) (**Figure 15.2**). In individualistic

Culture and attributional biases
• Figure 15.2

Westerners watching a baseball game in Japan who saw the umpire make a bad call would probably make a dispositional attribution ("He's a lousy umpire"), whereas Japanese spectators would tend to make a situational attribution ("He's under pressure"). What accounts for this difference?

Koji Sasahara/Associated Press

cultures, such as those of Canada and the United States, people are defined and understood as individual selves—largely responsible for their successes and failures. But in collectivistic cultures, such as those in China or Japan, people are primarily defined as members of their social network—responsible for doing as others expect. Accordingly, they tend to be more aware of situational constraints on behaviour, making the FAE less likely (Bozkurt & Aydin, 2004; Imada & Ellsworth, 2011; Mason & Morris, 2010).

The self-serving bias is also much less common in Eastern nations. In Japan, for instance, the ideal person is someone who is aware of his or her shortcomings and continually works to overcome them—not someone who thinks highly of himself or herself (Heine & Renshaw, 2002). In the East (as well as in other collectivistic cultures), self-esteem is not related to doing better than others but to fitting in with the group (Markus & Kitayama, 2003).

Attitudes: Learned Predispositions toward Others

When we observe and respond to the world around us, we are seldom completely neutral. Rather, our responses toward subjects as diverse as pizza, people, AIDS, and politics reflect our **attitudes**. We learn our attitudes both from direct experience and from watching others.

Social psychologists generally agree that most attitudes have three components (**Figure 15.3**): cognitive (thoughts and

> **attitudes** Learned predispositions to respond cognitively, affectively, and behaviourally to particular subjects in a particular way.

Three components of attitudes • Figure 15.3

When social psychologists study attitudes, they measure each of the three components: cognitive, affective, and behavioural.

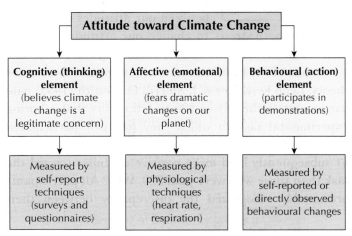

Attitude toward Climate Change

Cognitive (thinking) element (believes climate change is a legitimate concern)	**Affective (emotional) element** (fears dramatic changes on our planet)	**Behavioural (action) element** (participates in demonstrations)
Measured by self-report techniques (surveys and questionnaires)	Measured by physiological techniques (heart rate, respiration)	Measured by self-reported or directly observed behavioural changes

Visualizing

The cost of prejudice • Figure 15.6

a. Stereotypes on TV

TV shows often portray stereotyped views of groups. For example, *The Big Bang Theory* pokes fun at high achievers. We find this show funny because it reinforces the stereotype of high-IQ people as socially inept.

b. Harmless stereotypes?

Even seemingly positive forms of prejudice can have negative effects. For example, the stereotype that "Asian Canadians are good at math" might lead Asian Canadians to see few other routes to success.

c. Competition for resources

The "Occupy movement" and the slogan "We are the 99%," which spread across Canada and the United States in 2011–2012, emerged in part from a perception that a privileged outgroup was hoarding economic resources for themselves.

d. Prejudice and genocide

Prejudice can lead to atrocities. These skulls are from the recent acts of genocide in Sudan, where thousands of Africans have died from starvation, disease, and violence.

2007; Tropp & Mallett, 2011). People also learn prejudice through direct experience. For example, badmouthing others or receiving attention for expressing racist or sexist remarks can actually boost a person's self-esteem (Fein & Spencer, 1997; Plummer, 2001). Generalizing from a single negative experience with a specific member of a group also creates prejudice (Vidmar, 1997).

Mental shortcuts Prejudice may stem from normal attempts to simplify a complex social world (Kulik, 2005;

Sternberg, 2007, 2009). Stereotypes allow people to make quick judgements about others, thereby freeing up their mental resources for other activities (**Figure 15.6b**). In fact, stereotypes and prejudice can occur even without a person's conscious awareness or control. This process is known as "automatic" or "implicit" bias (Columb & Plant, 2011; Greenwald et al., 2009; Hofmann et al., 2008; von Hippel et al., 2008).

People use stereotypes to classify others in terms of their membership in a group. Given that people generally classify themselves as part of the preferred group, they also create ingroups and outgroups. An *ingroup* is any category that people see themselves as belonging to; an *outgroup* is any other category.

Compared with how they see outgroup members, people tend to see ingroup members as being more attractive, having better personalities, and so on—a phenomenon known as **ingroup favouritism** (Ahmed, 2007; DiDonato et al., 2011; Harth et al., 2008). People also tend to recognize greater diversity among members of their ingroup than they do among members of outgroups (Cehajic et al., 2008; Ryan et al., 2010; Wegener et al., 2006). This "they all look alike to me" tendency is termed the **outgroup homogeneity effect**. A danger with such outgroup homogeneity bias is that when members of minority groups are not recognized as varied and complex individuals, it is easier to perceive them as faceless objects and to treat them in discriminatory ways (Spears, 2011). A good example is war: viewing the people on the other side as simply faceless enemies makes it easier to kill large numbers of soldiers and civilians. This type of dehumanization and anonymity also helps perpetuate the high levels of fear and anxiety associated with terrorism (Dunham, 2011; Haslam et al., 2007; Hodson & Costello, 2007; Hutchison & Rosenthal, 2011; Zimbardo, 2007).

Competition for limited resources Some theorists think that prejudice develops and is maintained because it offers significant economic and political advantages to the dominant group (Esses et al., 2001; Schaefer, 2008) (**Figure 15.6c**).

Displaced aggression As we discuss in the next section, frustration often leads people to attack the source of that frustration. As history has shown, when the cause of frustration is ambiguous, or too powerful and capable of retaliation, people often redirect their aggression toward an alternative, innocent target, known as a *scapegoat* (**Figure 15.6d**).

Understanding the causes of prejudice is a first step toward overcoming it. Later in this chapter, we will consider several methods that psychologists have developed to reduce prejudice. In the section that follows, we examine the positive side of our feelings about others.

Interpersonal Attraction

What causes us to feel admiration, liking, friendship, intimacy, lust, or love? All these social experiences are reflections of **interpersonal attraction**. Psychologists have found three compelling factors in interpersonal attraction: physical attractiveness, proximity, and similarity. Each influences our attraction in different ways.

> **interpersonal attraction** Positive feelings toward another.

Physical attractiveness (size, shape, facial characteristics, and manner of dress) is one of the most important factors in our initial liking of others (Andreoni & Petrie, 2008; Buss, 2003, 2007, 2011; Cunningham et al., 2008; Lippa, 2007; Maner et al., 2008). Attractive individuals are seen as more poised, interesting, cooperative, achieving, sociable, independent, intelligent, healthy, and sexually warm than unattractive people (Fink & Penton-Voak, 2002; Swami & Furnham, 2008; Willis et al., 2008). Even children show such a bias: children who are physically attractive tend to be more popular than those who are less attractive (Langlois et al., 2000). Such stereotypes, moreover, may begin to operate very early: even very young infants can discriminate between attractive and unattractive faces and show a preference for faces that are attractive (Quinn et al., 2008; Ramsey et al., 2004).

Many cultures around the world share similar standards of attractiveness, especially for women—for example, youthful appearance and facial and body symmetry (Fink et al., 2004; Jones et al., 2007). From an evolutionary perspective, these findings may reflect the fact that good looks generally indicate good health, sound genes, and high fertility. However, what is considered beautiful also varies from era to era and from culture to culture (**Figure 15.7**).

How do those of us who are not "superstar beautiful" manage to find mates? The good news is that perceived attractiveness for *known* people, in contrast to *unknown* people, is strongly influenced by non-physical traits. This means that such factors as respect, positive interactions, similarity, and familiarity increase our judgements of beauty in friends and family (Barelds et al., 2011; Kniffin & Wilson, 2004; Lewandowski et al., 2007; Morry et al.,

Culture and attraction • Figure 15.7

Which of these women do you find most attractive? Can you see how your cultural background might train you to prefer one look over the others?

2011; Reis et al., 2011). Also, what people judge as "ideally attractive" may be quite different from what they eventually choose for a mate. According to the *matching hypothesis,* men and women tend to select partners whose physical attractiveness approximately matches their own (Regan, 1998; Sprecher & Regan, 2002; Taylor et al., 2011). People also use non-verbal flirting behaviour to increase their attractiveness and to signal interest to a potential romantic partner (Lott, 2000; Moore, 1998). Although both men and women flirt, in heterosexual couples women generally initiate courtship.

Attraction also depends on two people being in the same place at the same time. Such proximity promotes attraction, largely because of *mere exposure*—that is, repeated exposure increases liking (Monin, 2003; Rhodes et al., 2001) (**Figure 15.8**).

The major cementing factor for both liking and loving relationships is similarity. We tend to prefer and stay with people who are most like us, those who share our ethnic background, social class, interests, and attitudes (Böhm et al., 2011; Caprara et al., 2007; Morry et al., 2011). In fact, as we saw in Chapter 10, the importance of similarity to

The face in the mirror • Figure 15.8

We even like ourselves better when we see ourselves in a familiar way. People presented with pictures of themselves and reversed images of themselves strongly prefer the reversed images, which they are used to seeing in the mirror. Close friends prefer the unreversed images (Mita et al., 1977).

What a Psychologist Sees

✓ THE PLANNER

Love over the Lifespan

Even in the most devoted couples, the intense attraction and excitement of **romantic love** generally begin to fade 6 to 30 months after the relationship begins (Hatfield & Rapson, 1996; Livingston, 1999). This is because romantic love is largely based on mystery and fantasy—people often fall in love with others, not necessarily as they are, but as what they want them to be (Fletcher & Kerr, 2010; Fletcher & Simpson, 2000; Levine, 2001). These illusions usually fade with the realities of everyday living.

Intensity

— Romantic love
— Companionate love

Years of relationship

Companionate love is a strong, lasting attraction based on admiration, respect, trust, deep caring, and commitment. Studies of close friendships show that satisfaction grows with time as we come to recognize the value of companionship and intimacy (Gottman, 2011; Kim & Hatfield, 2004). One tip for maintaining companionate love is to overlook each other's faults. People are more satisfied with relationships when they have a somewhat idealized perception of their partner or the relationship (Barelds & Dijkstra, 2009, 2011; Campbell et al., 2001; Fletcher & Simpson, 2000). This makes sense in light of research on cognitive dissonance: idealizing our mates allows us to believe we have a "good deal."

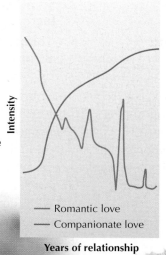

a-wrangler/iStockphoto

Johnny Hetfield/iStockphoto

---

the development of close relationships begins in childhood (Bukowski et al., 2009; Graham et al., 2009).

We can think of interpersonal attraction as a fundamental building block of how we feel about others. But how do we make sense of love? Many people find the subject to be alternately mysterious, exhilarating, comforting—and even maddening. In this section, we explore three perspectives on love: liking versus loving, romantic love, and companionate love.

Love often develops from initial feelings of friendship and liking. Using a questionnaire measure of liking and loving, Zick Rubin (1970) found that liking involves a favourable evaluation reflected in greater feelings of admiration and respect. Love, a more intense experience, involves caring, attachment to the other person, and intimacy. For more about love over the lifespan, see *What a Psychologist Sees: Love over the Lifespan*.

Couples who scored highest on Rubin's love scale spent more time looking into each other's eyes. Although both partners tended to match each other on their love scores, women liked their dating partners significantly more than they were liked in return (Rubin, 1970).

CONCEPT CHECK STOP

1. **What** factors contribute to the development of prejudice?

2. **What** process accounts for someone saying that members of another ethnic group "all look alike"?

3. **What** are the major factors that affect our attraction to others?

Our Actions toward Others

LEARNING OBJECTIVES

1. **Identify** the factors that contribute to conformity and obedience.

2. **Explain** how groups affect behaviour and decision-making.

3. **Summarize** the biological and psychosocial factors believed to be involved in aggression.

4. **Compare** the egoistic model with the empathy–altruism hypothesis.

K urt Lewin (1890–1947), often considered the "father of social psychology," was among the first to suggest that all behaviour results from interactions between the individual and the environment. In this section we consider several examples of such interaction, including social influence, group processes, and aggression.

Social Influence: Conformity and Obedience

Our society and culture teach us to believe certain things, feel certain ways, and act in accordance with these beliefs and feelings. These influences are so strong and so much a part of who we are that we rarely recognize them. In this section, we discuss two kinds of social influence: conformity and obedience.

Conformity: Going along with others Imagine that you've volunteered for a psychology experiment on perception. You're seated around a table with six other students. You are all shown a card with three lines labelled A, B, and C, as in **Figure 15.9**. You are then asked to select the line that is closest in length to a fourth line, X.

Solomon Asch's study of conformity
• Figure 15.9

Which line (A, B, or C) is most like line X in the bottom box? Could anyone convince you otherwise?

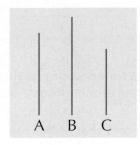

At first, everyone agrees on the correct line. On the third trial, however, the first participant selects line A, obviously a wrong answer. When the second, third, fourth, and fifth participants also say line A, you really start to wonder: "What's going on here? Are they blind? Or am I?"

What do you think you would do at this point in the experiment? Would you stick with your convictions and say line B, regardless of what the others have answered? Or would you go along with the group? In the original version of this experiment, conducted by Solomon Asch (1951), six of the seven participants were actually *confederates* of the experimenter (that is, they were working with the experimenter and purposely gave wrong answers). Their incorrect responses were designed to test the participant's degree of **conformity**.

> **conformity** The act of changing our behaviour as a result of real or imagined group pressure.

More than one-third of Asch's participants conformed—they agreed with the group's obviously incorrect choice. (Participants in a control group experienced no group pressure and almost always chose correctly.) Asch's study has been conducted dozens of times, in at least 17 countries, and always with similar results (Baumeister & Vohs, 2011; Bond & Smith, 1996; Jung, 2006; Takano & Sogon, 2008).

Why would so many people conform? To the onlooker, conformity is often difficult to understand. Even the conformer sometimes has a hard time explaining his or her behaviour. Let's look at three factors that drive conformity:

• *Normative social influence*. Often, people conform to group pressure out of a need for approval and acceptance by the group. **Norms** are expected behaviours that are adhered to by members of a group (*Psychological Science: Cultural Norms for Personal Space*). Most often, norms are quite subtle and implicit. Have you ever asked what

Cultural Norms for Personal Space

Culture and socialization have a lot to do with shaping norms for personal space. If someone invades the invisible "personal bubble" around our bodies, we generally feel very uncomfortable. People from Mediterranean, Muslim, and Latin American countries tend to maintain smaller interpersonal distances than do Northern Europeans and Canadians of European descent (Axtell, 2007; Steinhart, 1986). Children also tend to stand very close to others until they are socialized to recognize and maintain a greater personal distance. Furthermore, friends stand closer than strangers, women tend to stand closer than men, and violent prisoners prefer approximately three times the personal space of non-violent prisoners (Axtell, 1998, 2007; Gilmour & Walkey, 1981; Lawrence & Andrews, 2004).

Bassem Tellawi/Associated Press

Think Critically

1. Does it bother you when someone stands "too close" to you?
2. If this happens in a crowded bus or an elevator, does it make a difference?
3. If men and women have different norms for personal space, what effect might this have on their relationships?

others are wearing to a party or watched the person seated next to you at dinner to be sure you pick up the right fork? Such behaviour reflects your desire to conform and the power of normative social influence.

- *Informational social influence.* Have you ever bought a specific product simply because of friends' recommendations? You conform not necessarily to gain their approval (the *normative social influence* described above) but because you assume they have more information than you do. Participants in Asch's experiment observed all the other participants giving unanimous decisions on the length of the lines, so they may have logically conformed because they believed the others had more information.

- *Reference groups.* The third major factor in conformity is the power of **reference groups**—people we most

admire, like, and want to resemble. Attractive actors and popular sports stars are paid millions of dollars to endorse products because advertisers know that we want to be as cool as Canadian mixed martial arts champion Georges "Rush" St. Pierre or as beautiful as Canadian actress Elisha Cuthbert. Of course, we also have more important reference groups in our lives—parents, friends, family members, teachers, religious leaders, and so on.

Obedience: Following orders

As we've seen, conformity involves going along with the group. A second form of social influence, **obedience**, involves going along with a direct command, usually from someone in a position of authority.

> **obedience** The act of following a direct command, usually from an authority figure.

The advantages of conformity and obedience • Figure 15.10

Damian Dovarganes/Associated Press

These people willingly obey the firefighters who order them to evacuate a building, and many lives are saved. What would happen to our everyday functioning if people did not go along with the crowd or generally did not obey orders?

Conformity and obedience aren't always bad (**Figure 15.10**). In fact, most people conform and obey most of the time because it is in their own best interest (and everyone else's) to do so. Like most Canadians, you stand in line at the movie theatre instead of pushing ahead of others. This allows an orderly purchasing of tickets. Conformity and obedience allow social life to proceed with safety, order, and predictability.

However, on some occasions it is important not to conform or obey. We don't want teenagers (or adults) engaging in risky sex or drug use just to be part of the crowd. And we don't want soldiers (or anyone else) mindlessly following orders just because they were told to do so by an authority figure. Because recognizing and resisting destructive forms of obedience are important to our society, we'll explore this material in greater depth at the end of this chapter.

Imagine that you've responded to a newspaper ad that is seeking volunteers for a study on memory. At the Yale University laboratory, an experimenter explains to you and another participant that he is studying the effects of punishment on learning and memory. You are selected to play the role of the "teacher." The experimenter leads you into a room where he straps the other participant—the "learner"—into a chair. He applies electrode paste to the learner's wrist "to avoid blisters and burns" and attaches an electrode that's connected to a shock generator.

You are led into an adjacent room and told to sit in front of this same shock generator, which is wired through the wall to the chair of the learner. The shock generator consists of 30 switches representing successively higher levels of shock, from 15 volts to 450 volts. Written labels appear below each group of switches, ranging from "Slight Shock" to "Danger: Severe Shock," all the way to "XXX." The experimenter explains that it's your job to teach the learner a list of word pairs and to punish any errors by administering a shock. With each wrong answer, you are to increase the shock by one level. The setup for the experiment is illustrated in *What a Psychologist Sees*.

You begin teaching the word pairs, but the learner's responses are often wrong. Before long, you're inflicting shocks that you can only assume must be extremely painful. After you administer 150 volts, the learner begins to protest: "Get me out of here. . . . I refuse to go on."

You hesitate, but the experimenter tells you to continue. He insists that even if the learner refuses to answer, you must keep increasing the shock levels. But the other person is obviously in pain. What should you do?

Actual participants in this research—the "teachers"—suffered real conflict and distress when confronted with this problem. They sweated, trembled, stuttered, laughed nervously, and repeatedly protested that they did not want to hurt the learner. But they still obeyed.

What a Psychologist Sees

What Influences Obedience?

Milgram conducted a series of studies to discover the specific conditions that either increased or decreased obedience to authority.

From the film, *Obedience* © 1968 by Stanley Milgram; © renewed 1993 by Alexandra Milgram and distributed by Alexander Street Press.

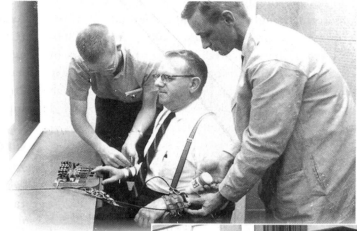

From the film, *Obedience* © 1968 by Stanley Milgram; © renewed 1993 by Alexandra Milgram and distributed by Alexander Street Press.

From the film, *Obedience* © 1968 by Stanley Milgram; © renewed 1993 by Alexandra Milgram and distributed by Alexander Street Press.

Milgram's Learner ▲

Under orders from an experimenter, would you shock a man with a known heart condition who is screaming and begging to be released? Few people believe they would. But research shows otherwise.

Milgram's Shock Generator ▶

From the film, *Obedience* © 1968 by Stanley Milgram; © renewed 1993 by Alexandra Milgram and distributed by Alexander Street Press.

Bar graph

Percentage of participants who gave 450-volt shocks

Condition	Bar
Milgram's original study	A
Orders given by ordinary person or experimenter gives orders by phone	B
Learner 11/2, (0.5 m) away	C
Teacher holds learner's hand on shock plate	D
Teacher reads list of words while another delivers shock	E
Teacher chooses level of shock	F
Teacher watches two others disobey	G
Teacher watches two others continue	H

Scale: 10 20 30 40 50 60 70 80 90 100

As you can see in the first bar on the graph (**A**), 65 percent of the participants in Milgram's original study gave the learner the full 450-volt level of shocks.

In the second bar (**B**), when orders came from an ordinary person, or from the experimenter by phone (versus in person), obedience dropped to 20 percent.

Now look at the third and fourth bars (**C** and **D**). Note how the physical closeness of the victim affected obedience. In the original experiment, the learner was seated behind a wall in another room, and 65 percent of the teachers gave the full 450-volt level of shocks. But obedience dropped to 40 percent when the learner was only 1 1/2 feet (0.5 m) away, and dropped even further to 30 percent when the teacher was required to hold the learner's hand on the shock plate.

Looking at bars (**E**) and (**F**), how does the teacher's level of responsibility affect obedience? In the original experiment, the teacher was required to actually pull the lever that supposedly delivered shocks to the learner. When the teacher only read the list of words, while another person delivered the shock, obedience increased to 92 percent. In contrast, when the teacher was allowed to choose the level of shock, obedience dropped to 2 percent.

Finally, looking at bars (**G**) and (**H**), note how modelling and imitation affected obedience. When teachers watched two other supposed teachers disobey the experimenter's orders, their own obedience dropped to 10 percent. However, when they watched other teachers follow the experimenter's orders, their obedience increased to more than 70 percent (Milgram 1963, 1974).

Self-Test

(Check your answers in Appendix A.)

1. The study of how other people influence our thoughts, feelings, and actions is called _____.
   a. sociology
   b. social science
   c. social psychology
   d. ethology

2. Which of the following are two major attribution mistakes?
   a. the fundamental attribution error and the self-serving bias
   b. situational attributions and dispositional attributions
   c. the actor bias and the observer bias
   d. prejudice and discrimination

3. When some people see homeless individuals, they think of them as lazy and unmotivated, failing to take into account the environments or situations that may have led to their condition. What explains people's tendency to focus on only this one aspect of the situation?
   a. self-serving bias
   b. cognitive dissonance
   c. groupthink
   d. saliency bias

4. Gaston thought his excellent qualifications and pleasant interpersonal style were the reasons he was hired for his new job. He then thought back to his recent firing from his previous job and how the boss was a miserable person who did not recognize his many talents. Which form of bias underlies Gaston's feelings?
   a. self-attribution bias
   b. self-serving bias
   c. actor bias
   d. saliency bias

5. Label the three components of attitudes on the figure below.

6. Which theory states that contradictions between our attitudes and behaviour can motivate us to change our attitudes to agree with our behaviour?
   a. social learning theory
   b. cognitive dissonance theory
   c. defence mechanisms theory
   d. power of inconsistencies theory

7. _____ is a learned, generally negative attitude toward specific people solely because of their membership in an identified group.
   a. Discrimination
   b. Stereotyping
   c. Cognitive biasing
   d. Prejudice

8. A number of studies have suggested that low levels of _____ may be associated with aggressive behaviour.
   a. frustration
   b. serotonin and GABA
   c. adrenaline
   d. blood sugar

9. The degree of positive feelings you have toward others is called _____.
   a. affective relations
   b. interpersonal attraction
   c. interpersonal attitudes
   d. affective connections

10. A strong and lasting attraction characterized by trust, caring, tolerance, and friendship is called _____.
    a. companionate love
    b. intimate love
    c. passionate love
    d. all of these options

11. What is the term given to the act of changing behaviour as a result of real or imagined group pressure?
    a. norm compliance
    b. obedience
    c. conformity
    d. mob rule

12. What was Stanley Milgram investigating in his classic teacher-learner shock study?
    a. the effects of punishment on learning
    b. the effects of reinforcement on learning
    c. obedience to authority
    d. all of these options

13. During _____ a person who feels anonymous within a group or crowd experiences an increase in arousal and a decrease in self-consciousness, inhibitions, and personal responsibility.

   a. groupthink

   b. group polarization

   c. authoritarianism

   d. deindividuation

14. Faulty decision-making that is the result of a highly cohesive group striving for agreement to the point of avoiding inconsistent information is known as _____.

   a. the risky shift

   b. group polarization

   c. groupthink

   d. destructive conformity

15. Zimbardo's research in which students played roles of prison inmates and guards showed that

   a. roles can influence social behaviour.

   b. because the roles were hypothetical, the students did not take them seriously.

   c. roles have little influence on social behaviour.

   d. social behaviour likely affects the roles people choose.

16. Actions that are designed to help others with no obvious benefit to the helper are referred to as _____.

   a. empathy

   b. sympathy

   c. altruism

   d. egoism

17. Cézar came upon the scene of a serious car accident and found a number of people standing around, yet no one had called 911. What is a likely reason why no one had called for help?

   a. altruism

   b. diffusion of responsibility

   c. egoistic model

   d. antisocial behaviour

18. Label the three major explanations for helping on the figure below.

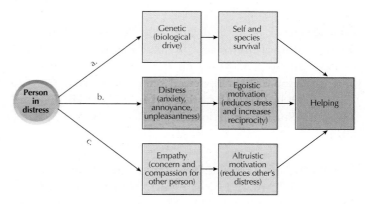

19. Research suggests that one of the best ways to decrease prejudice is to encourage _____.

   a. cooperation

   b. friendly competition

   c. reciprocity of liking

   d. conformity

20. Which of the following is most likely to decrease obedience?

   a. power of the situation

   b. foot-in-the-door

   c. socialization

   d. None of the above, as these are all ways to increase obedience.

THE PLANNER ✓

Review your Chapter Planner on the chapter opener and check off your completed work.

Chapter 1 1. d; 2. d; 3. c; 4. c; 5. b; 6. a; 7. b; 8. d; 9. Step 1: Literature review; Step 2: Operationally defined hypothesis; Step 3: Research design; Step 4: Statistical analysis; Step 5: Peer-reviewed scientific journal; Step 6: Theory; 10. b; 11. d; 12. a; 13. d; 14. b; 15. c; 16. b; 17. b; 18. d; 19. Survey, Question, Read, Recite, Review, wRite; 20. b.

Chapter 2 1. b; 2. d; 3. a; 4. a; 5. see Figure 2.6; 6. c; 7. b; 8. d; 9. b; 10. c; 11. see Figure 2.8; 12. a; 13. d; 14. c; 15. a; 16. see Figure 2.16; 17. see Figure 2.18; 18. a; 19. a. left, b. right, c. right, d. left; 20. b.

Chapter 3 1. c; 2. c; 3. d; 4. b; 5. d; 6. c; 7. b; 8. see Figure 3.3; 9. d; 10. a; 11. b; 12. d; 13. c; 14. c; 15. b; 16. c; 17. a; 18. b; 19. d; 20. b.

Chapter 4 1. c; 2. c; 3. d; 4. b; 5. see Figure 4.6; 6. c; 7. d; 8. see Figure 4.7; 9. c; 10. a; 11. b; 12. a; 13 a. photo 1, b. photo 2; 14. c; 15. b; 16. a; 17. b; 18. c; 19. b; 20. d.

Chapter 5 Critical and creative thinking question 8: the drug is alcohol 1. b; 2. c; 3. b; 4. c; 5. d; 6. a; 7. see Figure 5.2; 8. d; 9. c; 10. c; 11. c; 12. d; 13. a; 14. c; 15. a-2, b-1, c-4, d-3; 16. c; 17. b; 18. d; 19. d; 20. c.

Chapter 6 1. c; 2. c; 3. d; 4. d; 5. d; 6. c; 7. c; 8. a-2, b-1; 9. a; 10. c; 11. d; 12. a; 13. c; 14. b; 15. d; 16. c; 17. d; 18. c; 19. c; 20. d.

Chapter 7 1. a. encoding, b. retrieval, c. storage; 2. a. sensory memory, b. short-term memory (STM), c. long-term memory (LTM); 3. d; 4. a; 5. a, explicit and declarative, b, implicit and nondeclarative; 6. c; 7. d; 8. b; 9. c; 10. c; 11. c; 12. a. retrograde amnesia, b. anterograde amnesia (bottom); 13. a; 14. a. decay, b. interference, c. encoding failure, d. retrieval failure, e. motivated forgetting; 15. b; 16. b; 17. a; 18. d; 19. b; 20. c.

Chapter 8 1. b; 2. c; 3. a. preparation, b. identify given facts, c. separate relevant from irrelevant facts; 4. b; 5. a; 6. c; 7. c; 8. d; 9. d; 10. a. phonemes, b. morphemes, c. grammar; 11. b; 12. b; 13. d; 14. a; 15. b; 16. a; 17. b; 18. d; 19. b; 20. c.

Chapter 9 1. c; 2. c; 3. a. cross-sectional research, b. longitudinal research; 4. d; 5. d; 6. a; 7. c; 8. c; 9. b; 10. c;

11. d; 12. a. sensorimotor, b. preoperational, c. concrete operations, d. formal operations; 13. d; 14. c; 15. c; 16. d; 17. c; 18. b; 19. a; 20. a.

Chapter 10 1. c; 2. a; 3. c; 4. a; 5. c; 6. b; 7. a. trust, b. autonomy, c. initiative, d. industry; 8. a. identity, b. intimacy, c. generativity, d. ego integrity; 9. b; 10. c; 11. c; 12. b; 13. a; 14. a; 15. c; 16. a; 17. c; 18. d; 19. d; 20. a.

Chapter 11 1. a; 2. a; 3. c; 4. d; 5. b; 6. d; 7. d; 8. a; 9. c; 10. a. excitement, b. plateau, c. orgasm, d. resolution; 11. b; 12. c; 13. a; 14. c; 15. b; 16. c; 17. d; 18. d; 19. c; 20. c.

Chapter 12 1. b; 2. a. openness, b. conscientiousness, c. extroversion, d. agreeableness, e. neuroticism (OCEAN); 3. a. conscious, b. preconscious, c. unconscious; 4. d; 5. b; 6. c; 7. a. oral, b. anal, c. phallic, d. latency, e. genital; 8. b; 9. d; 10. d; 11. c; 12. b; 13. b; 14. c; 15. c; 16. d; 17. c; 18. c; 19. a; 20. b.

Chapter 13 1. d; 2. b; 3. Axis I. clinical disorders, Axis II. personality disorders and mental retardation, Axis III. General medical conditions, Axis IV. psychosocial and environmental problems, Axis V. global assessment of functioning; 4. a; 5. a. generalized anxiety disorder, b. panic disorder, c. phobias, d. obsessive-compulsive disorder, e. post-traumatic stress disorder; 6. d; 7. a; 8. b; 9. d; 10. a; 11. a; 12. d; 13. a. paranoid, b. catatonic, c. disorganized, d. undifferentiated, e. residual; 14. a; 15. c; 16. b; 17. a; 18. c; 19. c; 20. d.

Chapter 14 1. a; 2. c; 3. c; 4. b; 5. c; 6. c; 7. b; 8. c; 9. d; 10. a; 11. b; 12. d; 13. c; 14. c; 15. a. antianxiety drugs, b. antipsychotic drugs, c. mood stabilizer drugs, d. antidepressant drugs; 16. c; 17. b; 18. a. disturbed thoughts, b. disturbed emotions, c. disturbed behaviours, d. interpersonal and life situation difficulties, e. biomedical disturbances; 19. c; 20. b.

Chapter 15 1. c; 2. a; 3. d; 4. b; 5. a. cognitive, b. affective, c. behavioural; 6. b; 7. d; 8. b; 9. b; 10. a; 11. c; 12. c; 13. d; 14. c; 15. a; 16. c; 17. b; 18. a. evolutionary model, b. egoistic model, c. empathy-altruism model; 19. a; 20. d.

Statistics Module 1. c; 2. a; 3. c; 4. c; 5. b.

Statistics and Psychology Module: Using Numbers to Describe and Interpret Research Results

LEARNING OBJECTIVES

1. **Explain** the function and uses of statistics.
2. **Define** and describe the descriptive statistics.
3. **Understand** and interpret frequency histograms and frequency polygons.
4. **Describe** and calculate the three measures of central tendency.
5. **Describe** and calculate the three measures of spread.
6. **Explain** the function and relevance of inferential statistics.

We are constantly being bombarded with numbers: "Save 30 percent," "70 percent chance of rain," "9 out of 10 dentists recommend. . . ." Politicians use numbers to try to convince us that the economy is healthy (or unhealthy) (**Figure B.1**). Advertisers use numbers to convince us of the effectiveness of their products. Charitable organizations use numbers to convince us how badly they need our money. Psychologists and other scientists use numbers to summarize their results and support or refute their research findings. When people use numbers in these ways, they are using statistics. **Statistics** is a branch of applied mathematics that uses numbers to describe, analyze, interpret, and present information on a subject.

> **statistics**
> A branch of applied mathematics that uses numbers to describe, analyze, interpret, and present information.

Statistics make it possible for psychologists to quantify the information they obtain from their studies. They can then critically analyze and evaluate their results. Statistical analysis is imperative for researchers to describe, predict, or explain behaviour. For instance, Canadian psychologist Albert Bandura proposed that watching violence on television causes aggressive behaviour in children (Bandura & Walters, 1963). In carefully controlled experiments, he gathered numerical information and analyzed it according to specific statistical methods. The statistical analysis helped him demonstrate that the aggression of his subjects and the aggressive acts they had seen on television were related and that the relationship was causal and not mere coincidence (Chapter 6) (**Figure B.2**).

You don't have to be a math whiz to use statistics. Simple arithmetic is all you need to do most of the calculations and for more complex statistics, computer programs are readily available. A basic understanding of statistics is essential to critical thinking and real-world applications. Although the mathematical computations and formulas are important, what is more important is developing an understanding when and why each type of statistic is used.

Statistics and politics • Figure B.1 _____

Politicians routinely use statistics and statistical language to influence our beliefs and perceptions. Do you think statistics can be portrayed in ways that the original research might not have intended? Does this make statistics more or less useful?

Sean Kilpatrick/The Canadian Press

Violence and learning: The Bobo doll • Figure B.2 _____

In a related set of experiments, Bandura had children watch an adult act violently toward a large blow-up clown. Bandura then observed the behaviour of the children with the same clown. By using statistics he could make powerful research conclusions that aggressive behaviours in children can be caused by watching others behave aggressively.

With permission of Albert Bandura

The purpose of this section, then, is to help you understand the significance of the most commonly used statistics.

Organizing and Summarizing Research Results

Psychologists design their studies to gather information in order to answer research questions. The information they obtain from subjects in their studies is known as *data* (*data* is plural; its singular is *datum*). When the data are gathered, they are generally in the form of numbers; if they aren't, they are converted to numbers. After they are gathered, the data must be organized in such a way that statistical analysis is possible.

Variables

A **variable** is simply a factor or a thing that varies. In effect, a variable is anything that can assume more than one value. Height, weight, sex, eye colour, and scores on an

> **variable** Anything that can assume more than one value.

IQ test or video game are all factors that can assume more than one value in a population and are therefore variables. Number of noses is not considered a variable as it typically does not vary in a population. Anything that does not vary is called a **constant**. If researchers use only francophone Canadians in a study, then linguistic background is a constant and

> **constant** Anything that does not vary.

not a variable. Some variables will vary between people, such as sex (generally, a person is either male or female but not both at the same time). Some may vary within one person, such as scores on a video game; the same person might get 85,350 points one time and 163,410 when playing the game again (**Figure B.3**).

In non-experimental studies, variables can be factors that are merely observed and recorded through naturalistic observation or case studies, or they can be factors about which people are questioned in a test or survey. In experimental studies, the two variables of interest are the independent variable and the dependent variable. In correlational research, the variables are the linked (or related) things the researcher is studying. Beware here: do not confuse the independent variable and dependent variable of experimental designs with the related variables of correlational research. These are two completely different designs and the terms are not interchangeable. Consider this similar to the lack of interchangeability between, say, a spoon and a toaster.

Frequency Distributions

After conducting a study and obtaining measures of the variable(s) being studied, psychologists need to organize

Gaming and statistics • Figure B.3

Scores on a video game can be used as a variable. Variables like this can also be manipulated. Imagine an experiment in which an attractive confederate compliments male players in the experimental group on their gaming skills while another group of male gamers get no such compliment. What do you think might be the results of such a study? What would be the independent and dependent variables in an experiment like this?

Frederic J. Brown/AFP/Getty Images

the data in a meaningful way. **Table B.1** presents test scores from a statistics aptitude test collected from 50 college students. We use the letter n to represent the sample size. In this case $n = 50$. This information is called *raw data* because there is no order to the numbers and it has not been summarized in any way. The data are presented as they were collected.

The lack of order in raw data makes them very difficult to assess directly. Thus, the first step in understanding the results of an experiment is to impose some order on the raw

Statistics aptitude test scores for 50 college students Table B1				
73	57	63	59	50
72	66	50	67	51
63	59	65	62	65
62	72	64	73	66
61	68	62	68	63
59	61	72	63	52
59	58	57	68	57
64	56	65	59	60
50	62	68	54	63
52	62	70	60	68

frequency distribution
A summary of the number of times each score in a data set occurs.

data. This can be done in several ways. One of the simplest is to create a **frequency distribution**, which allows us to look at the number of times (or frequency) a score or an event occurs. The simplest way to make a frequency distribution is to list all the possible test scores and then tally the number of people who received those scores. **Table B.2** presents a frequency distribution using the raw data from Table B.1. As you can see, the data are now easier to read. From looking at the frequency distribution, you can see that most of the test scores lie in the middle, with only a few at the very high or very low ends of the distribution. This was not at all

Personality test scores for 50 college students
Table B.3

1350	750	530	540	750
1120	410	780	1020	430
720	1080	1110	770	610
1130	620	510	1160	630
640	1220	920	650	870
930	660	480	940	670
1070	950	680	450	990
690	1010	800	660	500
860	520	540	880	1090
580	730	570	560	740

evident when looking at the raw data and neither were the test marks that no one scored, such as 71, 69, 55, and 53.

This type of frequency distribution is practical when the number of possible scores is 20 or fewer. However, when there are more than 20 possible scores, it can be very difficult to make sense of. This difficulty can be seen in **Table B.3**, which presents the scores of 50 students who completed a hypothetical personality test. Notice that if we were to include all the test marks, including the marks that no one scored—that is, *all* the values between the highest score of 1,350 and the lowest score of 410—we would have 940 entries in the frequency distribution, making it extremely difficult to read, let alone interpret. So, when there are more than 20 possible scores, a group frequency distribution is normally used.

In a *group frequency distribution*, individual scores are clustered together in a range of scores (see **Table B.4**).

Frequency distribution of 50 students on the Statistics Aptitude Test   Table B.2

Score	Frequency
73	2
72	3
71	0
70	1
69	0
68	5
67	1
66	2
65	3
64	2
63	5
62	5
61	2
60	2
59	5
58	1
57	3
56	1
55	0
54	1
53	0
52	2
51	1
50	3
Total = 3,100*	n = 50

*Each score is multiplied by its frequency (e.g. 73 × 2 = 146), and all of these scores are added up to total 3,100.

Group frequency distribution of personality test scores for 50 college students   Table B.4

Class Interval	Frequency
1300–1390	1
1200–1290	1
1100–1190	4
1000–1090	5
900–990	5
800–890	4
700–790	7
600–690	10
500–590	9
400–490	4
Total	50

A histogram • Figure B.4

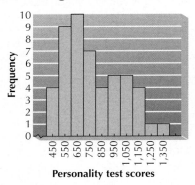

These groups are called *class intervals*. Grouping scores like this makes it much easier to make sense out of the distribution. As you can see, it is far easier to understand Table B.4 than Table B.3. Group frequency distributions are also easier to represent in a graph.

Information can be presented in the form of a bar graph, called a *histogram*, or in the form of a point or line graph, called a *polygon*. Both frequency histograms and frequency polygons allow us to picture the data and look at the shape of the distribution. **Figure B.4** shows a histogram created with the data from Table B.4. Note that the class intervals are represented along the bottom line of the graph (the *x*-axis). The width of the bar stands for the width of the class interval, and the height of the bar stands for the frequency in that interval. Look at the third bar from the left in Figure B.4. This bar represents the interval "600 to 690 personality scores," which has a frequency of 10. You can see that this directly corresponds to the same class interval in Table B.4, since graphs and tables are merely alternative ways to illustrate the same information. Now look at **Figure B.5**. The information presented here is exactly the same as that in Figure B.1 but is represented in the form of

A polygon • Figure B.5

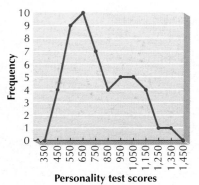

a polygon rather than a histogram. Notice that each point represents a class interval and is placed at the centre of the interval and the height corresponding to the frequency of that interval. To make the graph easier to read, straight lines connect the points. Can you see how both histograms and polygon graphs illustrate the same information? In fact, if we were to imagine a curve that touches the top of each histogram bar, it would look exactly the same as the polygon.

Graphs and Misrepresenting Data

As you have just learned, every graph has several major parts, including labels; axes; and points, lines, or bars. Find these parts in Figure B.4 and Figure B.5.

Important things to notice when interpreting a graph are the axes, labels, and values because they tell what the data are portraying. Labels should be clear, short, and easily understood. For example, in Figure B.4 the horizontal axis is clearly labelled "Personality test scores," and the vertical or *y*-axis is labelled "Frequency." If a graph is not labelled, as we sometimes see in TV commercials or magazine ads, it is impossible to interpret and should be ignored. Even when a graph is labelled, the labels can be misleading. For example, if graph designers want to distort the information, they can elongate one of the two axes. Thus, it is important to pay careful attention to the graph axes. Do not be misled by a graph that has been drawn to prove a point or sell a product (**Figure B.6**).

Displaying the data in a frequency distribution or in a graph can be especially helpful when researchers are trying to find relationships between certain variables. However, as we explained earlier, if psychologists want to make predictions or explanations about behaviour, they need to perform mathematical computations on the data.

Graphs can be used to mislead • Figure B.6

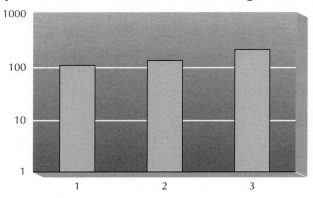

Can you identify three errors in this graph?

[Answers: No title, no axis lables, *y*-axis numerical units are not consistent.]

Numerically Describing the Data in a Distribution

Once the study has been completed and the data have been collected, the researcher must then organize the data. Along with collapsing data into meaningful graphs, the researcher must also condense them into meaningful summary numbers. This process of describing the data is formally known as **descriptive statistics**. Descriptive statistics are the numbers used to describe the data set. They can be used to describe the characteristics of a population (an entire group, such as all people living in Canada) or a sample (a part of a group, such as a randomly selected group of 250 students from McGill University). The major descriptive statistics include the measures of central tendency and the measures of spread.

descriptive statistics The summary numbers used to describe the results of a study.

Measures of Central Tendency

Descriptive statistics indicating the centre or middle of the distribution are called **measures of central tendency** and include the mean, median, and mode. They are all scores that are typical of the centre of the distribution. The *mean* is what most of us think of when we hear the word "average." The *median* is the middle value when the data set is rank ordered. The *mode* is the score that occurs most often.

measures of central tendency Descriptive statistics used to indicate the centre or middle of the distribution.

Mean Each measure of central tendency has different advantages, but in psychological research, the mean is used most often. The mean or arithmetic average is obtained by adding all the raw scores and then dividing this number by the total number of scores in the sample (n). The mean is represented by an x with a bar above it ($\overline{X}$, pronounced "x bar"). If we wanted to compute the $\overline{X}$ of the raw statistics test scores in Table B.2, we would sum all the x's and divide by n. In Table B.2, the sum of all the scores is 3,100 and there are 50 scores. Therefore, the mean of these scores is 62.

$$\overline{X} = \frac{3,100}{50} = 62$$

Although the mean is probably the most widely used measure of central tendency, it has one important problem: it is exquisitely sensitive to extreme scores or outliers. Take a look at the example in **Table B.5**. The values represent

Mean household income for streets A, B, and C
Table B.5

Street A($)	Street B($)	Street C($)
66,000	65,000	63,000
72,000	80,000	69,000
78,000	79,000	82,000
67,000	3,000,000	71,000
79,000	58,000	73,000
65,000	77,000	65,000
80,000	71,000	68,000
$\overline{X} = 72,428$	$\overline{X} = 490,000$	$\overline{X} = 70,142$

household incomes in 2012 for three small streets in Anytown, Canada. Notice how the means differ among the streets. What accounts for the difference you see between street A and C compared with B? If you did not have access to the raw data, you might wrongly conclude that Street B was far more affluent than A and C. It turns out that one extreme score is artificially inflating the mean in Street B. Without this score the mean for this street would be much closer to the means of the other two streets; calculate it and see. In such cases, when the data set contains extreme scores, the mean is tricky as a measure of central tendency and can properly be considered only with the measures of spread and the other measures of central tendency (**Figure B.7**).

Which house has the owner with the $3,000,000 salary? • Figure B.7 _____

Using the mean as a measure of central tendency can distort data interpretation severely. If a local government determined property taxes based only on mean income in a street, which street would you want to live on?

Digital Paws Inc./iStockphoto

Median The median is the middle score in the distribution once all the scores have been ranked from lowest to highest. If the total number of scores is odd, then there actually is a middle score and that middle score is the median. When *n* is an even number, the median is the mean of the two middle scores. **Table B.6** shows the computation of the median for two different sets of scores, one set with an odd number of scores (15) and one with an even number of scores (10).

Mode Of all the measures of central tendency, the easiest to compute is the mode, which is the most frequent score or the score that occurs most often.

Measures of Spread

When describing a distribution, it is not sufficient to give only the measures of central tendency; it is also necessary to give a **measure of spread**, which is a measure of the variation of the scores in the distribution. By examining the spread, we can determine whether the scores are bunched tightly around

> **measures of spread** Measures of the amount of variation of the scores in the distribution.

Computation of median for odd and even numbers of IQ scores Table B.6	
IQ	**IQ**
139	137
130	135
121	121
116	116
107	108 ← middle score
101	106 ← middle score
98	105
96 ← middle score	101
84	98
83	97
82	*n* = 10
75	*n* is even
75	
68	Median = $\frac{106 + 108}{2}$ = 107
65	
n = 15	
n is odd	
Median = 96	

Squished together or spread out? Measure of spread • Figure B.8

Three distributions with the same mean but different variability or measure of spread. Notice that the mean of 50 is the same for all three distributions.

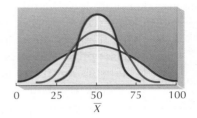

the middle value or tend to extend far from the middle value. **Figure B.8** shows three different distributions, all with the same mean but with different spreads of scores. Notice that different spreads correspond to different distribution shapes. To measure spread, we use one of three calculations.

Range The simplest measure of spread is the range. It is calculated by subtracting the highest score in the data set from the lowest score. The range gives a measure of total spread, but its biggest limitation is that it is extremely sensitive to outliers. This sensitivity occurs because the formula for calculating the range requires that the two most extreme scores be used—the biggest and the smallest value. Because extreme scores are often not representative values in the data set, the range has limited usefulness and is not widely used as a measure of spread.

Variance As you have just seen, using extreme scores to calculate a measure of spread is problematic. A better spread measure—the variance—calculates how far and every score in the data set deviates (or differs) from the middle score (usually the mean). Both the variance and the standard deviation are calculated by using these deviation scores.

$$s^2 = \frac{\sum (X - \overline{X})^2}{n}$$

Dismantling the Sample Variance Formula: Explaining It in Words

Step 1: Subtract the mean from each score in the data set. This provides a set of deviation scores.

Step 2: Square each deviation score.

Step 3: Add all the squared deviation scores to get one overall total deviation score.

Step 4: Divide the total deviation score by the sample size.

The result is an average squared deviation score or the sample variance, which is represented by s^2. After you have calculated the variance, the standard deviation is very easy.

Standard Deviation You might notice that the standard deviation is simply the square root of the variance. The standard deviation is the most widely used measure of variation and is represented by a lowercase s. The standard deviation is a standard measurement of how much the scores in a distribution deviate on average from the mean. The formula for the standard deviation is shown below. **Table B.7** shows how to compute standard deviation and a variance.

$$s = \sqrt{\frac{\sum (X - \overline{X})^2}{n}}$$

Most distributions of psychological data are bell shaped. That is, most of the scores are grouped around the mean, and the farther the scores are from the mean in either direction,

Computation of the standard deviation for 10 IQ scores
Table B.7
Mean = 110; n = 10

IQ Scores X Score	X − X̄ Score − mean = deviation score	(X − X̄)² Deviation score squared
143	143 − 110 = 33	1089
127	17	289
116	6	36
98	−12	144
85	−25	625
107	−3	9
106	−4	16
98	−12	144
104	−6	36
116	6	36
$\sum x = 1100$		$\sum (X - \overline{X})^2 = 2424$

Standard Deviation = s

$$= \sqrt{\frac{\sum (X - \overline{X})^2}{n}} = \sqrt{\frac{2424}{10}}$$

$$\sqrt{242.4} = 15.569$$

Variance = s^2 = 242.4

Normal distributions • Figure B.9

The normal distribution forms a symmetrical bell-shaped curve. In a normal distribution, two-thirds of the scores lie between one standard deviation above and one standard deviation below the mean.

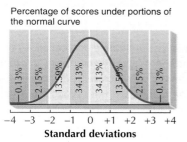

Percentage of scores under portions of the normal curve

the fewer the scores. Notice the bell shape of the distribution in **Figure B.9.** Such distributions as this are called *normal* distributions. In normal distributions, approximately two-thirds of the scores fall within a range that is one standard deviation below the mean to one standard deviation above the mean. For example, the Wechsler IQ tests (Chapter 8) have a mean of 100 and a standard deviation of 15. This means that approximately two-thirds of the people taking these tests will have scores between 85 and 115.

Inferential Statistics: Using the Sample to Generalize to the Larger Population

Descriptive statistics do just that—describe the data obtained from the study. Although descriptive statistics have many uses in numerically summarizing the results, they do not allow a researcher to make conclusions about the larger population. After all, who really cares about the results of a study of 50 people when the population might be a million or more? The use of **inferential statistics** allows psychologists and scientists to take a sample result and draw reliable conclusions about the larger population. By using a variety of different statistical tools, researchers can say with some degree of certainty what the results would have been if they had tested the entire population (which they can obviously never do). Inferential statistics also allow researchers to assess the probability of random or chance findings in their study and make comparisons between different study groups. As you can imagine, this is a very valuable statistical tool that provides the ability to draw powerful conclusions from study results (**Figure B.10**).

> **inferential statistics** Sample statistics used to make reliable claims about the larger population.

Radu Razvan/iStockphoto

Statistics and research • Figure B.10 _____

Descriptive statistics summarize and collapse raw data into manageable and representative numbers. Inferential statistics allows researchers to extrapolate from sample results to the entire population of interest. Both types are widely used in many different scientific arenas.

CONCEPT CHECK STOP

1. **What** is the main problem with using the mean as a measure of central tendency?

2. **How** is the variance different from the standard deviation?

3. **What** purpose do inferential statistics serve?

Summary

1 Organizing and Summarizing Research Results 440

- **Statistics** make it possible for psychologists to quantify the information they gather from their studies. Research results are obtained by measuring **variables** of interest. These are then numerically organized for statistical analysis and interpretation by using **frequency distributions**. Frequency polygons and frequency histograms allow us to look at the shape of the research results and draw conclusions. Care must be taken in interpreting graphs as they can be used to misrepresent data.

2 Numerically Describing the Data in a Distribution 443

- **Descriptive statistics** (which are not the same as descriptive studies) are used to numerically organize and summarize research results. The **measures of central tendency** provide information about the middle values. The **measures of spread** numerically quantify the shape of the distribution.

3 Inferential Statistics: Using the Sample to Generalize to the Larger Population 445

- **Inferential statistics** allow us to generalize sample results to the larger population.

Key Terms

- constant p. 440
- descriptive statistics p. 443
- frequency distribution p. 441
- inferential statistics p. 445
- measures of central tendency p. 443
- measures of spread p. 444
- statistics p. 439
- variable p. 440

Self-Test

(Check your answers in Appendix A.)

1. The measure of central tendency that requires adding all the values and dividing by *n* is the _____.
   a. median
   b. mode
   c. mean
   d. middle value

2. The primary problem with the mean is that it _____.
   a. is sensitive to outliers
   b. is not sensitive to outliers
   c. is complicated and difficult to calculate
   d. does not include all the values in the data set

3. One measure of spread is the _____.
   a. independent variable
   b. mode
   c. standard deviation
   d. standard median

4. The standard deviation is the _____.
   a. square of the variance
   b. middle value in an ordered data set
   c. square root of the variance
   d. least commonly used measure of spread

5. _____ allow(s) us to take a sample result and draw research conclusions about the larger population.
   a. Descriptive statistics
   b. Inferential statistics
   c. Correlational research
   d. Experimental research

abnormal behaviour Patterns of emotion, thought, and action that are considered pathological (diseased or disordered) for one or more of these reasons: statistical infrequency, disability or dysfunction, personal distress, or violation of norms (Davison et al., 2010).

accommodation In Piaget's theory, the process of adjusting old schemas or developing new ones to better fit with new information.

achievement motivation A desire to excel, especially when in competition with others.

action potential The voltage change across an axon membrane when an impulse is transmitted.

activity theory of aging Successful aging is fostered by a full and active commitment to life.

addiction A broad term referring to a condition in which a person has an overwhelming commitment to the drug of choice that supplants all other activities.

aggression Any behaviour intended to harm someone.

agonistic drug A drug that mimics or enhances the activity of neurotransmitters.

algorithm A logical step-by-step procedure that, if followed correctly, will eventually solve the problem.

altered state of consciousness (ASC) Mental states found generally during sleep, dreaming, psychoactive drug use, and hypnosis.

altruism Actions designed to help others with no obvious benefit to the helper.

Alzheimer's disease (AD) A degenerative brain disease characterized by progressive mental deterioration and pathological memory loss.

anorexia nervosa An eating disorder characterized by a pathological drive to be thin, excessive food restriction, extreme weight loss, and a distorted body image.

antagonistic drug A drug that blocks or inhibits the activity of neurotransmitters.

anxiety disorder A type of abnormal behaviour characterized by unrealistic, irrational fear.

applied research Research designed to solve practical real-world problems.

assimilation In Piaget's theory, the process of absorbing new information into existing schemas.

assumption Something taken for granted to be true.

attachment A strong affectional bond with primary caretakers that endures over time.

attitudes Learned predispositions to respond cognitively, affectively, and behaviourally to particular subjects in a particular way.

attributions Our explanations for the causes of our own and others' actions.

autonomic nervous system (ANS) Subdivision of the peripheral nervous system (PNS) that controls involuntary functions of tissues, organs, and glands. It is subdivided into the *sympathetic* nervous system and the *parasympathetic* nervous system.

basic research Research conducted to advance scientific knowledge and test scientific theories.

behaviour therapy A group of techniques based on learning principles that is used to change maladaptive behaviours.

behavioural genetics The study of the relative contributions of genetic influences and environment factors on behaviour and mental processes.

bias When a belief prevents fair judgement of an issue.

binge drinking When a man consumes five or more drinks in a row or a woman consumes four or more drinks in a row on at least three occasions during the previous two weeks.

biological preparedness Innate (built-in) readiness to form associations between certain stimuli and responses.

biological research Scientific studies of the brain and other parts of the nervous system.

biomedical therapy The use of physiological interventions (drugs, electroconvulsive therapy, and psychosurgery) to reduce or alleviate symptoms of psychological disorders.

biopsychosocial model A unifying theme of modern psychology that considers biological, psychological, and social processes.

bipolar disorder Repeated episodes of mania (unreasonable elation and hyperactivity) and depression.

bulimia nervosa An eating disorder characterized by the consumption of large quantities of food (bingeing), followed by vomiting, extreme exercise, or laxative use (purging) to prevent weight gain.

central nervous system (CNS) The brain and spinal cord.

cerebral cortex The thin surface layer on the cerebral hemispheres that regulates most complex behaviour, including processing sensations, motor control, and higher mental processes.

chunking The act of grouping separate pieces of information into a single unit (or chunk).

circadian [ser-KAY-dee-an] **rhythms** Biological, biochemical, and behavioural changes that occur in living organisms on a 24-hour cycle (in Latin, *circa* means "about," and *dies* means "day").

classical conditioning Learning that occurs when a neutral stimulus (NS) is paired (associated) with an unconditioned stimulus (UCS) to elicit a conditioned response (CR).

cognition The mental activities involved in acquiring, storing, retrieving, and using knowledge.

cognitive dissonance A feeling of discomfort caused by a discrepancy between an attitude and a behaviour or between two attitudes.

cognitive therapy Therapy that focuses on changing faulty thought processes and beliefs to treat problem behaviours.

cognitive-social theory A perspective that emphasizes the roles of thinking and social learning in behaviour.

collectivistic cultures Cultures in which the needs and goals of the group are emphasized over the needs and goals of the individual.

concrete operational stage Piaget's third stage (roughly ages 7 to 11) in which the child can perform mental operations on concrete objects and understand reversibility and conservation, although abstract thinking is not yet present.

conditioning The process of learning associations between environmental stimuli and behavioural responses.

conduction deafness (middle-ear deafness) Deafness resulting from problems with the mechanical system that conducts sound waves to the inner ear.

conformity The act of changing our behaviour as a result of real or imagined group pressure.

confound variables Nuisance variables that can affect the outcome of the study and lead to erroneous conclusions about the effects of the independent variable on the dependent variable.

conscious Freud's term for thoughts or motives that a person is currently aware of or is remembering.

consciousness An organism's awareness of its own self and surroundings (Damasio, 1999).

constant Anything that does not vary.

control group The group that does not receive the experimental manipulations but is treated in the same way as the experimental group in all other areas.

conventional level Kohlberg's second level of moral development in which moral judgements are based on compliance with the rules and values of society.

coping Adaptive or compensatory strategies designed to reduce the effects of a stressor.

correlational research A research method in which variables are observed or measured (without manipulation) to identify possible relationships between them.

creativity The ability to produce valued outcomes in a novel way.

critical period A time of special sensitivity to specific experiences that shapes the capacity for future development.

critical thinking The ability to accurately analyze information and be able to draw rational, fact-based conclusions based on the empirical evidence provided.

cross-sectional method Research design that compares individuals of various ages at one point in time to provide information about age differences.

debriefing Informing participants after a study about the purpose of the study, the nature of the anticipated results, and any deception used.

defence mechanisms In Freudian theory, the ego's protective method of reducing anxiety by self-deception and the distortion of reality.

deindividuation Increased arousal and reduced self-consciousness, inhibition, and personal responsibility that may occur in a group.

delusions Mistaken beliefs based on misrepresentations of reality.

dependent variable (DV) A variable that is measured; it is affected by (or dependent on) the independent variable and is the outcome or effect variable.

depressants Drugs that slow or depress nervous system activity.

descriptive research Research methods used to observe, record, and describe behaviour (without producing cause-effect explanations).

descriptive statistics The summary numbers used to describe the results of a study.

developmental psychology The study of age-related changes in behaviour and mental processes from conception to death.

Diagnostic and Statistical Manual of Mental Disorders (DSM-IV-TR) The classification system developed by the American Psychiatric Association used to describe abnormal behaviours; the *IV-TR* indicates that it is the text revision (TR) of the fourth major edition *(IV)*.

discrimination Negative behaviour directed at members of a group.

disengagement theory Successful aging is characterized by mutual withdrawal between the aging person and society.

dissociative disorders Amnesia, fugue, or multiple personalities resulting from avoidance of painful memories or situations.

drug abuse Drug use that is necessary for feelings of continued well-being; use continues despite adverse consequence.

dyssomnias Problems in the amount, timing, and quality of sleep, including insomnia, sleep apnea, and narcolepsy.

elaborative rehearsal The process of linking new information to previously stored material.

electroconvulsive therapy (ECT) Biomedical therapy in which electrical current is passed through the brain.

embryonic period The second stage of prenatal development, which begins after uterine implantation and lasts through the eighth week.

emotion A state of physiological arousal and tendency toward action involving changes in behaviour, cognitions, facial expressions, and subjective feelings.

emotion-focused forms of coping Coping strategies based on changing one's perceptions of stressful situations.

empirical evidence Information acquired by formal observation, experimentation, and measurement by using systematic scientific methods.

encoding Processing information into the memory system.

encoding specificity principle Retrieval of information is improved when the conditions of recovery are similar to the conditions that existed when the information was first encoded.

eustress Pleasant, beneficial, or curative stress.

evolutionary psychology A branch of psychology that studies the ways in which natural selection and evolution can help to explain behaviour and mental processes.

evolutionary/circadian theory As a part of circadian rhythms, sleep evolved to conserve energy and to serve as protection from predators.

experiment A carefully controlled scientific procedure that determines whether variables manipulated by the experimenter have a causal effect on the experiment result.

experimental group The group that receives the experimental manipulation.

explicit/declarative memory The subsystem within long-term memory that consciously stores facts, information, and personal life experiences.

extrinsic motivation Motivation based on obvious external rewards or threats of punishment.

family therapy Treatment to change maladaptive interaction patterns within a family.

feature detectors Specialized brain cells that respond only to certain sensory information.

fetal period The third and final stage of prenatal development (eight weeks to birth), which is characterized by rapid weight gain in the fetus and the fine detailing of bodily organs and systems.

five-factor model (FFM) The trait theory that explains personality in terms of the "Big Five" dimensions of openness, conscientiousness, extroversion, agreeableness, and neuroticism.

formal operational stage Piaget's fourth stage (around age 11 and beyond), which is characterized by abstract and hypothetical thinking.

frequency distribution A summary of the number of times each score in a data set occurs.

fundamental attribution error (FAE) The tendency to attribute people's behaviour to internal (dispositional) causes rather than external (situational) factors.

gate-control theory The theory that pain sensations are processed and altered by mechanisms within the spinal cord.

gender Psychological and sociocultural meanings added to biological maleness or femaleness.

gender roles Societal expectations for normal and appropriate male and female behaviour.

general adaptation syndrome (GAS) Selye's three-part generalized model of how organisms characteristically react physiologically to stressors.

germinal period The first stage of prenatal development, which begins with conception and ends with implantation in the uterus (the first two weeks).

glial cell A nervous system cell that supports, nourishes, insulates, and protects neurons.

grammar Rules that specify how phonemes, morphemes, words, and phrases should be combined to express thoughts; these rules include syntax and semantics.

group polarization A group's movement toward either riskier or more conservative behaviour depending on the members' initial dominant tendencies.

group therapy A form of therapy in which a number of people meet together to work toward therapeutic goals.

groupthink Faulty decision-making that occurs when a highly cohesive group strives for agreement and avoids inconsistent information.

habituation The tendency of the brain to ignore environmental factors that remain constant.

hallucinations Imaginary sensory perceptions that occur without an external stimulus.

hardiness A personality factor that produces resilient optimism by having a strong commitment to personal goals, feeling in control over life, and viewing change as a challenge rather than a threat.

health psychology The study of how biological, psychological, and social factors interact in health and illness.

heuristic A simple rule or shortcut for problem solving that does not guarantee a solution but does narrow the alternatives.

hierarchy of needs Maslow's theory of motivation that some motives (such as physiological and safety needs) must be met before going on to higher needs (such as belonging and self-actualization).

homeostasis A body's tendency to maintain a relatively stable state, such as a constant internal temperature, blood glucose level, oxygen level, or water balance.

hormones Chemicals synthesized by endocrine glands that are released into the bloodstream to bind to target tissues and organs, producing bodily changes or maintaining normal function.

human sexual response cycle Masters and Johnson's influential description of the four physiological stages of sexual arousal: excitement, plateau, orgasm, and resolution.

humanistic therapy Therapy that seeks to maximize personal growth through affective restructuring (emotional readjustment).

hypnosis A trancelike state of heightened suggestibility, deep relaxation, and intense focus.

implicit/nondeclarative memory The subsystem within long-term memory that consists of non-conscious procedural skills, simple classically conditioned responses (Chapter 6), and priming.

independent variable (IV) A variable that is manipulated by the researcher to determine its effect on the dependent variable. The IV is the cause variable.

individualistic cultures Cultures in which the needs and goals of the individual are emphasized over the needs and goals of the group.

inferential statistics Sample statistics used to make reliable claims about the larger population.

informed consent A participant's agreement to take part in a study after being told what to expect.

insight Sudden understanding of a problem that implies the solution.

instinctive drift The tendency of some conditioned responses to shift (or drift) back toward innate response patterns.

instincts Behavioural patterns that are unlearned (inborn), always expressed in the same way, and are universal in a species.

intelligence quotient (IQ) An individual's mental age divided by his or her chronological age and multiplied by 100.

intelligence The global capacity to think rationally, act purposefully, and deal effectively with the environment.

interpersonal attraction Positive feelings toward another.

intrinsic motivation Motivation resulting from personal enjoyment of a task or an activity.

labelled lines The way the brain interprets the type of sensory information based on its neural origin in the body and its destination in the brain.

language A form of communication that uses sounds and symbols combined according to specified rules.

latent learning Hidden learning that exists without behavioural signs.

law of effect Thorndike's rule that the probability of an action being repeated is strengthened when followed by a pleasant or satisfying consequence.

learning A relatively permanent change in behaviour or mental processes because of practice or experience.

localization of function Specialization of various parts of the brain for particular functions.

longitudinal method A research design that follows a group of same-aged individuals over time to provide information about age changes.

long-term memory (LTM) This third memory stage stores information for long periods. Its capacity is limitless; its duration is relatively permanent.

long-term potentiation (LTP) Long-lasting increase in neural excitability caused by repeated neural input. Believed to be the biological basis of learning and memory.

maintenance rehearsal Repeating information to keep it active and reverberating in short-term memory.

major depressive disorder Long-lasting depressed mood that interferes with the ability to function, feel pleasure, or maintain interest in life.

maturation Development governed by automatic, genetically predetermined signals.

measures of central tendency Descriptive statistics used to indicate the centre or middle of the distribution.

measures of spread Measures of the amount of variation of the scores in the distribution.

medical model The perspective that diseases (including mental illness) have physical causes that can be diagnosed, treated, and possibly cured.

meditation A group of techniques designed to refocus attention, block out all distractions, and produce an altered state of consciousness.

memory An internal record or representation of some prior event or experience.

meninges The triple-layered set of membranes that envelop the CNS to provide support and protection.

mindfulness A moment-to-moment non-judgmental awareness of one's experience.

misinformation effect Distortion of a memory by misleading post-event information.

modelling therapy A learning technique in which the subject watches and imitates models who demonstrate desirable behaviours.

morpheme [MOR-feem] The smallest meaningful unit of language, formed from a combination of phonemes.

motivation An internal state that activates, directs, and maintains behaviour, usually toward a goal or away from an unfavourable situation.

myelin sheath The fatty insulation that segmentally wraps an axon and serves to speed neural transmission.

natural selection The process by which genetically linked traits that confer a survival or reproductive advantage will increase in the population.

nature-nurture controversy The historical dispute over the relative contributors of nature (heredity) and nurture (environment) in the development of behaviour and mental processes.

nerve deafness (inner-ear deafness) Deafness resulting from damage to the cochlea, hair cells, or auditory nerve.

neurogenesis The process by which new neurons are generated.

neuron A nervous system cell that receives and conducts electrochemical impulses.

neuroplasticity The brain's remarkable malleability to reorganize and change its structure and function across the lifespan.

neuroscience An interdisciplinary field that studies how biological processes interact with behaviour and mental processes.

neurotransmitters Chemicals that neurons release in response to the arrival of an action potential, which affect other cells, including other neurons.

nociceptor A special type of sensory receptor that signals the spinal cord and brain in response to potentially damaging stimuli.

non-rapid-eye-movement (NREM) sleep Stages 1 to 4 of sleep.

obedience The act of following a direct command, usually from an authority figure.

objective personality tests Standardized questionnaires that require written responses, usually to multiple-choice or true-false questions.

observational learning The learning of new behaviour or information by watching others (also known as social learning or modelling).

operant conditioning Learning in which voluntary responses are controlled by their consequences (also known as instrumental or Skinnerian conditioning).

opiates Drugs derived from opium or synthetically derived and molecularly similar to opium that relieve pain and induce sleep.

opponent-process theory The theory that colour perception is based on three systems of colour receptors, each of which responds in an on-off fashion to opposite-colour stimuli: blue or yellow, red or green, and black or white.

parasomnias Abnormal disturbances occurring during sleep, including nightmares, night terrors, sleepwalking, and sleep talking.

perception The higher-level process of selecting, organizing, and interpreting sensory data into useful mental representations of the world.

perceptual constancy The tendency for the environment to be perceived as remaining the same, even with changes in sensory input.

peripheral nervous system (PNS) All other neurons connecting the CNS to the rest of the body.

personality disorders Inflexible, maladaptive personality traits that cause significant impairment of social and occupational functioning.

personality Relatively stable and enduring patterns of thoughts, feelings, and actions.

phoneme [FO-neem] The smallest basic unit of speech or sound (the English language has about 40 phonemes).

physical dependence Changes in physical or bodily processes that make the drug necessary for daily functioning.

plagiarism A form of academic dishonesty in which a person takes credit for the work or ideas of another person or fails to cite a source or an idea.

postconventional level Kohlberg's highest level of moral development in which individuals develop personal standards for right and wrong, and they define morality in terms of abstract principles and values that apply to all situations and societies.

post-traumatic stress disorder (PTSD) An anxiety disorder that develops following exposure to a life-threatening or other extreme event that evoked great horror or helplessness. It is characterized by flashbacks, nightmares, and impaired daily functioning.

preconscious Freud's term for thoughts, motives, or memories that exist just beneath the surface of awareness and that can be easily brought to mind.

preconventional level Kohlberg's first level of moral development in which morality is based on rewards, punishment, and the exchange of favours.

prejudice A learned, generally negative attitude directed toward specific people solely because of their membership in an identified group.

preoperational stage Piaget's second stage (roughly ages 2 to 7 years), which is characterized by the ability to employ significant language and to think symbolically although the child lacks operations (reversible mental processes) and thinking is egocentric and animistic.

problem-focused forms of coping Coping strategies that use problem-solving strategies to decrease or eliminate the source of stress.

projective tests Psychological tests that use ambiguous stimuli, such as inkblots or drawings, onto which the test taker is believed to project his or her unconscious thoughts and conflicts.

psychiatry The branch of medicine that deals with the diagnosis, treatment, and prevention of mental disorders.

psychoactive drugs Chemicals that alter perception, conscious awareness, or mood.

psychoanalysis Freudian therapy designed to bring unconscious conflicts, which usually date back to early childhood experiences, into consciousness. Also refers to Freud's theoretical school of thought, which emphasizes unconscious processes.

psychodynamic therapy A modern form of psychoanalysis that emphasizes internal conflicts, motives, and unconscious forces.

psychology The scientific study of behaviour and mental processes.

psychoneuroimmunology The interdisciplinary field in which researchers study the interaction among the mind, the nervous system, and the immune system.

psychopharmacology The study of drug effects on the brain and behaviour.

psychosexual stages In Freudian theory, the five developmental periods (oral, anal, phallic, latency, and genital) during which particular kinds of pleasures must be gratified if personality development is to proceed normally.

psychosocial stages In Erikson's theory, the eight developmental stages, each of which involves a crisis that must be successfully resolved.

psychosurgery Operative procedures on the brain designed to relieve severe mental symptoms that have not responded to other forms of treatment.

psychotherapy Techniques employed to improve psychological functioning and promote adjustment to life.

punishment A consequence that weakens a response, making the response less likely to occur again.

random assignment Everyone selected to be in the study has an equal chance of being put in either the control group or the experimental group.

random selection Everyone in the population of interest has an equal chance of being in the sample.

rapid-eye-movement (REM) sleep Stage of sleep marked by rapid eye movements, high-frequency brain waves, paralysis of large muscles, and dreaming.

reciprocal determinism Bandura's belief that cognitions, behaviours, and the environment interact to produce personality.

reflexes or reflex arcs Involuntary, automatic behaviour initiated by the spinal cord in response to some stimulus.

reinforcement A consequence that strengthens a response, making the response more likely to occur again.

reliability A measure of the consistency and stability of test scores when a test is re-administered.

repair/restoration theory A theory proposing that we sleep because it serves a recuperative function, allowing organisms to repair or replenish key cognitive and physiological factors.

retrieval Recovering information from memory storage.

retrieval cue A clue or prompt that helps stimulate recall and retrieval of a stored piece of information from long-term memory.

savant syndrome A condition in which a person who has an intellectual disability exhibits exceptional skill or brilliance in some limited field.

schemas Cognitive structures or patterns consisting of a number of organized ideas that grow and differentiate with experience.

schizophrenia A group of psychotic disorders involving major disturbances in perception, language, thought, emotion, and behaviour.

scientific method A systematic and orderly procedure for understanding and learning about the world.

selective attention Filtering out distractions and attending only to important sensory messages.

self-concept Rogers' term for all the information and beliefs that individuals have about their own nature, qualities, and behaviour.

self-efficacy Bandura's term for the learned belief that you are capable of producing desired results, such as mastering new skills and achieving personal goals.

sensation The process of receiving, translating, and transmitting raw sensory data from the external and internal environments to the brain.

sensorimotor stage Piaget's first stage (birth to approximately age 2), in which schemas are developed through sensory and motor activities.

sensory adaptation Repeated or constant stimulation decreases the number of sensory messages sent to the brain from the sense receptors.

sensory memory This first memory stage holds sensory information and has a relatively large capacity but a duration of only a few seconds.

sensory transduction The process by which a physical stimulus is converted into neural impulses.

sex Biological maleness and femaleness, including chromosomal sex. Also activities related to sexual behaviours, such as masturbation and intercourse.

sexual orientation The direction of a person's sexual attraction toward persons of the same sex (gay or lesbian), the other sex (heterosexual), or both sexes (bisexual).

shaping The reinforcement of successively closer and closer approximations to the desired response.

short-term memory (STM) This second memory stage temporarily stores encoded sensory information and decides whether to send it on to long-term memory (LTM). Its capacity is limited to five to nine items, and its duration is about 30 seconds.

social psychology The study of how other people influence a person's thoughts, feelings, and actions.

socioemotional selectivity theory A natural decline in social contact as older adults become more selective with their time.

somatic nervous system (SNS) Subdivision of the peripheral nervous system (PNS). The SNS transmits incoming sensory information and controls the skeletal muscles.

standardization The establishment of the norms and uniform procedures for giving and scoring a test.

statistics A branch of applied mathematics that uses numbers to describe, analyze, interpret, and present information.

stem cells Precursor (immature) cells that can develop into any type of new specialized cells; a stem cell holds all information it needs to make bone, blood, brain—any part of a human body—and can also copy itself to maintain a stock of stem cells.

stereotype threat Negative stereotypes about minority groups that cause some members to doubt their abilities.

stimulants Drugs that speed up nervous system activity.

storage Retaining information over time.

stress The body's non-specific response to any demand made on it; the physical and mental arousal to circumstances that we perceive as threatening or challenging.

stressor An event that places demands on an organism that tax its resources.

substance-related disorders Abuse of or dependence on a mood- or behaviour-altering drug.

tolerance A state reached when the physiological reaction to the drug decreases, such that increasing doses are necessary for the same effect.

trait A relatively stable and consistent characteristic that can be used to describe someone.

trichromatic theory The theory that colour perception results from mixing three distinct colour systems: red, green, and blue.

unconditional positive regard Rogers' term for positive behaviour toward a person without attaching any requirements or prerequisites.

unconscious Freud's term for thoughts, motives, or memories blocked from normal awareness but that still exert great influence.

validity The ability of a test to measure what it was designed to measure.

variable Anything that can assume more than one value.

withdrawal Characteristic signs that appear in a person when a drug is discontinued after prolonged use.

Chapter 1

Table 1.2, Figure 1.5, from Huffman, Karen. *Psychology in Action, 9e*. Reprinted with permission of John Wiley & Sons, Inc. Study Organizer 1.1, text from Huffman, Karen. *Psychology in Action, 9e*. Reprinted with permission of John Wiley & Sons, Inc.

Chapter 2

Figure 2.1 from Huffman, Karen. *Psychology in Action, 8e*. Reprinted with permission of John Wiley & Sons, Inc. Figure 2.7 from Tortora & Derrickson, *Principles of Anatomy and Physiology, 12e*. Reprinted with permission of John Wiley & Sons, Inc.*What a Psychologist Sees: How Toxins Affect Our Brain*, text from *Psychology in Action, 8e*. Reprinted with permission of John Wiley & Sons, Inc. *Psychological Science: The Brain Isn't Necessary for an Erection* adapted from Fig. 4.9 in Le Vay, S., & Baldwin, J. (2009). *Human Sexuality* (3rd ed.). Sunderland, MA: Sinauer Associates Inc., p. 103. Figure 2.8, Figure 2.9, Figure 2.11, Figure 2.13, Figure 2.14, Figure 2.15, Figure 2.16, Figure 2.18, Figure 2.20, Figure 2.22 (illustrations), Figure 2.23, and Figure 2.24 from Huffman, Karen. *Psychology in Action, 9e*. Reprinted with permission of John Wiley & Sons, Inc.

Chapter 3

Figure 3.1 from Huffman, Karen. *Psychology in Action, 9e*. Reprinted with permission of John Wiley & Sons, Inc. Table 3.1 from Hobson, C. J., Kamen, J., Szostek, J., Nethercut, C. M., Tiedmann, J. W., &Wojnarowicz, S. (1998). Stressful life events: A revision and update of the Social Readjustment Rating Scale. *International Journal of Stress Management, 5*(1), 1–23. Figure 3.4, Figure 3.5, and Figure 3.13, from Huffman, Karen *Psychology in Action, 9e*. Reprinted with permission of John Wiley & Sons, Inc. Table 3.2 from Statistics Canada. (2012a). Leading causes of death, by sex, 2009. Retrieved from www.statcan.gc.ca/tables-tableaux/sum-om/l01/cst01/hlth36a-eng.htm. Figure 3.10 from Statistics Canada. (2012b). Smokers, by sex, provinces and territories, 2011. Statistics Canada, CANSIM, table 105-0501and Catalogue no. 82-221-X. Data retrieved from www.statcan.gc.ca/tables-tableaux/sum-som/l01/cst01/health74b-eng.htm.

Chapter 4

Figure 4.1, Figure 4.3, text, Figure 4.7, Figure 4.8, Figure 4.11, and *What a Psychologist Sees: Four Visual Perceptual Constancies*, drawing of Ames room from Huffman, Karen. *Psychology in Action, 9e*. Reprinted with permission of John Wiley & Sons, Inc. Figure 4.8 (bottom) from Huffman, Karen, *Psychology in Action, 10e*. Reprinted with permission of John Wiley & Sons, Inc.

Chapter 5

Figure 5.1 and 5.2 from Huffman, Karen. *Psychology in Action, 9e*. Reprinted with permission of John Wiley & Sons, Inc. *Applying Psychology: A Wake-Up Call: Are You Sleep Deprived?* quiz from "Sleep for Success!" Maas, James and Robbins, Rebecca, AuthorHouse 2011. Reproduced by permission.Figure 5.3 and Figure 5.13 from Huffman, Karen, *Psychology in Action, 10e*. Reprinted with permission of John Wiley & Sons, Inc. Figure 5.14 from Paglia-Boak, A., Adlaf, E., & Mann, R.(2011). Drug use among Ontario students 1977–2011: Detailed OSDUHS findings. Centre forAddiction and Mental Health. Retrievedfrom http://www.camh.net/ Research/Areas_of_research/Population_Life_Course_Studies/ OSDUS/2011OSDUHS_Detailed_DrugUseReport_2.pdf. Reprinted with permission from the Centre for Addiction and Mental Health. *What a Psychologist Sees: Meditation and the Brain*, drawings of the brain from Huffman, Karen. *Psychology in Action, 9e*. Reprinted with permission of John Wiley & Sons, Inc.

Chapter 6

Figure 6.1, Figure 6.4, Figure 6.12 from Huffman, Karen. *Psychology in Action, 9e*. Reprinted with permission of John Wiley & Sons, Inc.

Chapter 7

Figure 7.1, Figure 7.2, Figure 7.3, Figure 7.4, Study Organizer7.1, *Applying Psychology: Mnemonic Devices, Psychological Science: Brain and Memory Formation*, Figure 7.9, and Figure 7.11 from Huffman, Karen. *Psychology in Action, 9e*. Reprinted with permission of John Wiley & Sons, Inc. Figure 7.7c, graph, from Bahrick, H. P., Bahrick, P. O., & Wittlinger, R. P. (1974). Long-term memory: Those unforgettable high-school days. *Psychology Today*, 8, 50–56. Reprinted with permission from *Psychology Today* magazine, Copyright © 1978 Sussex Publishers, LLC.

Chapter 8

Figure 8.3, Figure 8.5, *Applying Psychology: Are You Creative*, drawing, Figure 8.7, Study Organizer 8.1, and Table 8.3 from Huffman, Karen. *Psychology in Action, 9e*. Reprinted with permission of John Wiley & Sons, Inc. Table 8.4 from Sternberg: Beyond IQ. © 1985 Cambridge University Press. Reprinted with permission of the Cambridge University Press. Figure 8.13, *What a Psychologist Sees: Family Studies of Intelligence*, graph, *Psychological Science: Stereotype Threat: Potential Pitfall for Minorities?* diagram, solution to the nine-dot problem and solution to the coin problem from Huffman, Karen. *Psychology in Action, 9e*. Reprinted with permission of John Wiley & Sons, Inc.

Chapter 9

Figure 9.1 from Comer & Gould, *Psychology Around Us*, 2e. Reprinted with permission of John Wiley & Sons, Inc. Figure 9.2 from Huffman, Karen. *Psychology in Action, 9e*. Reprinted with permission of John Wiley & Sons, Inc. Figure 9.3 from Schaie: *The life course of Adult intellectual abilities, AmericanPsychologist*, American Psychological Association. Reprinted with permission. Figure 9.5 (1): From Huffman, Karen. *Psychology in Action, 9e*. Reprinted with permission of John Wiley & Sons, Inc. Figure 9.8 from *Pediatrics*, Vol 89, Issue 1, pages 91–97, Copyright 1992. *What a Psychologist Sees: How an Infant Perceives the World*, graph from Huffman, Karen. *Psychology in Action, 9e*. Reprinted with permission of John Wiley & Sons, Inc. Figure 9.13 reproduced from Tanner J. M. Whitehouse, R. N. and Takaislu, M. "Standards from birth to maturity for height, weight height velocity, and weight velocity: British children, 1965." *Archives of Diseases in Childhood*, 41, 454–471, 1966. Reprinted with permission from BMJ Publishing Group Ltd. Figure 9.14 from Comer & Gould, *Psychology Around Us*, 2e. Reprinted with permission of John Wiley & Sons, Inc. Figure 9.16 © Diagram Visual Information, "The Brain, A User's Manual." Reprinted by permission. Study Organizer 9.1 from Huffman, Karen. *Psychology in Action, 10e*. Reprinted with permission of John Wiley & Sons, Inc. *Applying Psychology: Putting Piaget to the Test*, From Huffman, Karen. *Psychology in Action, 9e*. Reprinted with permission of John Wiley & Sons, Inc.

Chapter 10

What a Psychologist Sees: Attachment the Power of Touch, Figure 10.2 from Huffman, Karen. *Psychology in Action, 9e*. Reprinted with permission of John Wiley & Sons, Inc. Figure 10.4 adapted from Kohlberg, L. "Stage and Sequence: The Cognitive Developmental Approach to Socialization." in D.A. Goslin, *The Handbook of Socialization Theory and Research*. Chicago: Rand McNally, 1969, p. 376 (Table 6.2). Table 10.3 adapted and reproduced by special permission of the Publisher, Psychological Assessment Resources, Inc., 16204 North Florida Avenue, Lutz, Florida, 33549, from the Self-Directed Search by John L. Holland, Ph.D., Copyright 1985, 1987, 1994. Further reproduction is prohibited without permission from PAR, Inc. Figure 10.13 from The Social Context of Emotional Experience, *Annual Review of Geriatrics & Gerontology*, from Laura L. Carstensen, James J. Gross, and Helen H. Fung, Reproduced with the permission of Springer Publishing Company, LLC, New York, NY 10036.

Chapter 11

Figure 11.3, *Applying Psychology: Overcoming Test Anxiety* from Huffman, Karen. *Psychology in Action, 9e*. Reprinted with permission of John Wiley & Sons, Inc. Figure 11.11 adapted from Masters, W. H., & Johnson, V. E. (1966). *Human sexual response*. Boston: Little, Brown. Figure 11.14, graph, Extrinsic versus intrinsic rewards Copyright © 1973 by the American Psychological Association. Adapted with permission. Lepper, Mark R; Greene, David; Nisbett, Richard E. "Undermining children's intrinsic interest with intrinsic reward: A Test of the 'Overjustification' Hypothesis." *Journal of Personality and Social Psychology*. No further reproduction or distribution is permitted without written permission from the American Psychological Association. Figure 11.17 from Huffman, Karen. *Psychology in Action, 9e*. Reprinted with permission of John Wiley & Sons, Inc. Figure 11.20 from Comer & Gould, *Psychology Around Us*, 2e. *What a Psychologist Sees: Polygraph Testing, graph* from Huffman, Karen. *Psychology in Action, 9e*. Reprinted with permission of John Wiley & Sons, Inc. *What a Psychologist Sees: Polygraph Testing*, three fMRI images courtesy of Daniel Langleben, MD and Kosha Ruparel, MS, University of Pennsylvania. Data from Telling truth from lie in individual subjects with fast event-related fMRI. Langleben DD, Loughead JW, Bilker WB, Ruparel K, Childress AR, Busch SI, Gur RC. *Human Brain Mapping*. 2005 December; 26(4):262–72 and Davatzikos C, Ruparel K, Fan Y, Shen DG, Acharyya M, Loughead JW, Gur RC, Langleben DD. Classifying spatial patterns of brain activity with machine-learning methods: application to lie detection. *Neuroimage*. 2005 November 15; 28(3):663–8.

Chapter 12

Applying Psychology: Love and the Big Five, "Mate preferences around the world" from Buss et al., "*International Preferences in Selecting Mates*," Journal of Cross-Cultural Psychology, 21, pp. 5–47 © 1990. Reprinted by permission of SAGE Publications, Inc. Figure 12.3, Figure 12.5, Figure 12.7, *What a Psychologist Sees: Congruence, Mental Health, and Self-Esteem*, charts, Figure 12.13, *Psychological Science: Multiple Influences on Personality*, pie chart from Huffman, Karen. *Psychology in Action, 9e*. Reprinted with permission of John Wiley & Sons, Inc.

Chapter 13

Figure 13.1 from Huffman, Karen. *Psychology in Action, 9e*. Reprinted with permission of John Wiley & Sons, Inc. Study Organizer 13.1 from the *Diagnostic and Statistical Manual of Mental Disorders*, fourth edition text revision, Washington, DC, © 2000 American Psychiatric Association. Reprinted with permission from the Diagnostic and Statistical Manual of Mental Disorders, Text Revision, Fourth Edition, (Copyright 2000). American Psychiatric Association. Figure 13.6, Figure 13.7 from Huffman, Karen. *Psychology in Action, 9e*. Reprinted with permission of John Wiley & Sons, Inc. Figure 13.11 graph 'Genetics and schizophrenia' from the book, Schizophrenia Genesis by I. I. Gottesman. Copyright © 1991 by W. H. Freeman and Company. Reprinted by arrangement with Henry Holt and Company, LLC. Figure 13.19 from Huffman, Karen. *Psychology in Action, 9e*. Reprinted with permission of John Wiley & Sons, Inc.

Chapter 14

Figure 14.2 and Figure 14.3 from Huffman, Karen. *Psychology in Action, 9e*. Reprinted with permission of John Wiley & Sons, Inc. Figure 14.4 from Beck, Judith S. *Cognitive Therapy: Basics and Beyond* © 1993. Dysfunctional Thought Record, Figure 9.1, page 126. Reprinted with permission of Guilford Publications, Inc. *Applying Psychology: Client-Centred Therapy in Action* from Shea, S.C., (1988) *Psychiatric Interviewing: the art of understanding*, Philadelphia: PA, Saunders (publisher), p.32–33; Figure 14.9 and Figure 14.11 from Huffman, Karen. *Psychology in Action, 10e*. Reprinted with permission of John Wiley & Sons, Inc. Figure 14.12 from Huffman, Karen. *Psychology in Action, 9e*. Reprinted with permission of John Wiley & Sons, Inc.

Chapter 15

Figure 15.3 from Huffman, Karen, *Psychology in Action, 10e*. Reprinted with permission of John Wiley & Sons, Inc. Figure 15.4 and Figure 15.5 from Huffman, Karen. *Psychology in Action*, 9. Reprinted with permission of John Wiley & Sons, Inc. Graph in *What a Psychologist Sees: Love over the Lifespan*, Figure 15.9, chart in *What a Psychologist Sees: What Influences Behaviour?* and Figure 15.18 from Huffman, Karen. *Psychology in Action, 9e*. Reprinted with permission of John Wiley & Sons, Inc.

A

Aalsma, M. C., Lapsley, D. K., & Flannery, D. K. (2006). Personal fables, narcissism, and adolescent adjustment. *Psychology in the Schools, 43*, 481–491.

Aarts, H. (2007). Unconscious authorship ascription: The effects of success and effect-specific information priming on experienced authorship. *Journal of Experimental Social Psychology, 43*, 119–126.

Abadinsky, H. (2008). *Drug use and abuse: A comprehensive introduction* (6th ed.). Belmont, CA: Cengage.

Abbott, A. (2004). Striking back. *Nature, 429*(6990), 338–339.

Abdul Ahad, H., Suresh Kumar, C., Kumar Reddy, K., Mahesh, K., Kumar, S., & Kumar, A. (2010). Somnambulism—Sleep walking disease. *Journal of Innovative Trends in Pharmaceutical Sciences, 1*(4), 175–180.

Aboa-Éboulé, C. (2008). Job strain and recurrent coronary heart disease events—Reply. *Journal of the American Medical Association, 299*, 520–521.

Aboa-Éboulé, C., Brisson, C., Maunsell, E., Benoît, M., Bourbonnais, R., Vézina, M., Milot, A., Théroux, P., & Dagenais, G. R. (2008). Job strain and risk of acute recurrent coronary heart disease events. *Journal of the American Medical Association, 298*, 1652–1660.

About James Randi. (2002). Detail biography. Retrieved from http://www.randi.org/jr/bio.html

Acarturk, C., de Graaf, R., van Straten, A., ten Have, M., & Cuijpers, P. (2008). Social phobia and number of social fears, and their association with comorbidity, health-related quality of life and help seeking: A population- based study. *Social Psychiatry and Psychiatric Epidemiology, 43*, 273–279.

Adelmann, P. K., & Zajonc, R. B. (1989). Facial efference and the experience of emotion. *Annual Review of Psychology, 40*, 249–280.

Adler, A. (1964). The individual psychology of Alfred Adler. In H. L. Ansbacher & R. R. Ansbacher (Eds.), *The individual psychology of Alfred Adler*. New York, NY: Harper & Row.

Adler, A. (1998). *Understanding human nature*. Center City, MN: Hazelden Information Education.

Adolphs, R., Gosselin, F., Buchanan, T., Tranel, D., Schyns, P., & Damasio, A. (2005). A mechanism for impaired fear recognition after amygdala damage. *Nature, 433*(7021), 68–72.

Afshar, A., Santhanam, G., Yu, B., Ryu, S., Sahani, M., & Shenoy, K. (2011). Single-trial neural correlates of arm movement preparation. *Neuron, 71*(3), 555–564.

Ahlsén, E. (2008). Embodiment in communication–Aphasia, apraxia, and the possible role of mirroring and imitation. *Clinical Linguistics & Phonetics, 22*, 311–315.

Ahmadi, S., Zarrindast, M. R., Nouri, M., Haeri-Rohini, A., & Rezayof, A. (2007). N-Methyl-D-aspartate receptors in the ventral tegmental area are involved in retrieval of inhibitory avoidance memory of nicotine. *Neurobiology of Learning and Memory, 88*, 352–358.

Ahmed, A. M. (2007). Group identity, social distance, and intergroup bias. *Journal of Economic Psychology, 28*, 324–337.

Ainsworth, M. D. S. (1967). *Infancy in Uganda: Infant care and the growth of love*. Baltimore: Johns Hopkins University Press.

Ainsworth, M. D. S., Blehar, M., Waters, E., & Wall, S. (1978). *Patterns of attachment: Observations in the strange situation and at home*. Hillsdale, NJ: Erlbaum.

Al'absi, M., Hugdahl, K., & Lovallo, W. R. (2002). Adrenocortical stress responses and altered working memory performance. *Psychophysiology, 39*(1), 95–99.

Alan Guttmacher Institute. (2002). *In their own right: Addressing the sexual and reproductive health needs of American men*. New York, NY: AGI.

Alberts, A., Elkind, D., & Ginsberg, S. (2007). The personal fable and risk-taking in early adolescence. *Journal of Youth and Adolescence, 36*, 71–76.

Alden, L. E., & Regambal, M. J. (2011). Interpersonal processes in the anxiety disorders. In L. M. Horowitz & S. Strack (Eds.), *Handbook of interpersonal psychology: Theory, research, assessment, and therapeutic interventions* (pp. 449–469). Hoboken, NJ: Wiley.

Alegre, A. (2011). Parenting styles and children's emotional intelligence: What do we know? *The Family Journal, 19*(1), 56–62.

Alexander, B. K. (1990). *Peaceful measures: Canada's way out of the "war on drugs."* Toronto, ON: University of Toronto Press.

Alexander, B. K. (1997). *Peaceful measures: Canada's way out of the war on drugs* (2nd ed.). Toronto, ON: University of Toronto Press.

Allan, K., & Gabbert, F. (2008). I still think it was a banana: Memorable "lies" and forgettable "truths." *Acta Psychologica, 127*, 299–308.

Allik, J., & McCrae, R. R. (2004). Toward a geography of personality traits: Patterns of profiles across 36 cultures. *Journal of Cross-Cultural Psychology, 35*(1), 13–28.

Alloy, L. B., Abramson, L. Y., Whitehouse, W. G., Hogan, M. E., Tashman, N. A., Steinberg, D. L., Rose, D. T., & Donovan, P. (1999). Depressogenic cognitive styles: Predictive validity, information processing and personality characteristics, and developmental origins. *Behavior Research and Therapy, 37*, 503–531.

Alloy, L. B., Wagner, C. A., Black, S. K., Gerstein, R. K., & Abramson, L. Y. (2011). The breakdown of self-enhancing and self-protecting cognitive biases in depression. In M. D. Alicke & C. Sedikides (Eds.), *Handbook of self-enhancement and self-protection* (pp. 358–379). New York, NY: Guilford Press.

Allport, G. W. (1937). *Personality: A psychological interpretation*. New York, NY: Holt, Rinehart and Winston.

Allport, G. W., & Odbert, H. S. (1936). Trait-names: A psycho-lexical study. *Psychological Monographs: General and Applied, 47*, 1–21.

Almeida, O. P., Burton, E. J., Ferrier, N., McKeith, I. G., & O'Brien, J. T. (2003). Depression with late onset is associated with right frontal lobe atrophy. *Psychological Medicine, 33*(4), 675–681.

Altintas, M., Nayer, B., Walford, E., Johnson, K., Gaidosh, G., Reiser, J., … Nayer, A. (2012). Leptin deficiency-induced obesity affects the density of mast cells in abdominal fat depots and lymph nodes in mice. *Lipids in Health and Disease, 11*, 21.

Amato, P. R. (2006). Marital discord, divorce, and children's well-being: Results from a 20-year longitudinal study of two generations. In A. Clarke-Stewart & J. Dunn (Eds.), *Families count: Effects on child and adolescent development* (pp. 179–202). New York, NY: Cambridge University Press.

Amato, P. R. (2007). Transformative processes in marriage: Some thoughts from a sociologist. *Journal of Marriage and Family, 69*, 305–309.

Amato, P. R., & Dorius, C. (2010). Fathers, children, and divorce. In M. E. Lamb (Ed.), *The role of the father in child development* (5th ed., pp. 177–200). Hoboken, NJ: Wiley.

American Counseling Association. (2006). Crisis fact sheet: 10 ways to recognize post-traumatic stress disorder. Retrieved from http://www.counseling.org/zPressRoom/PressReleases.aspx?AGuid=69c6fad2-c05e-4be3-af4e-3a1771414044

American Medical Association. (2008). Alcohol and other drug abuse. Retrieved from http://www.ama-assn.org/ama/pub/category/3337.html

American Psychiatric Association. (2000). *Diagnostic and statistical manual of mental disorders* (4th ed. TR). Washington, DC: American Psychiatric Press.

American Psychiatric Association. (2002). APA: Let's talk facts about posttraumatic stress disorder. Retrieved from http://www.psych.org/disasterpsych/fs/ptsd.cfm

American Psychological Association. (1984). *Behavioral research with animals*. Washington, DC: Author.

American Psychological Association. (2010). *Publication manual of the American Psychological Association* (6th ed.). Washington, DC: Author.

Amir, N., Cobb, M., & Morrison, A. S. (2008). Threat processing in obsessive-compulsive disorder: Evidence from a modified negative priming task. *Behaviour Research and Therapy, 46*, 728–736.

Amir, O., Biederman, I., & Hayworth, K. J. (2011). The neural basis for shape preferences. *Vision Research, 51*(20), 2198–2206.

Amundson, J. K., & Nuttgens, S. A. (2008). Strategic eclecticism in hypnotherapy: Effectiveness research considerations. *American Journal of Clinical Hypnosis, 50*, 233–245.

Anderson, C. A. (2001). Heat and violence. *Current Directions in Psychological Science, 10*(1), 33–38.

Anderson, C. A. (2004). An update on the effects of playing violent video games. *Journal of Adolescence, 27*(1), 113–122.

Anderson, C. A., Buckley, K. E., & Carnegey, N. L. (2008). Creating your own hostile environment: A laboratory examination of trait aggressiveness and the violence escalation cycle. *Personality and Social Psychology Bulletin, 34*, 462–473.

Anderson, C. A., Carnagey, N. L., Flanagan, M., Benjamin, A. J., Eubanks, J., & Valentine, J. C. (2004). Violent video games: Effects of violent content on aggressive thoughts and behavior. *Advances in Experimental Social Psychology, 36*, 199–249.

Anderson, C. A., Gentile, D. A., & Buckley, K. E. (2007). *Violent video game effects on children and adolescents: Theory, research, and public policy*. New York, NY: Oxford University Press.

Anderson, C. A., Shibuya, A., Ihori, N., Swing, E. L., Bushman, B. J., Sakamoto, A., Rothstein, H. R., & Saleem, M. (2010). Violent videogame effects on aggression, empathy, and prosocial behavior in Eastern and Western countries: A meta-analytic review. *Psychological Bulletin, 136*, 151–173.

Anderson, L. E., & Silver, J. M. (2008). Neurological and medical disorders. In R. I. Simon & K. Tardiff (Eds.), *Textbook of violence assessment and management* (pp. 185–209). Arlington, VA: American Psychiatric Publishing.

Anderson, M. C., Ochsner, K. N., Kuhl, B., Cooper, J., Robertson, E., Gabrieli, S. W., Glover, G. H., & Gabrieli, J. D. E. (2004). Neural systems underlying the suppression of unwanted memories. *Science, 303*(5655), 232–235.

Andrade, T. G. C. S., & Graeff, F. G. (2001). Effect of electrolytic and neurotoxic lesions of the median raphe nucleus on anxiety and stress. *Pharmacology, Biochemistry & Behavior, 70*(1), 1–14.

Andrasik, F. (2006). Psychophysiological disorders: Headache as a case in point. In F. Andrasik (Ed.), *Comprehensive handbook of personality and psychopathology: Vol. 2: Adult Psychopathology* (pp. 409–422). Hoboken, NJ: Wiley.

Andreasen, N. C., Calage, C. A., & O'Leary, D. S. (2008). Theory of mind and schizophrenia: A positron emission tomography study of medication-free patients. *Schizophrenia Bulletin, 34*(4), 708–719.

Andreoni, J., & Petrie, R. (2008). Beauty, gender and stereotypes: Evidence from laboratory experiments. *Journal of Economic Psychology, 29,* 73–93.

Anglin, J. M. (1993). Vocabulary development: A morphological analysis. *Monographs of the Society for Research in Child Development, 58* (10, Serial No. 238), 1–165.

Angrilli, A., Bianchin, M., Radaelli, S., Bertagnoni, G., & Pertile, M. (2008). Reduced startle reflex and aversive noise perception in patients with orbitofrontal cortex lesions. *Neuropsychologia, 46*(4), 1179–1184.

Angrilli, A., Mauri, A., Palomba, D., Flor, H., Birbaumer, N., Sartori, G., & di Paola, F. (1996). Startle reflex and emotion modulation impairment after a right amygdala lesion. *Brain: A Journal of Neurology, 119*(6), 1991–2000.

Angus Reid Public Opinion. (2009). Canada more open to same-sex marriage than U.S., UK. Retrieved from http://www.angus-reid.com/polls/37148/canada_more_open_to_same_sex_marriage_than_us_uk/

Anis, A. H., Zhang, W. W., Bansback, N. N., Guh, D. P., Amarsi, Z. Z., & Birmingham, C. L. (2010). Obesity and overweight in Canada: An updated cost-of-illness study. *Obesity Reviews, 11*(1), 31–40.

Anisman, H., Merali, Z., & Stead, J. D. H. (2008). Experiential and genetic contributions to depressive- and anxiety-like disorders: Clinical and experimental studies. *Neuroscience & Biobehavioral Reviews, 32,* 1185–1206.

Ansell, E. B., & Grilo, C. M. (2008). Personality disorders. In M. Hersen, S. M. Turner, & D. C. Beidel (Eds.), *Adult psychopathology and diagnosis* (5th ed., pp. 633–678). Hoboken, NJ: Wiley.

Antony, M. M., & Roemer, L. (2011). Behavior therapy: Traditional approaches. In S. B. Messer & A. S. Gurman (Eds.), *Essential psychotherapies: Theory and practice* (3rd ed., pp. 107–142). New York, NY: Guilford.

Aou, S. (2006). Role of medial hypothalamus on peptic ulcer and depression. In C. Kubo & T. Kuboki (Eds.), *Psychosomatic medicine: Proceedings of the 18th World Congress on Psychosomatic Medicine*. New York, NY: Elsevier Science.

Appel, M., & Richter, T. (2007). Persuasive effects of fictional narratives increase over time. *Media Psychology, 10,* 113–134.

Appiah, K. A. (2008). *Experiments in ethics*. Cambridge, MA: Harvard University Press.

Arbib, M. A., & Mundhenk, T. N. (2005). Schizophrenia and the mirror system: An essay. *Neuropsychologia, 43,* 268–280.

Arkes, H., & Kajdasz, J. (2011). Intuitive theories of behavior. In National Research Council (Ed.), *Intelligence analysis: Behavioral and social scientific foundations* (pp. 143–168). Washington, DC: National Academies Press.

Arnedt, J., Owens, J., Crouch, M., Stahl, J., & Carskadon, M. (2005). Neurobehavioral performance of residents after heavy night call vs after alcohol ingestion. *JAMA: Journal of the American Medical Association, 294*(9), 1025–1033.

Arriagada, O., Constandil, L., Hernández, A., Barra, R., Soto-Moyano, R., & Laurido, C. (2007). Brief communication: Effects of interleukin-1B on spinal cord nociceptive transmission in intact and propentofylline-treated rats. *International Journal of Neuroscience, 117,* 617–625.

Arriola, L., Martinez-Camblor, P., Larrañaga, N., Basterretxea, M., Amiano, P., Moreno-Iribas, … Dorronsoro, M. (2010). Alcohol intake and the risk of coronary heart disease in the Spanish EPIC cohort study. *Heart, 96*(2), 124–130.

Arumugam, V., Lee, J-S., Nowak, J. K., Pohle, R. J., Nyrop, J. E., Leddy, J. J., & Pelkman, C. L. (2008). A high-glycemic meal pattern elicited increased subjective appetite sensations in overweight and obese women. *Appetite, 50,* 215–222.

Asch, S. E. (1951). Effects of group pressure upon the modification and distortion of judgment. In H. Guetzkow (Ed.), *Groups, leadership, and men*. Pittsburgh: Carnegie Press.

Asghar, A. U. R., Chiu, Y-C., Hallam, G., Liu, S., Mole, H., Wright, H., & Young, A. W. (2008). An amygdala response to fearful faces with covered eyes. *Neuropsychologia, 46,* 2364–2370.

Atchley, R. C. (1997). *Social forces and aging* (8th ed.). Belmont, CA: Wadsworth.

Atkinson, R. C., & Shiffrin, R. M. (1968). Human memory: A proposed system and its control processes. In K. W. Spence & J. T. Spence (Eds.), *The psychology of learning and motivation* (Vol. 2). New York, NY: Academic Press.

Atlas, R. S., & Pepler, D. J. (1998). Observations of bullying in the classroom. *Journal of Educational Research, 92,* 86–99.

Aubert, A., & Dantzer, R. (2005). The taste of sickness: Lipopolysaccharide-induced finickiness in rats. *Physiology & Behavior, 84*(3), 437–444.

Aune, D., Lau, R., Chan, D., Vieira, R., Greenwood, D., Kampman, E., & Norat, T. (2011). Nonlinear reduction in risk for colorectal cancer by fruit and vegetable intake based on meta-analysis of prospective studies. *Gastroenterology, 141*(1), 106–118.

Auyeung, B., Baron-Cohen, S., Ashwin, E., Knickmeyer, R., Taylor, K., Hackett, G., & Hines, M. (2009). Fetal testosterone predicts sexually differentiated childhood behavior in girls and in boys. *Psychological Science, 20,* 144–148.

Axtell, R. E. (1998). *Gestures: The do's and taboos of body language around the world* (Rev. and expanded ed.). New York, NY: Wiley.

Axtell, R. E. (2007). *Essential do's and taboos: The complete guide to international business and leisure travel*. Hoboken, NJ: Wiley.

Ayers, S., Baum, A., McManus, C., Newman, S., Wallston, K., Weinman, J., & West, R. (Eds.). (2007). *Cambridge handbook of psychology, health, and medicine*. New York, NY: Cambridge University Press.

Azizian, A., & Polich, J. (2007). Evidence for attentional gradient in the serial position memory curve from event-related potentials. *Journal of Cognitive Neuroscience, 19,* 2071–2081.

B

Baby Signs Canada. (2006). Retrieved from http://www.babysigns.ca

Baddeley, A. D. (1992). Working memory. *Science, 255,* 556–559.

Baddeley, A. D. (1998). Recent developments in working memory. *Current Opinion in Neurobiology, 8,* 234–238.

Baddeley, A., & Jarrold, C. (2007). Working memory and Down syndrome. *Journal of Intellectual Disability Research, 51,* 925–931.

Badge, J. L., Cann, A. J., & Scott, J. (2007). To cheat or not to cheat? A trial of the JISC plagiarism detection service with biological science students. *Assessment and Evaluation in Higher Education, 32*(4), 1–7.

Baer, J. (1994). Divergent thinking is not a general trait: A multi-domain training experiment. *Creativity Research Journal, 7,* 35–36.

Bagermihl, B. (1999). *Biological exuberance: Animal homosexuality and natural diversity*. New York, NY: St Martins Press.

Bailey, J. M., Dunne, M. P., & Martin, N. G. (2000). Genetic and environmental influences on sexual orientation and its correlates in an Australian twin sample. *Journal of Personality and Social Psychology, 78*(3), 524–536.

Bailey, K. R., & Mair, R. G. (2005). Lesions of specific and nonspecific thalamic nuclei affect prefrontal cortex-dependent aspects of spatial working memory. *Behavioral Neuroscience, 119*(2), 410–419.

Bailey, S., & Covell, K. (2011). Pathways among abuse, daily hassles, depression, and substance use in adolescents. *The New School Psychology Bulletin, 8*(2), 4–14.

Baillargeon, R., Lee, J., Gertner, Y., & Wu, D. (2011). How do infants reason about physical events? In U. Goswami (Ed.), *The Wiley-Blackwell handbook of childhood cognitive development, second edition* (pp. 11–48). Chichester, England: Blackwell Publishing Ltd.

Baird, A. D., Scheffer, I. E., & Wilson, S. J. (2011). Mirror neuron system involvement in empathy: A critical look at the evidence. *Social Neuroscience, 6,* 327–335.

Baker, D., & Nieuwenhuijsen, M. J. (Eds.). (2008). *Environmental epidemiology: Study methods and application*. New York, NY: Oxford University Press.

Baker, R. R., & Pickren, W. E. (2007). *Psychology and the Department of Veterans Affairs: A historical analysis of training, research, practice, and advocacy*. Washington, DC: American Psychological Association.

Bakker, J., Brand, T., Van Ophemert, J., & Slob, A. (1993). Hormonal regulation of adult partner preference behavior in neonatally ATD-treated male rats. *Behavioral Neuroscience, 107*(3), 480–487.

Baldessarini, R. J., & Hennen, J. (2004). Genetics of suicide: An overview. *Harvard Review of Psychiatry, 12*(1), 1–13.

Ball, H. A., McGuffin, P., & Farmer, A. E. (2008). Attributional style and depression. *British Journal of Psychiatry, 192*, 275–278.

Ballantyne, J., & Shin, N. (2008). Efficacy of opioids for chronic pain: a review of the evidence. *Clinical Journal of Pain, 24*(6), 469–478.

Ballard, T., Knoflach, F., Prinssen, E., Borroni, E., Vivian, J., Basile, J., ... Hernandez, M. (2009). RO4938581, a novel cognitive enhancer acting at GABAA alpha5 subunit-containing receptors. *Psychopharmacology, 202*(1–3), 207–223.

Bamer, A. M., Johnson, K. L., Amtmann, D. D., & Kraft, G. H. (2008). Prevalence of sleep problems in individuals with multiple sclerosis. *Multiple Sclerosis, 14*(8), 1127–1130.

Bandura, A. (1969). *Principles of behavior modification.* New York, NY: Holt, Rinehart and Winston.

Bandura, A. (1986). *Social foundations of thought and action: A social cognitive theory.* Englewood Cliffs, NJ: Prentice Hall.

Bandura, A. (1991). Social cognitive theory of moral thought and action. In W. M. Kurtines & J. L. Gewirtz (Eds.), *Handbook of moral behavior and development: Vol. 1. Theory.* Hillsdale, NJ: Erlbaum.

Bandura, A. (1997). *Self-efficacy: The exercise of control.* New York, NY: Freeman.

Bandura, A. (2000). Exercise of human agency through collective efficacy. *Current Directions in Psychological Science, 9*(3), 75–83.

Bandura, A. (2003). On the psychosocial impact and mechanisms of spiritual modeling: Comment. *International Journal of Psychology of Religion, 13*(3), 167–173.

Bandura, A. (2006). Going global with social cognitive theory: From prospect to paydirt. In D. E. Berger & K. Pezdek (Eds.), *The rise of applied psychology: New frontiers and rewarding careers.* Mahwah, NJ: Erlbaum.

Bandura, A. (2008). Reconstrual of "free will" from the agentic perspective of social cognitive theory. In J. Baer, J. C. Kaufman, & R. F. Baumeister (Eds.), *Are we free? Psychology and free will* (pp. 86–127). New York, NY: Oxford University Press.

Bandura, A. (2011). The social and policy impact of social cognitive theory. In M. Mark, S. Donaldson, & B. Campbell (Eds.), *Social psychology and evaluation* (pp. 33–70). New York, NY: Guilford Press.

Bandura, A., & Walters, R. H. (1963). *Social learning and personality development.* New York, NY: Holt, Rinehart and Winston.

Bandura, A., Ross, D., & Ross, S. (1961). Transmission of aggression through imitation of aggressive models. *Journal of Abnormal & Social Psychology, 63*, 575–582.

Banich, M. T., & Compton, R. J. (2011). *Cognitive neuroscience* (3rd ed.). Belmont, CA: Cengage.

Banko, K. M. (2008). Increasing intrinsic motivation using rewards: The role of the social context. *Dissertation Abstracts International: Section B: The Sciences and Engineering, 68*(10-B), 7005.

Banks, M. S., & Salapatek, P. (1983). Infant visual perception. In M. M. Haith & J. J. Campos (Eds.), *Handbook of child psychology* (pp. 435–572). New York, NY: Wiley.

Bao, A., & Swaab, D. F. (2011). Sexual differentiation of the human brain: Relation to gender identity, sexual orientation and neuropsychiatric disorders. *Frontiers in Neuroendocrinology, 32*(2), 214–216.

Bard, C. (1934). On emotional expression after decortication with some remarks on certain theoretical views. *Psychological Review, 41*, 309–329.

Barelds, D. P. H., & Dijkstra, P. (2009). Positive illusions about a partner's physical attractiveness and relationship quality. *Personal Relationships, 16*, 263–283.

Barelds, D. P. H., & Dijkstra, P. (2011). Positive illusions about a partner's personality and relationship quality. *Journal of Research in Personality, 45*(1), 37–43.

Barelds, D., Dijkstra, P., Koudenburg, K., & Swami, V. (2011). An assessment of positive illusions of the physical attractiveness of romantic partners. *Journal of Social and Personal Relationships, 28*, 706–719.

Bargai, N., Ben-Shakar, G., & Shalev, A. Y. (2007). Posttraumatic stress disorder and depression in battered women: The mediating role of learned helplessness. *Journal of Family Violence, 22*(5), 267–275.

Barlett, C. P., Harris, R. J., & Bruey, C. (2008). The effect of the amount of blood in a violent video game on aggression, hostility, and arousal. *Journal of Experimental Social Psychology, 44*, 539–546.

Barlow, D. H. (Ed.). (2008). *Clinical handbook of psychological disorders: A step-by-step treatment manual* (4th ed.). New York, NY: Guilford Press.

Barlow, D. H., & Durand, V. M. (2009). *Abnormal psychology: An integrative approach* (5th ed.). Belmont, CA: Cengage.

Barner, D., Wood, J., Hauser, M., & Carey, S. (2008). Evidence for a non-linguistic distinction between singular and plural sets in rhesus monkeys. *Cognition, 107*, 603–622.

Barnow, S., Ulrich, I., Grabe, H-J., Freyberger, H. J., & Spitzer, C. (2007). The influence of parental drinking behaviour and antisocial personality disorder on adolescent behavioural problems: Results of the Greifswalder family study. *Alcohol and Alcoholism, 42*, 623–628.

Barriga, A. Q., Sullivan-Cosetti, M., Gibbs, J. C. (2009). Moral cognitive correlates of empathy in juvenile deliquents. *Criminal Behaviour and Mental Health, 19*, 253–264.

Barton, D. A., Esler, M. D., Dawood, T., Lambert, E. A., Haikerwal, D., Brenchley, C., ... Lambert, G. W. (2008). Elevated brain serotonin turnover in patients with depression: Effect of genotype and therapy. *Archives of General Psychiatry, 65*, 38–46.

Barton, J. J. S. (2008). Prosopagnosia associated with left occipitotemporal lesion. *Neuropsychologia, 46*, 2214–2224.

Basow, A. A. (2010). Gender in the classroom. In J. Chrisler & D. R. McCreary (Eds.), *Handbook of gender research in psychology: Vol. 1: Gender research in general and experimental psychology* (pp. 277–295). New York, NY: Springer.

Bates, A. L. (2007). How did you get in? Attributions of preferential selection in college admissions. *Dissertation Abstracts International: Section B: The Sciences and Engineering, 68*(4-B), 2694.

Batson, C. D. (1998). Altruism and prosocial behavior. In D. T. Gilbert, S. T. Fiske, & G. Lindzey (Eds.), *The handbook of social psychology, Vol. 2* (4th ed., pp. 282–316). Boston, MA: McGraw-Hill.

Batson, C. D. (2006). "Not all self-interest after all": Economics of empathy-induced altruism. In D. De Cremer, M. Zeelenberg, & J. K. Murnighan (Eds.), *Social psychology and economics* (pp. 281–299). Mahwah, NJ: Erlbaum.

Batson, C. D. (2011). *Altruism in humans.* New York, NY: Oxford University Press.

Baumeister, R. F., & Bushman, B. (2011). *Social psychology and human nature: Comprehensive edition* (2nd ed.). Belmont, CA: Cengage.

Baumeister, R., & Vohs, K. (2011). *New directions in social psychology.* Thousand Oaks, CA: Sage.

Baumrind, D. (1980). New directions in socialization research. *American Psychologist, 35*, 639–652.

Baumrind, D. (1991). Effective parenting during the early adolescent transition. In P. A. Cowan & E. M. Hetherington (Eds.), *Family transition* (pp. 111–163). Hillsdale, NJ: Erlbaum.

Baumrind, D. (1995). *Child maltreatment and optimal caregiving in social contexts.* New York, NY: Garland.

Bayley, T. M., Dye, L., & Hill, A. J. (2009). Taste aversions in pregnancy. In T. R. Schachtman, S. Reilly, & T. R. Schachtman (Eds.), *Conditioned taste aversion: Behavioral and neural processes* (pp. 497–512). New York, NY: Oxford University Press.

Bearer, C. F., Stoler, J. M., Cook, J. D., & Carpenter, S. J. (2004–2005). Biomarkers of alcohol use in pregnancy. *Alcohol Research & Health, 28*(1), 38–43.

Beaton, E. A., Schmidt, L. A., Schulkin, J., Antony, M. M., Swinson, R. P., & Hall, G. B. (2008). Different neural responses to stranger and personally familiar faces in shy and bold adults. *Behavioral Neuroscience, 122*, 704–709.

Beck, A. T. (1976). *Cognitive therapy and the emotional disorders.* New York, NY: International Universities Press.

Beck, A. T. (2000). *Prisoners of hate.* New York, NY: Harper Perennial.

Beck, A. T., & Grant, P. M. (2008). Negative self-defeating attitudes: Factors that influence everyday impairment in individuals with schizophrenia. *American Journal of Psychiatry, 165*, 772.

Becker, A. J., McCulloch, E. A., & Till, J. E. (1963). Cytological demonstration of the clonal nature of spleen colonies derived from transplanted mouse marrow cells. *Nature, 197*, 452–454.

Becker, K. A. (2003). *History of the Stanford-Binet intelligence scales: Content and psychometrics* (5th ed., Stanford-Binet Intelligence Scales, Assessment Service Bulletin No. 1). Itasca, IL: Riverside Publishing.

Becker, S. I. (2008). The mechanism of priming: Episodic retrieval or priming of popout? *Acta Psychologica, 127*, 324–339.

Begg, I. M., Needham, D. R., & Bookbinder, M. (1993). Do backward messages unconsciously affect listeners? No. *Canadian Journal of Experimental Psychology, 47*, 1–14.

Behar, R. (2007). Gender related aspects of eating disorders: A psychosocial view. In J. S. Rubin (Ed.), *Eating disorders and weight loss research* (pp. 39–65). Hauppauge, NY: Nova Science Publishers.

Beilin, H. (1992). Piaget's enduring contribution to developmental psychology. *Developmental Psychology, 28*, 191–204.

Bélanger, L., LeBlanc, M., & Morin, C. M. (2012). Cognitive behavioral therapy for insomnia in older adults. *Cognitive and Behavioral Practice, 19*(1), 101–115.

Bell, B., & Dittmar, H. (2011). Does media type matter? The role of identification in adolescent girls' media consumption and the impact of different thin-ideal media on body image. *Sex Roles, 65*(7/8), 478–490.

Belsky, J., & Fearon, R. M. P. (2008). Precursors of attachment security. In J. Cassidy & P. R. Shaver (Eds.), *Handbook of attachment: Theory, research, and clinical applications* (2nd ed., pp. 295–316). New York, NY: Guilford.

Benagiano, G., & Mori, M. (2009). The origins of human sexuality: Procreation or recreation? *Reproductive Biomedicine Online, 18*(Suppl.), 150–59.

Benarroch, E. (2010). Neural control of feeding behavior: Overview and clinical correlations. *Neurology, 74*(20), 1643–1650.

Bendersky, M., & Sullivan, M. W. (2007). Basic methods in infant research. In A. Slater & M. Lewis (Eds.), *Introduction to infant development* (2nd ed.). New York, NY: Oxford University Press.

Ben-Eliyahu, S., Page, G. G., & Schleifer, S. J. (2007). Stress, NK cells, and cancer: Still a promissory note. *Brain, Behavior, & Immunity, 21*, 881–887.

Bensafi, M., Sobel, N., & Khan, R. M. (2007). Hedonic-specific activity in piriform cortex during odor imagery mimics that during odor perception. *Journal of Neurophysiology, 98*, 3254–3262.

Beran, T. N., Ramirez-Serrano, A., Kuzyk, R., Fior, M., & Nugent, S. (2011). Understanding how children understand robots: Perceived animism in child-robot interaction. *International Journal of Human-Computer Studies, 69*, 539–550.

Berenbaum, S. A., Martin, C. L., & Ruble, D. N. (2008). Gender development. In W. Damon & R. M. Lerner (Eds.), *Child and adolescent development: An advanced course* (pp. 647–695). Hoboken, NJ: Wiley.

Berenbaum, S., & Beltz, A. (2011). Sexual differentiation of human behavior: Effects of prenatal and pubertal organizational hormones. *Frontiers in Neuroendocrinology, 32*(2), 183–200.

Berger, M., Speckmann, E.-J., Pape, H. C., & Gorji, A. (2008). Spreading depression enhances human neocortical excitability in vitro. *Cephalalgia, 28*, 558–562.

Bergh, C., Sjöstedt, S., Hellers, G., Zandian, M., & Södersten, P. (2003). Meal size, satiety and cholecystokinin in gastrectomized humans. *Physiology & Behavior, 78*(1), 143–147.

Bergstrom-Lynch, C. A. (2008). Becoming parents, remaining childfree: How same-sex couples are creating families and confronting social inequalities. *Dissertation Abstracts International Section A: Humanities and Social Sciences, 68*(8-A), 3608.

Berlin, L. J., Cassidy, J., & Appleyard, K. (2008). The influence of early attachments on other relationships. In J. Cassidy & P. R. Shaver (Eds.), *Handbook of attachment: Theory, research, and clinical applications* (2nd ed., pp. 333–347). New York, NY: Guilford.

Bernard, L. L. (1924). *Instinct*. New York, NY: Holt.

Berndt, T. J. (1988). The nature and significance of children's friendships. In R. Vasta (Ed.), *Annals of child development* (Vol. 5). Greenwich, CT: JAI Press.

Bernstein, M. J., Sacco, D. F., Brown, C. M., Young, S. G., & Claypool, H. M. (2010). A preference for genuine smiles following social exclusion. *Journal of Experimental Social Psychology, 46*(1), 196–199.

Berntson, G. G., Bechara, A., Damasio, H., Tranel, D., & Cacioppo, J. T. (2007). Amygdala contribution to selective dimensions of emotion. *Social Cognitive and Affective Neuroscience, 2*(2), 123–129.

Berreman, G. (1971). *Anthropology today*. Del Mar, CA: CRM Books.

Berry, J., Poortinga, Y., Breugelmans, S., Chasiotis, A., & Sam, D. (2011). *Cross-cutural psychology: Research and applications* (3rd ed.). Cambridge, England: Cambridge University Press.

Berthoud, H. (2002). Multiple neural systems controlling food intake and body weight. *Neuroscience & Biobehavioral Reviews, 26*(4), 393–428.

Berthoud, H., & Morrison, C. (2008). The brain, appetite, and obesity. *Annual Review of Psychology, 59*, 55–92.

Berthoud, H., & Münzberg, H. (2011). The lateral hypothalamus as integrator of metabolic and environmental needs: From electrical self-stimulation to opto-genetics. *Physiology & Behavior, 104*(1), 29–39.

Berzoff, J. (2008). Psychosocial ego development: The theory of Erik Erikson. In J. Berzoff, L. M. Flanagan, & P. Hertz (Eds.), *Inside out and outside in: Psychodynamic clinical theory and psychopathology in contemporary multicultural contexts* (2nd ed., pp. 99–120). Lanham, MD: Jason Aronson.

Besedovsky, L., Lange, T., & Born, J. (2012). Sleep and immune function. *Pflugers Archiv European Journal of Physiology, 463*(1), 121–137.

Best, J. B. (1999). *Cognitive psychology* (5th ed.). Belmont, CA: Wadsworth.

Bhattacharya, S. K., & Muruganandam, A. V. (2003). Adaptogenic activity of Withania somnifera: An experimental study using a rat model of chronic stress. *Pharmacology, Biochemistry & Behavior, 75*(3), 547–555.

Bialystok, E. (2007). Cognitive effects of bilingualism: How linguistic experience leads to cognitive change. *International Journal of Bilingual Education and Bilingualism, 10*, 210–223.

Bialystok, E. (2011). Reshaping the mind: The benefits of bilingualism. *Canadian Journal of Experimental Psychology, 65*, 229–235.

Biehl, M., Matsumoto, D., Ekman, P., Hearn, V., Heider, K., Kudoh, T., & Ton, V. (1997). Matsumoto and Ekman's Japanese and Caucasian facial expressions of emotion (JACFEE): Reliability data and cross-national differences. *Journal of Nonverbal Behavior, 21*, 3–21.

Billiard, M. (2007). Sleep disorders. In L. Candelise, R. Hughes, A. Liberati, B. M. J. Uitdehaag, & C. Warlow (Eds.), Evidence-based neurology: Management of neurological disorders (pp. 70–78). *Evidence-based medicine*. Malden, MA: Blackwell Publishing.

Binks, G. (2008, November 19). Student binge drinking: A problem well past the tipping point. CBC News. Retrieved from http://www.cbc.ca/canada/story/2008/11/19/f-student-drinking.html

Birkenhäger, T. K., Renes, J., & Pluijms, E. M. (2004). One-year follow-up after successful ECT: A naturalistic study in depressed inpatients. *Journal of Clinical Psychiatry, 65*(1), 87–91.

Bjorklund, D. F., & Pellegrini, A. D. (2011). Evolutionary perspectives on social development. In P. K. Smith & K. H. Hart (Eds.). *The Wiley-Blackwell handbook of childhood social development* (2nd ed., pp. 64–81). Hoboken, NJ: Wiley.

Bjorklund, D. F., & Pellegrinin, A. D. (2011). Evolutionary perspectives on social development. In P. K. Smith & K. H. Hart (Eds.). *The Wiley-Blackwell handbook of childhood social development* (2nd ed., pp. 64–81). Hoboken, NJ: Wiley.

Blaesi, S., & Wilson, M. (2010). The mirror reflects both ways: Action influences perception of others. *Brain & Cognition, 72*(2), 306–309.

Blaine, B. E. (2009). Obesity, binge eating, and psychological distress: The moderating role of self-concept disturbance. *Current Psychiatry Reviews, 5*(3), 175–181.

Blakemore, C., & Cooper, G. F. (1970). Development of the brain depends on the visual environment. *Nature, 228*, 477–478.

Blanton, C. (2003). From intellectual deficiency to cultural deficiency: Mexican Americans, testing, and public school policy in the American southwest, 1920–1940. *Pacific Historical Review, 72*(1), 39.

Blashfield, R. K., Flanagan, E., & Raley, K. (2010). Themes in the evolution of the 20th century DSMs. In T. Millon, R. F. Krueger, & E. Simonsen (Eds.), *Contemporary directions in psychopathology: Scientific foundations of the DSM-V and ICD-11* (pp. 53–71). New York, NY: Guilford Press.

Blonigen, D. M., Carlson, M. D., Hicks, B. M., Kreuger, R. F., & Iacono, W. G. (2008). Stability and change in personality traits from late adolescence to early childhood: A longitudinal twin study. *Journal of Personality, 76*, 229–266.

Blum, H. P. (2011). To what extent do you privilege dream interpretation in relation to other forms of mental representations? *The International Journal of Psychoanalysis, 92*(2), 275–277.

Blumenthal, R. S., & Margolis, S. (2009). Causes of heart attacks: *Heart attack prevention*. Baltimore, MD: Johns Hopkins Medicine, pp. 5–9.

Boardman, J., Alexander, K., & Stallings, M. (2011). Stressful life events and depression among adolescent twin pairs. *Biodemography and Social Biology, 57*(1), 53–66.

Bob, P. (2008). Pain, dissociation and subliminal self-representations. *Consciousness and Cognition: An International Journal, 17*, 355–369.

Boccato, G., Capozza, D., Falvo, R., & Durante, F. (2008). Capture of the eyes by relevant and irrelevant onsets. *Social Cognition, 26*, 224–234.

Bock, G. R., & Goode, J. A. (Eds.). (1996). *Genetics of criminal and antisocial behavior*. Chichester, England: Wiley.

Bodnar, R. J. (2011). Endogenous opiates and behavior: 2010. *Peptides, 32*(12), 2522–2552.

Bohart, A. C., & Watson, J. C. (2011). Person-centered psychotherapy and related experiential approaches. In S. B. Messer & A. S. Gurman (Eds.), *Essential psychotherapies: Theory and practice* (3rd ed., pp. 223–260). New York, NY: Guilford.

Böhm, R., Schütz, A., Rentzsch, K., Körner, A., & Funke, F. (2010). Are we looking for positivity or similarity in a partner's outlook on life? Similarity predicts perceptions of social attractiveness and relationship quality. *Journal of Positive Psychology, 5*(6), 431–438.

Bohm-Starke, N., Brodda-Jansen, G., Linder, J., & Danielsson, I. (2007). The result of treatment on vestibular and general pain thresholds in women with provoked vestibulodynia. *Clinical Journal of Pain, 23*(7), 598–604.

Bohus, M., Haaf, B., Simms, T., Limberger, M. F., Schmahl, C., Unckel, C., Lieb, K., & Linehan, M. M. (2004). Effectiveness of in-patient dialectical behavioral therapy for borderline personality disorder: A controlled trial. *Behaviour Research & Therapy, 42*(5), 487–499.

Bonafini, B. A., & Pozzilli, P. P. (2011). Body weight and beauty: The changing face of the ideal female body weight. *Obesity Reviews, 12*(1), 62–65.

Bond, F. W., & Bunce, D. (2000). Mediators of change in emotion-focused and problem-focused worksite stress management intervention. *Journal of Occupational Health Psychology, 5*, 153–163.

Bond, M. H., & Smith, P. B. (1996). Culture and conformity: A meta-analysis of studies using Asch's (1952b, 1956) line judgment task. *Psychological Bulletin, 119*, 111–137.

Booth-Laforce, C., & Kerns, K. A. (2009). Child-parent attachment relationships, peer relationships, and peer-group functioning. In K. H. Rubin, W. M. Bukowski, & B. Laursen (Eds.), *Handbook of peer interactions, relationships, and groups* (pp. 490–507). New York, NY: Guilford.

Bor, D., Billington, J., & Baron-Cohen, S. (2007). Savant memory for digits in a case of synaesthesia and Asberger Syndrome is related to hyperactivity in the lateral prefrontal cortex. *Neurocase, 13*, 311–319.

Borba, M. (2001). *Building moral intelligence: The seven essential virtues that teach kids to do the right thing.* San Francisco, CA: Jossey-Bass.

Borbely, A. A. (1982). Circadian and sleep-dependent processes in sleep regulation. In J. Aschoff, S. Daan, & G. A. Groos (Eds.), *Vertebrate circadian rhythms* (pp. 237–242). Berlin, Germany: Springer/Verlag.

Borenstein, A. R., Copenhaver, C. I., & Mortimer, J. A. (2006). Early-life risk factors for Alzheimer disease. *Alzheimer Disease and Associated Disorders, 20*(1), 63–72.

Borrego, J., Ibanez, E. S., Spendlove, S. J., & Pemberton, J. R. (2007). Treatment acceptability among Mexican American parents. *Behavior Therapy, 38*(3), 218–227.

Bosacki, S. L., Marini, Z. A., & Dane, A. V. (2006). Voices from the classroom: Pictorial and narrative representations of children's bullying experiences. *Journal of Moral Education, 35*, 231–245.

Bouchard, T. J., Jr. (1994). Genes, environment, and personality. *Science, 264*, 1700–1701.

Bouchard, T. J., Jr. (1997). The genetics of personality. In K. Blum & E. P. Noble (Eds.), *Handbook of psychiatric genetics.* Boca Raton, FL: CRC Press.

Bouchard, T. J., Jr. (1999). The search for intelligence. *Science, 284*, 922–923.

Bouchard, T. J., Jr. (2004). Genetic influence on human psychological traits: A survey. *Current Directions in Psychological Science, 13*(4), 148–151.

Bouchard, T. J., Jr., & McGue, M. (1981). Familial studies of intelligence: A review. *Science, 212*(4498), 1055–1059.

Bouchard, T. J., Jr., McGue, M., Hur, Y., & Horn, J. M. (1998). A genetic and environmental analysis of the California Psychological Inventory using adult twins reared apart and together. *European Journal of Personality, 12*, 307–320.

Boucher, L., & Dienes, Z. (2003). Two ways of learning associations. *Cognitive Science, 27*(6), 807–842.

Bourne, L. E., Dominowski, R. L., & Loftus, E. F. (1979). *Cognitive processes.* Englewood Cliffs, NJ: Prentice Hall.

Bouton, M. E. (1994). Context, ambiguity, and classical conditioning. *Current Directions in Psychological Science, 2*, 49–53.

Bowers, K. S., & Woody, E. Z. (1996). Hypnotic amnesia and the paradox of intentional forgetting. *Journal of Abnormal Psychology, 105*, 381–390.

Bowlby, J. (1969). *Attachment and loss: Vol. 1. Attachment.* New York, NY: Basic Books.

Bowlby, J. (1973). *Attachment and loss: Vol. 2. Separation and anxiety.* New York, NY: Basic Books.

Bowlby, J. (1982). Attachment and loss: Retrospect and prospect. *American Journal of Orthopsychiatry, 52*, 664–678.

Bowlby, J. (1989). *Secure attachment.* New York, NY: Basic Books.

Bowlby, J. (2000). *Attachment.* New York, NY: Basic Books.

Bowling, A. C., & Mackenzie, B. D. (1996). The relationship between speed of information processing and cognitive ability. *Personality & Individual Differences, 20*(6), 775–800.

Boyle, S. H., Williams, R. B., Mark, D. B., Brummett, B. H., Siegler, I. C., Helms, M. J., & Brady, S. S. (2007). Young adults' media use and attitudes toward interpersonal and institutional forms of aggression. *Aggressive Behavior, 33*(6), 519–525.

Boysen, G. A., & Vogel, D. L. (2007). Biased assimilation and attitude polarization in response to learning about biological explanations of homosexuality. *Sex Roles, 56*, 755–762.

Bozkurt, A. S., & Aydin, O. (2004). Temel yükleme hatasinin degisik yas ve iki alt kültürde incelenmesi (A developmental investigation of fundamental attribution error in two subcultures). *Türk Psikoloji Dergisi, 19*, 91–104.

Brabender, V. (2011). Group psychotherapies. In S. B. Messer & A. S. Gurman (Eds.), *Essential psychotherapies: Theory and practice* (3rd ed., pp. 460–493). New York, NY: Guilford.

Brackett, M., Rivers, S., & Salovey, P. (2011). Emotional intelligence: Implications for personal, social, academic, and workplace success. *Social and Personality Psychology Compass, 5*(1), 88–103.

Bradley, R., Conklin, C. Z., & Westen, D. (2007). Borderline personality disorder. In W. O'Donohue, K. A. Fowler, & S. O. Lilienfeld (Eds.), *Personality disorders: Toward the DSM-V* (pp. 167–201). Thousand Oaks, CA: Sage.

Brady, I. (2004). *Illustrating nature: Right-brain art in a left-brain world.* Talent, OR: Nature Works Press.

Brandon, T. H., Collins, B. N., Juliano, L. M., & Lazev, A. B. (2000). Preventing relapse among former smokers: A comparison of minimal interventions through telephone and mail. *Journal of Consulting and Clinical Psychology, 68*(1), 103–113.

Brannon, L. (2011). *Gender: Psychological perspectives* (6th ed.). Boston, MA: Pearson.

Braun, K. A., Ellis, R., & Loftus, E. F. (2002). Make my memory: How advertising can change our memories of the past. *Psychology & Marketing, 19*(1), 1–23.

Breeding, J. (2011). Thomas Szasz: Philosopher of liberty. *Journal of Humanistic Psychology, 51*(1), 112–128.

Breland, K., & Breland, M. (1961). The misbehavior of organisms. *American Psychologist, 16*, 681–684.

Bremner, J. D., Vythilingam, M., Vermetten, E., Anderson, G., Newcomer, J. W., & Charney, D. S. (2004). Effects of glucocorticoids on declarative memory function in major depression. *Biological Psychiatry, 55*(8), 811–815.

Breslau, N., Paneth, N., Lucia, V., & Paneth-Pollak, R. (2005). Maternal smoking during pregnancy and offspring IQ. *International Journal of Epidemiology, 34*, 1047–1053.

Bressan, R. A., & Crippa, J. A. (2005). The role of dopamine in reward and pleasure behaviour-review of data from preclinical research. *Acta Psychiatrica Scandinavica, 111*, 14–21.

Brett, M. A., Roberts, L. F., Johnson, T. W., & Wassersug, R. J. (2007). Eunuchs in contemporary society: Expectations, consequences, and adjustments to castration (part II). *Journal of Sexual Medicine, 4*(1), 946–955.

Brewer, J. B., Zhao, Z., Desmond, J. E., Glover, G. H., & Gabrieli, J. D. (1998). Making memories: Brain activity that predicts how well visual experience will be remembered. *Science, 281*, 1185–1187.

Bright, C. N., & Penrod, B. (2009). An evaluation of the overjustification effect across multiple contingency arrangements. *Behavioral Interventions, 24*(3), 185–194.

Brim, O. (1999). *The MacArthur Foundation study of midlife development.* Vero Beach, FL: MacArthur Foundation.

Brislin, R. W. (1997). *Understanding culture's influence on behavior* (2nd ed.). San Diego: Harcourt Brace.

Brislin, R. W. (2000). *Understanding culture's influence on behavior.* Ft. Worth, TX: Harcourt.

Brkich, M., Jeffs, D., & Carless, S. A. (2002). A global self-report measure of person-job fit. *European Journal of Psychological Assessment, 18*(1), 43–51.

Brody, A., Olmstead, R. E., London, E. D., Farahi, J., Meyer, J. H., Grossman, P., Lee, G. S., Huang, J., Hahn, E. L., & Mandelkern, M. A. (2004). Smoking-induced ventral striatum dopamine release. *American Journal of Psychiatry, 161*(7), 1211–1218.

Brody, L. R., & Hall, J. A. (2010). Gender, emotion, and socialization. In J. Chrisler & D. R. McCreary (Eds.), *Handbook of gender research in psychology: Vol. 1: Gender research in general and experimental psychology* (pp. 429–454). New York, NY: Springer.

Brondel, L. L., Romer, M. M., Van Wymelbeke, V. V., Pineau, N. N., Jiang, T. T., Hanus, C. C., & Rigaud, D. D. (2009). Variety enhances food intake in humans: Role of sensory-specific satiety. *Physiology & Behavior, 97*(1), 44–51.

Broughton, R. J., Billings, R. R., Cartwright, R. R., & Doucette, D. D. (1994). Homicidal somnambulism: A case report. *Sleep: Journal of Sleep Research & Sleep Medicine, 17*(3), 253–264.

Brown, D. (2000). Human universals and their implications. In N. Roughley (Ed.), *Being humans: anthropological universality and particularity in transdisciplinary perspectives* (pp. 1546–174). Berlin, Germany: Walter de Gruyter & Co.

Brown, L. S. (2011). Guidelines for treating dissociative identity disorder in adults, third revision: A tour de force for the dissociation field. *Journal of Trauma & Dissociation, 12*(2), 113–114.

Brown, P. K., & Wald, G. (1964). Visual pigments in single rods and cones of the human retina. Direct measurements reveal mechanisms of human night and color vision. *Science, 144*, 45–52.

Brown, R., & Kulik, J. (1977). Flashbulb memories. *Cognition, 5*, 73–99.

Bugg, J. M., Zook, N. A., DeLosh, E. L., Davalos, D. B., & Davis, H. P. (2006). Age differences in fluid intelligence: Contributions of general slowing and frontal decline. *Brain and Cognition, 62*, 9–16.

Bukowski, W. M., Motzoi, C., & Meyer, F. (2009). Friendship as process, function, & outcome. In K. H. Rubin, W. M. Bukowski, & B. Laursen (Eds.), *Handbook of peer interactions, relationships, and groups* (pp. 217–231). New York, NY: Guilford.

Bullough, V. L. (1998). Alfred Kinsey and the Kinsey Report: Historical overview and lasting contributions. *Journal of Sex Research, 35*(2), 127–131.

Bunde, J., & Suls, J. (2006). A quantitative analysis of the relationship between the Cook-Medley Hostility Scale and traditional coronary artery disease risk factors. *Health Psychology, 25*, 493–500.

Buontempo, G., & Brockner, J. (2008). Emotional intelligence and the ease of recall judgment bias: The mediating effect of private self-focused attention. *Journal of Applied Social Psychology, 38*, 159–172.

Burghardt, G. M. (2009). Ethics and animal consciousness: How rubber the ethical ruler? *Journal of Social Issues, 65*(3), 499–521.

Burns, S. M. (2008). Unique and interactive predictors of mental health quality of life among men living with prostate cancer. *Dissertation Abstracts International: Section B: The Sciences and Engineering, 68*(10-B), 6953.

Bushman, B. B., & Huesmann, L. R. (2010). Aggression. In S. T. Fiske, D. T. Gilbert, & G. Lindzey (Eds.), *Handbook of social psychology* (Vol. 2, pp. 833–863). Hoboken, NJ: Wiley.

Bushman, B. J., & Anderson, C. A. (2009). Comfortably numb: Desensitizing effects of violent media on helping others. *Psychological Science, 21*, 273–277.

Buss, D. M. (1989). Sex differences in human mate preferences: Evolutionary hypotheses tested in 37 cultures. *Behavioral and Brain Sciences, 12*, 1–49.

Buss, D. M. (2003). *The evolution of desire: Strategies of human mating.* New York, NY: Basic Books.

Buss, D. M. (2007). The evolution of human mating. *Acta Psychologica Sinica, 39*, 502–512.

Buss, D. M. (2011). *Evolutionary psychology: The new science of the mind* (4th ed.). Upper Saddle River, NJ: Prentice-Hall.

Buss, D. M. and 40 colleagues. (1990). International preferences in selecting mates: A study of 37 cultures. *Journal of Cross-Cultural Psychology, 21*, 5–47.

Bussey, K., & Bandura, A. (2004). Social cognitive theory of gender development and functioning. In A. H. Eagly, A. E. Beall, & R. J. Sternberg

(Eds.), *The psychology of gender* (2nd ed., pp. 92–119). New York, NY: Guilford Press.

Buswell, B. N. (2006). The role of empathy, responsibility, and motivations to respond without prejudice in reducing prejudice. *Dissertation Abstracts International: Section B: The Sciences and Engineering, 66*, 6968.

Butcher, J. N. (2000). Revising psychological tests: Lessons learned from the revision of the MMPI. *Psychological Assessment, 12*(3), 263–271.

Butcher, J. N. (2011). *A beginner's guide to the MMPI-2* (3rd ed.). Washington, DC: American Psychological Association.

Butcher, J. N., & Perry, J. N. (2008). *Personality assessment in treatment planning: Use of the MMPI-2 and BTPI.* New York, NY: Oxford University Press.

Butler, R. A. (1954, February). Curiosity in monkeys. *Scientific American, 190*, 70–75.

Butler, R., Sati, S., & Abas, M. (2011). Assessing mental health in different cultures. In M. Abou-Saleh, C. Katona, & A. Kumar (Eds.), *Principles and practice of geriatric psychiatry* (3rd ed., pp. 711–716). Hoboken, NJ: Wiley.

Butterweck, V. (2003). Mechanism of action of St John's wort in depression: What is known? *CNS Drugs, 17*(8), 539–562.

Byne, W. (2007). Biology and sexual minority status. In I. H. Meyer & M. E. Northridge (Eds.), *The health of sexual minorities: Public health perspectives on lesbian, gay, bisexual, and transgender populations* (pp. 65–90). New York, NY: Springer Science + Business Media.

Byne, W., Dracheva, S., Chin, B., Schmeidler, J. M., Davis, K. L., & Haroutunian, V. (2008). Schizophrenia and sex associated differences in the neuronal and oligodendrocyte specific genes in individual thalamic nuclei. *Schizophrenia Research, 98*, 118–128.

C

Cadinu, M., Maass, A., Rosabianca, A., & Kiesner, J. (2005). Why do women underperform under stereotype threat? Evidence for the role of negative thinking. *Psychological Science, 16*, 572–578.

Cai, W-H., Blundell, J., Han, J., Greene, R. W., & Powell, C. M. (2006). Postreactivation glucocorticoids impair recall of established fear memory. *Journal of Neuroscience, 26*(37), 9560–9566.

Cain, A., Epler, A., Steinley, D., & Sher, K. (2011). Concerns related to eating, weight, and shape: Typologies and transitions in men during the college years. *International Journal of Eating Disorders, 45*(6), 768–775.

Cairns, R. B., & Cairns, B. D. (2006). The making of developmental psychology. In R. M. Lerner (Ed.), *Handbook of child psychology, volume one: Theoretical models of human development* (6th ed., pp. 89–65). Hoboken, NJ: Wiley.

Calvete, E., Orue, I., Estevez, A., Villardon, L., & Padilla, P. (2010). Cyberbullying in adolescents: Modalities and aggressors' profile. *Computers in Human Behavior, 26*, 1128–1135.

Cameron, L., Rutland, A., & Brown, R. (2007). Promoting children's positive intergroup attitudes towards stigmatized groups: Extended contact and multiple classification skills training.

International Journal of Behavioral Development, 31, 454–466.

Camfield, D. A., Sarris, J., & Berk, M. (2011). Nutraceuticals in the treatment of obsessive compulsive disorder (OCD): A review of mechanistic and clinical evidence. *Progress in Neuro-Psychopharmacology & Biological Psychiatry, 35*(4), 887–895.

Campbell, A., & Muncer, S. (2008). Intent to harm or injure? Gender and the expression of anger. *Aggressive Behavior, 34*, 282–293.

Campbell, L., Simpson, J. A., Kashy, D. A., & Fletcher, G. J. O. (2001). Ideal standards, the self, and flexibility of ideals in close relationships. *Personality & Social Psychology Bulletin, 27*(4), 447–462.

Canadian Association of Cognitive and Behavioural Therapies. (2011). Canadian Association of Cognitive and Behavioural Therapies. Retrieved from http://cacbt.ca

Canadian Cancer Society. (2012). Smoking and cancer. Retrieved from http://www.cancer.ca/Canada-wide/Prevention/Smoking%20and%20tobacco/Why%20should%20I%20quit/Smoking%20and%20cancer.aspx?sc_lang=EN

Canadian Centre on Substance Abuse. (2007). Reducing alcohol-related harm in Canada: Toward a culture of moderation. Retrieved from http://www.ccsa.ca/2007%20CCSA%20Documents/ccsa-023876-2007.pdf

Canadian Centre on Substance Abuse. (2004). Canadian addiction survey. Retrieved from http://www.ccsa.ca/Eng/Priorities/Research/CanadianAddiction/Pages/default.aspx

Canadian Council on Animal Care. (2005). Guidelines for the treatment of animals in behavioural research and teaching. (2005). *Animal Behaviour, 69*(1), i–vi.

Canadian Council on Learning. (2007). *Lessons in Learning: French Immersion Education in Canada.* Ottawa, ON: Author. Retrieved from http://www.ccl-cca.ca/CCL/Reports/LessonsInLearning/LinL20070517_French_Immersion_programs.htm

Canadian Institute of Health Research & Institute of Population and Public Health. (2002). Sleepiness and the health and performance of adolescent students. Retrieved from http://www.css.to/pdf/sleep/Workshop_CIHR.pdf

Canadian Institutes of Health Research. (2011). The tri-agency framework: Responsible conduct of research. Retrieved from http://www.cihr-irsc.gc.ca/e/44574.html

Canadian Lung Association. (2011). Smoking and tobacco: Facts about smoking. Retrieved from http://www.lung.ca/protect-protegez/tobacco-tabagisme/facts-faits/index_e.php

Canadian Lung Association. (2008). Smoking and tobacco: Facts about smoking. Retrieved from http://www.lung.ca/protect-protegez/tobacco-tabagisme/facts-faits/index_e.php

Canadian Mental Health Association. (2009). News release: Canadian musician Matthew Good headlines Vancouver mental health conference. Retrieved from http://www.cmha.bc.ca/get-informed/news/media/2-18-09

Canadian Network for Mood and Anxiety Treatments. (2009). Canadian Network for Mood and Anxiety Treatments. Retrieved from http://www.canmat.org

Canadian Neurocritical Care Group. (1999). Guidelines for the diagnosis of brain death. *Canadian Journal of Neurological Sciences, 26*(1), 64–66.

Canadian Paediatric Society. (2009). Fetal alcohol spectrum disorder: What you should know about drinking during pregnancy. Retrieved from http://www.caringforkids.cps.ca/pregnancy&babies/FASpregnancy.htm

Canadian Parents for French. (2012). Annual FSL enrolment in Canada 2006–2011: National summary statistics. Retrieved from http://cpf.ca/en/files/CPF-FSL-Enrolment-Stats.pdf.

Canadian Psychological Association. (2000). *Canadian code of ethics for psychologists* (3rd ed.). Ottawa, ON: Author.

Canadian Society for Exercise Physiology. (2011). Canadian physical activity guidelines. Retrieved from http://www.csep.ca/english/view.asp?x=804

Cannon, W. B. (1927). The James-Lange theory of emotions: A critical examination and an alternative theory. *American Journal of Psychology, 39*, 106–124.

Cannon, W. B., Lewis, J. T., & Britton, S. W. (1927). The dispensability of the sympathetic division of the autonomic nervous system. *Boston Medical Surgery Journal, 197*, 514.

Caprara, G. V., Vecchione, M., Barbaranelli, C., & Fraley, R. C. (2007). When likeness goes with liking: The case of political preference. *Political Psychology, 28*, 609–632.

Carballo, J. J., Harkavy-Friedman, J., Burke, A. K., Sher, L., Baca-Garcia, E., Sullivan, G. M., ... Oquendo, M. A. (2008). Family history of suicidal behavior and early traumatic experiences: Addictive effect on suicidality and course of bipolar illness? *Journal of Affective Disorders, 109*, 57–63.

Carels, R. A., Konrad, K., Young, K. M., Darby, L. A., Coit, C., Clayton, A. M., & Oemig, C. K. (2008). Taking control of your personal eating and exercise environment: A weight maintenance program. *Eating Behaviors, 9*, 228–237.

Carey, B. (2008, October 1). Psychoanalytic therapy wins backing. *The New York Times*. Retrieved from http://www.nytimes.com/2008/10/01/health/01psych.html

Carey, B. (2009). A dream interpretation: Tune ups for the brain. *The New York Times*, p. 159.

Carlson, L. E., Speca, M., Faris, P., & Patel, K. D. (2007). One year pre-post intervention follow-up of psychological, immune, endocrine and blood pressure outcomes of mindfulness-based stress reduction (MBSR) in breast and prostate cancer outpatient. *Brain, Behavior, and Immunity, 21*, 1038–1049.

Carlson, N. R. (2008). *Foundations of physiological psychology* (International ed.). Boston, MA: Allyn & Bacon.

Carnagey, N. L., Anderson, C. A., & Bartholow, B. D. (2007). Media violence and social neuroscience: New questions and new opportunities. *Current Directions in Psychological Science, 16*, 178–182.

Carnagey, N. L., Anderson, C. A., & Bushman, B. J. (2007). The effect of video game violence on physiological desensitization to real-life violence. *Journal of Experimental Social Psychology, 43*, 489–496.

Carr, A. (2011). Social and emotional development in middle childhood. In Skuse, D., Bruce, L., Dowdney, L., & Mrazek, D., (Eds.), *Child psychology and psychiatry: Frameworks for practice* (2nd ed., pp. 56–59). Chichester, England: John Wiley & Sons, Ltd.

Carretié, L., Albert, J., López-Martín, S., & Tapia, M. (2009). Negative brain: An integrative review on the neural processes activated by unpleasant stimuli. *International Journal of Psychophysiology, 71*(1), 57–63.

Carretti, B., Borella, E., & De Beni, R. (2007). Does strategic memory training improve the working memory performance of younger and older adults? *Experimental Psychology, 54*(4), 311–320.

Carson, G., Cox, L. V., Crane, J., Croteau, P., Graves, L., Kluka., ... Wood, R. (2010). Alcohol use and pregnancy consensus clinical guidelines. *Journal of Obstetrics and Gynaecology in Canada, 32* (Supplement 3), S1–S33.

Carstensen, L. L., Turan, B., Scheibe, S., Ram, N., Ersner-Hershfield, H., Samanez-Larkin, G. R., Brooks, K., & Nesselroade, J. R. (2011). Emotional experience improves with age: Evidence based on over 10 years of experience sampling. *Psychology and Aging, 26*, 21–33.

Caruso, E. M. (2008). Use of experienced retrieval ease in self and social judgments. *Journal of Experimental Social Psychology, 44*, 148–155.

Carvalho, C., Mazzoni, G., Kirsch, I., Meo, M., & Santandrea, M. (2008). The effect of posthypnotic suggestion, hypnotic suggestibility, and goal intentions on adherence to medical instructions. *International Journal of Clinical and Experimental Hypnosis, 56*, 143–155.

Cassidy, J. (2008). The nature of the child's ties. In J. Cassidy & P. R. Shaver (Eds.), *Handbook of attachment: Theory, research, and clinical applications* (2nd ed., pp. 3–22). New York, NY: Guilford.

Cathers-Schiffman, T. A., & Thompson, M. S. (2007). Assessment of English- and Spanish-speaking students with the WISC-III and Leiter-R. *Journal of Psychoeducational Assessment, 25*, 41–52.

Cattell, R. B. (1950). *Personality: A systematic, theoretical, and factual study*. New York, NY: McGraw-Hill.

Cattell, R. B. (1963). Theory of fluid and crystallized intelligence: A critical experiment. *Journal of Educational Psychology, 54*, 1–22.

Cattell, R. B. (1965). *The scientific analysis of personality*. Baltimore, MD: Penguin.

Cattell, R. B. (1971). *Abilities: Their structure, growth, and action*. Boston, MA: Houghton Mifflin.

Cattell, R. B. (1990). Advances in Cattellian personality theory. In L. A. Pervin (Ed.), *Handbook of personality: Theory and research*. New York, NY: Guilford Press.

CBC News. (2003). Hell to pay: The "satanic sex scandal." *The Fifth Estate*. Retrieved from http://www.cbc.ca/fifth/martin/scandal.html

CBC News. (2007). The fight for the right to die. Retrieved from http://www.cbc.ca/news/background/assistedsuicide/

CBC News. (2009a). Girl watched skinhead videos and talked of how to kill, hearing told. Retrieved from http://www.cbc.ca/canada/manitoba/story/2009/05/25/mb-swastika-parents-winnipeg.html

CBC News. (2009b). Sask. MD's Wikipedia posting of ink blots angers psychologists. Retrieved from http://www.cbc.ca/canada/saskatchewan/story/2009/07/31/rorschach-test.html#socialcomments

CBC News. (2009c). The fight for the right to die. Retrieved from http://www.cbc.ca/canada/story/2009/02/09/f-assisted-suicide.html

CBC News. (2010). Williams's murder victims pleaded for their lives. Retrieved from http://www.cbc.ca/news/canada/story/2010/10/19/russell-williams-day-2.html

CBC News. (2011a, October 28). Alberta health services sued over baby Isaiah's death. Retrieved from http://www.cbc.ca/news/canada/edmonton/story/2011/10/28/edmonton-baby-lawsuit.html

CBC News. (2011b, October 4). B.C. woman describes 49-day ordeal in Nevada. Retrieved from http://www.cbc.ca/news/canada/british-columbia/story/2011/10/04/bc-rita-chretien-nevada.html

CBC News. (2012a). Body of missing B.C. man Albert Chretien found in Nevada. Retrieved from http://www.cbc.ca/news/canada/british-columbia/story/2012/10/01/albert-chretien-body-found.html

CBC News. (2012b). Oxycontin officially replaced by new drug. Retrieved from http://www.cbc.ca/news/health/story/2012/03/01/ottawa-oxycontin-off-shelf-pharmacy.html

CBC News Online. (2004, March 10). *Baby signing*. Retrieved from http://www.cbc.ca/news/background/babysign/

Cehajic, S., Brown, R., & Castano, E. (2008). Forgive and forget? Antecedents and consequences of intergroup forgiveness in Bosnia and Herzegovina. *Political Psychology, 29*, 351–367.

Centre for Addiction and Mental Health. (2008). Cognitive behavioural therapy (CBT) clinic. Retrieved from http://www.camh.net/About_CAMH/Guide_to_CAMH/Mental_Health_Programs/Mood_and_Anxiety_Program/guide_cognitive_behavtherapy.html

Ceschi, G., & Scherer, K. R. (2001). Contrôler l'expression faciale et changer l'émotion: Une approche développementale (The role of facial expression in emotion: A developmental perspective). *Enfance, 53*(3), 257–269.

Chalmers, L., & Milan, A. (2005). *Marital satisfaction during the retirement years* (Cat. no. 11-008). Retrieved from http://www.statcan.gc.ca/pub/11-008-x/2004004/article/7776-eng.pdf

Chambers, N. (2009). *Binge eating: Psychological factors, symptoms and treatment*. Hauppauge, NY: Nova Science Publishers.

Chandrashekar, J., Hoon, M. A., Ryba, N. J. P., & Zuker, C. S. (2006). The receptors and cells for mammalian taste. *Nature, 444*, 288–294.

Chang, G., Orav, J., McNamara, T. K., Tong, M. Y., & Antin, J. H. (2005). Psychosocial function after hematopoietic stem cell transplantation. *Psychosomatics: Journal of Consultation Liaison Psychiatry, 46*(1), 34–40.

Chao, H., Digruccio, M., Chen, P., & Li, C. (2012). Type 2 corticotropin-releasing factor receptor in the ventromedial nucleus of hypothalamus is critical in regulating feeding and lipid metabolism in white adipose tissue. *Endocrinology, 153*(1), 166–176.

Chapman, A. L., Leung, D. W., & Lynch, T. R. (2008). Impulsivity and emotion dysregulation in borderline personality disorder. *Journal of Personality Disorders, 22*, 148–164.

Charach, A., Pepler, D., & Ziegler, S. (1995). Bullying at school. *Education Canada, 37,* 12–18.

Charles, E. P. (2007). Object permanence, an ecological approach. *Dissertation Abstracts International: Section B: The Sciences and Engineering, 67*(8-B), 4737.

Charles, S. T., & Carstensen, L. L. (2007). Emotion regulation and aging. In J. J. Gross (Ed.), *Handbook of emotion regulation.* New York, NY: Guilford Press.

Charney, D., & Nestler, E. (2011). *The neurobiology of mental illness* (3rd ed.). New York, NY. Oxford University Press.

Chartrand, T., Pinckert, S., & Burger, J. M. (1999). When manipulation backfires: The effects of time delay and requester on the foot-in-the-door technique. *Journal of Applied Social Psychology, 29,* 211–221.

Chavez, C. M., McGaugh, J. L., & Weinberger, N. M. (2009). The basolateral amygdala modulates specific sensory memory representations in the cerebral cortex. *Neurobiology of Learning and Memory, 91*(4), 382–392.

Chellappa, S. L., Frey, S., Knoblauch, V., & Cajochen, C. (2011). Cortical activation patterns herald successful dream recall after NREM and REM sleep. *Biological Psychology, 87*(2), 251–256.

Cheng, C., & Chartrand, T. L. (2003). Self-monitoring without awareness: Using mimicry as a nonconscious affiliation strategy. *Journal of Personality & Social Psychology, 85*(6), 1170–1179.

Cheng, R. F., Borrett, D. S., Weyland, C., Kwan, H. C., & Cheng, R. S. (2010). Human prefrontal cortical response to the meditative state: A spectroscopy study. *International Journal of Neuroscience, 120* (7), 483–488.

Cheung, M. S., Gilbert, P., & Irons, C. (2004). An exploration of shame, social rank, and rumination in relation to depression. *Personality & Individual Differences, 36*(5), 1143–1153.

Chida, Y., & Steptoe, A. (2010). Greater cardiovascular responses to laboratory mental stress are associated with poor subsequent cardiovascular risk status. *Hypertension, 55*(4), 1026–1032.

Chida, Y., Hamer, M., Wardle, J., & Steptoe, A. (2008). Do stress-related psychosocial factors contribute to cancer incidence and survival? *Nature Clinical Practice Oncology, 5*(8), 466–475.

Chiou, W-B. (2007). Customers' attributional judgments towards complaint handling in airline service: A confirmatory study based on attribution theory. *Psychological Reports, 100,* 1141–1150.

Chiricozzi, F. R., Clausi, S., Molinari, M., & Leggio, M. G. (2008). Phonological shortterm store impairment after cerebellar lesion: A single case study. *Neuropsychologia, 46,* 1940–1953.

Choi, I., & Nisbett, R. E. (2000). Cultural psychology of surprise: Holistic theories and recognition of contradiction. *Journal of Personality and Social Psychology, 79*(6), 890–905.

Chomsky, N. (1968). *Language and mind.* New York, NY: Harcourt, Brace, World.

Chomsky, N. (1980). *Rules and representations.* New York, NY: Columbia University Press.

Christensen, D. (2000). Is snoring a diZZZease? Nighttime noises may serve as a wake-up call for future illness. *Science News, 157,* 172–173.

Christensen, H., Anstey, K. J., Leach, L. S., & Mackinnon, A. J. (2008). Intelligence, education, and the brain reserve hypothesis. In F. I. M. Craik & T. A. Salthouse (Eds.), *The handbook of aging and cognition* (3rd ed., pp. 133–188). New York, NY: Psychology Press.

Christopher, K., Lutz-Zois, C. J., & Reinhardt, A. R. (2007). Female sexual-offenders: Personality pathology as a mediator of the relationship between childhood sexual abuse history and sexual abuse. *Child Abuse & Neglect, 31,* 871–883.

Chu, J. (2011). *Rebuilding shattered lives: Treating complex PTSD and dissociative disorders* (2nd ed.). Hoboken, NJ: Wiley.

Chudley, A., Conry, J., Cook, J., Loock, C., Rosales, T., & Leblanc, N. (2005). Fetal alcohol spectrum disorder: Canadian guidelines for diagnosis. *Canadian Medical Association Journal, 172*(5 supp), S3–S21.

Chung, J. C. C. (2006). Measuring sensory processing patterns of older Chinese people: Psychometric validation of the adult sensory profile. *Aging & Mental Health, 10,* 648–655.

Cialdini, R. B. (2009). *Influence: Science and practice* (5th ed.). Boston, MA: Allyn & Bacon.

Cicchetti, D. (2010). Developmental psychopathology. In R. Lerner (Ed.), *Handbook of lifespan development,* Vol. 2: Social and emotional development (pp. 511–589). Hoboken, NJ: Wiley.

Clark, A. J. (2007). *Empathy in counseling and psychotherapy: Perspectives and practices.* Mahwah, NJ: Erlbaum.

Clark, D., & Beck, A. T. (2009). *Cognitive therapy of anxiety disorders: Science and practice.* New York, NY: Guilford.

Clark, K. B., & Clark, M. P. (1939). The development of consciousness of self and the emergence of racial identification in Negro preschool children. *Journal of Social Psychology, 10,* 591–599.

Clark, R., & Hatfield, E. (1989). Gender differences in receptivity to sexual offers. *Journal of Psychology & Human Sexuality, 2*(1), 39–55.

Clay, R. (2003). An empty nest can promote freedom, improved relationships. *Monitor on Psychology, 34*(4), 40.

Clay, S., Allen, J., & Parran, T. (2008). A review of addiction. *Postgraduate Medicine, 120*(2), E01-7.

Cleeremans, A., & Sarrazin, J. C. (2007). Time, action, and consciousness. *Human Movement Science, 26,* 180–202.

Clifford, A., Franklin, A., Davies, I. L., & Holmes, A. (2009). Electrophysiological markers of categorical perception of color in 7-month old infants. *Brain & Cognition, 71*(2), 165–172.

Clifford, J. S., Boufal, M. M., & Kurtz, J. E. (2004). Personality traits and critical thinking: Skills in college students: empirical tests of a two-factor theory. *Assessment, 11*(2), 169–176.

Clinton, S. M., & Meador-Woodruff, J H. (2004). Thalamic dysfunction in schizophrenia: Neurochemical, neuropathological, and in vivo imaging abnormalities. *Schizophrenia Research, 69*(2–3), 237–253.

Cochran, H. (2009). Shaping a form: The evolution of the feminine ideal. *Intersections, 7,* 41–55.

Cohen, D., Mason, K., & Farley, T. A. (2004). Beer consumption and premature mortality in Louisiana: An ecologic analysis. *Journal of Studies on Alcohol, 65*(3), 398–403.

Cohen, S., & Lemay, E. P. (2007). Why would social networks be linked to affect and health practices? *Health Psychology, 26,* 410–417.

Cohen, S., Hamrick, N., Rodriguez, M. S., Feldman, P. J., Rabin, B. S., & Manuck, S. B. (2002). Reactivity and vulnerability to stress associated risk for upper respiratory illness. *Psychosomatic Medicine, 64*(2), 302–310.

Cohidon, C., Santin, G., Imbernon, E., & Goldberg, M. (2010). Working conditions and depressive symptoms in the 2003 decennial health survey: The role of the occupational category. *Social Psychiatry & Psychiatric Epidemiology, 45*(12), 1135–1147.

Colcombe, S., & Kramer, A. F. (2003). Fitness effects on the cognitive function of older adults: A meta-analytic study. *Psychological Science, 14*(2), 125–130.

Cole, M., & Gajdamaschko, N. (2007). Vygotsky and culture. In H. Daniels, J. Wertsch, & M. Cole (Eds.), *The Cambridge companion to Vygotsky* (pp. 193–211). New York, NY: Cambridge University Press.

Coleborne, C., & MacKinnon, D. (2011). *Exhibiting madness in museums: Remembering psychiatry through collection and display.* New York, NY: Routledge.

Collet, C. C., Guillot, A. A., & Petit, C. C. (2010). Phoning while driving II: A review of driving conditions influence. *Ergonomics, 53*(5), 602–616.

Collins, R. L. (2011). Content analysis of gender roles in the media: Where are we now and where should we go? *Sex Roles, 64,* 290–298.

Colrain, I. M. (2011). Sleep and the brain. *Neuropsychology Review, 21*(1), 1–4.

Colson, M. (2010). Female orgasm: Myths, facts and controversies. *Sexologies, 19*(1), 39–47.

Columb, C., & Plant, E. A. (2011). Revisiting the Obama effect: Exposure to Obama reduces implicit prejudice. *Journal of Experimental Social Psychology, 47*(2), 499–501.

Combrink-Graham, L., & McKenna, S. B. (2006). Families with children with disrupted attachments. In L. Combrinck-Graham (Ed.), *Children in family contexts: Perspectives on treatment* (pp. 242–264). New York, NY: Guilford Press.

Combs, D. R., Basso, M. R., Wanner, J. L., & Ledet, S. N. (2008). Schizophrenia. In M. Hersen & J. Rosqvist (Eds.), *Handbook of psychological assessment, case conceptualization, and treatment, Vol 1: Adults* (pp. 352–402). Hoboken, NJ: Wiley.

Comer, R., Gould, E., Ogden, N., & Boyes, M. (2012). *Psychology around us* (Canadian edition). Mississauga, ON: John Wiley & Sons Canada.

Comstock, G., & Scharrer, E. (2006). Media and popular culture. In K. A. Renninger, I. E. Sigel, W. E. Damon, & R. M. Lerner (Eds.), *Handbook of child psychology: Vol 4, Child psychology in practice* (6th ed., pp. 817–863). Hoboken, NJ: Wiley.

Conley, T. D., Moors, A. C., Matsick, J. L., Ziegler, A., & Valentine, B. A. (2011). Women, men, and the bedroom: Methodological and conceptual insights that narrow, reframe, and eliminate gender differences in sexuality. *Current Directions In Psychological Science, 20*(5), 296–300.

Conn, P., & Rantin, F. (2010). Ethical research as the target of animal extremism: An international problem. *Brazilian Journal of Medical and Biological Research, 43*(2), 124–126.

Connolly, S. (2000). *LSD (just the facts).* Baltimore: Heinemann Library.

Connor, D. F. (2004). *Aggression and antisocial behavior in children and adolescents: Research and treatment.* New York, NY: Guilford.

Connor, K. M., & Davidson, J. R. T. (2002). A placebo-controlled study of Kava kava in generalized anxiety disorder. *International Clinical Psychopharmacology, 17*(4), 185–188.

Constantino, M. J., Manber, R., Ong, J., Kuo, T. F., Huang, J. S., & Arnow, B. A. (2007). Patient expectations and therapeutic alliance as predictors of outcome in group cognitive-behavioral therapy for insomnia. *Behavioral Sleep Medicine, 5*, 210–228.

Cook, M., & Mineka, S. (1989). Observational conditioning of fear to fear-relevant versus fear-irrelevant stimuli in rhesus monkeys. *Journal of Abnormal Psychology, 98*, 448–459.

Cooper, C., Bebbington, P. E., Meltzer, H., Bhugra, D., Brugha, T., Jenkins, R., Farrell, M., & King, M. (2008). Depression and common mental disoders in lone parents: Results of the 2000 National Psychiatric Morbidity Survey. *Psychological Medicine, 38*, 335–342.

Cooper, J., & Hogg, M. A. (2007). Feeling the anguish of others: A theory of vicarious dissonance. In M. P. Zanna (Ed.), *Advances in experimental social psychology* (pp. 359–403). San Diego, CA: Elsevier.

Cooper, R. (2004). What is wrong with the *DSM? History of Psychiatry, 15*(1), 5–25.

Cooper, W. E. Jr., Pérez-Mellado, V., Vitt, L. J., & Budzinsky, B. (2002). Behavioral responses to plant toxins in two omnivorous lizard species. *Physiology & Behavior, 76*(2), 297–303.

Coplan, R. J., Arbeau, K. A., & Armer, M. (2008). Don't fret, be supportive! Maternal characteristics linking child shyness to psychosocial and school adjustment in kindergarten. *Journal of Abnormal Child Psychology, 36*, 359–371.

Coppens, E., Van Paesschen, W., Vandenbulcke, M., & Vansteenwegen, D. (2010). Fear conditioning following a unilateral anterior temporal lobectomy: Reduced autonomic responding and stimulus contingency knowledge. *Acta Neurologica Belgica, 110*(1), 36–48.

Corey, G. (2012). *Theory and practice of group counseling* (8th ed.). Belmont, CA: Cengage.

Corkin, S. (2002). What's new with the amnesic patient H. M.? *Nature Reviews Neuroscience, 3*, 153–160.

Cornelius, J. R., & Clark, D. B. (2008). Depressive disorders and adolescent substance use disorders. In Y. Kaminer & O. G. Bukstein (Eds.), *Adolescent substance abuse: Psychiatric comorbidity and high-risk behaviors* (pp. 221–242). New York, NY: Routledge/Taylor & Francis Group.

Corr, C. A., Nabe, C. M., & Corr, D. M. (2009). *Death and dying: Life and living* (6th ed.). Belmont, CA: Wadsworth.

Corrigan, J., Selassie, A., & Orman, J. (2010). The epidemiology of traumatic brain injury. *Journal of Head Trauma Rehabilitation, 25*(2), 72–80.

Cosci, F., & Fava, G. A. (2011). New clinical strategies of assessment of comorbidity associated with substance use disorders. *Clinical Psychology Review, 31*(3), 418–427.

Costa, P. T. Jr., & McCrae, R. R. (1992). *NEO PI-R professional manual.* Odessa, FL: Psychological Assessment Resources.

Costa, P. T. Jr., & McCrae, R. R. (2011). The five-factor model, five-factor theory, and interpersonal psychology. In L. M. Horowitz & S. Strack (Eds.), *Handbook of interpersonal psychology: Theory, research, assessment, and therapeutic interventions* (pp. 91–104). Hoboken, NJ: John Wiley.

Cowperthwaite, B., Hains, S. M., & Kisilevsky, B. S. (2007) Fetal behavior in smoking compared to non-smoking pregnant women. *Infant Behavior and Development, 30*, 422–430.

Coyne, S. M., Archer, J., & Eslea, M. (2004). Cruel intentions on television and in real life: Can viewing indirect aggression increase viewers' subsequent indirect aggression? *Journal of Experimental Child Psychology , 88*(3), 234–253.

Craig, A. D., & Bushnell, M. C. (1994). The thermal grill illusion: Unmasking the burn of cold pain. *Science, 265*, 252–255.

Craig, C. L., Russell, S. J., Cameron, C., & Beaulieu, A. (1999). *Foundation for joint action: Reducing physical inactivity.* Ottawa, ON: Canadian Fitness and Lifestyle Research Institute.

Craig, W., & Pepler, D. (1995). Peer processes in bullying and victimization: An observational study. *Exceptionality Education Canada, 5*, 81–95.

Craig, W., & Pepler, D. (2003). Identifying and targeting risk for involvement in bullying and victimization. *Canadian Journal of Psychiatry, 48*, 577–582.

Craig, W., Pepler, D., & Blais, J. (2007). Responding to bullying: What works. *School Psychology International, 28*, 465–477.

Craik, E. I. M., & Tulving, E. (1975). Depth of processing and retention of words in episodic memory. *Journal of Experimental Psychology: General, 104*, 268–294.

Craik, F. I., Bialystok, E., & Freedman, M. (2010). Delaying the onset of Alzheimer disease: Bilingualism as a form of cognitive reserve. *Neurology, 75*, 1726–1729.

Crain, W. (2011). *Theories of development: Concepts and applications* (6th ed.). Upper Saddle River, NJ: Pearson.

Crawford, C. S. (2008). Ghost in the machine: A genealogy of phantom-prosthetic relations (amputation, dismemberment, prosthetic). *Dissertation Abstracts International Section A: Humanities and Social Sciences, 68*(7-A), 3173.

Crespo-Facorro, B., Barbadillo, L., Pelayo-Terán, J., Rodríguez-Sánchez, J. M., & Teran, J. M. (2007). Neuropsychological functioning and brain structure in schizophrenia. *International Review of Psychiatry, 19*, 325–336.

Cresswell, M. (2008). Szasz and his interlocutors: Reconsidering Thomas Szasz's "Myth of mental illness" thesis. *Journal for the Theory of Social Behaviour, 38*, 23–44.

Crews, F. T., Collins, M. A., Dlugos, C., Littleton, J., Wilkins, L., Neafsey, E. J., Pentney, R., Snell, L. D., Tabakoff, B., Zou, J., & Noronha, A. (2004). Alcohol-induced neurodegeneration: When, where and why? *Alcoholism: Clinical & Experimental Research, 28*(2), 350–364.

CRI English. (2012). Memory champion Wang Feng. Retrived from http://english.cri.cn/7146/2012/05/11/2702s698871.htm

Crick, N. R., Ostrov, J. M., & Yawabata, Y. (2007). Relational aggression and gender: An overview. In D. J. Flannery, A. T. Vazsonyi, & I. D.

Waldman (Eds.), *The Cambridge handbook of violent behavior and aggression* (pp. 245–259). New York, NY: Cambridge University Press.

Cristinzio, C., N'Diaye, K., Seeck, M., Vuilleumier, P., & Sander, D. (2010). Integration of gaze direction and facial expression in patients with unilateral amygdala damage. *Brain: A Journal of Neurology, 133*(Pt 1), 248–261.

Cristofalo, V. J. (1996). Ten years later: What have we learned about human aging from studies of cell cultures? *Gerontology, 36,* 737–741.

Crone, C. C., & Gabriel, G. (2002). Herbal and nonherbal supplements in medical-psychiatric patient populations. *Psychiatric Clinics of North America, 25*(1), 211–230.

Crooks, R. L., & Baur, K. (2011). *Our sexuality* (11th ed.). Belmont, CA: Cengage.

Crosby, B. (2003). Case studies in rational emotive behavior therapy with children and adolescents. *Journal of Cognitive Psychotherapy, 17*(3), 289–291.

Cross, T. P., & Saxe, L. (1992). A critique of the validity of polygraph testing in child sexual abuse cases. *Journal of Child Sexual Abuse: Research, Treatment, & Program Innovations for Victims, Survivors, & Offenders, 1*(4), 19–33.

Crowell, S. E., Beauchaine, T. P., & Lenzenweger, M. F. (2008). The development of borderline personality disorder and self-injurious behavior. In T. P. Beauchaine & S. P. Hinshaw (Eds.), *Child and adolescent psychopathology* (pp. 510–539). Hoboken, NJ: Wiley.

CTV. (2008). Calgary man makes it to top of Everest on 3rd try. Retrieved from http://www.ctv.ca/servlet/ArticleNews/story/CTVNews/20080523/everest_brash_080523?s_name=&no_ads

Cubelli, R., & Della Sala, S. (2008). Flashbulb memories: Special but not iconic. *Cortex, 44,* 908–909.

Cui, Y., Jin, J., Zhang, X., Xu, H., Yang, L., Du, D., … Cao, X. (2011). Forebrain NR2B overexpression facilitating the prefrontal cortex long-term potentiation and enhancing working memory function in mice. *Plos One, 6*(5), e20312.

Cullen, D., & Gotell, L. (2002). From orgasms to organizations: Maslow, women's sexuality and the gendered foundations of the needs hierarchy. *Gender, Work & Organization, 9*(5), 537–555.

Cully, J. A., & Stanley, M. A. (2008). Assessment and treatment of anxiety in later life. In K. Laidlaw & B. Knight (Eds.), *Handbook of emotional disorders in later life: Assessment and treatment.* New York, NY: Oxford University Press.

Cummings, D. E. (2006). Ghrelin and the short- and long-term regulation of appetite and body weight. *Physiology & Behavior, 89,* 71–84.

Cunningham, G. B. (2002). Diversity and recategorization: Examining the effects of cooperation on bias and work outcomes. *Dissertation Abstracts International Section A: Humanities and Social Sciences, 63,* 1288.

Cunningham, G. B., Fink, J. S., & Kenix, L. J. (2008). Choosing an endorser for a women's sporting event: The interaction of attractiveness and expertise. *Sex Roles, 58,* 371–378.

Curtiss, S. (1977). *Genie: A psycholinguistic study of a modern-day "wild child."* New York, NY: Academic Press.

D

D'Amato, B. (2009). Mary Shelley's *Frankenstein*: An orphaned author's dream and journey toward integration. *Modern Psychoanalysis, 34*(1), 117–135.

Daan, S. (2011). How and why? The lab versus the field. *Sleep and Biological Rhythms, 9*(1), 1–2.

Dackis, C. A., & O'Brien, C. P. (2001). Cocaine dependence: A disease of the brain's reward centers. *Journal of Substance Abuse Treatment, 21*(3), 111–117.

Daffner, K. R. (2010). Promoting successful cognitive aging: A comprehensive review. *Journal of Alzheimer's Disease, 19*(4), 1101–1122.

Dakof, G. A., Godley, S. H., & Smith, J. E. (2011). The adolescent community reinforcement approach and multidimensional family therapy: Addressing relapse during treatment. In Y. Kaminer & K. C. Winters (Eds.), *Clinical manual of adolescent substance abuse treatment* (pp. 239–268). Arlington, VA: American Psychiatric Publishing.

Dale, A., & DeCicco, T. L. (2011). Content and discovery in the dreams of Canadian male university students: A pilot study. *Dreaming, 21*(4), 257–276.

Dalenberg, C., Loewenstein, R., Spiegel, D., Brewin, C., Lanius, R., Frankel, S., ... Paulson, K. (2007). Scientific study of the dissociative disorders. *Psychotherapy and Psychosomatics, 76*, 400–401.

Dalley, J. W., Fryer, T. D., Brichard, L., Robinson, E. S. J., Theobald, D. E. H., Lääne, K., ... Robbins, T. W. (2007). Nucleus accumbens D2/3 receptors predict trait impulsivity and cocaine reinforcement. *Science, 315*, 1267–1270.

Damasio, A. R. (1999). *The feeling of what happens: Body and emotion in the making of consciousness.* New York, NY: Harcourt Brace.

Damasio, A. R. (2006). From Descartes' error: Emotion, reason, and the human brain. In G. Marcus (Ed.), *The Norton Psychology Reader* (pp. 58–69). New York, NY: Norton.

Daniels, K., Toth, J., & Jacoby, J. (2006). The aging of executive functions. In E. Bialystok & F. I. M. Craik (Eds.), *Lifespan cognition: Mechanisms of change.* New York, NY: Oxford University Press.

Dantzer, R., O'Connor, J. C., Freund, G. C., Johnson, R. W., & Kelley, K. W. (2008). From inflammation to sickness and depression: When the immune system subjugates the brain. *Nature Reviews Neuroscience, 9*, 46–57.

Danziger, K. (1994). Does the history of psychology have a future? *Theory and Psychology, 4*(4), 467–484.

Dapretto, M., Davies, M. S., Pfeifer, J. H., Scott, A. A., Sigman, M., Bookheimer, S. Y., & Iacoboni, M. (2006). Understanding emotions in others: Mirror neuron dysfunction in children with autism spectrum disorders. *Nature Neuroscience, 9*, 28–30.

Darmani, N. A., & Crim, J. L. (2005) Delta9-tetrahydrocannabinol prevents emesis more potently than enhanced locomotor activity produced by chemically diverse dopamine D2/D3 receptor agonists in the least shrew (Cryptotis parva). *Pharmacology Biochemistry and Behavior, 80*, 35–44.

Darwin, C. (1859). *On the origin of species.* London, England: Murray.

Darwin, C. (1872). *The expression of the emotions in man and animals.* London, England: Murray.

Dasi, C., Soler, M. J., Cervera, T., & Ruiz, J. C. (2008). Influence of articulation rate on two memory tasks in young and older adults. *Perceptual and Motor Skills, 106*, 579–589.

Dastani, Z., Pajukanta, P., Marcil, M., Rudzicz, N., Ruel, I., Bailey, S. D., ... Genest, J. (2010). Fine mapping and association studies of a high-density lipoprotein cholesterol linkage region on chromosome 16 in French-Canadian subjects. *European Journal of Human Genetics, 18*(3), 342–347.

Dattilio, F. M., & Nichols, M. P. (2011). Reuniting estranged family members: A cognitive-behavioral-systemic perspective. *American Journal of Family Therapy, 39*(2), 88–99.

Davidson, P. S. R., Anaki, D., Ciaramelli, E., Cohn, M., Kim, A. S. N., Murphy, K. J., ...Levine, B. (2008). Does lateral parietal cortex support episodic memory? Evidence from focal lesion patients. *Neuropsychologia, 46*, 1743–1755.

Davies, I. (1998). A study of colour grouping in three languages: A test of the linguistic relativity hypothesis. *British Journal of Psychology, 89*, 433–452.

Davies, J. M. (1996). Dissociation, repression and reality testing in the countertransference: the controversey over memory and false memory in the psychoanalytic treatment of adult survivors of childhood sexual abuse. *Psychoanalytic Dialogues, 6*, 189–218.

Davies, M. F. (2008). Irrational beliefs and unconditional self-acceptance. III. The relative importance of different types of irrational belief. *Journal of Rational-Emotive & Cognitive Behavior Therapy, 26*, 102–118.

Davis, D. M., & Hayes, J. A. (2011). Benefits of mindfulness? A practice review of psychotherapy-related research. *Psychotherapy, 48*(2), 198–208.

Davis, J. I., Senghas, A., Brandt, F., & Ochsner, K. N. (2010). The effects of Botox injections on emotional experience. *Emotion, 10*(3), 433–440.

Davison, G., Blankstein, K,,. Flett, G., & Neale, J. (2010). *Abnormal psychology* (4th Cdn ed.). Mississauga, ON: Wiley.

Dawson, K. A. (2004). Temporal organization of the brain: Neurocognitive mechanisms and clinical implications. *Brain & Cognition, 54*(1), 75–94.

De Coteau, T. J., Hope, D. A., & Anderson, J. (2003). Anxiety, stress, and health in northern plains Native Americans. *Behavior Therapy, 34*(3), 365–380.

De Graaf, C. (2006). Effects of snacks on energy intake: An evolutionary perspective. *Appetite, 47*(1), 18–23.

De Jong, M., Pieters, R., & Fox, J. (2010). Reducing social desirability bias through item randomized response: An application to measure underreported desires. *Journal of Marketing Research (JMR), 47*(1), 14–27.

De Oliveira-Souza, R., Moll, J., Ignácio, F. A., & Hare, R. D. (2008). Psychopathy in a civil psychiatric outpatient sample. *Criminal Justice and Behavior, 35*, 427–437.

De Ridder, D. & van den Bos, R. (2006). Evolutionary perspectives on overeating and overweight: Introduction to the special section of Appetite. *Appetite, 47*(1), 1–2.

De Waal, F. B. M. (2008). Putting the altruism back into altruism: The evolution of empathy. *Annual Review of Psychology, 59*, 279–300.

Deary, I. J., & Stough, C. (1996). Intelligence and inspection time: Achievements, prospects, and problems. *American Psychologist, 51*, 599–608.

Deary, I. J., & Stough, C. (1997). Looking down on human intelligence. *American Psychologist, 52*, 1148–1149.

Deary, I. J., Ferguson, K. J., Bastin, M. E., Barrow, G. W. S., Reid, L. M., Seckl, ... MacLullich, A. M. J. (2007). Skull size and intelligence, and King Robert Bruce's IQ. *Intelligence, 35*, 519–528.

Debarnot, U., Castellani, E., Valenza, G., Sebastiani, L., & Guillot, A. (2011). Daytime naps improve motor imagery learning. *Cognitive, Affective & Behavioral Neuroscience, 11*(4), 541–550.

DeCasper, A. J., & Fifer, W. D. (1980). Of human bonding: Newborns prefer their mother's voices. *Science, 208*, 1174–1176.

DeCasper, A. J., & Spence, M. J. (1986). Newborns prefer a familiar story over an unfamiliar one. *Infant Behavior and Development, 9*, 133–150.

Deci, E. L. (1995). *Why we do what we do: The dynamics of personal autonomy.* New York, NY: Putnam's Sons.

Deci, E. L., & Moller, A. C. (2005). The concept of competence: A starting place for understanding intrinsic motivation and selfdetermined extrinsic motivation. In A. J. Elliot & C. S. Dweck (Eds.), *Handbook of competence and motivation* (pp. 579–597). New York, NY: Guilford.

Deci, E. L., & Ryan, R. M. (2008). Facilitating optimal motivation and psychological well-being across life's domains. *Canadian Psychology/Psychologie Canadienne, 49*(1), 14–23.

Deci, E. L., Koestner, R., & Ryan, R. M. (1999). A meta-analytic review of experiments examining the effects of extrinsic rewards on intrinsic motivation. *Psychological Bulletin, 125*(6), 627–668.

Deci, E., & Ryan, R. (2010). Intrinsic motivation. In W. Edward Craighead & Charles B. Nemeroff (Eds.), *Corsini Encyclopedia of Psychology*, Vol. 2 (4th ed., p. 868). New York, NY: Wiley.

DeCicco, T. L. (2007). Dreams of female university students: Content analysis and the relationship to discovery using the Ullman method. *Dreaming, 17*(2), 98–112.

Deckers, L. (2005). *Motivation: Biological, psychological, and environmental* (2nd ed.). Boston, MA: Allyn & Bacon/Longman.

DeClue, G. (2003). The polygraph and lie detection. *Journal of Psychiatry & Law, 31*(3), 361–368.

Delgado, J. M. R. (1960). Emotional behavior in animals and humans. *Psychiatric Research Report, 12*, 259–271.

Delgado, P. L. (2004). How antidepressants help depression: Mechanisms of action and clinical response. *Journal of Clinical Psychiatry, 65*, 25–30.

Deller, T., Haas, C. A., Freiman, T. M., Phinney, A., Jucker, M., & Frotscher, M. (2006). Lesion induced axonal sprouting in the central nervous system. *Advances in Experimental Medicine and Biology, 557*, 101–121.

Delormier, T., Frohlich, K., & Potvin, L. (2009). Food and eating as social practice: Understanding eating patterns as social phenomena and implications for public health. *Sociology of Health & Illness, 31*(2), 215–228.

Delville, Y., Mansour, K. M., & Ferris, C. F. (1996). Testosterone facilitates aggression by modulating vasopressin receptors in the hypothalamus. *Physiology and Behavior, 60*, 25–29.

DeMaria, S. (2012). Club drugs. In Bryson, E. & Frost, E. (Eds.), *Perioperative addiction: Clinical management of the addicted patient* (pp. 111–128). New York, NY: Springer.

Dembe, A. E., Erickson, J. B., Delbos, R. G., & Banks, S. M. (2006). Nonstandard shift schedules and the risk of job-related injuries. *Scandinavian Journal of Work, Environment, & Health, 32*, 232–240.

Dement, W. (1997). Sleepless at Stanford: What all undergraduates should know about how their sleeping lives affect their waking lives. Retrieved from http//www.stanford.edu/~dement/sleepless.html

Dement, W. C., & Vaughan, C. (1999). *The promise of sleep*. New York, NY: Delacorte Press.

Dement, W. C., & Wolpert, E. (1958). The relation of eye movements, bodily motility, and external stimuli to dream content. *Journal of Experimental Psychology, 53*, 543–553.

Deng, W., Aimone, J. B., & Gage, F. H. (2010). New neurons and new memories: how does adult hippocampal neurogenesis affect learning and memory? *Nature Reviews Neuroscience, 11*(5), 339–350.

Depp, C. A., Vahia, I. V., & Jeste, D. V. (2012). Successful aging. In S. K. Whitbourne & M. J. Sliwinski (Eds.), *The Wiley-Blackwell handbook of adulthood and aging* (pp. 459–476). Chichester, England: Wiley.

Desmon, D., & MacLachlan, M. (2010). Prevalence and characteristics of phantom limb pain and residual limb pain in the long term after upper limb amputation. *International Journal of Rehabilitation Research, 33*(3), 279–282.

Dessalles, J. (2011). Sharing cognitive dissonance as a way to reach social harmony. *Social Science Information, 50*, 116–127.

DeValois, R. L. (1965). Behavioral and electro-physiological studies of primate vision. In W. D. Neff (Ed.). *Contributions to sensory physiology* (Vol. 1, pp. 137–178). New York, NY: Academic Press.

Dewan, M. J., Steenbarger, B. N., & Greenberg, R. P. (2011). Brief psychotherapies. In R. E. Hales, S. C. Yudofsky, & G. O. Gabbard (Eds.), *Essentials of psychiatry* (3rd ed., pp. 525–539). Arlington, VA: American Psychiatric Publishing.

Dhikav, V., Aggarwal, N., Gupta, S., Jadhavi, R., & Singh, K. (2008). Depression in Dhat syndrome. *Journal of Sexual Medicine, 5*, 841–844.

Dhikav, V., & Anand, K. (2011). Potential predictors of hippocampal atrophy in Alzheimer's disease. *Drugs & Aging, 28*(1), 1–11.

Di Chiara, G., & Bassareo, V. (2007). Reward system and addiction: what dopamine does and doesn't do. *Current Opinion in Pharmacology, 7*(1), 69–76.

Diaconis, P. (1985). Theories of data analysis: From magical thinking through classical statistics. In D. Haglin, F. Mosteller, & J. Tukey (Eds.), *Exploring data tables, trends and shapes* (pp. 1–36). New York, NY: Wiley.

Diamond, A., & Amso, D. (2008). Contributions of neuroscience to our understanding of cognitive development. *Current Directions in Psychological Science, 17*, 136–141.

Diaz-Berciano, C., de Vicente, F., & Fontecha, E. (2008). Modulating effects in learned helplessness of dyadic dominance-submission relations. *Aggressive Behavior, 34*(3), 273–281.

Dickens, W. T., & Flynn, J. R. (2001). Heritability estimates versus large environmental effects: The IQ paradox resolved. *Psychological Review, 108*(2), 346–369.

Dickens, W. T., & Flynn, J. R. (2006). Black Americans reduce the racial IQ gap: Evidence from standardization samples. *Psychological Science, 17*, 913–920.

Dickinson, D. J., O'Connell, D. Q., & Dunn, J. S. (1996). Distributed study, cognitive study strategies and aptitude on student learning. *Psychology: A Journal of Human Behavior, 33*(3), 31–39.

Dicks, J., & Kristmanson, P. (2008). French immersion: when and why? In *The State of French Second-Language Education in Canada 2008* (p. 16). Ottawa, ON: Canadian Parents for French. Retrieved from http://www.cpf.ca/eng/pdf/resources/reports/fsl/2008/FSL2008.pdf

DiDonato, T. E., Ullrich, J., & Krueger, J. I. (2011). Social perception as induction and inference: An integrative model of intergroup differentiation, ingroup favoritism, and differential accuracy. *Journal of Personality and Social Psychology, 100*(1), 66–83.

Diego, M. A., & Jones, N. A. (2007). Neonatal antecedents for empathy. In T. Farrow & P. Woodruff (Eds.), *Empathy in mental illness* (pp. 145–167). New York, NY: Cambridge University Press.

Dien, D. S. F. (1982). A Chinese perspective on Kohlberg's theory of moral development. *Developmental Review, 2*, 331–341.

Dienes, K. A., Torres-Harding, S., Reinecke, M. A., Freeman, A., & Sauer, A. (2011). Cognitive therapy. In S. B. Messer & A. S. Gurman (Eds.), *Essential psychotherapies: Theory and practice* (3rd ed., pp. 143–183). New York, NY: Guilford.

Dietz, P. M., England, L. J., Shapiro-Mendoza, C. K., Tong, V. T., Farr, S. L., & Callaghan, W. M. (2010). Infant morbidity and mortality attributable to prenatal smoking in the U.S. *American Journal of Preventive Medicine, 39*, 45–52.

Dijksterhuis, A., Aarts, H., & Smith, P. K. (2005). The power of the subliminal: On subliminal persuasion and other potential applications. In R. R. Hassin, J. S. Uleman, & J. A. Bargh (Eds.), The new unconscious (pp. 77–106). *Oxford series in social cognition and social neuro-science*. New York, NY: Oxford University Press.

DiLauro, M. D. (2004). Psychosocial factors associated with types of child maltreatment. *Child Welfare, 83*(1), 69–99.

Dill, K. E., & Thill, K. P. (2007). Video game characters and the socialization of gender roles: Young people's perceptions mirror sexist media depictions. *Sex Roles, 57*, 851–864.

Dimberg, U., & Thunberg, M. (1998). Rapid facial reactions to emotion facial expressions. *Scandinavian Journal of Psychology, 39*(1), 39–46.

Dimberg, U., Thunberg, M., & Elmehed, K. (2000). Unconscious facial reactions to emotional facial expressions. *Psychological Science, 11*(1), 86–89.

Dimsdale, J. E. (2008). Psychological stress and cardiovascular disease. *Journal of the American College of Cardiology, 51*(13), 1237–1246.

DiPietro, J. A. (2000). Baby and the brain: Advances in child development. *Annual Review of Public Health, 21*, 455–71.

Distel, M. A., Middeldorp, C. M., Trull, T. J., Derom, C. A, Willemsen, G., & Boomsma, D. I. (2011). Life events and borderline personality features: The influence of gene-environment interaction and gene-environment correlation. *Psychological Medicine, 41*(4), 849–860.

Dittmar, H. (2009). How do "body perfect" ideals in the media have a negative impact on body image and behaviors? Factors and processes related to self and identity. *Journal of Social & Clinical Psychology, 28*(1), 1–8.

Dobson, K. S. (2012). *Cognitive therapy*. Washington, DC: American Psychological Association Press.

Dodge, K. A., & Sherrill, M. R. (2007). The interaction of nature and nurture in antisocial behavior. In D. J. Flannery, A. T. Vazsonyi, & I. D. Waldman (Eds.), *The Cambridge handbook of violent behavior and aggression* (pp. 215–242). New York, NY: Cambridge University Press.

Dodge, K. A., Coie, J. D., & Lynam, D. (2008). Aggression and antisocial behaviour in youth. In W. Damon & R. M. Lerner (Eds.), *Child and adolescent development* (pp. 437–472). Hoboken, NJ: Wiley.

Doghramji, K. (2000, December). Sleepless in America: Diagnosing and treating insomnia. Retrieved from http://psychiatry.medscape.com/Medscape/psychiatry/ClinicalMgmt/CM.v02/public/indexCM.v02.html

Dolan, B. (1999). From the field: Cognitive profiles of First Nations and Caucasian children referred for psychoeducational assessment. *Canadian Journal of School Psychology, 15*, 63–71.

Dollard, J., Doob, L., Miller, N., Mowrer, O. H., & Sears, R. R. (1939). *Frustration and aggression*. New Haven, CT: Yale University Press.

Domhoff, G. W. (2004). Why did empirical dream researchers reject Freud? A critique of historical claims by Mark Solms. *Dreaming, 14*(1), 3–17.

Domhoff, G. W. (2005). A reply to Hobson (2005). *Dreaming, 15*(1), 30–32.

Domhoff, G. W. (2007). Realistic simulation and bizarreness in dream content: Past findings and suggestions for future research. In D. Barrett & P. McNamara (Eds.), *The new science of dreaming Volume 2. Content, recall, and personality correlates* (pp. 1–27). Praeger perspectives. Westport, CT: Praeger.

Domhoff, G. W. (2010). Dream content is continuous with waking thought, based on preoccupations, concerns, and interests. *Sleep Medicine Clinics, 5*(2), 203–215.

Dominguez-Salazar, E., Portillo, W., Baum, M. J., Bakker, J., & Paredes, R. G. (2002). Effect of prenatal androgen receptor antagonist or aromatase inhibitor on sexual behavior, partner preference and neuronal Fos responses to estrous female odors in the rat accessory olfactory system. *Physiology & Behavior, 75*(3), 337.

Domjan, M. (2005). Pavlovian conditioning: A functional perspective. *Annual Review of Psychology, 56*, 179–206.

Donini, L. M., Savina, C., & Cannella, C. (2003). Eating habits and appetite control in the elderly: The anorexia of aging. *International Psychogeriatrics, 15*(1), 73–87.

Donohue, R. (2006). Person-environment congruence in relation to career change and career persistence. *Journal of Vocational Behavior, 68*, 504–515.

Donovan, J. J., & Radosevich, D. J. (1999). A meta-analytic review of the distribution of practice effect: Now you see it, now you don't. *Journal of Applied Psychology, 84*, 795–805.

Doron, N., & Ledoux, J. (2000). Cells in the posterior thalamus project to both amygdala and temporal cortex: A quantitative retrograde double-labeling study in the rat. *The Journal of Comparative Neurology, 425*(2), 257–274.

Dougal, S., Phelps, E. A., & Davachi, L. (2007). The role of medial temporal lobe in item recognition and source recollection of emotional stimuli. *Cognitive, Affective & Behavioral Neuroscience, 7,* 233–242.

Dovidio, J. F., Eller, A., & Hewstone, M. (2011). Improving intergroup relations through direct, extended and other forms of indirect contact. *Group Processes & Intergroup Relations, 14*(2), 147–160.

Doyle, A., & Pollack, M. H. (2004). Long-term management of panic disorder. *Journal of Clinical Psychiatry. 65*(Suppl 5), 24–28.

Dozier, M., & Rutter, M. (2008). Challenges to the development of attachment relationships faced by young children in adoptive and foster care. In J. Cassidy & P. R. Shaver (Eds.), *Handbook of attachment: Theory, research, and clinical applications* (2nd ed., pp. 698–717). New York, NY: Guilford.

Dufresne, T. (2007). *Against Freud: Critics talk back.* Palo Alto, CA: Stanford University Press.

Dummies.com. (2012). Tasting Spain: Local cuisine. Retrieved from http://www.dummies.com/how-to/content/tasting-spain-local-cuisine.html

Dumont, F. (2010). *A history of personality psychology: Theory, science, and research from Hellenism to the twenty-first century.* New York, NY: Cambridge University Press.

Duncan, G. J., & Brooks-Gunn, J. (1997). *Consequences of growing up poor.* New York, NY: Russell Sage Foundation.

Duncan, G. J., & Brooks-Gunn, J. (2000). Family poverty, welfare reform, and child development. *Child Development, 71,* 188–196.

Duncan, G. J., & Magnuson, K. A. (2005). Can family socioeconomical resources account for racial and ethnic test score gaps? *The Future of Children, 15,* 35–54.

Dunham, Y. (2011). An angry outgroup effect. *Journal of Experimental Social Psychology, 47*(3), 668–671.

Dunn, J. (2007). Siblings and socialization. In J. E. Grusec & P. D. Hastings (Eds.), *Handbook of socialization: Theory and research* (pp. 309–327). New York, NY: Guilford.

Duparc, T., Naslain, D., Colom, A., Muccioli, G., Massaly, N., Delzenne, N., ... Knauf, C. (2011). Jejunum inflammation in obese and diabetic mice impairs enteric glucose detection and modifies nitric oxide release in the hypothalamus. *Antioxidants & Redox Signaling, 14*(3), 415–423.

Durham, M. D., & Dane, F. C. (1999). Juror knowledge of eyewitness behavior: Evidence for the necessity of expert testimony. *Journal of Social Behavior & Personality, 14,* 299–308.

Dutton, D. G., & Aron, A. P. (1974). Some evidence for heightened sexual attraction under conditions of high anxiety. *Journal of Personality and Social Psychology, 30,* 510–517.

Dworin, J., & Wyant, O. (1957). Authoritarian patterns in the mothers of schizophrenics. *Journal of Clinical Psychology, 13*(4), 332–338.

E

Eaker, E. D., Sullivan, L. M., Kelly-Hayes, M., D'Agostino, R. B., & Benajmin, E. J. (2007). Marital status, marital strain, and risk of coronary heart disease or total mortality: The Framingham offspring study. *Psychosomatic Medicine, 69,* 509–513.

Eap, S., Gobin, R. L., Ng, J., Hall, G. C., Nagayama, T. (2010). Sociocultural issues in the diagnosis and assessment of psychological disorders. In J. E. Maddux & J. P. Tangney (Eds.), *Social psychological foundations of clinical psychology* (pp. 312–328). New York, NY: Guilford Press.

Ebbinghaus, H. (1913). *Memory: A contribution to experimental psychology* (H. A. Ruger & C. E. Bussenius, Trans.). New York, NY: Teachers College, Columbia University. (Original work published in 1885)

Eddy, K. T., Hennessey, M., & Thompson-Brenner, H. (2007). Eating pathology in East African women: The role of media exposure and globalization. *Journal of Nervous and Mental Disease, 195,* 196–202.

Edelman, A., Fritsch, J., & Ollero, M. (2011). Twenty years after cystic fibrosis gene identification: Where are we and what are we up to? *Pathologie-Biologie, 59*(3), 131–133.

Edwards, B. (1999). *The new drawing on the right side of the brain.* Baltimore, MD: J P Tarcher.

Ehrenreich, B. (2004, July 15). All together now. *The New York Times.* Retrieved from http://select.nytimes.com/ gst/abstract. html?res=F00E16FA3C5E0C768 DDDAE0894DC404482

Eisenberger, R., & Armeli, S. (1997). Can salient reward increase creative performance without reducing intrinsic creative interest? *Journal of Personality and Social Psychology, 72,* 652–663.

Eisenberger, R., & Rhoades, L. (2002). Incremental effects of reward on creativity. *Journal of Personality and Social Psychology, 81*(4), 728–741.

Ekers, D., Richards, D., & Gilbody, S. (2008). A meta-analysis of randomized trials of behavioural treatment of depression. *Psychological Medicine, 38,* 611–623.

Ekman, P. (1989). The argument and evidence about universals in facial expressions of emotion. In H. Wagner & A. Manstead (Eds.), *Handbook of social psychophysiology* (pp. 143–164). Oxford, England: John Wiley & Sons.

Ekman, P. (1993). Facial expression and emotion. *American Psychologist, 48,* 384–392.

Ekman, P. (1994). Strong evidence for universals in facial expressions: A reply to Russell's mistaken critique. *Psychological Bulletin, 115,* 268–287.

Ekman, P. (1999). Basic emotions. In T. Dalgleish & T. Power (Eds.), *Handbook of cognition and emotion* (pp. 45–60). New York, NY: Wiley.

Ekman, P. (2004). *Emotions revealed: Recognizing faces and feelings to improve communication and emotional life.* Thousand Oaks, CA: Owl Books.

Ekman, P., & Keltner, D. (1997). Universal facial expressions of emotion: An old controversy and new findings. In U. C. Segerstrale & P. Molnar (Eds.), *Nonverbal communication: Where nature meets culture.* Mahwah, NJ: Erlbaum.

Ekman, P., Friesen, W. V., O'Sullivan, M., Chan, A., Diacoyanni-Tarlatzis, I., Heider, K., ... Tzavaras, A. (1987). Universals and cultural differences in the judgments of facial expressions of emotion. *Journal of Personality and Social Psychology, 53*(4), 712–717.

Elder, B., & Mosack, V. (2011). Genetics of depression: An overview of the current science. *Issues in Mental Health Nursing, 32*(4), 192–202.

Eley, M. G. (1992). Differential adoption of study approaches within individual students. *Higher Education, 23*(3), 231–254.

Elkind, D. (1967). Egocentrism in adolescence. *Child Development, 38,* 1025–1034.

Elkind, D. (2007). *The hurried child: Growing up too fast, too soon* (25th anniversary ed.). Cambridge, MA: De Capo Press.

Ellis, A. (1961). *A guide to rational living.* Englewood Cliffs, NJ: Prentice-Hall.

Ellis, A. (2003a). Early theories and practices of rational emotive behavior therapy and how they have been augmented and revised during the last three decades. *Journal of Rational-Emotive & Cognitive Behavior Therapy, 21*(3–4), 219–243.

Ellis, A. (2003b). Similarities and differences between rational emotive behavior therapy and cognitive therapy. *Journal of Cognitive Psychotherapy, 17*(3), 225–240.

Ellis, A. (2004). Why rational emotive behavior therapy is the most comprehensive and effective form of behavior therapy. *Journal of Rational Emotive & Cognitive Behavior Therapy, 22*(2), 85–92.

Ellis, A., & Ellis, D. J. (2011). *Rational emotive behavior therapy.* Washington, DC: American Psychological Association.

Ellis, B. J. (1992). The evolution of sexual attraction: Evaluative mechanisms in women. In J. H. Barkow, L. Cosmides, & J. Tooby (Eds.), *The adapted mind: Evolutionary psychology and the generation of culture* (pp. 267–288). New York, NY: Oxford University Press.

Ellis, L., Ficek, C., Burke, D., & Das, S. (2008). Eye color, hair color, blood type, and the rhesus factor: Exploring possible genetic links to sexual orientation. *Archives of Sexual Behavior, 37,* 145–149.

Ellis, S., Rogoff, B., & Cromer, C. C. (1981). Age segregation in children's social interactions. *Developmental Psychology, 17,* 399–407.

Ellman, L. M., & Cannon, T. D. (2008). Environmental pre- and perinatal influences in etiology. In K. T. Mueser & D. V. Jeste (Eds.), *Clinical handbook of schizophrenia* (pp. 65–73). New York, NY: Guilford.

Elmenhorst, D., Elmenhorst, E., Luks, N., Maass, H., Mueller, E., Vejvoda, M., Wenzel, J., & Samel, A. (2009). Performance impairment during four days partial sleep deprivation compared with the acute effects of alcohol and hypoxia. *Sleep Medicine, 10*(2), 189–197.

ElSohly, M. A., & Salamone, S. J. (1999). Prevalence of drugs used in cases of alleged sexual assault. *Journal of Analytical Toxicology, 23,* 141–146.

Emery, A. H. (2002). The muscular dystrophies. *Lancet, 359*(9307), 687.

Emery, R. E. (2004) *The truth about children and divorce.* New York, NY: Viking Press.

Endler, N. (1982). *Holiday of darkness: A psychologist's personal journey out of depression.* Toronto, ON: John Wiley & Sons Canada.

Endsley, M. R. (1993). A survey of situation awareness requirements in air-to-air combat fighters. *International Journal of Aviation Psychology, 3*(2), 157–168.

England, D. E., Descartes, L., & Collier-Meek, M. A. (2011). Gender role portrayal and the Disney princesses. *Sex Roles, 64,* 555–567.

Epley, N. (2008, January 31). Rebate psychology. *The New York Times.* Retrieved from http://select.

nytimes.com/mem/tnt.html?tntget=2008/01/31/opinion/31epley.html

Erickson, R. P. (2008). A study of the science of taste: On the origins and influence of the core ideas. *Behavioral and Brain Sciences, 31*(1), 59–75.

Erikson, E. (1950). *Childhood and society.* New York, NY: Norton

Erlacher, D., & Schredl, M. (2004). Dreams reflecting waking sport activities: A comparison of sport and psychology students. *International Journal of Sport Psychology, 35*(4), 301–308.

Ersche, K. (2011). The neuropsychology of stimulant and opiate dependence: Neuroimaging and neuropsychological studies. *Attention and Performance, 23*, 469–504.

Ertekin-Taner, N. (2007). Genetics of Alzheimer's disease: A centennial review. *Neurologic Clinics, 25*, 611–667.

Esses, V. M., Dovidio, J. F., Jackson, L. M., & Armstrong, T. L. (2001). The immigration dilemma: The role of perceived group competition, ethnic prejudice, and national identity. *Journal of Social Issues, 57*(3), 389–412.

Evans, J. S. B. T. (2003). In two minds: Dual-process accounts of reasoning. *Trends in Cognitive Sciences, 7*(10), 454–459.

Evans, M. A. (2010). Language performance, academic performance, and signs of shyness: A comprehensive review. In K. H. Rubin & R. J. Coplan (Eds.), *The development of shyness and social withdrawal* (pp. 179–212). New York, NY: Guilford.

Evans, S., Ferrando, S., Findler, M., Stowell, C., Smart, C., & Haglin, D. (2008). Mindfulness-based cognitive therapy for generalized anxiety disorder. *Journal of Anxiety Disorders, 22*, 716–721.

Eysenck, H. J. (1967). *The biological basis of personality.* Springfield, IL: Charles C Thomas.

Eysenck, H. J. (1982). *Personality, genetics, and behavior: Selected papers.* New York, NY: Prager.

Eysenck, H. J. (1990). Biological dimensions of personality. In L. A. Pervin (Ed.), *Handbook of personality: Theory and research.* New York, NY: Guilford Press.

F

Faddiman, A. (1997). *The spirit catches you and you fall down.* New York, NY: Straus & Giroux.

Faigman, D. L., Kaye, D., Saks, M. J., & Sanders, J. (1997). *Modern scientific evidence: The law and science of expert testimony.* St. Paul, MN: West.

FAIR. (2011). Protecting whistleblowers who protect the public interest: Pilot fatigue to blame for Air Canada dipping incident. Retrieved from http://fairwhistleblower.ca/content/pilot-fatigue-blame-air-canada-dipping-incident

Fairburn, C. G., Cooper, Z., Shafran, R., & Wilson, G. T. (2008). Eating disorders: A transdiagnostic protocol. In D. H. Barlow (Ed.), *Clinical handbook of psychological disorders: A step-by-step treatment manual* (4th ed., pp. 578–614). New York, NY: Guilford Press.

Fairburn, C., Cooper, Z., Doll, H., O'Connor, M., Bohn, K., Hawker, D., Wales, J., & Palmer, R. (2009). Transdiagnostic cognitive-behavioral therapy for patients with eating disorders: A two-site trial with 60-week follow-up. *American Journal of Psychiatry, 166*(3), 311–319.

Falleti, M., Maruff, P., Collie, A., Darby, D., & McStephen, M. (2003). Qualitative similarities in cognitive impairment associated with 24 h of sustained wakefulness and a blood alcohol concentration of 0.05%. *Journal of Sleep Research, 12*(4), 265–274.

Fang, M., & Gerhart, B. (2012). Does pay for performance diminish intrinsic interest? *International Journal of Human Resource Management, 23*(6), 1176–1196.

Fang, X., & Corso, P. S. (2007). Child maltreatment, youth violence, and intimate partner violence: Developmental relationships. *American Journal of Preventive Medicine, 33*, 281–290.

Fantz, R. L. (1956). A method for studying early visual development. *Perceptual and Motor Skills, 6*, 13–15.

Fantz, R. L. (1963). Pattern vision in newborn infants. *Science, 140*, 296–297.

Faraone, S. V. (2008). Statistical and molecular genetic approaches to developmental psychopathology: The pathway forward. In J. J. Hudziak (Ed.), *Developmental psychopathology and wellness: Genetic and environmental influences* (pp. 245–265). Arlington, VA: American Psychiatric Publishing.

Faraut, B., Boudjeltia, K., Dyzma, M., Rousseau, A., David, E., Stenuit, P., ... Kerkhofs, M. (2011). Benefits of napping and an extended duration of recovery sleep on alertness and immune cells after acute sleep restriction. *Brain, Behavior & Immunity, 25*(1), 16–24.

Farooqi, I., & O'Rahilly, S. (2009). Leptin: A pivotal regulator of human energy homeostasis. *American Journal of Clinical Nutrition, 89*(3), 980S–984S.

Farr, R. H., Forssell, S. L., & Patterson, C. J. (2010). Parenting and child development in adoptive families: Does parental sexual orientation matter? *Applied Developmental Science, 14*(3), 164–178.

Fassler, O., Lynn, S. J., & Knox, J. (2008). Is hypnotic suggestibility a stable trait? *Consciousness and Cognition: An International Journal, 17*, 240–253.

Fazel, S., Buxrud, P., Ruchkin, V., & Grann, M. (2010). Homicide in discharged patients with schizophrenia and other psychoses: A national case-control study. *Schizophrenia Research, 123*(2–3), 263–269.

Feeney, J. A. (2008). Adult romantic attachment: Developments in the study of couple relationships. In J. Cassidy & P. R. Shaver (Eds.), *Handbook of attachment: Theory, research, and clinical applications* (2nd ed., pp. 456–481). New York, NY: Guilford.

Fehr, C., Yakushev, I., Hohmann, N., Buchholz, H-G., Landvogt, C., Deckers, H., ... Schreckenberger, M. (2008). Association of low striatal dopamine D-sub-2 receptor availability with nicotine dependence similar to that seen with other drugs of abuse. *American Journal of Psychiatry, 165*, 507–514.

Fein, S., & Spencer, S. J. (1997). Prejudice as self image maintenance: Affirming the self through derogating others. *Journal of Personality and Social Psychology, 73*(1), 31–44.

Feng, S. Q., Zhou, X. F., Rush, R. A., & Ferguson, I. A. (2008). Graft of pre-injured sural nerve promotes regeneration of corticospinal tract and functional recovery in rats with chronic spinal cord injury. *Brain Research, 1209*, 40–48.

Fernández, J. R., Casazza, K., Divers, J., & LópezAlarcón, M. (2008). Disruptions in energy balance: Does nature overcome nurture? *Physiology & Behavior, 94*, 105–112.

Fernández, M. I., Bowen, G. S., Varga, L. M., Collazo, J. B., Hernandez, N., Perrino, T., & Rehbein, A. (2005). High rates of club drug use and risky sexual practices among Hispanic men who have sex with men in Miami, Florida. *Substance Use & Misuse, 40*(9–10), 1347–1362.

Ferrari, P. F., Rozzi, S., & Fogassi, L. (2005). Mirror neurons responding to observation of actions made with tools in monkey ventral premotor cortex. *Journal of Cognitive Neuroscience, 17*, 212–226.

Ferretti, P., Copp, A., Tickle, C., & Moore, G. (Eds.). (2006). *Embryos, genes, and birth defects* (2nd ed.). Hoboken, NJ: Wiley.

Festinger, L. A. (1957). *A theory of cognitive dissonance.* Palo Alto, CA: Stanford University Press.

Festinger, L. A., & Carlsmith, L. M. (1959). Cognitive consequences of forced compliance. *Journal of Abnormal and Social Psychology, 58*, 203–210.

Field, A. P. (2006). Is conditioning a useful framework for understanding the development and treatment of phobias? *Clinical Psychology Review, 26*, 857–875.

Field, K. M., Woodson, R., Greenberg, R., & Cohen, D. (1982). Discrimination and imitation of facial expressions by neonates. *Science, 218*, 179–181.

Field, T., Diego, M., & Hernandez-Reif, M. (2010). Preterm infant massage therapy research: A review. *Infant Behavior and Development, 33*, 115–124.

Fields, A., & Cochran, S. (2011). Men and depression: Current perspectives for health care professionals. *American Journal of Lifestyle Medicine, 5*(1), 92–100.

Fields, R. (2007). *Drugs in perspective* (6th ed.). New York, NY: McGraw-Hill.

Fields, W. M., Segerdahl, P., & Savage-Rumbaugh, S. (2007). The material practices of ape language research. In J. Valsiner & A. Rosa (Eds.), *The Cambridge handbook of socio-cultural psychology* (pp. 164–186). New York, NY: Cambridge University Press.

Figueredo, A., Jacobs, W., Burger, S., Gladden, P., & Olderbak, S. (2011). The biology of personality. In G. Terzis & R. Arp (Eds.), *Information and living systems: Philosophical and scientific perspectives* (pp. 371–406). Boston, MA: MIT Press.

Fink, B., & Penton-Voak, I. (2002). Evolutionary psychology of facial attractiveness. *Current Directions in Psychological Science, 11*(5), 154–158.

Fink, B., Manning, J. T., Neave, N., & Grammer, K. (2004). Second to fourth digit ratio and facial asymmetry. *Evolution and Human Behavior, 25*(2), 125–132.

Fiori, M., & Antonakis, J. (2011). The ability model of emotional intelligence: Searching for valid measures. *Personality and Individual Differences, 50*, 329–334.

First, M., & Tasman, A. (2004). *DSM-IV-TR mental disorders: Diagnosis, etiology, and treatment.* Hoboken, NJ: Wiley.

First patient dosed in cervical region in neuralstem ALS stem cell trial. (2011, November 23). PR Newswire US. Retrieved from http://www.prnewswire.com/news-releases/first-patient-dosed-in-cervical-region-in-neuralstem-als-stem-cell-trial-134388533.html

Fisher, J. O., & Kral, T. V. E. (2008). Super-size me: Portion size effects on young children's eating. *Physiology & Behavior, 94,* 39–47.

Fisk, J. E., Bury, A. S., & Holden, R. (2006). Reasoning about complex probabilistic concepts in childhood. *Scandinavian Journal of Psychology, 47,* 497–504.

Fiske, S. T. (1998). Stereotyping, prejudice, and discrimination. In D. T. Gilbert, S. T. Fiske, and G. Lindzey (Eds.), *The handbook of social psychology* (4th ed., Vol. 2, pp. 357–411). New York, NY: Oxford University Press.

Flaskerud, J. H. (2010). DSM proposed changes, part I: Criticisms and influences on changes. *Issues in Mental Health Nursing, 31*(10), 686–688.

Flegel, K., & Fletcher, J. (2012). Choosing when and how to die: Are we ready to perform therapeutic homicide? *Canadian Medical Association Journal, 184*(11).

Flegel, K., MacDonald, N., & Hebert, P. C. (2011). Binge drinking: All too prevalent and hazardous. *Canadian Medical Association Journal, 183*(4), 411.

Fleischmann, B. K., & Welz, A. (2008). Cardiovascular regeneration and stem cell therapy. *Journal of the American Medical Association, 299*(6), 700–701.

Fletcher, G. J. O., & Kerr, P. S. G. (2010). Through the eyes of love: Reality and illusion in intimate relationships. *Psychological Bulletin, 136*(4), 627–658.

Fletcher, G. J. O., & Simpson, J. A. (2000). Ideal standards in close relationships: Their structure and functions. *Current Directions in Psychological Science, 9,* 102–105.

Flett, G. (2007). *Personality theory and research.* Toronto, ON: John Wiley & Sons Canada.

Flynn, J. R. (1987). Massive IQ gains in 14 nations: What IQ tests really measure. *Psychological Bulletin, 101,* 171–191.

Flynn, J. R. (2006). The history of the American mind in the 20th century: A scenario to explain gains over time and a case for the irrelevance of g. In P. C. Kyllonen, R. D. Roberts, & L. Stankov (Eds.), *Extending intelligence.* Mahwah, NJ: Erlbaum.

Flynn, J. R. (2007). *What is intelligence? Beyond the Flynn effect.* New York, NY: Cambridge University Press.

Fogarty, A., Rawstorne, P., Prestage, G., Crawford, J., Grierson, J., & Kippax, S. (2007). Marijuana as therapy for people living with HIV/AIDS: Social and health aspects. *AIDS Care, 19,* 295–301.

Fogassi, L., Ferrari, P. F., Gesierich, B., Rozzi, S., Chersi, F., & Rizzolatti, G. (2005). Parietal lobe: From action understanding to intention understanding. *Science, 308,* 662–667.

Fok, H. K., Hui, C. M., Bond, M. H., Matsumoto, D., & Yoo, S. H. (2008). Integrating personality, context, relationship, and emotion type into a model of display rules. *Journal of Research in Personality, 42,* 133–150.

Folk, C. L., & Remington, R. W. (1998). Selectivity in distraction by irrelevant featural singletons: Evidence for two forms of attentional capture. *Journal of Experimental Psychology: Human Perception and Performance, 24,* 1–12.

Follette, W. C., & Callaghan, G. M. (2011). Behavior therapy: Functional-contextual approaches. In

S. B. Messer & A. S. Gurman (Eds.), *Essential psychotherapies: Theory and practice* (3rd ed., pp. 184–220). New York, NY: Guilford.

Fondell, E., Axelsson, J., Franck, K., Ploner, A., Lekander, M., Bälter, K., & Gaines, H. (2011). Short natural sleep is associated with higher T cell and lower NK cell activities. *Brain, Behavior & Immunity, 25*(7), 1367–1375.

Ford, T. E., Ferguson, M. A., Brooks, J. L., & Hagadone, K. M. (2004). Coping sense of humor reduces effects of stereotype threat on women's math performance. *Personality & Social Psychology Bulletin, 30*(5), 643–653.

Foulkes, D. (1993). Children's dreaming. In D. Foulkes & C. Cavallero (Eds.), *Dreaming as cognition* (pp. 114–132). New York, NY: Harvester Wheatsheaf.

Foulkes, D. (1999). *Children's dreaming and the development of consciousness.* Cambridge, MA: Harvard University Press.

Fox, N. A., & Reeb-Sutherland, B. C. (2010). Biological moderators of infant temperament and its relation to social withdrawal. In K. H. Rubin & R. J. Coplan (Eds.), *The development of shyness and social withdrawal* (pp. 84–103). New York, NY: Guilford.

Francis, G. (2012). Too good to be true: Publication bias in two prominent studies from experimental psychology. *Psychonomic Bulletin & Review, 19*(2), 151–156.

Fraser, J., Maticka-Tyndale, E., & Smylie, L. (2004). Sexuality of Canadian women at midlife. *Canadian Journal of Human Sexuality, 13,* 171–188.

Fredricks, J. A., & Eccles, J. S. (2005). Family socialization, gender, and sport motivation and involvement. *Journal of Sport & Exercise Psychology, 27*(1), 3–31.

Freeman, D., Pugh, K., Vorontsova, N., & Southgate, L. (2009). Insomnia and paranoia. *Schizophrenia Research, 108*(1–3), 280–284.

Frei, M. (2010). Party drugs—Use and harm reduction. *Australian Family Physician, 39*(8), 548–552.

Freiwald, W., Tsao, D., & Livingstone, M. (2009). A face feature space in the macaque temporal lobe. *Nature Neuroscience, 12*(9), 1187–1196.

French, E. G., & Thomas, F. H. (1958). The relation of achievement motivation to problem-solving effectiveness. *Journal of Abnormal and Social Psychology, 56*(1), 45–48.

Frick, W. B. (2000). Remembering Maslow: Reflections on a 1968 interview. *Journal of Humanistic Psychology, 40*(2), 128–147.

Friedman, H., & Schustack, M. (2006). *Personality: Classic theories and modern research* (3rd ed.). Boston, MA: Allyn & Bacon/Longman.

Friedman, R., & James, J. W. (2008). The myth of the stages of dying, death, and grief. *Skeptic, 14*(2), 37–41.

Fryer, S. L., Crocker, N. A., & Mattson, S. N. (2008). Exposure to teratogenic agents as a risk factor for psychopathology. In T. P. Beauchaine & S. P. Hinshaw (Eds.), *Child and adolescent psychopathology* (pp. 180–207). Hoboken, NJ: Wiley.

Fuentes, C. J., Armijo-Olivo, S., Magee, D. J., & Gross, D. P. (2011). A preliminary investigation into the effects of active interferential current therapy and placebo on pressure pain sensitivity: a random crossover placebo controlled study. *Physiotherapy, 97*(4), 291–301.

Funder, D. C. (2001). Personality. *Annual Review of Psychology, 52,* 197–221.

Funder, D. C., & Fast, L. A. (2010). Personality in social psychology. In S. T. Fiske, D. T. Gilbert, & G. Lindzey (Eds.), *Handbook of social psychology* (Vol. 2) (pp. 668–697). Hoboken, NJ: John Wiley & Sons.

Funk, J. B., Baldacci, H. B., Pasold, T., & Baumgardner, J. (2004). Violence exposure in real-life, video games, television, movies, and the internet: Is there desensitization? *Journal of Adolescence, 27,* 23–39.

Furman, E. (1990, November). Plant a potato, learn about life (and death). *Young Children, 46*(1), 15–20.

Furnham, A. (2009). The importance and training of emotional intelligence at work. In J. D. A. Parker, D. H. Saklofske, & C. Stough (Eds.), *Assessing emotional intelligence: Theory, research, and applications* (pp. 137–155). Boston, MA: Springer.

Fusar-Poli, P., Borgwardt, S., Crescini, A., Deste, G., Kempton, M. J., Lawrie, S., McGuire, P., & Sacchetti, E. (2011). Neuroanatomy of vulnerability to psychosis: A voxel-based meta-analysis. *Neuroscience and Biobehavioral Reviews, 35*(5), 1175–1185.

G

Gabbe, S. G., Niebyl, J. R., & Simpson, J. L. (2007). *Obstetrics: Normal and problem pregnancies.* Philadelphia, PA: Elsevier.

Gabry, K. E., Chrousos, G. P., Rice, K. C., Mostafa, R. M., Sternberg, E., Negrao, A. B., Webster, E. L., McCann, S. M., & Gold, P. W. (2002). Marked suppression of gastric ulcerogenesis and intestinal responses to stress by a novel class of drugs. *Molecular Psychiatry, 7*(5), 474–483.

Gacono, C. B., Evans, F. B., & Viglione, D. J. (2008). Essential issues in the forensic use of the Rorschach. In C. B. Gacono (Ed.), F. B. Evans (Ed.), N. Kaser-Boyd (Col.), & L. A. Gacono (Col.), *The handbook of forensic Rorschach assessment* (pp. 3–20). The LEA series in personality and clinical psychology. New York, NY: Routledge/Taylor & Francis Group.

Gadalla, T. (2009). Eating disorders in men: A community-based study. *International Journal of Men's Health, 8*(1), 72–81.

Gage, F. (2002). Neurogenesis in the adult brain. *Journal of Neuroscience, 22*(3), 612–613.

Gaither, G., Sellbom, M., & Meier, B. (2003). The effect of stimulus content on volunteering for sexual interest research among college students. *Journal of Sex Research, 40*(3), 240–248.

Galderisi, S., Quarantelli, M., Volpe, U., Mucci, A., Cassano, G. B., Invernizzi, G., … Maj, M. (2008). Patterns of structural MRI abnormalities in deficit and nondeficit schizophrenia. *Schizophrenia Bulletin, 34,* 393–401.

Galinsky, A. D., & Ku, G. (2004). The effects of perspective-taking on prejudice: The moderating role of self-evaluation. *Personality & Social Psychology Bulletin, 30*(5), 594–604.

Galinsky, A. D., & Moskowitz, G. B. (2000). Perspective-taking: Decreasing stereotype expression, stereotype accessibility, and in-group favoritism. *Journal of Personality and Social Psychology, 78*(4), 708–724.

Ganis, G., Posenfeld, J. P., Meixner, J., Klevit, R. A., & Schendan Haline, E. (2011). Lying in the scanner: Covert countermeasures disrupt deception detection by functional magnetic resonance imaging. *NeuroImage, 55*(1), 312–319.

Garb, H. N., Wood, J. M., Lilienfeld, S. O., & Nezworski, M. T. (2005). Roots of the Rorschach controversy. *Clinical Psychology Review, 25*, 97–118.

Garcia, G. M., & Stafford, M. E. (2000). Prediction of reading by Ga and Gc specific cognitive abilities for low-SES White and Hispanic English-speaking children. *Psychology in the Schools, 37*(3), 227–235.

Garcia, J. (2003). Psychology is not an enclave. In R. Sternberg (Ed.), *Psychologists defying the crowd: Stories of those who battled the establishment and won* (pp. 67–77). Washington, DC: American Psychological Association.

Garcia, J., & Koelling, R. S. (1966). Relation of cue to consequence in avoidance learning. *Psychonomic Science, 4*, 123–124.

Gardiner, H., & Kosmitzki, G. (2005). *Lives across cultures: Cross-cultural human development* (3rd ed.). Boston, MA: Allyn & Bacon/Longman.

Gardner, H. (1983). *Frames of mind.* New York, NY: Basic Books.

Gardner, H. (1999, February). Who owns intelligence? *Atlantic Monthly, 283*(2), 67–76.

Gardner, H. (2008). Who owns intelligence? In M. H. Immordino-Yang (Ed.), *Jossey-Bass Education Team. The Jossey-Bass reader on the brain and learning* (pp. 120–132). San Francisco, CA: Jossey-Bass.

Gardner, R. A., & Gardner, B. T. (1969). Teaching sign language to a chimpanzee. *Science, 165*, 664–672.

Garland, E. L. (2011). Trait mindfulness predicts attentional and autonomic regulation of alcohol cue-reactivity. *Journal of Psychophysiology, 25*(4), 180–189.

Garno, J. L., Gunawardane, N., & Goldberg, J. F. (2008). Predictors of trait aggression in bipolar disorder. *Bipolar Disorders, 10*, 285–292.

Garry, M., & Gerrie, M. P. (2005). When photographs create false memories. *Current Directions in Psychological Science, 14*, 321–324.

Gaser, C., Nenadic, I., Buchsbaum, B. R., Hazeltt, E. A., & Buchsbaum, M. S. (2004). Ventricular enlargement in schizophrenia related to volume reduction of the thalamus, striatum, and superior temporal cortex. *American Journal of Psychiatry, 161*(1), 154–156.

Gaskin, S., Tardif, M., & Mumby, D. (2009). Patterns of retrograde amnesia for recent and remote incidental spatial learning in rats. *Hippocampus, 19*(12), 1212–1221.

Gasser, S., & Raulet, D. H. (2006). Activation and self-tolerance of natural killer cells. *Immunology Review, 214*, 130–142.

Gaw, A. C. (2001). *Concise guide to cross-cultural psychiatry. Concise guides.* Washington, DC: American Psychiatric Association.

Gay, P. (2000). *Freud for historians.* Boston, MA: Replica Books.

Gebauer, H., Krempl, R., & Fleisch, E. (2008). Exploring the effect of cognitive biases on customer support services. *Creativity and Innovation Management, 17*, 58–70.

Gelder, B. D., Meeren, H. K., Righart, R., Stock, J. V., van de Riet, W. A., & Tamietto, M. (2006). Beyond the face: Exploring rapid influences of context on face processing. *Progress in Brain Research, 155*, 37–48.

Gellerman, D. M., & Lu, F. G. (2011). Religious and spiritual issues in the outline for cultural formulation. In J. R. Peteet, F. G. Lu, & W. E Narrow (Eds.), *Religious and spiritual issues in psychiatric diagnosis: A research agenda for DSM-V* (pp. 207–220). Washington, DC: American Psychiatric Association.

Genesee, F. (1987). *Learning through two languages: Studies of immersion and bilingual education.* Cambridge, MA: Newbury House.

Genesee, F., & Gandara, P. (1999). Bilingual education programs: A cross-national perspective. *Journal of Social Issues, 55*, 665–685.

Gentile, D. A., Lynch, P. J., Linder, J. R., & Walsh, D. A. (2004). The effects of violent video game habits on adolescent hostility, aggressive behaviors, and school performance. *Journal of Adolescence, 27*, 5–22.

Gerber, A. J., Posner, J., Gorman, D., Colibazzi, T., Yu, S., Wang, Z., … Peterson, B. S. (2008). An affective circumplex model of neural systems sub-serving valence, arousal, and cognitive overlay during the appraisal of emotional faces. *Neuropsychologia, 46*, 2129–2139.

Germo, G. R., Chang, E. S., Keller, M. A., & Goldberg, W. A. (2007). Child sleep arrangements and family life: Perspectives from mothers and fathers. *Infant and Child Development, 16*, 433–456.

Gershon, E. S., & Rieder, R. O. (1993). Major disorders of mind and brain. *Mind and brain: Readings from Scientific American Magazine* (pp. 91–100). New York, NY: Freeman.

Giacobbi, P. Jr., Foore, B., & Weinberg, R. S. (2004). Broken clubs and expletives: The sources of stress and coping responses of skilled and moderately skilled golfers. *Journal of Applied Sport Psychology, 16*(2), 166–182.

Gibbs, J. C. (2010). *Moral development and reality: Beyond the theories of Kohlberg and Hoffman* (2nd ed.). Boston, MA: Pearson Allyn & Bacon.

Gibson, E. J., & Walk, R. D. (1960). The visual cliff. *Scientific American, 202*(2), 67–71.

Giedd, J. N. (2008). The teen brain: Insights from neuroimaging. *Journal of Adolescent Health, 42*, 335–343.

Gignac, G. E., & Vernon, P. A. (2003). Biological approaches to the assessment of human intrelligence. In C. R. Reynolds & R. W. Kamphaus (Eds.), *Handbook of psychological and educational assessment of children: Intelligence, aptitude, and achievement* (2nd ed., pp. 325–342). New York, NY: Guilford.

Gill, R. K., Pant, N., Saksena, S., Singla, A., Nazirv, T. M., Vohwinkel, L., … Dudeja, P. K. (2008). Function, expression, and characterization of the serotonin transporter in the native human intestine. *American Journal of Physiology: Gastrointestinal & Liver Physiology, 57*(1), G254–G262.

Gilligan, C. (1977). In a different voice: Women's conception of morality. *Harvard Educational Review, 47*(4), 481–517.

Gilligan, C. (1990). Teaching Shakespeare's sister. In C. Gilligan, N. Lyons, & T. Hanmer (Eds.), *Mapping the moral domain* (pp. 73–86). Cambridge, MA: Harvard University Press.

Gilligan, C. (1993). Adolescent development reconsidered. In A. Garrod (Ed.), *Approaches to moral development: New research and emerging themes.* New York, NY: Teachers College Press.

Gilmour, D. R., & Walkey, F. H. (1981). Identifying violent offenders using a video measure of interpersonal distance. *Journal of Consulting and Clinical Psychology, 49*, 287–291.

Gitau, R., Modi, N., Gianakoulopoulos, X., Bond, C., Glover, V., & Stevenson, J. (2002). Acute effects of maternal skin-to-skin contact and massage on saliva cortisol in preterm babies. *Journal of Reproductive & Infant Psychology, 20*(2), 83–88.

Giumetti, G. W., & Markey, P. M. (2007). Violent video games and anger as predictors of aggression. *Journal of Research in Personality, 41*, 1234–1243.

Glamour. (2012). Retouching: How much is too much? Retrieved from http://www.glamour.com/health-fitness/2012/02/retouching-how-much-is-too-much

Glick, B., & Gibbs, J. C. (2011). *Aggression replacement training: A comprehensive intervention for aggressive youth* (3rd ed.). Champaign, IL: Research Press.

Gliga, T., Elsabbagh, M., Andravizou, A., & Johnson, M. (2009). Faces attract infants' attention in complex displays. *Infancy, 14*(5), 550–562.

Gluck, M. A. (2008). Behavioral and neural correlates of error correction in classical conditioning and human category learning. In M. A. Gluck, J. R. Anderson, & S. M. Kosslyn (Eds.), *Memory and mind: A festschrift for Gordon H. Bower* (pp. 281–305). Mahwah, NJ: Lawrence Erlbaum.

Godden, D. R., & Baddeley, A. D. (1975). Context-dependent memory in two natural environments: On land and underwater. *British Journal of Psychology, 66*, 325–331.

Goldberg, M. (2009). Beauty myths. Retrieved from http://prospect.org/article/beauty-myths-0

Goldberg, W. A., & Keller, M. A. (2007). Parent-infant co-sleeping: Why the interest and concern? *Infant and Child Development, 16*, 331–339.

Golden, W. L. (2006). Hypnotherapy for anxiety, phobias and psychophysiological disorders. In R. A. Chapman (Ed.), *The clinical use of hypnosis in cognitive behavior therapy: A practitioner's casebook* (pp. 101–137). New York, NY: Springer.

Goldstein, A. P. (2004). Skillstreaming: The behavioral component. In A. Goldstein, R. Nensen, B. Daleflod, & M. Kalt (Eds.), *New perspectives on aggression replacement training* (pp. 23–50). Chichester, England: Wiley.

Goldstein, E. G. (2008). *Cognitive psychology: Connecting mind, research, and everyday experience* (2nd ed.). Belmont, CA: Cengage.

Goleman, D. (1980, February). 1,528 little geniuses and how they grew. *Psychology Today, 13*(9), 28–53.

Goleman, D. (1995). *Emotional intelligence: Why it can matter more than IQ.* New York, NY: Bantam.

Goleman, D. (2000). *Working with emotional intelligence.* New York, NY: Bantam Doubleday.

Gómez-Laplaza, L. M., & Gerlai, R. (2010). Latent learning in zebra fish (Danio rerio). *Behavioral Brain Research, 208*, 509–515.

Goodman, G. S., Ghetti, S., Quas, J. A., Edelstein, R. S., Alexander, K. W., Redlich, A. D., Cordon, I. M., & Jones, D. P. H. (2003). A prospective study of memory for child sexual abuse: New findings relevant to the repressed memory controversy. *Psychological Science, 14*(2), 113–118.

Goodwin, C. J. (2011). *A history of modern psychology* (4th ed.). Hoboken, NJ: Wiley.

Goodwin, J. (2011). *Research in psychology: Methods and design* (6th ed.). Hoboken, NJ: Wiley.

Goodwyn, S. L., Acredolo, L. P., & Brown, C. A. (2000). Impact of symbolic gesturing on early language development. *Journal of Nonverbal Behavior, 24,* 81–103.

Gooren, L. (2006). The biology of human psychosexual differentiation. *Hormones and Behavior, 50,* 589–601.

Gorchoff, S. M., John, O. P., & Helson, R. (2008). Contextualizing change in marital satisfaction during middle age: An 18-year longitudinal study. *Psychological Science, 19,* 1194–1200.

Gotlieb, I. H., & Abramson, L. Y. (1999). Attributional theories of emotion. In T. Dalgleish & M. Power (Eds.), *Handbook of cognition and emotion.* New York, NY: Wiley.

Gottesman, I. I. (1991). *Schizophrenia genesis: The origins of madness.* New York, NY: Freeman.

Gottfredson, G. D., & Duffy, R. D. (2008). Using a theory of vocational personalities and work environments to explore subjective well-being. *Journal of Career Assessment, 16,* 44–59.

Gottman, J. M. (2011). *The science of trust: Emotional attunement for couples.* New York, NY: Norton.

Gottman, J. M., & Levenson, R. W. (2002). A two-factor model for predicting when a couple will divorce: Exploratory analyses using 14-year longitudinal data. *Family Process, 41*(1), 83–96.

Gottman, J. M., & Notarius, C. I. (2000). Decade review: Observing marital interaction. *Journal of Marriage & the Family, 62*(4), 927–947.

Gould, E., Tanapat, P., Hastings, N. B., & Shors, T. J. (1999). Neurogenesis in adulthood: A possible role in learning. *Trends in Cognitive Sciences, 3*(5), 186–191.

Gould, R. L. (1975, August). Adult life stages: Growth toward self-tolerance. *Psychology Today,* pp. 74–78.

Grabe, S., Ward, L., & Hyde, J. (2008). The role of the media in body image concerns among women: A meta-analysis of experimental and correlational studies. *Psychological Bulletin, 134*(3), 460–476.

Gracely, R. H., Farrell, M. J., & Grant, M. A. (2002). Temperature and pain perception. In H. Pashler & S. Yantis (Eds.), *Stevens' handbook of experimental psychology: Vol. 1. Sensation and perception* (3rd ed., pp. 619–653). Hoboken, NJ: Wiley.

Graham, S., & Juvonen, J. (1998). Self-blame and peer victimization in middle school: An attributional analysis. *Developmental Psychology, 34,* 587–599.

Graham, S., Taylor, A. Z., & Ho, A. Y. (2009). Race and ethnicity in peer relations research. In K. H. Rubin, W. M. Bukowski, & B. Laursen (Eds.), *Handbook of peer interactions, relationships, and groups* (pp. 394–413). New York, NY: Guilford.

Grant, J. A., Courtemanche, J., & Rainville, P. (2011). A non-elaborative mental stance and decoupling of executive and pain-related cortices predicts low pain sensitivity in Zen meditators. *Pain, 152*(1), 150–156.

Gratz, K. L., Latzman, R. D., Tull, M. T., Reynolds, E. K., & Lejuez, C.W. (2011). Exploring the association between emotional abuse and childhood borderline personality features: The moderating role of personality traits. *Behavior Therapy, 42,* 493–508.

Graziano, M. (2006). The organization of behavioral repertoire in motor cortex. *Annual Review of Neuroscience, 29,* 105–134.

Green, C. D. (2009). Darwinian theory, functionalism, and the first American psychological revolution. *American Psychologist, 64*(2), 75–83.

Greenberg, J. (2002). Who stole the money, and when? Individual and situational determinants of employee theft. *Organizational Behavior and Human Decision Processes, 89*(1), 985–1003.

Greene, E., & Ellis, L. (2008). *Decision making in criminal justice.* In D. Carson, R. Milne, F. Pakes, K. Shalev, & A. Shawyer (Eds.), *Applying psychology to criminal justice* (pp. 183–200). New York, NY: Wiley.

Greenwald, A. G., Poehlman, T. A., Uhlmann, E. L., & Banaji, M. R. (2009). Understanding and using the Implicit Association Test III: Meta-analysis of predictive validity. *Journal of Personality and Social Psychology, 97*(1), 17–41.

Gregory, R. J. (2011). *Psychological testing: History, principles, and applications* (6th ed.). Boston, MA: Allyn & Bacon.

Gringart, E., Helmes, E., & Speelman, C. (2008). Harnessing cognitive dissonance to promote positive attitudes toward older workers in Australia. *Journal of Applied Social Psychology, 38,* 751–778.

Grippo, A. J. (2011). The utility of animal models in understanding links between psychosocial processes and cardiovascular health. *Social and Personality Psychology Compass, 5*(4), 164–179.

Grondin, S., Ouellet, B., & Roussel, M. (2004). Benefits and limits of explicit counting for discriminating temporal intervals. *Canadian Journal of Experimental Psychology, 58*(1), 1–12.

Grossmann, K., Grossman, K. E., Kindler, H., & Zimmermann, P. (2008). A wider view of attachment and exploration: The influence of mothers and fathers on the development of psychological security from infancy to young adulthood. In J. Cassidy & P. R. Shaver (Eds.), *Handbook of attachment: Theory, research, and clinical applications* (2nd ed., pp. 857–879). New York, NY: Guilford.

Grover, K. E., Carpenter, L. L., Price, L. H., Gagne, G. G., Mello, A. F., Mello, M. F., & Tyra, A. R. (2007). The relationship between childhood abuse and adult personality disorder symptoms. *Journal of Personality Disorders, 21,* 442–447.

Guidelines for ethical conduct in the care and use of animals. (2008). Retrieved from http://www.apa.org/science/anguide.html

Guilford, J. P. (1967). *The nature of human intelligence.* New York, NY: McGraw-Hill.

Gunderson, J. G. (2011). Borderline personality disorder. *New England Journal of Medicine, 364*(21), 2037–2042.

Gunzerath, L., Faden, V., Zakhari, S., & Warren, K. (2004). National Institute on Alcohol Abuse and Alcoholism report on moderate drinking. *Alcoholism: Clinical & Experimental Research, 28*(6), 829–847.

Gustavson, C. R., & Garcia, J. (1974, August). Pulling a gag on the wily coyote. *Psychology Today,* pp. 68–72.

Guzzetta, A., Baldini, S., Bancale, A., Baroncelli, L., Ciucci, F., Ghirri, P., ... Maffei, L. (2009). Massage accelerates brain development and the maturation of visual functions. *Journal of Neuroscience, 29,* 6042–6051.

H

Haberstick, B. C., Schmitz, S., Young, S. E., & Hewitt, J. K. (2006). Genes and developmental stability of aggressive behavior problems at home and school in a community sample of twins aged 7–12. *Behavior Genetics, 36,* 809–819.

Haddad, R., Khan, R., Takahashi, Y., Mori, K., Harel, D., & Sobel, N. (2008). A metric for odorant comparison. *Nature Methods, 5*(5), 425–429.

Haddock, G., & Shaw, J. J. (2008). Understanding and working with aggression, violence, and psychosis. In K. T. Mueser & D. V. Jeste (Eds.), *Clinical handbook of schizophrenia* (pp. 398–410). New York, NY: Guilford Press.

Hadley, D., Anderson, B. S., Borckardt, J. J., Arana, A., Li, X., Nahas, Z., & George, M. S. (2011). Safety, tolerability, and effectiveness of high doses of adjunctive daily left prefrontal repetitive transcranial magnetic stimulation for treatment-resistant depression in a clinical setting. *The Journal of ECT, 27*(1), 18–25.

Hagenauer, M. H., Perryman, J. I., Lee, T. M., Carskadon, M. A. (2009). Adolescent changes in the homeostatic and circadian regulation of sleep. *Developmental Neuroscience, 31,* 276–284.

Hagger, M. S., & Chatzisarantis, N. D. (2011). Causality orientations moderate the undermining effect of rewards on intrinsic motivation. *Journal of Experimental Social Psychology, 47*(2), 485–489.

Hainline, L. (1998). The development of basic visual abilities. In A. Slater (Ed.), *Perceptual development: Visual, auditory, and speech perception in infancy.* Hove, England: Psychology Press.

Halbreich, U., & Kahn, L. S. (2007). A typical depression, somatic depression and anxious depression in women: Are they gender preferred phenotypes? *Journal of Affective Disorders, 102,* 245–258.

Haley, A. P. (2005). Effects of orally administered glucose on hippocampal metabolites and cognition in Alzheimer's disease. *Dissertation Abstracts International: Section B: The Sciences and Engineering, 66*(3-B), 1719.

Halgin, R. P., & Whitbourne, S. K. (2008). *Abnormal psychology: Clinical perspectives on psychological disorders.* New York, NY: McGraw-Hill.

Halim, M. L., & Ruble, D. (2010). Gender identity and stereotyping in early and middle childhood. In J. Chrisler & D. McCreary (Eds.), *Handbook of gender research in psychology: Vol. 1: Gender research in general and experimental psychology* (pp. 495–525). New York, NY: Springer.

Hall, K. (2007). Sexual dysfunction and childhood sexual abuse: Gender differences and treatment implications. In S. R. Leiblum (Ed.), *Principles and practice of sex therapy* (4th ed., pp. 350–378). New York, NY: Guilford.

Haller, S., Radue, E. W., Erb, M., Grodd, W., & Kircher, T. (2005). Overt sentence production in event-related fMRI. *Neuropsychologia, 43*(5), 807–814.

Halpern, D. F. (1998). Teaching critical thinking for transfer across domains. *American Psychologist, 53,* 449–455.

Halpern, D. F. (2012). *Sex differences in cognitive abilities* (4th ed.). New York, NY: Psychology Press.

Hamilton, J. P., & Gotlib, I. H. (2008). Neural substrates of increased memory sensitivity for negative stimuli in major depression. *Biological Psychiatry, 63*, 1155–1162.

Hammack, P. L. (2003). The question of cognitive therapy in a postmodern world. *Ethical Human Sciences & Services, 5*(3), 209–224.

Hammen, C. (2005). Stress and depression. *Annual Review of Clinical Psychology, 1*, 293–319.

Hammond, D. C. (2007). What is neurofeedback? *Journal of Neurotherapy, 10*, 25–36.

Hampton, T. (2006). Stem cells probed as diabetes treatment. *Journal of American Medical Association, 296*, 2785–2786.

Hampton, T. (2007). Stem cells ease Parkinson symptoms in monkeys. *Journal of American Medical Association, 298*, 165.

Hands-Free Info. (2012). Canadian distracted driving updates. Retrieved from http://handsfreeinfo.com/canadian-cell-phone-law-updates

Haney, C., Banks, C., & Zimbardo, P. (1978). Interpersonal dynamics in a simulated prison. *International Journal of Criminology and Penology, 1*, 69–97.

Hanley, S. J., & Abell, S. C. (2002). Maslow and relatedness: Creating an interpersonal model of self-actualization. *Journal of Humanistic Psychology, 42*(4), 37–56.

Hanon, A. (2010, January 20). Plug stays in for allegedly brain-dead baby. Retrieved from http://cnews.canoe.ca/CNEWS/Canada/2010/01/19/12544441-qmi.html?cid=rssnewslast24hours

Hansell, J. H., & Damour, L. K. (2008). *Abnormal psychology* (2nd ed.). Hoboken, NJ: Wiley.

Harati, H., Majchrzak, M., Cosquer, B., Galani, R., Kelche, C., Cassel, J.-C., & Barbelivien, A. (2011). Attention and memory in aged rats: Impact of lifelong environmental enrichment. *Neurobiology of Aging, 32*(4), 718–736.

Harlow, H. F., & Harlow, M. K. (1966). Learning to love. *American Scientist, 54*, 244–272.

Harlow, H. F., & Zimmerman, R. R. (1959). Affectional responses in the infant monkey. *Science, 130*, 421–432.

Harlow, H. F., Harlow, M. K., & Meyer, D. R. (1950). Learning motivated by a manipulation drive. *Journal of Experimental Psychology, 40*, 228–234.

Harper, F. D., Harper, J. A., & Stills, A. B. (2003). Counseling children in crisis based on Maslow's hierarchy of basic needs. *International Journal for the Advancement of Counselling, 25*(1), 10–25.

Harrington, A. (2012). The fall of the schizophrenogenic mother. *Lancet, 379*(9823), 1292–1293.

Harris, V. (2012). Intoxicating trends. *History Today, 62*(4), 3–4.

Harrison, E. (2005). *How meditation heals: Scientific evidence and practical applications* (2nd ed.). Berkeley, CA: Ulysses Press.

Harrison, M. A. (2011). College students' prevalence and perceptions of text messaging while driving. *Accident Analysis & Prevention, 43*(4), 1516–1520.

Hart, J. Jr., & Kraut, M. A. (2007). Neural hybrid model of semantic object memory (version 1.1). In J. Hart Jr. & M. A. Kraut (Eds.), *Neural basis of semantic memory* (pp. 331–359). New York, NY: Cambridge University Press.

Hartenbaum, N., Collop, N., Rosen, I. M., Phillips, B., George, C. F. P., Rowley, J. A., … Rosekind, M. R. (2006). Sleep apnea and commercial motor vehicle operators: Statement from the joint task force of the American College of Chest Physicians, American College of Occupational and Environmental Medicine, and the National Sleep Foundation. *Journal of Occupational & Environmental Medicine, 48*, S4–S37.

Harter, S. (2006). The development of self-esteem. In M. Kernis (Ed.), *Self-esteem: issues and answers: A sourcebook of current perspectives* (pp. 144–150). New York, NY: Psychology Press.

Harter, S. (2008). The developing self. In W. Damon & R. M. Lerner (Eds.), *Child and adolescent development: An advanced course* (pp. 216–260). Hoboken, NJ: Wiley.

Harth, N. S., Kessler, T., & Leach, C. W. (2008). Advantaged group's emotional reactions to intergroup inequality: The dynamics of pride, guilt, and sympathy. *Personality and Social Psychology Bulletin, 34*, 115–129.

Hartwell, C. (1996). The schizophrenogenic mother concept in American psychiatry. *Psychiatry: Interpersonal & Biological Processes, 59*(3), 274.

Hartwell, L. (2008). *Genetics* (3rd ed.). New York, NY: McGraw-Hill.

Haslam, N., Loughnan, S., Reynolds, C., & Wilson, S. (2007). Dehumanization: A new perspective. *Social and Personality Psychology Compass, 1*, 409–422.

Hatami, M., Mehrjardi, N., Kiani, S., Hemmesi, K., Azizi, H., Shahverdi, A., & Baharvand, H. (2009). Human embryonic stem cell-derived neural precursor transplants in collagen scaffolds promote recovery in injured rat spinal cord. *Cytotherapy, 11*(5), 618–630.

Hatfield, E., & Rapson, R. L. (1996). *Love and sex: Cross-cultural perspectives*. Needham Heights, MA: Allyn & Bacon.

Hatsukami, D. K. (2008). Nicotine addiction: Past, present and future. *Drug and Alcohol Dependence, 92*, 312–316.

Haugen, R., Ommundsen, Y., & Lund, T. (2004). The concept of expectancy: A central factor in various personality dispositions. *Educational Psychology, 24*(1), 43–55.

Hawkins, D. L., Pepler, D. J., & Craig, W. M. (2001). Naturalistic observations of peer interventions in bullying. *Social Development, 10*(5), 512–527.

Haworth, C. A., Plomin, R., Carnell, S., & Wardle, J. (2008). Childhood obesity: Genetic and environmental overlap with normal-range BMI. *Obesity, 16*(7), 1585–1590.

Hayflick, L. (1977). The cellular basis for biological aging. In C. E. Finch & L. Hayflick (Eds.), *Handbook of the biology of aging* (pp. 159–186). New York, NY: Van Nostrand Reinhold.

Hayflick, L. (1996). *How and why we age*. New York, NY: Ballantine Books.

Hays, W. S. T. (2003). Human pheromones: Have they been demonstrated? *Behavioral Ecology & Sociobiology, 54*(2), 89–97.

Hazan, C., & Shaver, P. (1987). Romantic love conceptualized as an attachment process. *Journal of Personality and Social Psychology, 52*, 511–524.

Hazan, C., & Shaver, P. (1994). Attachment as an organizational concept for research on close relationships. *Psychological Inquiry, 5*, 1–22.

Health Canada. (2002). *A report on mental illnesses in Canada*. Ottawa, ON: Health Canada. Retrieved from http://www.phac-aspc.gc.ca/publicat/miic-mmac/index-eng.php

Health Canada. (2006a). Safe use of energy drinks. Retrieved from http://www.hc-sc.gc.ca/hlvs/iyh-vsv/prod/energy-energie-eng.php

Health Canada. (2006b). Drug and health products: Medical use of marihuana. Retrieved from http://www.hc-sc.gc.ca/dhp-mps/marihuana/

Health Canada. (2007). Canadian tobacco use monitoring survey. Table 7. Smoking and pregnancy, women age 20–44 years. Retrieved from http://www.hc-sc.gc.ca/hc-ps/tobac-tabac/research-recherche/stat/_ctums-esutc_2007/ann-table7-eng.php

Health Canada. (2009a). Healthy living. Retrieved from http://www.hc-sc.gc.ca/hl-vs/index-eng.php

Health Canada. (2009b). Drugs and health products: Natural health products. Retrieved from http://www.hc-sc.gc.ca/dhp-mps/prodnatur/index-eng.php

Health Canada. (2010a). Summary of results from the 2008–09 Youth Smoking Survey. Retrieved from http://www.hc-sc.gc.ca/hc-ps/tobac-tabac/research-recherche/stat/_survey-sondage_2008-2009/result-eng.php

Health Canada. (2010b). Health Canada's marijuana supply. Retrieved from: http://www.hc-sc.gc.ca/dhp-mps/marihuana/supply-approvis/index-eng.php

Health Canada. (2010c). Information for health care professionals: Marihuana (marijuana, cannabis). Retrieved from http://www.hc-sc.gc.ca/dhp-mps/alt_formats/hecs-sesc/pdf/marihuana/how-comment/medpract/infoprof/marijuana-monograph-eng.php

Health Canada. (2011a). Harper government announces new measures to support families— New approach on energy drinks. Retrieved from: http://www.hc-sc.gc.ca/ahc-asc/media/nr-cp/_2011/2011-132-eng.php

Health Canada. (2011b). Drugs and health products: Natural health products. Retrieved from http://www.hc-sc.gc.ca/dhp-mps/prodnatur/index-eng.php

Health Canada. (2012). Speech for the Honourable Leona Aglukkaq, Minister of Health for the Summit on Healthy Weights. Retrieved from http://www.hc-sc.gc.ca/ahc-asc/minist/speeches-discours/_2012/2012_02_27-eng.php

Healy, A. F., Shea, K. M., Kole, J. A., & Cunningham, T. F. (2008). Position distinctiveness, item familiarity, and presentation frequency affect reconstruction of order in immediate episodic memory. *Journal of Memory and Language, 58*, 746–764.

Hebb, D. O. (1949). *The organization of behaviour: A neuropsychological theory*. New York, NY: Wiley.

Hedges, D., & Burchfield, C. (2006). *Mind, brain, and drug: An introduction to psychopharmacology*. Boston, MA: Allyn & Bacon/Longman.

Heffelfinger, A. K., & Newcomer, J. W. (2001). Glucocorticoid effects on memory function over the human life span. *Development & Psychopathology, 13*(3), 491–513.

Heider, F. (1958). *The psychology of interpersonal relations*. New York, NY: Wiley.

Heine, S. J., & Renshaw, K. (2002). Inter-judge agreement, self-enhancement, and liking: Cross-cultural divergences. *Personality & Social Psychology Bulletin, 28*(5), 578–587.

Heller, S. (2005). *Freud A to Z.* Hoboken, NJ: Wiley.

Helms, J. E., & Cook, D. A. (1999). *Using race and culture in counseling and psychotherapy: Theory and process.* Boston, MA: Allyn & Bacon.

Hennessey, B. A., & Amabile, T. M. (1998). Reward, intrinsic motivation, and creativity. *American Psychologist, 53,* 674–675.

Henrich, J., Heine, S., & Norenzayan, A. (2010). The weirdest people in the world? *The Behavioral and Brain Sciences, 33*(23–), 61–83.

Herman, C. P., & Polivy, J. (2008). External cues in the control of food intake in humans: The sensory-normative distinction. *Physiology & Behavior, 94,* 722–728.

Herman, L. M., Richards, D. G., & Woltz, J. P. (1984). Comprehension of sentences by bottlenosed dolphins. *Cognition, 16,* 129–139.

Hermans, E. J., Ramsey, N. F., & van Honk, J. (2008). Exogenous testosterone enhances responsiveness to social threat in the neural circuitry of social aggression in humans. *Biological Psychiatry, 63*(3), 263–270.

Herrnstein, R. J., & Murray, C. (1994). *The bell curve: Intelligence and class structure in American life.* New York, NY: Free Press.

Hetherington, E. M. (2006). The influence of conflict, marital problem solving, and parenting on children's adjustment in nondivorced, divorced, and remarried families. In A. Clarke-Stewart & J. Dunn (Eds.), *Families count: Effects on child and adolescent development* (pp. 203–237). New York, NY: Cambridge University Press.

Heyder, K., Suchan, B., & Daum, I. (2004). Cortico-subcortical contributions to executive control. *Acta Psychologica, 115*(2–3), 271–289.

Heyes, C. (2011). Automatic imitation. *Psychological Bulletin, 137*(3), 463–483.

Hilgard, E. R. (1978). Hypnosis and consciousness. *Human Nature, 1,* 42–51.

Hilgard, E. R. (1992). Divided consciousness and dissociation. *Consciousness and Cognition, 1,* 16–31.

Hill, E. L. (2004). Evaluating the theory of executive dysfunction in autism. *Developmental Review, 24*(2), 189–233.

Hinduja, S., & Patchin, J. W. (2010). Bullying, cyberbullying, and suicide. *Archives of Suicide Research, 14,* 206–221.

Hinton, E. C., Parkinson, J. A., Holland, A. J., Arana, F. S., Roberts, A. C., & Owen, A. M. (2004). Neural contributions to the motivational control of appetite in humans. *European Journal of Neuroscience, 20*(5), 1411–1418.

Hinton, G. E. (2010). Learning to represent visual input. *Philosophical Transactions of the Royal Society B: Biological Sciences, 365*(1537), 177–184.

Hobson, C. J., Kamen, J., Szostek, J., Nethercut, C. M., Tiedmann, J. W., & Wojnarowicz, S. (1998). Stressful life events: A revision and update of the Social Readjustment Rating Scale. *International Journal of Stress Management, 5*(1), 1–23.

Hobson, J. (2009). REM sleep and dreaming: Towards a theory of protoconsciousness. *Nature Reviews. Neuroscience, 10*(11), 803–813.

Hobson, J. A. (1988). *The dreaming brain.* New York, NY: Basic Books.

Hobson, J. A. (1999). *Dreaming as delirium: How the brain goes out of its mind.* Cambridge, MA: MIT Press.

Hobson, J. A. (2005). In bed with Mark Solms? What a nightmare! A reply to Domhoff. *Dreaming, 15*(1), 21–29.

Hobson, J. A., & McCarley, R. W. (1977). The brain as a dream-state generator: An activation-synthesis hypothesis of the dream process. *American Journal of Psychiatry, 134,* 1335–1348.

Hobson, J. A., & Silvestri, L. (1999). Parasomnias. *The Harvard Mental Health Letter, 15*(8), 3–5.

Hobson, J. A., Sangsanguan, S., Arantes, H., & Kahn, D. (2011). Dream logic—The inferential reasoning paradigm. *Dreaming, 21*(1), 1–15.

Hobson, J., Pace-Schott, E. F., & Stickgold, R. (2003). Dreaming and the brain: Toward a cognitive neuroscience of conscious states. In E. F. Pace-Schott, M. Solms, M. Blagrove, & S. Harnad (Eds.), *Sleep and dreaming: Scientific advances and reconsiderations* (pp. 1–50). New York, NY: Cambridge University Press.

Hodges, S. D., & Biswas-Diener, R. (2007). Balancing the empathy expense account: Strategies for regulating empathic response. In T. Farrow & P. Woodruff (Eds.), *Empathy in mental illness* (pp. 389–407). New York, NY: Cambridge University Press.

Hodson, G., & Costello, K. (2007). Interpersonal disgust, ideological orientations, and dehumanization as predictors of intergroup attitudes. *Psychological Science, 18,* 691–698.

Hoek, H. W., van Harten, P. N., Hermans, K. M. E., Katzman, M. A., Matroos, G. E., & Susser, E. S. (2005). The incidence of anorexia nervosa on Curacao. *American Journal of Psychiatry, 162,* 748–752.

Hofer, A., Siedentopf, C. M., Ischebeck, A., Rettenbacher, M. A., Verius, M., Golaszewski, S. M., Felber, S., & Fleischhacker, W. W. (2007). Neural substrates for episodic encoding and recognition of unfamiliar faces. *Brain and Cognition, 63,* 174–181.

Hoff, E. (2009). *Language development* (4th ed.). Belmont, CA: Wadsworth.

Hoffman, M. L. (2008). Empathy and prosocial behavior. In M. Lewis, J. M. Haviland-Jones, & L. M. Barrett (Eds.), *Handbook of emotions* (3rd ed., pp. 440–455). New York, NY: Guilford.

Hofmann, S. (2011). *An introduction to modern CBT: Psychological solutions to mental health problems.* Hoboken, NJ: Wiley-Blackwell.

Hofmann, W., Gschwendner, T., Castelli, L., & Schmitt, M. (2008). Implicit and explicit attitudes and interracial interaction: The moderating role of situationally available control resources. *Group Processes & Intergroup Relations, 11,* 69–87.

Hogan, T. P. (2006). *Psychological testing: A practical introduction* (2nd ed.). Hoboken, NJ: Wiley.

Holland, J. L. (1985). *Making vocational choices: A theory of vocational personalities and work environments* (2nd ed.). Englewood Cliffs, NJ: Prentice Hall.

Holland, J. L. (1994). *Self-directed search form R.* Lutz, FL: Psychological Assessment Resources.

Holmes, T. H., & Rahe, R. H. (1967). The social readjustment rating scale. *Journal of Psychosomatic Research, 11,* 213–218.

Holzel, B. K., Carmody, J., Vangel, M., Congleton, C., Yerramsetti, S. M., Gard, T., & Lazar, S. W. (2011). Mindfulness practice leads to increases in regional brain gray matter density. *Psychiatry Research: Neuroimaging, 191*(1) 36–43.

Honts, C. R., & Kircher, J. C. (1994). Mental and physical countermeasures reduce the accuracy of polygraph tests. *Journal of Applied Psychology, 79*(2), 252–259.

Hooley, J. M., & Hiller, J. B. (2001). Family relationships and major mental disorder: Risk factors and preventive strategies. In B. R. Sarason & S. Duck (Eds.), *Personal relationships: implications for clinical and community psychology.* New York, NY: Wiley.

Horiuchi, Y., Nakayama, K., Ishiguro, H., Ohtsuki, T., Detera-Wadleigh, S. D., Toyota, T., … Arinami, T. (2004). Possible association between a haplotype of the GABA-A receptor alpha 1 subunit gene (GABRA1) and mood disorders. *Biological Psychiatry, 55*(1), 40–45.

Horney, K. (1939). *New ways in psychoanalysis.* New York, NY: International Universities Press.

Horney, K. (1945). *Our inner conflicts: A constructive theory of neurosis.* New York, NY: Norton.

Horwath, E., & Gould, F. (2011). Epidemiology of anxiety disorders. In M. Tsuang, M. Tohen, & P. Jones (Eds.), *Textbook in psychiatric epidemiology* (3rd ed., pp. 311–328). Hoboken, NJ: Wiley.

Hosokawa, N., & Chiba, A. (2010). Androgen receptor blockade in the posterodorsal medial amygdala impairs sexual odor preference in male rats. *Hormones and Behavior, 58*(3), 493–500.

Houlfort, N. (2006). The impact of performance-contingent rewards on perceived autonomy and intrinsic motivation. *Dissertation Abstracts International Section A: Humanities and Social Sciences, 67*(2-A), 460.

Houtz, J. C., Matos, H., Park, M-K. S., Scheinholtz, J., & Selby, E. (2007). Problem-solving style and motivational attributions. *Psychological Reports, 101,* 823–830.

Hovland, C. I. (1937). The generalization of conditioned responses: II. The sensory generalization of conditioned responses with varying intensities of tone. *Journal of Genetic Psychology, 51,* 279–291.

Howard, M. A., & Marczinski, C. A. (2010). Acute effects of a glucose energy drink on behavioral control. *Experimental and Clinical Psychopharmacology, 18*(6), 553–561.

Howe, N., & Recchia, H. (2008). Siblings and sibling rivalry. In M. Haith & J. Benson (Eds.), *Encyclopaedia of infant and early childhood development* (pp. 154–164). Oxford, England: Elsevier.

Howe, N., Ross, H. S., & Recchia, H. (2011). Sibling relations in early and middle childhood. In P. K. Smith & K. H. Hart (Eds.), *The Wiley-Blackwell handbook of childhood social development* (2nd ed., pp. 356–372). Hoboken, NJ: Wiley.

Howell, K. K., Coles, C. D., & Kable, J. A. (2008). The medical and developmental consequences of prenatal drug exposure. In J. Brick (Ed.), *Handbook of the medical consequences of alcohol and drug abuse* (2nd ed., pp. 219–249). The Haworth Press series in neuropharmacology. New York, NY: Haworth Press/Taylor and Francis Group.

Howes, M. B. (2007). *Human memory: Structures and images.* Thousand Oaks, CA: Sage Publications.

Howland, R. H. (2010). Update on St. John's wort. *Journal of Psychosocial Nursing and Mental Health Services, 48*(11), 20–24.

Hsieh, P-H. (2005). How college students explain their grades in a foreign language course: The interrelationship of attributions, self-efficacy, language learning beliefs, and achievement. *Dissertation Abstracts International Section A: Humanities and Social Sciences, 65*(10-A), 3691.

Hubel, D. H., & Wiesel, T. N. (1965). Receptive fields and the functional architecture in two nonstriate visual areas (18 and 19) of the cat. *Journal of Neurophysiology, 28,* 229–289.

Hubel, D. H., & Wiesel, T. N. (1979). Brain mechanisms of vision. *Scientific American, 241,* 150–162.

Hubert, H., Bloch, D., Oehlert, J., & Fries, J. (2002). Lifestyle habits and compression of morbidity. *Journals of Gerontology: Series A: Biological Sciences and Medical Sciences, 57*(6), M347–M351.

Hudson, J., Hiripi, E., Pope, H., & Kessler, R. (2007). The prevalence and correlates of eating disorders in the national comorbidity survey replication. *Biological Psychiatry, 61*(3), 348–358.

Hudziak, J. J. (Ed.). (2008). *Developmental psychopathology and wellness: Genetic and environmental influences.* Arlington, VA: American Psychiatric Publishing.

Huesmann, L. R., & Kirwil, L. (2007). Why observing violence increases the risk of violent behavior by the observer. In D. J. Flannery, A. T. Vazsonyi, & I. D. Waldman (Eds.), *The Cambridge handbook of violent behavior and aggression* (pp. 545–570). New York, NY: Cambridge University Press.

Huijbregts, S. C., Séguin, J. R., Zoccolillo, M., Boivin, M., & Tremblay, R. E. (2008). Maternal prenatal smoking, parental antisocial behavior, and early childhood physical aggression. *Development and Psychopathology, 20,* 437–453.

Huijbregts, S., Séguin, J., Zelazo, P., Parent, S., Japel, C., & Tremblay, R. (2006). Interrelations between maternal smoking during pregnancy, birth weight and sociodemographic factors in the prediction of early cognitive abilities. *Infant and Child Development, 15,* 593–607.

Hulette, A., Freyd, J., & Fisher, P. (2011). Dissociation in middle childhood among foster children with early maltreatment experiences. *Child Abuse & Neglect, 35,* 123–126.

Hull, C. (1952). *A behavior system.* New Haven, CT: Yale University Press.

Human Resources and Social Development Canada. (2007). *National occupational classification* (Cat. no. MP53-25/2006E). Ottawa, ON: Government of Canada.

Hunsley, J., & Lee, C. M. (2010). *Introduction to clinical psychology* (2nd ed.). Toronto, ON: John Wiley & Sons Canada.

Hunsley, J., Lee, C. M., & Aubrey, T. (1999). Who uses psychological services in Canada? *Canadian Psychology, 40,* 232–240.

Hunt, E. (2011). *Human intelligence.* New York, NY: Cambridge University Press.

Hunter, J. P., Katz, J. J., & Davis, K. D. (2008). Stability of phantom limb phenomena after upper limb amputation: A longitudinal study. *Neuroscience, 156*(4), 939–949.

Hurley, S. (2008). The shared circuits model (SCM): How control, mirroring, and simulation can enable imitation, and deliberation, and mindreading. *Behavioral and Brain Sciences, 31,* 1–22.

Husain, M. M., & Lisanby, S. H. (2011). Repetitive transcranial magnetic stimulation (rTMS):

A noninvasive neuromodulation probe and intervention. *The Journal of ECT, 27*(1), 2.

Hutchinson-Phillips, S., Gow, K., & Jamieson, G. A. (2007). Hypnotizability, eating behaviors, attitudes, and concerns: A literature survey. *International Journal of Clinical and Experimental Hypnosis, 55,* 84–113.

Hutchison, P., & Rosenthal, H. E. S. (2011). Prejudice against Muslims: Anxiety as a mediator between intergroup contact and attitudes, perceived group variability and behavioural intentions. *Ethnic and Racial Studies, 34*(1), 40–61.

Hutson, M. (2008). Magical thinking. *Psychology Today.* Retrieved from http://www.psychologytoday.com/articles/200802/magical-thinking

Hyde, J. S. (2005). The genetics of sexual orientation. In J. S. Hyde (Ed.), *Biological substrates of human sexuality.* Washington, DC: American Psychological Association.

Hyde, J. S. (2007). *Half the human experience: The psychology of women* (7th ed.). Boston, MA: Houghton Mifflin.

Hyde, J. S., & DeLamater, J. D. (2011). *Understanding human sexuality* (11th ed.). New York, NY: McGraw-Hill.

Hyder, A. A., Wunderlich, C. A., Puvanachandra, P., Gururaj, G. G., & Kobusingye, O. C. (2007). The impact of traumatic brain injuries: A global perspective. *Neurorehabilitation, 22*(5), 341–353.

Hyman, R. (1981). Cold reading: How to convince strangers that you know all about them. In K. Fraizer (Ed.), *Paranormal borderlands of science* (pp. 232–244). Buffalo, NY: Prometheus.

Hyman, R. (1996). The evidence for psychic functioning: Claims vs. reality. *Skeptical Inquirer, 20,* 24–26.

Hyman, R. (2010). Meta-analysis that conceals more than it reveals: Comment on Storm et al. (2010). *Psychological Bulletin, 136*(4), 486–490.

Hypericum Depression Trial Study Group. (2002). Effect of *Hypericum performatum* (St John's wort) in major depressive disorder: A randomized controlled trial. *JAMA: Journal of the American Medical Association, 287*(14), 1807–1814.

I

Iacono, W. G., & Lykken, D. T. (1997). The validity of the lie detector: Two surveys of scientific opinion. *Journal of Applied Psychology, 82*(3), 426–433.

Iavarone, A., Patruno, M., Galeone, F., Chieffi, S., & Carlomagno, S. (2007). Brief report: Error pattern in an autistic savant calendar calculator. *Journal of Autism and Developmental Disorders, 37,* 775–779.

Ikeda, H., & Murase, K. (2004). Glial nitric oxide-mediated long-term presynaptic facilitation revealed by optical imaging in rat spinal dorsal horn. *Journal of Neuroscience, 24*(44), 9888–9896.

Imada, T., & Ellsworth, P. C. (2011). Proud Americans and lucky Japanese: Cultural differences in appraisal and corresponding emotion. *Emotion, 11*(2), 329–345.

Imada, T., & Kitayama, S. (2010). Social eyes and choice justification: Culture and dissonance revisited. *Social Cognition, 28*(5), 589–608.

International Human Genome Sequencing Consortium. (2004). Finishing the euchromatic

sequence of the human genome. *Nature, 431*(7011), 931–945.

Irwin, M., Mascovich, A., Gillin, J. C., Willoughby, R., Pike, J., & Smith, T. L. (1994). Partial sleep deprivation reduced natural killer cell activity in humans. *Psychosomatic Medicine, 56*(6), 493–498.

Isabelle Caro dies. (2010). *The Guardian.* Retrieved from http://www.guardian.co.uk/society/2010/dec/30/isabelle-caro-dies-model-anorexia

Ivanovic, D. M., Leiva, B. P., Pérez, H. T., Olivares, M. G., Díaz, N. S., Urrutia, … Larraín, C. G. (2004). Head size and intelligence, learning, nutritional status and brain development: Head, IQ, learning, nutrition and brain. *Neuropsychologia, 42*(8), 1118–1131.

Iwata, Y., Suzuki, K., Takei, N., Toulopoulou, T., Tsuchiya, K. J., Matsumoto, K., … Mori, N. (2011). Jiko-shisen-kyofu (fear of one's own glance), but not taijin-kyofusho (fear of interpersonal relations), is an east Asian culture-related specific syndrome. *Australian and New Zealand Journal of Psychiatry, 45*(2), 148–152.

Izard, C. E. (1977). Human emotions. New York, NY: Plenum Press.

Izard, C. E. (1992). Basic emotions, relations among emotions, and emotion-cognition relations. *Psychological Review, 99*(3), 561–565.

J

Jackendoff, R. (2003). Foundations of language, brain, meaning, grammar, evolution. *Applied Cognitive Psychology, 17*(1), 121–122.

Jackson, D. N. (1997). *Jackson Personality Inventory-Revised.* London, ON: Research Psychologists' Press.

Jackson, E. D. (2008). Cortisol effects on emotional memory: Independent of stress effects. *Dissertation Abstracts International: Section B: The Sciences and Engineering, 68*(11-B), 7666.

Jackson, L. M. (2011). *The psychology of prejudice: From attitudes to social action.* Washington, DC: American Psychological Association.

Jackson, P. B., & Williams, D. R. (2006). Culture, race/ethnicity, and depression. In C. L. M. Keyes & S. H. Goodman (Eds), *Women and depression: A handbook for the social, behavioral, and biomedical sciences* (pp. 328–359). New York, NY: Cambridge University Press.

Jacob, P. (2008). What do mirror neurons contribute to human social cognition? *Mind & Language, 23,* 90–223.

Jacobi, C., Hayward, C., de Zwaan, M., Kraemer, H. C., & Agras, W. S. (2004). Coming to terms with risk factors for eating disorders: Application of risk terminology and suggestions for a general taxonomy. *Psychological Bulletin, 130*(1), 19–65.

Jaffee, S. R., Caspi, A., Moffitt, T. E., Dodge, K. A., Rutter, M., Taylor, A., & Tully, L. A. (2005). Nature × nurture: Genetic vulnerabilities interact with physical maltreatment to promote conduct problems. *Development and Psychopathology, 17,* 67–84.

Jain, G., Kumar, V., Chakrabarti, S., & Grover, S. (2008). The use of electroconvulsive therapy in the elderly: A study from the psychiatric unit of a North Indian teaching hospital. *Journal of ECT, 24,* 122–127.

James Randi Educational Foundation. (2008). Retrieved from http://www.randi.org/joom/challenge-info.html

James, F. O., Cermakian, N., & Boivin, D. B. (2007). Circadian rhythms of melatonin, cortisol, and clock gene expression during simulated night shift work. *Sleep: Journal of Sleep and Sleep Disorders Research, 30*(11), 1427–1436.

James, G., Blakeley, C. J., Hashemi, K., Channing, K., & Duff, M. (2006). A case of self-inflicted craniocerebral penetrating injury. *Emergency Medicine Journal, 23*, e32.

James, W. (1890). *The principles of psychology* (Vol. 2). New York, NY: Holt.

Jamieson, G. A., & Hasegawa, H. (2007). New paradigms of hypnosis research. In G. A. Jamieson (Ed.), *Hypnosis and conscious states: The cognitive neuroscience perspective* (pp. 133–144). New York, NY: Oxford University Press.

Jang, K. L., Livesley, W. J., Anso, J., Yamagata, S., Suzuki, A., Angleitner, A., ... Spinath, F. (2006). Behavioral genetics of the higher-order factors of the Big Five. *Personality and Individual Differences, 41*, 261–272.

Janis, I. L. (1972). *Victims of groupthink: A psychological study of foreign-policy decisions and fiascoes.* Boston, MA: Houghton Mifflin.

Janis, I. L. (1989). *Crucial decisions: Leadership in policymaking and crisis management.* New York, NY: Free Press.

Jausovec, N., & Jausovec, K. (2012). Working memory training: Improving intelligence-changing brain activity. *Brain and Cognition, 79*(2), 96–106.

Jensen, M. P., Hakimian, S., Sherlin, L. H., & Fregni, F. (2008). New insights into neuromodulatory approaches for the treatment of pain. *The Journal of Pain, 9*, 193–199.

Johansson, L. E., Danielsson, A. H., Parikh, H., Klintenberg, M., Norström, F., Groop, L., & Ridderstråle, M. (2012). Differential gene expression in adipose tissue from obese human subjects during weight loss and weight maintenance. *American Journal of Clinical Nutrition, 96*(1), 196–207.

Johnson, D. M., Delahanty, D. L., & Pinna, K. (2008). The cortisol awakening response as a function of PTSD severity and abuse chronicity in sheltered battered women. *Journal of Anxiety Disorders, 22*, 793–800.

Johnson, S. (2008). Couple and family therapy: An attachment perspective. In J. Cassidy & P. R. Shaver (Eds.), *Handbook of attachment: Theory, research, and clinical applications* (2nd ed., pp. 811–832). New York, NY: Guilford.

Johnson, S. (2011). The attachment perspective on the bonds of love: A prototype for relationship change. In J. Furrow, B. Bradley, & S. Johnson (Eds.), *The emotionally focused casebook* (pp. 31–58). New York, NY: Brunner Routledge.

Johnson, W., Bouchard, T. J. Jr., Krueger, R. F., McGue, M., & Gottesman, I. I. (2004). Just one g: Consistent results from three test batteries. *Intelligence, 32*(1), 95–107.

Johnson, W., Bouchard, T. J. Jr., McGue, M., Segal, N. L., Tellegen, A., Keyes, M., & Gottesman, I. I. (2007). Genetic and environmental influences on the Verbal-Perceptual-Image Rotation (VPR) model of the structure of mental abilities in the Minnesota study of twins reared apart. *Intelligence, 35*, 542–562.

Johnston, J. C., Durieux-Smith, A., & Bloom, K. (2005). Teaching gestural signs to infants to advance child development: A review of the evidence. *First Language, 25*(2), 235–251.

Jolliffe, C. D., & Nicholas, M. K. (2004). Verbally reinforcing pain reports: An experimental test of the operant conditioning of chronic pain. *Pain, 107*, 167–175.

Jonas, E., Traut-Mattausch, E., Frey, D., & Greenberg, J. (2008). The path or the goal? Decision vs. information focus in biased information seeking after preliminary decisions. *Journal of Experimental Social Psychology, 44*, 1180–1186.

Jones, B. C., DeBruine, L. M., & Little, A. C. (2007). The role of symmetry in attraction to average faces. *Perception & Psychophysics, 69*, 1273–1277.

Jones, B. C., Little, A. C., Penton-Voak, I. S., Tiddeman, B. P., Burt, D. M., & Perrett, D. I. (2001). Facial symmetry and judgements of apparent health: Support for a "good genes" explanation of the attractiveness-symmetry relationship. *Evolution and Human Behavior, 22*(6), 417–429.

Jones, D. G., Anderson, E. R., & Galvin, K. A. (2003). Spinal cord regeneration: Moving tentatively towards new perspectives. *NeuroRehabilitation, 18*(4), 339–351.

Jones, E. (2008). Predicting performance in first-semester college basic writers: Revisiting the role of self-beliefs. *Contemporary Educational Psychology, 33*, 209–238.

Jones, S. R., & Fernyhough, C. (2007). A new look at the neural diathesis-stress model of schizophrenia: The primacy of social-evaluative and uncontrollable situations. *Schizophrenia Bulletin, 33*, 1171–1177.

Jonides, J., Lewis, R. L., Nee, D. E., Lustig, C. A., Berman, M. G., & Moore, K. S. (2008). The mind and brain of short-term memory. *Annual Review of Psychology, 59*, 193–224.

Jorenby, D., Leischow, S., Nides, M., Rennard, S., Johnston, J., Hughes, A., ... Baker, T. (1999). A controlled trial of sustained-release bupropion, a nicotine patch, or both for smoking cessation. *New England Journal of Medicine, 340*(9), 685–691.

Joy, L. A., Kimball, M. M., & Zabrack, M. L. (1986). Television and children's aggressive behavior. In T. M. Williams (Ed.), *The impact of television: A natural experiment in three communities* (pp. 303–360). Orlando, FL: Academic Press.

Juby, H., Billette, J. M., Laplante, B., & Le Bourdais, C. (2007). Nonresident fathers and children: Parents' new unions and frequency of contact. *Journal of Family Issues, 28*, 1220–1245.

Jung, C. (1969). The concept of collective unconscious. In *Collected Works*, Vol. 9, Part 1. Princeton, NJ: Princeton University Press. (Original work published 1936.)

Jung, C. G. (1946). *Psychological types.* New York, NY: Harcourt Brace.

Jung, C. G. (1959). The archetypes and the collective unconscious. In H. Read, M. Fordham, & G. Adler (Eds.), *The collected works of C.G. Jung,* Vol. 9. New York, NY: Pantheon.

Jung, H. (2006). Assessing the influence of cultural values on consumer susceptibility to social pressure for conformity: Self-image enhancing motivations vs. information searching motivation. In L. R. Kahle & C-H. Kim (Eds.), Creating images and the psychology of marketing communication (pp. 309–329). *Advertising and Consumer Psychology.* Mahwah, NJ: Erlbaum.

Jung, R. E., & Haier, R. J. (2007). The Parieto-Frontal Integration Theory (P-FIT) of intelligence: Converging neuroimaging evidence. *Behavioral and Brain Sciences, 30*, 135–154.

Juntii, S. A., Coats, J. K., & Shah, N. M. (2008). A genetic approach to dissect sexually dimorphic behaviors. *Hormones and Behavior, 53*, 627–637.

Juvonen, J., & Galván, A. (2008). Peer influence in involuntary social groups: Lessons from research on bullying. In M. Prinstein & K. Dodge (Eds.), *Understanding peer influence in children and adolescents* (pp. 225–244). New York, NY: Guilford Press.

Juvonen, J., & Gross, E. F. (2008). Extending the school grounds? Bullying experiences in cyberspace. *Journal of School Health, 78*(9), 496–505.

K

Kagan, J., & Fox, N. A. (2006). Biology, culture, and temperamental biases. In W. Damon & R. M. Lerner (Series Eds.) & N. Eisenberg (Vol. Ed.), *Handbook of child psychology: Vol. 3. Social, emotional, and personality development* (6th ed., pp. 167–225). Hoboken, NJ: Wiley.

Kahneman, D. (2003). Experiences of collaborative research. *American Psychologist, 58*(9), 723–730.

Kalodner, C. R. (2011). Cognitive-behavioral theories. In D. Capuzzi & D. R. Gross (Eds.), *Counseling and psychotherapy* (5th ed., pp. 193–213). Alexandria, VA: American Counseling Association.

Kamdar, B. B., Kaplan, K. A., Kezirian, E. J., & Dement, W. C. (2004). The impact of extended sleep on daytime alertness, vigilance, and mood. *Sleep Medicine, 5*(5), 441–448.

Kampen, J. K. (2011). A methodological note on the making of causal statements in the debate on anthropogenic global warming. *Theoretical & Applied Climatology, 104*(3/4), 423–427.

Kana, R. K., Wadsworth, H. M., & Travers, B. G. (2011). A systems level analysis of the mirror neuron hypothesis and imitation impairments in autism spectrum disorders. *Neuroscience and Biobehavioral Reviews, 35*(3), 894–902.

Kanner, A. D., Coyne, J. C., Schaefer, C., Lazarus, R. S. (1981). Comparison of two modes of stress measurement: Daily hassles and uplifts versus major life events. *Journal of Behavioral Medicine, 4*, 1–39.

Kaplan, L. E. (2006). Moral reasoning of MSW social workers and the influence of education. *Journal of Social Work Education, 42*, 507–522.

Kapner, D. A. (2004). Infofacts resources: Alcohol and other drugs on campus. Retrieved from http://www.edc.org/hec//hec/pubs/factsheets/scope.html

Kardong, K. (2008). *Introduction to biological evolution* (2nd ed.). New York, NY: McGraw-Hill.

Kareev, Y. (2000). Seven (indeed, plus or minus two) and the detection of correlations. *Psychological Review, 107*(2), 397–402.

Karmiloff, K, & Karmiloff-Smith, A. (2002). *Pathways to language: From fetus to adolescent.* Cambridge, MA: Harvard University Press.

Karon, B. P., & Widener, A. J. (1998). Repressed memories: The real story. *Professional Psychology: Research & Practice, 29*, 482–487.

Karremans, J. C., Stroebe, W., & Claus, J. (2006). Beyond Vicary's fantasies: The impact of subliminal priming and brand choice. *Journal of Experimental Social Psychology, 42*, 792–798.

Kaslow, N. J., Bhaju, J., & Celano, M. P. (2011). Family therapies. In S. B. Messer & A. S. Gurman (Eds.), *Essential psychotherapies: Theory and practice* (3rd ed., pp. 297–344). New York, NY: Guilford.

Kasper, S., Caraci, F., Forti, B., Drago, F., & Aguglia, E. (2010). Efficacy and tolerability of Hypericum extract for the treatment of mild to moderate depression. *European Neuropsychopharmacology, 20*(11), 747–765.

Kassin, S., Fein, S., & Markus, H. R. (2008). *Social psychology* (7th ed.). Belmont, CA: Cengage.

Kastenbaum, R. J. (2012). *Death, society, and human experience* (11th ed.). Upper Saddle River, NJ: Prentice-Hall.

Katz, I., Kaplan, A., Buzukashvily, T. (2011). The role of parents' motivation in students' autonomous motivation for doing homework. *Learning and Individual Differences, 21*(4), 376–386.

Katzmarzyk, P. T., Gledhill, N., & Shephard, R. J. (2000). The economic burden of physical inactivity in Canada. *Canadian Medical Association Journal, 163*(11), 1435–1440.

Kaye, W. (2008). Neurobiology of anorexia and bulimia nervosa. *Physiology & Behavior, 94*, 121–135.

Kaysen, D., Pantalone, D. W., Chawla, N., Lindgrren, K. P., Clum, G. A., Lee, C., & Resick, P. A. (2008). Posttraumatic stress disorder, alcohol use, and physical health concerns. *Journal of Behavioral Medicine, 31*, 115–125.

Kazdin, A. E. (1994). Methodology, design, and evaluation in psychotherapy research. In A. E. Bergin & S. L. Garfield (Eds.), *Handbook of psychotherapy and behavior change* (4th ed.). New York, NY: Wiley.

Kazdin, A. E. (2008). *Behavior modification in applied settings*. Long Grove, IL: Waveland Press.

Keats, D. M. (1982). Cultural bases of concepts of intelligence: A Chinese versus Australian comparison. In P. Sukontasarp, N. Yongsiri, P. Intasuwan, N. Jotiban, & C. Suvannathat (Eds.), *Proceedings of the Second Asian Workshop on Child and Adolescent Development* (pp. 67–75). Bangkok: Burapasilpa Press.

Keen, E. (2011). Emotional narratives: Depression as sadness—Anxiety as fear. *The Humanistic Psychologist, 39*(1), 66–70.

Keller, J., & Bless, H. (2008). The interplay of stereotype threat and regulatory focus. In Y. Kashima, K. Fiedler, & P. Freytag (Eds.), *Stereotype dynamics: Language-based approaches to the formation, maintenance, and transformation of stereotypes* (pp. 367–389). Mahwah, NJ: Erlbaum.

Kellogg, S. H., & Young, J. E. (2008). Cognitive therapy. In J. L. Lebow (Ed.), *Twenty-first century psychotherapies: Contemporary approaches to theory and practice* (pp. 43–79). Hoboken, NJ: Wiley.

Keltner, D., Ekman, P., Gonzaga, G. C., & Beer, J. (2003). Facial expression of emotion. In R. J. Davidson, K. R. Scherer, H. Goldsmith (Eds.), *Handbook of affective sciences* (pp. 415–432). New York, NY: Oxford University Press.

Keltner, D., Kring, A. M., & Bonanno, G. A. (1999). Fleeting signs of the course of life: Facial expression and personal adjustment. *Current Directions in Psychological Science, 8*(1), 18–22.

Kemeny, M. E. (2007). Psychoneuroimmunology. In H. S. Friedman & R. C. Silver (Eds.), *Foundations of health psychology*. New York, NY: Oxford University Press.

Kemker, B. E., Stierwalt, J. G., LaPointe, L. L., & Heald, G. R. (2009). Effects of a cell phone conversation on cognitive processing performances. *Journal of the American Academy of Audiology, 20*(9), 582–588.

Kenealy, P. M. (1997). Mood-state-dependent retrieval: The effects of induced mood on memory reconsidered. *Quarterly Journal of Experimental Psychology: Human Experimental Psychology, 50A*, 290–317.

Kennedy, M. M. (2010). Attribution error and the quest for teacher quality. *Educational Researcher, 39*(8), 591–598.

Keo, H., Baumgartner, I., Hirsch, A., Duval, S., Steg, P., Pasquet, B., Bhatt, D., & Roether, J. (2011). Carotid plaque and intima-media thickness and the incidence of ischemic events in patients with atherosclerotic vascular disease. *Vascular Medicine, 16*(5), 323–330.

Keppler, H., Dhooge, I., Maes, L., D'haenens, W., Bockstael, A., Philips, B., Swinnen, F., & Vinck, B. (2010). Short-term auditory effects of listening to an MP3 player. *Archives of Otolaryngology—Head and Neck Surgery, 136*(6), 538–548.

Kerns, K. A. (2008). Attachment in middle childhood. In J. Cassidy & P. R. Shaver (Eds.), *Handbook of attachment: Theory, research, and clinical applications* (2nd ed., pp. 366–382). New York, NY: Guilford.

Kerr, C. L., Letzen, B. S., Hill, C. M., Agrawal, G., Thakor, N. V., Sterneckert, J. L., Gearhart, J. D., & All, A. H. (2010). Efficient differentiation of human embryonic stem cells into oligodendrocyte progenitors for application in a rat contusion model of spinal cord injury. *International Journal of Neuroscience, 120*(4), 305–313.

Kerschreiter, R., Schulz-Hardt, S., Mojzisch, A., & Frey, D. (2008). Biased information search in homogeneous groups: Confidence as a moderator for the effect of anticipated task requirements. *Personality & Social Psychology Bulletin, 34*, 679–691.

Key, T. J. (2011). Fruit and vegetables and cancer risk. *British Journal of Cancer, 104*(1), 6–11.

Kezwer, G. (1998). Organic cigarettes new fad for "health conscious" smokers. *Canadian Medical Association Journal, 158*(1), 13.

Khalid, N., Atkins, M., Tredget, J., Giles, M., Champney-Smith, K., & Kirov, G. (2008). The effectiveness of electroconvulsive therapy in treatment-resistant depression. *Journal of ECT, 24*, 141–145.

Kibos, A., & Guerchicoff, A. (2011). Susceptibility genes for coronary heart disease and myocardial infarction. *Acute Cardiac Care, 13*(3), 136–142.

Kieffer, K. M., Schinka, J. A., & Curtiss, G. (2004). Person-environment congruence and personality domains in the prediction of job performance and work quality. *Journal of Counseling Psychology, 51*(2), 168–177.

Kihlstrom, J. F. (2004). An unbalanced balancing act: Blocked, recovered, and false memories in the laboratory and clinic. *Clinical Psychology: Science & Practice, 11*(1), 34–41.

Kihlstrom, J. F. (2005). Dissociative disorders. *Annual Review of Clinical Psychology, 1*, 227–253.

Killen, M., & Hart, D. (1999). *Morality in everyday life*. New York, NY: Cambridge University Press.

Kilpatrick, L. A., Suyenobu, B. Y., Smith, S. R., Bueller, J. A., Goodman, T. Creswell, J. D., … Naliboff, B. D. (2011). Impact of mindfulness-based stress reduction training on intrinsic brain connectivity. *NeuroImage, 56*(1), 290–298.

Kim, J., & Hatfield, E. (2004). Love types and subjective well-being: A cross cultural study. *Social Behavior & Personality, 32*(2), 173–182.

Kim, S. U. (2004). Human neural stem cells genetically modified for brain repair in neurological disorders. *Neuropathology, 24*(3), 159–171.

Kimball, M. M. (1986). Television and sex-role attitudes. In T. M. Williams (Ed.), *The impact of television: A natural experiment in three communities* (pp. 265–302). Orlando, FL: Academic Press.

Kimura, D. (2004). Human sex differences in cognition: Fact, not predicament. *Sexualities, Evolution, and Gender, 6*, 45–53.

Kinder, L. S., Bradley, K. A., Katon, W. J., Ludman, E., McDonnell, M. B., & Bryson, C. L. (2008). Depression, posttraumatic stress disorder, and mortality. *Psychosomatic Medicine, 70*, 20–26.

King, B. M. (2012). *Human sexuality today* (7th ed.). Boston, MA: Allyn & Bacon.

Kinsella, T., & Verhoef, M. (1999). Determinants of Canadian physicians' opinions about legalized physician-assisted suicide: A national survey. *Annals of the Royal College of Physicians and Surgeons of Canada, 32*, 211–215.

Kinsley, C. H., & Lambert, K. G. (2008). Reproduction-induced neuroplasticity: Natural behavioural and neuronal alterations associated with the production and care of offspring. *Journal of Neuroendocrinology, 20*(4), 515–525.

Kirby, M., Maggi, S., & D'Angiulli, A. (2011). School start times and the sleep-wake cycle of adolescents: A review and critical evaluation of available evidence. *Educational Researcher, 40*(2), 56–61.

Kiriakidis, S. P., & Kavoura, A. (2010). Cyberbullying: A review of the literature on harassment through the internet and other electronic means. *Family and Community Health, 33*(2), 82–93.

Kirk, K. M., Bailey, J. M., Dunne, M. P., & Martin, N. G. (2000). Measurement models for sexual orientation in a community twin sample. *Behavior Genetics, 30*(4), 345–356.

Kirsch, I., & Braffman, W. (2001). Imaginative suggestibility and hypnotizability. *Current Directions in Psychological Science, 10*(2), 57–61.

Kirsch, I., Mazzoni, G., & Montgomery, G. H. (2006). Remembrance of hypnosis past. *American Journal of Clinical Hypnosis, 49*, 171–178.

Kirschenbaum, H., & Jourdan, A. (2005). The current status of Carl Rogers and the person-centered approach. *Psychotherapy: Theory, Research Practice, Training, 42*(1), 37–51.

Kisilevsky, B. S., Hains, S. M. J., Brown, C. A., Lee, C. T., Cowperthwaite, B., Stutzman, S. S., … Wang, Z. (2009). Fetal sensitivity to properties of maternal speech and language. *Infant Behavior and Development, 32*, 59–71.

Kisilevsky, B. S., Hains, S. M. J., Lee, K., Xie, X., Huang, H., Ye, H., Zhang, K., & Wang, Z. (2003). Effects of experience on fetal voice recognition. *Psychological Science, 14*(3), 220–224.

Klatzky, R. L. (1984). *Memory and awareness.* New York, NY: Freeman.

Kleider, H. M., Pezdek, K., Goldinger, S. D., & Kirk, A. (2008). Schema-driven source misattribution errors: Remembering the expected from a witnessed event. *Applied Cognitive Psychology, 22,* 1–20.

Klein, O., Pohl, S., & Ndagijimana, C. (2007). The influence of intergroup comparisons on Africans' intelligence test performance in a job selection context. *Journal of Psychology: Interdisciplinary and Applied, 141,* 453–467.

Klimes-Dougan, B., Lee, C-Y. S., Ronsaville, D., & Martinez, P. (2008). Suicidal risk in young adult offspring of mothers with bipolar or major depressive disorder: A longitudinal family risk study. *Journal of Clinical Psychology, 64,* 531–540.

Knekt, P., Lindfors, O., Laaksonen, M. A., Raitasalo, R., Haaramo, P., Järvikoski, A., & The Helsinki Psychotherapy Study Group, Helsinki, Finland. (2008). Effectiveness of short-term and long-term psychotherapy on work ability and functional capacity—A randomized clinical trial on depressive and anxiety disorders. *Journal of Affective Disorders, 107,* 95–106.

Kniffin, K. M., & Wilson, D. S. (2004). The effect of nonphysical traits on the perception of physical attractiveness: Three naturalistic studies. *Evolution & Human Behavior, 25,* 88–101.

Knoblauch, K., Vital-Durand, F., & Barbur, J. L. (2000). Variation of chromatic sensitivity across the life span. *Vision Research, 41*(1), 23–36.

Kobal, G., Klimek, L., Wolfensberger, M., Gudziol, H., Temmel, A., Owen, C …. Hummel, T. (2000). Multicenter investigation of 1,036 subjects using a standardized method for the assessment of olfactory function combining tests of odor identification, odor discrimination, and olfactory thresholds. *European Archives of Oto-Rhino-Laryngology: Official Journal of the European Federation of Oto-Rhino-Laryngological Societies (EUFOS): Affiliated with the German Society for Oto-Rhino-Laryngology—Head and Neck Surgery, 257*(4), 205–211.

Kobasa, S. (1979). Stressful life events, personality, and health: An inquiry into hardiness. *Journal of Personality and Social Psychology, 37,* 1–11.

Kobeissi, J., Aloysi, A., Tobias, K., Popeo, D., & Kellner, C. H. (2011). Resolution of severe suicidality with a single electroconvulsive therapy. *Journal of ECT, 27*(1), 86–88.

Köfalvi, A. (Ed.). (2008). *Cannabinoids and the brain.* New York, NY: Springer Science & Business Media.

Kohlberg, L. (1964). Development of moral character and moral behavior. In L. W. Hoffman & M. L. Hoffman (Eds.), *Review of child development research* (Vol. 1). New York, NY: Sage.

Kohlberg, L. (1984). *The psychology of moral development: Essays on moral development* (Vol. 2). San Francisco, CA: Harper & Row.

Köhler, W. (1925). *The mentality of apes.* New York, NY: Harcourt, Brace.

Kohn, A. (2000). *Punished by rewards: The trouble with gold stars, incentive plans, A's, and other bribes.* New York, NY: Houghton Mifflin.

Kolb, B., & Whishaw, I. Q. (2009). *Fundamentals of human neuropsychology.* New York, NY: Worth Publishers.

Kolb, B., Muhammad, A., & Gibb, R. (2011). Searching for factors underlying cerebral plasticity in the normal and injured brain. *Journal of Communication Disorders, 44*(5), 503–514.

Köfalvi, A. (Ed.). (2008). *Cannabinoids and the brain.* New York, NY: Springer Science & Business Media.

Komiya, N., Good, G. E, & Sherrod, N. B. (2000). Emotional openness as a predictor of college students' attitudes toward seeking psychological help. *Journal of Counseling Psychology, 47*(1), 138–143.

Kondo, N. (2008). Mental illness in film. *Psychiatric Rehabilitation Journal, 31,* 250–252.

Konheim-Kalkstein, Y. L., & van den Broek, P. (2008). The effect of incentives on cognitive processing of text. *Discourse Processes, 45,* 180–194.

Konigsberg, R. D. (2011). *The truth about grief: The myth of its five stages and the new science of loss.* New York, NY: Simon & Schuster.

Koop, C. E., Richmond, J., & Steinfeld, J. (2004). America's choice: Reducing tobacco addiction and disease. *American Journal of Public Health, 94*(2), 174–176.

Korda, J., Goldstein, S., & Sommer, F. (2010). The history of female ejaculation. *The Journal of Sexual Medicine, 7*(5), 1965–1975.

Korman, M., Doyon, J., Doljansky, J., Carrier, J., Dagan, Y., & Karni, A. (2007). Daytime sleep condenses the time course of motor memory consolidation. *Nature Neuroscience, 10*(9), 1206–1213.

Kosslyn, S. M., & Thompson, W. L. (2000). Hypnotic visual illusions alters color processing in the brain. *American Journal of Psychiatry, 157*(8), 1279.

Kovacic, Z., Henigsberg, N., Pivac, N., Nedic, G., & Borovecki, A. (2008). Platelet serotonin concentration and suicidal behavior in combat related posttraumatic stress disorder. *Progress in Neuro-Psychopharmacology & Biological Psychiatry, 32,* 544–551.

Kowalski, R. M., & Westen, D. (2011). *Psychology* (6th ed.). Hoboken, NJ: Wiley.

Kowalski, R. M., Limber, S. P., & Agatston, P. W. (2012. *Cyber bullying: Bullying in the digital age* (2nd edition). Hoboken, NJ: Wiley.

Kraaij, V., Arensman, E., & Spinhoven, P. (2002). Negative life events and depression in elderly persons: A meta-analysis. *Journals of Gerontology: Series B: Psychological Sciences & Social Sciences, 57B*(1), 87–94.

Krahé, B., Möller, I., Huesmann, L. R., Kirwil, L., Felber, J., & Berger, A. (2011). Desensitization to media violence: Links with habitual media violence exposure, aggressive cognitions, and aggressive behavior. *Journal of Personality and Social Psychology, 100*(4), 630–646.

Kramer, A. F., Hahn, S., Irwin, D. E., & Theeuwes, J. (2000). Age differences in the control of looking behavior. *Psychological Science, 11*(3), 210–217.

Krantz, D. S., & McCeney, M. K. (2002). Effects of psychological and social factors on organic disease: A critical assessment of research on coronary heart disease. *Annual Review of Psychology, 1,* 341–369.

Kring, A. M., Johnson, S. L. Davison, G. C., & Neale, J. M. (2010). *Abnormal psychology* (11th ed.). Hoboken, NJ: Wiley.

Krishna, G. (1999). *The dawn of a new science.* Los Angeles, CA: Institute for Consciousness Research.

Kronenberger, W. G., Mathews, V. P., Dunn, D. W., Wang, Y., Wood, E. A., Larsen, J. J., … Lurito, J. T. (2005). Media violence exposure in aggressive and control adolescents: Differences in self- and parent-reported exposure to violence on television and in video games. *Aggressive Behavior, 31*(3), 201–216.

Krueger, J. I. (2007). From social projection to social behaviour. *European Review of Social Psychology, 18,* 1–35.

Krumpal, I. (2011). Determinants of social desirability bias in sensitive surveys: A literature review. *Quality & Quantity* (Online first).

Krusemark, E. A., Campbell, W. K., & Clementz, B. A. (2008). Attributions, deception, and event related potentials: An investigation of the self-serving bias. *Psychophysiology, 45,* 511–515.

Ksir, C. J., Hart, C. I., & Ray, O. S. (2008). *Drugs, society, and human behavior.* New York, NY: McGraw-Hill.

Kubiak, T., Vögele, C., Siering, M., Schiel, R., & Weber, H. (2008). Daily hassles and emotional eating in obese adolescents under restricted dietary conditions—The role of ruminative thinking. *Appetite, 51,* 206–209.

Kübler-Ross, E. (1983). *On children and death.* New York, NY: Macmillan.

Kübler-Ross, E. (1997). *Death: The final stage of growth.* New York, NY: Simon & Schuster.

Kübler-Ross, E. (1999). *On death and dying.* New York, NY: Simon & Schuster.

Kudo, E., & Numazaki, M. (2003). Explicit and direct self-serving bias in Japan. Reexamination of self-serving bias for success and failure. *Journal of Cross-Cultural Psychology, 34*(5), 511–521.

Kuffler, S. (1967). Neuroglial cells: physiological properties and a potassium mediated effect of neuronal activity on the glial membrane potential. *Proceedings of the Royal Society of London. Series B, Containing Papers of a Biological Character, 168*(10), 1–21.

Kuhn, C., Swartzwelder, S., & Wilson, W. (2003). *Buzzed: The straight facts about the most used and abused drugs from alcohol to ecstasy* (2nd ed.). New York, NY: Norton.

Kuhn, H., Dickinson-Anson, H., & Gage, F. (1996). Neurogenesis in the dentate gyrus of the adult rat: age-related decrease of neuronal progenitor proliferation. *Journal of Neuroscience, 16*(6), 2027–2033.

Kulik, L. (2005). Intrafamiliar congruence in gender role attitudes and ethnic stereotypes: The Israeli case. *Journal of Comparative Family Studies, 36*(2), 289–303.

Kumkale, G. T, & Albarracin, D. (2004). The sleeper effect in persuasion: A metaanalytic review. *Psychological Bulletin, 130*(1), 143–172.

Kuperstok, N. (2008). Effects of exposure to differentiated aggressive films, equated for levels of interest and excitation, and the vicarious hostility catharsis hypothesis. *Dissertation Abstracts International: Section B: The Sciences and Engineering 68*(7-B), 4806.

Kyle, A. (2009, August 1). Inkblot release sparks furor. *Regina Leader-Post.*

Kyriacou, C. P., & Hastings, M. H. (2010). Circadian clocks: genes, sleep, and cognition. *Trends in Cognitive Sciences*, *14*(6), 259–267.

L

Lachman, M. E. (2004). Development in midlife. *Annual Review of Psychology*, *55*, 305–331.

Lader, M. (2007). Limitations of current medical treatments for depression: Disturbed circadian rhythms as a possible therapeutic target. *European Neuropsychopharacology*, *17*, 743–755.

Lahav, O., & Mioduser, D. (2008). Haptic-feedback support for cognitive mapping of unknown spaces by people who are blind. *International Journal of Human-Computer Studies*, *66*, 23–35.

Lakein, A. (1998). *Give me a moment and I'll change your life: Tools for moment management.* New York, NY: Andrews McMeel Publishing.

Lamb, M. E., & Lewis, C. (2010). The development and significance of father-child relationships in two-parent families. In M. E. Lamb (Ed.), *The role of the father in child development* (5th ed., pp. 94–153). Hoboken, NJ: Wiley.

Lammers, J., & Stapel, D. (2011). Power increases dehumanization. *Group processes and intergroup relations*, *14*(1), 113–126.

Landeira-Fernandez, J. (2004). Analysis of the cold-water restraint procedure in gastric ulceration and body temperature. *Physiology & Behavior*, *82*(5), 827–833.

Lang, U. E., Bajbouj, M., Sander, T., & Gallinat, J. (2007). Gender-dependent association of the functional catechol-Omethyltransferase Val158Met genotype with sensation seeking personality trait. *Neuropsychopharmacology*, *32*, 1950–1955.

Langdon, K., & Corbett, D. (2012). Improved working memory following novel combinations of physical and cognitive activity. *Neurorehabilitation and Neural Repair*, *26*(5), 523–532.

Langenecker, S. A., Bieliauskas, L. A., Rapport, L. J., Zubieta, J-K., Wilde, E. A., & Berent, S. (2005). Face emotion perception and executive functioning deficits in depression. *Journal of Clinical & Experimental Neuropsychology*, *27*(3), 320–333.

Langlois, J. H., Kalakanis, L., Rubenstein, A. J., Larson, A., Hallam, M., & Smoot, M. (2000). Maxims or myths of beauty: A meta-analytic and theoretical review. *Psychological Bulletin*, *126*, 390–423.

Latané, B., & Darley, J. M. (1970). *The unresponsive bystander: Why doesn't he help?* New York, NY: Appleton-Century-Crofts.

Laungani, P. D. (2007). *Understanding cross-cultural psychology.* Thousand Oaks, CA: Sage.

Lavender, J., De Young, K., & Anderson, D. (2010). Eating Disorder Examination Questionnaire (EDE-Q): Norms for undergraduate men. *Eating Behaviors*, *11*(2), 119–121.

Lawrence, C., & Andrews, K. (2004). The influence of perceived prison crowding on male inmates' perception of aggressive events. *Aggressive Behavior*, *30*, 273–283.

Lawrence, M. (2008). Review of the bifurcation of the self: The history and theory of dissociation and its disorders. *American Journal of Clinical Hypnosis*, *50*, 281–282.

Lazar, S. W., Kerr, C. E., Wasserman, R. H., Gray, J. R., Greve, D. N., Treadway, M. T., ... Fischl, B. (2005). Meditation experience is associated with increased cortical thickness. *Neuroreport*, *16*(17), 1893–1897.

Le Moal, M. (2009). Drug abuse: Vulnerability and transition to addiction. *Pharmacopsychiatry*, *42*(0), S42–S55.

Leadbeater, B. (2008). Engaging community champions in the prevention of bullying. In D. Pepler & W. Craig, (Eds.), *Understanding and addressing bullying: An international perspective.* PREVNet Series (Vol. 1, pp.166–183). Bloomington, IN: AuthorHouse.

Leadbeater, B. (2010). The fickle fates of push and pull in the dissemination of mental health programs for children. *Canadian Psychology*, *51*, 221–230.

Leadbeater, B., & Hoglund, W. (2006). Changing the social contexts of peer victimization. *Journal of the Canadian Academy of Child and Adolescent Psychiatry*, *15*, 21–26.

Leaper, C., & Friedman, C. K. (2007). The socialization of gender. In J. Grusec & P. Hastings (Eds.), *Handbook of socialization: Theory and research* (pp. 561–587). New York, NY: Guilford Press.

Leaper, C., Breed, L., Hoffman, L., & Perlman, C. A. (2002). Variations in the gender-stereotyped content of children's television cartoons across genres. *Journal of Applied Social Psychology*, *32*, 1653–1662.

Leary, C. E., Kelley, M. L., Morrow, J., & Mikulka, P. J. (2008). Parental use of physical punishment as related to family environment, psychological well-being, and personality in undergraduates. *Journal of Family Violence*, *23*(1), 1–7.

Lecrubier, Y., Clerc, G., Didi, R., & Kieser, M. (2002). Efficacy of St. John's wort extract WS 5570 in major depression: A double-blind, placebo-controlled trial. *American Journal of Psychiatry*, *159*(8), 1361–1366.

LeDoux, J. (1996a). *The emotional brain: The mysterious underpinnings of emotional life.* New York, NY: Simon & Schuster.

LeDoux, J. E. (1996b). Sensory systems and emotion: A model of affective processing. *Integrative Psychiatry*, *4*, 237–243.

LeDoux, J. E. (1998). *The emotional brain.* New York, NY: Simon & Schuster.

LeDoux, J. E. (2002). *Synaptic self: How our brains become who we are.* New York, NY: Viking.

LeDoux, J. E. (2007). Emotional memory. *Scholarpedia, 2*, 180.

LeDoux, J. E., & Phelps, E. A. (2008). Emotional networks in the brain. In M. Lewis, J. M. Haviland-Jones, & L. Barrett (Eds.), *Handbook of emotions* (3rd ed., pp. 159–179). New York, NY: Guilford Press.

Lee, H., Lee, J., Lee, E., Lee, H., Kim, H., Lee, K., ... Ahn, K. (2009). Substance P and beta endorphin mediate electroacupuncture induced analgesic activity in mouse cancer pain model. *Acupuncture & Electro-Therapeutics Research*, *34*(1–2), 27–40.

Lee, J., Chen, L., Snieder, H., Chen, D., Lee, L., Liu, G., ... Hu, Y. (2010). Heritability of obesity-related phenotypes and association with adiponectin gene polymorphisms in the Chinese national twin registry. *Annals of Human Genetics*, *74*(2), 146–154.

Lee, J., Jiang, J., Sim, K., Tay, J., Subramaniam, M., & Chong, S. (2011). Gender differences in Singaporean Chinese patients with schizophrenia. *Asian Journal of Psychiatry*, *4*(1), 60–64.

Lee, J-H., Kwon, Y-D., Hong, S-H., Jeong, H-J., Kim, H-M., & Um, J-Y. (2008). Interleukin-1 beta gene polymorphism and traditional constitution in obese women. *International Journal of Neuroscience*, *118*, 793–805.

Lee, S. S. (2011). Deviant peer affiliation and antisocial behavior: Interaction with monoamine oxidase A (MAOA) genotype. *Journal of Abnormal Child Psychology*, *39*(3), 321–332.

Lee, S., Amis, T., Byth, K., Larcos, G., Kairaitis, K., Robinson, T., & Wheatley, J. (2008). Heavy snoring as a cause of carotid artery atherosclerosis. *Sleep*, *31*(9), 1207–1213.

Lee, W-Y. (2002). One therapist, four cultures: Working with families in Greater China. *Journal of Family Therapy*, *24*, 258–275.

Leffel, T. (2004). Eat where the locals eat. *Transitions Abroad.* Retrieved from http://www.transitionsabroad.com/publications/magazine/0405/eat_where_locals_eat.shtml

Lefley, H. P. (2000). Cultural perspectives on families, mental illness, and the law. *International Journal of Law and Psychiatry*, *23*, 229–243.

Leglise, A. (2008). *Progress in circadian rhythm research.* Hauppauge, NY: Nova Science.

Legrand, F. D., Gomà-i-freixanet, M., Kaltenbach, M. L., & Joly, P. M. (2007). Association between sensation seeking and alcohol consumption in French college students: Some ecological data collected in "open bar" parties. *Personality and Individual Differences*, *43*, 1950–1959.

Lehnert, G., & Zimmer, H. D. (2008). Modality and domain specific components in auditory and visual working memory tasks. *Cognitive Processing*, *9*, 53–61.

Lehto, S. M., Tolmunen, T., Joensuu, M., Saarinen, P. I., Valkonen-Korhonen, M., Vanninen, R., ... Lehtonen, J. (2008). Changes in midbrain serotonin transporter availability in atypically depressed subjects after one year of psychotherapy. *Progress in Neuro-Psychopharmacology & Biological Psychiatry*, *32*, 229–237.

Leichsenring, F., Leibing, E., Kruse, J., New, A., & Leweke, F. (2011). Borderline personality disorder. *The Lancet*, *377*(9759), 74–84.

Leichtman, M. D. (2006). Cultural and maturational influences on long-term event memory. In L. Balter & C. S. Tamis-LeMonda (Eds.), *Child psychology: A handbook of contemporary issues* (2nd ed., pp. 565–589). New York, NY: Psychology Press.

Lele, D. U. (2008). The influence of individual personality and attachment styles on romantic relationships (partner choice and couples' satisfaction). *Dissertation Abstracts International: Section B: The Sciences and Engineering*, *68*, 6316.

Leonard, B. E. (2003). *Fundamentals of psychopharmacology* (3rd ed.). Hoboken, NJ: Wiley.

Lepper, M. R., Greene, D., & Nisbett, R. E. (1973). Undermining children's intrinsic interest with extrinsic rewards: A test of the overjustification hypothesis. *Journal of Personality and Social Psychology*, *28*, 129–137.

Leri, A., Anversa, P., & Frishman, W. H. (Eds.). (2007). *Cardiovascular regeneration and stem cell therapy.* Hoboken, NJ: Wiley-Blackwell.

Lerner, H. D. (2008). Psychodynamic perspectives. In M. Hersen & A. M. Gross (Eds.), *Handbook of clinical psychology, vol 1: Adults* (pp. 127–160). Hoboken, NJ: Wiley.

Lerner, J. S., Gonzalez, R. M., Small, D. A., & Fischhoff, B. (2003). Effects of fear and anger on perceived risks of terrorism: A national field experiment. *Psychological Science, 14*, 144–150.

Leslie, M. (2000, July/August). The vexing legacy of Lewis Terman. *Stanford Magazine.* Retrieved from http://www.stanfordalumni.org/news/magazine/2000/julaug/articles/terman.html

Lett, D. (2009, March 6). Following voices. *National Post*, p. A7.

LeVay, S. (2003). Queer science: The use and abuse of research into homosexuality. *Archives of Sexual Behavior, 32*(2), 187–189.

LeVay, S., & Baldwin, J. (2012). *Human sexuality* (4th ed.). Sunderland, MA: Sinaeur Associates.

Levenson, R. W. (1992). Autonomic nervous system differences among emotions. *Psychological Science, 3*, 23–27.

Levenson, R. W. (2007). Emotion elicitation with neurological patients. In J. A. Coan & J. J. B. Allen (Eds.), *Handbook of emotion elicitation and assessment* (pp. 158–168). *Series in affective science.* New York, NY: Oxford University Press.

Leventhal, H., Weinman, J., Leventhal, E. A., & Phillips, L. A. (2008). Health psychology: The search for pathways between behavior and health. *Annual Review of Psychology, 59*, 477–505.

Levine, J. R. (2001). *Why do fools fall in love: Experiencing the magic, mystery, and meaning of successful relationships.* New York, NY: JosseyBass.

Levinson, D. J. (1977). The mid-life transition, *Psychiatry, 40*, 99–112.

Levinson, D. J. (1996). *The seasons of a woman's life.* New York, NY: Knopf.

Levinthal, C. (2008). *Drugs, behavior, and modern society* (5th ed.). Boston, MA: Allyn & Bacon.

Levitan, L. C. (2008). Giving prejudice an attitude adjustment: The implications of attitude strength and social network attitudinal composition for prejudice and prejudice reduction. *Dissertation Abstracts International: Section B: The Sciences and Engineering, 68*(8-B), 5634.

Levy, B., Wegman, D., Baron, S., & Sokas, R. (2011). *Occupational and environmental health: Recognizing and preventing disease and injury* (6th ed.). New York, NY: Oxford University Press.

Lew, A. R. (2011). Looking beyond the boundaries: Time to put landmarks back on the cognitive map? *Psychological Bulletin, 13*, 484–507.

Lewandowski, G. W. Jr., Aron, A., & Gee, J. (2007). Personality goes a long way: The malleability of opposite-sex physical attractiveness. *Personal Relationships, 14*, 571–585.

Lewis, C. (2009, August 29). Attempt to legalize euthanasia revived: Death by appointment. *National Post.*

Lewis, M. (2008). The emergence of human emotions. In M. Lewis, J. M. Haviland-Jones, & L. M. Barrett (Eds.) *Handbook of emotions* (3rd ed.) (pp. 304–319). New York, NY: Guilford.

Lewis, M. B., & Bowler, P. J. (2009). Botulinum toxin cosmetic therapy correlates with a more positive mood. *Journal of Cosmetic Dermatology, 8*(1), 24–26.

Lewis, S. (1963). *Dear Shari.* New York, NY: Stein & Day.

Libon, D. J., Xie, S. X., Moore, P., Farmer, J., Antani, S., McCawley, G., Cross, K., & Grossman, M. (2007). Patterns of neuropsychological impairment in fronto-temporal dementia. *Neurology, 68*, 369–375.

Library and Archives Canada. (2008). Famous Canadian physicians: Dr. Wilder Penfield. Retrieved from http://www.collectionscanada.gc.ca/physicians/030002-2400-e.html

Lieberman, P. (1998). *Eve spoke: Human language and human evolution.* New York, NY: Norton.

Lilienfeld, S. O., Lynn, S., Ruscio, J., & Beyerstein, B. L. (2010). 50 great myths of popular psychology: Shattering widespread misconceptions about human behavior. Oxford, England: Wiley-Blackwell.

Lin, Y., Reilly, M., & Mercer, V. S. (2010). Responses to a modified visual cliff by pre-walking infants born preterm and at term. *Physical & Occupational Therapy in Pediatrics, 30*(1), 66–78.

Lincoln, G. A. (1992). Biology of antlers. *Journal of Zoology, 226*(3), 517–528.

Linden, E. (1993). Can animals think? *Time, 141*(12), 54–61.

Links, P. S., Eynan, R., Heisel, M. J., & Nisenbaum, R. (2008). Elements of affective instability associated with suicidal behaviour in patients with borderline personality disorder. *Canadian Journal of Psychiatry, 53*, 112–116.

Linnet, J., Møller, A., Peterson, E., Gjedde, A., & Doudet, D. (2011). Dopamine release in ventral striatum during Iowa Gambling Task performance is associated with increased excitement levels in pathological gambling. *Addiction, 106*(2), 383–390.

Lippa, R. A. (2007). The preferred traits of mates in a cross-national study of heterosexual and homosexual men and women: An examination of biological and cultural influences. *Archives of Sexual Behavior, 36*, 193–208.

Lipsanen, T., Korkeila, J., Peltola, P., Järvinen, J., Langen, K., & Lauerma, H. (2004). Dissociative disorders among psychiatric patients: Comparison with a nonclinical sample. *European Psychiatry, 19*(1), 53–55.

Lissek, S., & Powers, A. S. (2003). Sensation seeking and startle modulation by physically threatening images. *Biological Psychology, 63*(2), 179–197.

Little, A., Jones, B., Waitt, C., Tiddeman, B., Feinberg, D., Perrett, D., Apicella, C., & Marlowe, F. (2008). Symmetry is related to sexual dimorphism in faces: Data across culture and species. *Plos One, 3*(5), e2106.

Liu, J. H., & Latané, B. (1998). Extremitization of attitudes: Does thought- and discussion-induced polarization cumulate? *Basic and Applied Social Psychology, 20*, 103–110.

Liu, Y.-F., Chen, H.-i., Wul, C.-L., Kuol, Y.-M., Yu, L., Huang, A.-M., ... Jen, C. J. (2009). Differential effects of treadmill running and wheel running on spatial or aversive learning and memory: Roles of amygdalar brain-derived neurotrophic factor and synaptotagmin I. *Journal of Physiology, 587*(13), 3221–3231.

Livesley, W. J., & Jackson, D. N. (2002). *Manual for the Dimensional Assessment of Personality Problems—Basic Questionnaire.* London, ON: Research Psychologists' Press.

Livingston, J. A. (1999). Something old and something new: Love, creativity, and the enduring relationship. *Bulletin of the Menninger Clinic, 63*, 40–52.

Livingston, R. W., & Drwecki, B. B. (2007). Why are some individuals not racially biased? Susceptibility to affective conditioning predicts nonprejudice toward Blacks. *Psychological Science, 18*, 816–823.

Lock, J., Agras, W. S., Bryson, S., & Kraemer, H. C. (2005). A comparison of short- and long-term family therapy for adolescent anorexia nervosa. *Journal of the American Academy of Child and Adolescent Psychiatry, 44*, 632–639.

Lodge, D. J., & Grace, A. A. (2011). Developmental pathology, dopamine, stress and schizophrenia. *International Journal of Developmental Neuroscience, 29*(3), 207–213.

Loehlin, J. C. (2000). Group differences in intelligence. In R. J. Sternberg (Ed.), *Handbook of intelligence.* New York, NY: Cambridge University Press.

Loewenthal, D., & Winter, D. (Eds.). (2006). *What is psychotherapeutic research?* London, England: Karnac Books.

Loftus, E. (1982). Memory and its distortions. In A. G. Kraut (Ed.), *The G. Stanley Hall Lecture Series Vol. 2* (pp. 123–154). Washington, DC: American Psychological Association.

Loftus, E. F. (2000). Remembering what never happened. In E. Tulving, et al. (Eds.), *Memory, consciousness, and the brain: The Tallinn Conference*, pp. 106–118. Philadelphia: Psychology Press/Taylor & Francis.

Loftus, E. F. (2001). Imagining the past. *Psychologist, 14*(11), 584–587.

Loftus, E. F. (2007). Memory distortions: Problems solved and unsolved. In M. Garry & H. Hayne (Eds.), *Do justice and let the skies fall.* Mahwah, NJ: Erlbaum.

Loftus, E. F., & Cahill, L. (2007). Memory distortion from misattribution to rich false memory. In J. S. Nairne (Ed.), *The foundations of remembering: Essays in honor of Henry L. Roediger, III* (pp. 413–425). New York, NY: Psychology Press.

Loftus, E., & Ketcham, K. (1994). *The myth of repressed memories: False memories and allegations of sexual abuse.* New York, NY: St. Martin's Press.

Loftus, G. (2010). What can a perception-memory expert tell a jury? *Psychonomic Bulletin & Review, 17*(2), 143–148.

Loo, C. K., Mahon, M., Katalinic, N., Lyndon, B., & Hadzi-Pavlovic, D. (2011). Predictors of response to ultra-brief right unilateral electroconvulsive therapy. *Journal of Affective Disorders, 130*(1–2), 192–197.

Lopez-Munoz, F., & Alamo, C. (2011). *Neurobiology of depression.* Boca Raton, FL: CRC Press.

Lorenz, K. Z. (1937). The companion in the bird's world. *Auk, 54*, 245–273.

Lores-Arnaiz, S., Bustamante, J., Czernizyniec, A., Galeano, P., Gervasoni, M. G., Martinez, A. R., Paglia, N., Cores, V, & Lores-Arnaiz, M. R. (2007) . Exposure to enriched environments increases brain nitric oxide synthase and improves cognitive performance in prepubertal but not in young rats. *Behavioural Brain Research, 184*, 117–123.

Loriaux, D. L. (2008). Historical note: Hans Hugo Bruno Seyle (1907–1982). *The Endocrinologist, 18*(2), 53–54.

Lott, D. A. (2000). *The new flirting game.* London, England: Sage.

Lottery Canada. (2011). *Lotto 6/49.* Retrieved from http://www.lotterycanada.com/lotto-649

Loxton, N. J., Nguyen, D., Casey, L., & Dawe, S. (2008) . Reward drive, rash impulsivity and punishment sensitivity in problem gamblers. *Personality & Individual Differences, 45,* 167–173.

Lu, Z. L., Williamson, S. J., & Kaufman, L. (1992). Behavioral lifetime of human auditory sensory memory predicted by physiological measures. *Science, 258,* 1668–1670.

Lubinski, D., & Benbow, C. P. (2000). States of excellence. *American Psychologist, 55*(1), 137–150.

Luecken, L. J., & Lemery, K. S. (2004). Early caregiving and physiological stress responses. *Clinical Psychology Review, 24*(2), 171–191.

Lung Association. (2011). Smoking and tobacco. Retrieved from http://lung.ca/protect-protegez/ tobacco-tabagisme/quitting-cesser/how-comment_e.php#proven

Lunn, J., Sakowski, S., Federici, T., Glass, J., Boulis, N., & Feldman, E. (2011). Stem cell technology for the study and treatment of motor neuron diseases. *Regenerative Medicine, 6*(2), 201–213.

Lupien, S., McEwen, B., Gunnar, M., & Heim, C. (2009). Effects of stress throughout the lifespan on the brain, behaviour and cognition. *Nature Reviews. Neuroscience, 10*(6), 434–445.

Luria, A. R. (1968). *The mind of a mnemonist: A little book about a vast memory.* New York, NY: Basic Books.

Lynn, S. J. (2007). Hypnosis reconsidered. *American Journal of Clinical Hypnosis, 49,* 195–197.

Lyons-Ruth, K., Holmes, B. M., Sasvari-Szekely, M., Ronai, Z., Nemoda, Z., & Pauls, D. (2007). Serotonin transporter polymorphism and borderline or antisocial traits among low-income young adults. *Psychiatric Genetics, 17,* 339–343.

Lyoo, I. K., Kim, M. J., Stoll, A. L., Demopulos, C. M., Parow, A. M., Dager, … Renshaw, P. F. (2004). Frontal lobe gray matter density decreases in bipolar I disorder. *Biological Psychiatry, 55*(6), 648–651.

Lyubimov, N. N. (1992). *Electrophysiological characteristics of sensory processing and mobilization of hidden brain reserves. 2nd Russian-Swedish Symposium New Research in Neurobiology.* Moscow: Russian Academy of Science Institute of Human Brain.

M

Maas, J. B. (1999). *Power sleep.* New York, NY: HarperPerennial.

Maas, J., B., Wherry, M. L., Axelrod, D. J., Hogan, B. R., & Bloomin, J. (1999). *Power sleep: The revolutionary program that prepares your mind for peak performance.* New York, NY: HarperPerennial.

Machelska, H., Cabot, P. J., Mousa, S. A., Zhang, Q., & Stein, C. (1998). Pain control in inflammation governed by selectins. *Nature Medicine, 4*(12), 1425.

Macmillan, M. B. (2000). *An odd kind of fame: Stories of Phineas Gage.* Cambridge, MA: MIT Press.

Maddi, S. R., Harvey, R. H., Khoshaba, D. M., Lu, J. L., Persico, M., & Brow, M. (2006). The personality construct of hardiness, III: Relationships with repression, innovativeness, authoritarianism, and performance. *Journal of Personality, 74,* 575–597.

Maehr, M. L., & Urdan, T. C. (2000). *Advances in motivation and achievement: The role of context.* Greenwich, CT: JAI Press.

Maisto, S. A., Galizio, M., & Connors, G. J. (2008). *Drug use and abuse* (5th ed.). Belmont, CA: Cengage.

Major, B., Spencer, S., Schmader, T., Wolfe, C., & Crocker, J. (1998). Coping with negative stereotypes about intellectual performance: The role of psychological disengagement. *Personality & Social Psychology Bulletin, 24*(1), 34–50.

Malo, A. F., Roldan, E. S., Garde, J., Soler, A. J., & Gomendio, M. (2005). Antlers honestly advertise sperm production and quality. *Royal Society of London. Proceedings: Biological Sciences, 272*(1559), 149–157.

Maner, J. K., DeWall, C. N., & Gailliot, M. T. (2008). Selective attention to signs of success: Social dominance and early stage interpersonal perception. *Personality and Social Psychology Bulletin, 34,* 488–501.

Manly, J. J., Byrd, D., Touradji, P., Sanchez, D., & Stern, Y. (2004). Literacy and cognitive change among ethnically diverse elders. *International Journal of Psychology, 39*(1), 47–60.

Manning, J. (2007). The use of meridian-based therapy for anxiety and phobias. *Australian Journal of Clinical Hypnotherapy and Hypnosis, 28,* 45–50.

Marchand, A., & Blanc, M. (2011). Occupation, work organisation conditions and the development of chronic psychological distress. *Work, 40*(4), 425–435.

Maren, S., Yap, S., & Goosens, K. (2001). The amygdala is essential for the development of neuronal plasticity in the medial geniculate nucleus during auditory fear conditioning in rats. *The Journal of Neuroscience: The Official Journal of the Society for Neuroscience, 21*(6), RC135.

Markham, J. A., & Koenig, J. I. (2011). Prenatal stress: Role in psychotic and depressive diseases. *Psychopharmacology, 214*(1), 89–106.

Markle, A. (2007). Asymmetric disconfirmation in managerial beliefs about employee motivation. *Dissertation Abstracts International Section A: Humanities and Social Sciences, 68*(5-A), 2051.

Markovitz, P. J. (2004). Recent trends in the pharmacotherapy of personality disorders. *Journal of Personality Disorders, 18*(1), 99–101.

Marks, L. D., Hopkins, K. C., Monroe, P. A., Nesteruk, O., & Sasser, D. D. (2008). "Together, we are strong": A qualitative study of happy, enduring African American marriages. *Family Relations, 57,* 172–185.

Markstrom, C. A., & Marshall, S. K. (2007). The psychosocial inventory of ego strengths: Examination of theory and psychometric properties. *Journal of Adolescence, 30,* 63–79.

Markus, H. R., & Kitayama, S. (1998). The cultural psychology of personality. *Journal of Cross-Cultural Psychology, 29,* 63–87.

Marques, L., Robinaugh, D., LeBlanc, N., & Hinton, D. (2011). Cross-cultural variations in the prevalence and presentation of anxiety disorders. *Expert Review of Neurotherapeutics, 11*(2), 313–322.

Marsh, H. W., Trautwein, U., Lüdtke, O., Köller, O., & Baumert, J. (2005). Academic self-concept, interest, grades, and standardized test scores: Reciprocal effects models of causal ordering. *Child Development, 76,* 397–416.

Marshall, K. (2006). *Converging gender roles* (Cat. no. 75-001-XIE). Ottawa, ON: Statistics Canada.

Marshall, L., & Born, J. (2007). The contribution of sleep to hippocampus-dependent memory consolidation. *Trends in Cognitive Sciences, 11,* 442–450.

Marshall, M., & Brown, J. D. (2008). On the psychological benefits of self-enhancement. In E. C. Chang (Ed.), *Self-criticism and self-enhancement: Theory, research, and clinical implications* (pp. 19–35). Washington, DC: American Psychological Association.

Martensville saga ends. (2006). *The StarPhoenix (Saskatoon).* Retrieved from http://www. canada.com/saskatoonstarphoenix/news/ story.html?id=9ec972d8-8782-41fc-ac78-ed9e29270ef9&k=48902&p=1

Martin, C. L., & Fabes, R. (2009). *Discovering child development* (2nd ed.). Belmont, CA: Cengage.

Martin, C. L., Ruble, D. N., & Szkrybalo, J. (2002). Cognitive theories of early gender development. *Psychological Bulletin, 128,* 903–933.

Martin, S. E., Snyder, L. B., Hamilton, M., Fleming-Milici, F., Slater, M. D., Stacy, A., Chen, M., & Grube, J. W. (2002). Alcohol advertising and youth. *Alcoholism: Clinical & Experimental Research, 26*(6), 900–906.

Martineau, J., Cochin, S., Magne, R., & Barthelemy, C. (2008). Impaired cortical activation in autistic children: Is the mirror neuron system involved? *International Journal of Psychophysiology, 68,* 35–40.

Marvin, R. S., & Britner, P. A. (2008). Normative development: The ontogeny of attachment. In J. Cassidy & P. R. Shaver (Eds.), *Handbook of attachment: Theory, research, and clinical applications* (2nd ed., pp. 269–294). New York, NY: Guilford.

Marx, D. M., Ko, S. J., & Friedman, R. A. (2009). The "Obama effect": How a salient role model reduces race-based performance differences. *Journal of Experimental Social Psychology, 45,* 953–956.

Maslow, A. H. (1954). *Motivation and personality.* New York, NY: Harper & Row.

Maslow, A. H. (1970). *Motivation and personality* (2nd ed.). New York, NY: Harper & Row.

Maslow, A. H. (1999). *Toward a psychology of being* (3rd ed.). New York, NY: Wiley.

Mason, M. F., & Morris, M. W. (2010). Culture, attribution and automaticity: A social cognitive neuroscience view. *Social Cognitive and Affective Neuroscience, 5*(2–3), 292–306.

Massicotte-Marquez, J., Décary, A., Gagnon, J. F., Vendette, M., Mathieu, A., Postuma, R. B., Carrier, J., & Montplaisir, J. (2008). Executive dysfunction and memory impairment in idiopathic REM sleep behavior disorder. *Neurology, 70,* 1250–1257.

Masters, W. H., & Johnson, V. E. (1961). Orgasm, anatomy of the female. In A. Ellis & A. Abarbonel (Eds.), *Encyclopedia of Sexual Behavior* (Vol. 2). New York, NY: Hawthorn.

Masters, W. H., & Johnson, V. E. (1966). *Human sexual response.* Boston, MA: Little, Brown.

Masters, W. H., & Johnson, V. E. (1970). *Human sexual inadequacy.* Boston, MA: Little, Brown.

Mathews, A., & MacLeod, C. (2005). Cognitive vulnerability to emotional disorders. *Annual Review of Clinical Psychology, 1,* 167–195.

Mathiesen, E. B., Johnsen, S. H., Wilsgaard, T., Bonaa, K. H., Lochen, M., & Njolstad, I. (2011). Cartoid plaque area and intima-media thickness in prediciton of first-ever ischemic stroke, A 10-year follow-up of 6584 men and women: The Tromso study. *Stroke, 42*, 972–978.

Mathy, F., & Feldman, J. (2012). What's magic about magic numbers? Chunking and data compression in short-term memory. *Cognition, 122*(3), 346–362.

Mateer, C. A., & Kerns, K. A. (2000). Capitalizing on neuroplasticity. *Brain and Cognition, 42*, 106–109.

Matlin, M. W. (2012). *The psychology of women* (7th ed.). Belmont, CA: Cengage.

Matlin, M. W., & Foley, H. J. (1997). *Sensation and perception* (4th ed.). Boston, MA: Allyn and Bacon.

Matos, G., Tufik, S., Scorza, F. A., Cavalheiro, E. A., & Andersen, M. L. (2011). Sleep, epilepsy and translational research: What can we learn from the laboratory bench? *Progress in Neurobiology, 95*(3), 396–405.

Matousek, R., Pruessner, J., & Dobkin, P. (2011). Changes in the cortisol awakening response (CAR) following participation in mindfulness-based stress reduction in women who completed treatment for breast cancer. *Complementary Therapies in Clinical Practice, 17*(2), 65–70.

Matsumoto, D. (2000). *Culture and psychology: People around the world.* Belmont, CA: Wadsworth.

Matsumoto, D., & Juang, L. (2008). *Culture and psychology* (4th ed.). Belmont, CA: Cengage.

Matthews, J. (2005). The political foundations of support for same-sex marriage in Canada. *Canadian Journal of Political Science, 38*(4), 841–866.

Matusov, E., & Hayes, R. (2000). Sociocultural critique of Piaget and Vygotsky. *New Ideas in Psychology, 18*(2–3), 215–239.

Maurer, D., & Lewis, T. L. (2001). Visual acuity and spatial contrast sensitivity: Normal development and underlying mechanisms. In C. A. Nelson & M. Luciana (Eds.), *Handbook of developmental cognitive neuroscience* (pp. 237–251). Cambridge, MA: MIT Press.

Maxson, S. C., & Canastar, A. (2007). The genetics of aggression in mice. In D. J. Flannery, A. T. Vazsonyi, & I. D. Waldman (Eds.), *The Cambridge handbook of violent behavior and aggression* (pp. 91–110). New York, NY: Cambridge University Press.

May, A., Hajak, G., Gänssbauer, S., Steffens, T., Langguth, B., Kleinjung, T., & Eichhammer, P. (2007). Structural brain alterations following 5 days of intervention: Dynamic aspects of neuroplasticity. *Cerebral Cortex, 17*, 205–210.

Mayer, J. D., Roberts, R. D., & Barsade, S. G. (2008). Human abilities: Emotional intelligence. *Annual Review of Psychology, 59*, 507–536.

Maynard, A. E, & Greenfield, P. M. (2003). Implicit cognitive development in cultural tools and children: Lessons from Maya Mexico. *Cognitive Development, 18*(4), 489–510.

Mazzoni, G., & Memon, A. (2003). Imagination can create false autobiographical memories. *Psychological Science, 14*, 186–188.

Mazzoni, G., & Vannucci, M. (2007). Hindsight bias, the misinformation effect, and false autobiographical memories. *Social Cognition, 25*, 203–220.

Mazzoni, G., Heap, M., & Scoboria, A. (2010). Hypnosis and memory: Theory, laboratory research, and applications. In S. Lynn, J. W. Rhue, & I. Kirsch (Eds.), *Handbook of clinical hypnosis* (2nd ed., pp. 709–741). Washington, DC: American Psychological Association.

McAllister-Williams, R. H., & Rugg, M. D. (2002). Effects of repeated cortisol administration on brain potential correlates of episodic memory retrieval. *Psychopharmacology, 160*(1), 74–83.

McAuliff, B. D., & Groscup, J. L. (2009). Daubert and psychological science in court: Judging validity from the bench, bar, and jury box. In J. L. Skeem and S. O. Lilienfeld (Eds.), *Psychological science in the courtroom: Consensus and controversy* (pp. 26–52). New York, NY: Guilford Press.

McCabe, C., & Rolls, E. T. (2007). Umami: A delicious flavor formed by convergence of taste and olfactory pathways in the human brain. *European Journal of Neuroscience, 25*, 1855–1864.

McClelland, D. C. (1958). Risk-taking in children with high and low need for achievement. In J. W. Atkinson (Ed.), *Motives in fantasy, action, and society.* Princeton, NJ: Van Nostrand.

McClelland, D. C. (1987). Characteristics of successful entrepreneurs. *Journal of Creative Behavior, 3*, 219–233.

McClelland, D. C. (1993). Intelligence is not the best predictor of job performance. *Current Directions in Psychological Science, 2*, 5–6.

McClintock, M. (1971). Menstrual synchrony and suppression. *Nature, 229*(5285), 244–245.

McClure, J., Meyer, L. H., Garisch, J., Fischer, R., Weir, K. F., & Walkey, F. H. (2011). Students' attributions for their best and worst marks: Do they relate to achievement? *Contemporary Educational Psychology, 36*(2), 71–81.

McCrae, R. R. (2004). Human nature and culture: A trait perspective. *Journal of Research in Personality, 38*(1), 3–14.

McCrae, R. R., & Costa, P. T. Jr. (1990). *Personality in adulthood.* New York, NY: Guilford Press.

McCrae, R. R., & Costa, P. T. Jr. (1999). A fivefactor theory of personality. In L. A. Pervin & O. P. John (Eds.), *Handbook of personality: Theory and research.* New York, NY: Guilford Press.

McCrae, R. R., & Sutin, A. R. (2007). New frontiers for the five-factor model: A preview of the literature. *Social and Personality Psychology Compass, 1*, 423–440.

McCrae, R. R., Costa, P. T. Jr., Hrebicková, M., Urbánek, T., Martin, T. A., Oryol, V. E., Rukavishnikov, A. A., & Senin, I. G. (2004). Age differences in personality traits across cultures: Self-report and observer perspectives. *European Journal of Personality, 18*(2), 143–157.

McCrae, R. R., Costa, P. T. Jr., Martin, T. A., Oryol, V. E., Rukavishnikov, A. A., Senin, I. G., Hrebicková, M., & Urbánek, T. (2004). Consensual validation of personality traits across cultures. *Journal of Research in Personality, 38*(2), 179–201.

McCrae, R. R., Costa, P. T. Jr., Ostendorf, F., Angleitner, A., Hrebickova, M., Avia, M. D., … Smith, P. B. (2000). Nature over nurture: Temperament, personality, and life span development. *Journal of Personality and Social Psychology, 78*(1), 173–186.

McDonald, J. W., Liu, X. Z., Qu, Y., Liu, S., Mickey, S. K., Turetsky, D., Gottlieb, D. I., & Choi, D. W. (1999). Transplanted embryonic stem cells survive, differentiate, and promote recovery in injured rat spinal cord. *Nature & Medicine, 5*, 1410–1412.

McDougall, W. (1908). *Social psychology.* New York, NY: Putnam's Sons.

McEvoy, P. M. (2007). Effectiveness of cognitive behavioural group therapy for social phobia in a community clinic: A benchmarking study. *Behaviour Research and Therapy, 45*, 3030–3040.

McFarlane, W. R. (2006). Family expressed emotion prior to onset of psychosis. In S. R. H. Beach, M. Z. Wamboldt, N. J. Kaslow, R. E. Heyman, M. B. First, L. G. Underwood, & D. Reiss (Eds.), *Relational processes and DSM-V: Neuroscience, assessment, prevention, and treatment* (pp. 77–87). Washington, DC: American Psychiatric Association.

McGrath, J. (2011). Environmental risk factors for schizophrenia. In D. Weinberger & P. Harrison (Eds.), *Schizophrenia* (3rd ed., pp. 226–244). Hoboken, NJ: Wiley.

McGrath, J. M. (2009). Touch and massage in the newborn period. Effects on biomarkers and brain development. *Journal of Perinatal and Neonatal Nursing, 23*, 304–306.

McGrath, P. (2002). Qualitative findings on the experience of end-of-life care for hematological malignancies. *American Journal of Hospice & Palliative Care, 19*(2), 103–111.

McGue, M., Bouchard, T. J., Iacono, W. G., & Lykken, D. T. (1993). Behavioral genetics of cognitive ability: A life-span perspective. In R. Plomin & G. McClearn (Eds.), *Nature, nurture, and psychology.* Washington, DC: American Psychological Association.

McHale, S. M., Crouter, A. C., & Whiteman, S. D. (2003). The family contexts of gender development in childhood and adolescence. *Social Development, 12*, 125–148.

McHale, S. M., Updegraff, K. A., Helms-Erikson, H., & Crouter, A. C. (2001). Sibling influences on gender development in middle childhood and early adolescence: A longitudinal study. *Developmental Psychology, 37*, 115–125.

McIntyre, M. (2009a, March 5). Fateful meeting on Greyhound. *Winnipeg Free Press.* Retrieved from http://www.winnipegfreepress.com/local/fateful_meeting_on_greyhound-40702917.html

McIntyre, M. (2009b, March 6). Li found not criminally responsible. *National Post*, p. A7.

McKellar, P. (1972). Imagery from the standpoint of introspection. In P. W. Sheehan (Ed.), *The function and nature of imagery* (pp. 35–61). New York, NY: Academic Press.

McKenna, J. J., & Volpe, L. E. (2007). Sleeping with baby: An internet-based sampling of parental experiences, choices, perceptions, and interpretations in a Western industrialized context. *Infant and Child Development, 16*, 359–385.

McKeown, B. (Writer) & Rumak, O. (Director). (2010). Above suspicion: The shocking case of Russell Williams (Television series episode). In J. Williamson (Executive producer), *The Fifth Estate.* Toronto, ON: CBC. Retrieved from http://www.cbc.ca/fifth/2010-2011/abovesuspicion/

McKim, W. A. (2002). *Drugs and behavior: An introduction to behavioral pharmacology* (5th ed.). Englewood Cliffs, NJ: Prentice Hall.

McKinney, W. (2001). Overview of the past contributions of animal models and their changing place in psychiatry. *Seminars in Clinical Neuropsychiatry, 6*(1), 68–78.

McNeil, R., & Guirguis-Younger, M. (2012). Illicit drug use as a challenge to the delivery of end-of-life care services to homeless persons. *Palliative Medicine, 26,* 350–359.

McNicholas, W. T, & Javaheri, S. (2007). Pathophysiologic mechanisms of cardiovascular disease in obstructive sleep apnea. *Sleep Medicine Clinics, 2,* 539–547.

McReynolds, J. R., Donowho, K., Abdi, A., McGaugh, J. L., Roozendaal, B., & McIntyre, C. K. (2010). Memory-enhancing corticosterone treatment increases amygdala norepinephrine and Arc protein expression in hippocampal synaptic fractions. *Neurobiology of Learning & Memory, 93*(3), 312–321.

Medina, J. J. (1996). *The clock of ages: Why we age.* Cambridge, MA: Cambridge University Press.

Meijer, E. H., & Verschuere, B. (2010). The polygraph and the detection of deception. *Journal of Forensic Psychology Practice, 10*(4), 325–338.

Metcalf, P., & Huntington, R. (1991). *Celebrations of death: The anthropology of mortuary ritual* (2nd ed.). Cambridge, England: Cambridge University Press.

Meltzoff, A. N., & Moore, M. K. (1985). Cognitive foundations and social functions of imitation and intermodal representation in infancy. In J. Mehler & R. Fox (Eds.), *Neonate cognition: Beyond the blooming buzzing confusion* (pp. 139–156). Hillsdale, NJ: Erlbaum.

Meltzoff, A. N., & Moore, M. K. (1994). Imitation, memory, and the representation of persons. *Infant Behavior and Development, 17,* 83–99.

Meltzer, G. (2000). Genetics and etiology of schizophrenia and bipolar disorder. *Biological Psychiatry, 47*(3), 171–178.

Meltzer, L. (2004). Resilience and learning disabilities: Research on internal and external protective dynamics. *Learning Disabilities Research & Practice, 19*(1), 1–2.

Meltzoff, A. N., & Moore, M. K. (1977). Imitation of facial and manual gestures by human neonates. *Science, 198,* 75–78.

Melzack, R. (1999). Pain and stress: A new perspective. In R. J. Gatchel & D. C. Turk (Eds.), *Psychosocial factors in pain: Critical perspectives.* New York, NY: Guilford Press.

Melzack, R., & Wall, P. D. (1965). Pain mechanisms: A new theory. *Science, 150,* 971–979.

Menezes, A., Lavie, C., Milani, R., O'Keefe, J., & Lavie, T. (2011). Psychological risk factors and cardiovascular disease: Is it all in your head? *Postgraduate Medicine, 123*(5), 165–176.

Merabet, L. B., & Pascual-Leone, A. (2010). Neural reorganization following sensory loss: The opportunity of change. *Nature Reviews Neuroscience, 11*(1), 44–52.

Merrill, D. A., & Small, G. W. (2011). Prevention in psychiatry: Effects of healthy lifestyle on cognition. *Psychiatric Clinics of North America, 34*(1), 249–261.

Mertens, R., & Allen, J. B. (2008). The role of psychophysiology in forensic assessments: Deception detection, ERPs, and virtual reality mock crime scenarios. *Psychophysiology, 45*(2), 286–298.

Meyer, J. F, Parsons, P., & Dunne, T. T. (1990). Individual study orchestrations and their association with learning outcome. *Higher Education, 20*(1), 67–89.

Meyer, U., Nyffeler, M., Schwendener, S., Knuesel, I., Yee, B. K., & Feldon, J. (2008). Relative prenatal and postnatal maternal contributions to schizophrenia-related neurochemical dysfunction after in utero immune challenge. *Neuropsychopharmacology, 33,* 441–456.

Michaels, K. B. (2000). Prospective study of fruit and vegetable consumption and incidence of colon and rectal cancers. *Journal of the National Cancer Institute, 92*(21), 1740–1752.

Michon, C. C., O'Sullivan, M. G., Delahunty, C. M., & Kerry, J. P. (2009). The investigation of gender-related sensitivity differences in food perception. *Journal of Sensory Studies, 24*(6), 922–937.

Mignot, E. (2010). Narcolepsy: Genetic predisposition and pathophysiology. In M. Goswami, S. R. Pandi-Perumal, & M. J. Thorpy (Eds.), *Narcolepsy: A clinical guide* (pp. 3–21). Totowa, NJ: Humana Press.

Migueles, M., & Garcia-Bajos, E. (1999). Recall, recognition, and confidence patterns in eyewitness testimony. *Applied Cognitive Psychology, 13,* 257–268.

Mikulincer, M., & Goodman, G. S. (Eds.). (2006). *Dynamics of romantic love: Attachment, caregiving, and sex.* New York, NY: Guilford Press.

Milgram, S. (1963). Behavioral study of obedience. *Journal of Abnormal and Social Psychology, 67,* 371–378.

Milgram, S. (1974). *Obedience to authority: An experimental view.* New York, NY: Harper & Row.

Miller, G. A. (1956). The magical number seven, plus or minus two: Some limits on our capacity for processing information. *Psychological Review, 63,* 81–97.

Miller, G. E., Chen, E., & Parker, K. J. (2011). Psychological stress in childhood and susceptibility to the chronic diseases of aging: Moving toward a model of behavioral and biological mechanisms. *Psychological Bulletin, 137*(6), 959–997.

Miller, G. E., Chen, E., Sze, J., Marin, T., Arevalo, J. G., Doll, R., Ma, R., & Cole, S. W. (2008). A functional genomic fingerprint of chronic stress in humans: Blunted glucocorticoid and increased NF-κ signaling. *Biological Psychiatry, 64*(4), 266–272.

Miller, J. G. (2006). Insights into moral development from cultural psychology. In M. Killen & J. G. Smetana (Eds.), *Handbook of moral development* (pp. 375–398). Mahwah, NJ: Erlbaum.

Miller, J. G., & Bersoff, D. M. (1998). The role of liking in perceptions of the moral responsibility of help: A cultural perspective. *Journal of Experimental Social Psychology, 34,* 443–469.

Miller, L. K. (2005). What the savant syndrome can tell us about the nature and nurture of talent. *Journal for the Education of the Gifted, 28,* 361–373.

Millon, T. (2004). *Masters of the mind: Exploring the story of mental illness from ancient times to the new millennium.* Hoboken, NJ: Wiley.

Miltenberger, R. G. (2011). *Behavior modification: Principles and procedures* (5th ed.). Belmont, CA: Cengage.

Milton, J., & Wiseman, R. (1999). Does psi exist? Lack of replication of an anomalous process of information transfer. *Psychological Bulletin, 125,* 387–391.

Milton, J., & Wiseman, R. (2001). Does psi exist? Reply to Storm and Ertel 2000. *Psychological Bulletin, 127*(3), 434–438.

Mineka, S., & Oehlberg, K. (2008). The relevance of recent developments in classical conditioning to understanding the etiology and maintenance of anxiety disorders. *Acta Psychologica, 127,* 567–580.

Mineka, S., & Ohman, A. (2002). Phobias and preparedness: The selective, automatic, and encapsulated nature of fear. *Biological Psychiatry, 51*(9), 927–937.

Ming, G., & Song, H. (2005). Adult neurogenesis in the mammalian central nervous system. *Annual Review of Neuroscience, 28,* 223–250.

Mingo, C., Herman, C. J., & Jasperse, M. (2000). Women's stories: Ethnic variations in women's attitudes and experiences of menopause, hysterectomy, and hormone replacement therapy. *Journal of Women's Health and Gender Based Medicine, 9,* S27–S38.

Mingroni, M. A. (2004). The secular rise in IQ. *Intelligence, 32,* 65–83.

Mirescu, C., Peters, J. D., Noiman, L., & Gould, E. (2006). Sleep deprivation inhibits adult neurogenesis in the hippocampus by elevating glucocorticoids. *PNAS Proceedings of the National Academy of Sciences of the United States of America, 103*(50), 19170–19175.

Mischel, W., Shoda, Y., & Ayduk, O. (2008). *Introduction to personality: Toward an integrative science of the person* (8th ed.). Hoboken, NJ: Wiley.

Mita, T. H., Dermer, M., & Knight, J. (1977). Reversed facial images and the mere-exposure hypothesis. *Journal of Personality and Social Psychology, 35*(8), 597–601.

Mitchell, B. A., & Lovegreen, L. D. (2009). The empty nest syndrome in midlife families: A multimethod exploration of parental gender differences and cultural dynamics. *Journal of Family Issues, 30,* 1651–1670.

Mitchell, E. A., & Milerad, J. (2006). Smoking and sudden infant death syndrome. *Reviews on Environmental Health, 21,* 81–103.

Mitchell, J. P., Dodson, C. S., & Schacter, D. L. (2005). fMRI evidence for the role of recollection in suppressing misattribution errors: The illusory truth effect. *Journal of Cognitive Neuroscience, 17,* 800–810.

Mitchell, R. (2003). Ideological reflections on the *DSM-IV-R* (or pay no attention to that man behind the curtain, Dorothy!). *Child & Youth Care Forum, 32*(5), 281–298.

Mithoefer, A. T., Jerome, L., & Doblin, R. (2011). The safety and efficacy of ±3, 4-methylenedioxymethamphetamine-assisted psychotherapy in subjects with chronic, treatment-resistant posttraumatic stress disorder: the first randomized controlled pilot study. *Journal of Psychopharmacology, 25*(4), 439–452.

Mittag, O., & Maurischat, C. (2004). Die CookMedley Hostility Scale (Ho-Skala) im Vergleich zu den Inhaltsskalen "Zynismus," "Ärger," sowie "Typ A" aus dem MMPI-2: Zur zukünftigen Operationalisierung von Feindseligkeit (A comparison of the Cook-Medley Hostility Scale (Ho-scale) and the content scales "cynicism," "anger," and "type A" out of the MMPI-2: On the future assessment of hostility). *Zeitschrift für Medizinische Psychologie, 13*(1), 7–12.

Miyake, N., Thompson, J., Skinbjerg, M., & Abi-Dargham, A. (2011). Presynaptic dopamine in schizophrenia. *CNS Neuroscience & Therapeutics, 17*(2), 104–109.

Mogil, J. S., Davis, K. D., & Derbyshire, S. W. (2010). The necessity of animal models in pain research. *Pain, 151*(1), 12–17.

Mograss, M. A., Guillem, F., & Godbout, R. (2008). Event-related potentials differentiates the processes involved in the effects of sleep on recognition memory. *Psychophysiology, 45*, 420–434.

Mohan, A., Sharma, R., & Bijlani, R. L. (2011). Effect of meditation on stress-induced changes in cognitive functions. *Journal of Alternative & Complementary Medicine, 17*(3), 207–212.

Möhler, H., Rudolph, U., Boison, D., Singer, P., Feldon, J., & Yee, B. K. (2008). Regulation of cognition and symptoms of psychosis: Focus on GABA-sub(A) receptors and glycine transporter 1. *Pharmacology, Biochemistry & Behavior, 90*, 58–64.

Mondimore, F., & Kelly, P. (2011). *Borderline personality disorder: New reasons for hope.* Baltimore, MD: Johns Hopkins University Press.

Moneta, G. B., & Siu, C. M. Y. (2002). Trait intrinsic and extrinsic motivations, academic performance, and creativity in Hong Kong college students. *Journal of College Student Development, 43*(5), 664–683.

Monin, B. (2003). The warm glow heuristic: When liking leads to familiarity. *Journal of Personality and Social Psychology, 85*(6), 1035–1048.

Monks, C. P., Ortega-Ruiz, R., & Rodriguez-Hidalgo, A. J. (2008). Peer victimization in multicultural schools in Spain and England. *European Journal of Developmental Psychology, 5*, 507–535.

Montgomery, S. A. (2008). The under-recognized role of dopamine in the treatment of major depressive disorder. *International Clinical Psychopharmacology, 23*, 63–69.

Moore, M. M. (1998). The science of sexual signaling. In G. C. Brannigan, E. R. Allgeier, & A. R. Allgeier (Eds.), *The sex scientists* (pp. 61–75). New York, NY: Longman.

Moore, S., Grunberg, L., & Greenberg, E. (2004). Repeated downsizing contact: The effects of similar and dissimilar layoff experiences on work and well-being outcomes. *Journal of Occupational Health Psychology, 9*(3), 247–257.

Morewedge, C. K., & Norton, M. J. (2009). When dreaming is believing: The (motivated) interpretation of dreams. *Journal of Personality and Social Psychology, 96*, 249–264.

Morgenthaler, T. I., Lee-Chiong, T., Alessi, C., Friedman, L., Aurora, R. N., Boehlecke, B., ... Standards of Practice Committee of the AASM. (2007). Practice parameters for the clinical evaluation and treatment of circadian rhythm sleep disorders: An American academy of sleep medicine report. *Sleep: Journal of Sleep and Sleep Disorders Research, 30*, 1445–1459.

Morris, S. G. (2007). Influences on childrens' narrative coherence: Age, memory breadth, and verbal comprehension. *Dissertation Abstracts International: Section B: The Sciences and Engineering, 68*(6-B), 4157.

Morrison, C., & Westman, A. S. (2001). Women report being more likely than men to model their relationships after what they have seen on TV. *Psychological Reports, 89*(2), 252–254.

Morry, M. M., Kito, M., & Ortiz, L. (2011). The attraction–similarity model and dating couples: Projection, perceived similarity, and psychological benefits. *Personal Relationships, 18*(1), 125–143.

Moss, D. (2004). Biofeedback. *Applied Psychophysiology & Biofeedback, 29*(1), 75–78.

Moulton, S. T., & Kosslyn, S. M. (2011). Imagining predictions: Mental imagery as mental emulation. In M. Bar (Ed.), *Predictions in the brain: Using our past to generate a future* (pp. 95–106). New York, NY: Oxford University Press.

Muchnik, C., Amir, N., Shabtai, E., & Kaplan-Neeman, R. (2012). Preferred listening levels of personal listening devices in young teenagers: Self reports and physical measurements. *International Journal of Audiology, 51*(4), 287–293.

Muehlenkamp, J. J., Ertelt, T. W., Miller, A. L., & Claes, L. (2011). Borderline personality symptoms differentiate non-suicidal and suicidal self-injury in ethnically diverse adolescent outpatients. *Journal of Child Psychology and Psychiatry, 52*(2), 148–155.

Mueser, K. T., & Jeste, D. V. (Eds.). (2008). *Clinical handbook of schizophrenia.* New York, NY: Guilford Press.

Murayama, K., Matsumoto, M., Izuma, K., & Matsumoto, K. (2010). Neural basis of the undermining effect of monetary reward on intrinsic motivation. *Proceedings of the National Academy of Sciences of the United States of America, 107*(49), 20911–20916.

Murdoch, S. (2007). *IQ: A smart history of a failed idea.* Hoboken, NJ: Wiley.

Murray, B. M. (2010). You have to be mental to be a fighter pilot. *Canadian Air Force Journal, 3*(4), 44–51.

Murray, H. A. (1938). *Explorations in personality.* New York, NY: Oxford University Press.

Murray-Close, D., Ostrov, J. M., & Crick, N. R. (2007). A short-term longitudinal study of growth of relational aggression during middle childhood: Associations with gender, friendship intimacy, and internalizing problems. *Development and Psychopathology, 19*, 187–203.

Mychasiuk, R., Gibb, R., & Kolb, B. (2011). Prenatal bystander stress induces neuroanatomical changes in the prefrontal cortex and hippocampus of developing rat offspring. *Brain Research, 1412*, 55–62.

Myerson, J., Rank, M. R., Raines, F. Q., & Schnitzler, M. A. (1998). Race and general cognitive ability: The myth of diminishing returns to education. *Psychological Science, 9*, 139–142.

N

Nabi, R. L., Moyer-Gusé, E., & Byrne, S. (2007). All joking aside: A serious investigation into the persuasive effect of funny social issue messages. *Communication Monographs, 74*, 29–54.

Naglieri, J. A., & Ronning, M. E. (2000). Comparison of White, African American, Hispanic, and Asian children on the Naglieri Nonverbal Ability Test. *Psychological Assessment, 12*(3), 328–334.

Naisch, P. L. N. (2007). Time to explain the nature of hypnosis? *Contemporary Hypnosis, 23*, 33–46.

Nakamura, K. (2006). The history of psychotherapy in Japan. *International Medical Journal, 13*, 13–18.

Nash, M. (1987). What, if anything, is regressed about hypnotic age regression? A review of the empirical literature. *Psychological Bulletin, 102*, 42–52.

Nash, M., & Barnier, A. (Eds.). (2008). *The Oxford handbook of hypnosis.* New York, NY: Oxford University Press.

Näslund, E., & Hellström, P. M. (2007). Appetite signaling: From gut peptides and enteric nerves to brain. *Physiology & Behavior, 92*, 256–262.

Natarajan, D., & Caramaschi, D. (2010). Animal violence demystified. *Frontiers in Behavioral Neuroscience, 4*, 9.

National Eating Disorders Association. (2004). Factors that may contribute to eating disorders. Retrieved from http://www.nationaleatingdisorders.org/uploads/file/information-resources/Factors%20that%20may%20Contribute%20to%20Eating%20Disorders.pdf

National Eating Disorders Association. (2005). Know dieting: Risks and reasons to stop. Retrieved from http://www.nationaleatingdisorders.org/uploads/file/information-resources/kNOw%20Dieting%20Reasons.pdf

National Institute on Drug Abuse. (2005). NIDA infofacts: Club drugs. Retrieved from http://www.nida.nih.gov/infofacts/clubdrugs.html

National Organization on Fetal Alcohol Syndrome. (2008). Facts about FAS and FASD. Retrieved from http://www.nofas.org/family/facts.aspx

National Research Council. (1991). *Science, Medicine, and Animals* . Washington, DC: National Academies Press. Retrieved from http://www.nap.edu/openbook.php?record_id=10089&page=14

National Sleep Foundation. (2007). Myths and facts about sleep. Retrieved from http://www.sleepfoundation.org/article/hot-topics/myths-and-facts-about-sleep

Neal, D. T. & Chartrand, T. L. (2011) *Social psychological and personality science*, published online 21 April 2011. Retrieved from http://www.cuclasses.com/stat1001/lectures/classnotes/EmbodiedEmotionPerception.pdf

Neale, J. M., Oltmanns, T. F., & Winters, K. C. (1983). Recent developments in the assessment and conceptualization of schizophrenia. *Behavioral Assessment, 5*, 33–54.

Neher, A. (1991). Maslow's theory of motivation: A critique. *Journal of Humanistic Psychology, 31*, 89–112.

Neisser, U. (1967). *Cognitive psychology.* New York, NY: Appleton-Century-Crofts.

Nelson, C. A. III, Zeanah, C. H., & Fox, N. A. (2007). The effects of early deprivation on brain-behavioral development: The Bucharest early intervention project. In D. Romer & E. F. Walker (Eds.), *Adolescent psychopathology and the developing brain: Integrating brain and prevention science* (pp. 197–215). New York, NY: Oxford University Press.

Nemer, M. (2008). Genetic insights into normal and abnormal heart development. *Cardiovascular Pathology, 17*(1), 48–54.

Nemoda, Z., Szekely, A., & Sasvari-Szekely, M. (2011). Psychopathological aspects of dopaminergic gene polymorphisms in adolescence and young adulthood. *Neuroscience and Biobehavioral Reviews, 35*, 1665–1686.

Ness, R. C. (1978). The old hag phenomenon as sleep paralysis: A biocultural interpretation. In R. C. Simons & C. C. Hughes (Eds.), *The culture-bound syndromes* (pp. 123–145). Dordrecht, Holland: D. Reidel Publishing Company.

Nesse, R. M. (2000). Is depression an adaptation? *Archives of General Psychiatry, 57*, 14–20.

Nesse, R. M., & Ellsworth, P. C. (2009). Evolution, emotions, and emotional disorders. *American Psychologist, 64*(2), 129–139.

Nesse, R. M., & Jackson, E. D. (2006). Evolution: Psychiatric nosology's missing biological foundation. *Clinical Neuropsychiatry: Journal of Treatment Evaluation, 3*, 121–131.

Neto, F., & Furnham, A. (2005). Gender-role portrayals in children's television advertisements. *International Journal of Adolescence & Youth, 12*(1–2), 69–90.

Nettle, D. (2011). Normality, disorder, and evolved function: The case of depression. In P. Adriaens & A. de Block (Eds.), *Maladapting minds: Philosophy, psychiatry, and evolutionary theory* (pp.198–215). New York, NY: Oxford University Press.

Neubauer, A. C., Grabner, R. H., Freudenthaler, H. H., Beckmann, J. F., & Guthke, J. (2004). Intelligence and individual differences in becoming neurally efficient. *Acta Psychologica, 116*(1), 55–74.

Niaura, R., Todaro, J. F., Stroud, L., Spiro, A., Ward, K. D., & Weiss, S. (2002). Hostility, the metabolic syndrome, and incident cornary heart disease. *Health Psychology, 21*(6), 598–593.

Nickerson, R. (1998). Confirmation bias: A ubiquitous phenomenon in many guises. *Review of General Psychology, 2*, 175–220.

Niclas, K., Elisabet, Å., Michèle, T., Svitlana, V., Anongnad, N., Erik, S., … Elena N. K. (2011). Forced Runx1 expression in human neural stem/progenitor cells transplanted to the rat dorsal root ganglion cavity results in extensive axonal growth specifically from spinal cord–derived neurospheres. *Stem Cells & Development, 20*(11), 1847–1857.

Nicotra, A., Critchley, H. D., Mathias, C. J., & Dolan, R. J. (2006). Emotional and autonomic consequences of spinal cord injury explored using functional brain imaging. *Brain: A Journal of Neurology, 129*, 718–728.

Nielsen, M., Subiaul, F., Galef, B., Zentall, T., & Whiten, A. (2012). Social learning in humans and nonhuman animals: Theoretical and empirical dissections. *Journal of Comparative Psychology, 126*(2), 109–113.

Nielsen, T. A., Zadra, A., Simard, V., Saucier, S., Stenstrom, P., Smith, C., & Kuiken, D. (2003). The typical dreams of Canadian university students. *Dreaming, 13*(4), 216.

Nirmala, A., Reddy, B. M. & Reddy, P. P. (2008). Genetics of human obesity: An Overview. *International Journal of Human Genetics, 8*, 217–226.

Nishimoto, R. (1988). A cross-cultural analysis of psychiatric symptom expression using Langer's twenty-two item index. *Journal of Sociology and Social Welfare, 15*, 45–62.

Nishino, S., Ripley, B., Overeem, S., Lammers, G. L., & Mignot E. (2000). Hypocretin (orexin) transmission in human narcolepsy. *Lancet, 355*, 39–40.

Nogueiras, R., & Tschöp, M. (2005). Separation of conjoined hormones yields appetite rivals. *Science, 310*, 985–986.

Nolen-Hoeksema, S., Larson, J., & Grayson, C. (2000). Explaining the gender difference in depressive symptoms. *Journal of Personality and Social Psychology, 77*, 1061–1072.

Norcross, J. C., & Wampold, B. E. (2011). Evidence-based therapy relationships: Research conclusions and clinical practices. *Psychotherapy, 48*(1), 98–102.

Norton, K. L., Olds, T. S., Olive, S., & Dank, S. (1996). Ken and Barbie at life size. *Sex Roles, 34*, 287–294.

Nouchi, R., & Hyodo, M. (2007). The congruence between the emotional valences of recalled episodes and mood states influences the mood congruence effect. *Japanese Journal of Psychology, 78*, 25–32.

O

O'Farrell, T. J. (2011). Family therapy. In M. Galanter & H. D. Kleber (Eds.), *Psychotherapy for the treatment of substance abuse* (pp. 329–350). Arlington, VA: American Psychiatric Publishing.

O'Tuathaigh, C. M., Babovic, D., O'Meara, G., Clifford, J. J., Croke, D. T., & Waddingion, J. L. (2006). Susceptibility genes for schizophrenia: Characterisation of mutant mouse models at the level of phenotypic behaviour. *Neuroscience and Biobehavioral Reviews, 31*(1), 60–78.

Oei, T. P. S., & Dingle, G. (2008). The effectiveness of group cognitive behaviour therapy for unipolar depressive disorders. *Journal of Affective Disorders, 107*, 5–21.

Ogeil, R. P., Rajaratnam, S. W., Phillips, J. G., Redman, J. R., & Broadbear, J. H. (2011). Ecstasy use and self-reported disturbances in sleep. *Human Psychopharmacology: Clinical & Experimental, 26*(7), 508–516.

Ohman, O., & Mineka, S. (2001). Fears, phobias, and preparedness: Toward an evolved module of fear and fear learning. *Psychological Review, 108*, 483–522.

Oishi, K., Ohkura, N., Sei, H., Matsuda, J., & Ishida, N. (2007). CLOCK regulates the circadian rhythm of kaolin-induced writhing behavior in mice. *Neuroreport: For Rapid Communication of Neuroscience Research, 18*, 1925–1928.

Okajima, I., Komada, Y., & Inoue, Y. (2011). A meta-analysis on the treatment effectiveness of cognitive behavioral therapy for primary insomnia. *Sleep & Biological Rhythms, 9*(1), 24–34.

Olds, J., & Milner, P. M. (1954). Positive reinforcement produced by electrical stimulation of septal area and other regions of rat brains. *Journal of Comparative and Physiological Psychology, 47*, 419–427.

Olfson, M., Marcus, S., Pincus, H. A., Zito, J. M., Thompson, J. W., & Zarin, D. A. (1998). Antidepressant prescribing practices of outpatient psychiatrists. *Archives of General Psychiatry, 55*, 310, 316.

Olweus, D. (2001). Peer harassment: A critical analysis and some important issues. In J. Juvonen & S. Graham (Eds.), *Peer harassment in school: The plight of the vulnerable and victimized.* New York, NY: Guilford.

Omori, M., & Ingersoll, G. M. (2005). Health-endangering behaviours among Japanese college students: A test of psychosocial model of risk-taking behaviours. *Journal of Adolescence, 28*, 17–33.

Ong, J., & Sholtes, D. (2010). A mindfulness-based approach to the treatment of insomnia. *Journal of Clinical Psychology, 66*(11), 1175–1184.

Ontario Lottery and Gaming Corporation. (2009). Payout levels of slot machines at OLG gaming facilities: Fact sheet. Retrieved from http://www.olg.ca/assets/documents/media/slots_payout_fact_sheet_2009.pdf

Oppenheimer, D. M. (2004). Spontaneous discounting of availability in frequency judgment tasks. *Psychological Science, 15*(2), 100–105.

Orangutan Foundation International. (2011). Dr. Biruté Mary Galdikas Bio. Retrieved from http://www.orangutan.org/dr-galdikas-bio

Orne, M. T. (2006). The nature of hypnosis, artifact and essence: An experimental study. *Dissertation Abstracts International: Section B: The Sciences and Engineering, 67*(2-B), 1207.

Orth-Gomer, K. (2007). Job strain and risk of recurrent coronary events. *Journal of the American Medical Association, 298*, 1693–1694.

Orzel-Gryglewska, J. (2010). Consequences of sleep deprivation. *International Journal of Occupational Medicine and Environmental Health, 23*(1), 95–114.

Osadchy, A., Kazmin, A., & Koren, G. (2009). Nicotine replacement therapy during pregnancy: Recommended or not. *Journal of Obstetrics and Gynaecology in Canada, 31*, 744–747.

Oscar-Berman, M. (1980). Neuropsychological consequences of long-term chronic alcoholism. *American Scientist, 68*(4), 410–419.

Ostrov, J. M., & Crick, N. R. (2007). Forms and functions of aggression during early childhood: A short-term longitudinal study. *School Psychology Review, 36*, 22–43.

Ostrov, J. M., & Keating, C. F. (2004). Gender differences in preschool aggression during free play and structured interactions: An observational study. *Social Development, 13*(2), 255–277.

Overmier, J. B., & Murison, R. (2000). Anxiety and helplessness in the face of stress predisposes, precipitates, and sustains gastric ulceration. *Behavioural Brain Research, 110*(1–2), 161–174.

Owens, J., & Massey, D. S. (2011). Stereotype threat and college academic performance: A latent variables approach. *Social Science Research, 40*, 150–166.

Ozawa-de Silva, C. (2007). Demystifying Japanese therapy: An analysis of Naikan and the Ajase complex through Buddhist thought. *Ethos, 35*, 411–446.

P

Paglia-Boak, A., Adlaf, E., & Mann, R. (2011). Drug use among Ontario students 1977–2011: Detailed OSDUHS findings. Centre for Addiction and Mental Health. Retrieved from http://www.camh.net/Research/Areas_of_research/Population_Life_Course_Studies/OSDUS/2011OSDUHS_Detailed_DrugUseReport_2.pdf

Panksepp, J. (2005). Affective consciousness: Core emotional feelings in animals and humans. *Consciousness & Cognition: An International Journal*, 14(1), 30–80.

Papadelis, C., Chen, Z., Kourtidou-Papadeli, C., Bamidis, P. D., Chouvarda, I., Bekiaris, E., & Maglaveras, N. (2007). Monitoring sleepiness with on-board electrophysiological recordings for preventing sleep-deprived traffic accidents. *Clinical Neurophysiology, 118*, 1906–1922.

Papageorgiou, G., Cañas, F., Zink, M., & Rossi, A. (2011). Country differences in patient characteristics and treatment in schizophrenia: Data from a physician-based survey in Europe. *European Psychiatry, 26*(1, Suppl 1), 17–28.

Paris, J. (2002). Chronic suicidality among patients with borderline personality disorder. *Psychiatric Services, 53*, 738–742.

Park, C. (2007). In other (people's) words: Plagiarism by university students—literature and lessons. *Assessment and Evaluation in Higher Education, 28*(5), 231–241.

Parke, R. D., & Clarke-Stewart, A. (2011). *Social development*. Hoboken, NJ: Wiley & Sons.

Parker, G. (1982). Researching the schizophrenogenic mother. *The Journal of Nervous and Mental Disease, 170*(8), 452–462.

Parker, J. D. A, Saklofske, D. H., Wood, L. M., & Collin, T. (2009). The role of emotional intelligence in education. In J. D. A. Parker, D. H. Saklofske, & C. Stough (Eds.), *Assessing emotional intelligence: Theory, research, and applications* (pp. 239–255). Boston, MA: Springer.

Parker, K., Bradshaw, A., Kahn, S., Acreman, M., & Peters, R. (2010). *Early primary school outcomes associated with maternal use of alcohol and tobacco during pregnancy and with exposure to parent alcohol and tobacco use postnatally*. Ottawa, ON: Public Health Agency of Canada. Retreived from http://www.phac-aspc.gc.ca/hp-ps/dca-dea/prog-ini/fasd-etcaf/publications/epso-edp/pdf/epso-edp-eng.pdf

Parker-Oliver, D. (2002). Redefining hope for the terminally ill. *American Journal of Hospice & Palliative Care, 19*(2), 115–120.

Parrott, A., Morinan, A., Moss, M., & Scholey, A. (2004). *Understanding drugs and behavior*. Hoboken, NJ: Wiley.

Parsons, T., & Otto, T. (2010). Time-limited involvement of dorsal hippocampus in unimodal discriminative contextual conditioning. *Neurobiology of Learning and Memory, 94*(4), 481–487.

Patrick, C. J., & Verona, E. (2007). The psychophysiology of aggression: Autonomic, electrocortical, and neuro-imaging findings. In D. J. Flannery, A. T. Vazsonyi, & I. D. Waldman (Eds.), *The Cambridge handbook of violent behavior and aggression* (pp. 111–150). New York, NY: Cambridge University Press.

Patterson, C. J. (2009). APA online public interest. Lesbian and gay parenting: Children of lesbian and gay parents. Retrieved from http://www.apa.org/pi/lgbc/publications/1gpchildren.html

Patterson, F., & Linden, E. (1981). *The education of Koko*. New York, NY: Holt, Rinehart and Winston.

Patterson, J. M., Holm, K. E., & Gurney, J. G. (2004). The impact of childhood cancer on the family: A qualitative analysis of strains, resources, and coping behaviors. *Psycho-Oncology, 13*(6), 390–407.

Patterson, P. (2002). *Penny's journal: Koko wants to have a baby*. Retrieved from http://www.koko.org/world/journal.phtml?

Paul, D. B., & Blumenthal, A. L. (1989). On the trail of little Albert. *The Psychological Record, 39*, 547–553.

Payne, J. D. (2011). Learning, memory, and sleep in humans. *Sleep Medicine Clinics, 6*(1), 15–30.

Pearce, M. E., Christian, W. M., Patterson, K., Norris, K., Moniruzzaman, A., Craib, K. J. P., Schechter, M. T., & Spittal, P. M. (2008). The Cedar Project: Historical trauma, sexual abuse and HIV risk among young Aboriginal people who use injection and non-injection drugs in two Canadian cities. *Social Science and Medicine, 66*(11), 2185–2194.

Pearson, N. J., Johnson, I. M., & Nahin, R. L. (2006). Insomnia, trouble sleeping, and complementary and alternative medicine: Analysis of the 2002 National Health Interview Survey data. *Archives of Internal Medicine, 166*, 1775–1782.

Pedrazzoli, M., Pontes, J. C., Peirano, P., & Tufik, S. (2007). HLA-DQB1 genotyping in a family with narcolepsy-cataplexy. *Brain Research, 1165*, 1–4.

Peleg, G., Katzir, G., Peleg, O., Kamara, M., Brodsky, L., Hel-Or, H., Keren, D., & Nevo, E. (2006). Hereditary family signature of facial expression. *Proceedings of the National Academy of Sciences, 103*, 15921–15926.

Pellegrino, J. E., & Pellegrino, L. (2008). Fetal alcohol syndrome and related disorders. In P. J. Accardo (Ed.), *Caputo and Accardo's neurodevelopmental disabilities in infancy and childhood: Vol 1: Neurodevelopmental diagnosis and treatment* (3rd ed., pp. 269–284). Baltimore, MD: Paul H Brookes.

Pelletier, J. G., & Paré, D. (2004). Role of amygdale oscillations in the consolidation of emotional memories. *Biological Psychiatry, 55*(6), 559–562.

Penfield, W. (1947). Some observations in the cerebral cortex of man. *Proceedings of the Royal Society, 134*, 349.

Pepler, D., & Craig, W. (2000). *Making a difference in bullying*. LaMarsh Research Programme, Report Series, Report # 60. Toronto, ON: LaMarsh Centre for Research on Violence and Conflict Resolution. Retrieved from http://www.arts.yorku.ca/lamarsh/pdf/Making_a_Difference_in_Bullying.pdf

Pérez-Mata, N., & Diges, M. (2007). False recollections and the congruence of suggested information. *Memory, 15*, 701–717.

Persson, J., Lind, J., Larsson, A., Ingvar, M., Sleegers, K., Van Broeckhoven, C., … Nyberg, L. (2008). Altered deactivation in individuals with genetic risk for Alzheimer's disease. *Neuropsychologia, 46*, 1679–1687.

Peterson, C., Mitchell, J., Crow, S., Crosby, R., & Wonderlich, S. (2009). The efficacy of self-help group treatment and therapist-led group treatment for binge eating disorder. *American Journal of Psychiatry, 166*(12), 1347–1354.

Peterson, C., Warren, K. L., & Short, M. M. (2011). Infantile amnesia across the years: A 2-year follow-up of children's earliest memories. *Child Development, 82*(4), 1092–1105.

Petrides, K. V. (2011). Ability and trait emotional intelligence. In A. Furnham, S. von Stumm, & T. Chamorro-Pemruzic (Eds.), *The Wiley-Blackwell handbook of individual differences* (pp. 656–677). Hoboken, NJ: Wiley.

Petry, Y. (2012). 'Many things surpass our knowledge': An early modern surgeon on magic, witchcraft and demonic possession. *Social History of Medicine, 25*, 47–64.

Pettigrew, T. F. (1998). Reactions towards the new minorities of Western Europe. *Annual Review of Sociology, 24*, 77–103.

Pevet, P., & Challet, E. (2011). Melatonin: Both master clock output and internal time-giver in the circadian clocks network. *Journal of Physiology, 105*(4–6), 170–182.

Pham, T. M., Winblad, B., Granholm, A-C., & Mohammed, A. H. (2002). Environmental influences on brain neurotrophins in rats. *Pharmacology, Biochemistry & Behavior, 73*(1), 167–175.

Phares, V. (2008). *Understanding abnormal child psychology* (2nd ed.). Hoboken, NJ: Wiley.

Phillips, S. T., & Ziller, R. C. (1997). Toward a theory and measure of the nature of non-prejudice. *Journal of Personality and Social Psychology, 72*, 420–434.

"Phone now," said CBC subliminally—but nobody did. (1958, February 10). *Advertising Age*, p. 8.

Piaget, J. (1962). *Play, dreams and imitation in Childhood*. New York, NY: Norton.

Pierce, J. P. (2007). Tobacco industry marketing, population-based tobacco control, and smoking behavior. *American Journal of Preventive Medicine, 33*, 327–334.

Pigeon, W. R. (2010). Diagnosis, prevalence, pathways, consequences & treatment of insomnia. *Indian Journal of Medical Research, 131*(2), 321–332.

Pinker, S. (2007). *The language instinct: How the mind creates language* (PS ed.). New York, NY: Harper-Collins.

Pinker, S., & Jackendoff, R. (2005) What's special about the human language faculty? *Cognition, 95*(2), 201–236.

Pittenger, D. J. (2005). Cautionary comments regarding the Myers-Briggs Type Indicator. *Consulting Psychology Journal: Practice and Research, 57*, 210–221.

Plomin, R. (1990). The role of inheritance in behavior. *Science, 248*, 183–188.

Plomin, R. (1999). Genetics and general cognitive ability. *Nature, 402*, C25–C29.

Plomin, R., DeFries, J. C., & Fulker, D. W. (2007). *Nature and nurture during infancy and early childhood*. New York, NY: Cambridge University Press.

Plummer, D. C. (2001). The quest for modern manhood: Masculine stereotypes, peer culture and the social significance of homophobia. *Journal of Adolescence, 24*(1), 15–23.

Plutchik, R. (1962). *The emotions: Facts, theories, and a new model*. New York, NY: Random House.

Plutchik, R. (1984). Emotions: A general psychoevolutionary theory. In K. R. Scherer & P. Ekman (Eds.), *Approaches to emotion*. Hillsdale, NJ: Erlbaum.

Plutchik, R. (1994). *The psychology and biology of emotion*. New York, NY: HarperCollins.

Plutchik, R. (2000). *Emotions in the practice of psychotherapy: Clinical implications of affect theories*. Washington, DC: American Psychological Association.

Plutchik, R. (2005). The nature of emotions. In P. W. Sherman & J. Alcock (Eds.), *Exploring animal* behavior: Readings from American Scientist (4th ed., pp. 85–91). Sunderland, MA: Sinauer Associates.

Poirier, P., Giles, T., Bray, G., Hong, Y., Stern, J., Pi-Sunyer, F., & Eckel, R. (2006). Obesity and cardiovascular disease: Pathophysiology, evaluation, and effect of weight loss. *Arteriosclerosis, Thrombosis, and Vascular Biology, 26*(5), 968–976.

Pomponio, A. T. (2002). *Psychological consequences of terror.* New York, NY: Wiley.

Ponzi, A. (2008). Dynamical model of salience gated working memory, action selection and reinforcement based on basal ganglia and dopamine feedback. *Neural Networks, 21,* 322–330.

Pope, H. G. Jr., Barry, S., Bodkin, J. A., & Hudson, J. (2007). "Scientific study of the dissociative disorders": Reply. *Psychotherapy and Psychosomatics, 76,* 401–403.

Popma, A., Vermeiren, R., Geluk, C. A. M. L., Rinne, T., van den Brink, W., Knol, D. L., … Doreleijers, T. A. H. (2007). Cortisol moderates the relationship between testosterone and aggression in delinquent male adolescents. *Biological Psychiatry, 61,* 405–411.

Portnuff, C. F., Fligor, B. J., & Arehart, K. H. (2011). Teenage use of portable listening devices: A hazard to hearing? *Journal of the American Academy of Audiology, 22*(10), 663–677.

Post, J. M. (2011). Crimes of obedience: "Groupthink" at Abu Ghraib. *International Journal of Group Psychotherapy, 61*(1), 49–66.

Posthuma, D., de Geus, E. J. C., & Boomsma, D. I. (2001). Perceptual speed and IQ are associated through common genetic factors. *Behavior Genetics, 31*(6), 593–602.

Posthuma, D., Neale, M. C., Boomsma, D. I., & de Geus, E. J. C. (2001). Are smarter brains running faster? Heritability of alpha peak frequency, IQ, and their interrelation. *Behavior Genetics, 31*(6), 567–579.

Potlatch. (2011). In *Columbia Electronic Encyclopedia* (6th ed.), 1.

Poulin-Dubois, D., & Serbin, L. A. (2006). La connaissance des catégories de genre et des stéréotypes sexués chez le jeune enfant. *Enfance, 58,* 283–310.

Powell, D. H. (1998). *The nine myths of aging: Maximizing the quality of later life.* San Francisco, CA: Freeman.

Prabhu, V., Sutton, C., & Sauser, W. (2008). Creativity and certain personality traits: Understanding the mediating effect of intrinsic motivation. *Creativity Research Journal, 20,* 53–66.

Prakash, R., Dubey, I., Abhishek, P., Gupta, S., Rastogi, P., & Siddiqui, S. (2010). Long-term Vihangam yoga meditation and scores on tests of attention. *Perceptual & Motor Skills, 110*(3), 1139–1148.

Preuss, U. W., Zetzsche, T., Jäger, M., Groll, C., Frodl, T., Bottlender, R., … Meisenzahl, E. M. (2005). Thalamic volume in firstepisode and chronic schizophrenic subjects: A volumetric MRI study. *Schizophrenia Research, 73*(1), 91–101.

Priess, H. A., & Hyde, J. S. (2010). Gender and academic abilities and preferences. In J. Chrisler & D. R. McCreary (Eds.), *Handbook of gender research in psychology: Vol. 1: Gender research in general and experimental psychology* (pp. 297–316). New York, NY: Springer.

Prigatano, G. P., & Gray, J. A. (2008). Predictors of performance on three developmentally sensitive neuropsychological tests in children with and without traumatic brain injury. *Brain Injury, 22,* 491–500.

Primavera, L. H., & Herron, W. G. (1996). The effect of viewing television violence on aggression. *International Journal of Instructional Media, 23,* 91–104.

Pring, L., Woolf, K., & Tadic, V. (2008). Melody and pitch processing in five musical savants with congenital blindness. *Perception, 37,* 290–307.

Prkachin, K. M. (2005). Effects of deliberate control on verbal and facial expressions of pain. *Pain, 114,* 328–338.

Prkachin, K. M., & Silverman, B. E. (2002). Hostility and facial expression in young men and women: Is social regulation more important than negative affect? *Health Psychology, 21*(1), 33–39.

Pro-Test. (2006). Benefits. Retrieved from http://www.pro-test.org.uk/facts.php?lt=c.

Pruett, M. K., & Barker, R. (2009). Children of divorce: New trends and ongoing dilemmas. In J. H. Bray & M. Stanton (Eds.), *The Wiley-Blackwell handbook of family psychology* (pp. 463–474). Hoboken, NJ: Wiley.

Public Health Agency of Canada. (2006a). Awareness of the effects of alcohol use during pregnancy and awareness of fetal alcohol spectrum disorder: Results of a national survey (PN4568). Retrieved from http://www.phac-aspc.gc.ca/publicat/fas-saf-natsurv-2006/pdf/ap-ag-finalreport06_e.pdf

Public Health Agency of Canada. (2006b). *The Human Face of Mental Health and Mental Illness in Canada.* Ottawa, ON: Government of Canada. Retrieved from http://www.phac-aspc.gc.ca/publicat/human-humain06/pdf/human_face_e.pdf

Public Health Agency of Canada. (2007). Fetal alcohol spectrum disorder (FASD). Retrieved from http://www.phac-aspc.gc.ca/fasd-etcaf/faq_e.html#7

Public Health Agency of Canada. (2008). Common questions about smoking and pregnancy. Retrieved from http://www.phac-aspc.gc.ca/hp-gs/faq/smoke-fumer-eng.php

Public Health Agency of Canada. (2009). What mothers say: The Canadian maternity experiences survey. Retrieved from http://www.phac-aspc.gc.ca/rhs-ssg/pdf/survey-eng.pdf

Public Health Agency of Canada. (2011). Physical activity guidelines. Retrieved from http://www.phac-aspc.gc.ca/hp-ps/hl-mvs/pa-ap/03paap-eng.php

Puhl, A. A., Reinhart, C. J., Rok, E. R., & Injeyan, H. (2011). An examination of the observed placebo effect associated with the treatment of low back pain—A systematic review. *Pain Research & Management, 16*(1), 45–52.

Pullum, G. K. (1991). *The great Eskimo vocabulary hoax and other irreverent essays on the study of language.* Chicago, IL: University of Chicago Press.

Q

Querna, B. (2006). Paul McCartney and "Yesterday". *U.S. News & World Report, 140*(18), 60.

Quinn, P. C., Kelly, D. J., Lee, K., Pascalis, O., & Slater, A. M. (2008). Preference for attractive faces in human infants extends beyond conspecifics. *Developmental Science, 11,* 76–83.

Quintanilla, Y. T. (2007). Achievement motivation strategies: An integrative achievement motivation program with first year seminar students. *Dissertation Abstracts International Section A: Humanities and Social Sciences, 68* (6-A), 2339.

R

Raevuori, A., Keski-Rahkonen, A., Hoek, H. W., Sihvola, E., Rissanen, A., & Kaprio, J. (2008). Lifetime anorexia nervosa in young men in the community: Five cases and their co-twins. *International Journal of Eating Disorders, 41,* 458–463.

Rahman, S. A., Kayumov, L., Tchmoutina, E. A., & Shapiro, C. M. (2009). Clinical efficacy of dim light melatonin onset testing in diagnosing delayed sleep phase syndrome. *Sleep Medicine, 10*(5), 549–555.

Ramachandran, V. S., & Altschuler, E. L. (2010). Reflections on hand. *Pain, 149*(2), 171–172.

Ramachandran, V., Brang, D., & McGeoch, P. (2009). Size reduction using mirror visual feedback (MVF) reduces phantom pain. *Neurocase (Psychology Press), 15*(5), 357–360.

Ramirez, G., Zemba, D., & Geiselman, R. E. (1996). Judges' cautionary instructions on eyewitness testimony. *American Journal of Forensic Psychology, 14,* 31–66.

Ramsey, J. L., Langlois, J. H., Hoss, R. A., Rubenstein, A. J., & Griffin, A. G. (2004). Origins of a stereotype: Categorization of facial attractiveness by 6-month-old infants. *Developmental Science, 7,* 201–211.

Ramstedt, M. (2006). Is alcohol good or bad for Canadian hearts? A time-series analysis of the link between alcohol consumption and IHD mortality. *Drug & Alcohol Review, 25*(4), 315–320.

Ran, M. (2007). Experimental research on the reliability of the testimony from eyewitnesses. *Psychological Science (China), 30,* 727–730.

Randall, J., & Rodgers, R. (1988). Adaptive pain inhibition in murine resident-intruder interactions. *International Journal of Neuroscience, 41*(3–4), 251–259.

Randall, S., Roehrs, T. A., & Roth, T. (2008). Over-the counter sleep aid medications and insomnia. *Primary Psychiatry, 15*(5), 52–58.

Ranganath, C., Flegal, K. E., & Kelly, L. L. (2011). Can cognitive training improve episodic memory? *Neuron, 72*(5), 688–691.

Rankinen, T., Zuberi, A., Chagnon, Y., Weisnagel, S., Argyropoulos, G., Walts, B., Pérusse, L., & Bouchard, C. (2006). The human obesity gene map: The 2005 update. *Obesity, 14*(4), 529–644.

Raskauskas, J., & Stoltz, A. D. (2007). Involvement in traditional and electronic bullying among adolescents. *Developmental Psychology, 43,* 564–575.

Rattaz, C., Goubet, N., & Bullinger, A. (2005). The calming effect of a familiar odor on full-term newborns. *Journal of Developmental & Behavioral Pediatrics, 26,* 86–92.

Rauer, A. J. (2007). Identifying happy, healthy marriages for men, women, and children. *Dissertation Abstracts International: Section B: The Sciences and Engineering, 67*(10-B), 6098.

Ravindran, L., & Kennedy, S. H. (2007). Are antidepressants as effective as claimed? Yes, but … *Canadian Journal of Psychiatry, 52*, 98–99.

Rechtschaffen, A., & Bergmann, B. M. (2002). Sleep deprivation in the rat: An update of the 1989 paper. *Sleep, 25*(1), 18–24.

Rechtschaffen, A., & Siegel, J. M. (2000). Sleep and dreaming. In E. R. Kandel, J. H. Schwartz, & T. M. Jessel (Eds.), *Principles of Neuroscience* (4th ed., pp. 936–947). New York, NY: McGraw-Hill.

Reed, L., Zeglen, K. N., & Schmidt, K. L. (2012). Facial expressions as honest signals of cooperative intent in a one-shot anonymous prisoner's dilema game. *Evolution and Human Behavior, 33*(3), 200–209.

Reeve, J. (2005). *Understanding motivation and emotion* (4th ed.). Hoboken, NJ: Wiley.

Regan, P. (1998). What if you can't get what you want? Willingness to compromise ideal mate selection standards as a function of sex, mate value, and relationship context. *Personality and Social Psychology Bulletin, 24*, 1294–1303.

Rehm, J., Baliunas, D., Borges, G. G., Graham, K., Irving, H., Kehoe, T., . . . Taylor, B. (2010). The relation between different dimensions of alcohol consumption and burden of disease: An overview. *Addiction, 105*(5), 817–843.

Reich, D. A. (2004). What you expect is not always what you get: The roles of extremity, optimism, and pessimism in the behavioral confirmation process. *Journal of Experimental Social Psychology, 40*(2), 199–215.

Reid, G. J., Seidelin, P. H., Kop, W. J., Irvine, M., Strauss, B. H., Nolan, R. P., Lau, H.K., & Yeo, E. L. (2009). Mental stress-induced platelet activation among patients with coronary artery disease. *Psychosomatic Medicine, 71*(4), 438–445.

Reid, K., McGee-Koch, L., & Zee, P. (2011). Cognition in circadian rhythm sleep disorders. *Progress In Brain Research, 190*, 3–20.

Reifman, A. (2000). Revisiting the bell curve. *Psychology, 11*, 21–29.

Reis, H. T., Maniaci, M. R., Caprariello, P. A., Eastwick, P. W., & Finkel, E. J. (2011). Familiarity does indeed promote attraction in live interaction. *Journal of Personality and Social Psychology, 101*, 557–570.

Reissig, C. J., Strain, E. C., & Griffiths, R. R. (2009). Caffeinated energy drinks: A growing problem. *Drug and Alcohol Dependence, 99*(1–3), 1–10.

Renzetti, C., Curran, D., & Kennedy-Bergen, R. (2006). *Understanding diversity*. Boston, MA: Allyn & Bacon/Longman.

Responsible Gambling Council. (2012). Safe or sorry. Retrieved from http://www.safeorsorry.ca/odds.php

Rest, J., Narvaez, D., Bebeau, M., & Thoma, S. (1999). A neo-Kohlbergian approach: The DIT and schema theory. *Educational Psychology Review, 11*(4), 291–324.

Revonsuo, A. (2006). *Inner presence: Consciousness as a biological phenomenon*. Cambridge, MA: MIT Press.

Rhee, S. H., & Waldman, I. D. (2007). Behavior-genetics of criminality and aggression. In D. J. Flannery, A. T. Vazsonyi, & I. D. Waldman (Eds.), *The Cambridge handbook of violent behavior and aggression* (pp. 77–90). New York, NY: Cambridge University Press.

Rhee, S. H., & Waldman, I. D. (2011). Genetic and environmental influences on aggression. In P. R. Shaver & M. Mikulincer (Eds.), *Human aggression and violence: Causes, manifestations, and consequences* (pp. 143–163). Washington, DC: American Psychological Association.

Rhodes, G., Halberstadt, J., & Brajkovich, G. (2001). Generalization of mere exposure effects to averaged composite faces. *Social Cognition, 19*(1), 57–70.

Richards, J. E. (2010). The development of attention to simple and complex visual stimuli in infants: Behavioral and psychophysiological measures. *Developmental Review, 30*(2), 203–219.

Ridley, R. M., Baker, H. F., Cummings, R. M., Green, M. E., & Leow-Dyke, A. (2005). Mild topographical memory impairment following crossed unilateral lesions of the mediodorsal thalamic nucleus and the inferotemporal cortex. *Behavioral Neuroscience, 119*(2), 518–525.

Riemann, D., & Voderholzer, U. (2003). Primary insomnia: a risk factor to develop depression? *Journal of Affective Disorders, 76*(1–3), 255–259.

Rigby, K. (2008). *Children and bullying: How parents and educators can reduce bullying at school*. Malden, MA: Blackwell.

Riley, B., & Kendler, K. (2011). Classical genetic studies of schizophrenia. In D. Weinberger & P. Harrison (Eds.), *Schizophrenia* (3rd ed., pp. 245–268). Hoboken, NJ: Wiley.

Rizzolatti, G., & Fabbri-Destro, M. (2009). The mirror neuron system. In G. Berntson & J. Caciopppo (Eds.), *Handbook of neuroscience for the behavioral sciences, Vol 1*. (pp. 337–357). Hoboken, NJ: Wiley.

Rizzolatti, G., Fadiga, L., Fogassi, L., & Gallese, V. (2002). From mirror neurons to imitation: Facts and speculations. In A. N. Meltzoff & W. Prinz (Eds.), *The imitative mind: Development, evolution, and brain bases*. Cambridge, MA: Cambridge University Press.

Rizzolatti, G., Fogassi, L., & Gallese, V. (2006, November). In the mind. *Scientific American*, 54–61.

Roane, B., & Taylor, D. (2008). Adolescent insomnia as a risk factor for early adult depression and substance abuse. *Sleep, 31*(10), 1351–1356.

Robbins, C., Schick, V., Reece, M., Herbenick, D., Sanders, S., Dodge, B., & Fortenberry, J. (2011). Prevalence, frequency, and associations of masturbation with partnered sexual behaviors among US adolescents. *Archives of Pediatrics & Adolescent Medicine, 165*(12), 1087–1093.

Roberts, W. W., & Nagel, J. (1996). First-order projections activated by stimulation of hypothalamic sites eliciting attack and flight in rats. *Behavioral Neuroscience, 110*, 509–527.

Robinson, F. P. (1970). *Effective study* (4th ed.). New York, NY: Harper & Row.

Robinson, T., & Berridge, K. (2010). The incentive sensitization theory of addiction: Some current issues. In T. Robbins, B. Everitt, & D. Nutt (Eds.), *The neurobiology of addiction* (pp. 45–59). New York, NY: Oxford University Press.

Rodrigues, A., Assmar, E. M., & Jablonski, B. (2005). Social-psychology and the invasion of Iraq. *Revista de Psicologia Social, 20*, 387–398.

Rogers, C. R. (1961). *On becoming a person*. Boston, MA: Houghton Mifflin.

Rogers, C. R. (1980). *A way of being*. Boston, MA: Houghton Mifflin.

Rogosch, F. A., & Cicchetti, D. (2004). Child maltreatment and emergent personality organization: Perspectives from the five-factor model. *Journal of Abnormal Child Psychology, 32*(2), 123–145.

Roid, G. H. (2003). *Stanford-Binet Intelligence Scales* (5th ed.). Itasca, IL: Riverside Publishing.

Romero, S. G., McFarland, D. J., Faust, R., Farrell, L., & Cacace, A. T. (2008). Electrophysiological markers of skill-related neuroplasticity. *Biological Psychology, 78*, 221–230.

Rosch, E. (1978). Principles of organization. In E. Rosch & H. L. Lloyd (Eds.), *Cognition and categorization* (pp. 27–48). Hillsdale, NJ: Erlbaum.

Rosch, E. H. (1973). Natural categories. *Cognitive Psychology, 4*, 328–350.

Rose, A. J., & Rudolph, K. D. (2006). A review of sex differences in peer relationship processes: Potential tradeoffs for the emotional development of girls and boys. *Psychological Bulletin, 132*, 98–131.

Rose, A. J., & Smith, R. L. (2009). Sex differences in peer relationships. In K. H. Rubin, W. M. Bukowski, & B. Laursen (Eds.), *Handbook of peer interactions, relationships, and groups* (pp. 379–393). New York, NY: Guilford.

Roselli, C., & Stormshak, F. (2010). The ovine sexually dimorphic nucleus, aromatase, and sexual partner preferences in sheep. *The Journal of Steroid Biochemistry and Molecular Biology, 118*(4–5), 252–256.

Rosenfeld, J. P., Shue, E., & Singer, E. (2007). Single versus multiple probe blocks of P300-based concealed information tests for self-referring versus incidentally obtained information. *Biological Psychology, 74*(3), 396–404.

Rosenfeld, J., Soskins, M., Bosh, G., & Ryan, A. (2004). Simple, effective countermeasures to P300-based tests of detection of concealed information. *Psychophysiology, 41*(2), 205–219.

Rosenthal, C. J., & Gladstone, J. (2007). *Grand-parenthood in Canada*. Ottawa, ON: The Vanier Institute of the Family. Retrieved from http://www.vifamily.ca/library/cft/grandparenthood.html

Rosenzweig, M. R., & Bennett, E. L. (1996). Psychobiology of plasticity: Effects of training and experience on brain and behavior. *Behavioral Brain Research, 78*(1), 57–65.

Rosenzweig, M. R., Bennett, E. L., & Diamond, M. C. (1972). Brain changes in response to experience. *Scientific American, 226*, 22–29.

Rossi, S., Nistor, G., Wyatt, T., Yin, H., Poole, A., Weiss, J., . . . Keirstead, H. (2010). Histological and functional benefit following transplantation of motor neuron progenitors to the injured rat spinal cord. *Plos One, 5*(7), e11852.

Rossignol, S., Barrière, G., Frigon, A., Barthélemy, D., Bouyer, L., Provencher, J., Leblond, H., & Bernard, G. (2008). Plasticity of locomotor sensorimotor interactions after peripheral and/or spinal lesions. *Brain Research Reviews, 57*, 228–240.

Roth, M. L., Tripp, D. A., Harrison, M. H., Sullivan, M., & Carson, P. (2007). Demographic and psychosocial predictors of acute perioperative pain for total knee arthroplasty. *Pain Research & Management, 12*, 185–194.

Rotter, J. B. (1954). *Social learning and clinical psychology*. Englewood Cliffs, NJ: Prentice Hall.

Rotter, J. B. (1990). Internal versus external control of reinforcement: A case history of a variable. *American Psychologist, 45,* 489–493.

Rowe, R., Maughan, B., Worthman, C. M., Costello, E. J., & Angold, A. (2004). Testosterone, antisocial behavior, and social dominance in boys: Pubertal development and biosocial interaction. *Biological Psychiatry, 55*(5), 546–552.

Rozencwajg, P., Cherfi, M., Ferrandez, A. M., Lautrey, J., Lemoine, C., & Loarer, E. (2005). Age related differences in the strategies used by middle aged adults to solve a block design task. *International Journal of Aging & Human Development, 60*(2), 159–182.

Rubin, K. H., Coplan, R. J., & Bowker, J. (2009). Social withdrawal and shyness in childhood and adolescence. *Annual Review of Psychology, 60,* 141–171.

Rubin, K. H., Bukowski, W. M., & Parker, J. G. (2006). Peer interactions, relationships, and groups. In N. E. Eisenberg, W. Damon, & R. M. Lerner (Eds.), *Handbook of child psychology, Vol. 3: Social, emotional, and personality development* (6th ed., pp. 571–645). Hoboken, NJ: Wiley.

Rubin, Z. (1970). Measurement of romantic love. *Journal of Personality and Social Psychology, 16,* 265–273.

Rubinstein, E. (2008). Judicial perceptions of eyewitness testimony. *Dissertation Abstracts International: Section B: The Sciences and Engineering, 68*(8-B), 5592.

Ruble, D. N., Martin, C. L., & Berenbaum, S. A. (2006). Gender development. In N. E. Eisenberg, W. E. Damon, & R. M. Lerner (Eds.), *Handbook of child psychology. Vol. 3: Social, emotional, and personality development* (6th ed., pp. 858–932). Hoboken, NJ: Wiley.

Rumbaugh, D. M., von Glasersfeld, E. C., Warner, H., Pisani, P., & Gill, T. V. (1974). Lana (chimpanzee) learning language: A progress report. *Brain & Language, 1*(2), 205–212.

Rushton, J. P., & Jensen, A. R. (2005). Thirty years of research on race differences in cognitive ability. *Psychology, Public Policy, and Law, 11,* 235–294.

Russo, N. F., & Tartaro, J. (2008). Women and mental health. In F. L. Denmark & M. A. Paludi (Eds.), *Psychology of women: A handbook of issues and theories* (2nd ed., pp. 440–483). *Women's psychology.* Westport, CT: Praeger/Greenwood.

Rust, J., Golombok, S., Hines, M., & Johnston, K. (2000). The role of brothers and sisters in the gender development of preschool children. *Journal of Experimental Child Psychology, 77,* 292–303.

Ruthig, J. C., Chipperfield, J. G., Perry, R. P., Newall, N. E., & Swift, A. (2007). Comparative risk and perceived control: Implications for psychological and physical well-being among older adults. *Journal of Social Psychology, 147,* 345–369.

Rutter, M. (2007). Gene-environment interdependence. *Developmental Science, 10,* 12–18.

Ryan, A. M. (2001). The peer group as a context for the development of young adolescent motivation and achievement. *Child Development, 72,* 1135–1150.

Ryan, C. S., Casas, J. F., & Thompson, B. K. (2010). Interethnic ideology, intergroup perceptions, and cultural orientation. *Journal of Social Issues, 66*(1), 29–44.

Ryback, D., Ikemi, A., & Miki, Y. (2001). Japanese psychology in crisis: Thinking inside the (empty) box. *Journal of Humanistic Psychology, 41*(4), 124–136.

Rymer, R. (1993). *Genie: An abused child's first flight from silence.* New York, NY: HarperCollins.

S

Sabini, J., & Silver, M. (1993). Critical thinking and obedience to authority. In J. Chaffee (Ed.), *Critical thinking* (2nd ed., pp. 367–376). Palo Alto, CA: Houghton Mifflin.

Sacchetti, B., Sacco, T., & Strata, P. (2007). Reversible inactivation of amygdala and cerebellum but not perirhinal cortex impairs reactivated fear memories. *European Journal of Neuroscience, 25*(9), 2875–2884.

Sachdev, P., Mondraty, N., Wen, W., & Gulliford, K. (2008). Brains of anorexia nervosa patients process self-images differently from non-self-images: An fMRI study. *Neuropsychologia, 46,* 2161–2168.

Sack, R. L., Auckley, D., Auger, R. R., Carskadon, M. A., Wright, Jr., K. P., Vitiello, M. V., & Zhdanova, I. V. (2007). Circadian rhythm sleep disorders: Part I, basic principles, shift work and jet lag disorders: An American Academy of Sleep Medicine review. *Sleep: Journal of Sleep and Sleep Disorders Research, 30,* 1460–1483.

Sacks, O. (1995). *An anthropologist on Mars.* New York, NY: Vintage Books.

Salgado-Pineda, P., Fakra, E., Delaveau, P., McKenna, P. J., Pomarol-Clotet, E., & Blin, O. (2011). Correlated structural and functional brain abnormalities in the default mode network in schizophrenia patients. *Schizophrenia Research, 125*(2–3), 101–109.

Salmina, A. B., Inzhutova, A. I., Malinovskaya, N. A., & Petrova, M. M. (2010). Endothelial dysfunction and repair in Alzheimer-type neurodegeneration: Neuronal and glial control. *Journal of Alzheimer's Disease, 22*(1), 17–36.

Salmivalli, C., Peets, K., & Hodges, E. V. (2011). Bullying. In P. K. Smith & K. H. Hart (Eds.), *The Wiley-Blackwell handbook of childhood social development* (2nd ed., pp. 510–528). Hoboken, NJ: Wiley.

Salois, K. (1999). A comparative study of the Wechsler Intelligence Scale for Children-Third Edition (WISC-III) test performance: Northern Cheyenne and Blackfeet reservation Indian children with the standardization sample. *Dissertation Abstracts International: Section B: The Sciences and Engineering, 60*(4-B), p. 1909.

Salvatore, P., Ghidini, S., Zita, G., De Panfilis, C., Lambertino, S., Maggini, C., & Baldessarini, R. J. (2008). Circadian activity rhythm abnormalities in ill and recovered bipolar I disorder patients. *Bipolar Disorders, 10,* 256–265.

Sampselle, C. M., Harris, V., Harlow, S. D., & Sowers, M. F. (2002). Midlife development and menopause in African American and Caucasian women. *Health Care for Women International, 23*(4), 351–363.

Sanders, J. L., & Buck, G. (2010). A long journey: Biological and non-biological parents' experiences raising children with FASD. *Journal of Population Therapeutics and Clinical Pharmacology, 17,* e308–e322.

Sangwan, S. (2001). Ecological factors as related to I.Q. of children. *Psycho-Lingua, 31*(2), 89–92.

Sarafino, E. P. (2008). *Health psychology: Biopsychosocial interactions* (6th ed.). Hoboken, NJ: Wiley.

Sarris, J., & Byrne, G. J. (2011). A systematic review of insomnia and complementary medicine. *Sleep Medicine Reviews, 15*(2), 99–106.

Sassenberg, K., Moskowitz, G. B., Jacoby, J., & Hansen, N. (2007). The carry-over effect of competition: The impact of competition on prejudice towards uninvolved outgroups. *Journal of Experimental Social Psychology, 43,* 529–538.

Satcher, N. D. (2007). Social and moral reasoning of high school athletes and non-athletes. *Dissertation Abstracts International Section 7A: Humanities and Social Sciences, 68*(3-A), 928.

Sathyaprabha, T. N., Satishchandra, P., Pradhan, C., Sinha, S., Kaveri, B., Thennarasu, K., Murthy, B. T. C., & Raju, T. R. (2008). Modulation of cardiac autonomic balance with adjuvant yoga therapy in patients with refractory epilepsy. *Epilepsy & Behavior, 12,* 245–252.

Sato, S. M., Schulz, K. M., Sisk, C. L., & Wood, R. I. (2008). Adolescents and androgens, receptors and rewards. *Hormones and Behavior, 53,* 647–658.

Sattler, J. M. (1988). *Assessment of children* (3rd ed.). San Diego, CA: Jerome M. Sattler Publisher.

Sattler, J. M., & Hoge, R. D. (2006). *Assessment of children: Behavioral, social, and clinical foundations* (5th ed.). San Diego, CA: Jerome M. Sattler Publisher.

Saucier, D., & Ehresman, C. (2010). The physiology of sex differences. In J. Chrisler & D. R. McCreary (Eds.), *Handbook of gender research in psychology: Vol. 1: Gender research in general and experimental psychology* (pp. 215–233). New York, NY: Springer.

Saudino, K. J. (1997). Moving beyond the heritability question: New directions in behavioral genetic studies of personality. *Current Directions in Psychological Science, 6,* 86–90.

Savage-Rumbaugh, E. S. (1990). Language acquisition in a nonhuman species: Implications for the innateness debate. *Developmental Psychobiology, 23,* 599–620.

Savic, I., Berglund, H., & Lindström, P. (2007). Brain response to putative pheromones in homosexual men. In G. Einstein (Ed.), *Sex and the brain* (pp. 731–738). Cambridge, MA: MIT Press.

Savin-Williams, R. (2009). How many gays are there? It depends. In D. A. Hope (Ed.), *Contemporary perspectives on lesbian, gay, and bisexual identities* (pp. 5–41). New York, NY: Springer Science + Business Media.

Scarpa, A., & Raine, A. (2007). Biosocial bases of violence. In D. J. Flannery, A. T. Vazsonyi, & I. D. Waldman (Eds.), *The Cambridge handbook of violent behavior and aggression* (pp. 151–159). New York, NY: Cambridge University Press.

Schachter, S., & Singer, J. E. (1962). Cognitive, social, and physiological determinants of emotional state. *Psychological Review, 69,* 379–399.

Schaefer, R. T. (2008). Power and power elite. In V. Parrillo (Ed.), *Encyclopedia of social problems.* Thousand Oaks, CA: Sage.

Schaie, K. W. (1994). The life course of adult intellectual development. *American Psychologist, 49*, 304–313.

Schaie, K. W. (2008). A lifespan developmental perspective of psychological ageing. In K. Laidlaw & B. Knight (Eds.), *Handbook of emotional disorders in later life: Assessment and treatment.* New York, NY: Oxford University Press.

Schank, J. C. (2001). Menstrual-cycle synchrony: Problems and new directions for research. *Journal of Comparative Psychology, 115*(1), 3–15.

Schatzkin, A., Lanza, E., Corle, D., Lance, P., Iber, F., Caan, B., … the Polyp Prevention Trial Study Group. (2000). Lack of effect of a low-fat, high fiber diet on the recurrence of colorectal adenomas. *New England Journal of Medicine, 342*, 1149–1155.

Schenck, C., Milner, D., Hurwitz, T., Bundlie, S., & Mahowald, M. (1989). A polysomnographic and clinical report on sleep-related injury in 100 adult patients. *The American Journal of Psychiatry, 146*(9), 1166–1173.

Schifferstein, H. N. J., & Hilscher, M. C. (2010). Multisensory images for everyday products: How modality importance, stimulus congruence, and emotional context affect image descriptions and modality vividness ratings. *Journal of Mental Imagery, 34*, 63–98.

Schmader, T. (2010). Stereotype threat deconstructed. *Current Directions in Psychological Science, 19,*14–18.

Schmader, T., & Johns, M. (2003). Converging evidence that stereotype threat reduces working memory capacity. *Journal of Personality and Social Psychology, 85*, 440–452.

Schmader, T., Johns, M., & Forbes, C. (2008). An integrated process model of stereotype threat effects on performance. *Psychological Review, 115*, 336–356.

Schmidt, U. (2004). Undue influence of weight on self-evaluation: A population-based twin study of gender differences. *International Journal of Eating Disorders, 35*(2), 133–135.

Schmidt, U., Lee, S., Beecham, J., Perkins, S., Treasure, J., Yi, I., … Eisler, I. (2007). A randomized controlled trial of family therapy and cognitive behavior therapy guided self-care for adolescents with bulimia nervosa and related disorders. *American Journal of Psychiatry, 164*(4), 591–598.

Schopp, L. H., Good, G. E., Mazurek, M. O., Barker, K. B., & Stucky, R. C. (2007). Masculine role variables and outcomes among men with spinal cord injury. *Disability and Rehabilitation: An International, Multidisciplinary Journal, 29*, 625–633.

Schunk, D. H. (2008). Attributions as motivators of self-regulated learning. In D. H. Schunk & B. J. Zimmerman (Eds.), *Motivation and self-regulated learning: Theory, research, and applications* (pp. 245–266). Mahwah, NJ: Erlbaum.

Schweckendiek, J., Klucken, T., Merz, C. J., Tabbert, K., Walter, B., Ambach, W., Vaitl, D., & Stark, R. (2011). Weaving the (neuronal) web: Fear learning in spider phobia. *NeuroImage, 54*(1), 681–688.

Scribner, S. (1977). Modes of thinking and ways of speaking: Culture and logic reconsidered. In P. N. Johnson-Laird & P. C. Wason (Eds.), *Thinking: Readings in cognitive science* (pp. 324–339). New York, NY: Cambridge University Press.

Scully, J. A., Tosi, H., & Banning, K. (2000). Life event checklists: Revisiting the Social Readjustment Rating Scale after 30 years. *Educational & Psychological Measurement, 60*(6), 864–876.

Sebre, S., Sprugevica, I., Novotni, A., Bonevski, D., Pakalniskiene, V., Popescu, D., Turchina, T., Friedrich, W., & Lewis, O. (2004). Crosscultural comparisons of child-reported emotional and physical abuse: Rates, risk factors and psychosocial symptoms. *Child Abuse & Neglect, 28*(1), 113–127.

Seedat, S., Scott, K. M., Angermeyer, M. C., Berglund, P., Bromet, E. J., Brugha, T. S., … Kessler, R. C. (2009). Cross-national associations between gender and mental disorders in the World Health Organization World Mental Health surveys. *Archives of General Psychiatry, 66*, 785–795.

Seeman, P. (2011). All roads to schizophrenia lead to dopamine supersensitivity and elevated dopamine D2High receptors. *CNS Neuroscience & Therapeutics, 17*(2), 118–132.

Segal, Z., Bieling, P., Young, T., MacQueen, G., Cooke, R., Martin, L., Bloch, R., & Levitan, R. (2010). Antidepressant monotherapy vs sequential pharmacotherapy and mindfulness-based cognitive therapy, or placebo, for relapse prophylaxis in recurrent depression. *Archives of General Psychiatry, 67*(12), 1256–1264.

Segerdahl, P., Fields, W., & Savage-Rumbaugh, E. S. (2006). *Kanzai's primal language: The cultural initiation of primates into language.* New York, NY: Palgrave Macmillan.

Segerstrom, S. C., & Miller, G. E. (2004). Psychological stress and the human immune system: A meta-analytic study of 30 years of inquiry. *Psychological Bulletin, 130*(4), 601–630.

Ségin, J. R., Sylvers, P., & Lielenfeld, S. O. (2007). The neuropsychology of violence. In D. J. Flannery, A. T. Vazsonyi, & I. D. Waldman (Eds.), *The Cambridge handbook of violent behavior and aggression* (pp. 187–214). New York, NY: Cambridge University Press.

Seligman, M. E. P. (1971). Phobias and preparedness. *Behavior Therapy, 2*, 307–321.

Seligman, M. E. P. (1975) *Helplessness: On depression, development, and death.* San Francisco, CA: Freeman.

Seligman, M. E. P. (1994). *What you can change and what you can't.* New York, NY: Alfred A. Knopf.

Seligman, M. E. P. (2007). Coaching and positive psychology. *Australian Psychologist, 42*, 266–267.

Selye, H. (1936). A syndrome produced by diverse nocuous agents. *Nature, 138*, 32.

Selye, H. (1974). *Stress without distress.* New York, NY: Harper & Row.

Şendağ, S., Duran, M., & Fraser, M. (2012). Surveying the extent of involvement in online academic dishonesty (e-dishonesty) related practices among university students and the rationale students provide: One university's experience. *Computers in Human Behavior, 28*(3), 849–860.

Senko, C., Durik, A. M., & Harackiewicz, J. M. (2008). Historical perspectives and new directions in achievement goal theory: Understanding the effects of mastery and performance-approach goals. In J. Y. Shah & W. L. Gardner (Eds.), *Handbook of motivation science* (pp. 100–113). New York, NY: Guilford Press.

Sequeira, A., Mamdani, F., Lalovic, A., Anguelova, M., Lesage, A., Seguin, M., …Turecki, G. (2004). Alpha 2A adrenergic receptor gene and suicide. *Psychiatry Research, 125*(2), 87–93.

Shah, V. S., & Ohlsson, A. (2007). Venepuncture versus heel lance for blood sampling in term neonates. *Cochrane Database of Systematic Reviews, 4*, CD001452.

Sharma, V., & Mazmanian, D. (2003). Sleep loss and postpartum psychosis. *Bipolar Disorders, 5*(2), 98–105.

Sharot, T., Shiner, T., Brown, A. C., Fan, J., & Dolan, R. J. (2009). Dopamine enhances expectation of pleasure in humans. *Current Biology: CB, 19*(24), 2077–2080.

Sharps, M. J., Hess, A. B., Casner, H., Ranes, B., & Jones, J. (2007). Eyewitness memory in context: Toward a systematic understanding of eyewitness evidence. *The Forensic Examiner, 16*, 20–27.

Shatkin, J., & Janssen, A. (2012). Atypical psychopharmacologic strategies. In D. Rosenberg, P. Davanzo, & S. Gershon (Eds.), *Pharmacotherapy of child and adolescent psychiatric disorders* (pp. 365–398). West Sussex, England: John Wiley & Sons.

Shaver, P. R., & Mikulincer, M. (2005). Attachment theory and research: Resurrection of the psychodynamic approach to personality. *Journal of Research in Personality, 39*(1), 22–45.

Shea, S. C. (1988). *Psychiatric interviewing: The art of understanding.* Philadelphia, PA: Saunders.

Shear, K., Halmi, K. A., Widiger, T. A., & Boyce, C. (2007). Sociocultural factors and gender. In W. E. Narrow, M. B. First, P. J. Sirovatka, & D. A. Regier (Eds.), *Age and gender considerations in psychiatric diagnosis: A research agenda for DSM-V* (pp. 65–79). Arlington, VA: American Psychiatric Publishing.

Sheehan, C. (2011). Making the jurors the "experts": The case for eyewitness identification jury instructions. Retrieved from http://lawdigitalcommons.bc.edu/bclr/vol52/iss2/10

Sheehy, G. (1976). *Passages. Predictable crises of adult life.* New York, NY: Dutton.

Sheppard, L. D., & Vernon, P. A. (2008). Intelligence and speed of information-processing: A review of 50 years of research. *Personality and Individual Differences, 44*, 535–551.

Shepperd, J., Malone, W., & Sweeny, K. (2008). Exploring causes of the self-serving bias. *Social and Personality Psychology Compass, 2*, 895–908.

Sher, K. J., Grekin, E. R., & Williams, N. A. (2005). The development of alcohol use disorders. *Annual Review of Clinical Psychology, 1*, 493–523.

Sheridan, C., Draganova, R., Ware, M., Murphy, P., Govindan, R., Siegel, E. R., … Preissl, H. (2010). Early development of brain responses to rapidly presented auditory stimulation: A magnetoencephalographic study. *Brain and Development, 32*, 642–657.

Sherif, M. (1966). *In common predicament: Social psychology of intergroup conflict and cooperation.* Boston, MA: Houghton Mifflin.

Sherif, M. (1998). Experiments in group conflict. In J. M. Jenkins, K. Oatley, & N. L. Stein (Eds.), *Human emotions: A reader* (pp. 245–252). Malden, MA: Blackwell.

Sheth, J. N., Newman, B. I., & Gross, B. L. (1991). Why we buy what we buy: A theory of

consumption values. *Journal of Business Research*, 22(2), 159–170.

Shields, M., Carroll, M., & Ogden, C. (2011). *Adult obesity prevalence in Canada and the United States.* NCHS data brief, no 56. Hyattsville, MD: National Center for Health Statistics.

Shin, R.-M., Tully, K., Li, Y., Cho, J.-H., Higuchi, M., Suhara, T., & Bolshakov, V. Y. (2010). Hierarchical order of coexisting pre- and postsynaptic forms of long-term potentiation at synapses in amygdala. *PNAS Proceedings of the National Academy of Sciences of the United States of America, 107*(44), 19073–19078.

Shiraishi, J., Tanizawa, H., Fujita, M., Kawakami, S., & Bungo, T. (2011). Localization of hypothalamic insulin receptor in neonatal chicks: Evidence for insulinergic system control of feeding behavior. *Neuroscience Letters, 491*(3), 177–180.

Siccoli, M. M., Rölli-Baumeler, N., Achermann, P., & Bassetti, C. L. (2008). Correlation between sleep and cognitive functions after hemispheric ischaemic stroke. *European Journal of Neurology, 15,* 565–572.

Sideridis, G. D., & Kaplan, A. (2011). Achievement goals and persistence across tasks: The roles of failure and success. *Journal of Experimental Education, 79*(4), 429–451.

Siegala, M., & Varley, R. (2008). If we could talk to the animals. *Behavioral & Brain Sciences, 31,* 146–147.

Siegel, A. (2004). *The neurobiology of aggression and rage.* Boca Raton, FL: CRC Press.

Siegel, J. M. (2000, January). Narcolepsy. *Scientific American*, pp. 76–81.

Siegel, J. M. (2008). Do all animals sleep? *Trends in Neurosciences, 31,* 208–213.

Siever, L. J. (2008). Neurobiology of aggression and violence. *American Journal of Psychiatry, 165,* 429–442.

Sigall, H., & Johnson, M. (2006). The relationship between facial contact with a pillow and mood. *Journal of Applied Social Psychology, 36,* 505–526.

Silventoinen, K., Magnusson, P. K., Tynelius, P., Kaprio, J., & Rasmussen, F. (2008). Heritability of body size and muscle strength in young adulthood: A study of one million Swedish men. *Genetic Epidemiology, 32*(4), 341–349.

Silverman, W. K., Pina, A. A., & Viswesvaran, C. (2008). Evidence-based psychosocial treatments for phobic and anxiety disorders in children and adolescents. *Journal of Clinical Child and Adolescent Psychology, 37,* 105–130.

Silvestri, A. J., & Root, D. H. (2008). Effects of REM deprivation and an NMDA agonist on the extinction of conditioned fear. *Physiology & Behavior, 93,* 274–281.

Simpson, J. A., & Beckes, L. (2010). Evolutionary perspectives on prosocial behavior. In M. Mikulincer & P. R. Shaver (Eds.), *Prosocial motives, emotions, and behavior: The better angels of our nature* (pp. 35–53). Washington, DC: American Psychological Association.

Sinason, V. (Ed.). (2011). *Attachment, trauma, and multiplicity: Working with dissociative identity disorder* (2nd ed.). New York, NY: Routledge.

Singelis, T. M., Triandis, H. C., Bhawuk, D. S., & Gelfand, M. (1995). Horizontal and vertical dimensions of individualism and collectivism: A theoretical and measurement refinement. *Cross-Cultural Research, 29,* 240–275.

Skelhorn, J., Griksaitis, D., & Rowe, C. (2008). Colour biases are more than a question of taste. *Animal Behaviour, 75,* 827–835.

The Skeptics Dictionary. (2012). Retrieved from http://skepdic.com/randi.html

Skinner, B. F. (1948). Superstition in the pigeon. *Journal of Experimental Psychology, 38,* 168–172.

Skinner, B. F. (1953). *Science and human behavior.* New York, NY: Macmillan.

Skinner, B. F. (1961). Diagramming schedules of reinforcement. *Journal of the Experimental Analysis of Behavior, 1,* 67–68.

Skinner, B. F. (1992). "Superstition" in the pigeon. *Journal of Experimental Psychology: General, 121*(3), 273–274.

Skoczenski, A. M., & Norcia, A. M. (2002). Late maturation of visual hyperacuity. *Psychological Science, 13,* 537–541.

Slagter, H. A., Lutz, A., Greischar, L. L., Francis, A. D., Nieuwenhuis, S., Davis, J. M., & Davidson, R. J. (2007). Mental training affects distribution of limited brain resources. *PLoS Biology, 5*(6), e138.

Slováčková, B., & Slováček, L. (2007). Moral judgement competence and moral attitudes of medical students. *Nursing Ethics, 14,* 320–328.

Small, M. F. (1992). The evolution of female sexuality and mate selection in humans. *Human Nature, 3*(2), 133–156.

SMARTRISK. (2009). *The economic burden of injury in Canada.* Toronto, ON: Author.

Smeesters, D., Mussweiler, T., & Mandel, N. (2010). The effects of thin and heavy media images on overweight and underweight consumers: Social comparison processes and behavioral implications. *Journal of Consumer Research, 36*(6), 930–949.

Smith, E. E. (1995). Concepts and categorization. In E. E. Smith & D. N. Osherson (Eds.), *Thinking: An invitation to cognitive science* (2nd ed., Vol. 3, pp. 3–33). Cambridge: MIT Press.

Smith, K., Berridge, K., & Aldridge, J. (2011). Disentangling pleasure from incentive salience and learning signals in brain reward circuitry. *Proceedings of the National Academy of Sciences of the United States of America, 108*(27), E255–E264.

Smith, M. T., Huang, M. I., & Manber, R. (2005). Cognitive behavior therapy for chronic insomnia occurring within the context of medical and psychiatric disorders. *Clinical Psychology Review, 25,* 559–592.

Smith, P., Frank, J., Bondy, S., & Mustard, C. (2008). Do changes in job control predict differences in health status? Results from a longitudinal national survey of Canadians. *Psychosomatic Medicine, 70,* 85–91.

Smith, R. A. (2002). *Challenging your preconceptions: Thinking critically about psychology* (2nd ed.). Toronto, ON: Nelson.

Smolak, L. (1996). *National Eating Disorders Association/Next Door Neighbors Puppet Guide Book.* Seattle, WA: NEDA.

Smoller, J. W., Gardner-Schuster, E., & Covino, J. (2008). The genetic basis of panic and phonic anxiety disorders. *American Journal of Medical Genetics Part C (Seminars in Medical Genetics), 148C,* 118–126.

Snarey, J. R. (1985). Cross-cultural universality of social-moral development: A critical review of Kohlbergian research. *Psychological Bulletin, 97,* 202–233.

Snarey, J. R. (1995). In communitarian voice: The sociological expansion of Kohlbergian theory, research, and practice. In W. M. Kurtines & J. L. Gewirtz (Eds.), *Moral development: An introduction* (pp. 109–134). Boston, MA: Allyn & Bacon.

Snyder, C. R., Lopez, S. J., & Pedrotti, J. T. (2011). *Positive psychology: The scientific and practical explorations of human strengths* (2nd ed.). Los Angeles, CA: Sage.

Snyder, J. S., & Alain, C. (2007). Sequential auditory sense analysis is preserved in normal aging adults. *Cerebral Cortex, 17,* 501–512.

Snyder, J., Soumier, A., Brewer, M., Pickel, J., & Cameron, H. (2011). Adult hippocampal neurogenesis buffers stress responses and depressive behaviour. *Nature, 476*(7361), 458–461.

Soares, M. M., Jacobs, K., Korunka, C., Kubicek, B., Prem, R., & Cvitan, A. (2012). Recovery and detachment between shifts, and fatigue during a twelve-hour shift. *Work, 41,* 3227–3233.

Solan, H. A., & Mozlin, R. (2001). Children in poverty: Impact on health, visual development, and school failure. *Issues in Interdisciplinary Care, 3*(4), 271–288.

Sollod, R. N., Monte, C. F., & Wilson, J. P. (2009). *Beneath the mask: An introduction to theories of personality* (8th ed.). Hoboken, NJ: Wiley.

Solms, M. (1997). *The neuropsychology of dreams.* Mahwah, NJ: Lawrence Erlbaum.

Solomon, L. (2008). *The Deniers.* Bloomington, MN: Richard Vigilante Books Inc.

Sood, A. K., Armaiz-Pena, G. N., Halder, J., Nick, A. M., Stone, R. L., Wei, H., ... Lutgendorf, S. K. (2010). Adrenergic modulation of focal adhesion kinase protects human ovarian cancer cells from anoikis. *Journal of Clinical Investigation, 120*(5), 1515–1523.

Sowell, E. R., Mattson, S. N., Kan, E., Thompson, P. M., Riley, E. P., Edward, P., & Toga, A. W. (2008). Abnormal cortical thickness and brain-behavior correlation patterns in individuals with heavy prenatal alcohol exposure. *Cerebral Cortex, 18,* 136–144.

Spearman, C. (1923). *The nature of "intelligence" and the principles of cognition.* London: Macmillan.

Spears, R. (2011). Group identities: The social identity perspective. In S. Schwartz, K. Luyckx, & V. Vignoles (Eds.), *Handbook of identity theory and research* (Vols. 1–2, pp. 201–224). New York, NY: Springer.

Sperling, G. (1960). The information available in brief visual presentations. *Psychological Monographs, 74* (Whole No. 498).

Spiegel, D., & Maldonado, J. R. (1999). Dissociative disorders. In R. E. Hales, S. C. Yudofsky, & J. C. Talbott (Eds.), *American psychiatric press textbook of psychiatry.* Washington, DC: American Psychiatric Press.

Spitz, R. A., & Wolf, K. M. (1946). The smiling response: A contribution to the ontogenesis of social relations. *Genetic Psychology Monographs, 34,* 57–123.

Spokane, A. R., Meir, E. I., & Caialano, M. (2000). Person-environment congruence and Holland's theory: A review and reconsideration. *Journal of Vocational Behavior, 57*(2), 137–187.

Sprecher, S., & Regan, P. C. (2002). Liking some things (in some people) more than others: Partner preferences in romantic relationships

and friendships. *Journal of Social & Personal Relationships, 19*(4), 463–481.

Sroufe, L. A., Egeland, B., Carlson, E. A., & Collins, W. A. (2005). *The development of the person: The Minnesota study of risk and adaptation from birth to adulthood.* New York, NY: Guilford.

Stafford, J., & Lynn, S. J. (2002). Cultural scripts, memories of childhood abuse, and multiple identities: A study of role-played enactments. *International Journal of Clinical & Experimental Hypnosis, 50*(1), 67–85.

Stanley, J. T., & Isaacowitz, D. M. (2012). Socioemotional perspectives on adult development. In S. K. Whitbourne & M. J. Sliwinski (Eds.), *The Wiley-Blackwell handbook of adulthood and aging* (pp. 236–253). Chichester, UK: Wiley.

Statistics Canada. (2004). Canadian community health survey: Mental health and well-being. Retrieved from http://www.statcan.gc.ca/pub/82-617-x/index-eng.htm

Statistics Canada. (2005a). Work-life balance of shift workers. Retrieved from http://www.statcan.gc.ca/pub/75-001-x/2008108/article/10677-eng.htm

Statistics Canada. (2005b). Divorces. *The Daily,* March 9. Retrieved from http://www.statcan.ca/Daily/English/050309/d050309b.htm

Statistics Canada. (2007). 2006 Census: Immigration, citizenship, language mobility, and migration. *The Daily,* December 4. Retrieved from http://www.statcan.ca/Daily/English/071204/td071204.htm

Statistics Canada. (2008). Study: Sedentary behaviour and obesity. *The Daily,* June 18. Retrieved from http://www.statcan.gc.ca/daily-quotidien/080618/dq080618b-eng.htm

Statistics Canada. (2012a). Leading causes of death, by sex, 2009. Retrieved from www.statcan.gc.ca/tables-tableaux/sum-som/l01/cst01/hlth36a-eng.htm.

Statistics Canada. (2012b). Smokers, by sex, provinces and territories, 2011. CANSIM, table 105-0501. Catalogue no. 82-221-X. Retrieved from http://www.statcan.gc.ca/tables-tableaux/sum-som/l01/cst01/health74b-eng.htm

Statistics Canada. (2012c). 2011 census of population: Linguistic characteristics of Canadians. *The Daily,* October 24. Retrieved from http://www.statcan.gc.ca/daily-quotidien/121024/dq121024a-eng.htm

Statistics Canada. (2012d). Portrait of families and living arrangements in Canada. Retrieved from http://www12.statcan.gc.ca/census-recensement/2011/as-sa/98-312-x/98-312-x2011001-eng.cfm

Steele, C. M. (2003). Through the back door to theory. *Psychological Inquiry, 14*(3–4), 314–317.

Steele, C. M., & Aronson, J. (1995). Stereotype threat and the intellectual test performance of African Americans. *Journal of Personality and Social Psychology, 69,* 797–811.

Steele, J., James, J. B., & Barnett, R. C. (2002). Learning in a man's world: Examining the perceptions of undergraduate women in male-dominated academic areas. *Psychology of Women Quarterly, 26*(1), 46–50.

Steenkamp, J., de Jong, M., & Baumgartner, H. (2010). Socially desirable response tendencies in survey research. *Journal of Marketing Research (JMR), 47*(2), 199–214.

Stein, D. J., & Matsunaga, H. (2006). Specific phobia: A disorder of fear conditioning and extinction. *CNS Spectrums, 11*(4), 248–251.

Steinberg, L. (2008). A social neuroscience perspective on adolescent risk-taking. *Developmental Review, 28,* 78–106.

Steinhart, P. (1986, March). Personal boundaries. *Audubon,* pp. 8–11.

Sternberg, R. J. (1985). *Beyond IQ: A triarchic theory of human intelligence.* New York, NY: Cambridge University Press.

Sternberg, R. J. (1998). Principles of teaching for successful intelligence. *Educational Psychologist, 33,* 65–72.

Sternberg, R. J. (1999). The theory of successful intelligence. *Review of General Psychology, 3,* 292–316.

Sternberg, R. J. (2004). Culture and intelligence. *American Psychologist, 59,* 325–338.

Sternberg, R. J. (2005). The importance of converging operations in the study of human intelligence. *Cortex. 41*(2), 243–244.

Sternberg, R. J. (2007). Developing successful intelligence in all children: A potential solution to underachievement in ethnic minority children. In M. C. Wang & R. D. Taylor (Eds.), *Closing the achievement gap.* Philadelphia: Laboratory for Student Success at Temple University.

Sternberg, R. J. (2008). The triarchic theory of human intelligence. In N. Salkind (Ed.), *Encyclopedia of educational psychology* (Vol. 2, pp. 988–994). Thousand Oaks, CA: Sage.

Sternberg, R. J. (2009a). Sketch of a componential subtheory of human intelligence. In J. C. Kaufman & E. L. Grigorenko (Eds.), *The essential Sternberg: Essays on intelligence, psychology, and education* (pp. 3–32). New York, NY: Springer Publishing Co.

Sternberg, R. J. (2009b). The nature of creativity. In J. C. Kaufman & E. L. Grigorenko (Eds.) *The essential Sternberg: Essays on intelligence, psychology, and education* (pp. 103–118). New York, NY: Springer Publishing Co.

Sternberg, R. J. (2009c). The theory of successful intelligence. In J. C. Kaufman & E. L. Grigorenko (Eds.), *The essential Sternberg: Essays on intelligence, psychology, and education* (pp. 71–100). New York, NY: Springer Publishing Co.

Sternberg, R. J. (2009d). Toward a triarchic theory of intelligence. In J. C. Kaufman & E. L. Grigorenko (Eds.), *The essential Sternberg: Essays on intelligence, psychology, and education* (pp. 33–70). New York, NY: Springer Publishing Co.

Sternberg, R. J. (2012). *Cognitive psychology* (6th ed.). Belmont, CA: Cengage.

Sternberg, R. J., & Grigorenko, E. L. (2008). Ability testing across cultures. In L. Suzuki (Ed.), *Handbook of multicultural assessment* (3rd ed.). New York, NY: Jossey-Bass.

Sternberg, R. J., Grigorenko, E. L., & Kidd, K. C. (2005). Intelligence, race, and genetics. *American Psychologist, 60,* 46–59.

Sternberg, R. J., & Hedlund, J. (2002). Practical intelligence, g, and work psychology. *Human Performance, 15*(1–2), 143–160.

Sternberg, R. J., & Lubart, T. I. (1992). Buy low and sell high: An investment approach to creativity. *Current Directions in Psychological Science, 1*(1), 1–5.

Sternberg, R. J., & Lubart, T. I. (1996). Investing in creativity. *American Psychologist, 51*(7), 677–688.

Sternberg, R. J., Grigorenko, E. L., & Kidd, K. C. (2005). Intelligence, race, and genetics. *American Psychologist, 60,* 46–59.

Stiles, W. B., Barkham, M., Mellor-Clark, J., & Connell, J. (2008). Effectiveness of cognitive-behavioural, person-centered, and psychodynamic therapies in UK primary-care routine practice: Replication in a larger sample. *Psychological Medicine, 38,* 677–688.

Stokes, D., & Lappin, M. (2010). Neurofeedback and biofeedback with 37 migraineurs: A clinical outcome study. *Behavioral and Brain Functions, 6,* Article ID 9.

Stompe, T. G., Ortwein-Swoboda, K., Ritter, K., & Schanda, H. (2003). Old wine in new bottles? Stability and plasticity of the contents of schizophrenic delusions. *Psychopathology, 36*(1), 6–12.

Stone, J., & Focella, E. (2011). Post-decisional self-enhancement and self-protection: The role of the self in cognitive dissonance processes. In M. D. Alicke & C. Sedikides (Eds.), *Handbook of self-enhancement and self-protection* (pp. 192–210). New York, NY: Guilford Press.

Stone, K. L., & Redline, S. (2006). Sleep-related breathing disorders in the elderly. *Sleep Medicine Clinics, 1*(2), 247–262.

Stone, S., Teixeira, C., Devito, L., Zaslavsky, K., Josselyn, S., Lozano, A., & Frankland, P. (2011). Stimulation of entorhinal cortex promotes adult neurogenesis and facilitates spatial memory. *Journal of Neuroscience, 31*(38), 13469–13484.

Stoner, J. A. (1961). *A comparison of individual and group decisions involving risk.* Unpublished master's thesis, School of Industrial Management, MIT, Cambridge, MA.

Strack, F., Martin, L. L., & Stepper, S. (1988). Inhibiting and facilitating conditions of the human smile: A nonobstrusive test of the facial feedback hypothesis. *Journal of Personality and Social Psychology, 54,* 768–777.

Strahan, E., Panayiotou, G., Clements, R., & Scott, J. (2011). Beer, wine, and social anxiety: Testing the "self-medication hypothesis" in the US and Cyprus. *Addiction Research & Theory, 19*(4), 302–311.

Strassmann, B. I. (1999). Menstrual synchrony pheromones: Cause for doubt. *Human Reproduction, 14,* 579–580

Stratton, G. M. (1896). Some preliminary experiments on vision without inversion of the retinal image. *Psychological Review, 3,* 611–617.

Straub, R. O. (2007). *Health psychology: A biopsychosocial approach* (2nd ed.). New York, NY: Worth.

Strayer, D., Drews, F., & Crouch, D. (2006). A comparison of the cell phone driver and the drunk driver. *Human Factors, 48*(2), 381–391.

Streissguth, A. P., & Connor, P. D. (2001). Fetal alcohol syndrome and other effects of prenatal alcohol: Developmental cognitive neuroscience implications. In C. A. Nelson & M. Luciana (Eds.), *Handbook of developmental cognitive neuroscience* (pp. 505–518). Cambridge, MA: MIT Press.

Strickland, B. R. (1995). Research on sexual orientation and human development: A commentary. *Developmental Psychology, 31*(1), 137–140.

Striegel-Moore, R., Rosselli, F., Perrin, N., DeBar, L., Wilson, G., May, A., & Kraemer, H. (2009). Gender difference in the prevalence of eating disorder symptoms. *The International Journal of Eating Disorders, 42*(5), 471–474.

Sue, D. W., & Sue, D. (2008). *Counseling the culturally diverse: Theory and practice* (5th ed.). Hoboken, NJ: Wiley.

Sue, D. W., & Sue, D. (2012). *Counseling the culturally diverse: Theory and practice* (6th ed.). Hoboken, NJ: Wiley.

Sugarman, H., Impey, C., Buxner, S., & Antonellis, J. (2011). Astrology beliefs among undergraduate students. *Astronomy Education Review, 10*(1).

Sullivan, M. J. L. (2008). Toward a biopsychomotor conceptualization of pain: Implications for research and intervention. *Clinical Journal of Pain, 24*, 281–290.

Sullivan, M. J. L., Tripp, D. A., & Santor, D. (1998). *Gender differences in pain and pain behavior: The role of catastrophizing.* Paper presented at the annual meeting of the American Psychological Association, San Francisco, CA.

Sullivan, T. P., & Holt, L. J. (2008). PTSD symptom clusters are differentially related to substance use among community women exposed to intimate partner violence. *Journal of Traumatic Stress, 21* , 173–180.

Sundram, F., Deeley, Q., Sarkar, S., Daly, E., Latham, R., Barker, G., & Murphy, D. (2011). White matter microstructural abnormalities in antisocial personality disorder: A pilot diffusion tensor imaging study. *European Psychiatry, 26*(1), 957.

Sünram-Lea, S., Owen-Lynch, J., Robinson, S., Jones, E., & Hu, H. (2012). The effect of energy drinks on cortisol levels, cognition and mood during a fire-fighting exercise. *Psychopharmacology, 219*(1), 83–97.

Suomi, S. J. (1991). Adolescent depression and depressive symptoms: Insights from longitudinal studies with rhesus monkeys. *Journal of Youth and Adolescence, 20*, 273–287.

Suzuki, L. A., & Valencia, R. (1997). Race-ethnicity and measured intelligence. *American Psychologist, 52*, 1103–1114.

Suzuki, W. A., & Amaral, D. G. (2004). Functional neuroanatomy of the medial temporal lobe memory system. *Cortex, 40*(1), 220–222.

Swami, V., & Furnham, A. (2008). *The psychology of physical attraction.* New York, NY: Routledge/ Taylor & Francis Group.

Swanson, S. A., Crow, S. J., Le Grange, D., Swendsen, J., & Merikangas, K. R. (2011). Prevalence and correlates of eating disorders in adolescents: Results from the national comorbidity survey replication adolescent supplement. *Archives of General Psychiatry, 68*(7), 714–723.

Swartz, K. L. (2008). *Depression and anxiety.* Johns Hopkins White Papers. Baltimore, MD: Johns Hopkins Medical Institutions.

Szasz, T. (1960). The myth of mental illness. *American Psychologist, 15*, 113–118.

Szasz, T. (2000). Second commentary on "Aristotle's function argument." *Philosophy, Psychiatry, & Psychology, 7*, 3–16.

Szasz, T. (2004). The psychiatric protection order for the "battered mental patient." *British Medical Journal, 327*(7429), 1449–1451.

T

Takano, Y., & Sogon, S. (2008). Are Japanese more collectivistic than Americans? Examining conformity in in-groups and the reference-group effect. *Journal of Cross-Cultural Psychology, 39*, 237–250.

Talarico, J. M., & Rubin, D. C. (2007). Flashbulb memories are special after all; in phenomenology, not accuracy. *Applied Cognitive Psychology, 21*, 557–578.

Tal-Or, N., & Papirman, Y. (2007). The fundamental attribution error in attributing fictional figures' characteristics to the actors. *Media Psychology, 9*, 331–345.

Tanaka, T., Yoshida, M., Yokoo, H., Tomita, M., & Tanaka, M. (1998). Expression of aggression attenuates both stress-induced gastric ulcer formation and increases in noradrenaline release in the rat amygdala assessed intracerebral microdialysis. *Pharmacology, Biochemistry & Behavior, 59*(1), 27–31.

Tandon, R., Keshavan, M. S., & Nasrallah, H. A. (2008). Schizophrenia, "just the facts": What we know in 2008. Part 2. Epidemiology and etiology. *Schizophrenia Research, 102*, 1–18.

Tang, Y.-P., Wang, H., Feng, R., Kyin, M., & Tsien, J. Z. (2001). Differential effects of enrichment on learning and memory function in NR2B transgenic mice. *Neuropharmacology, 41*(6), 779–790.

Tarbox, R. S. F., Ghezzi, P. M., & Wilson, G. (2006). The effects of token reinforcement on attending in a young child with autism. *Behavioral Interventions, 21*, 155–164.

Taub, E. (2004). Harnessing brain plasticity through behavioral techniques to produce new treatments in neurorehabilitation. *American Psychologist, 59*(8), 692–704.

Taylor, D. J., Lichstein, K. L., & Durrence, H. H. (2003). Insomnia as a risk factor. *Behavioral Sleep Medicine, 1*, 227–247.

Taylor, L., Fiore, A., Mendelsohn, G., & Cheshire, C. (2011). "Out of my league": A real-world test of the matching hypothesis. *Personality and Social Psychology Bulletin, 37*(7), 942–954.

Taylor, R. C., Harris, N. A., Singleton, E. G., Moolchan, E. T., & Heishman, S. J. (2000). Tobacco craving: Intensity-related effects of imagery scripts in drug abusers. *Experimental and Clinical Psychopharmacology, 8*(1), 75–87.

Tebartz van Elst, L., Hesslinger, B., Thiel, T., Geiger, E., Haegele, K., Lemieux, L., … Ebert, D. (2003). Frontolimbic brain abnormalities in patients with borderline personality disorder: A volumetric magnetic resonance imaging study. *Biological Psychiatry, 54*(2), 163–171.

Tecchio, F., Zappasodi, F., Pasqualetti, P., De Gennaro, L., Pellicciari, M. C., Ercolani, M., Squitti, R., & Rossini, P. M. (2008). Age dependence of primary motor cortex plasticity induced by paired associative stimulation. *Clinical Neurophysiology, 119*, 675–682.

Tellegen, A. (1985). Structures of mood and personality and their relevance to assessing anxiety with an emphasis on self-report. In A. H. Tuma & J. D. Maser (Eds.), *Anxiety and the anxiety disorders* (pp. 681–706). Hillsdale, NJ: Erlbaum.

Terman, L. M. (1916). *The measurement of intelligence.* Boston, MA: Houghton Mifflin.

Terman, L. M. (1954). Scientists and nonscientists in a group of 800 gifted men. *Psychological Monographs, 68*(7), 1–44.

Terrace, H. S. (1979, November). How Nim Chimpsky changed my mind. *Psychology Today, 13*(6), 65–76.

Terry, S. W. (2009). *Learning and memory* (4th ed.). Boston, MA: Allyn and Bacon.

Tetlock, P. E., Peterson, R. S., McGuire, C., Chang, S., & Feld, P. (1992). Assessing political group dynamics: A test of the groupthink model. *Journal of Personality and Social Psychology, 63*, 403–425.

Tett, R. P., & Murphy, P. J. (2002). Personality and situations in co-worker preference: Similarity and complementarity in worker compatibility. *Journal of Business & Psychology, 17*(2), 223–243.

Thanh, N. X., & Jonsson, E. (2010). Drinking alcohol during pregnancy: Evidence from Canadian community health survey 2007/2008. *Journal of Population Therapeutics and Clinical Pharmacology, 17*, e302–e307.

Thomas, N., Rossell, S., Farhall, J., Shawyer, F., & Castle, D. (2011). Cognitive behavioural therapy for auditory hallucinations: Effectiveness and predictors of outcome in a specialist clinic. *Behavioural and Cognitive Psychotherapy, 39*(2), 129–138.

Thomas, S. E., Randall, P. K., Book, S. W., & Randall, C. L. (2008). The complex relationship between co-occurring social anxiety and alcohol use disorders: What effect does treating social anxiety have on drinking? *Alcoholism: Clinical and Experimental Research, 32*, 77–84.

Thompson, R. A. (2008). Early attachment and later development: Familiar questions, new answers. In J. Cassidy & P. R. Shaver (Eds.), *Handbook of attachment: Theory, research, and clinical applications* (2nd ed., pp. 348–365). New York, NY: Guilford.

Thompson, R. A., & Meyer, S. (2007). The socialization of emotion regulation in the family. In J. Gross (Ed.), *Handbook of emotion regulation* (pp. 249–268). New York, NY: Guilford Press.

Thompson, R. F. (2005). In search of memory traces. *Annual Review of Clinical Psychology, 56*, 1–23.

Thomson, A. (2000). Mechanisms of vitamin deficiency in chronic alcohol misusers and the development of the Wernicke-Korsakoff syndrome. *Alcohol and Alcoholism 35*(Suppl. 1), 2–7.

Thomson, E. (2007). *Mind in life: Biology, phenomenology, and the sciences of mind.* Cambridge, MA: Belknap Press.

Thorndike, E. L. (1898). Animal intelligence. *Psychological Review Monograph, 2*(8).

Thorndike, E. L. (1911). *Animal intelligence.* New York, NY: Macmillan.

Thornhill, R., Gangestad, S. W., Miller, R., Scheyd, G., McCollough, J. K., & Franklin, M. (2003). Major histocompatibility complex genes, symmetry, and body scent attractiveness in men and women. *Behavioral Ecology, 14*(5), 668–678.

Thurstone, L. L. (1938). *Primary mental abilities.* Chicago, IL: University of Chicago Press.

Tilley, E., Walmsley, J., Earle, S., & Atkinson, D. (2012). "The silence is roaring": Sterilization, reproductive rights and women with intellectual disabilities. *Disability & Society, 27*(3), 413–426.

Tindale, S., & Posavac, E. (2011). The social psychology of stakeholder processes: Group processes and interpersonal relations. In M. Mark, S. Donaldson, & B. Campbell (Eds.), *Social*

psychology and evaluation (pp. 189–209). New York, NY: Guilford Press.

Tirodkar, M. A., & Jain, A. (2003). Food messages on African American television shows. *American Journal of Public Health, 93*(3), 439–441.

Todd, A. R., Bodenhausen, G. V., Richeson, J. A., & Galinsky, A. D. (2011). Perspective taking combats automatic expressions of racial bias. *Journal of Personality and Social Psychology, 100*(6), 1027–1042.

Tolin, D. F., Robison, J. T., Gaztambide, S., Horowitz, S., & Blank, K. (2007). *Ataques de nervios* and psychiatric disorders in older Puerto Rican primary care patients. *Journal of Cross-Cultural Psychology, 38,* 659–669.

Tolman, E. C., & Honzik, C. H. (1930). Introduction and removal of reward and maze performance in rats. *University of California Publications in Psychology, 4,* 257–275.

Tomkins, S. S. (1962). *Affect, imagery, consciousness: Vol. 1. The positive affects.* New York, NY: Springer.

Tonstad, S., Tønnesen, P., Hajek, P., Williams, K., Billing, C., & Reeves, K. (2006). Effect of maintenance therapy with varenicline on smoking cessation: a randomized controlled trial. *JAMA: Journal of the American Medical Association, 296*(1), 64–71.

Tooby, J., & Cosmides, L. (2008). The evolutionary psychology of the emotions and their relationship to internal regulatory variables. In M. Lewis, J. M. Haviland-Jones, & L. Barrett (Eds.), *Handbook of emotions* (3rd ed., pp. 114–137). New York, NY: Guilford Press.

Torges, C. M., Stewart, A. J., & Duncan, L. E. (2008). Achieving ego-integrity: Personality development in late midlife. *Journal of Research in Personality, 42,* 1004–1019.

Torre P. (2008). Young adults' use and output level settings of personal music systems. *Ear Hear, 29*(5), 791–799.

Torta, D. M., & Castelli, L. (2008). Reward pathways in Parkinson's disease: Clinical and theoretical implications. *Psychiatry and Clinical Neurosciences, 62*(2), 303–313.

Tough Mudder. (n.d.). Retrieved from http://toughmudder.com

Trainor, B. C., Bird, I. M., & Marler, C. A. (2004). Opposing hormonal mechanisms of aggression revealed through short-lived testosterone manipulations and multiple winning experiences. *Hormones & Behavior, 45*(2), 115–121.

Tremaine, R., Dorrian, J., Lack, L., Lovato, N., Ferguson, S., Zhou, X., & Roach, G. (2010). The relationship between subjective and objective sleepiness and performance during a simulated night-shift with a nap countermeasure. *Applied Ergonomics, 42*(1), 52–61.

Tremblay, P. F., Graham, K., & Wells, S. (2008). Severity of physical aggression reported by university students: A test of the interaction between trait aggression and alcohol consumption. *Personality and Individual Differences, 45,* 3–9.

Triandis, H. C. (2007). Culture and psychology: A history of the study of their relationship. In S. Kitayama & D. Cohen (Eds.), *Handbook of cultural psychology* (pp. 59–76). New York, NY: Guilford.

Troll, S. J., Miller, J., & Atchley, R. C. (1979). *Families in later life.* Belmont, CA: Wadsworth.

Tropp, L. R., & Mallett, R. K. (2011). *Moving beyond prejudice reduction: Pathways to positive intergroup relations.* Washington, DC: American Psychological Association.

Tryon, W. W. (2008). Whatever happened to symptom substitution? *Clinical Psychology Review, 28,* 963–968.

Tsao, D. Y., & Livingstone, M. S. (2008). Mechanisms of face perception. *Annual Review of Neuroscience, 31,* 411–437.

Tseng, W. (2004). Culture and psychotherapy: Asian perspectives. *Journal of Mental Health, 13*(2), 151–161.

Tsien, J. Z. (2000, April). Building a brainier mouse. *Scientific American,* pp. 62–68.

Tulving, E. (2000). Concepts of memory. In E. Tulving & F. I. M. Craik (Eds.), *The Oxford handbook of memory* (pp. 33–44). New York, NY: Oxford University Press.

Tulving, E., & Schacter, D. (1990). Priming and human memory systems. *Science, 247*(4940), 301–306.

Tulving, E., & Thompson, D. M. (1973). Encoding specificity and retrieval processes in episodic memory. *Psychological Review, 80,* 352–373.

Tversky, A., & Kahneman, D. (1974). Judgment under uncertainty: Heuristics and biases. *Science, 185,* 1124–1131.

Tversky, A., & Kahneman, D. (1993). Probabilistic reasoning. In A. I. Goldman (Ed.), *Readings in philosophy and cognitive science* (pp. 43–68). Cambridge, MA: The MIT Press.

Twenge, J. M., Baumeisier, R. F., Tice, D. M., & Siucke, T. S. (2001). If you can't join them, beat them: Effects of social exclusion on aggressive behavior. *Journal of Personality and Social Psychology, 81*(6), 1058–1069.

U

Ueno, M., Uchiyama, I., Campos, J., Dahl, A., & Anderson, D. (2011). The organization of wariness of heights in experienced crawlers. *Infancy.* 1–17.

Ulrich, R. E., Stachnik, T. J., & Stainton, N. R. (1963). Student acceptance of generalized personality interpretations. *Psychological Reports, 13,* 831–834.

V

Vaillancourt, T., Hymel, S., & McDougall, P. (2003). Bullying is power: Implications for school-based intervention strategies. *Journal of Applied School Psychology, 19,* 157–176.

Vaillend, C., Poirier, R., & Laroche, S. (2008). Genes, plasticity and mental retardation. *Behavioural Brain Research, 192*(1), 88–105.

Valeo, T., & Beyerstein, L. (2008). Curses! In T. Gordon (Eds.), *Your brain on Cubs: Inside the players and fans* (pp. 59–74, 139–140). Washington, DC: Dana Press.

Van Bokhoven, P., Oomen, C., Hoogendijk, W., Smit, A., Lucassen, P., & Spijker, S. (2011). Reduction in hippocampal neurogenesis after social defeat is long-lasting and responsive to late antidepressant treatment. *European Journal of Neuroscience, 33*(10), 1833–1840.

Van de Carr, F. R., & Lehrer, M. (1997). *While you are expecting: Your own prenatal classroom.* New York, NY: Humanics Publishing.

van de Mortel, T. F. (2008). Faking it: Social desirability response bias in self-report research. *Australian Journal of Advanced Nursing, 25*(4), 40–48.

van Heck, G. L., & den Oudsten, B. L. (2008). Emotional intelligence: Relationships to stress, health, and well-being. In A. Vingerhoets & I. Nyklícek (Eds.), *Emotion regulation: Conceptual and clinical issues* (pp. 97–121). New York, NY: Springer Science Business Media.

van Lier, P., Boivin, M., Dionne, G., Vitaro, F., Brendgen, M., Koot, H., Tremblay, R. E., & Pérusse, D. (2007). Kindergarten children's genetic variabilities interact with friends' aggression to promote children's own aggression. *Journal of the American Academy of Child & Adolescent Psychiatry, 46,* 1080–1087.

van Stegeren, A. H. (2008). The role of the noradrenergic system in emotional memory. *Acta Psychologica, 127,* 532–541.

Verhoeckx, K., Voortman, T., Balvers, M., Hendriks, H., Wortelboer, H., & Witkamp, R. (2011). Presence, formation and putative biological activities of N-acyl serotonins, a novel class of fatty-acid derived mediators, in the intestinal tract. *Biochimica Et Biophysica Acta, 1811*(10), 578–586.

Verschuere, B., Crombez, G., Koster, E. W., & Uzieblo, K. (2006). Psychopathy and physiological detection of concealed information: A review. *Psychologica Belgica, 46*(1–2), 99–116.

Vertosick, F. T. (2000). *Why we hurt: The natural history of pain.* New York, NY: Harcourt.

Vickers, J. C., Dickson, T. C., Adlard, P. A., Saunders, H. L., King, C. E., & McCormack, G. (2000). The cause of neuronal degeneration in Alzheimer's disease. *Progress in Neurobiology, 60*(2), 139–165.

Vidmar, N. (1997). Generic prejudice and the presumption of guilt in sex abuse trials. *Law and Human Behavior, 21*(1), 5–25.

Vijgen, S. M. C., van Baal, P. H. M., Hoogenveen, R. T., de Wit, G. A., & Feenstra, T. L. (2008). Cost-effectiveness analyses of health promotion programs: A case study of smoking prevention and cessation among Dutch students. *Health Education Research, 23,* 310–318.

Vitaro, F., Boivin, M., & Bukowski, W. M. (2009). The role of friendship in child and adolescent psychosocial development. In K. H. Rubin, W. M. Bukowski, & B. Laursen (Eds.), *Handbook of peer interactions, relationships, and groups* (pp. 568–585). New York, NY: Guilford.

Vogt, D. S., Rizvi, S. L., Shipherd, J. C., & Resick, P. A. (2008). Longitudinal investigation of reciprocal relationship between stress reactions and hardiness. *Personality and Social Psychology Bulletin, 34,* 61–73.

von Hippel, W., Brener, L., & von Hippel, C. (2008). Implicit prejudice toward injecting drug users predicts intentions to change jobs among drug and alcohol nurses. *Psychological Science, 19,* 7–11.

Vorria, P., Vairami, M., Gialaouzidis, M., Kotroni, E., Koutra, G., Markou, N., Marti, E., & Pantoleon, I. (2007). Romantic relationships, attachment syles, and experiences of childhood. *Hellenic Journal of Psychology, 4,* 281–309.

W

Wachtel, P. L. (2011). *Inside the session: What really happens in psychotherapy.* Washington, DC: American Psychological Association.

Wagg, J. (2008, October 30). Challenge application: $1M challenge. Retrieved from http://www.randi.org/site/index.php/1m-challenge/challenge-application.html

Wahlstrom, K. L. (2002). Accommodating the sleep patterns of adolescents within current educational structures: An uncharted path. In M. A. Carskadon (Ed.), *Adolescent sleep patterns: Biological, social, and psychological influences* (pp. 172–197). New York, NY: Cambridge University Press.

Wakefield, M., Flay, B., Nichter, M., & Giovino, G. (2003). Role of the media in influencing trajectories of youth smoking. *Addiction, 98*(Suppl 1), 79–103.

Walker, E., Kestler, L., Bollini, A., & Hochman, K. M. (2004). Schizophrenia: Etiology and course. *Annual Review of Psychology, 55,* 401–430.

Walker, L. J. (1991). Sex differences in moral reasoning. In W. M. Kurtines & J. L. Gewirtz (Eds.), *Handbook of moral behavior and development: Vol. 2: Research.* Hillsdale, NJ: Erlbaum.

Walker, L. J. (2006). Gender and morality. In M. Killen & J. G. Smetana (Eds.), *Handbook of moral development* (pp. 93–115). Mahwah, NJ: Lawrence Erlbaum.

Wallace, D. C. (1997, August). Mitochondrial DNA in aging and disease. *Scientific American,* 40–47.

Wallen, K. (2005). Hormonal influences on sexually differentiated behavior in nonhuman primates. *Frontiers in Neuroendocrinology, 26,* 7–26.

Wallen, K., & Lloyd, E. A. (2011). Female sexual arousal: Genital anatomy and orgasm in intercourse. *Hormones and Behavior, 59*(5), 780–792.

Waller, M. R., & McLanahan, S. S. (2005). "His" and "her" marriage expectations: Determinants and consequences. *Journal of Marriage & Family, 67*(1), 53–67.

Waller, N. G., & Ross, C. A. (1997). The prevalence and biometric structure of pathological dissociation in the general population: Taxometric and behavior genetics findings. *Journal of Abnormal Psychology, 106,* 499–510.

Wallerstein, G. (2008). *The pleasure instinct: Why we crave adventure, chocolate, pheromones, and music.* New York, NY: Wiley.

Wallis, C. (2011). Performing gender: A content analysis of gender display in music videos. *Sex Roles, 64,* 160–172.

Wamsley, E. J., Hirota, Y., Tucker, M. A., Smith, M. R. , & Antrobus, J. S. (2007). Circadian and ultradian influences on dreaming: A dual rhythm model. *Brain Research Bulletin, 71,* 204–211.

Wamsley, E. J., Tucker, M. A., Payne, J. D., & Stickgold, R. (2010). A brief nap is beneficial for human route-learning: The role of navigation experience and EEG spectral power. *Learning & Memory, 17*(7), 332–336.

Wang, Q. (2008). Emotion, knowledge and autobiographical memory across the preschool years: A cross-cultural longitudinal investigation. *Cognition, 108,* 117–135.

Wangensteen, O. H., & Carlson, H. A. (1931). Hunger sensations in a patient after total gastrectomy. *Proceedings of the Society for Experimental Biology & Medicine, 28,* 545–547.

Wansink, B. (2004). Environmental factors that increase the food intake and consumption volume of unknowing consumers. *Annual Review of Nutrition, 24,* 455–479.

Wansink, B., & Payne, C. R. (2008). Eating behavior and obesity at Chinese buffets. *Obesity, 16*(8), 1957–1960.

Ward, N. S., & Frackowiak, R. S. (2006). The functional anatomy of cerebral reorganization after focal brain injury. *Journal of Physiology, Paris, 99,* 425–436.

Ward, P., & Walker, J. (2008). The influence of study methods and knowledge processing on academic success and long-term recall of anatomy learning by first-year veterinary students. *Anatomical Sciences Education, 1*(2), 68–74.

Wardlaw, G. M., & Hampl, J. (2007). *Perspectives in nutrition* (7th ed.). New York, NY: McGraw-Hill.

Warneken, F., & Tomasello, M. (2008). Extrinsic rewards undermine altruistic tendencies in 20-month-olds. *Developmental Psychology, 44*(6), 1785–1788.

Warr, P., Butcher, V., & Robertson, I. (2004). Activity and psychological well-being in older people. *Aging & Mental Health, 8*(2), 172–183.

Wason, P. C. (1968). Reasoning about a rule. *Quarterly Journal of Experimental Psychology, 20*(3), 273–281.

Wass, T. S. (2008). Neuroanatomical and neurobehavioral effects of heavy prenatal alcohol exposure. In J. Brick (Ed.), *Handbook of the medical consequences of alcohol and drug abuse* (2nd ed., pp. 177–217). *The Haworth Press series in neuropharmacology.* New York, NY: Haworth Press/Taylor and Francis Group.

Watson, C. N., Watt-Watson, J., & Chipman, M. (2010). The long-term safety and efficacy of opioids: A survey of 84 selected patients with intractable chronic noncancer pain. *Pain Research & Management, 15*(4), 213–217.

Watson, H., Raykos, B., Street, H., Fursland, A., & Nathan, P. (2011). Mediators between perfectionism and eating disorder psychopathology: Shape and weight overvaluation and conditional goal-setting. *International Journal of Eating Disorders, 44*(2), 142–149.

Watson, J. (1913). Psychology as the behaviorist views it. *Psychological Review, 20,* 158–177.

Watson, J. B., & Rayner, R. (1920). Conditioned emotional reactions. *Journal of Experimental Psychology, 3,* 1–14.

Watson, J. C. & Greenberg, L. S. (1996). Emotion and cognition in experiential therapy: A dialectical-constructivist position. In H. Rosen & K. Kuelwein (Eds.), *Constructing realities: Meaning-making perspectives for psychotherapists* (pp. 253–276). San Francisco, CA: Jossey-Bass.

Watson, J. C., Goldman, R. N., & Greenberg, L. S. (2011). Humanistic and experiential theories of psychotherapy. In H. Rosen & K. Kuelwein (Eds.), *Constructing realities: Meaning-making perspectives for psychotherapists* (pp. 141–172). San Francisco, CA: Jossey-Bass.

Waye, K. P. (2004). Effects of low-frequency noise on sleep. *Noise Health, 6,* 87–91.

Waye, K. P., Bengtsson, J., Rylander, R., Hucklebridge, F., Evans, P., & Clow, A. (2002). Low-frequency noise enhances cortisol among noise-sensitive subjects during work performance. *Life Sciences, 70*(7), 745–758.

Weaver, M. F., & Schnoll, S. H. (2008). Hallucinogens and club drugs. In M. Galanter & H. D. Kleber (Eds.), *The American Psychiatric Publishing textbook of substance abuse treatment* (4th ed., pp. 191–200). Arlington, VA: American Psychiatric Publishing.

Weber, B. R. (2010). Talking sex, talking Kinsey. *Australian Feminist Studies, 25*(64), 189–198.

Webster's Revised Unabridged Dictionary. (1913). Springfield, MA: C. & G. Merriam Co. Retrieved from http://www.webster-dictionary.org

Wechsler, D. (1944). *The measurement of adult intelligence* (3rd ed.). Baltimore: Williams & Wilkins.

Wechsler, D. (1977). *Manual for the Wechsler Intelligence Scale for Children* (Rev. ed.). New York, NY: Psychological Corporation.

Weeks, S., Anderson-Barnes, V., & Tsao, J. (2010). Phantom limb pain: theories and therapies. *The Neurologist, 16*(5), 277–286.

Wegener, D. T., Clark, J. K., & Petty, R. E. (2006). Not all stereotyping is created equal: Differential consequences of thoughtful versus nonthoughtful stereotyping. *Journal of Personality and Social Psychology, 90,* 42–59.

Wei, R. (2007). Effects of playing violent video games on Chinese adolescents' proviolence attitudes, attitudes toward others, and aggressive behavior. *CyberPsychology & Behavior, 10,* 371–380.

Weiner, B. (1972). *Theories of motivation.* Chicago, IL: Rand-McNally.

Weiner, B. (1982). The emotional consequences of causal attributions. In M. S. Clark & S. T. Fiske (Eds.), *Affect and cognition.* Hillsdale, NJ: Erlbaum.

Weiner, G. (2008). *Handbook of personality assessment.* Hoboken, NJ: Wiley.

Weiner, M. F. (2008). Perspective on race and ethnicity in Alzheimer's disease research. *Alzheimer's & Dementia, 4,* 233–238.

Weinfield, N. S., Sroufe, L. A., Egeland, B., & Carlson, E. (2008). Individual differences in infant-caregiver attachment: Conceptual and empirical aspects of security. In J. Cassidy & P. R. Shaver (Eds.), *Handbook of attachment: Theory, research, and clinical applications* (2nd ed., pp. 78–101). New York, NY: Guilford.

Weiss, A., Bates, T. C., & Luciano, M. (2008). Happiness is a personal(ity) thing: The genetics of personality and well-being in a representative sample. *Psychological Science, 19,* 205–210.

Weitlauf, J. C., Cervone, D., Smith, R. E., & Wright, P. M. (2001). Assessing generalization in perceived self-efficacy: Multidomain and global assessments of the effects of self-defense training for women. *Personality & Social Psychology Bulletin, 27*(12), 1683–1691.

Wenger, A., & Fowers, B. J. (2008). Positive illusions in parenting: Every child is above average. *Journal of Applied Social Psychology, 38,* 611–634.

Wentz, E., Mellström, D., Gillberg, I. C., Gillberg, C. , & Råstam, M. (2007). Brief report: Decreased bone mineral density as a long-term complication of teenage-onset anorexia nervosa. *European Eating Disorders Review, 15,* 290–295.

Werner, J. S., & Wooten, B. R. (1979). Human infant color vision and color perception. *Infant Behavior and Development, 2*(3), 241–273.

Werner, K. H., Roberts, N. A., Rosen, H. J., Dean, D. L., Kramer, J. H., Weiner, M. W., Miller, B. L., & Levenson, R. W. (2007). Emotional reactivity and emotion recognition in frontotemporal lobar degeneration. *Neurology, 69,* 148–155.

Werth, J. L. Jr., Wright, K. S., Archambault, R. J., & Bardash, R. (2003). When does the "duty to protect" apply with a client who has anorexia nervosa? *Counseling Psychologist, 31*(4), 427–450.

Westen, D. (1998). Unconscious thought, feeling, and motivation: The end of a century-long debate. In R. F. Bornstein & J. M. Masling (Eds.), *Empirical perspectives on the psychoanalytic unconscious.* Washington, DC: American Psychological Association.

Wheat, A. L., & Larkin, K. T. (2010). Biofeedback of heart rate variability and related physiology: A critical review. *Applied Psychophysiology and Biofeedback, 35*(3), 229–242.

Whitbourne, S. K., & Whitbourne, S. B. (2011). *Adult development and aging: Biopsychosocial perspectives.* Hoboken, NJ: Wiley.

White, T., & Hilgetag, C. C. (2011). Gyrification and neural connectivity in schizophrenia. *Development and Psychopathology, 23*(1), 339–352.

White, T., Andreasen, N. C., & Nopoulos, P. (2002). Brain volumes and surface morphology in monozygotic twins. *Cerebral Cortex, 12*(5), 486–493.

Whitworth, B., & Ryu, H. (2009). A comparison of human and computer information processing. In M. Pagaini (Ed.), *Encyclopedia of Multimedia Technology and Networking* (pp. 230–239). Hershey, PA: Information Science Reference.

Whorf, B. L. (1956). Science and linguistics. In J. B. Carroll (Ed.), *Language, thought and reality* (pp. 207–219). Cambridge, MA: MIT Press.

Wickett, J. C., Vernon, P. A., & Lee, D. H. (2000). Relationships between factors of intelligence and brain voume. *Personality and Individual Differences, 29,* 1095–1122.

Wickramasekera, I. II. (2008). Review of how can we help witnesses to remember more? It's an eyes open and shut case. *American Journal of Clinical Hypnosis, 50,* 290–291.

Wiederman, M. W. (1999). Volunteer bias in sexuality research using college student participants. *Journal of Sex Research, 36*(1), 59–66.

Wieseler-Frank, J., Maier, S. F., & Watkins, L. R. (2005). Immune-to-brain communication dynamically modulates pain: Physiological and pathological consequences. *Brain, Behavior, & Immunity, 19*(2), 104–111.

Wilfley, D. E., Kolko, R. P., & Kass, A. E. (2011). Cognitive-behavioral therapy for weight management and eating disorders in children and adolescents. *Child and Adolescent Psychiatric Clinics of North America, 20*(2), 271–285.

Williams, A. L., Haber, D., Weaver, G. D., & Freeman, J. L. (1998). Altruistic activity: Does it make a difference in the senior center? *Activities, Adaptation and Aging, 22*(4), 31–39.

Williams, G., Cai, X. J., Elliott, J. C., & Harrold, J. A. (2004). Anabolic neuropeptides. *Physiology & Behavior, 81*(2), 211–222.

Williams, S. S. (2001). Sexual lying among college students in close and casual relationships. *Journal of Applied Social Psychology, 31*(11), 2322–2338.

Williamson, A. M., & Feyer, A. M. (2000). Moderate sleep deprivation produces impairments in cognitive and motor performance equivalent to legally prescribed levels of alcohol intoxication. *Occupational and Environmental Medicine, 57*(10), 649–655.

Willingham, D. B. (2001). *Cognition: The thinking animal.* Upper Saddle River, NJ: Prentice Hall.

Willis, M. S., Esqueda, C. W., & Schacht, R. N. (2008). Social perceptions of individuals missing upper front teeth. *Perceptual and Motor Skills, 106,* 423–435.

Wilson, E. O. (1975). *Sociobiology: The new synthesis.* Cambridge, MA: Harvard University Press.

Wilson, E. O. (1978). *On human nature.* Cambridge, MA: Harvard University Press.

Wilson, F. A., & Stimpson, J. P. (2010). Trends in fatalities from distracted driving in the United States, 1999 to 2008. *American Journal of Public Health, 100*(11), 2213–2219.

Wilson, K. G., Chochinov, H. W., McPherson, C. J., Graham, M., Allard, P., Chary, S., … Clinch, J. J. (2007). Desire for euthanasia or physician-assisted suicide in palliative cancer care. *Health Psychology, 26,* 314–323.

Wilson, R. S., Gilley, D. W., Bennett, D. A., Beckett, L. A., & Evans, D. A. (2000). Person-specific paths of cognitive decline in Alzheimer's disease and their relation to age. *Psychology & Aging, 15*(1), 18–28.

Wilson, S., & Nutt, D. (2008). *Sleep disorders.* Oxford, England: Oxford University Press.

Winterich, J. A. (2003). Sex, menopause, and culture: Sexual orientation and the meaning of menopause for women's sex lives. *Gender & Society, 17*(4), 627–642.

Winterowd, C., Beck, A. T., & Gruener, D. (2003). *Cognitive therapy with chronic pain patients.* New York, NY: Springer.

Winters, B. D., Saksida, L. M., & Bussey, T. J. (2010). Implications of animal object memory research for human amnesia. *Neuropsychologia, 48*(8), 2251–2261.

Wise, D., & Rosqvist, J. (2006). Explanatory style and well-being. In J. C. Thomas, D. L. Segal, & M. Hersen (Eds.), *Comprehensive handbook of personality and psychopathology, Vol. 1: Personality and everyday functioning* (pp. 285–305). Hoboken, NJ: Wiley.

Wiste, A. K., Arango, V., Ellis, S. P., Mann, J. J., & Underwood, M. D. (2008). Norepinephrine and serotonin imbalance in the locus coeruleus in bipolar disorder. *Bipolar Disorders, 10,* 349–359.

Witelson, S. F., Kigar, D. L., & Harvey, T. (1999). The exceptional brain of Albert Einstein. *The Lancet, 353,* 2149–2153.

Witherington, D. C., Campos, J. J., Anderson, D. I., Lejeune, L., & Seah, E. (2005). Avoidance of heights on the visual cliff in newly walking infants. *Infancy, 7*(3), 285–298.

Withrow, D. D., & Alter, D. A. (2011). The economic burden of obesity worldwide: A systematic review of the direct costs of obesity. *Obesity Reviews, 12*(2), 131–141.

Wolf, G. (2008). Want to remember everything you'll ever learn? Surrender to this algorithm. *Wired Magazine.* Retrieved from http://www.wired.com/print/medtech/ health/magazine/16-05/FF_Wozniak

Wolf, S. L., Winstein, C. J., Miller, J. P., Thompson, P. A., Taub, E., Uswatte, G., … Clark, P. C. (2008). Retention of upper limb function in stroke survivors who have received constraint-induced movement therapy: The EXCITE randomized trial. *Lancet Neurology, 7*(1), 33–40.

Wolitzky, D. L. (2011). Psychoanalytic theories of psychotherapy. In J. C. Norcross, G. R. VandenBos, & D. K. Freedhelm (Eds.), *History of psychotherapy: Continuity and change* (2nd ed., pp. 65–100). Washington, DC: American Psychological Association.

Wolpe, J., & Plaud, J. J. (1997). Pavlov's contributions to behavior therapy. *American Psychologist, 52*(9), 966–972.

Woods, T., Coyle, K., Hoglund, W., & Leadbeater, B. (2007). Changing the contexts of peer victimization: The effects of a primary prevention program on school and classroom levels of victimization. In J. E. Zins, M. J. Elias, & C. A. Maher (Eds.), *Bullying, victimization, and peer harassment: A handbook of prevention and intervention* (pp. 369–388). New York, NY: Haworth Press.

Workman, L., & Reader, W. (2008). *Evolutionary psychology: An introduction.* New York, NY: Cambridge University Press.

World Health Organization. (2007). Cultural diversity presents special challenges for mental health. Retrieved from http://www.paho.org/English/DD/PIN/pr071010.htm

World Health Organization. (2008). Mental health and substance abuse. Retrieved from http://www.searo.who.int/en/section1174/section1199/section1567_6741.htm

World Memory Sports Council. (n.d.). World memory statistics. Retrieved from http://www.world-memory-statistics.com/competitor.php?id=797

Worldometers. (n.d). Real time world statistics. Retrieved from http://www.worldometers.info/weight-loss/

Worthen, J. B. (2006). Resolution of discrepant memory strengths: An explanation of the effects of bizarreness on memory. In R. Hunt and J. B. Worthen (Eds.), *Distinctiveness and memory* (pp. 133–156). New York, NY: Oxford University Press.

Wright, M. J., & Myers, C. R. (1982). *History of academic psychology in Canada.* Toronto, ON: Hogrefe.

Wright, W. G., Gurfinkel, V. S., King, L. A., Nutt, J. G., Cordo, P. J., & Horak, F. B. (2010). Axial kinesthesia is impaired in Parkinson's disease: Effects of levodopa. *Experimental Neurology, 225*(1), 202–209.

Wu, C., Chang, Y., Yu, L., Chen, H., Jen, C. J., Wu, S., Lo, C, & Kuo, Y. (2008). Exercise enhances the proliferation of neural stem cells and neurite growth and survival of neuronal progenitor cells in dentate gyms of middle-aged mice. *Journal of Applied Physiology, 105*(5), 1585–1594.

Wu, J. C., Huang, W. C., Tsai, Y. A., Chen, Y. C., & Cheng, H. (2008). Nerve repair using acidic fibroblast growth factor in human cervial spinal cord: A preliminary Phase I clinical study. *Journal Neurosurgery of the Spine, 8,* 208–214.

Wu, Z., & Schimmele, C. (2009). Divorce and repartnering. In M. Baker (Ed.), *Families: Changing trends in Canada.* Toronto, ON: McGraw-Hill Ryerson.

Wyman, A. J., & Vyse, S. (2008). Science versus the stars: A double-blind test of the validity of the NEO Five Factor Inventory and computer-generated astrological natal charts. *Journal of General Psychology, 135,* 287–300.

Wynne, C. D. L. (2007). What the ape said. *Ethology, 113,* 411–413.

X

Xu, Y., Hill, J., Fukuda, M., Gautron, L., Sohn, J., Kim, K., ... Elmquist, J. (2010). PI3K signaling in the ventromedial hypothalamic nucleus is required for normal energy homeostasis. *Cell Metabolism, 12*(1), 88–95.

Xue, W., Hu, J., Yuan, Y., Sun, J., Li, B., Zhang, D., Li, C., & Chen, N. (2009). Polygalasaponin XXXII from Polygala tenuifolia root improves hippocampal-dependent learning and memory. *Acta Pharmacologica Sinica, 30*(9), 1211–1219.

Y

Yacoubian, G. S. Jr., Green, M. K., & Peters, R. J. (2003). Identifying the prevalence and correlates of Ecstasy and other club drug (EOCD) use among high school seniors. *Journal of Ethnicity in Substance Abuse, 2*(2), 53–66.

Yamada, H. (1997). *Different games, different rules: Why Americans and Japanese misunderstand each other.* London, England: Oxford University Press.

Yang, Y. K., Yao, W. J., Yeh, T. L., Lee, I. H., Chen, P. S., Lu, R. B, & Chiu, N. T. (2008). Decreased dopamine transporter availability in male smokers—A dual isotope SPECT study. *Progress in Neuro-Psychopharmacology & Biological Psychiatry, 32,* 274–279.

Yaniv, I. (2011). Group diversity and decision quality: Amplification and attenuation of the framing effect. *International Journal of Forecasting, 27*(1), 41–49.

Yarmey, A. D. (2004). Eyewitness recall and photo identification: A field experiment. *Psychology, Crime & Law, 10*(1), 53–68.

Yegneswaran, B., & Shapiro, C. (2007). Do sleep deprivation and alcohol have the same effects on psychomotor performance? *Journal of Psychosomatic Research, 63,* 569–572.

Yeh, S. J., & Lo, S. K. (2004). Living alone, social support, and feeling lonely among the elderly. *Social Behavior & Personality, 32*(2), 129–138.

Yokoyama, H., Uchida, H., Kuroiwa, H., Kasahara, J., & Araki, T. (2011). Role of glial cells in neurotoxin-induced animal models of Parkinson's disease. *Neurological Sciences, 32*(1), 1–7.

Yoo, S-S., Hu, P. T., Gujar, N., Jolesz, F. A., & Walker, M. P. (2007). A deficit in the ability to form new human memories without sleep. *Nature Neuroscience, 10,* 385–392.

Young, J. D., & Taylor, E. (1998). Meditation as a voluntary hypometabolic state of biological estivation. *News in Physiological Science, 13,* 149–153.

Young, M. E., Mizzau, M., Mai, N. T., Sirisegaram, A., & Wilson, M. (2009). Food for thought: What you eat depends on your sex and eating companions. *Appetite, 53*(2), 268–271.

Young, M. M., Saewyc, E., Boak, A., Jahrig, J., Anderson, B., Doiron, Y., ... Clark, H. (Student Drug Use Surveys Working Group). (2011). *Cross-Canada report on student alcohol and drug use: Technical report.* Ottawa, ON: Canadian Centre on Substance Abuse.

Young, T. (1802). Color vision. *Philosophical Transactions of the Royal Society,* p. 12.

Younger, A. J., Adler, S. A., & Vasta, R. (2012). *Child psychology: A Canadian perspective* (3rd ed.). Toronto, ON: John Wiley & Sons, Canada.

Z

Zalaquett, C. P., Fuerth, K. M., Stein, C., Ivey, A. E., & Ivey, M. B. (2008). Reframing the *DSM-IV-TR* from a multicultural/social justice perspective. *Journal of Counseling & Development, 86,* 364–371.

Zarrindast, M-R., Fazli-Tabaei, S., Khalilzadeh, A., Farahmanfar, M., & Yahyavi, S-Y. (2005). Cross state-dependent retrieval between histamine and lithium. *Physiology & Behavior, 86,* 154–163.

Zarrindast, M-R., Shendy, M. M., & Ahmadi, S. (2007). Nitric oxide modulates states dependency induced by lithium in an inhibitory avoidance task in mice. *Behavioural Pharmacology, 18,* 289–295.

Zeifman, D. M., & Hazan, C. (2008). Pair bonds as attachments: Reevaluating the evidence. In J. Cassidy & P. R. Shaver (Eds.), *Handbook of attachment: Theory, research, and clinical applications* (2nd ed., pp. 436–455). New York, NY: Guilford.

Zelinski, E. L., Hong, N. S., Tyndall, A. V, Halsall, B., & McDonald, R. J. (2010). Prefrontal cortical contributions during discriminative fear conditioning, extinction, and spontaneous recovery in rats. *Experimental Brain Research, 203*(2), 285–297.

Zillmer, E. A., Spiers, M. V., & Culbertson, W. (2008). *Principles of neuropsychology* (2nd ed.). Belmont, CA: Cengage.

Zimbardo, P. (2007). *The Lucifer effect: Understanding how good people turn evil.* New York, NY: Random House.

Zimbardo, P. G. (1993). Stanford prison experiment: A 20-year retrospective. Invited presentation at the meeting of the Western Psychological Association, Phoenix, AZ.

Zimbardo, P. G., Ebbeson, E. B., & Maslach, C. (1977). *Influencing attitudes and changing behavior.* Reading, MA: Addison-Wesley.

Zubrzycka, M., & Janecka, A. (2000). Substance P: transmitter of nociception (Minireview). *Endocrine Regulations, 34*(4), 195–201.

Zucker, K. J. (2008). Special issue: Biological research on sex-dimorphic behavior and sexual orientation. *Archives of Sexual Behavior, 37,* 1.

Zuckerman, L., & Weiner, I. (2005). Maternal immune activation leads to behavioral and pharmacological changes in the adult offspring. *Journal of Psychiatric Research, 39*(3), 311–323.

Zuckerman, M. (1979). *Sensation seeking: Beyond the optimal level of arousal.* Hillsdale, NJ: Erlbaum.

Zuckerman, M. (1994). *Behavioral expressions and biosocial bases of sensation seeking.* New York, NY: Cambridge University Press.

Zuckerman, M. (2004). The shaping of personality: Genes, environments, and chance encounters. *Journal of Personality Assessment, 82*(1), 11–22.

Zuckerman, M. (2008). Rose is a rose is a rose: Content and construct validity. *Personality and Individual Differences, 45,* 110–112.

Zweig, R., & Leahy, R. (2012). *Treatment plans and interventions for bulimia and binge-eating disorder.* New York, NY: Guilford Press.

Name Index

A

Aalsma, M. C., 260
Aarts, H., 121
Abadinsky, H., 86, 146, 246
Abbott, A., 52
Abdul Ahad, H., 138
Abell, S. C., 300
Aboa-Éboulé, C., 72, 77, 79
Abramson, L. Y., 365
Acarturk, C., 360
Acredolo, L. P., 221
Adelmann, P. K., 315
Adler, A., 334
Adler, S. A., 246, 249, 347
Adolphs, R., 311
Ahlsén, E., 170
Ahmadi, S., 194
Ahmed, A. M., 417
Ainsworth, M. D. S., 270
Al'absi, M., 195
Alain, C., 253
Alamo, C., 364
Albarracín, D., 201
Alberts, A., 260
Alden, L. E., 360
Alegre, A., 228
Alexander, B. K., 83, 142, 144, 146
Allan, K., 200, 203
Allen, J. B., 320
Allik, J., 329
Alloy, L. B., 365, 376, 413
Allport, G. W., 326
Almeida, O. P., 364
Alter, D. A., 303
Altintas, M., 301
Altschuler, E. L., 101
Amabile, T. M., 309
Amaral, D. G., 190
Amato, P. R., 283, 284
Amir, N., 190, 194
Amir, O., 297
Amso, D., 198
Amundson, J. K., 150
Anderson, C. A., 166, 176–177, 427, 428
Anderson, L. E., 427
Anderson, M. C., 205
Andrade, T. G. C. S., 82
Andrasik, F., 175
Andreasen, N. C., 59, 231
Andreoni, J., 417
Andrews, K., 421
Anglin, J. M., 219
Angrilli, A., 311
Anis, A. H., 303
Anisman, H., 364
Ansell, E. B., 374
Antonakis, J., 228
Antony, M. M., 390, 396, 397, 398
Aou, S., 82
Appel, M., 201
Appiah, K. A., 16
Arbib, M. A., 171
Arendt, H., 433
Aristotle, 240
Arkes, H., 412
Armeli, S., 310

Arnedt, J., 131
Aron, A. P., 316
Aronson, J., 233
Arriagada, O., 43
Arriola, L., 86
Arumugam, V., 301
Asch, S. E., 420, 421
Asghar, A. U. R., 59
Atchley, R. C., 287
Atkinson, R. C., 185
Atlas, R. S., 428, 429
Aubert, A., 172
Aubry, T., 402
Aune, D., 79
Auyeung, B., 280
Axtell, R. E., 319, 421
Aydin, O., 413
Ayers, S., 78, 79
Azizian, A., 200

B

Baddeley, A. D., 188, 194
Badge, J. L., 16
Baer, J., 216
Bagermihl, B., 307
Bailey, J. M., 307
Bailey, K. R., 58
Bailey, S., 372
Baillargeon, R., 261
Baird, A. D., 170
Baker, D., 246
Baker, R. R., 17
Bakker, J., 307
Baldessarini, R. J., 364
Baldwin, J., 41
Baldwin, J. M., 9
Ball, H. A., 365
Ballantyne, J., 144
Ballard, T., 195
Bamer, A. M., 137
Bandura, A., 168–169, 276, 281, 340, 397
Banich, M. T., 212
Banks, C., 424–425
Banks, M. S., 115
Bao, A., 307
Barbur, J. L., 118
Bard, P., 313
Barelds, D. P. H., 417, 419
Bargai, N., 166
Barker, R., 283
Barker, C. P., 428
Barlow, D. H., 426
Barner, D., 222
Barnett, R. C., 233
Barnier, A., 149, 150
Barnow, S., 374
Barriga, A. Q., 428
Bartholow, B. D., 177, 428
Barton, D. A., 364
Barton, J. J. S., 113
Basow, A. A., 281
Bassareo, V., 144
Bates, A. L., 233
Batson, C. D., 430
Baumeister, R. F., 412, 414, 420
Baumrind, D., 270

Bayley, T. M., 108
Bearer, C. F., 23
Beck, A. T., 390
Becker, A. J., 52
Becker, K. A., 227
Becker, S. I., 190, 194
Beckes, L., 430
Begg, I. M., 121
Behar, R., 305
Beilin, H., 261
Bélanger, L., 137
Bell, B., 305
Belsey, B., 429
Belsky, J., 270
Beltz, A., 307
Ben-Eliyahu, S., 77, 79
Benagiano, G., 306
Benarroch, E., 302
Benbow, C. P., 309
Bendersky, M., 251
Bennett, E. L., 170
Bensafi, M., 212
Beran, T. N., 258
Berenbaum, S., 307
Berenbaum, S. A., 176
Berger, M., 195
Bergh, C., 301
Berglund, H., 108
Bergmann, B. M., 131
Bergstrom-Lynch, C. A., 308
Berlin, L. J., 269
Bernard, L. L., 296
Berndt, T. J., 273
Bernstein, M. J., 313
Berntson, G. G., 311
Berreman, G., 375
Berridge, K., 298
Berry, J., 223, 376, 414
Bersoff, D. M., 276
Berthoud, H., 302
Berzoff, J., 276
Besedovsky, L., 79
Best, J. B., 187
Beyerstein, L., 121
Bhattacharya, S. K., 82
Bialystock, E., 220, 221
Biehl, M., 318
Billiard, M., 137, 138, 139
Binet, A., 224, 226
Binks, G., 87
Birkenhäger, T. K., 400
Biswas-Diener, R., 392
Bjorklund, D. F., 7, 279
Blaine, B. E., 304
Blais, J., 429
Blakemore, C., 113
Blanton, C., 17
Blashfield, R. K., 357
Bless, H., 232, 233
Bleuler, E., 366
Blonigen, D. M., 230
Bloom, K., 221
Blum, H. P., 135
Blumenthal, R. S., 80
Boardman, J., 364
Bob, P., 149
Boccato, G., 121

Subject Index

Cerebrum, 50, 58
Chemical senses, 108
Chemical signal, 45
Children
    abused/neglected, 329
    achievement motivation in, 309
    adopted, 40
    and aggression, 279
    behavioural genetics and, 40
    brains, 248–249
    and bullying, 428–429
    cognitive development, 257–260
    conditioning in, 160
    and death/dying, 287
    divorce and, 283
    and friendships, 273
    in gay families, 308
    and language, 219–220
    memories, 190
    moral development, 273–275
    motor development, 250
    parenting styles and, 270
    and peers, 273
    REM sleep and, 132
    sense of taste, 108–109
    and siblings, 271–273
    and sleep disorders, 139
    smoking and, 83–84, 246
    unconditional positive regard and, 338
    victimization by, 428–429
Chromosomes, 38
Chronic stressors, 72
Chunking, 187
Circadian rhythms
    about, 128
    control of, 130
    disruption of, 128
    and evolutionary/circadian theory, 135
Civil Marriage Act, 307–308
Clairvoyance, 120
Classical conditioning, 156–160, 173–174
    and anxiety disorders, 361–362
    in behaviour therapy, 395–397
Classically conditioned memory, 190
Client-centred therapy, 392, 393
Climacteric, male, 253
Clitoris, 53, 306
Cochlea, 105
Cochlear fluid, 105
Cochlear implants, 106
Cognition
    building blocks, 212–213
    defined, 212
    environment and, 340
    gender differences in, 278–279
Cognitive appraisal, and coping, 89
Cognitive attitudes, 413–414
Cognitive development
    about, 255–261
    concrete operational stage, 256, 258, 259
    formal operational stage, 256, 260–261
    and gender-role development, 281
    Piaget's four stages, 255, 256, 257–261
    preoperational stage, 256, 257–258, 259
    sensorimotor stage, 256, 257
Cognitive dissonance, 414, 419, 432
Cognitive expectancies, 340
Cognitive maps, 168
Cognitive perspective, 10

Cognitive prejudice, 415
Cognitive restructuring, 388, 389
Cognitive retraining, 432
Cognitive therapy, 388–392
Cognitive-behaviour therapy
    about, 390
    faulty thinking and, 391
    for sleep, 137
Cognitive-social learning, 167–170, 176–177
Cognitive-social theory, 167
Cohort effects, 243
Collective unconscious, 334, 335
Collectivist cultures, 281–282, 413
Colour perception, 118–119
Committed relationships, 283. *See also*
        Marriage
Comorbidity, 371–372
Competition
    achievement and, 309
    for limited resources, 417
    and prejudice, 431–432
Concepts
    formation, 213–214
    hierarchies, 213
Concrete operational stage of cognitive
        development, 256, 258, 259
Conditioned emotional responses, 158, 174,
        190
Conditioned response (CR), 156, 157, 174
Conditioned stimulus (CS), 156, 157
Conditioning, 10
    classical, 156–160, 173–174
    defined, 156
    in everyday life, 173–177
    higher-order, 160
    operant, 161–166, 174–176, 223
Conduction deafness, 106
Cones, 104
Confirmation bias, 121–122, 215
Conflict, and stress, 74
Conformity, 420–421
Confound variables, 20
Congruence, between self-esteem and
        experiences, 337, 338
Conscientiousness, 326, 328, 329
Consciousness. *See also* Awareness
    about, 128
    brain and, 129
    Freud's levels of, 330–333
    mind-body issue and, 129
Continuous reinforcement, 162
Control group, 19
Conventional level of moral development, 274,
        275, 276
Convolutions, 60
Cooperation, 431–432
Coping, 88–89, 91
Cornea, 104
Coronary heart disease, 79
Corpus callosum, 56, 63, 64
Correlation, 226
    coefficients, 22
Correlational research, 22–24
Cortisol, 49, 76, 78, 80, 195
Cramming, 201
Creativity, and problem solving, 216–217
Criterion-related validity, 226
Critical periods, 240
Critical thinking, 4–8

Cross-sectional method of research, 242–243
CT (computed tomography) scans, 25
Culture-bound symptoms, 377
Culture-general symptoms, 377
Culture(s)
    and aggression, 427
    and aging, 287
    and anxiety disorders, 362
    and attractiveness, 417
    and attributional biases, 413
    and children's motivation, 309
    and cognitive dissonance, 414
    collective, 281–282, 413
    and death, 288
    and development, 281–282
    and development of self, 282
    and eating, 302, 303, 305
    and emotions, 319
    and hierarchy of needs, 300
    individualistic, 281, 413
    and IQ testing, 232
    and moral development, 276
    and norms, 421
    and personality, 329
    and personality assessment, 347
    and psychological disorders, 376–378
    and schizophrenia, 376
    and self-esteem, 413, 414
    and sense of taste, 109
    and therapies, 403–404
Curiosity, 297–298
Cystic fibrosis, 40

D

Damage theory, 254
Dark adaptation, 103
Deafness. *See* Hearing: loss
Death/dying
    about, 287–289
    alcohol and, 86
    causes of, 79
    physician-assisted suicide, 289
Debriefing, 15
Decibels, 106, 107
Defence mechanisms, 331–333
Deindividuation, 425
Deinstitutionalization, 406
Delusions, 366, 368
    of grandeur, 363, 366
    of persecution, 366
    of reference, 368
Dendrites, 43
Denial, 332
Deoxyribonucleic acid. *See* DNA
Dependent variable (DV), 18
Depersonalization disorder, 372
Depolarization, 44
Depressants, 142, 143
Depression
    biopsychosocial model and, 376
    clinical, 363
    gender differences in, 375–376
    major depressive disorder, 363
    maladaptive thinking and, 390
    stem cells and, 52
    unipolar, 363
Depth perception, 115, 117–118
Descriptive research, 21–22